SOFTWARE ARCHITECTURE

Foundations, Theory, and Practice

Richard N. Taylor
University of California, Irvine

Nenad Medvidović
University of Southern California

Eric M. Dashofy
The Aerospace Corporation

WILEY

John Wiley & Sons, Inc.

To Lily May, Lyrica, and Richard
—*Richard N. Taylor*

To Pavle and Sasha
—*Nenad Medvidović*

To Mom and Keith
—*Eric M. Dashofy*

Vice President & Publisher	Donald Fowley
Acquisitions Editor	Daniel Sayre
Senior Editorial Assistant	Carolyn Weisman
Executive Marketing Manager	Christopher Ruel
Senior Production Editor	Sandra Dumas
Production Manager	Dorothy Sinclair
Design Director	Jeof Vita
Designer	Lee Goldstein
Cover Designer	James O'Shea
Senior Media Editor	Lauren Sapira
Production Management Services	Elm Street Publishing Services

This book was set in 10/12 Goudy by Thomson Digital

ISBN-13   978-0470-16774-8

About the Cover

THE ARCHITECT'S DREAM, THOMAS COLE, 1840

In *The Architect's Dream*, Thomas Cole painted a vision of the history of Western civilization as a succession of buildings through time and space. A massive Egyptian pyramid and temple, Roman aqueduct, and Greek and Roman temples demonstrate his knowledge of architectural history, likely taken from architectural pattern books given to the artist as partial payment for the commission, showing the range of forms that inspired 19th-century architects. Geographical and historical contrasts separate the right and left sides of the composition. Tall trees mirror the cathedral's steeple, pointing towards Heaven, indicating the inspiration of nature in the architectural form of the church. A sacred place in harmony with nature and God, the shaded church contrasts with the towering classical structures that appear artificial and warn against fleeting power. Inspired by Salisbury Cathedral and Chapter House in England, the cathedral suggests the 19th-century Gothic architectural revival in America. Symmetrical capitals frame the sides of the canvas, their forms taken from Salisbury Chapter House, creating a Gothic window. We gaze through the theatrical window, to behind the cathedral spire, where the setting sun shines brilliant light through the windows, creating the impression of stained glass, and evoking divine light. Cole's youth and travels in England may have contributed to a sense of national pride that influenced his reference to an English Gothic cathedral, an architectural style from shared American and English history, thereby extending American history back in time. With his face turned towards the radiant light emanating through the cathedral steeple, the architect reclines on gigantic pattern books, the catalyst of this vision of creative imagination. By including architectural tools, books, and plans alongside the dreaming architect, the artist indicates the importance of engineering and design in growing American commerce, elevating the artist and architect's roles. The extraordinary variety and enduring beauty of Thomas Cole's painting celebrates human creativity.

The painting provides an apt illustration for a textbook on software architecture. Many contemporary software systems have designs that draw heavily from the designs of prior applications. Others take fresh inspiration from social systems or nature. Just as Cole's architect is surrounded by past structures, books, and plans, so the skilled software architect has existing systems and, importantly, a vast store of styles, techniques, processes, and tools from which to choose when confronting a design challenge.

—*LET & RNT*

Credits

Figures 1-4, 1-5, 1-6, and 1-7 courtesy Royal Philips N.V.

Figure 2-13 adapted from Figure 1 from: Weaving Together Requirements and Architectures, Bashar Nuseibeh. IEEE Computer 34 (2):115–117. 2001. © IEEE. Used by permission.

Ch. 4 Sidebar: "Styling with Perry and Wolf" Text excerpt from Dewayne E. Perry and Alexander L. Wolf. Foundations for the Study of Software Architecture. ACM SIGSOFT Software Engineering Notes 17 (4): 40–52. 1992. © Dewayne E. Perry and Alexander L. Wolf. Used by permission.

Figure 6-1 adapted from Maier and Rechtin, The Art of Software Architecting, 2nd. Ed. Copyright © CRC Press. Used with permission.

Figure 7-18 used by permission of Jeff Magee.

Figures 8-4, 12-4, and 12-5 adapted from Figures 1, 5: Bowman, R.T. et al, "Linux as a Case Study: Its Extracted Software Architecture," Proceedings of the 21st ACM/IEEE Conference on Software Engineering (ICSE'99), pp. 555–563. DOI: http://doi.acm.org/10.1145/302405.302691: Copyright © 1999 ACM, Inc. Reprinted by permission.

The ATAM Figure located at page 320 in this publication has been adapted from the ATAM diagram © 2008 by Carnegie Mellon University and is reproduced in its adapted form in this publication with special permission from the Software Engineering Institute of Carnegie Mellon University. ® Architecture Tradeoff Analysis Method and ATAM are registered in the U.S. Patent and Trademark Office by Carnegie Mellon University.

ANY CARNEGIE MELLON UNIVERSITY AND SOFTWARE ENGINEERING INSTITUTE MATERIAL IS FURNISHED ON AN "AS-IS" BASIS. CARNEGIE MELLON UNIVERSITY MAKES NO WARRANTIES OF ANY KIND, EITHER EXPRESSED OR IMPLIED, AS TO ANY MATER INCLUDING, BUT NOT LIMITED TO, WARRANTY OF FITNESS FOR PURPOSE OR MERCHANTIBILITY, EXCLUSIVITY, OR RESULTS OBTAINED FROM USE OF THE MATERIAL. CARNEGIE MELLON UNIVERSITY DOES NOT MAKE ANY WARRANTY OF ANY KIND WITH RESPECT TO FREEDOM FROM PATENT, TRADEMARK OR COPYRIGHT INFRINGEMENT.

Neither Carnegie Mellon University nor the Software Engineering Institute directly or indirectly endorse this publication. Accuracy and interpretation of figure 8-12 are the responsibility of Eric Dashofy. The Software Engineering Institute has not participated in the creation of Figure 8-12.

Figure 10-1 adapted from Figure 1; Figure 11-12 adapted from Figure 4; both from Reconceptualizing a Family of Heterogeneous Embedded Systems via Explicit Architectural Support. Sam Malek, Chiyoung Seo, Sharmila Ravula, Brad Petrus, and Nenad Medvidović. Proceedings of the Twenty-Ninth International Conference on Software Engineering, IEEE Computer Society, pp. 591–601. 2007. © IEEE. Used by permission.

Figure 10-2 from Figure 1 of Software Architectural Support for Handheld Computing. Medvidović, N.; Mikic-Rakic, M.; Mehta, N.R.; Malek, S. IEEE Computer, 36 (9):66–73, 2003. © IEEE. Used by permission.

Figure 10-9 used by permission of Antonio Carzaniga.

Ch. 11 Sidebar: "Skype on Skype" © 2008 Skype Limited. Used by permission.

Figure 13-1 from Table 1 in A Call to Action: Look Beyond the Horizon. J. M Wing, IEEE Security & Privacy, 1 (6): 62–67, 2003. © IEEE Used by permission.

Figure 14-1 Diagram by Donald Ryan, from HOW BUILDINGS LEARN by Stewart Brand, copyright © 1994 by Stewart Brand. Used by permission of Viking Penguin, a division of Penguin Group (USA) Inc.

Figure 14-5 from Figure 2 of An Architecture-Based Approach to Self-Adaptive Software. Peyman Oreizy, Michael M. Gorlick, Richard N. Taylor, Dennis Heimbigner, Greg Johnson, Nenad Medvidović, Alex Quilici, David S. Rosenblum, and Alexander L. Wolf. IEEE Intelligent Systems 14 (3): 54–62. 1999 © IEEE. Used by permission.

Ch. 14 Sidebar: Autonomic Computing. Reprint Courtesy of International Business Machines Corporation, copyright 2001 © International Business Machines Corporation.

Ch. 14 Sidebar: Quiescence. Text excerpt from Kramer, J. and Magee, J., "Change Management of Distributed Systems," Proceedings of the 3rd ACM SIGOPS European Workshop: Autonomy or interdependence in distributed systems? (1988) http://doi.acm.org/10.1145/504092.504113: Copyright © 1988 ACM, Inc. Reprinted by permission.

Portion of Figure 15-14 from Apollo Operations Handbook, Lunar Module LM5 and Subsequent, Volume 1 Subsystems Data (Document LMA790-3-LM5), 1968.

Figures 16-6 & 16-7 Copyright © The Open Group. Used with permission. TOGAF™ is a Trademark of The Open Group.

Figure 16-14 Kroll/Krutchen, RATIONAL UNIFIED PROCESS MADE EASY: PRACT, (figure 1.2) © Pearson Education, Inc. Reproduced by permission of Pearson Education, Inc.

Contents

6 Modeling

185

7 Visualization

249

12 Designing for Non-Functional Properties 447

13 Security and Trust 487

16 Standards   621

17 People, Roles, and Teams   655

Preface

Software architecture is the centerpiece of modern system development. The goal of architecture-centric development is the effective, efficient, competitive development of software *products*. The activities of development are anchored in the architecture. The goal of this text is to provide both student and professional a comprehensive treatment of architecture-centric development, instructing how to develop products and serving as a reference for the panoply of techniques, modeling notations, standards, and methods comprising the approach.

The text is intended for upper-division undergraduate and graduate courses in software architecture, software design, component-based software engineering, and distributed systems; the text may also be used in introductory as well as advanced software engineering courses. The targeted courses can be of different lengths, from a single ten-week quarter, to a fifteen-week semester, to a two-semester sequence. Both the breadth and depth of topics covered will vary depending on the exact nature of the course. Specific recommendations for instructors are provided below.

With such an ambitious goal, the text is extensive and may be approached in different ways. In this preface we guide the reader in the use of the book. Hence we briefly present here:

- The general view of software architecture taken by the book.
- The scope of the book.
- The intended audiences.
- Our assumptions regarding the technical maturity/background of the professionals and students who will use the book.
- Thoughts regarding selection of materials for use in the classroom, and by professionals, including systems engineers, software architects, and managers of software systems development.
- How instruction in the material may be supported by tools.
- A summary of each chapter.

SOFTWARE ARCHITECTURE

The text adopts a particular definition of software architecture: the set of principal design decisions governing a system. This definition is broad and stakeholder-centric. Nonetheless, a decidedly technical view of software architecture pervades the book. We believe that software architecture must help developers create real implemented systems. Software architecture without a tie to implementation, deployment, and long-term adaptation misses its potential by a wide mark and risks being irrelevant busywork; tolerated perhaps, but not treasured.

The comprehensive character of software architecture as presented in the text makes it, in our estimation, the central focus of software engineering. The text attempts to show architecture's critical role in software engineering, yet the text does not attempt to be a general software engineering reference. There are, for example, many important parts of software engineering not treated at all, such as source-code testing strategies, general project management, and development environments.

THE SCOPE OF THE BOOK

This book is characterized by breadth. Rather than focus on one method, notation, tool, or process, the book attempts to widely survey software development from an architectural perspective, putting many of these elements in context, comparing and contrasting them with one another. A reader should expect to gain a broad appreciation for the role of software architecture across the wide variety of activities that characterize the development of large, software-intensive systems.

Our assumption is that readers seek fundamental insights and knowledge to supplement their own experience, rather than canned solutions to specific problems (those, if they do exist, can most likely be found elsewhere). The text therefore focuses on overarching principles, general strategies, and broadly applicable techniques. It illustrates them with many specific examples from various domains. The text does not advocate a single approach and it is not a manual or advertisement for one—even the authors' own.

Audiences

The book attempts to address the needs of several audiences.

The *instructor* audience is supported by a detailed treatment of a broad spectrum of software architecture-related topics, from which different subsets can be selected for use in courses with specific foci. An instructor will be able to tailor the material provided in the book to both the length and the objective of a course. To date, the authors have used this text in five quarter-long (ten-week) courses and two semester-long (fifteen-week) courses, at both the undergraduate and graduate levels. The courses have focused on software engineering, software architecture, software design, software interoperability, and distributed systems. Both semester-long courses have used the entire text, while the quarter-long courses have relied on different selections of the chapters. The instructor using the text will be able to rely on a comprehensive set of lecture slides, solutions to end-of-chapter exercises, sample exams with solutions, and a tool suite that will be described below.

The *student* audience is supported with a presentation that is comprehensive, making relatively few assumptions about background knowledge and experience. We do assume that the student is generally familiar with the most basic elements of software engineering and programming. The order of the text and the way the material is presented makes the student the primary audience of the book—the other audiences will pick and choose material from various parts of the text.

The *professional* audience is supported with, for example, comprehensive treatment of the major modeling techniques, architectural description standards, and the way they are directly tied to the implementation of software products. Our perspective is not confined to some presumed ivory tower: The standards and notations include commercial, government, *and* research products. The text also attempts to provide, in the majority of chapters, specific guidance on how to achieve various goals, such as how to design to achieve specific system properties. References and examples draw from a wide range of industrial experience.

Professionals should expect to encounter realistic and frank assessments of the techniques, notations, and tools with which they are already familiar, while also being exposed to projects and approaches that provide valuable insights but are nonetheless not well-known in practitioners' circles.

The *systems engineer* will find that this book's perspective, while still focused on software, has implications that are quite a bit broader. Insights in this book will enable better understanding of the unique issues involved in the development of large *software* systems. Many of the insights, however, are applicable to *systems* development in general. Insights, notations, and methods from the systems engineering and systems architecture community are not ignored, and this book explores overlap between systems and software engineering throughout.

The systems and/or software development *manager* will find substantial material here that addresses the way in which architecture-centric development can shape and improve processes and organizations, especially with regard to the development of product families.

ASSUMPTIONS AND BACKGROUND

Depending on the sections of the book used for reference or in class, the necessary background varies. As a whole, however, the book assumes familiarity with the basics of software development. This includes the core ideas of software development activities and processes, notions of requirements, design, programming, and analysis and testing. The level of maturity required is, in some sense, only what would be acquired in a single, quarter- or semester-long introduction to software development/engineering. Appreciation for the problems of large-scale development is very useful. Proficiency in any particular programming language, development environment, or modeling tool such as UML is not required.

Additional experience will likely make it possible for certain readers to develop a deeper understanding and appreciation of specific topics. For example, the implementation chapter will be of most value to those with substantive training and experience in programming. Similarly, appreciating the discussion of deployment or product lines demands some level of understanding of how commercial development and product-and-revenue focused businesses work. However, none of the chapters presuppose an extensive background in the area on which they focus.

HOW THE BOOK CAN BE USED

The text is designed to be used as a textbook in formal classroom settings, both at the undergraduate and graduate levels. It can also be used as a reference for systems engineers, software architects, managers, and programmers. Chapters 1 through 5 present the critical concepts of software architecture. Chapter 5 also bridges to the next section, the nuts and bolts of applying the concepts, which encompasses Chapters 6 through 10. Chapters 11 through 17 treat associated issues: topics that may be critical in one development context, but not in another.

Classroom Usage

There is adequate material in the book for a year-long class at the master's degree level. The presentation does not presuppose that this is the normative case however. The authors have used material from the book in quarter-long and semester-long courses, including, as a primary text, an undergraduate software engineering course and a graduate software engineering course. The book, in its preprint form, has also been used at several other universities, including Drexel University, Southern Methodist University, Seattle University, and the University of Zurich.

Clearly, material has to be chosen based upon the level of the instruction and the length of the class. Nonetheless, a few comments are in order. The concepts section—Chapters 1 through 5—is essential to use of the book. The material in the subsequent chapters depends on these core concepts. How long it will take to cover those initial chapters, however, will vary significantly. The first chapter, for instance, will be a very quick read for the experienced. Similarly, Chapter 2 will be relatively quick for those with experience in software engineering, but will take a bit longer in an undergraduate class that has minimal prerequisites. Chapter 4 is a long chapter, but it covers a single, critical topic: how to go about designing a system. This chapter may thus be a major focus over many class sessions, especially for those with little training or experience in design.

Selection of materials from Chapters 6 through 10 will depend upon the level of the class, the course objectives, and the length of the class. The authors recommend a shallow treatment of all of them over a deep look at any individual chapters, but this is up to the instructor.

Several suggested pathways through the book, depending on course type and length, are as follows:

- A fifteen-week software architecture course—Chapters 1 through 17
- A ten-week software architecture course—Chapters 1 through 9, 11, 12, and 15
- A ten-week distributed systems course—Chapters 1 through 6, 7 through 15, and 17
- A fifteen-week software engineering course—Chapters 1 through 15 and 17
- A ten-week software engineering course—Chapters 1 through 6, 8, 9, 11, and 12

If the book is used as a primary text for a software engineering course, the instructor may want to supplement it with material covering topics such as software testing, OO design patterns, software engineering economics, and project management. The book can also be used as a companion text in a software analysis and quality assurance course; the relevant chapters would be Chapters 8, 12, 13 and 14.

A key issue the instructor will have to deal with is use of the exercises. Each chapter has a number of exercises listed. Software architecture is not a topic like algebra where numerous simple questions can be posed and the answers given in the back of the book. Software architecture concerns itself with design, with complex systems, and with long-lived products. Hence it is difficult to pose exercises that fit nicely into the constraints of a modern college class. Many of the exercises included in the text could be assigned as mini-projects. The instructor will thus have to tailor the scope of the assignments and provide guidance to the students regarding the level of detail expected in the answers. Assessing the answers similarly will require thought and discretion.

Use by Professionals

The authors have tried to include substantial material to make the book a superior reference for the professional. A theme running through the entire book is software reuse and, more generally, reuse of corporate and domain knowledge. Similarly, there is explicit reliance in the presented techniques on the use of frameworks to help achieve rapid system implementation. A wide range of modeling notations is discussed, and a complete chapter on standards is included to provide a thoughtful basis for choosing a notation or approach for a project. Similarly, the discussion of designing for non-functional properties is targeted at providing proven techniques capable of addressing these difficult issues. Chapter 4 on designing similarly will be useful as a reference to the professional. Without being a handbook of field techniques, it nevertheless presents a wide range of architectural styles and design techniques, with the styles summarized individually and in a comparison table to aid the professional in choosing the right technique for the job at hand.

Tool Support

Use of the book in the classroom or by professionals in practice does not require the use of any particular tool or programming language. Clearly, however, the subject is designing and building applications—products—and that only happens effectively in the presence of good tools. The professional may be constrained by the choice of the modeling notation required in a particular development context. If AADL, for example, is mandated as the architecture description language for a project, then the die is cast.

For those contexts where external constraints do not dictate, the instructor or reader is encouraged to use technologies that not only help model an architecture, but build implementations based upon those models. If modeling alone is supported, then the value of a tool over a simple boxes-and-arrows drawing tool rests upon the value obtained from analyses that can be performed on the model. If building real products is the goal, then a tool suite that addresses the full range of developers' needs is required.

To this latter end we encourage the book's users to use the ArchStudio tool suite, as it has been developed for this purpose. The tool can benefit faculty, students, and even professionals using this text. The tool is free, is integrated with the Eclipse development environment, and has been used in the classroom and in industry. A community of developers and users has formed around this project, with dozens of projects around the world using and contributing. Further details can be found on the project's Web site: www.isr.uci.edu/projects/archstudio/.

Chapter Summaries

Chapter 1: The Big Idea
The chapter introduces software architecture through discussion of three primary examples of its application: in the very large (the architecture of the World Wide Web), in the very small (pipe-and-filter on the desktop), and in the product/in the many (the Philips/Koala architecture for consumer electronics).

Chapter 2: Architectures in Context: The Reorientation of Software Engineering
The role of software architecture in the major activities of software engineering is explored, including application conception, design, implementation, and analysis. An architecture-centric perspective on development is presented.

Chapter 3: Basic Concepts
Definitions of the key terms and concepts are presented. The definitions build from the examples in the preceding chapters and form the foundation for the subsequent chapters.

Chapter 4: Designing Architectures

The concepts of the preceding chapters are made productive in this one. This chapter presents, at length, techniques and approaches for designing applications from an architecture-centric perspective. The central focus is on the ways in which refined experience may be used to guide new developments.

Chapter 5: Connectors

Connectors play a distinguished role in architecture-centric development. They are also, perhaps, the most unfamiliar concept to those unskilled in the art of system design. This chapter reveals the breadth and depth of the concept, and includes an extensive guide to the numerous techniques available.

Chapter 6: Modeling

This chapter surveys an extensive range of modeling notations used for capturing the design decisions that make up architecture. Notations from research and practice are examined, and the distinctive aspects of each notation are called out. A consistent running example application is used throughout the chapter to demonstrate each notation.

Chapter 7: Visualization

This chapter draws a distinction between how architectures are modeled—the syntax and semantics of how design decisions are documented—from how they are visualized. Visualization encompasses both depiction—how design decisions are presented—and interaction—the "user interface" through which stakeholders interact with those depictions. Various visualization approaches are surveyed and compared, along with techniques for constructing and integrating new visualizations.

Chapter 8: Analysis

One of the primary benefits of software architecture is that it can enable early assessment of a given system, before significant resources are invested in the system's implementation and deployment. This chapter provides a broad overview of the various analysis techniques that can be applied at the architectural level, their strengths, and limitations.

Chapter 9: Implementation

This chapter describes the problem of moving from architectural design decisions to implementation artifacts. Special attention is paid to the use of *architecture implementation frameworks*, special-purpose middleware that bridges the gap between architectural styles and existing platform services. Two complete implemented applications in alternative frameworks are presented with commentary.

Chapter 10: Deployment and Mobility

This chapter addresses deployment and mobility, two related topics that have become important in contemporary distributed, embedded, and pervasive systems. The objective of the chapter is not to provide a complete treatment of these two topics, but rather to isolate and focus on their characteristics from an explicit software architectural perspective.

Chapter 11: Applied Architectures and Styles

Several examples from "the practice" are explored, showing how various of the ideas in the preceding chapters have been applied to solve deep and commercially important problems. The architectures of the World Wide Web, Napster, Gnutella, Skype, BitTorrent, robotics systems, Google, and Akamai are discussed. The pedagogical goal is showing how multiple simple architectural approaches can effectively be combined.

Chapter 12: Designing for Non-Functional Properties

This chapter selects a set of non-functional properties that are frequently required of large and complex software systems: efficiency, complexity, scalability, adaptability, and dependability. The role of software architecture in achieving the desired level of each property is discussed, and many specific architectural design guidelines are provided and discussed.

Chapter 13: Security and Trust

Architecture-based techniques are presented for coping with security and trust needs in application system design. After a general introduction to security issues, attention is focused on architecture-based access control and reputation-based trust systems.

Chapter 14: Architectural Adaptation

The theme of this chapter is use of an architectural model to guide long-term system adaptation. A comprehensive conceptual framework for adaptation is presented, followed by consideration of numerous specific techniques for effecting adaptation and for designing applications to be accommodating of post-release adaptation.

Chapter 15: Domain-Specific Software Engineering

Architecture-centric development is perhaps most valuable when applied in the context of a specific domain, where reuse of hard-won engineering knowledge and principles can substantially reduce the amount of effort, cost, and risk involved in system development. This chapter surveys a variety of techniques for applying architecture-centric development within a domain, and ends with an extensive treatment of product-line architectures.

Chapter 16: Standards

A practicing architect or system developer is faced with a panoply of de facto and de jure standards—IEEE 1471, UML, SysML, DoDAF, RM-ODP, and so on. The chapter opens with a discussion of standards, how they are created and evolved, and how they can add value to development efforts. The remainder of the chapter surveys the most influential standards and attempts to put them in perspective, identifying their strengths and weaknesses explicitly.

Chapter 17: People, Roles, and Teams

An effective architect may need to possess many different skills, beyond just being a good software designer. An architect is an integral part of a larger organization, and may be one of several architects working on a project. The context within which software architects operate, and therefore their job description, can get quite complex. This chapter overviews the various roles software architects may play in a project and, more broadly, an organization.

Acknowledgments

The authors want to express their sincere appreciation to the large number of people who have been instrumental in bringing this text to fruition.

Hazel Asuncion was instrumental in the development of the various Lunar Lander examples, the domain model for the Lander, and was indefatigable as a reviewer. Girish Suryanarayana and Jie Ren were key contributors to the chapter on security and trust. Sam Malek and Marija Mikic-Rakic supplied several figures and a number of key insights in our discussions of deployment and mobility. Chris Mattmann provided the material for data-intensive connectors presented in Chapter 5. Joshua Garcia and Brian D'Souza contributed to the connector compatability matrix in the same chapter. George Edwards provided the example approach used in illustrating scenario-driven analysis in Chapter 8. John Georgas provided essential material for the discussion of robotics architectures in Chapter 11.

Kari Nies was an especially helpful and careful reviewer of the entire manuscript. The students of UC Irvine's Fall 2006 and Fall 2007 graduate classes in software engineering (Informatics 211) and USC's Spring 2007 and Spring 2008 graduate classes in software architectures (CSci 578) were early reviewers and commentators on key parts of the manuscript; their help is gratefully acknowledged. The undergraduates in UC Irvine's Spring 2008 class in Software Architectures, Distributed Systems, and Interoperability also were helpful. Similarly, the comments of Peyman Oriezy, Justin Erenkrantz, Roy Fielding, Scott Hendrickson, Michael Gorlick, David Woollard, Roshanak Roshandel, Daniel Popescu, George Edwards, and Chris Mattmann were very much appreciated.

Dan Sayre of John Wiley and Sons was instrumental in shepherding three first-time authors through the harrowing and often confusing process of developing and writing a textbook. Our interactions with him convinced us that Wiley was the right place for this book. Our subsequent interactions with the editorial and production staff confirmed this positive experience. Heather Johnson and the copy editor provided pleasant and extremely helpful service, Lee Goldstein's book design skills were much appreciated and she was a pleasure to work with. Special thanks to Lyrica Taylor for recommending the painting by Thomas Cole for the cover and writing the explanatory text.

External reviewers included Professors George Heineman (Worcester Polytechnic Institute) and Anthony I. Wasserman (Carnegie-Mellon West), both of whom provided particularly helpful suggestions and recommendations. Professors André van der Hoek (UC Irvine), Jeff Kramer (Imperial College London), Hans van Vliet (Vrije Universiteit), Alexander Wolf (Imperial College London), LiGuo Huang (Southern Methodist University), Hossein Saiedian (University of Kansas), Giuseppe Valetto (Drexel University), Tony Sullivan (University of Texas, Dallas), and John McGregor (Clemson University) also provided important guidance. Several anonymous reviewers also contributed key insights for the work, as did MIT Press's Robert Prior.

University College London deserves special thanks for hosting Taylor's sabbatical in 2005–2006, during which time the initial manuscript was substantially developed. A wonderful flat in Hampstead helped, too.

From the technical side, production of the book was dependent upon the services of Subversion for close to 1,000 commits of the manuscript. OmniGraffle was used for the majority of the diagrams; Skype kept us in touch while the authors were separated by thousands of miles.

The support of the National Science Foundation through grants CNS-0438996, CCF-0430066, CCF-0524033, CCR-9985441, ITR-0312780, and CSR-0509539, The Boeing Company, Bosch, the Jet Propulsion Laboratory, and IBM is gratefully acknowledged. Eric Dashofy would like to express his personal thanks to Dr. Michael and Julie Penley and the ARCS Foundation, Orange County Chapter, for their generous support.

—Richard N. Taylor, Nenad Medvidović, and Eric M. Dashofy

About the Authors

Richard N. Taylor is a Professor of Information and Computer Sciences at the University of California, Irvine, in the Department of Informatics. He received a Ph.D. degree in computer science from the University of Colorado at Boulder in 1980. Professor Taylor is Director of the Institute for Software Research, which is dedicated to fostering innovative basic and applied research in software and information technologies through partnerships with industry and government. He has taught courses at the graduate and undergraduate levels in software engineering, software design, project development, and software engineering environments. He is the author of more than 100 journal and conference publications and has chaired the dissertation committees of over twenty Ph.D. graduates. He has served as chairman of ACM's Special Interest Group on Software Engineering, SIGSOFT, and as chairman of the steering committee for the International Conference on Software Engineering (ICSE). He has served as an expert witness in several intellectual property disputes. Taylor was a 1985 recipient of a Presidential Young Investigator Award. In 1998, he was recognized as an ACM Fellow and in 2005 was awarded the ACM SIGSOFT Distinguished Service Award.

Nenad Medvidović is an Associate Professor in the Computer Science Department at the University of Southern California. He received his Ph.D. in 1999 from the Department of Information and Computer Science at the University of California, Irvine. As of January 1, 2009, he is the Director of the USC Center for Systems and Software Engineering (CSSE). Medvidović has taught undergraduate, graduate, and industry courses in software engineering, software architecture, software engineering for embedded systems, and formal methods. He has published more than 100 journal and conference papers and has chaired the dissertation committees of seven Ph.D. graduates. Along with Richard N. Taylor and Peyman Oreizy, he co-authored the ICSE 1998 paper titled, "Architecture-Based Runtime Software Evolution," which in 2008 was named that conference's most influential paper. Professors Medvidović and Taylor's paper, "A Classification and Comparison Framework for Software Architecture Description Languages," was recognized by the Elsevier Information and Software Technology Journal as the most cited journal article in software engineering published in 2000. Medvidović served as a consultant to NASA's Jet Propulsion Laboratory in creating their software architect training program (SWAP). He is a recipient of the National Science Foundation CAREER award, the Okawa Foundation Research Grant, and the IBM Real-Time Innovation Award.

Eric M. Dashofy is a senior member of the technical staff in the Computer Systems Research Department at The Aerospace Corporation in El Segundo, CA. He received his Ph.D. in 2007 from the Donald Bren School of Information and Computer Sciences at the University of California, Irvine. He has written numerous technical publications in software engineering and architecture. He is the lead developer of the ArchStudio architecture-centric software development environment, an open-source, Eclipse-based tool set for modeling, visualizing, analyzing, and implementing architecture-based software systems. He also co-authored the xADL 2.0 architecture description language, upon which ArchStudio is based. His current work focuses on software architecture, high-performance computing, and wireless sensor networks of embedded devices.

1

The Big Idea

The study of software architecture is the study of how software systems are designed and built. A system's architecture is the set of principal design decisions made during its development and any subsequent evolution. As a subject, architecture is the proper primary focus of software engineering, for the production of high-quality, successful products is dependent upon those principal decisions.

An architecture-centric approach to software development places an emphasis on *design* that pervades the activity from the very beginning. Design quality correlates well with software quality—it would be extremely unusual to find a high-quality software system with a poor design. The practice of architecture-centric development can also enable the creation of cost-effective families of software products that can dominate an application sector over an extended period of time. Good design practices can leverage the lessons of experience and provide strategies for effectively meeting a wide range of needs.

This chapter introduces the central ideas of software architecture. It does so by first exploring the analogy between the architecture of buildings and the architecture of software. Software architecture, and the power that comes from making it the centerpiece of system development, is then illustrated three ways. First, the architectural ideas underpinning the World Wide Web are explored—software architecture "in the very large." Second, the ideas are explored on the desktop—software architecture in the small. Third, the central role of architectures in enabling successful product families is explored, using consumer electronics as the application domain. We deliberately omit most technical details, seeking rather to instill a sense of "the big idea."

1.1 THE POWER OF ANALOGY: THE ARCHITECTURE OF BUILDINGS

The discipline of architecture, that is, the design and construction of buildings, offers a rich base of concepts from which software architecture, and more generally, software engineering has drawn. The analogy between the design and construction of buildings and the design and construction of software is strong and readily apprehended, since we all have substantial experience in living in and around buildings and in seeing them built.

Software engineering textbooks typically use this analogy to motivate the phases of the traditional software life cycle. In a highly simplified and idealized conception of architecture, requirements for a building are collected, a design is created to satisfy those requirements, the design is refined to yield elaborate blueprints, construction is based on the blueprints, and the resulting structure is then occupied and used. So, notionally, in the software domain, requirements are specified, a high-level design is created, detailed algorithms are developed based upon that design, code is written to implement the algorithms, and finally the system is deployed and used.

The idealized summary above of how buildings come to be is almost trivial, but offers several insights reflected in the software domain. For instance, the architectural process has as its focus the satisfaction of the future occupant's needs. It allows for specialization of labor: The designer of the structure need not be the contractor who performs the actual construction. The process has many intermediate points where plans and progress may be reviewed. Thus there is the corresponding simplistic view of software development: Specification of a system's requirements precedes its design; that design is created by specialists, not by the ultimate users of a system. Actual programming may be contracted out, even sent offshore. Prototypes and mock-ups created at various points during development enable the customer to periodically assess whether the emerging system will indeed meet identified needs.

A more serious consideration of architecture, however, reveals deeper insights. First and perhaps foremost is the very conception of a building having an architecture, where that architecture is a concept separate from, but inextricably linked to, the physical structure itself. A building's architecture, that is, its major elements, their composition, and arrangement, can be described, discussed, and compared with those of other buildings. The architecture that was in the mind of the architect early in the development process can be compared with the architecture of whatever physical structure emerged from the construction process. So, too, as we will shortly describe, the principal design decisions characterizing a software application—that is, its architecture—exist independently from, but linked to, the code that ostensibly implements that architecture.

In the first century AD, the Roman author Marcus Vitruvius Pollio, best known as Vitruvius, produced a famous treatise on architecture, entitled *De Architectura*. This handbook contains numerous admonitions, opinions, and observations about architecture and architects that remain, two thousand years later, insightful and worth considering. He begins his treatise in a remarkable place, considering the practice and the theory of architecture. Both are necessary for the professional. Consider his words:

> Practice is the frequent and continued contemplation of the mode of executing any given work, or of the mere operation of the hands, for the conversion of the material in the best and readiest way. Theory is the result of that reasoning which demonstrates and explains that the material wrought has been so converted as to answer the end proposed. Vitruvius I, 1, 1

(All Vitruvius quotes in this text are from Pollio)
Note that practice is not the mere "doing," but involves contemplation of what is done.

Practice *and* Theory

A second insight is that properties of structures are induced by the design of their architectures. For instance, a medieval castle with high, thick walls and narrow or nonexistent windows is designed that way so that it has excellent defensive properties (as long as attackers are armed only with swords and arrows). So, too, as we will see, properties of software applications, such as resilience in the face of particular types of security attacks, are determined by the design of their architectures.

All these should possess strength, utility, and beauty. Strength arises from carrying down the foundations to a good solid bottom, and from making a proper choice of materials without parsimony. Utility arises from a judicious distribution of the parts, so that their purposes be duly answered, and that each have its proper situation. Beauty is produced by the pleasing appearance and good taste of the whole, and by the dimensions of all the parts being duly proportioned to each other. Vitruvius I, 3, 2

Strength, Utility, and Beauty: The Qualities Obtained from Good Architecture

A third insight is recognition of the distinctive role and character of an architect, the person responsible for the creation of the architecture. The discipline of architecture has long recognized that architects require very broad training. While competence in aspects of engineering is necessary, much more than that is required. A fine sense of aesthetics and a deep understanding of how people work, play, eat, and live are essential in creating buildings that are enjoyed, satisfy their occupants, and perform effectively over the seasons and through the years. In a like manner, simple skill in programming is not sufficient for the creation of complex software applications that people can effectively employ.

An architect should be ingenious, and apt in the acquisition of knowledge. Deficient in either of these qualities, he cannot be a perfect master. He should be a good writer, a skillful draftsman, versed in geometry and optics, expert at figures, acquainted with history, informed on the principles of natural and moral philosophy, somewhat of a musician, not ignorant of the sciences

Vitruvius on Qualifications of an Architect

both of law and physic, nor of the motions, laws, and relations to each other, of the heavenly bodies. Vitruvius, I, 1, 3

A fourth insight is that process is not as important as architecture. This is not to say that process is unimportant. On the contrary, architects and construction companies clearly follow and depend upon standard processes to guide their daily activities and ensure that all aspects of the design and build activities are addressed. But there is never any question that the product—the architecture—is the central focus. Simply following a standard process will not guarantee that a successful building will emerge, meeting the needs of its owners and occupants. The architects and engineers responsible for the structure must keep its design and qualities at the forefront; process is present to serve those ends, not to be an end in itself.

A fifth insight is that architecture has matured over the years into a discipline: A body of knowledge exists about how to create a wide range of buildings to meet many types of needs. It is not simply a discipline of basic principles and generic development processes, however. If every building had to be designed from first principles and the properties of materials had to be rediscovered for each new project, then most of us would be wet and shivering with the sky for our roof.

The discipline of architectural engineering has captured the experiences and lessons of previous generations so that the process of designing, for instance, a new suburban home is much like the process of designing a thousand other homes. This is not to say that the homes are identical; rather, within the broad concept of "suburban home" some basics are established and points of allowable variation are known. Where there is commonality between two homes, great efficiencies can be realized through reuse of knowledge, reuse of subsystem design, reuse of tools, and the benefits that come from standardized materials, parts, and sizes. While anyone who has ever endeavored to build a custom home would certainly dispute that the process is efficient compared to the activity of designing from a truly clean slate, the craft works very well. So, too, as the ensuing chapters of this book will demonstrate, software architecture is quickly maturing into a robust discipline, leveraging the knowledge gained through a myriad of system development experiences.

One fundamental way in which the experiences and lessons from previous generations of architects and building-dwellers has been captured is summed up in the notion of *architectural styles*—an insight that has powerful application in the domain of software. The phrases "Roman villa," "Gothic cathedral," "ranch-style tract home," "Swiss chalet," and "New York skyscraper" each characterize types of buildings that have various features in common. Ranch-style tract homes, for instance, are single-story residences with low roofs; Swiss chalets are usually two to four stories, traditionally made of timber, have steep roofs, and large sheltered balconies. New York skyscrapers have many dozens of stories, have steel frames, make superb use of small footprint building areas, and offer hundreds of thousands of square meters of floor space. Roman villas suit a Mediterranean climate, and so on.

The development of an architectural style over time reflects the knowledge and experience gained by the builders and occupants as they try to meet a common set of requirements and accommodate the constraints of the local topography, weather, available building materials, tools, and labor. Ranch-style houses, such as those prevalent in Southern California, can be inexpensively built if lumber for framing is readily available, function very well in earthquake-prone areas, and are excellent for individuals who cannot climb stairs. Swiss chalets work well in areas with heavy snowfall, with the steep roofs assisting in minimizing the structural load caused by the snow. Therefore an approach that works well for providing homes in Southern California is not necessarily going to be appropriate for providing homes in Switzerland, or vice versa. But within Southern California a wide variety of site-suitable houses can be successfully built in a cost-effective manner by those architects skilled in the local idioms and materials.

> [Private buildings] are properly designed, when due regard is had to the country and climate in which they are erected. For the method of building which is suited to Egypt would be very improper in Spain, and that in use in Pontus would be absurd at Rome: so in other parts of the world a style suitable to one climate, would be very unsuitable to another: for one part of the world is under the sun's course, another is distant from it, and another, between the two, is temperate. Vitruvius, VI, 1, 1

Vitruvius on Styles

One way architectural styles can be summed up is as a set of constraints—constraints put upon development in order to elicit particular desirable qualities. For example, the Swiss chalet style has a constraint that the roofs have steep slopes; the quality elicited is that chalets tend to do well in areas of heavy snowfall. The suburban ranch style has a constraint that commodity components be used; the quality being that the houses are cheaper to build and easier to fix than custom homes. The Gothic style constrains one to building with stone, stained glass, and high fluted vaults; the qualities elicited are that the buildings are long-lived, instructional, and inspirational.

Characterized in more constructive terms, styles offer the architect a wide range of solutions, techniques, and palettes of compatible materials, colors, and sizes. Rather than spending a large amount of time searching through an unbounded space of alternatives, by working within a style an architect can spend that same amount of time refining, customizing, and perfecting a particular design.

The concept of architectural styles carries over very powerfully into the domain of software. As we will illustrate in the remainder of this chapter and then throughout the book, styles are essential tools for architects to master, for they are a major point of intellectual leverage in the task of creating complex software systems.

1.1.1 Limitations of the Analogy

Before pressing on to the detailed consideration of architectures, styles, and their use in software systems development, a few cautionary words are in order with regard to the use of the analogy to building architectures. As with any analogy, it has limitations.

First, we know a lot about buildings. That is, since birth we all have experienced and learned about buildings. As a result, we have a well-developed intuition as to what kinds of buildings can and cannot be built, and what is appropriate for a given need and situation. Our intuitions for software are not nearly so well-developed and hence we must be more methodical and more analytical in our approach.

Second, the essential nature of the software medium is fundamentally different from the materials and media of building architecture. You can discern much of a building's architecture just by looking at it. With software the problem is much more difficult. Software is intrinsically intangible; at core it is an abstract entity and we only work with various representations of it. This implies that software is more difficult to measure and analyze, making it more difficult to evaluate the various qualities of designs and measure progress towards completion.

Third, software is more malleable than physical building materials, offering the possibility of types of change unthinkable in a physical domain. The building analogy is thus a poor source of ideas for dealing with change, since buildings accommodate change with difficulty[1].

There are additional problems with the analogy:

- There is no software construction industry in the same degree that there is for buildings. The building industry has substantial substructure, reflecting numerous specializations, skill sets, training paths, corporate organizations, standards bodies, and regulations. While the software industry has some structure, including that seen in offshore development practices, it is much less differentiated than the building industry.

- The discipline of architecture does not have anything akin to the issue of deployment as found in software: Software is built one place, but deployed for use in many places, often with specialization and localization. Manufactured buildings, otherwise known as trailers, are somewhat similar, but still there is no corresponding notion to dynamic distributed, mobile architectures, as there is with software.

- Software is a machine; buildings are not (notwithstanding Le Corbusier's declaration that, "A house is a machine for living in"). The dynamic character of software—the observation that led to Edsger Dijkstra's famous "**goto** statement considered harmful" paper (Dijkstra 1968), provides a profoundly difficult challenge to designers, for which there is no counterpart in building design.

Despite these limitations—and others—the analogy between the architecture of buildings and software is strong and instructive. The focus on architecture is critical in the design of buildings; such a focus is similarly powerful for software. Subsequent sections of this chapter will demonstrate this in the large, in the small, and in the crucible of industry. Before considering these examples, however, we summarize our main themes in the next section.

1.1.2   So, What's the Big Idea?

The big idea is that software architecture must be at the very heart of software systems design and development. It must be in the foreground, more than process, more than analysis, and certainly more than programming. Only by giving adequate attention and prominence to the architecture of a software system, over its entire lifespan, can that system's development and long-term evolution be effective or efficient in any meaningful sense. Indeed, we will see that for any application of significant size or complexity, its architecture must be considered in advance, just as the successful creation of a large building requires consideration of its architecture in advance of construction.

---

[1] This topic will be explored in more detail in Chapter 14. See also (Brand, 1994).

Furthermore, the insights presented above about architecture, architects, and especially, architectural styles offer substantial intellectual leverage in the creation of software systems, but demand careful study, good tools, and disciplined use to yield their substantial potential benefits.

Giving preeminence to architecture offers the potential for realizing:

- Intellectual control
- Conceptual integrity
- An adequate and effective basis for reuse—of knowledge, experience, designs, and code
- Effective project communication
- Management of a set of related variant systems

Note the phrase above about directing "attention and prominence to the architecture of a software system, *over its entire lifespan.*" A limited-term focus on software architecture will not yield significant benefits. Just as the concept of architecture, or the involvement of an architect, in a building project is no guarantee that a successful building will be created, so it is for software. Shortcomings in the construction process—whether of buildings or of software—can cause the built system to deviate from its intended architecture, possibly with disastrous consequences. Such shortcomings can be avoided, however, and we will discuss techniques specifically intended to ensure that the implemented system is, and remains, faithful to its intended architecture.

Finally, note that by saying adequate attention must be given to a software system's architecture we are not advocating the creation of something wholly new: All software systems have an architecture. Just as every building has an architecture and at least one architect, so does software. Simply stating that a building or a program has an architecture or an architect does not imply much. There are good architectures, bad architectures, elegant ones, and curious ones. So it is with software. An application's structure may be elegant and effective or clumsy and dysfunctional. Our objective in the coming pages is to give the reader the skills necessary to ensure that applications have good, elegant, and effective architectures. The following sections proceed by considering some outstanding examples of the discipline of software architecture, well applied.

1.2 THE POWER AND NECESSITY OF BIG IDEAS: THE ARCHITECTURE OF THE WEB

A primary example of the power of architecture can be seen in an application all readers of this book are familiar with: the World Wide Web. Think for a moment: What *is* the Web? How is it built? How do you explain the Web to a child? If you have a business and want to have a Web-based e-commerce presence, how do you go about designing the software for your site, including determining how your site will interact with your customers' machines? It is *architecture* that offers the vocabulary and the means for answering these questions. It is the particular *architectural style* of the Web that constrains (and thereby helps) you in producing an e-commerce system that "plays well" with others.

Let's answer some of the questions above. What is the Web? In one view, focusing on the user's perception, the Web is a dynamic set of relationships among collections of

Figure 1-1.
*A document
hypertext.*

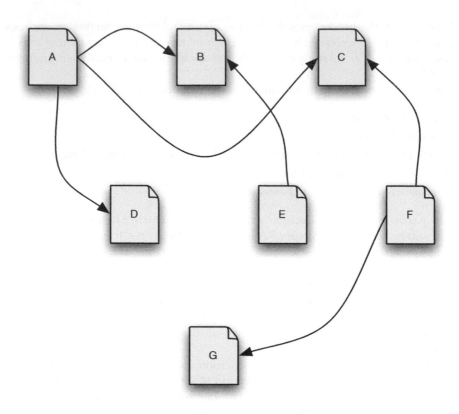

information. In another view, focusing on coarse-grained aspects of the Web's structure, the Web is a dynamic collection of independently owned and operated machines, located around the world, which interact across computer networks. In another view, taking the perspective of an application developer, it is a collection of independently written programs that interact with each other according to rules specified in the HTTP, URI, MIME, and HTML standards.

Considering these perspectives in turn, the view of the Web as a collection of interrelated pieces of information is illustrated in Figure 1-1.

In the figure documents labeled A to G are shown as independent entities, but with explicit relationships among them. For instance, if document A is a biography of the author C. S. Lewis, then the arrow to document D might represent a view of The Kilns, the house in Oxford where Lewis lived for many years, as imaged by a webcam. The arrow to document C from document A might represent a reference to a description of Oxfordshire, the county in which The Kilns is found. The other documents shown might represent the text of some of the many books that Lewis wrote, such as *The Lion, the Witch and the Wardrobe*. We, as users of the Web, can understand Figure 1-1's mini-Web as set of interrelated documents and a Web browser, such as Safari or Internet Explorer, as a vehicle for viewing the documents and navigating among them. In short, this mini-Web is known as a *hypertext* and the viewing and shifting of focus from one document to the next as browsing, or surfing, this hypertext.

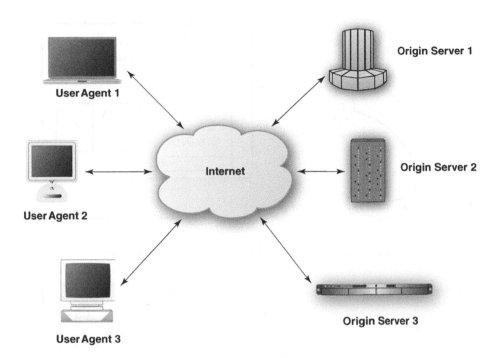

Figure 1-2.
*A machine view
of a small part of
the World Wide
Web.*

The view illustrated in Figure 1-1 is one in which the data of the Web and the relationships among the data are shown. In contrast, Figure 1-2 shows the Web as a collection of computers interconnected through the Internet. The machines are shown here as being of two kinds: *user agents* and *origin servers*. User agents are, for instance, desktop and laptop machines on which a Web browser is running. Origin servers are machines that serve as the permanent repositories of information, such as the aforementioned documents pertaining to C. S. Lewis. In this view, the Web is understood as a physical set of machines whereby a user at a user agent computer can access information from the origin servers. The view is quite sketchy, however, and does not present any real insight into how the information is obtained by the user agents or how the information in one document is related to information in another. Nonetheless, the abstraction it presents is accurate insofar as it goes, and can be useful in explaining some Web concepts.

A third view of the Web is shown in Figure 1-3. In this view, the user agents and origin servers of Figure 1-2 are once again shown, but now the location of documents A to G are shown. The figure also shows a set of specific interactions among two of the user agents and two of the origin servers, corresponding to a particular pattern of accessing the C. S. Lewis hypertext. In this example, User Agent 1 requests, by means of the HTTP method GET, a copy of document A, a biography of Lewis. This interaction is shown in the diagram by the arrow marked 1. A representation, or "copy," of the biography is returned, shown as the arrow marked 2. Since the biography has within it a hypertext reference (href) to document D, a JPEG of The Kilns, User Agent 1 issues another GET, this time to machine.usc.edu, to obtain the picture. This request is marked 3 in the diagram. A copy of the image is returned, as shown by the arrow marked 4. Further interactions between user agents and servers are shown in the diagram as interactions 5 and 6.

Figure 1-3.
*Agents and origin
servers
interacting
according to the
HTTP protocol,
as users peruse
the Web.*

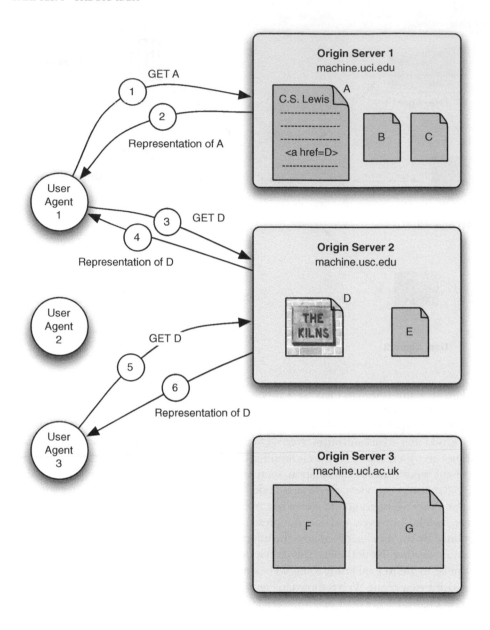

These three diagrams illustrate the Web and provide an indication of how it works, but clearly there is much, much more to it. These diagrams use a very simple, limited set of information to represent the billions of pages of information available on the Web, and a set of less than a dozen machines to represent the millions of machines interacting at any given instant over the Internet. So, can we really say that these diagrams explain how the Web works? Clearly not. A much more general understanding of the Web can be given as a set of definitions and constraints on how these billions of documents interrelate and millions of machines interact,[2] as follows:

- The Web is a collection of *resources*, each of which can be identified by a uniform resource locator, or URL. A standard specifies the legal syntax of a URL.
- Each resource denotes, informally, some information. The information may be, for example, a document, an image, a time-varying service (for example, "today's weather in Los Angeles"), a collection of other resources, and so on.
- URLs can be used to determine the identity of a machine on the Internet, known as an *origin server*, where the value of the resource may be ascertained.
- Communication is initiated by clients, known as *user agents* who make requests of servers. Web browsers are common instances of user agents.
- Resources can be manipulated through their *representations*. For instance, a resource may be updated by a user agent sending a new representation of that resource to the origin server that holds that information. Similarly a resource may be viewed by a user agent obtaining a representation of that resource from an origin server and displaying that representation on a monitor. HTML is a very common representation language used on the Web.
- All communication among user agents and origin servers must be performed in accordance with a simple, common protocol (HTTP). Communicating according to HTTP requires that the parties implement a few primitive operations, such as GET and POST.
- All communication between user agents and origin servers must be context-free. That is, an origin server must be able to respond correctly to a user agent's request based solely on information contained in the request, and not require maintenance of a history of interactions between that user agent and the origin server. (This is sometimes known as "stateless interactions.")

To illustrate, in the example above, documents A to G are resources; machines machine.uci.edu and machine.usc.edu running the Apache Web server are example origin servers. User agents could be personal laptops running a Web browser such as Internet Explorer. Representations include a copy of the HTML of Lewis's biography, and a JPEG of the current view of The Kilns as imaged by a webcam.

Describing the rules by which the various parts of the Web work and interact—its architectural *style*—provides the basis for understanding the Web independent of its configuration or actions at any particular instant. Such description enables us to effectively reason about how the Web works and guides in determining what must be done to incorporate new information or new machines into the Web. While the list above is not complete (more details are provided later in Chapter 11 and in various references) it is nonetheless representative and substantive. This approach to understanding the Web is clearly superior to one based upon the code—trying to state every detail of every machine and every piece of software engaged in the Web at one particular time.

A number of critical observations are apparent:

- The architecture of the Web is wholly separate from the code that implements its various elements. Indeed, to understand the Web, the architecture is the *only* effective

---

[2] This characterization still omits many details! A more comprehensive description appears in Chapter 11.

reference point. The architecture is the set of principal design decisions that determine the key elements of the Web and their interrelationships. These decisions are at an abstraction level above that of the source code, and are thus conducive to understanding the entire system at the application level.

- There is no single piece of code that "implements the architecture." The Web is "implemented" by Web servers of various design, browsers of various design, proxies, routers, and network infrastructure. Just looking at any single piece of code, or even all the code on any single machine, will not explain the Web's structure; rather, the architecture is the only adequate guide to understanding the whole.
- There are multiple equivalent (with respect to the architecture) pieces of code that exist and implement the various components of the architecture. The architectural style of the Web constrains the code in some respects, saying how a given piece must work with respect to the other elements of the architecture, but substantial freedom for coding the internals of an element is present. Thus, we see many different browsers from different vendors, offering a variety of individual advantages, but insofar as the browsers relate to the rest of the Web, they are equivalent.
- The stylistic constraints that constitute the definition of the Web's style are not necessarily apparent in the code, but the effects of the constraints as implemented in all the components are evident in the Web.

These observations are profound, and begin to indicate the role of architecture in the Web. But the most important questions of all remain:

- Why were these particular decisions made?
- Why were these decisions important and not others?
- Why did similar systems that made slightly different decisions fail, when the Web is such a wild success?

These questions can be answered only when looking at the Web from an architectural perspective, and indeed they cut straight to the heart of architecture. Chapter 11 discusses how the Web's designers targeted a particular set of qualities—the ones that make the Web so successful—and then made decisions specifically to imbue the Web with those qualities. That chapter will discuss the Web and its underlying style, REST (REpresentational State Transfer), in more detail, and show how the style is based upon and derivative from a large set of simpler styles.

The take-away message here is that one of the world's most successful software systems is understood adequately only from an architectural vantage point. The development of the Web, the maturation of the HTTP/1.1 protocol, and the implementation of its core elements were all driven by architectural understandings and principles. Without the rock of this abstraction it is unlikely the Web would have survived past its first two or three years of existence.

1.3 THE POWER OF ARCHITECTURE IN THE SMALL: ARCHITECTURE ON THE DESKTOP

One need not look at large complex applications, such as the Web, to find interesting architectures or to find applications where a focus on architectures has a big payoff.

Architectures underlie the simplest applications, and architectural concepts provide the conceptual power behind, for example, the nearly ubiquitous command-line shell programs. Found on virtually every platform, including Mac OS X, Linux, Windows, and the Unix platforms where the concepts originated, such scripts enable the user to quickly and easily compose new applications from preexisting components called filters (which happen to be complete executable programs in their own right), just by following some simple rules. For example, the following application creates a sorted list of all the files in the directory named invoices whose names include the character string "August":

```
ls invoices | grep —e August | sort
```

At first blush this may not seem to be an application, since we can visually discern how the functionality is provided from piece-parts, but that is indeed what it is. To understand how this application works and how it is built, one must understand in general what filters and pipes are, understand what the specific filters used in building this application do, and finally, reason about how these particular filters are configured, using the pipes, to form this application.

First, a *filter* is a program that takes a stream of text characters as its input and produces a stream of characters as its output. A filter's processing may be controlled by a set of parameters. A *pipe* is a way of connecting two filters, in which the character stream output from the first filter is routed to the character stream input of the second filter.

In the application above, three filter programs are used: `ls`, `grep`, and `sort`. The `sort` filter examines its input stream, noting how the stream is divided into lines of text by an end-of-line character, and produces on its output stream those same lines of text, but in sorted order. While `sort` may be given optional parameters to control, for instance, whether the lines are sorted in ascending or descending order, in the application above no parameters are provided, so the default behavior is to sort in ascending order.

The `grep` filter examines its input character stream for lines (that is, portions of the input character stream demarcated by end-of-line characters) that contain a substring matching a string value provided as a parameter. In the application above, the —e parameter is used to provide the string value ("August") for which `grep` is to search. `grep` produces as its output stream only those lines that contain the designated search string.

The `ls` filter does not process an incoming stream of characters; instead it communicates with the operating system to obtain the names of files in a named directory (or "folder"). `ls` then produces, as its output stream, a sequence of characters that are the textual names of the files in the directory designated by the command-line parameters to `ls`, with each file name followed by an end-of-line character.

With this understanding of filters as programs that read and produce character streams, pipes as ways of hooking up filters by routing the character streams, and the functioning of each of the three filters used (listing file names, looking for the presence of a particular substring, and sorting), it is easy to understand how the application above works. `ls` produces a textual list of files found in the `invoices` directory. A pipe (shown on the command line as a vertical bar) routes this output to the input of `grep`. `grep` then examines those names to identify any containing the substring "August," and produces only those names as its output stream. A second pipe routes that output stream on to `sort`, which then sorts the file names in ascending order, producing that ordered listing as its (and the application's) output.

The critical observation here is that this application's structure can be understood on the basis of a very few rules. Given understanding of that structure and knowledge of the functioning of the individual filters, the function of the complete application can be understood. Knowledge of those same rules and of the functioning of a few dozen, preexisting, basic filter programs allows one to understand hundreds of other useful applications. Similarly, a developer may readily create new applications based upon those same rules and knowledge of the filters.

Common Unix Filter Programs

These commonly used Unix filter programs can be used individually or combined into pipe-and-filter architectures to create many useful applications. Consult your system's manual pages for detailed instructions on how to use them (try ``man man`` in a terminal window).

ls: List the names of files within a directory.

grep: Produce lines on output that match a specified pattern, where that pattern is described as a regular expression.

sort: Sort all input lines according to a set of parameters (for example, for ascending or descending order).

cat: Concatenate files specified by parameters to the output stream.

sed: Read the input stream, modify (edit) it according to specified parameters, and write the result to the output.

awk: Match patterns in the input stream and perform specified operations upon a match.

head: List the first n lines of the input on the output.

tail: List the last n lines of the input.

uniq: Copy unique input lines to the output.

less: Incrementally list the input on the output, with controls determining how much information to list at a given time.

lpr: Send input to the printer.

cut: Select portions of each input line and write them to the output.

man: Format and display the on-line manual pages for a specified command to the output.

tee: Copy the input to the output, plus make a copy in zero or more specified files.

A complex example:

```
grep HTTP_USER_AGENT httpd_state_log | cut -f 2- |
grep -v 'via Gateway' | grep -v 'via proxy gateway'
| sort | uniq -c | sort -nr | head -5
```

This produces the top five browsers (user agents) from a WWW state log called "httpd_state_log" eliminating all proxy user agent strings.

The particular set of rules at work here defines an architectural style known, not surprisingly, as pipe-and-filter. Part of the beauty of pipe-and-filter is that because of its simplicity end users can develop applications without ever being trained as programmers. It is akin to working with Lego blocks, or Tinker Toys: Once you understand how to fit the parts together and the different kinds of functions that the various piece-parts are capable of performing, the creative task of assembling the pieces into a new design can proceed quickly and effectively. Training in the details of programming is not required; the power of a simple architectural concept can be comprehended and applied by a broad audience.

Though the style is very simple, note that use of it is not confined to the use of the standard filter programs found in Unix, Linux, and the other operating systems that support pipe-and-filter; a developer may create a program that operates by reading and writing a character stream and then use that filter/program in conjunction with others in a pipe-and-filter–based application. Similarly, the style is not confined to applications written in the command-line notation, though that notation is certainly common.

In addition to pipe-and-filter, a wide variety of other simple architectural styles exist. Most of these will be familiar to experienced developers: layered system, main program and subroutines, object-oriented, implicit invocation, and blackboard. A detailed discussion appears in Chapter 4. Developers can choose among these styles, and a vast array of others, based upon the nature of the problem to be solved and the qualities desired in the solution. For instance, pipe-and-filter applications are readily understandable, run on almost any operating system, and run efficiently when the problem (and its structuring in pipe-and-filter) admits concurrency. On the other hand, pipe-and-filter requires all communication between filters to be serialized into character streams; thus, if a graph data structure has to be passed from one filter to another it must first be serialized into a textual stream, transferred across the pipe, and then rebuilt into the graph data structure by the next filter. The pipes ensure syntactic compatibility between the filters, but do nothing to ensure semantic compatibility.

1.4 THE POWER OF ARCHITECTURE IN BUSINESS: PRODUCTIVITY AND PRODUCT LINES

The discussion of the World Wide Web in Section 1.2 illustrated how architecture is a critical enabler for the development of large-scale, complex systems. The discussion of the pipe-and-filter style in Section 1.3 showed how architectural concepts can make effective the development of even online applications, providing the leverage needed for exploiting the power of a library of reusable components (in particular, Unix filters). Architectures are also critical enablers for developing *product families*, a key element of many business strategies.

Product families are sets of independent programs that have a significant measure of commonality in their constituent components and structure. The key concepts are shown in the following example. Any purchaser of consumer electronics, such as televisions, is aware that myriad choices are available. Even from a single manufacturer, the consumer is faced with a range of sizes and features that allows one to purchase a device meeting a very particular set of requirements. Perhaps a purchaser wants a 35-inch HDTV with a built-in DVD player for the North American market. Such a device might contain upwards of a million lines of embedded software. This particular television/DVD player will be very similar to a 35-inch HDTV without the DVD player, and also to a 35-inch HDTV with a built-in DVD player for the European market, where the TV must be able to handle DVB-T broadcasts, rather than North America's ATSC format. Each of these closely related televisions will have a million or more lines of code embedded within them.

The economic challenge from the manufacturer's point of view is to produce the wide range of products that a worldwide market of sophisticated consumers demands while simultaneously exploiting the commonalities among members of a product family. Reusing structure, behaviors, and component implementations is increasingly important to successful business practice because:

- It simplifies the software development task: Existing design- and implementation-level solutions can be either directly applied or easily adapted to multiple products within a family.
- It reduces the development time and cost: Part of the functionality needed for a new product will already exist within previous products within the same family.
- It improves the overall system reliability: Any functionality that is reused from a previous product will have been used and tested more extensively than if developed anew.

Software architecture provides the critical abstractions that enable variation and commonality within a product family to be simultaneously managed. We will provide an extensive treatment of this subject in Chapter 15. Here, we discuss a representative example that demonstrates the power of product families and the benefits accrued via an explicit, and extensive, software architectural focus.

The business case for exploiting software architecture for this task has been recognized by one of the world's leading consumer electronics manufacturers, Philips. Since the late 1990s, Philips progressively has developed and applied their Koala technology for specifying and implementing the architectures of their mid- and high-end television sets, and has hundreds of software engineers exploiting the concepts.

The motivation for Koala came directly from the nature of and advances in the consumer electronics domain, as shown in the case of Philips television sets in Figure 1-4. While early televisions supported a very small number of simple functions, over time they became more powerful with increasingly sophisticated hardware and, eventually, software capabilities. The resulting growth in complexity carried with it the risks of ever-increasing costs and lengthened time-to-market. Of course, this is precisely the opposite of what modern consumers have come to expect: Fierce competition has forced Philips, as well as its rivals, to produce a steady stream of new products and variations on existing products, while containing their costs.

Figure 1-4.
More sophisticated products carry with them increased complexity, which in turn implies increased cost and worse time-to-market unless the problem is addressed. (Figure courtesy Royal Phillips N.V.)

Complexity

A Television Product Family

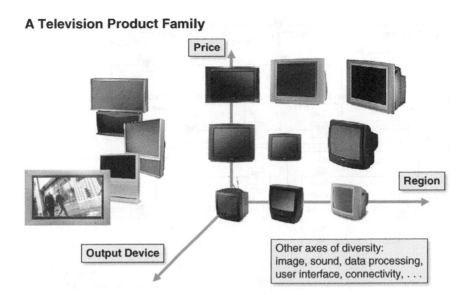

Figure 1-5.
*Philips TVs as a
product family,
varying along
three dimensions.
(Figure courtesy
Royal Phillips
N.V.)*

Philips addressed the problem by formulating a product family, as shown in Figure 1-5, in which its many different types of TV sets varied along three dimensions—price, output device, and geographical region—while they shared their basic purpose and much of their functionality. The same approach was applied to other Philips products including VCRs, DVD players, and audio equipment.

In order to support its product families adequately, Philips had to be able to address two key issues: *commonality* and *variability* across products. The key observation that the Philips engineers made, and one that is of particular relevance to this book, was that the product family notion extended to the growing amounts of *software* embedded in the different devices. To exploit the commonality and manage the variability across the different embedded software product families, Philips developed an architectural methodology, called Koala. A more extensive treatment of Koala is provided in Chapters 6 and 15; here we only highlight its key features.

Koala models and implements a software system as a collection of interacting components. Each component exports a set of services via a set of *provides* interfaces. Additionally, each component explicitly defines its dependencies on its environment (either the hardware or other software components) via a set of *requires* interfaces. For illustration, a software architecture for a Philips TV platform modeled in Koala's graphical notation is shown in Figure 1-6.

This approach allows an engineer to construct and analyze an architecture with relative ease: Each component is essentially akin to a Lego block with well-defined "pins" for composing with other components; in order for such compositions to be legal, the *provides* and *requires* interfaces of the respective components must match according to a set of rigorously defined rules. Moreover, a given assembly of components in Koala can be treated as a *compound* component, which can then be used as a single unit. For example, the architecture shown in Figure 1-6 is a compound component with three *provides* and two

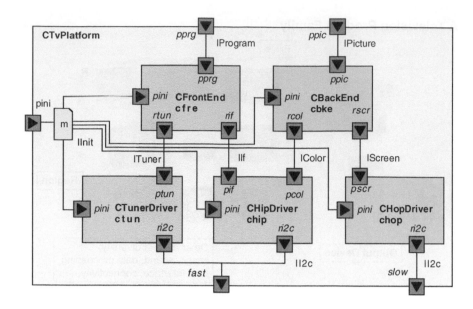

Figure 1-6.
An example software architecture for a TV set. The architecture consists of five interacting components with various incoming and outgoing interfaces. (Figure courtesy Royal Phillips N.V.)

requires interfaces. This allows components of arbitrary complexity to become reusable assets across Koala architectures (that is, across Philips products).

Our previous examples of the use of software architecture, the Web and pipe-and-filter applications, hint that a focus on architecture is a focus on reuse: reuse of ideas, knowledge, patterns, and well-worn experience. In turn, product family architectures facilitate a higher-order level of reuse: reusing structure, behaviors, implementations, and so on, across many related products.

In addition to its ability to exploit commonalities within a product family via reusable assets, Koala also provides explicit support for managing variability across products. Three separate mechanisms are used to this end.

1. *Diversity interfaces* are a mechanism for parameterizing a component. Diversity interfaces allow a component to import configuration-specific properties from Koala's specialized interface implementation elements, which are external to the component and are contained within the architecture encompassing the component.

2. *Switches* are connecting elements that allow a single component to interact with one of a set of components, depending on the value of a given run-time parameter.

3. *Optional interfaces* allow a component of a given type either to provide or to require additional functionality that may be specialized for certain, but not all, products within a family.

The combination of Koala's support for sharing reusable assets of arbitrary complexity and managing diversity across products in a family has made it possible for Philips to explore combining components from different families in novel and interesting ways. Some of those are depicted in Figure 1-7. The resulting *product populations* are a further extension of the technical challenges inherent in product families. For example, the presence of

Composition

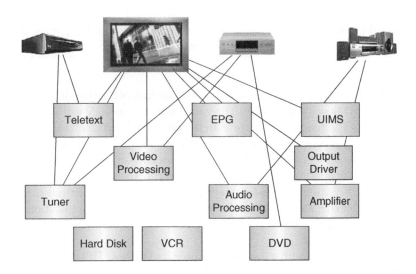

Figure 1-7.
An ever-expanding range of possibilities opens by combining existing consumer electronics products. This provides an even broader and longer-term motivation for product families. (Figure courtesy Royal Phillips N.V.)

variation induces requirements for extensive configuration management of the individual components and of entire architectures.

Koala has directly helped Philips to conquer these challenges and turn them into a competitive advantage. We should note that while architecture has played a central role in this process, product families and populations also require broader changes to processes and business organization practices. The standard approach to software development as found in most businesses does not effectively support product families. One common reason is that a development team often has little incentive to expend its already scarce resources and produce more widely (re)usable assets that will benefit other teams and projects in the future. Therefore, introduction of a robust strategy to support product families also demands changes in how development organizations are structured and operate internally, and how they interact with other parts of a company's business, including marketing, hardware engineering, and finance.

Apart from the obvious cost savings from the reuse of components and the ability to quickly craft yet another new television configuration, the Philips example reveals another critical benefit of the software architecture abstraction: Koala is the concrete manifestation of the company's corporate experience, knowledge, and competitive advantage. Without a specific way of representing such knowledge, companies are left relying on the memories of their employees and the verbal conveyance of past experience to retain and pass along "our company's way" of solving problems and creating new products. With increasing trends of employee mobility from company to company, reliance on a social structure to maintain such understanding is an increasingly shaky policy. Software architecture offers not only a solution to a socially induced problem, but, with its substantial technical support, the ability to achieve much higher levels of productivity than have heretofore been seen. This is a critical observation and further explication of it will be provided throughout the remainder of this book.

1.5 END MATTER

> Architecture depends on fitness (ordinatio) and arrangement (dispositio), . . .; it also depends
> on proportion, uniformity, consistency, and economy, . . . Vitruvius I, 2, 1

This chapter began with an extended discussion of an analogy of how buildings are designed and constructed and how software is designed and built; the analogy will appear again in following chapters. The fundamental role of architecture has been emphasized throughout the chapter, showing its essential role in the World Wide Web, and then, at the other end of the size spectrum, in quickly composed desktop applications. Software architecture has been presented as the set of *principal design decisions* made during the system's conceptualization and development. Knowing and understanding these decisions is essential to successful system evolution. Making such decisions determines the course of an application: whether it will be effective, elegant, and successful or a costly, error-prone thorn in the side of all who come in contact with it.

The chapter concluded with a discussion of product families. This concluding focus is particularly appropriate as it echoes closely a lesson from the world of buildings, namely the critical role of architecture and architects in carrying forward lessons, experiences, and reusable elements to new projects.

In 1979, architect Christopher Alexander's book, *The Timeless Way of Building*, showed how patterns of solutions to common architectural needs have developed over the years, and how combinations of patterns can be made to yield structures that address complex needs and constraints. Software architecture not only supplies the intellectual means for applying such reuse of knowledge in the software domain, enabling engineers to efficiently address needs for new systems, but also provides the framework for reusing substantial functional components in the production of new members of a product family.

The vision of architecture-centric software engineering is very compelling. It prefigures a world where complex software systems are engineered, rather than crafted, drawing from extensive experience in past projects to form the basis for new ones. System designs are modeled in a variety of notations, each optimized for depicting particular aspects of the architecture. Powerful tools automate the process of maintaining consistency between these models. Each project stakeholder has a panoply of visualizations available for looking at the architecture in ways that are most natural or convenient. Capable analysis tools provide deep insights into the nature of the designed system long before implementation activities begin—stakeholders are able to assess the qualities of a software system from its design before costly mistakes are introduced. The design serves as the basis for system deployment and evolution as well, informing future engineers as to exactly how to evolve the system in ways that are consistent with its original design principles and goals. The architecture (and the qualities induced by it) accompanies the system through its lifetime to its eventual retirement. This vision is not fully a reality today. However, as this book will show, today's foundations, theory, and practice of software architecture can achieve vastly superior results to those of traditional development practices, while also providing a rich basis for achieving the stated vision.

The coming chapters will supply the missing details in our discussion. To apply the techniques of software architecture one must have adequate conceptual foundations, notations, analysis techniques, tools, and processes, all of which will be discussed. We will begin this examination in the next chapter by considering how a software architecture-centric approach to development radically reshapes the other tasks and processes of software engineering. The emphasis will be on recognizing that principal design decisions are made throughout a system's life cycle, and that by focusing on such decisions, capturing the knowledge they represent, the development process is improved. Chapter 3 then sets the concepts of software architecture in precise terms, while subsequent chapters show how to design, develop, deploy, and adapt systems based on these principles.

1.6 REVIEW QUESTIONS

1. What are the principal insights from the discipline of building architecture that are applicable to the construction of software systems?

2. Recognizing the limitations of an analogy—where it does not apply—can be as instructive as considering the situations where it does apply. What's wrong with the building architecture analogy? In what ways is constructing software fundamentally different from building a physical structure? Do a Web search for "software construction analogy is broken." Do you agree or disagree with the opinions posted online?

3. Philips's use of software architecture for supporting product lines is targeted at consumer electronics, such as televisions. What other industries or markets could benefit from the commonalities and efficiencies of a software product-line approach?

1.7 EXERCISES

1. Architects use hand-drawn sketches, prose, and blueprints to describe buildings. What do these correspond to in software development?

2. When a software developer begins a new development task by directly starting to program, what kind of development activity would that correspond to in building?

3. Look up several definitions of "software design." Do any of these definitions correspond to what architects (or industrial designers) term "design"?

4. What corresponds in software development to a building architect's concern for aesthetics?

5. Interview an architect and find what his or her key vocabulary items are. From your knowledge of software engineering, what analogs do those terms have in software?

6. Is X a better analogy for the construction of software? Why or why not? Let X =(law, medicine, automotive engineering, oil painting). For example, in law, consider the process by which laws are made and enforced. For oil painting, consider the commissioned works that artists such as Michelangelo produced. What process did he follow? For medicine, consider whether the "product" of medicine is tangible or not, and what that implies for medical knowledge.

7. Perform a Web search for "software architecture." Are the top hits deserving of the billing? Are the terms used on those Web sites consistent with the terms as used in this textbook?

8. Write a pipe-and-filter application that prints a sorted list of every unique word in a file. That is, each unique word should appear only once on the output.

1.8 FURTHER READING

The works of Vitruvius have been translated into English many times and should be readily available in a good library. Free, online translations are also available; see, for example, Bill Thayer's Web site (Pollio).

Many excellent books on architecture have been written, of course, but few provide substantive insights for software developers. A significant exception is Stewart Brand's *How Buildings Learn* (Brand, 1994). Brand chronicles how a wide range of kinds of buildings have been changed over the many years since their initial construction. A discussion of some of the principles from this book and how they relate to software architecture is found in Chapter 14 of this text. Another architecture text that has had substantial impact on software development is Alexander's *The Timeless Way of Building* (Alexander, 1979). This work has influenced thinking on patterns for object-oriented programming, and more generally, software architecture styles.

An interesting chronicle of the construction of a New York City skyscraper can be found in (Sabbagh, 1989).

The processes the designers and builders follow, and the problems they encounter, are eerily similar to those in large-scale software development.

A detailed discussion of the architecture of the World Wide Web can be found in (Fielding and Taylor 2002). Key points from this work are discussed in detail in Chapter 11. The standards that govern the operation of the Web are available from the Internet Engineering Task Force (IETF) and the World Wide Web Consortium (W3C) Web sites: www.ietf.org and www.w3.org, respectively. Tim Berners-Lee's description of the Web from 1994 can be found at (Berners-Lee, et al. 1994).

Further information on Koala and how it has been used to support development of product families is available at (van Ommering et al. 2000) and (van Ommering 2002).

2

Architectures in Context: The Reorientation of Software Engineering

The preceding chapter introduced the concept of software architecture and illustrated its power in establishing the contemporary World Wide Web. It also showed how software architecture provides a technical foundation for the exploitation of the notion of product families. This chapter shows how software architecture relates to the concepts of software engineering that traditionally are the most prominent.

What emerges from this consideration is a reorientation of those concepts away from their typical understanding, for the power of architecture demands a primacy of place. As a result the very character of key software engineering activities, such as requirements analysis and programming, are altered and the technical approaches taken during various software engineering activities are changed.

The focus of this chapter is showing the role of architecture in the whole of the software engineering enterprise, so it is somewhat cursory—most of the major topics of software engineering are discussed, but each individual topic is only allotted a few pages. Subsequent chapters will take up the major points in turn, treating them in substantial detail. The reader will be able to understand the role of software architecture in the larger development context, and could apply the ideas in broad terms, but without the specific techniques and tools covered in subsequent chapters effective application of the ideas will be elusive.

2.1 FUNDAMENTAL UNDERSTANDINGS

There are three fundamental understandings of architecture, the recognition of which helps situate architecture with respect to the rest of software engineering:

1. Every application has an architecture.
2. Every application has at least one architect.
3. Architecture is not a phase of development.

By architecture we mean the set of principal design decisions made about a system; it is a characterization of the essence and essentials of the application. Referring back to the analogy to buildings discussed at the beginning of Chapter 1, it is evident that every building has an architecture. That is not to say that every building has an honorable, or elegant, or effective architecture: Sadly, many buildings evince architectures that ill-serve their occupants and shame their designers. But those buildings *have* architectures, just as much as the beautiful, elegant buildings that are a delight to see and to work within. So it is with software. An application's fundamental structure can be characterized, and the principal design decisions made during its development can be laid out. For example, as described in the previous chapter, the architecture of the World Wide Web is characterized by the set of decisions referred to as the REST architectural style. The Unix shell script we saw in the previous chapter has an architecture characterized by the pipe-and-filter style. All applications do have architectures because they all result from key design decisions.

The contribution of this observation is that it immediately raises questions: Where did the architecture of an application come from? How can that architecture be characterized? What are its properties? Is it a "good architecture" or a "bad architecture?" Can its shortcomings be easily remedied?

The second understanding follows naturally from the first: Every application has an architect, though perhaps not known by that title or recognized for what is done.[3] The architect is the person or, in most cases, group who makes the principal decisions about the application, who establishes and (it is hoped) maintains the foundational design. As with

---

[3]Conversely, just because a company bestows a title such as "chief software architect" on someone does not necessarily mean that the individual possesses any particular credentials or ability to responsibly create good or effective software architectures, or indeed to know anything about software technology.

the first understanding, this observation also immediately raises some questions, including: Were the architects always aware when they had made a fundamental design decision? Can they articulate those foundational design decisions to others? Can they maintain the conceptual integrity of the design over time? Were alternatives considered at the various decision points?

The third understanding is the most profound, and which provides the focus for the majority of this chapter. Architecture refers to the conceptual essence of an application, the principal decisions regarding its design, the key abstractions that characterize the application. If it is agreed that every application has an architecture, then the question arises, Where did it come from? How does it change?

In a simplistic, traditional, and *inaccurate* understanding, the architecture is a specific product of a particular phase in the development process that succeeds identification of requirements and that precedes detailed design. In elaborate software engineering waterfall processes, or in the spiral model, such phases are often explicitly labeled, using such terms as "preliminary design," "high-level design," "product design," or "software product design." Thinking of architecture as the product of such a phase—especially an early phase—confines architecture to consist of only a few design decisions, a subset of those that fully characterize the application, and, unfortunately in many cases, to the decisions most likely to be contravened by subsequent decisions. While the creation and maintenance of the architecture may begin or have special prominence in a particular phase, these activities pervade the development process.

To show how software architecture relates to the broader traditional picture of software engineering, we discuss architecture in the context of traditional phases and activities of software engineering. For convenience and familiarity, we organize the following discussion around the notional waterfall process. Our discussion is predicated on a recognition that a system's architecture should result from a conscious, deliberate activity by an individual or group recognized as having responsibility for the architecture. Those unfortunate situations where the architecture is not explicit and not the result of conscious choice or effort simply reflect poor engineering practice.

2.2 REQUIREMENTS

Consideration of architecture rightly and properly begins at the outset of any software development activity. Notions of structure, design, and solution are quite appropriate during the requirements analysis activity. To understand why, it is appropriate to begin with a short exploration of the traditional software engineering approach. We contrast that view with the practice in actual software development, the practice in (building) architecture, and then consider the role of design and decision making in the initial phase of application conception.

In the waterfall model, indeed in most process models, the initial phase of activities is focused on developing the requirements for an application—the statement of what the application is supposed to do. The traditional academic view of requirements analysis and specification is that the activity, and the resulting requirements document, should remain unsullied by any consideration for a design that might be used to satisfy the identified requirements. Indeed, some researchers in the requirements community are rather strident on this point: "The central part of this paper sketches an approach to problem analysis and structuring that aims to avoid the magnetic attraction of solution-orientation" (Jackson 2000); similar quotes can be found throughout the literature. (More recent work in requirements engineering has moved away from such a viewpoint, as will be discussed at the end of the chapter.)

The focus on isolating requirements and delaying any thought of solution goes back to antiquity. Pappus, the Greek mathematician from the fourth century wrote, "In analysis we start from what is required, we take it for granted, and we draw consequences from it, till we reach a point that we can use as [a] starting point in synthesis." Synthesis is here the design, or solution, activity. More recently, the twentieth-century American mathematician George Polya wrote an influential treatise on "How to Solve It" (Polya 1957). The essence of his approach is as follows.

- First, understand the problem.
- Second, find the connection between the data and the unknown. You should obtain eventually a plan of the solution.
- Third, carry out your plan.
- Fourth, examine the solution obtained.

In both these approaches, a full understanding of the requirements precedes any work toward solution. Most software engineering writers have taken this essential stance, as we have seen in the quote above, and argued that any thought about how to solve a problem must follow a full exploration and understanding of the requirements.

One of the stories used to illustrate the wisdom of this approach concerns the development of washing machines. If in designing washing machines we simply automated the manual solution of ages past we would have machines that banged clothes on rocks down by the riverside. In contrast, focusing on the requirements (namely, cleaning clothes) independent of any "magnetic attraction of solution-orientation" allows novel, creative solutions to be obtained: rotating drums with agitators.

This ideal view of isolating requirements first, then designing afterward, is in substantial contrast to the typical practice of software engineering. While it is not something that developers write academic papers about, the practice indicates that, apart from government-contracted development and some specialized applications, substantive requirements documents are seldom produced in advance of development. Requirements analysis, which ostensibly produces requirements documents, is often done in a quick, superficial manner, if at all. Explanations for such deviation of actual practice from putative "best practices" include schedule and budget pressures, inferior processes, denigration of the responsible engineers' qualifications and training, and so on.

We believe the real reasons are different, and that these differences begin to indicate the role of architecture and solution considerations at the very outset of a development process. The differences have to do with human limitations in abstract reasoning, economics, and perhaps most importantly, "evocation."

Consider once again the analogy to buildings. When we decide we need a new house or apartment, or a modification to our current dwelling, we do not begin a process of reasoning about our needs independently of how they may be satisfied. We think, and talk, in terms of how many rooms, what style of windows, whether we want a gas or electric stove—not in terms of "means for providing shelter from inclement weather, means for providing privacy, means for supplying adequate illumination, means for preparing hot food" and so on. We have extensive experience with housing, and that experience allows us to reason quickly and articulately about our desires, and to do efficient approximate analyses of cost and schedule for meeting the needs. Seeing other houses or buildings inspires our imagination and sparks creative thought as to what "might be." Our needs start to encompass particular styles of houses that we find charming or cutting edge. Thus our understanding of the architecture of our current dwelling and the architecture of the other people's dwellings enables us to envision our "needs" in a way that is likely to lead to their satisfaction (or revision downward to reality!)

So it is with software. Specifying requirements independently of any concern for how those requirements might be met leads to difficulty in even articulating the requirements. Aside from limited domains, such as numerical analysis, it is exceptionally difficult to reason in purely abstract terms. Without reference to existing architectures it becomes difficult to assess practicality, schedules, or cost. Seeing what can be done in other systems, on the other hand, what kind of user interfaces are available, what new hardware is capable of, what kind of services can be provided, evokes "requirements" that reflect our imagination and yet are grounded in reasonable understandings of possibility. Current practice reflects this approach, showing the practicality of reasoning about structure and solution hand-in-hand with requirements.

This observed experience with software practice is consistent with that found in other engineering disciplines. Henry Petroski, the popular chronicler of the modern history of engineering, has observed that failure is the driver of engineering and the basis for innovation. That is, innovation and new products come from observation of existing solutions and their limitations. Reference to those prior designs is intrinsically part of work toward new solutions and products.

The nearly ubiquitous zipper followed a typical engineering development path. Rather than starting from a design-free functional specification—something like "means for joining edges of a jacket"—the zipper appeared in the early 1900s as an incremental successor to a long line of patented inventions. The earliest of these go back to the problem of buttoning high-top boots. From the C-curity hook-and-eye fastener to the Plako to the hidden hook and then to the still-common nested, cup-shaped fasteners we refer to as zippers, the history is one of repeated invention, failure, and new innovation. In addition to the technical challenges of getting a fastener to function reliably and be aesthetically acceptable, the developers of the zipper also faced the equally daunting challenge of developing a demand for the product.

Henry Petroski tells the story in detail in, *The Evolution of Useful Things* (Petroski 1992). He concludes his chapter on the zipper with the following insight, "... like the form of many a now familiar artifact, that of what has come to be known as the zipper certainly did not follow directly from function. The form clearly followed from the correction of failure after failure."

The Development of Zippers

Similarly, if we consider the behavior of corporations, or especially of venture capitalists, we see a focus from the outset on structures and designs, rather than requirements. That is, one does not successfully approach a venture capitalist and simply enumerate a great list of requirements for some product. Requirements do not create value; products do. Successful new ventures are begun on the basis of a potential solution—possibly even without a conception of what requirement it might be meeting. Marketing organizations within companies have as their charter the responsibility to match existing products to needs, to create needs, or, especially, to identify how existing products need to be modified in order to address emerging customer needs. In all this, solution and structure are equal partners with requirements in a conversation about needs. The core observations from this reflection are:

- Existing designs and architectures provide the vocabulary for talking about what might be.
- Our understanding of what works now, and how it works, affects our wants and perceived needs, typically in very solution-focused terms.
- The insights from our experiences with existing systems helps us imagine what might work and enables us to assess, at an early stage, how long we must be willing to wait for it, and how much we will need to pay for it.

The simple conclusion then, is that analysis of requirements and consideration of design—concerning oneself with the decisions of architecture—are naturally and properly pursued cooperatively and contemporaneously.

The starting point for a new development activity thus includes knowledge of what exists now, how the extant systems fail or fail to provide all that is desired, and knowledge of what about those systems can or cannot be changed. In many ways, therefore, the current architectures drive the requirements. Indeed, requirements can be thought of as the articulation of improvements needed to existing architectures—desired changes to the principal design decisions of the current applications. Architectures provide a frame of reference, a vocabulary, a basis for describing properties, and a basis for effective analysis. New architectures can be created based upon experience with and improvement to pre-existing architectures.

The overwrought objection to this approach is that it will limit innovation and guide development down unfruitful paths. After all, that is the point of the washing machine story mentioned earlier. The problem is, while the anecdote is amusing, it does not reflect how modern washing machines were developed. Engineers at Maytag did not begin by stating abstract requirements for the "removal of particulate matter greater than n microns in size from fabrics composed of cotton fibers, to an effective level of only k residual particles per gram of fabric after t seconds of processing." Rather, history shows an incremental progression of machines that largely draw from automation of formerly human actions, but with innovative progressions.

Developers, nonetheless, do have to be concerned about having their vision limited by current designs. An analogy used by professors David Garlan and Mary Shaw makes the point well: To ascend to the top of a house a ladder may be used. To ascend to the top of a small building, a fire truck ladder may be used. But to ascend to the top of a skyscraper a ladder of any variety will be insufficient; an elevator (which bears no physical relationship to a ladder) is effective. To ascend to the moon requires yet another totally different technology. In this analogy, the concept of ascension is constant across the different situations, but the specifics of the situations end up implying the need for distinctly different solution architectures.

The point is this: Predecessors, that is, existing architectures, provide the surest base for the *vast* majority of new developments; in such situations requirements should be stated using the terminology and structural concepts of existing systems. In situations where an adequate ("physical") predecessor is *unknown*, conceptual predecessors or analogies (for example, "things used before to ascend") may provide a terminological basis for describing the new needs, but caution must be exercised in drawing any architectural notions from such predecessors. Conceptual predecessors may provide a vision but frequently offer little help beyond that.[4]

Perhaps most dangerous is so-called greenfield development: one for which there is no immediate architectural predecessor. In such cases the temptation is to believe that new conceptual ground is being broken and hence no effort need be or should be undertaken to examine existing systems and architectures for framing the development. The risk is a directionless development; better is the strategy to first extensively search for existing architectures that might provide the efficient basis for framing the new requirements and solution. Greenfields are often minefields in disguise.

Lastly, the admonition to always consider architectural predecessors and to base development on improvements to existing systems is not absolute. Not all architectures are worthy of further work and may be incapable of serving as the basis for additional development. As further chapters will illustrate, some architectural styles are much more effective at supporting change and enhancement than others; some architectures deserve to be abandoned.

This section has called for a new understanding and approach toward requirements engineering which provides substantial prominence to the role of architectures and solution considerations. Architectures provide the language for discussion of needs—not only a glossary of terms, but a language of structures, mechanisms, and possibilities. With this architectural underpinning preliminary analyses can proceed. Requirements documents still serve an important role in the engineering process, for instance as the basis for contracts and setting out the precise objectives for new work, but these documents should be strongly informed by architectural considerations. Chapter 15 will elaborate an advanced application of these ideas known as reference requirements, under the banner of "domain specific software architectures." Later in this chapter, we briefly return to the relationship between requirements and development, when in the section on processes we consider the Twin Peaks model and agile development methods.

2.3 DESIGN

Designing is, by definition, the activity that creates a system's software architecture—its set of principal *design* decisions. As the preceding sections have indicated, these decisions are not confined, for instance, to high-level notions of a system's structure. Rather the decisions span issues that arise throughout the development process. Nonetheless, there is a time during development when more attention is paid to making many of those principal decisions than at other times—an architectural design "phase." Our points for this section

---

[4]Nonetheless, the considerable inspiration that can come from considering an analogy from a different domain of knowledge should not be underestimated. An example *par excellence* is the invention of hypertext: Vannevar Bush in his article, "As We May Think" (Bush 1996) conceived of the notion of hypertext through explicit analogy to how the human brain operates associatively. His conception for a device for making and recalling information associatively, however, had nothing to do with biology or cells, but rather with extrapolations from mechanical devices of the 1940s.

are simply as follows:

- The traditional design phase is not *exclusively* "the place or the time" when a system's architecture is developed—for that happens over the course of development—but it is a time when particular emphasis is placed on architectural concerns.
- Since principal design decisions are made throughout development, designing must be seen as an aspect of many other development activities.
- Architectural decisions are of many different kinds, requiring a rich repertoire of design techniques.

In traditional formulations of software engineering, the activity of design is confined to the "design phase." In the notional waterfall model, the abstract requirements produced by the requirements phase are examined, a design process is followed, and, at completion of the phase, a design is produced and handed to programmers for implementation. Most often those decisions concern a system's structure, including identification of its primary components and how they are connected. (Hence such a design denotes a particular set of design decisions that *partially* comprise the architecture.) To the extent that, during the design phase, some portion of the requirements are found to be infeasible, those requirements issues are referred back to the requirements phase for reconsideration. (And, in the extreme purist view, without passing back any solution information!) If any portions of the design are found to be infeasible or undesirable during the implementation phase, those issues are referred back to the design phase for reconsideration.

With an architecture-centric approach to development, these artificial and counterproductive phase boundaries are diminished or eliminated. As the previous section discussed, the analysis of requirements is properly bound up with notions of architecture and design, with these notions providing the context and vocabulary for describing the new capabilities desired. The activities of analysis, design, and implementation proceed, but in an enriched and more integrated fashion. The principal decisions governing an application—its architecture—are informed from many sources and typically made throughout the process of development.

Last, a rich repertoire of design techniques is needed to assist the architect in making the wide range of design decisions comprising an architecture. The architect must deal, for example, with:

- Stakeholder issues, such as choices concerning the use of proprietary, commercial off-the-shelf or open-source components, with their attendant and varying licensing obligations.
- Over arching style and structure.
- Types of connectors for composing subelements.
- Package and primary class structure (that is, low-level style and structure when working in an object-oriented development context).
- Distributed and decentralized system concerns.
- Deployment issues.
- Security and other nonfunctional properties.
- Postimplementation issues (means for supporting upgrade and adaptation).

Clearly, a simple one-size-fits-all design strategy will not suffice. The following subsection considers the topic of design techniques in a little more detail. In many ways, however, everything in the rest of this book is an exploration of the many facets of software design; this section provides only the briefest introduction.

2.3.1 Design Techniques

A variety of strategies exist for helping the designer develop an architecture. Chapter 4 will discuss several of them in substantial detail, including the use of basic conceptual tools, architectural styles and patterns, and strategies for dealing with unprecedented systems. For the purposes of this chapter, namely relating an architecture-centric approach with classical software engineering, we only consider two strategies for use in development of a solution architecture: object-oriented design and the use of domain-specific architectures, just to illustrate the spectrum of approaches, issues, and concerns.

Object-oriented design is perhaps the most common design approach taught and close consideration of it helps reveal why a wide repertoire of techniques is necessary. A similar analysis could be developed for other traditional approaches to design, such as functional decomposition.

Object-Oriented Design

Object-oriented design (OOD) is usually taught in the context of object-oriented programming, that is, the reduction of an algorithm to machine-executable form. The essence of OOD is the identification of so-called objects, which are encapsulations of state with functions for accessing and manipulating that state. Numerous variations are found in different object-oriented programming languages regarding the way objects are specified, related to one another, created, destroyed, and so on. Given the prevalence of the technique it will not be further summarized here; numerous excellent references are widely available (Larman 2002; Schach 2007).

While object-oriented design can be used as a strategy when developing an architecture, it is not a complete approach and is not effective in all situations. This is not to say that it is an ineffective design technique. On the contrary, OOD is exceptionally effective in a wide variety of development situations! It is just important to realize its limitations, so that other additional or alternative techniques can be brought to bear on those portions of the task.

First, clearly, OOD is not a complete design approach, for it fails to address myriad stakeholder concerns. OOD says nothing about deployment issues, security and trust, or use of commercial components, for instance. Similarly, OOD, as a practice, has no intrinsic means for carrying forward domain knowledge and solutions from previous architectures to new products. While code reuse techniques may be employed or higher-level representations such as Unified Modeling Language (UML) used, no facility is available for explicitly indicating points of variation or other aspects of program families.

Second, OOD is not effective in all situations. For instance, some of its limitations are as follows:

- OOD views all applications as consisting, solely, of one software species (namely, "object"), regardless of purpose. Forcing all concepts and entities into a single mold can obfuscate important differences. The REST style, for instance, maintains distinct notions of "user agent," "origin server," and "cache." Apart from using programming language types to try to characterize these distinct elements, OOD does not offer any helpful modeling mechanism.

- OOD provides only one kind of encapsulation (the object), one notion of interface, one type of explicit connector (procedure call), no real notion of structure (objects are constantly created and destroyed), and no notion of required interfaces. This implies that all the richness of a given solution approach has to be mapped down or transformed to this level of single choice. Some architectures—such as pipe-and-filter—may not be at all effective after such a transformation.

- OOD is so closely related to programming language concerns and choices that it tends to have the forest obscured by the trees. For instance, the vagaries of type inheritance may obscure identification of the principal objects critical to the design. Similarly, it is so bound with programming language issues that the language may start dictating what the important decisions are.

- The typical OOD approach assumes a shared address space and adequate support for heap-and-stack management. OOD typically assumes a single thread of control; support for multiple threads is accommodated in languages largely as an afterthought. Concern for concurrent, distributed, or decentralized architectures is largely outside the OOD purview. Support for distributed objects, such as that provided by CORBA-style middleware, attempts to hide the presence of network boundaries. Architectures that must deal with the realities of networks and their unavoidable characteristics of introducing failures, latency, and authority domains will not be directly supportable with an OOD approach.

One positive step in the object-oriented design world has been the creation of the UML notation. This has helped lift the discussion of object-oriented designs above the programming language level. In 2003, the UML notation was enhanced with some simple notions of software architecture, further improving its contribution. UML is covered in Chapters 6 and 16.

Also helping to lift object-oriented design closer to a richer notion of architecture is the extensive work in patterns, as exemplified in the work of computer scientists Erich Gamma, Richard Helm, Ralph Johnson, and John Vlissides (Gamma et al. 1995). Patterns are explicitly designed to enable the carry-forward of knowledge and experience from previous work into new applications. As such, patterns represent an excellent, "in the small," OO-particular application of an important concept from software architecture.

Extending the idea of patterns to a broad, application-encompassing level yields a design approach known as domain-specific software architectures. This approach exemplifies how architecture-centric design may be supported, and how significant technical and business benefits can consequently be achieved.

Domain-Specific Software Architectures (DSSAs)

The approach known as domain specific software architectures, or DSSAs, is appropriate when prior experience and prior architectures are able to strongly influence new projects. The key notion is that if a developer or company has worked within a particular application domain for many years, it is likely that a best approach or best general solution for applications within that domain will have been identified. Future applications in that domain can leverage this knowledge, with those applications having their fundamental architecture determined by the architectures of the past generations of applications. Indeed, the new architectures will likely be variations on the previous applications. The technical essence of the domain-specific software engineering approach is to capture and characterize the best solutions and best practices from past projects within a domain in such a way that production of new applications can focus more or less exclusively on the points of novel variation. For those points where commonality with past systems is present, reuse of those corresponding parts of the architecture, and indeed reuse of corresponding parts of the implementation, is done. The DSSA approach to system development is thus consistent with the development of product lines as introduced in Chapter 1, and can be the technical centerpiece of a product-line approach.

For instance, if a company is in the business of producing television sets for the world market, such as the example of Philips discussed in Chapter 1, a backbone software architecture can be identified that can be used in televisions destined for sale in North America, Europe, and the Far East. Different tuners for the different markets can be written, and if the backbone architecture has identified variation points and interfaces for the tuner component, the various market-specific tuners can be slotted in, enabling customization in a very cost-effective manner.

To effectively follow the DSSA approach, good technical support is required: The architecture of the previous generation of applications must be captured and refined for reuse; the points of allowable variation must be identified and isolated, the interfaces between the points of variation and the core architecture must be made explicit, the dependencies between multiple points of variation must be identified, and so on. A particularly important element of the DSSA approach is creation and use of a standard way of describing products and systems within the domain of interest. Use of regularized terminology enables an engineer to determine the degree to which a new product concept fits within the company's existing DSSA. These issues and more are explained in Chapter 15, where the DSSA concept and product lines are explored in depth; suffice it to say here that the DSSA approach to design enables the many advantages of an architecture-centric development approach to be realized.

2.4 IMPLEMENTATION

The task of the implementation activity is to create machine-executable source code that is faithful to the architecture and that fully develops all outstanding details of the application. This is true whether speaking from the perspective of classical software engineering or from the software architecture-centric view of software engineering set forth in this book. Architecture-centric development somewhat changes our understanding of the implementation activity and its responsibilities, however. It also emphasizes some particular approaches to implementation.

First, the implementation activity may add to or modify the architecture—if key design decisions are made while working with the source code, they are part of the architecture as much as any principal decision made much earlier in the process. Second, there is no presumption that architecture is completed before implementation begins. Indeed there may be substantial iteration and revision of the architecture as the code is developed, depending on the development process followed. What the architecture approach empha-sizes is keeping all the recorded decisions constituting the architecture consistent with the code as the application is fully developed. That is, the implementation activity cannot turn its back upon the preceding decisions and proceed to modify, for example, the application's structure without making corresponding changes to the recorded architecture.

With regard to implementation strategies, architecture-based development recognizes the enormous cost and quality benefits that accrue from generative and reuse-based imple-mentation strategies. In those cases where full automatic generation is not possible—by far the dominant case—a set of supportive techniques are emphasized. These include appli-cation frameworks and other types of code reuse, which provide significant parts of the implementation prebuilt.

The watchword for the creation of the implementation is its being faithful to, or con-sistent with, the architecture. The simplest understanding of a faithful implementation is that all of the structural elements found in the architecture are implemented in the source code, and that all of the source code corresponds to various parts of the explicit archi-tecture. It is fair for the source code to contain more details, such as low-level algorithms for implementing a higher-level concept described in the architecture, but the source code:

- Must not utilize major new computational elements that have no corresponding ele-ments in the architecture.
- Must not contain new connections between elements of the architecture (for exam-ple, such as might be motivated by efficiency concerns) that are not found in the architecture.

This initial conception of the relationship between the architecture and the source code is not fully adequate, however, for it does not accommodate some of the legitimate char-acteristics of reuse-oriented engineering. For instance, an architecture may require the presence of a component to perform some mathematical functions—a sine and cosine routine perhaps. The most cost-effective and quality-focused approach to providing an implementation for that component may be to acquire and use a general math library, one providing not only sine and cosine functions, but tangent, inverse trig functions, and so on. Such a component may have interfaces in addition to those required by the architecture, and will certainly contain subfunctions that do not correspond to anything identified in the architecture.

Further issues may come into this notion of faithfulness between the implementation and the architecture as it existed before the implementation began. Examination of a candidate mathematics library may reveal that it provides 98 percent of the functionality required by the architecture, for a very low price, and at a very high quality level. Analysis of the consequences of the missing 2 percent of the functionality may lead the designers to conclude that the missing functionality will be acceptable under most usage situations, and for the cost savings realized, (1) choose to use the library, and (2) revise the specifications of the system, including the architecture, in accordance with the reduced functionality. The critical point is that the architecture is always kept in a consistent state with the implementation.

2.4.1 Implementation Strategies

A variety of techniques are available to assist in the faithful development of the implementation from the design, including generation technologies, frameworks and middleware, and reuse. Choice of the techniques is largely determined by availability. Generative techniques, when available, are often the best: The implementation is generated automatically and is of very high quality. The reuse-based techniques come next: Implementation time is significantly less than programming the entire implementation from scratch and quality is similarly better. Least desirable is writing all the code manually: The project cost goes up significantly due to extended development and quality-assurance time. These various approaches are discussed below.

The use of generation technologies is the easiest and most straightforward way of ensuring complete consistency between the architecture and the implementation. The concept is simple: For some narrow application domains, sufficient intelligence can be encoded in a tool such that a formal specification of the architecture can be input to the tool, and the tool will generate a complete program to perform the functions as specified. One example of such technology is parser generators. Given the specification of the syntax of a programming language, a parser generator will generate a program capable of recognizing programs written in the language specified by the grammar. Choice of the parser generator determines the required form of the language specification and determines the structure of the generated parser, such as recursive descent or SLR(1) (for a list of such tools, consult online resources such as (*The Catalog of Compiler Construction Tools* 2006) or (Heng). Bear in mind, of course, that this technique does not generate a compiler; rather only the front end that handles lexical and syntactic issues. The point is that the development engineer's labor can be directed to semantic issues concerning what to do when a sentence in the language is recognized by the generated parser.

The great attraction of generative technologies is, of course, that no human labor need be spent on programming. The limitation of the technique is just as obvious: The approach is only applicable in those limited situations where the domain is so thoroughly understood and bounded that generation is feasible.

For domains that do not satisfy the rigorous requirements of generative technologies, an effective approach is the use of frameworks. An architecture-implementation framework is a piece of software that acts as a bridge between a particular architectural style and a set of implementation technologies. It provides key elements of the architectural style in code, in a way that assists developers in implementing systems that conform to the prescriptions and constraints of the style. Frameworks may be extensive, requiring only minor portions to be completed by hand, or may be very basic, only offering help in implementing the most generic aspects of an architecture or architectural style. In any case, the places where hand work must be done are defined in advance. The developer need not, indeed must not, stray from doing work only in those locations, and must do the work in those locations in such a way that it does not violate the design of the framework or of the architecture.

The role of frameworks in the implementation of an architecture is placed in context in Figure 2-1. Framework selection and development is an integral part of architecture-based system implementation, because the framework provides the bridge between concepts from the architecture and concepts from the platform (that is, programming language and operating system). If a framework does not exist for a particular combination of architectural style

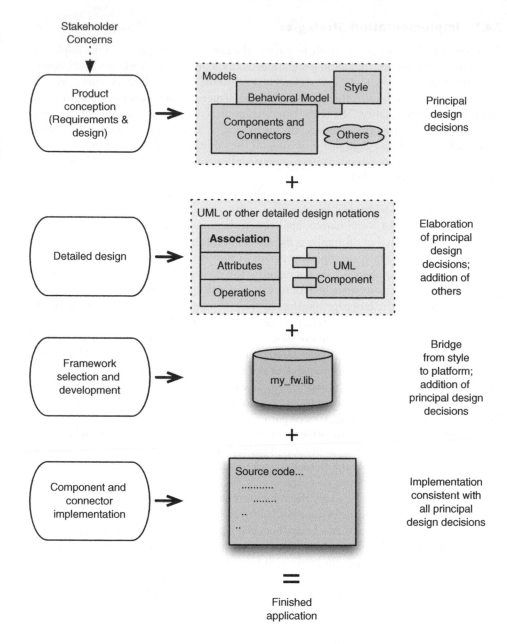

Figure 2-1.
*Frameworks and
the implemen-
tation activity in
the context of
development.
Activities are
shown in the left
column; artifacts
are in the central
column; notes
are on the right.*

and platform, conscientious developers will generally end up implementing one anyway because of the general software engineering principles of abstraction and modularity—frameworks encapsulate key features effective in mapping architectures to implementations.

As examples, common frameworks in extensive use are those targeted at supporting implementation of user interfaces. Both the Microsoft Foundation Classes (MFC) and the Java Swing library represent frameworks that provide the user with common user interface widgets and interaction methods in object-oriented libraries. More than simply providing a set of facilities that users can take advantage of, these frameworks fundamentally influence the architectures of systems that employ them. For example, both frameworks (to some degree) manage concurrency and threading—the frameworks themselves create and manage the threads of control responsible for gathering user input events from the operating system and dispatching them to processing code developed by the user.

Related to frameworks, as aids for assisting in the implementation of architectures, are middleware technologies. Middleware comes in several varieties, some of which provide an extensive range of services, but as a whole they typically support communication between software components. As such, middleware facilitates the implementation of connectors—the architectural elements responsible for providing communication between components. The developer has complete responsibility for implementing an architecture's components' business logic, but relies on middleware for implementation of connectors.

Commonly found middleware includes CORBA and Microsoft's DCOM (for supporting communication between remote objects), RPC (for remote procedure calls), and message-oriented middleware (for delivery of asynchronous messages between remote components).

Generative technologies, frameworks, and middleware thus represent a spectrum of generic and widely used technologies for assisting in the faithful implementation of an architecture. These technologies progress from fully automatic, to partially automatic, to providing help with the implementation of connectors.

Less generic, but no less important, is the reuse of software components, whether commercial off-the-shelf, open-source, or in-house proprietary software. The key issue of such reuse, as it pertains to the faithful implementation of an architecture, is the degree to which the functionality, interfaces, and nonfunctional properties of a candidate component for reuse match those required by an architecture. In the (unfortunately) unlikely event that a perfect match exists, the job is done. In the common case, namely involving some degree of mismatch, the issues and choices are difficult. One strategy, which preserves the architecture as specified, is to encapsulate the preexisting component inside a new interface so that the thus-modified component exactly meets the requirements of the architecture. While this technique can be successful, a more likely circumstance is that performing such encapsulation still will not be economically or technically viable. In such cases, a decision needs to be made: whether to revise the architecture in such a way as to enable the reuse of the component, or to abandon this particular preexisting code and either search for alternatives or create a new component from scratch. This choice is a difficult one.

In absence of any technology to assist the developer in creating source code faithful to the architecture, the implementation must be developed manually. In such circumstances, the programmer must rely upon discipline and great care, for this can be the "great divide." To the extent that the implementation differs from the architecture that resulted from preceding development activities, that architecture does not characterize the application. The implementation *does* have an architecture: It is latent, as opposed to what is documented. Failure to recognize this distinction:

- Robs one of the ability to reason about the implemented application's architecture in the future.

- Misleads all stakeholders regarding what they believe they have as opposed to what they really have.
- Makes any development or evolution strategy that is based on the documented but inaccurate architecture doomed to failure.

Chapter 9 takes up these various issues in detail.

2.5 ANALYSIS AND TESTING

Analysis and testing are activities undertaken to assess the qualities of an artifact. In the traditional waterfall, analysis and testing are conducted after the code has been written, in the testing phase. In this context, the artifact being examined is the code; usually the quality being assessed is functional correctness, though properties such as performance may be examined as well. Analysis and testing activities do not have to be confined to occur after programming, of course, and many excellent development processes integrate these activities within the development activity. As long as an artifact exists that is susceptible to analysis for a defined property, that analysis can proceed—whether the artifact is a requirements document, a description of the application's structure, or something else. One of the virtues of conducting analysis before code exists is cost savings: The earlier an error is detected and corrected, the lower the aggregate cost.

Given that early detection of errors is a good thing, one must ask why conventional analysis and testing is almost always confined to simply testing source code. Moreover, why is such testing performed only against the most basic of specifications, namely the system functional requirements? The answer is almost always because of the nonexistence of any sufficiently rigorous representation of an application apart from source code. Rigorous representations are required so that precise questions can be asked and so that definitive answers can be obtained—preferably by means of automated analysis aids.

A technically based, architecture-centric approach to software development offers significant opportunity for early analysis and for improved analysis of source code. Additionally, the prospect for analyzing properties other than just functional correctness is present. In this approach to development, technically rich architectural models are present long before source code, and hence serve as the basis for and subject of early analysis. (Chapter 8 will present substantial details on architectural analysis, Chapter 12 will extend that discussion to non-functional properties, and Chapter 13 will delve in particular to architectural support for security and trustworthiness.) In the few paragraphs below we simply outline some of the approaches; details will come after our presentation of architectures and architectural models is on a more precise footing.

First, the structural architecture of an application can be examined for consistency, correctness, and exhibition of desired nonfunctional properties. If the architecture upon which the implementation is (later) based is of high quality, the prospects for a high-quality implementation are significantly raised.

As a formal artifact, the architectural model can be examined for internal consistency and correctness: Syntactic checks of the model can identify, for instance, mismatched components, incomplete specification of properties, and undesired communication patterns. Data flow analysis can be applied to determine definition/use mismatches, similar to how such analysis is performed on source code. More significantly, flow analysis can be used to detect security flaws. Model-checking techniques can analyze for problems with deadlock. Estimates of the size of the final application can be based upon analysis of the architecture. Simulation techniques can be applied to perform some simple forms of dynamic analysis.

Second, the architectural model may be examined for consistency with requirements. Regardless of whether the requirements were developed in the classical way (that is, before any development of solution notions), or in the modern sense, in which the two are developed in concert, the two must be consistent. Such examination may be limited to manually performed analysis if the requirements are stated in natural language. Nevertheless, such comparisons are essential in guaranteeing that the two specifications are in agreement.

Third, the architectural model may be used in determining and supporting analysis and testing strategies applied to the source code. The architecture, of course, provides the design for the source code, so consistency between them is essential. Concretely, as the specification for the implementation, the architecture serves as the source of information for governing specification-based testing at all levels: unit, subsystem, and system level.

The architect can prioritize analysis and testing activities based upon the architecture, focusing activities on the most critical components and subassemblies. For example, in the development of a family of software products, special attention should be paid to those components that are part of every member of the product family: An error in one of them will affect all of the products. Conversely, a component that only implements a rarely used and noncritical feature of one member of the family may be judged to not merit nearly as much scrutiny. Testing costs money, and organizations must have a means for determining the priorities for their testing budget; architecture can provide the basis for some of that guidance.

In a similar vein, architecture provides a means for carrying forward analysis results from previous testing activities, with accompanying cost savings. For instance, if a particular component is reused in a new architecture, the degree of its unit testing can be reduced if examination of the architecture confirms that the context and conditions of use are the same as (or more constrained than) the earlier use.

Architecture can provide guidance and economies in the development of test harnesses. Test harnesses are small programs used to test components and subassemblies of larger applications. They provide the analyst with the ability to conveniently and effectively test the internal parts of an application. It can be difficult, for instance, to use system-level inputs to fully and economically exercise the boundary conditions of an internal component. For instance, if an architecture is designed to support a product family, and a small set of components are changed to customize the product for a particular market, a test harness can be constructed to focus testing on those components that comprise the change set. Each customized product can thus have a testing regimen emphasizing only those parts that have changed.

Architecture can also provide guidance in directing the analyst's attention to the connectors in a system's implementation. As will be discussed in Chapter 5, connectors play a particularly important role in some systems' structures, being tasked with supporting all intercomponent communication. The architecture provides an effective way for identifying those points of special leverage, and hence can aid in shaping the analysis and testing activity. Additionally, some connectors offer particularly effective opportunities for nonintrusive monitoring and logging of applications, which can play a key role in helping an engineer develop an understanding of how a system works, as well as assisting in analysis and testing.

Fourth, the architectural model can be compared to a model derived from the source code of an application. This is a form of checking your answer. Stated abstractly, suppose program P is derived from architecture A. A separate team of engineers, with no access to A, could, by reading and analyzing P, develop an architectural model A'—a model of the architecture that P implements. If all is well, A will be consistent with A'. If not, either P does not faithfully implement A, or else A' does not faithfully reflect the architecture of P. Either way, an important inconsistency can be detected. This issue will be discussed in more detail in Chapter 3.

This abstract characterization is not very practical, as it would likely involve substantial human labor. But particular features of implementations can be readily extracted and compared with the architecture. For instance, it is straightforward to extract a model from source code that shows which components communicate with which others. That communication pattern can be compared to the corresponding communication pattern in the architecture and any discrepancies noted. An example of this type of analysis appears in the following chapter.

As noted above, substantive consideration of the analysis of architectures must wait until later in this text. Techniques for representing architectures must first be presented (see Chapter 6). It is sufficient for now to note that architecture-centric development provides a variety of new and significant opportunities for assessing and hence improving the quality of systems.

2.6 EVOLUTION AND MAINTENANCE

Software evolution and software maintenance—the terms are synonymous—refer to all manner of activities that chronologically follow the release of an application. These range from bug fixes to major additions of new functionality to creation of specialized versions of the application for specific markets or platforms.

The typical software engineering approach to maintenance is largely ad hoc. In a best-practices situation, each type of change causes the software process to return to whatever phase that issue is usually considered in, and the development process restarts from that point. Thus, if new functionality is requested, that requires returning to the requirements analysis phase and then moving forward in sequence from there. If the change is thought to be a minor bug fix, then perhaps only the coding phase and its successors are revisited.

The major risk presented by evolution is degradation of the quality of the application. Intellectual control of the application may degrade if changes may be made anywhere, by whatever means are most expedient. In practice, this is precisely what happens. Rather than following best practices, it is common for only the coding phase to be revisited. The code is modified in whatever way is easiest. Over time, the quality of the application degrades significantly, and making successive changes becomes increasingly difficult as complex dependencies between ill-considered earlier changes come to light.

An architecture-centric approach to development offers a solid basis for effective evolution. The key is a sustained focus on an explicit, substantive, modifiable, faithful architectural model.

The evolution process can be understood as consisting of the following stages:

- Motivation
- Evaluation or assessment
- Design and choice of approach
- Action, which includes preparation for the next round of adaptation

The motivations for evolution are many, as noted above. We draw special attention to the creation of new versions of a product. This motivation does not often appear in traditional treatments of software evolution, but is common in the commercial software industry. This kind of change raises the topic of software product families, and as discussed in Chapter 1, supporting product families can be a particular strength of architecture-centric approaches.

Whatever the motivation for evolution may be, the next step is assessment. The proposed change, as well as the existing application, must be examined to determine, for example, whether the desired change can be achieved and, if so, how. Put another way, this stage requires deep understanding of the existing product.

It is at this point that the architecture-centric approach emerges as a superior engineering strategy. If an explicit architectural model that is faithful to the implementation is available, then understanding and analysis can proceed efficiently. A good architectural model offers the basis for maintaining intellectual control of the application. If no architectural model is available, or if the model in existence is not consistent with the implementation, then the activity of understanding the application must proceed in a reverse-engineering fashion. That is, understanding the application will require examination of the source code and recovery of a model that provides adequate intellectual basis for determining how the needed changes can be made. This is time-consuming and costly, especially when the personnel involved are new to the project.

Errors in maintenance often arise from shortchanging this activity. If there is insufficient understanding of the existing structure, then plans to modify that structure will likely fail—at the points of misunderstanding. In contrast, a good architectural model offers a principled basis for deciding whether a desired modification is reasonable. A proposed change may be found to be too costly or detrimental to system properties to warrant development. Only with a good intellectual grip on the existing architecture, as well as the proposed change, can such a determination sensibly be made. The net effect of this principled approach will be the maintenance of architectural integrity and the attenuation of requirements volatility.

The next stage in evolution is development of an approach to satisfy whatever requirement motivated the activity. Several courses of action likely will be identified, so a further step of choosing among alternatives is required. Once a course of action is determined, it must be put into action. For changes of even moderate significance, the first artifact to be modified should be the model of the architecture. In particular, if the change needed pertains to the architecture, then changing the architecture is the place to begin. After changing the architecture corresponding changes to code can be made. The critical matter, of course, is maintaining consistency between the architecture and the implementation. Tools can help with this task.

A mistake to avoid is changing the code first and then planning to revise the architectural description to match. Following up afterward on that good intention seldom takes place.

Making the various changes needed to accommodate whatever motivated the evolution activity should not considered complete until all elements of an application—architecture and code—are consistent. The reason is simple: Additional needs for evolution will be identified in the future. If the application is left inconsistent it will sabotage those future evolution activities.

Software will evolve, whether one is using an architecture-centric development process or not. The question is whether such evolution will proceed efficiently and whether it will result in the degradation of the quality and intellectual integrity of the product. Architecture provides the bedrock for maintenance of coherence, quality, and control. These issues are discussed in greater detail in Chapter 14.

2.7 PROCESSES

A key theme of this chapter has been that architecture concerns properly permeate the entire software development and evolution activity. The set of decisions comprising the architecture forms in concert with the requirements and continues to expand through maintenance. The architecture is thus under constant change.

Architecture, correspondingly, is not a phase in a software engineering process; it is a core, evolving body of information. Indeed, the development of this body of information may reach back and out to preceding applications and other applications.

The centrality of architecture to software development, and the insights that arise from a focus on architecture, are unfortunately totally obscured in traditional characterizations of the software development activity. Traditional software process discussions make the process activities the focal point; the architecture (and hence the product!) is often nowhere to be found. Equally bad, the standard software development processes encourage, if not enforce, sharp divisions between various types of development activities. For instance, the waterfall and spiral models both separate the activity of requirements determination from the activity of design development. As we have seen, such boundaries are not warranted and indeed are counterproductive.

Simply stating, however, that software development processes should be architecture-centric does not by any means say that there is a single correct way to proceed in application development. Different organizations and engineers will want to adopt particular strategies to best take advantage of their particular organizational strengths and preferences. Equally important, different development settings (for example, knowledge, preexisting developments, component libraries, codified architectures) will demand that different prominence be given to the various types of development activities, and those activities will vary in the amount of time required for their completion.

Comparing, or even understanding, different strategies for software development requires a means for describing those strategies. A good descriptive formalism for characterizing strategies will provide a way of not only showing what activities are occurring when, but will give appropriate and effective prominence to the central role of architecture (and all other project artifacts) in the formation of the software product. Accordingly, we now present the *turbine visualization of software development*, and use it to portray a variety of development strategies.

2.7.1   The Turbine Visualization

The turbine visualization is a means for depicting an integrated set of software development activities in which the central role of software architecture in the evolution of the product can be prominently shown—if indeed it is central. The visualization accounts for the following independent aspects of software development:

- Time
- Kinds of activities active at any given time
- Effort (for example, labor hours expended) at any given time
- Product state (for example, total content of product development, or knowledge, at any given time).

The visualization also shows a variety of combined factors, such as investment (cumulative effort over time-demarcated phases).

Spatially, the visualization consists of a set of variable-width, variable-thickness rings stacked around a core. The axis of the core is time; the core represents the software product (the architecture plus all the other artifacts comprising the product); the rings represent time-demarcated phases of activity—all aspects of development or evolution.

The simple, unidirectional waterfall is as simple in the three-dimensional turbine visualization as it is in its traditional depiction—save that the role of the software product is now evident. A nominal waterfall process is shown in three-dimensional perspective in Figure 2-2. An annotated side view of the same process is illustrated in Figure 2-3.

The bottom ring of the waterfall turbine example begins with a null core, consists solely of the requirements analysis activity, and finishes at t_1 with a core consisting solely of the requirements document. The second ring begins at t_2, consists solely of the design activity, and completes at t_3, with the core now consisting of both the requirements document (unchanged since t_1) and the design document. The third ring consists solely of the coding activity, and the fourth solely of the testing activity. Each ring adds one more element to the core. The added value of the turbine model is that, by portraying the growing core, the set of existing product elements is made clear. The testing phase, for instance, visibly has reference to not only the subject of the tests (the code) but the requirements that the code is supposed to satisfy—including any acceptance tests developed during the requirements phase.

A cross-section shows the state of the project at a given point in time. The area of the ring is proportional to the number of labor hours currently being invested in the project. The area of the core indicates the content of the product at that same time. Subregions of the core show the relative development of different parts of the product. An example is shown in Figure 2-4, at time t_i from Figure 2-3. The only activity is Design and the core consists of only the two documents shown.

The thickness of a ring denotes the time period during which the (possibly multiple, concurrent) activities of that ring are active, that is, its duration. Consequently, the volume of a ring (thickness multiplied by area) represents the investment made during that ring: the product of the time that ring was active and the investment made during

Figure 2-2.
*The
unidirectional
waterfall model
as depicted by a
turbine, shown
from an angled
perspective.*

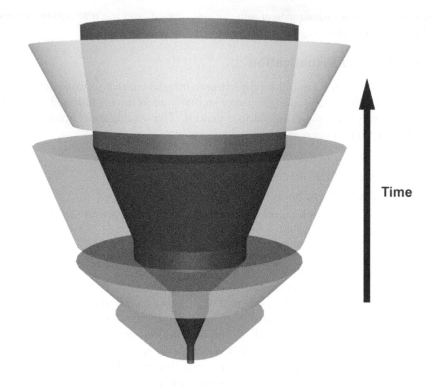

Time

Figure 2-3.
*Side view,
annotated, of the
simple process
depicted in
Figure 2-2.*

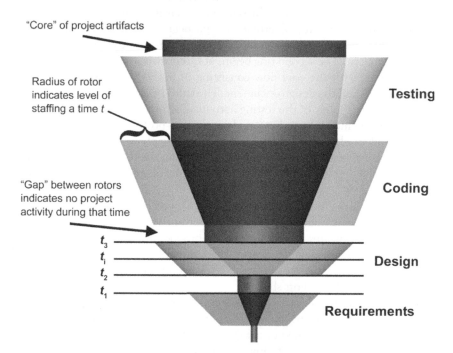

"Core" of project artifacts

Radius of rotor
indicates level of
staffing a time *t*

Testing

"Gap" between rotors
indicates no project
activity during that time

Coding

t_3

t_i

Design

t_2

t_1

Requirements

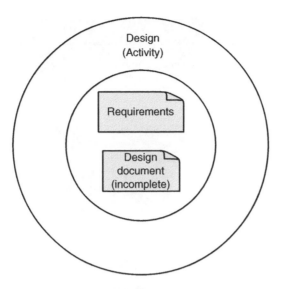

Figure 2-4.
*Cross-section of
turbine from
Figure 2-3 at
time t_i.*

that ring. (Rings do not need to have the same cross-sectional area at t_i as they do at time t_{i+1}, but we will make that simplifying assumption for the moment.)

Not all projects proceed in an uninterrupted fashion, so gaps between rings represent periods of inactivity in a project. During such gaps the core is nominally constant—though if project data gets lost, the core would shrink correspondingly. Rings may be divided into subareas, each of which represents a type of activity going on at that time. The activities shown in the subareas are *concurrent*. The relative size of the subareas denotes the share of the labor directed at that type of activity at that particular point in time.

A more complicated and more realistic illustration that involves multiple concurrent activities is shown in Figure 2-5; a side view for this nominal project is shown in Figure 2-6.

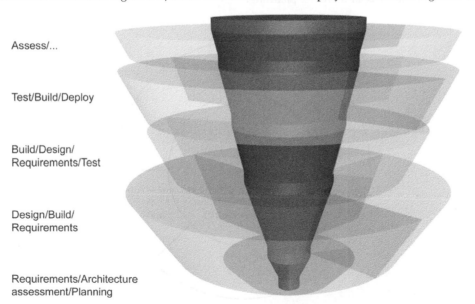

Figure 2-5.
*Example turbine
visualization,
shown in a
three-dimensional
perspective view,
with rings shaded
by type of
activity.
Transparency is
used to enable
seeing activities
otherwise
obscured.*

Figure 2-6.
*Side view of the
project shown in
Figure 2-5.*

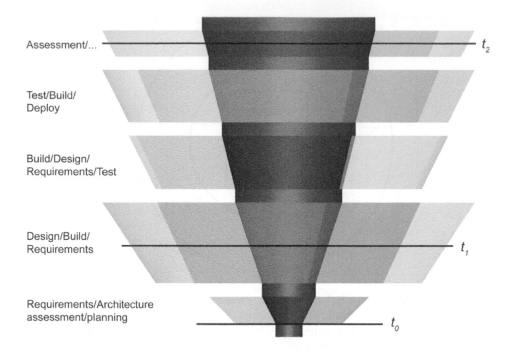

Cross-section S_0, shown in Figure 2-7, represents the state of the project at its beginning. The diameter of the core of the project is significant, representing substantial knowledge and resources carried forward from previous projects. The activities at time t_0 include architecture assessment (that is, evaluation of architectures from previous projects), requirements analysis, and project planning.

Figure 2-7.
*Cross-section of
turbine at time t_0.*

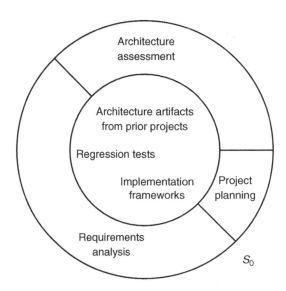

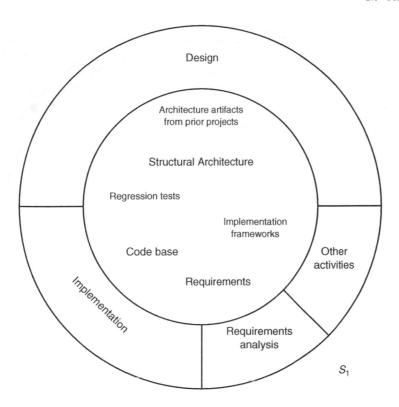

Figure 2-8.
*Cross-section of
turbine at time t_1.*

Cross-section S_1, shown in Figure 2-8, represents the state of the project at time t_1. The core of the project has grown significantly, and particular subelements of the core are shown. The relative mix of the activities at t_1 has changed also: A preponderance of the activity is devoted to design of the application's structure. A small amount of requirements analysis is still active, and some implementation is underway.

Cross-section S_n, shown in Figure 2-9, represents the state of the project near the time of its formal conclusion: The core shows a robust architecture, implementation, deployment processes, testing scripts, test results, and so on. The activity level is low, with remaining activities focused on capturing lessons learned.

Viewed as a whole (Figure 2-5), it is evident that the purpose of the rings is to build the core. In other words, the purpose of the development activities is to create the product, in all its various details. These details and structures are abundant at the end of the development activities. This also highlights how a wise organization must treat this core: It is a composite asset of considerable size and value, and should be managed, post-project, accordingly.

Before going on, a few comments on the analogy used in naming the visualization are in order. Turbines are, of course, the engines that propel aircraft, generate hydroelectricity, and power myriad other devices. The core of such turbines is the fluid that flows through them. With jet turbines the fluid is air; the "rings" of a jet turbine include the compressors with their fan blades whose job it is to compress the air, pushing it into the combustion

Figure 2-9.
*Cross-section
of turbine at
time t_n.*

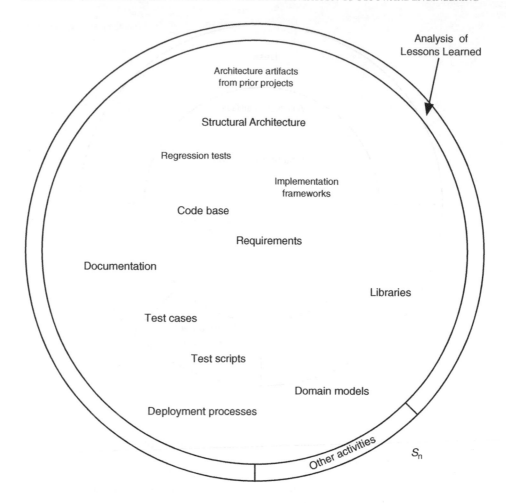

chamber, where fuel is added and ignited. Other rings behind the combustion chamber contribute to the overall process, in which the air, now in large volume and at high speed, exits the engine.

The analogy to software development is only a mild one and should not be pressed very far. But the product is the focus of the turbine; each ring and element contributes to that product. The air flows through the turbine, and is touched by each of the various rings. So, too, does the software product and the architecture, in particular, represents the core of software development. It is touched and (it is hoped) enhanced by each aspect of software development. In contrast to a physical turbine, however, each ring of software development genuinely adds to the core, not just heating it up. (Other difficulties—or advantages—of the analogy, such as the rings spinning in circles and the product just being hot air, are strictly unauthorized!)

2.7.2 Example Process Depictions

Two further examples are shown now, where use of the turbine visualization technique highlights distinctive aspects of these approaches to software development.

A Robust Domain-Specific Software Architecture-based Project

Figure 2-10 shows a turbine visualization of a notional project that was based upon a preexisting domain-specific software architecture, that is, a project similar to the Philips television example of Chapter 1. At the project outset, the core is quite large; it contains a multitude of reusable artifacts from preceding projects. The activities are thus (1) to assess the artifacts to ensure that the current project fits within the constraints imposed by those artifacts, (2) to parameterize those artifacts to meet the new project's needs and to perform any customization necessary, and (3) to integrate, assess, and deploy the product.

Agile Development

The turbine visualization can be used in analyzing alternative approaches to software development. For example, Figure 2-11 shows a notional agile development process. Agile processes are positive in showing, and emphasizing, concurrency between a variety of kinds of development activities; requirements elicitation and development of tests, for instance. As the development progresses those activities do not cease, for example, once code development is begun. Indeed all of these activities continue throughout the project.

As the skinny core of the turbine model indicates, however, the agile process denies development of any explicit architecture; rather for the agile developer the code *is* the architecture. The visualization indicates that the agile process starts with a core that is devoid of any architecture and terminates similarly. A large body of code may be present, along with, perhaps, requirements documents or user guides, but no explicit record of the fundamental design decisions, such as the application's architectural style.

Deployment
Capture of
new work
Other

Customization

Parameterization

Assessment

Figure 2-10.
*A development
process based on
an existing
domain-specific
software
architecture and
reuse library.*

Figure 2-11.
Turbine
visualization of a
notional agile
development
process.

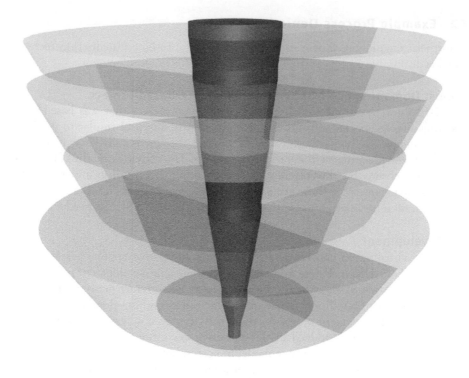

The problems with this approach are made clear when a follow-on project is required. That is, if at some point after the first agile project completes its development, a follow-on project is required to have the application meet some new demand. Unless the same development team—with excellent memories—is employed on the subsequent project, an initial project model such as shown in Figure 2-12 may be anticipated. In particular,

Figure 2-12.
Initial portion of
a turbine model
of a phase 2 agile
process.

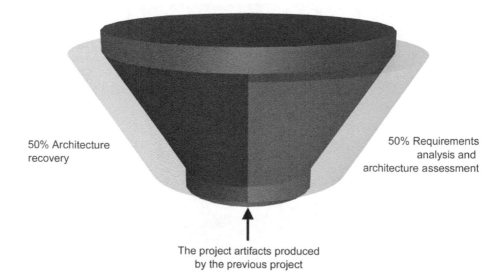

50% Architecture
recovery

50% Requirements
analysis and
architecture assessment

The project artifacts produced
by the previous project

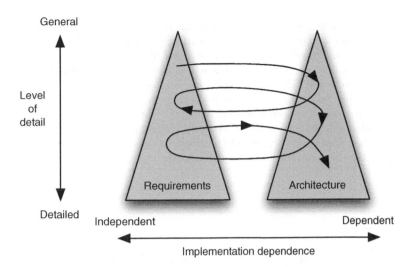

Figure 2-13.
*Twin Peaks
model of
development.*
© *IEEE 2001.*

a significant ring of activity will be required at the beginning of the project to simply understand the existing code base and partially recover the latent architecture so that planning for how to meet the new needs can proceed.

Other Processes and Process Models

A variety of researchers and organizations have promulgated processes that, to a greater or lesser extent, show the special role of architecture in development. One of the best of these is Professor Bashar Nuseibeh's Twin Peaks model Nuseibeh (Nuseibeh 2001). Twin Peaks emphasizes the co-development of requirements and architectures, incrementally elaborating details. The model is illustrated in Figure 2-13, which is derived from the Twin Peaks paper.

It is left as an exercise for the reader to create a turbine visualization of the Twin Peaks process shown in the figure. It should also be noted that the Twin Peaks work is representative of recent work in requirements engineering that is now giving much more prominence to the role of design and existing architectures in the activity of product conception.

"Brooks' law: Adding people to a late software project makes it later."

This adage is one of the best known in software engineering. Yet the reasons why it is so often true are seldom explained. Fred Brooks gave those reasons in an interview:

"Brooks' law depends heavily on the amount of information that has to be communicated. So the argument is that if you add people to a project that you already know is late, which means you're at least in the middle of the project, you have to repartition the work. That's a job in itself: Just deciding who is going to do what means that instead of having the thing divided into the units you had it divided into, you have to divide it into more units. Sometimes that can be done by subdividing the existing units, but sometimes you have to move boundaries."

(Fred Brooks, quoted in *Fortune*, December 12, 2005.)

**Brooks'
Law and
Software
Architecture**

Additional impacts include training of the new people on the team—that takes the time and energy of the existing staff, removing them from productive work. Then when the new people start working they are relatively unproductive at first, and likely to make errors.

Note that Brooks did not say that his law is true because we have immature processes or poor management ability. The law is true because the intellectual substance of software is profound and weighty. An architecture-centric perspective on development therefore gives some advantage in coping with problems in schedule slippage and project management: It provides a technically substantive basis for reasoning about the nascent product that is at a higher level of abstraction than source code, and provides a vehicle for conveying to new project members the principal design decisions that characterize the system.

2.8 END MATTER

This chapter has shown how a proper view of software architecture affects every aspect of the classical software engineering activities and reorients those activities. Any practitioner can have his work informed and changed by an understanding of software architecture, to the project's benefit. In summary,

- The requirements activity is seen as a co-equal partner with design activities, wherein previous products and designs provide the vocabulary for articulating new requirements, and wherein new design insights provide the inspiration for detailed product strategies and requirements.

- The design activity is enriched by techniques that exploit knowledge gained in previous product developments. Designing infuses the entire development and evolution process, instead of being confined to a stand-alone activity.

- The implementation activity is centered on creating a faithful implementation of the architecture and utilizes a variety of techniques to achieve this in a cost-effective manner, ranging from generation of the source code to utilizing implementation frameworks to reuse of preexisting code.

- Analysis and testing activities can be focused on and guided by the architecture, offering the prospect of earlier detection of errors and more efficient and effective examinations of the product. Higher quality at a lower price should be the result.

- Evolution activities revolve around the conceptual bedrock of the product's architecture. Critically, it provides the means for reasoning about possible changes and for conveying essential understandings of the product to engineers who are new to the project.

- An equal focus on process and product results from a proper understanding of the role of software architecture in the development activity. The turbine visualization enables insight into a development process's full character, as it can reveal the extent to which activities are intermingled (likely a very good thing) and especially the extent to which the corpus of project artifacts changes over time.

Despite these insights, attempting to appropriate and apply these ideas without further detail and technical support is difficult and subject to the limitations of a designer's organization and self-discipline. It is the purpose of the following chapters to provide the representational basis for describing architectures effectively and the technological basis for incorporating architecture into a professional approach to the development of software applications. Chapter 3 proceeds to put the concepts on a firm definitional footing; Chapter 4 then proceeds to describe how to design systems from an architectural perspective.

The Business Case for Architecture-centric Development

Sales of a product provide revenue for a company. For a company to grow, sales typically must expand through offering a range of products. For a company to retain its customer base it must be responsive to requests for altered versions of current products, as well as new offerings.

While these observations are almost trivial, the question arises as to what enables a company to perform these tasks successfully over an extended period. Again, the almost trivial answer is a sustained focus on the company's processes as well as a focus on the company's products.

What is remarkable is that over the past twenty years or so this dual focus seems to have been lost in a large number of software organizations. For many, the focus has been solely a focus on process and its improvement. The results of this myopia have been rather mixed. Clearly, there have been many examples of companies improving their processes and also being successful in producing high-quality, successful products. But there are also companies—much less publicized—that have achieved high levels of process improvement but that fail to produce successful, market-leading products. The correlation between process improvement and product success is not absolute, to say the least.

In contrast, consider the relationship between a product's architecture and its quality. It is difficult to have a bad architecture and great product, a product that remains a leader after successive versions and releases. Similarly, it is difficult to have a great architecture and a bad product. Unless the implementation activity is deeply flawed, a great architecture—one that emerges from design that considers all stakeholder concerns and that exhibits intellectual clarity and vision—typically will result in great products.

The correlation between a great architecture and a successful product family is perhaps even stronger. A cost-effective strategy for delivering a good product family demands intellectual coherence across the members of the product family and cost-savings resulting from commonalities and shared infrastructure across the line.

An architecture-centric approach to software development thus puts primacy on the products that are sold and that provide a company's revenue. If process is allowed to become the primary focus, then the focus is on something that does not intrinsically generate revenue for the company. A good process is an asset—a critical one at that—but architecture, at the heart of great products, must be of primary attention.

2.9 REVIEW QUESTIONS

1. Does object-oriented design impose an architecture on an application? Why or why not?

2. Is an architecture-centric viewpoint more consistent with the waterfall model or Boehm's spiral model of software development (Boehm 1988)? Why?

3. Suppose a feature-addition request is given to a development team that has not previously worked on the product in question. How might the team proceed if it is not in possession of the product's architecture? If it is in possession of an accurate, rich architecture?

2.10 EXERCISES

1. For some application that you have developed, describe its architecture, as built. Is that the same as the design you originally developed for the application? What accounts for any differences you observed?

2. Describe an application for which you can develop a complete, adequate requirements document without any recourse to thinking about how the system might be built. Describe an application for which you think it would be difficult, if not impossible, to describe the requirements without recourse to architectural ("how to") concerns.

3. Investigate the history of an influential software product, such as spreadsheets (for example, VisiCalc, Lotus 1-2-3, or Excel), or a service product (for example, eBay or Google). What role did requirements analysis play in the development of the product? How early were design prototypes created?

4. Develop three alternative architectures for a sample problem (such as a simple video game like Tetris or an address book). What makes them different and how did you arrive at the architectures?

5. Consider the application domain of video games, in particular very simple games based on the idea of landing a spacecraft on the moon by controlling the amount of descent thrust. Create a glossary for use in requirements descriptions, including such key terms as descent rate, controls, display, and score. Do notions of solution structure affect development of the definitions? If so, how?

6. Do Exercise 5, but for the domain of spreadsheets. Make sure your glossary includes all the terms needed to fully characterize the spreadsheet's concepts.

7. How does a company build market niche? How could that affect the company's approach to software processes?

8. Is it easier to build a parser for a programming language by manually programming in an object-oriented language, such as Java, or use a parser generator, such as ANTLR or Bison? What assumptions does your analysis make?

9. With regard to Exercise 8, what does implementing a parser using a parser generator entail? Where did the architecture of the (generated) parser come from?

10. With regard to Exercises 8 and 9, if you were responsible for testing both a manually written parser and a parser generated by a parser tool, how would your testing concerns and strategies vary between the two products? Why?

11. Abstract requirements may work on small problems wherein the engineer can, after specification, devise many solutions quickly, or there may only be a small number of solutions, *and* the total time involved in finding one solution starting from scratch is not so great as to matter. But above a certain threshold, it appears that it becomes either economically inefficient to pursue this course of action or it is intellectually too difficult to pursue this practice, or both. Describe a small domain where you illustrate this point. In which domains do you think that the use of abstract requirements have been most effective? To what do you attribute the success?

12. The chapter described how the width of a rotor in the turbine visualization should be proportional to the amount of labor directed at the development activity at a given point in time. For example, the width could be a function of the number of labor hours per day devoted to development. What should the width of the turbine's core be? It should be a measure of the information space of the project. Consider the relative merits of measuring: the number of megabytes of project artifacts, the number of project artifact files, and the number of source lines of code or text documents. What other measures could be used?

13. Draw a turbine visualization of a notional Twin Peaks software development process.

14. Draw a turbine visualization of a notional software project that follows the Unified Process [see (Kruchten 2000; Larman 2002; Schach 2007) for example explications].

2.11 FURTHER READING

Substantive presentations of software engineering and software development processes can be found in any of several excellent textbooks, such as those by Ghezzi et al. (Ghezzi, Jazayeri, and Mandrioli 2003), and van Vliet (van Vliet 2000).

Problem solving and design in general has been addressed by many authors. Design is the focus of Chapter 4, and a variety of readings are listed at the end of that chapter. Polya's original book on problem solving—which largely focuses on the solving of problems in mathematics—is readily available (Polya 1957). Some general reflections on design and the design process include Schön's classic *The Reflective Practitioner* (Schön 1983), Don Norman's insightful book on *The Design of Everyday Things* (Norman 2002), and Nelson's treatment of the traditions and practices of design (Nelson and Stolterman 2003). For the engineer in all of us, Henry Petroski's books are a delight, exploring the design of things from bridges to paperclips, but they are especially valuable in revealing the role of failure in achieving new designs (Petroski 1985, 1992, 1994, 1996). Several detailed stories of how design of the F-15, F-16, and A-10 aircraft were, or nearly were, subverted due to loss of focus on the core architecture are told in *Boyd: The Fighter Pilot Who Changed the Art of War* (Coram 2002). The history of the design of washing machines, mentioned briefly in the text, is presented online in a variety of Web sites, including www.sciencetech.technomuses.ca/english/collection/wash1.cfm and www.historychannel.com/exhibits/hometech/wash.html.

Excellent presentation of contemporary thinking on the process of requirements analysis can be found in the works of Jackson, van Lamsweerde, and Nuseibeh (Jackson 1995; Jackson 2001; Nuseibeh and Easterbrook 2000; van Lamsweerde 2000). Object-oriented design is explained in most modern software engineering textbooks, such as those listed above. Software analysis and testing is explained in detail in Pezzè and Young's textbook (Pezzè and Young 2007).

The Twin Peaks model of development was presented in a short paper in *IEEE Computer* (Nuseibeh 2001). Subsequent work has explored more deeply the relationship between requirements and architecture; see for example (Rapanotti et al. 2004).

3

Basic Concepts

The preceding chapters informally discussed a number of software architectural notions, such as software components and connectors; their configurations in a given system; relationships between a system's requirements, its architecture, and its implementation; and software product lines. These ideas served to provide context for the field of software architecture, situate it within other facets of software engineering, and motivate its unique role and importance. Indeed, we have generally avoided definitions of terms in the hope that the reader will more readily recognize many of the discussed concepts within his own experience, or be able to relate the architectural concepts to those with which he is already familiar.

While informal terms have a useful role in introducing concepts, the uncertainties that result can hinder deeper understanding. Hence, the objective of this chapter is to define the key terms and ideas from the field of software architecture, providing a uniform basis for their discussion in the remainder of the book. Key elements of architecture-centric design and their interrelationships, basic techniques and processes for developing a software system's architecture, and the relevant stakeholders and their roles in architecture-based software development are presented and illustrated with simple examples.

Outline of Chapter 3

3.1 TERMINOLOGY

We begin presentation of the field's key terms with an exploration of software architecture itself and several concepts tied to it, such as architectural degradation. The major constituent elements of architectures are then explored, including components, connectors, and configurations. Two important types of potentially deep architectural knowledge—architectural patterns and styles—are then defined and examined.

3.1.1   Architecture

At its essence, software architecture is defined quite simply, as follows.

> *Definition.* **A software system's *architecture* is the set of principal design decisions made about the system.**

Put another way, software architecture is the blueprint for a software system's construction and evolution. The notion of *design decision* is central to software architecture and to all of the concepts based on it. For example, the special notion of *product family architectures* was briefly introduced Chapter 1. Product family architectures are anchored on the idea of reference architecture, defined as follows.

> *Definition.* **A *reference architecture* is the set of principal design decisions that are simultaneously applicable to multiple related systems, typically within an application domain, with explicitly defined points of variation.**

Design decisions encompass every aspect of the system under development, including:

- Design decisions related to system *structure*—for example, "The architectural elements should be organized and composed exactly like this . . ."
- Design decisions related to *functional behavior*—for example, "Data processing, storage, and visualization will be performed in strict sequence."
- Design decisions related to *interaction*—for example, "Communication among all system elements will occur only using event notifications."
- Design decisions related to the system's *nonfunctional properties*—for example, "The system's dependability will be ensured by replicated processing modules."
- Design decisions related to the system's *implementation*—for example, "The user interface components will be built using the Java Swing toolkit."

Note that in the preceding discussion and examples we have used terms such as *element* and *module*, which we have not yet defined. You can think of them simply as building blocks (akin to bricks in the construction of physical structures) from which the architecture is composed. We soon will address them more rigorously.

Another important term that appears in the above definitions is *principal*. It implies a degree of importance and topicality that grants a design decision architectural status, that is, that makes it an *architectural design decision*. It also implies that not all design decisions are architectural. In fact, many of the design decisions made in the process of engineering a system (for example, the details of the selected algorithms or data structures) will not impact a system's architecture. How one defines principal will depend on the system goals. Ultimately, the system's stakeholders (including, but not restricted only to the architect) will decide which design decisions are or are not important enough to include in the architecture.

Based on this, note that architecture is at least in part determined by context, that nontechnical considerations may end up driving it, and that different sets of stakeholders may deem different sets of design decisions principal (that is, architectural). We discuss this further below and elsewhere in the text.

Another observation following from the definition of software architecture is that every set of principal design decisions can be thought of as a different architecture. Over the lifetime of a system, these design decisions will be made and unmade; they will change, evolve, "fork," converge, and so on. As the architecture of a large, complex, long-lived system is developed and evolved, the corresponding set of architectural design decisions will be changed hundreds of times. The outcome will, in effect, be hundreds of different (though related) architectures, rather than a single architecture. In that sense, architecture has a temporal aspect.

Prescriptive Architecture versus Descriptive Architecture

At any time, t, during the process of engineering a software system, that system's architects will have made a set of architectural design decisions, P, that reflect their intent. These design decisions comprise the system's *prescriptive architecture*. In other words, these design decisions represent the prescription for the system's construction. The prescriptive architecture is thus the system's as-intended or as-conceived architecture. The prescriptive architecture need not necessarily exist in any tangible form. For example, it may be entirely in the architects' minds. Alternatively, the prescriptive architecture may have been captured in a notation such as an architecture description language (such as those presented in Chapter 6) or another form of documentation.

It is important to note that documenting the prescriptive architecture is not enough. The reader should recall that architecture is not just a phase in the process of developing a software system, but rather forms the critical underpinning for the system from its inception through retirement. Thus, at any point during this process, the architectural design decisions that are part of the prescriptive architecture (that is, of the set P) will putatively be refined and *realized* with a set of artifacts, A. These artifacts may include refinements of architectural design decisions in a notation such as the Unified Modeling Language or their implementations in a programming language. The artifacts may also include models of architectural styles and patterns used in the architecture, previously existing off-the-shelf software components that will be used in the desired system, implementation frameworks and middleware infrastructures that will aid the system's construction, specifications of standards to which the architecture needs to adhere, and so on.

While many of the artifacts in A may have existed prior to and independently of the architecture under consideration, each embodies certain design decisions that the architects find desirable and relevant to the current system. The full set of principal design decisions, D, embodied in the set of artifacts, A, is referred to as the system's *descriptive architecture*. The descriptive architecture is referred to as such because it describes how the system has been realized. The descriptive architecture is thus the system's as-realized architecture.

The reader should note that, in the early stages of a system's life cycle, the number of artifacts that realize the architecture will typically be smaller than during later stages when more of the system's architecture has been elaborated and possibly implemented.

In fact, if we consider time t_1 to indicate the inception of the initial set P_1 of architectural design decisions for a given system, the sets A_1, and thus D_1, may be empty. This will typically be the case in so-called greenfield development, where the system is designed and implemented from scratch. In the case of brownfield development, many artifacts partially realizing the architecture for a given system may exist before the architecture is even conceived; in other words, at the start of a project, t_0, the set D_0 is nonempty while P_0 may be an empty set. This is the case if the new system is a member of a closely related application family, the architectural styles and/or patterns that will be used are known ahead of time, the middleware platforms and/or implementation languages have been selected, and so on. Another situation in which P_0 may be empty while D_0 is large is development involving a legacy system whose architectural intent has been lost over time. Such discrepancies between sets P and D can be indications of problems with a system's software architecture, and will be discussed further below.

Prescriptive and Descriptive Architectures in Action: An Example

Let us illustrate the above discussion with a simple example. At this point, the reader is not expected to understand all the nuances and implications of this example, but only to follow along with the argument as it pertains to prescriptive and descriptive architecture.

Figure 3-1 shows a graphical view of the prescriptive architecture of a simple logistics application. In other words, the diagram in the figure is a model of the architecture in a graphical architecture description language. The architecture is designed using a set of components, which implement the application's functionality, and connectors, which enable the components to call each other's operations and exchange data. (Components and connectors will be defined more formally later in this chapter.)

This application controls the routing of cargo from a set of incoming Delivery Ports to a set of Warehouses via a set of Vehicles. The Cargo Router component tries to optimize the use of vehicles and deliver the cargo to its proper destination (that is, warehouse). The Clock component provides the time and helps the ports, vehicles, and warehouses to synchronize as necessary. Finally, the Graphics Binding component provides a graphical user interface that allows a human operator to assess the state of the system during its execution. The components in the system interact via three connectors—Clock Conn, Router Conn, and Graphics Conn—by exchanging requests and replies. The lines connecting the component and connector elements in the architecture represent the elements' interaction paths.

The cargo routing application is useful in this discussion for three reasons. First, its simplicity suggests that its architects should have been able to evaluate all of the architectural decisions and their trade-offs before the application was implemented. Second, the architecture was carefully implemented with the help of an architectural framework (see Chapter 9 for a discussion of architectural frameworks), which allowed the application's developers to realize all of the architectural design decisions directly in the code. Third, aside from a graphical user interface (GUI) library, no other off-the-shelf functionality was used in the implementation, which allowed for a carefully controlled mapping between the architecture and its implementation (that is, between the sets P and D).

A graphical view of the descriptive (that is, as-realized) architecture of the cargo routing application is depicted in Figure 3-2. While there are many artifacts in the set A of this application (including the architectural style used to realize the architecture, the implementation framework, the off-the-shelf GUI toolkit, and the implementation code itself), we have deliberately elided many of these and extracted the simplified view of the descriptive architecture, D, from them.

It can be noticed immediately that the extracted view of the descriptive architecture is not identical to the prescriptive architecture: the Vehicle component is not connected to the Clock Conn connector, while the Router Conn and Clock Conn connectors are connected, allowing two-hop routing of requests and replies in the architecture. It is thus possible for the Clock component to interact directly with the Cargo Router component via the two connectors. The application-specific reasons behind these changes are unimportant to this discussion. What is important is the fact that the programmers and architects together discovered that, even in the case of such a simple application, they had not properly thought through all of the architectural design decisions. It is, then, reasonable to expect that such issues would only be exacerbated in larger, more complex systems. In such systems, the prescriptive and descriptive architectures may not look nearly as similar to one another. This is an issue that will be revisited several times throughout the book.

Let us take this discussion a step further. We can ask several questions about the prescriptive and descriptive architectures of the cargo routing application. Again, the reader is not yet expected to be able to provide complete answers to these questions. Instead, the purpose is to illustrate certain issues that will be revisited and sensitize the reader to the difficulties inherent in the architectural design of even moderately complex software systems.

1. Which architecture is "correct?" The prescriptive architecture reflects the architects' intent, but the descriptive architecture reflects the added experience of actually implementing the system.

2. Are the two architectures consistent with one another? In this example, the differences were relatively easy to spot. However, architectural inconsistencies can be much more complex and/or insidious.

3. What criteria are used to establish the consistency between the two architectures? Again, in this example a simple structural comparison sufficed, but more sophisticated techniques may be needed.

4. On what information is the answer to the preceding questions based? The two diagrams in Figure 3-1 and Figure 3-2 represent very small subsets of different concerns that may be captured and/or visualized in an architectural model. Even if these two diagrams were identical, the amount of architectural information they represent is insufficient to make any guarantees about the two architectures' relationship.

Architectural Degradation

During the lifespan of a typical software system, a large number of prescriptive and descriptive architectures will be created. Each corresponding pair of such architectures represents the system's software architecture at a given time, t. As the set of principal design decisions, P, the set of artifacts, A, and the corresponding principal design decisions, D, embodied in the artifacts, grow, so the system's software architecture becomes more complete. The system's stakeholders will decide the state at which P and A (and thus D) can be considered sufficiently complete and sufficiently consistent with one another for the system to be released into operation.

In an ideal scenario, the two sets of architectural design decisions, P and D, would always be identical; in other words, D would always be a perfect realization of P. However,

Figure 3-1.
*A high-level
graphical view of
the prescriptive
(that is,
as-designed or
as-intended)
architecture of
the cargo routing
application.*

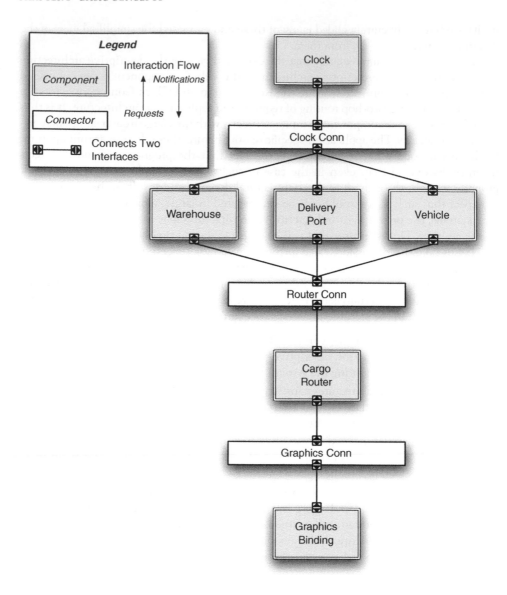

this need not be the case. For example, an off-the-shelf component or middleware platform will likely embody a number of design decisions that may, in turn, impact the architectural design decisions made for the system under construction. Thus, the exact relationship between sets P and D may vary depending on the system in question, the requirements imposed by system stakeholders, the point in the system's lifespan, and so on. However, it is imperative that the stakeholders, and architects in particular, understand this relationship and be precise about the allowed differences between P and D.

Note that, given sets of design decisions in P and D at time t, it is possible for these sets to remain stable to time $t + n$. This simply means that though the set A may have enlarged as implementation progresses, the addition of more artifacts or the further development of

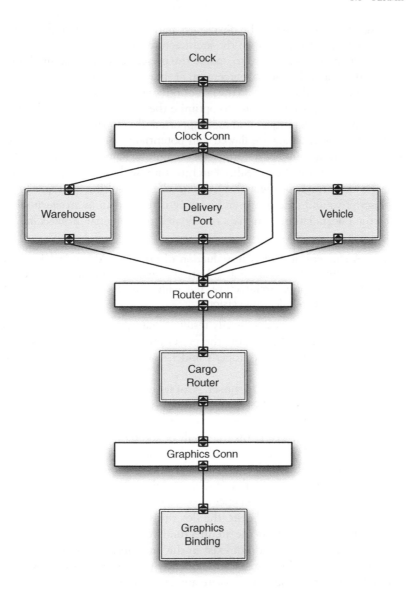

Figure 3-2.
A high-level,
graphical view of
the descriptive
(that is,
as-implemented
or as-realized)
architecture of
the cargo routing
application.

existing artifacts did not introduce any new principal design decisions. It is also possible that P changes while D remains the same (for instance, when architectural design concerns are elaborated but the artifacts realizing the system have not yet been updated); similarly, D may change while P remains the same.

When a system is initially developed or when the already implemented system is evolved, ideally its prescriptive architecture is first modified appropriately, and then the corresponding changes to the descriptive architecture follow. Unfortunately, this does not always happen in practice. Instead, the system (and thus its descriptive architecture) is often directly modified, without accounting for the impact relative to the prescriptive architecture.

In the cargo routing example, the developers may not have bothered to inform the architects that they decided to change the architecture in several places—even if those changes were warranted. Such failure to update the prescriptive architecture happens for several reasons: developer sloppiness, perception of short deadlines that prevent thinking through and documenting the impact on the prescriptive architecture, lack of a documented prescriptive architecture, need or desire to optimize the system "which can be done only in the code," inadequate techniques and tool support, and so forth.

Whatever the reasons, they are flawed and potentially dangerous, especially if one considers that software systems are notorious for containing many errors (that is, for being "buggy"). Do we really want the as-realized architecture, with all of its potentially latent faults, to be the final arbiter of the architects' *intent*? The resulting discrepancy between a system's prescriptive and descriptive architecture is referred to as *architectural degradation*. Architectural degradation comprises two related phenomena: *architectural drift* and *architectural erosion*.

> **Definition.** **Architectural drift is introduction of principal design decisions into a system's descriptive architecture that (a) are not included in, encompassed by, or implied by the prescriptive architecture, but which (b) do not violate any of the prescriptive architecture's design decisions.**

Architectural drift does not necessarily result in outright violations of the prescriptive architecture. Instead, it circumvents the prescriptive architecture and may involve decisions whose implications are not properly understood and which may affect the given system's future adaptability.

Drift is a result of direct changes to the set, A, of system artifacts. These changes may, in turn, result in changes to the set, D, of corresponding principal design decisions. Note that all expansions of the set D do not necessarily result in architectural drift. New principal design decisions may be added to D (as the result of adding or changing elements of A) that are consistent with all the decisions in P and that are implied by or encompassed by decisions in P. For instance, P may require encryption to be used in any communication over an open network; D may state that public-key algorithms be used to support such encrypted communication—a decision encompassed by P.

As an example of architectural drift, the descriptive architecture in the cargo routing application (Figure 3-2) reflects the architectural design decision to introduce a link between two connectors, which did not exist in the prescriptive architecture. Assuming that the system's original architects did not explicitly prohibit the direct linking of two connectors, adding the link would not violate any of the architectural decisions made in the prescriptive architecture. However, it does not mean that adding this link is a harmless or proper thing to do.

Architectural drift may also cause violations of architectural style rules. In other words, architectural drift reflects the engineers' insensitivity to the system's architecture and can lead to a loss of clarity of form and system understanding (Perry and Wolf 1992). If not properly addressed, architectural drift will eventually result in architectural erosion.

> **Definition.** **Architectural erosion is the introduction of architectural design decisions into a system's descriptive architecture that violate its prescriptive architecture.**

In terms of the architectural design decision sets, P and D, architectural erosion can be thought of as the result of direct changes to the system artifact set, A, which introduces a principal design decision in D that invalidates or violates one or more design decisions that already exist in *P*. Erosion renders a system difficult to understand and adapt, and also frequently leads to system failure.

Architectural erosion can easily occur when a system has drifted too far, in that it is easy to violate important architectural decisions if those decisions are obscured by many small, intermediate changes. Note that an architecture can certainly erode without previous drift. However, this is both less likely to happen (since there has been no drift yet, the prescriptive and descriptive architectures are consistent at the time the erroneous changes are made) and easier to recover from (since fewer decisions are involved). Note also that architectural erosion may be caused by design decisions that are sound when considered in isolation. However, in combination with other decisions that have been made, but perhaps not properly documented, a new design decision may have unforeseen and undesired consequences.

In the cargo routing application example, the removal of the link between the Vehicle component and its adjacent connector in the descriptive architecture would have resulted in architectural erosion had it not been justified and had the prescriptive architecture not been properly updated. The removal of this link introduces the potential danger that the vehicles controlled by the system are unable to synchronize properly with the rest of the system and deliver their cargo on time. In this case, the system developers realized that Vehicles do not need to keep track of time internally so long as the Cargo Router component gives them appropriate instructions. They discussed this observation with the architects, who agreed and updated the prescriptive architecture accordingly.

Both architectural drift and architectural erosion can be dangerous and expensive, and should be avoided. This requires a certain discipline on the part of architects and developers, but in the long run it saves effort and money, while helping to preserve the important system properties.

Architectural Perspectives

The notion of an architectural perspective is to highlight some aspects of an architecture while eliding others.

> **Definition.** An *architectural perspective* is a nonempty set of types of architectural design decisions.

As the preceding discussion indicated, software architectures encompass decisions made by a variety of stakeholders at varying levels of detail and abstraction. The purpose of an architectural perspective is to direct attention, for example, for purposes of analysis, to a subset of the decisions. Figure 3-1 and Figure 3-2, for example, provide only the *structural* perspective of the cargo routing application, and say nothing about its behavior, interactions, rationale, and so on.

Another example perspective is *deployment*. A software system cannot fulfill its purpose until it is deployed, that is, until its executable modules are physically placed on the hardware devices on which they are intended to run. The deployment perspective of an architecture can be critical in assessing whether the system will be able to satisfy its requirements. For example, placing many large components on a small device with limited memory and CPU power, or transferring high volumes of data over a network link with low bandwidth will negatively impact the system, much like incorrectly implementing its functionality will. An example deployment perspective on the cargo routing application's architecture is shown in Figure 3-3.

Figure 3-3.
*A deployment
view of the cargo
routing
application's
architecture
distributed across
five devices. It is
assumed that the
Warehouse,
Delivery Port,
and Vehicle
components
interact with the
corresponding
physical objects in
order to be able to
maintain their
state in real-time.
However, those
interactions are
not depicted here.*

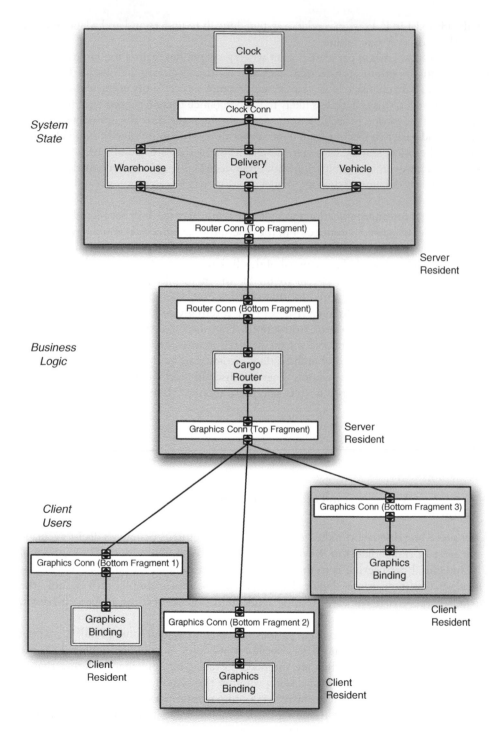

To further illustrate, recall that architecture has a temporal dimension, that is, that a system's architecture will likely change over time. However, at any given point in time, the system has only *one* architecture. That architecture may be thought of, modeled, visualized, and discussed from different perspectives. For example, the perspective of the system's modules and their interconnections that is unencumbered with any aspects of the hardware on which the system will run might be referred to as the *structural* view; if we were talking about the prescriptive architecture of a system, then we would say that this is the *structural view of the prescriptive architecture*; if, on the other hand, we were to postulate the hardware topology on which this architecture may (or should) run once implemented, then we would be talking about the *deployment view of the prescriptive architecture*; if we are discussing the distribution of implemented system modules on the different hardware hosts, we would say that this is the *deployment view of the descriptive architecture*; and so on.

Architectural perspectives and views will be discussed in more detail in Chapters 6 and 7. We continue the discussion below with definitions of key architectural building blocks and several other key concepts derived from the concept of software architecture.

Dewayne Perry and Alexander Wolf (Perry and Wolf 1992) provide a useful characterization of software architecture as a triple:

Other Definitions of Software Architecture

> *Definition.* Architecture = {*elements, form, rationale*}

In other words, the architecture defines the system's key elements, and their relationships to each other and to their environment. Furthermore, the architecture reflects the rationale behind the system's structure, functionality, interactions, and resulting properties.

Elements capture the system's building blocks, and help to answer the What questions about the architecture. The questions you may ask about the architecture's elements include the following: What are the system's building blocks? What is a given element's primary purpose in the system? What system services does each element (help to) provide?

Perry and Wolf identify three types of building blocks:

- Processing elements
- Data elements
- Connecting elements

These three types are usually consolidated into two major architectural concepts, components and connectors, which will be discussed below. The one notable exception is the REST architectural style (introduced in Chapter 1 and further discussed in Chapter 11). REST not only gives data elements first-class status, they surpass in importance both processing and connecting elements.

The form captures the way in which the system elements are organized in the architecture. Form represents the structure of individual architectural elements, the manner in which they are composed in the system (that is, the architecture's configuration or topology), the characteristics of their interaction, as well as their relationship to their operating environment (for example, deployment of specific software elements onto specific hardware hosts). The form helps to answer the How questions about the architecture, which may include the following: How is the overall architecture organized? How are the elements composed to accomplish the system's key tasks? How are the elements distributed over a network?

Finally, rationale represents the system designers' intent, assumptions, subtle choices, external (perhaps nontechnical) constraints, selected design patterns and styles, and any other information that may not be obvious or easily derivable from the architecture. Rationale helps to answer the Why questions about the architecture. These questions may include the following: Why are particular elements used? Why are they combined in a particular way? Why is the system distributed in the given manner?

Although in their seminal paper Perry and Wolf acknowledge the key role of software architecture in a system's evolution, note that their definition does not explicitly capture evolution. However, their definition does suggest that capturing the design rationale is a prerequisite to successfully making any subsequent changes to the system's architecture.

Another useful definition of architecture, which explicitly addresses system evolution, is that provided by the *ANSI/IEEE Standard 1471-2000, Recommended Practice for Architectural Description of Software-Intensive Systems*:

> **Definition.** **Architecture is the fundamental organization of a system, embodied in its components, their relationships to each other and the environment, and the principles governing its design and evolution.**

Note that this definition does not specifically refer to software, suggesting that the architecture of a software system is fundamentally similar to architectures of other types of complex systems.

Another interesting, and frequently cited definition of software architecture is attributed to Chris Verhoef (Klusener et al. 2005):

> **Definition.** **The software architecture of deployed software is determined by those aspects that are the hardest to change.**

This is a different perspective on how to define software architecture: The definition tells us what *effect* architecture will have on a software system in terms of that system's stability and modifiability. However, the definition does not say what architecture *is*. Furthermore, it is a fair question to ask whether just because something is principal it must be the most difficult to change. In fact, in many cases, architectural design decisions will be explicit enablers of system modification. Examples of this will be provided throughout the book, and in particular in the discussion of architecture-driven software system adaptation discussed in Chapter 14.

3.1.2 Component

The decisions comprising a software system's architecture encompass a rich interplay and composition of many different elements. These elements address key system concerns, including:

- Processing, which may also be referred to as functionality or behavior.
- State, which may also be referred to as information or data.
- Interaction, which may also be referred to as interconnection, communication, coordination, or mediation.

In this section, we will address architectural elements dealing with the first two concerns—processing and data; interaction is covered in the next section.

Elements that encapsulate processing and data in a system's architecture are referred to as *software components*.

Definition. A *software component* is an architectural entity that (1) encapsulates a subset of the system's functionality and/or data, (2) restricts access to that subset via an explicitly defined interface, and (3) has explicitly defined dependencies on its required execution context.

Put another way, a software component is a locus of computation and state in a system (Shaw et al. 1995). A component can be as simple as a single operation or as complex as an entire system, depending on the architecture, the perspective taken by the designers, and the needs of the given system. The key aspect of any component is that it can be "seen" by its users, whether human or software, from the outside only, and only via the interface it (or, rather, its developer) has chosen to make public. Otherwise it appears as a "black box." Software components are thus embodiments of the software engineering principles of *encapsulation*, *abstraction*, and *modularity*. In turn, this has a number of positive implications on a component's composability, reusability, and evolvability.

Another critical facet of software components that makes them usable and reusable across applications is their explicit treatment of the execution context that a component assumes and on which it depends. The extent of the context captured by a component can include:

- The component's *required* interface, that is, the interface to services provided by other components in a system on which this component depends for its ability to perform its operations.
- The availability of specific resources, such as data files or directories, on which the component relies.
- The required system software, such as programming language run time environments, middleware platforms, operating systems, network protocols, device drivers, and so on.
- The hardware configurations needed to execute the component.

Another aspect of a software component, and one that helps to distinguish it further from the connectors discussed below, is a component's relationship to the specific application to which it belongs. Components are often targeted at the processing and data capture needs of a particular application; that is, they are said to be *application-specific*. For example, Vehicle and Warehouse in the cargo routing system are application-specific components: While they may be useful in other similar systems, they were specifically designed and implemented to address the needs of that application.

This need not be always the case, however. Sometimes components are designed to address the needs of multiple applications within a particular class of applications or problem domain. For example, Web servers are an integral part of any Web-based system; one will probably download, install, and configure an existing Web server rather than develop one's own. Another example involves components such as CTunerDriver, CFrontEnd, and CBackEnd, introduced in the product-line discussion in Chapter 1, Figure 1-6, which are intended to be reused across different systems within the consumer electronics domain.

Finally, certain software components are utilities that are needed and can be reused across numerous applications, without regard for the specific application characteristics or domain. Common examples of reusable utility components are math libraries and GUI toolkits, such as Java's Swing toolkit. Another example of arbitrarily reusable components includes common off-the-shelf applications such as word processors, spreadsheets, or drawing packages. While they usually provide a large superset of any one system's particular needs, architects may choose to integrate them rather than reimplement the exact needed functionality. As the reader will recall, this is the very reason why a system's prescriptive and descriptive architectures need not be identical.

Other Definitions of Software Component	Clemens Szyperski provides another, widely cited definition of software component (Szyperski 1997). He approaches components from a somewhat different perspective:

> *Definition.* **A software component is a unit of composition with contractually specified interfaces and explicit context dependencies only. A software component can be deployed independently and is subject to composition by third parties.**

This definition does not tell us what a component is, but rather how it is to be structured and used, both by software developers (by composing the component into a system and deploying it) and by other components (by interacting with it through explicit interfaces). This definition also reflects the vision that, once engineered, the component's interior becomes invisible to the outside world. At the same time, the definition does not capture the role a component plays in a system, so that the same definition could, in fact, be used to define a software connector. Below we will define what a software connector is, and how it fundamentally differs from a component.

Szyperski's definition is similar to several other definitions of software components [for example, see Heineman and Councill's book (Heineman and Councill 2001)] in that it does not separate processing from data components as suggested by Perry and Wolf. It is possible that this failure to separate data from computation in software systems' architectures is a side effect of the popularity of object-orientation and particularly object-oriented languages, in which all system elements are treated as objects, regardless of their purpose. One of the primary goals of software architectures is to illuminate and improve understanding of software systems, however, and it may be argued that different concerns (in this case, processing components and data components) should be treated separately. Even though our definition does identify the dual purpose of software components, we should point out that we have rarely found the two addressed separately (the REST architectural style being one notable exception); instead, most frequently a single component will perform a portion of the system's functionality and maintain a part of its state. The distinction will, then, be made according to the component's primary purpose in the system.

3.1.3 Connector

Components are in charge of *processing* or *data*, or both simultaneously. Another fundamental aspect of software systems is *interaction* among the system's building blocks. Many modern systems are built from large numbers of complex components, distributed across multiple, possibly mobile hosts, and dynamically updated over long time periods. In such systems, ensuring appropriate interactions among the components may become even more important and challenging to developers than the functionality of the individual components. In other words, the interactions in a system become a principal (that is, architectural) concern. Software connectors are the architectural abstraction tasked with managing component interactions.

> *Definition.* **A *software connector* is an architectural element tasked with effecting and regulating interactions among components.**

In traditional desktop software systems, connectors usually have manifested themselves as simple procedure calls or shared data accesses, and have typically been treated as ephemeral or invisible in terms of architecture. This is emblematic of boxes-and-lines diagrams, where the boxes, that is, components, dominate, while connectors are relegated to a minor role and accordingly are represented as lines without identity or any unique or important properties. Furthermore, these simple connectors are usually restricted to enabling the interaction of pairs of components. However, as software systems have become more complex, so have connectors, with their own separate identities, roles, and bodies of implementation-level code, as well as ability to simultaneously service many different components.

Connectors are such a critical, rich, and yet largely underappreciated element of software architectures that we have decided to dedicate Chapter 5 to them. Here, we just briefly illustrate some of the connectors with which the reader may be familiar.

The simplest and most widely used type of connector is *procedure call*. Procedure calls are directly implemented in programming languages, where they typically enable synchronous exchange of data and control between pairs of components: The invoking component (the caller) passes the thread of control, as well as data in the form of invocation parameters, to the invoked component (the callee); after it completes the requested operation, the callee returns the control, as well as any results of the operation, to the caller.

Another very common connector type is *shared data access*. This connector type is manifested in software systems in the form of nonlocal variables or shared memory. Connectors of this type allow multiple software components to interact by reading from and writing to the shared facilities. The interaction is distributed in time, that is, it is asynchronous: The writers need not have any temporal dependencies or place any temporal constraints on the readers and vice versa.

An important class of connectors in modern software systems is *distribution* connectors. These connectors typically encapsulate network library application programming interfaces (APIs) to enable components in a distributed system to interact. A distribution connector is usually coupled with a more basic connector to insulate the interacting components from the system distribution details. Thus, for example, remote procedure call (RPC) connectors couple distribution support with procedure calls.

Many software systems are constructed from preexisting components, which may not have been tailor-made for the given system. In such cases, the components may need help with integrating and interacting with one another. *Adaptor* connectors are employed to this end. Depending on their characteristics and the context within which they are used, wrappers and glue code are two common kinds of adaptor connectors with which the reader may be familiar.

Note that while components mostly provide application-specific services, connectors are typically application-independent. We can discuss the characteristics of a procedure call, distributor, adaptor, and so forth independently of the components they service. Notions that have entered our collective dialect, such as "publish-subscribe," "asynchronous event notification," and "remote procedure call," have associated meanings and characteristics that are largely independent of the context within which they are used. Such connectors can be built without a specific purpose in mind, and then used in applications repeatedly (possibly after some customization).

3.1.4 Configuration

Components and connectors are composed in a specific way in a given system's architecture to accomplish that system's objective. That composition represents the system's configuration, also referred to as topology. We define configurations as follows.

> *Definition.* An *architectural configuration* is a set of specific associations between the components and connectors of a software system's architecture.

A configuration may be represented as a graph wherein nodes represent components and connectors, and whose edges represent their associations (topology or interconnectivity).

As an example, Figure 3-1 shows the architectural configuration of the example cargo routing system. In the figure, Delivery Port and Cargo Router are examples of components, while Router Conn is a connector between them. The configuration shown in the diagram implies that it is possible for these two components to interact with one another; that is, that there is a possible interaction *path* between the components. However, the displayed information does not guarantee their actual ability to interact. In addition to the appropriate connectivity, the components must have compatible interfaces; note that interfaces are not shown in the diagram in Figure 3-1. Incompatible interfaces are one source of *architectural mismatch*, which we further discuss below.

3.1.5 Architectural Style

As software engineers have built many different systems across a multitude of application domains they have observed that, under given circumstances, certain design choices regularly result in solutions with superior properties. Compared to other possible alternatives, these solutions are more elegant, effective, efficient, dependable, evolvable, and scalable. For example, it has been observed that the following set of design choices ensures effective provision of services to multiple system users in a distributed setting. These choices are intentionally stated here informally, to illustrate the point.

1. Physically separate the software components used to request services from the components that provide the needed services, to allow for proper distribution and scaling up, both in the numbers of service providers and service requesters.
2. Make the service providers unaware of the requesters' identity to allow the providers to service transparently many, possibly changing requesters.
3. Insulate the requesters from one another to allow for their independent addition, removal, and modification. Make the requesters dependent only on the service providers.
4. Allow for multiple service providers to emerge dynamically to off-load the existing providers should the demand for services increase above a given threshold.

Note that the above list does not comprise architectural design decisions for a particular system (or class of systems). Rather, these architectural decisions are applicable to any system that shares the distributed service provision context. These decisions do not specify the components (or component types), the interaction mechanisms among those components, or their specific configuration. The architect will have to elaborate further on these decisions and turn them into application-specific architectural decisions when designing a system. These higher-level architectural decisions do, however, state the rationale that underlies them, so that the architect can justify choosing them for his system.

> *Definition*. An *architectural style* is a named collection of architectural design decisions that (1) are applicable in a given development context, (2) constrain architectural design decisions that are specific to a particular system within that context, and (3) elicit beneficial qualities in each resulting system.

The above example is an informal and partial specification of the popular client-server style. Many other styles are in use regularly in software systems, including REST and pipe-and-filter styles introduced in Chapter 1 and others that will be revisited throughout the book. Chapters 4 and 11 provide detailed discussions of architectural styles.

3.1.6 Architectural Pattern

Architectural styles provide general design decisions that both constrain and may need to be refined into additional, usually more specific design decisions in order to be applied to a system. In contrast, an architectural pattern provides a set of specific design decisions that have been identified as effective for organizing certain classes of software systems or, more typically, specific subsystems. These design decisions can be thought of as configurable in that they need to be instantiated with the components and connectors particular to an application. In other words:

> *Definition*. An *architectural pattern* is a named collection of architectural design decisions that are applicable to a recurring design problem, parameterized to account for different software development contexts in which that problem appears.

On the surface, this definition is reminiscent of the definition of architectural style. In fact, the two notions are similar and it is not always possible to identify a crisp boundary between them. However, in general styles and patterns differ in at least three important ways:

1. *Scope*: An architectural style applies to a development *context* (for example, "highly distributed systems" or "GUI-intensive") while an architectural pattern applies to a specific design *problem* (for example, "The system's state must be presented in multiple ways" or "The system's business logic must be separated from data management"). A problem is significantly more concrete than a context. Put more concisely, architectural styles are *strategic* while patterns are *tactical* design tools.

2. *Abstraction*: A style helps to constrain the architectural design decisions one makes about a system. However, styles require human interpretation in order to relate design guidelines captured to reflect the general characteristics of the development context to the design problems pertaining to the specific system at hand. By themselves, styles are too abstract to yield a concrete system design. In contrast, patterns are parameterized architectural fragments that can be thought of as concrete pieces of a design.

3. *Relationship*: Patterns may not be usable "as is" in that they are parameterized to account for the different contexts in which a given problem appears. This means that a single pattern could be applied to systems designed according to the

Figure 3-4.
*Graphical view
of the three-
tier system
architectural
pattern.*

guidelines of multiple styles. Conversely, a system designed according to the rules of a single style may involve the use of multiple patterns.

An example pattern that is used widely in modern distributed systems is the *three-tier system* pattern. The three-tier pattern is applicable to many types of systems in which distributed users need to process, store, and retrieve significant amounts of data, such as science (for example, cancer research, astronomy, geology, weather), banking, electronic commerce, and reservation systems across widely different domains (for example, travel, entertainment, medical care). Figure 3-4 shows an informal graphical view of this pattern.

In this pattern, the first tier, often referred to as the *front* or *client* tier, contains the functionality needed to access the system's services, typically by a human user. The front tier would thus contain the system's GUI, and possibly be able to cache data and perform some minor local processing. It is assumed that the front tier is deployed on a standard host (for example, a desktop PC), possibly with limited computing and storage capacity. It is also assumed that the front tier will be replicated to allow independent, simultaneous access to multiple users.

The second tier, also referred to as the *middle, application,* or *business logic* tier contains the application's major functionality. The middle tier is in charge of all significant process-ing, servicing requests from the front tier and accessing and processing data from the back tier. It is assumed that the middle tier will be deployed on a set of powerful and capacious server hosts. However, the number of middle-tier hosts is usually significantly smaller than the number of front-tier hosts.

Finally, the third tier, also referred to as the *back, back-end,* or *data* tier contains the application's data access and storage functionality. Typically, this tier will host a powerful database that is capable of servicing many data access requests in parallel.

The interactions among the tiers in principle obey the request-reply paradigm. At the same time, the pattern does not prescribe those interactions further. For example, it may be possible to design and implement a three-tier-compliant system to strictly adhere to synchronous, request-triggered, single-request–single-reply interaction; alternatively, it may be possible to allow multiple requests to result in a single reply, multiple replies to be issued in response to a single request, periodic updates to be issued from the back and middle tiers to the front tier, and so forth.

The three-tier architectural pattern can be used to determine the architecture of a specific distributed software system. The things the architect needs to specify are:

1. Which application-specific user interface, processing, and data access and storage facilities are needed and how they should be organized within each tier.
2. Which mechanisms should be used to enable interaction across the tiers.

Use of architectural styles to solve the same problem requires, in contrast, more attention from the system's architect, and provides less direct support. In fact, the three-tier architectural pattern can be thought of as two specific architectures that are designed according to the client-server style and overlaid on top of each other: The front tier is the client to the middle tier, while the middle tier is the client to the back tier; the middle tier is thus a server in the first client-server architecture and a client in the second. Indeed, systems adhering to the client-server style are sometimes referred to as two-tier systems.

As an example, Figure 3-5 shows architectures of two different three-tier systems. At this point, the reader should be able to identify some architectural traits the two systems have in common, and those that differ. Further discussion and additional examples of architectural patterns can be found in Chapter 4, which also discusses the fuzzy boundary between patterns and styles. While the definitions above distinguish the concepts, in practice the two notions can become blurred.

3.2 MODELS

A software system's architecture is captured in an architectural *model* using a particular modeling *notation*.

> *Definitions.* **An architectural *model* is an artifact that captures some or all of the design decisions that comprise a system's architecture. Architectural *modeling* is the reification and documentation of those design decisions.**

A model is a result of the activity of modeling, which constitutes a significant portion of a software architect's responsibilities. One system may have many distinct models associated with it. Models may vary in the amount of detail they capture, the specific architectural perspective they capture (for instance, structural versus behavioral, static versus dynamic, entire system versus a particular component or subsystem), the type of notation they use, and so forth.

> *Definition.* **An architectural modeling *notation* is a language or means of capturing design decisions.**

For example, the two diagrams shown in Figure 3-5 represent models captured in two different visual modeling notations. The notations for modeling software architectures are frequently referred to as architecture description languages (ADLs). ADLs can be textual or graphical, informal (such as PowerPoint diagrams), semi-formal, or formal, domain-specific or general-purpose, proprietary or standardized, and so on.

Architectural models are used as the foundation for most other activities in architecture-based software development processes, such as analysis, system implementation, deployment, and dynamic adaptation. Models and modeling are critical facets of software architecture and are discussed in depth in Chapter 6.

3.3 PROCESSES

As discussed at length in Chapter 2, software architecture is not a software engineering life cycle phase that follows requirements elicitation and precedes low-level design and system implementation. Instead, it permeates, is an integral element of, and is continually

Figure 3-5.
*Two example
three-tier system
architectures.
Simply
"Googling" the
phrase will yield
many hits.*

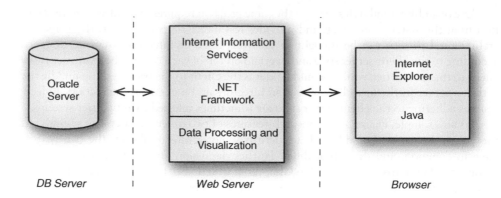

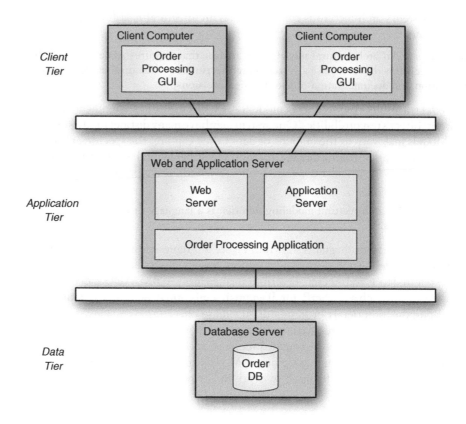

impacted by, all facets of software systems development. In that sense, software architecture helps to anchor the processes associated with different development activities. Each of these activities is covered separately in this book; with one exception, we will only name them here and state in which chapter they are discussed:

- The activity of architectural *design* (Chapter 4)
- Architecture *modeling* (Chapter 6) and *visualization* (Chapter 7)
- Architecture-driven system *analysis* (Chapter 8)
- Architecture-driven system *implementation* (Chapter 9)
- Architecture-driven system *deployment*, run-time *redeployment*, and *mobility* (Chapter 10)
- Architecture-based *design for nonfunctional properties* (Chapter 12), including security and trust (Chapter 13)
- Architectural *adaptation* (Chapter 14)

The one activity on which we will focus in this section is *architectural recovery*, which is again revisited in Chapter 4, in the context of architectural design processes, and in Chapter 8, in the context of architectural analysis.

Recall the above discussion of architectural degradation (that is, architectural drift and/or erosion). If degradation is allowed to occur, a software development organization is likely to be forced to *recover* the system's architecture sooner or later. This happens when, at time t during a system's life, changes to the system become too expensive to implement and their effects too unpredictable because the documented prescriptive (that is, as-intended) architecture is so outdated as to be useless or, sometimes even worse, misleading.

> **Definition.** **Architectural recovery is the process of determining a software system's architecture from its implementation artifacts.**

Implementation artifacts can be source code, executable files, Java.class files, and so forth. As an illustration, Figure 3-6 shows the dependencies among the Java objects that implement the cargo routing application introduced in earlier. This diagram has been automatically generated from the application's source code using an off-the-shelf source code analysis tool. At this magnification the figure is used for illustration only; we do not expect the reader to understand its details, other than that the rectangles, which are mostly on the left, represent objects and the lines, extending to the right, represent dependencies between them (for example, Java method calls).

Figure 3-6 reflects many details, including architectural design decisions, low-level design decisions, implementation-level decisions, the Java libraries used by the system, the implementation framework, and so on. From derived artifacts such as this, the system's architecture is recovered by the process of isolating and extracting only the architectural— that is, principal—design decisions.

By its very nature, the process of architectural recovery extracts a system's *descriptive* architecture. That architecture, if complemented with a statement of the architects' original intent, can in principle be used to recover the system's *prescriptive* architecture. However, since the original architects may be unavailable, and their original intent may not have been recorded (or, even if it was recorded originally, may have been repeatedly violated

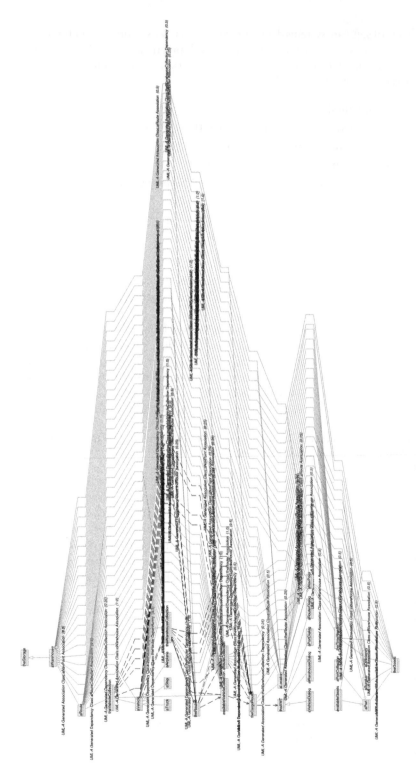

Figure 3-6. *Implementation-level view of the cargo routing application.*

over time), it is often impossible to recover a system's prescriptive architecture. Instead, the recovered descriptive architecture is treated as the closest approximation of the system's prescriptive architecture, and thus the system's architectural evolution clock is effectively reset.

Even though the specifics of the architectural recovery tools and techniques used in practice are beyond the scope of this chapter, the reader should appreciate that recovery is a very time-consuming and complex process. Furthermore, the sheer complexity of most software systems—with their myriad explicit, implicit, intended, and unintended module interdependencies—makes the task of assessing a given implementation's compliance to its purported architecture very difficult. This is why it is critical for software architects and engineers to maintain architectural integrity at *every* step throughout the system's life span. Once the architecture degrades, all subsequent solutions to stem that degradation will be more costly and more error-prone by comparison.

3.4 STAKEHOLDERS

The preceding sections have introduced the reader to the what, the how, and the why of software architecture. This section rounds out the chapter by briefly introducing the who—that is, several key architectural stakeholders.

The software *architect* is one obvious stakeholder. The architect conceives the system's architecture, and then models, assesses, prototypes, and evolves it. Architects maintain a system's conceptual integrity and are thus the system's critical stakeholders.

Software *developers* are the primary consumers of an architect's product (that is, the architecture). They will realize the principal design decisions embodied in the architecture by producing a system implementation.

The role of software *managers* from an architectural standpoint is to provide project oversight and support for the software architects. As will be detailed in Chapter 17, in an organization architects often bear much of the responsibility for a system's success without the accompanying authority. This is why it is critical for architects and managers to work closely together, and for the managers to buy into the key architectural decisions and, if necessary, exert their authority on behalf of the architects. Managers are thus key stakeholders as well.

The bottom-line objective for a given system's *customers*—the ultimate stakeholders—is that a high-quality system satisfying their requirements be delivered on time and within budget. A significant determinant of a project's ability to meet that objective will be the system's architecture. Simply put, an effective architecture will result in a successful project, while an ineffective one will seriously hamper the project's success. A more complete treatment of architectural stakeholders will be provided in Chapter 17.

3.5 END MATTER

Any mature engineering field must be accompanied by a shared, precise understanding of its basic concepts, commonly used models, and processes. This chapter has defined the notions that underlie the field of software architecture. While a less-experienced reader may not yet be able to fully appreciate some of the definitions and accompanying discussion, in subsequent chapters we return to these concepts as we study them in greater depth. We expect that the reader will also find it useful to return to these concepts and this chapter. In fact, right away, Chapter 4 uses many of the concepts introduced here in the discussion of how software architectures are designed and, in particular, in providing an overview of a large number of commonly used architectural styles. In turn, Chapter 5 will elaborate on the many different classes of software connectors and their properties.

The Business Case

Software architecture is a field of study that is characterized by an unusual diversity of views and understandings of some fundamental concepts. For example, a quick search of the Internet will yield many definitions of architecture. Similarly, there is a diversity of views on the role and importance of connectors, and even whether they deserve a separate treatment from components. The reader will also find arguments (even explicitly embodied in component models such as Microsoft DCOM's component model) that components are exclusively executable entities, which would go against many of the motivations and underpinnings of software architecture.

Simply put, imprecise and inconsistent use of poorly defined—and sometimes undefined—terms is counter to success in a highly competitive environment such as software product development. The ability to build quality products and amass and train a skilled workforce requires precise use of concrete terminology with specific meanings.

A specific instance of this issue would be an organization intending to hire and/or train a software architect. Without a shared technical language, hiring such an individual would be difficult and risky. Without a precise understanding of the foundational concepts in the field of software architecture, training software architects would be expensive and ultimately unproductive.

3.6 REVIEW QUESTIONS

1. Software architects often are asked what the difference is between architecture and design. Given the definition of software architecture provided in this chapter, can you distinguish between the two?

2. What are the key differences between a software component and a software connector?

3. Can connectors simply be treated as special-purpose components? Should they?

4. Should architects and engineers be expected to accept architectural degradation as a fact of life? What, if any, dangers are inherent in doing that?

5. What is the difference between an architectural style and an architectural pattern?

6. Can multiple patterns be used to realize a style?

7. Why should architects concern themselves with the needs of the customers?

3.7 EXERCISES

1. Identify components, connectors, topology in a well-known system's architecture. This can be something Web-based, something described in a publication, or even one of the examples introduced in the book so far, but for which this question has not been answered as part of the chapter.

   a. How can you tell components apart from connectors?

   b. Is the architecture descriptive or prescriptive?

2. The section that defined architectural styles provides a set of architectural guidelines corresponding to client-server systems. Select a distributed application scenario of your choice and show how you would turn these guidelines into specific design decisions. How easy are the guidelines to apply correctly? How easy are they to violate? Try to violate the second guideline and discuss the immediate and potential impact on your architecture.

3. Try to solve the above problem by applying the three-tier system pattern. Compare this solution to the previous one. Discuss which approach was easier to apply and why.

3.8 FURTHER READING

The first explicit treatment of software architecture and the concepts that underlie it was provided by Perry and Wolf (Perry and Wolf 1992). This seminal paper introduced several definitions that have inspired those we have provided in this chapter. Several years later, Shaw and Garlan's book (Shaw and Garlan 1996) provided their collection of definitions, summaries of several industrial and research projects in which the authors were involved, and early architectural insights from those projects. Several subsequent books offered their respective authors' takes on different facets of software architecture: modeling (Hofmeister, Nord, and Soni 1999), evaluation (Clements, Kazman, and Klein 2002), architectural patterns (Buschmann et al. 1996), product lines (Bosch 2000), and component-based system development (Heineman and Council 2001; Szyperski 2002).

A large number of conference and journal articles accompanied these books, and several specialized venues emerged. Initially, the SIGSOFT International Software Architecture Workshop (ISAW) was the primary venue for researchers and practitioners in the field of software architecture to exchange their ideas and develop common understandings. A more narrowly focused workshop series, the Role of Software Architecture for Testing and Analysis (ROSATEA), followed soon thereafter. ISAW

was eventually supplanted by the Working IEEE/IFIP Conference on Software Architecture (WICSA). More recently, the European Conference on Software Architecture (ECSA) and the International Conference on the Quality of Software Architectures (QoSA) have emerged. The on-going conference series on Component-Based Software Engineering (CBSE) has naturally had a significant architectural dimension. Finally, the Elsevier Journal on Systems and Software has recently introduced a regular section on software architecture.

While this wealth of books, papers, workshops, conferences, and journals has helped the field of software architecture to mature relatively quickly, it did not result in a convergence of understanding of the principal architectural concepts. One example of this lack of convergence is the use by the software engineering community of a very large and divergent collection of different definitions of software architecture, gathered by the Software Engineering Institute (www.sei.cmu.edu/architecture/definitions.html). While collecting all those definitions may be useful as a sort of historical record, actually relying on all of them is not a hallmark of a mature engineering field. That realization was one of the primary motivators for this book, and this chapter in particular.

4

Designing Architectures

The preceding chapters have laid the foundation for software architecture. Chapter 1 presented motivations for focusing on architectures and the benefits that result. Chapter 2 positioned software architecture with respect to the major activities of software engineering. Chapter 3 took the informal notions of the first two chapters and set them on a firm basis.

So far, however, we have largely neglected the question of *how* architectures are created. Returning to the analogy of building architectures, simply having a set of power tools and a lofty vision for a skyscraper, for example, is not a fully adequate basis for creating a fifty-story building that successfully houses businesses, provides the base for a television broadcast tower, and which effectively integrates with a city's electrical, water, data, and wastewater infrastructures. The small matter of design stands between raw materials and tools and realization of the vision. The design of a skyscraper is the product of a cadre of architects and engineers who labor to meet all the goals for the building while simultaneously satisfying all the constraints placed upon it, and upon them.

But how are designs such as this created? How are engineers and architects taught to approach the problem?

For many serious engineers and building architects, design is viewed as something that cannot be taught as a method. Rather, students are apprenticed: One "sits by the feet of the master" and the hope is that by some mysterious process of osmosis the student eventually acquires some smidgen of the master's ability. For others, the ability to design is simply something one either is or is not born with. We disagree with both of these views.

First, as human beings we all have the ability to design. We are all innately designers, and in fact engage that ability regularly in our daily lives, from cooking to decorating to painting to writing. It is just how we are created.

Second, design is subject to rigorous, methodical examination, like any other endeavor—there is nothing about it that renders it incapable of study. The outcome of such study is a set of approaches and techniques for designing that can be described, taught, applied, evaluated, and refined. Examination of existing designs helps identify good strategies for tackling various kinds of problems and helps develop a sense for associated costs and qualities. At a very minimum, students can be taught the use of design tools and simple design methods. Be assured, however, that study of design methods does not imply that there is no place, or need, for creativity. Far from it; one outcome of disciplined study of design is a focusing of design effort and creativity on those aspects of problems that demand it.

The goal of this chapter, therefore, is to set forth a variety of approaches for helping the student learn how to design software systems. We begin with considering some basics of design processes and then move on to foundational conceptual tools; easy to understand, but perhaps hard to apply. To provide a more concrete grip on the task, we then examine in detail a variety of techniques that exploit the most useful software design tool of all, that of refined experience. This discussion briefly reviews the subject of domain-specific software architectures, as introduced in Chapters 1 and 2, putting this particular technique in context with others. The chapter then introduces a wide gamut of architectural patterns and styles that capture and exploit the experience of preceding designs. The section concludes with a discussion of design recovery, the process of making the design of an existing system explicit in such a way that it becomes useful in the tasks of extending or modifying that system or using that architecture as a basis for a new system. This, of course, reinforces one of this text's primary themes: Architecture is the centerpiece of system development and evolution. While designing the architecture is the focus of this chapter, extending and maintaining the architecture is something that occurs throughout a system's lifespan.

When refined experience proves inadequate or is unavailable for solving a new design problem, we describe a variety of techniques for dealing with such design challenges. The techniques presented draw from industrial product design, building architectures, and other sources, as well as from software engineering.

The chapter concludes by briefly returning to the topic of design processes, tying the whole discussion together. Since this is a long chapter, with a multitude of techniques and approaches described, this section helps to put all the details into perspective.

A designer may come to a problem from many starting points—with no prior relevant experience, with much directly relevant experience, or with a goal of simply recovering a design. This chapter provides insights for each.

4.1 THE DESIGN PROCESS

The typical assumption of software design is that the process can proceed in the general manner of architectural design or engineering design, which can be summarized (Jones 1970) as consisting of the following four stages.

1. Feasibility stage: Identifying a set of feasible concepts
2. Preliminary design stage: Selection and development of the best concept
3. Detailed design stage: Development of engineering descriptions of the concept
4. Planning stage: Evaluating and altering the concept to suit the requirements of production, distribution, consumption and product retirement

Of these processes, Jones comments, "... designing begins (stage 1) by the taking-in of information. From this *a set of alternative arrangements for the design as a whole is quickly derived.* Stage 2 is to select one of these alternatives for further development. When this design has reached the point of satisfying the chief designer the work is split up for detailed design by many people working in parallel (stages 3 and 4)" [(Jones 1970), p. 24, emphasis added]. Jones here is echoing Vitruvius in stating that good architecture depends on fitness and arrangement.

The reader will quickly recognize that this approach to design is completely consistent with common, broader notions of software engineering processes, such as the waterfall and spiral models of development. It is similarly consistent with more specific approaches to design, such as the Unified Process, Jackson System Development, and Microsoft's Code Complete. Such universal use indicates that it is a very effective strategy in many situations.

The viewpoint represented by this process so pervades the software development world that it is hard to realize that the use of this process represents a choice—that, indeed, other approaches are possible. This is an important recognition because the standard approach does not always work. Even in those situations where it does work, it may not yield the best results. At a minimum, designers must be aware of some of the conditions under which the traditional approach is likely to be insufficient.

We will consider first the conditions under which this process may not work:

- More than anything else, success of the standard process is predicated on the success of the first step: identifying a set of feasible concepts for the overall structure of the system. If the designer is unable to produce such a set, progress stops.
- While not intrinsically part of the standard approach, in history and in typical current practice, the first step (or two) is performed by an individual. As problems and products increase in size and complexity, the probability that any one individual can successfully perform the first steps decreases. Merely saying that those steps should be performed by a design team does not resolve the issue: the existence of a team generates new problems. These problems can be resolved, or at least mitigated, but honesty demands that their existence be explicitly acknowledged.
- In a similar vein, the standard approach does not directly address the situation where *system* design is at stake, that is, when relationships between a *set* of products is at issue. The issue is again complexity. As complexity of the problem increases, the likelihood of an individual successfully performing the first step of the typical process decreases.

The common thread in these remarks is complexity of the application being designed. As complexity increases or, as we shall see later, the experience of the designer is not sufficient for the challenge, alternative approaches to the design process must be adopted. As Jones puts it, ". . . the principle of deciding the form of the whole before the details have been explored outside the mind of the chief designer does not work in novel situations for which the necessary experience cannot be contained within the mind of one person."

The good news is that there are many design strategies to choose from—essentially they are process models applied at the level of design:

- Standard: The linear model described above.
- Cyclic: As problems or infeasible approaches are identified in stages 2 to 4 of the standard model, the process reverts to an earlier stage.
- Parallel: After stage 1 of the standard model, independent alternatives are explored in parallel; at suitable times selection is made between the identified viable alternatives. A related strategy is to parallelize at stage 1: Multiple independent attempts at design are initiated, with no dependencies between them.
- Adaptive ("lay tracks as you go"): The design strategy to follow in the next stage of the design activity is decided at the end of a given stage, based upon insights gained during that stage.
- Incremental: Design at each stage of development is treated as a task of incrementally improving whatever design or previous product exists after a preceding stage.

Sensible management of the design process also yields another "strategy": The process is observed as it proceeds and the methods and approach used are modified as needed to focus on the best strategy and to avoid unpromising developments.

Now that we have identified conditions under which the standard approach to design does not work as well as alternative approaches, we now focus on the critical first step of design: identifying a candidate set of feasible concepts.

4.2 ARCHITECTURAL CONCEPTION

The standard approach to architectural and engineering design says that the first major step consists of identifying a feasible set of "alternative arrangements for the design as a whole," choosing one of those arrangements, and then proceeding to refine and elaborate it. What the standard approach does not tell, however, is *how* to identify that set of viable arrangements—or even one viable arrangement.

A facile answer to the question is to simply state, "Apply the fundamental design tools of software engineering: abstraction and modularity." While the utility, even the necessity, of such intellectual tools is unquestionable, they are only tools. As very basic tools—principles, really—one must decide where and how to wield them. One can carve with those knives, but to what design?

An equally facile answer is just to say, "Inspiration." Creative inspiration is needed, to be sure, but it is not a reliable magic wand to be blithely waved over a complex design challenge. A more effective strategy is to minimize and isolate those parts of a design for which creative inspiration is required, and to apply more prosaic and predictable techniques elsewhere. In other words, focus the creative efforts. Still, however, one has to know where creativity is and is not required.

A common, effective, and appropriate answer to the question of how to identify a feasible set of "alternative arrangements for the design as a whole" is applying experience. This is not a shallow answer to the problem. There is substantial sophistication to the use of experience. It is not foolproof and does not always suffice—but treatment of such issues comes later in the chapter.

We proceed by first discussing the most basic design tools of software engineering, then begin an extended discussion of how the lessons of experience may be used to tackle new design problems.

4.2.1 Fundamental Conceptual Tools

The most basic design tools are separation of concerns, abstraction, modularity, and other "first principles of software engineering" such as anticipation of change and design for generality. As noted above, however, they are hard to apply straight out of the box; fortunately it is usually not necessary to do so. These concepts are familiar, so we provide only a brief discussion.

Abstraction and the Simple Machines

Abstraction is the selection of a set of concepts to represent a more complex whole. One view of this definition sees abstraction as a process that moves upward, from details to summarizing concepts. As it relates to design, however, abstraction is usually employed as a tool to be used when moving downward: A set of concepts is chosen to allow discussion of an idea—an arrangement of abstract parts that (it is hoped) constitutes a solution, though still at a high level. The design then moves further downward as the concepts of the abstraction are reified into more concrete structures—a more complex whole. Ultimately, the reification process ends with the production of source code. While refinement or deduction might be more accurate and appropriate terms for this activity, *abstraction* is often used because the intent from the outset is to create source code for which the abstraction is an accurate and useful characterization.

The question remains, though, what concepts should be chosen at the outset of a design task? One good answer, and one that helps support the use of the term *abstraction* is, "Search for a simple machine that serves as an abstraction of a potential system that will perform the required task."

The simple machines of software design are many. For instance, what kind of simple machine makes a spreadsheet program? It is "just a graph of relationships, and when one node is changed, the relationships are all reevaluated to bring everything back into synch." What makes up a parser? "Essentially, it is just a push-down automaton." How does fax machine software work? "At core, it is basically just a little state machine." How does an avionics system work? "You just read all the sensors, calculate the control laws, write values out to the displays and actuators, and then do it all over again."

While these answers may seem trivial and inadequate—and they are in many ways— the point is that they provide a plausible first conception of how an application might be built. That is, they provide the first clues into designing a system's architecture.

Every application domain has its common simple machines. The commonness of these simple machines reflects, of course, experience in designing applications within those domains. Some examples are shown in Figure 4-1. Choice of a simple machine can enable further exploration of the feasibility of that design concept.

Figure 4-1.
Common simple machines.

Domain	Simple Machines
Graphics	Pixel arrays Transformation matrices Widgets Abstract depiction graphs
Word processing	Structured documents Layouts
Industrial process control	Finite state machines
Income tax return preparation	Hypertext Spreadsheets Form templates
Web pages	Hypertext Composite documents
Scientific computing	Matrices Mathematical functions
Financial accounting	Spreadsheets Databases Transactions

Choosing the Level and Terms of Discourse

Whether or not the approach of attempting to identify simple machines is adopted, any attempt to use abstraction as a tool requires choice of a field of discourse, and once that is chosen, the selection of the terms used in discourse is needed. Often the two choices are virtually inseparable.

The linear, or standard approach, to architectural concept formation demands that the initial subject of discourse be that of the application as a whole. For example, the old technique of stepwise refinement begins at that level.

Two alternatives exist, however. The first is to choose to work, initially, at a level lower than that of the whole application. That is, the subject of discourse might be something that is optimistically assumed to be a part of a solution to the larger problem. Design is performed at that level in the hope that once several such subproblems are solved they can be composed together to form an overall solution, where the means of composition does not impinge upon their internal structure. Success with this approach need not demand great foresight; sometimes just whittling away at parts of a problem makes later tackling of the overall problem easier. Good foresight certainly helps, of course.

The occasion when this approach is particularly appropriate is when there exists a body of preexisting components that are available for reuse in the development of a new application. (Note this is almost *always* the case!) Thorough understanding of what those components are capable of, and how they may be composed, can provide critical insights into how the whole application should be structured so as to enable the potential reuse.

The second alternative is to choose to work, initially, at a level *above* that of the desired application. In some cases, this may mean solving a more general problem. This has worked well in handling complicated input to programs. Rather than building a custom component for processing an application's simple, restricted user input language, it can be very effective to employ a generic parser tool. Though the parser may end up being far more powerful than what the specific application requires, the maturity of technology development in that domain, coupled with an abundance of reusable packages embodying that technology, will likely result in a smaller, faster, off-the-shelf component being used.

In other cases, this may simply mean understanding the core issues of an application in a more fundamental way. To use a physical example, building a guitar may suggest thinking about choosing strings, wood for the fingerboard, side, top, bridge, and so on. Moving up a level of abstraction, however, would involve thinking about the physics of vibrating strings, wave propagation, and so forth [see, for example (Vogel)]. The benefit is to identify in advance what the key design factors are.

To use a software example, consider the challenge of designing an application to help in the preparation of income tax returns. For any given year, the nation's tax laws determine the information that must be reported, the calculations that must be done, and how the information must be reported on various forms. Publications from the taxing authority provide instructions and explanations. A custom application could, of course, be designed to perform those functions as required. But if the problem is reconsidered at a higher, more abstract level, it can be formulated as a spreadsheet problem coupled with a formatting (text-layout) problem coupled with hypertext. The spreadsheet includes within it the particular formulas required in a given year. The text layout can be viewed in a similarly generic way, with rules specifying the particular layout required for a particular year. Hypertext associates instructions with the portions of the forms to which the instructions apply. Built in this way (that is, using a generic spreadsheet engine, a generic form layout engine, and a hypertext engine), a tax software application can be created and updated efficiently from year to year, enabling a profitable business.

Separation of Concerns

Separation of concerns is the subdivision of a problem into independent parts. For instance, the visual interface that a customer sees at a bank's automatic teller machine is independent from the logic used to control operation on that customer's accounts. If the concepts at issue are genuinely independent, then using this technique is straightforward. The difficulties arise when the issues are either actually or apparently intertwined.

When such interrelationships are found their causes should be identified. Sometimes interrelationships may be present just because of use, or abuse, of language. For example, a single, common word such as "account" may be used to describe what are, in fact, different entities in different parts of an application. In other cases, concepts may be intertwined because of (past or prospective) solution efficiency. For example, the presence of numeric keys in user records may simply reflect prior database implementation strategies, and not be intrinsic information about the user.

A primary example of separation of concerns at work in software architecture is the separation of a system's structure into components (loci of computation) and connectors (loci of communication). This separation reflects the independence of the issues and is at the heart of the chapter on connectors. The myriad details and concerns addressed in that chapter reveals that, like many applications of the principle, numerous trade-offs and alternatives must be considered.

Separation of concerns frequently involves many trade-offs; total independence of concepts may not be possible. The designer is thus left with the substantial obligation of assessing performance, cost, appearance, or functional trade-offs between competing conceptions.

4.2.2 The Grand Tool: Refined Experience

While the intellectual tools of abstraction and separation of concerns are of undeniable use in the process of designing an architecture, in and of themselves they provide scant guidance to the designer. Experience can be a masterful teacher, however, and can provide the guidance necessary to wield the basic tools in an effective fashion. Raw experience by itself, though, does not provide the mature guidance that enables effective tackling of new problems. Experience must be reflected upon and refined to the point where the designer understands the essential issues and lessons from prior work, enabling judicious choice of context-appropriate techniques.

The lessons from prior work include not only the lessons of successes, but also the lessons arising from failure. In either case, it is only reflection that can indicate the root causes for the success or failure, and hence the critical knowledge that can be carried forward. (This is not to say that every failure has the seeds of valuable technical advice. Regrettably, too many projects fail for reasons independent of technology.) Lessons from prior work need not only come from one's own experience, of course. One virtue of reading widely in a technical field or attending technical conferences is to benefit from the experiences of others. There is no virtue in reinventing wheels, broken or otherwise.

When valuable technical experience is possessed, however, substantial efficiencies result. Experience can provide that initial feasible set of "alternative arrangements for the design as a whole" called for at the beginning of Section 4.1. One need not devote valuable design time to topics for which one already has a validated solution in hand. Similarly, communication between development team members is enhanced: when others have experience with the same or similar preexisting systems, it is easier to describe use of or modifications to an established approach, as compared to conveying a completely new concept.

Applying established approaches is not an entirely risk-free strategy however. Once one has a favorite hammer, everything starts to look like a nail. Pursuing such a strategy may yield a working application, but can easily yield one that is seriously deficient in some respect or is at least suboptimal. Not only are the benefits of previous systems imported by reusing an approach, but so are the limitations. Innovation is certainly inhibited by mindlessly following one's standard approach. That said, it is nonetheless clear that refined experience is indeed the Grand Tool for designers to apply in creating new applications.

Software engineering literature is replete with surefire approaches to design—tools and techniques that are assured to always work and provide that needed solution. Some of these mistaken approaches to design confuse a notation or language with a design method. UML, for instance, is a notation, not an approach. So, too, is Java. Other approaches confuse a tool or technology with a design method. Thus some have said that CORBA provides all the needed guidance for building robotic systems; others have assured us that rule-based expert systems are all we need. Most assuredly, there is no magic potion, and an adequate approach to design problems demands care, thought, creativity, discipline, experience, and method.	**Silver Bullets and Other Misfires**

The software designer of the twenty-first century has a wide basis of experience from which to draw. Reflection on the development of thousands of systems has yielded a wide variety of approaches and lessons, ranging from broadly encompassing domain-specific architectures to simple programming language-level design patterns. The following section presents key lessons from this experience base in considerable detail.

4.3 REFINED EXPERIENCE IN ACTION: STYLES AND ARCHITECTURAL PATTERNS

The distilled architectural wisdom that has arisen from a vast body of experience comes in many shapes and flavors. As a whole, we are treating them under the rubric of styles and patterns. As introduced in Chapter 1, the notion of architectural styles is an ancient one, dating back at least to Vitruvius. Styles are designed to capture knowledge of effective designs for achieving specified goals within a particular application context. For building architecture, the combination of goals and context might be providing a house for a single family in a Mediterranean climate using stone and tile as principal building materials. The correspondingly appropriate style might be a single-story villa. For software, the goals and context might be providing a secure instant messaging system to operate between remote sites of a global company; the appropriate style might be client-server.

Patterns and styles can be characterized for large problems as well as small. Again, with regard to buildings, one can characterize a pattern for determining the appropriate overhang of a tiled roof over an entryway; similarly, one can characterize a (much more complicated) pattern for provision of elevator service in a ninety-story skyscraper. So it is with software architecture; patterns and styles have been developed that are appropriate for small as well as large and complex applications.

Not surprisingly, the lessons of experience in software architecture have arisen from several different software development communities, with each having its own contribution to make. Unfortunately, this has resulted in a variety of terms for characterizing this experience, not all of which describe distinct concepts. As an aid to teasing out the various issues and as a means to provide structure for the rest of this section, see Figure 4-2 for a summary of the main types of architectural styles and patterns.

The horizontal axis of Figure 4-2 refers to the scope of applicability of the body of knowledge—the domain of discourse. For instance, design patterns exemplified by those

Figure 4-2.
Domain knowledge versus scope in showing the relationship between styles and patterns. Beware! The boundaries between the concepts are not precise.

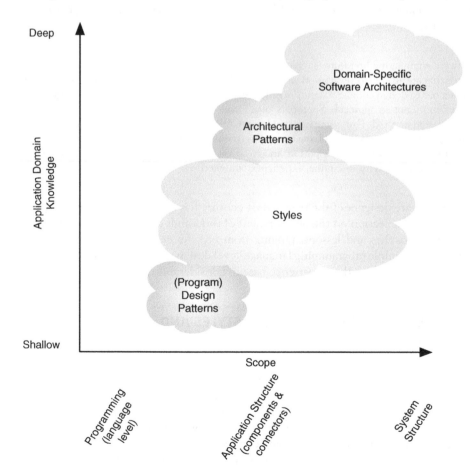

presented in the book by Gamma (Gamma et al. 1995), are focused on the programming of object-oriented solutions to program design problems. Such patterns are inapplicable to enterprise-level system design, which is at the other end of the horizontal axis.

The vertical axis reflects the amount of domain knowledge represented by (or encoded within) the body of knowledge. Program design patterns are shown at the shallow end of this scale, reflecting that they are very generally applicable and are not restricted to use within a particular application domain. At the other end of the scale are domain-specific software architectures. Such styles are applicable to the design of very large applications and concomitantly encode substantial knowledge about the design of applications within a domain. Thus, for instance, a domain-specific software architecture for retail banking might specify all major parts of the application; it is unlikely, however, that such a structure would be appropriate for any other kind of application apart from retail banking.

The diagram has fuzzy boundaries, however, and should only be taken as a rough guide. Programming languages exist at many levels of abstraction; applications range from very simple to extraordinarily complex. The scope axis should not, therefore, be taken as genuinely linear or fully ordered. The concept clouds in the diagram similarly have fuzzy boundaries; what one architect may term an architectural pattern might be called a style by another. The following sections will bring a little more precision to the discussion. While the topic of domain-specific architectures was introduced in Chapter 2 and will be dealt with at substantial length in Chapter 15, we begin the following exposition by a brief consideration of such architectures, as they are a powerful way of exploiting experience in the task of developing the architecture for a new system. We then consider architectural patterns and styles at length. These topics were introduced and defined in the preceding chapters; here, a wide variety of specific instances are presented. This chapter does not include any further discussion of program design patterns. As Figure 4-2 indicates, such patterns deal with concepts at the level of programming languages, and most often only for object-oriented languages. As such, they offer little guidance to the architect seeking to identify a feasible set of "alternative arrangements for the design as a whole." (They do, of course, offer significant guidance to a programmer charged with implementing a chosen architecture in an object-oriented language, but that is not the topic of this chapter.)

4.3.1 Domain-Specific Software Architectures

Domain-specific software architectures (DSSAs) encode substantial knowledge, acquired through extensive experience, about how to structure complete applications within a particular domain. A useful operational definition of DSSAs is the combination of (1) a *reference architecture* for an application domain (as defined in Chapter 3), (2) a library of software components for that architecture containing reusable chunks of domain expertise, and (3) a method of choosing and configuring components to work within an instance of the reference architecture (Hayes-Roth et al. 1995). As such, a DSSA represents the most valuable type of experience useful in identifying a feasible set of "alternative arrangements for the design as a whole."

In terms of our familiar building analogy, DSSAs are akin to the generic design of tract houses, that is, house designs that are instantiated dozens or hundreds of times to yield individual homes in a housing development. Such homes are not identical to one another; they typically vary in terms of cabinetry, banister styles, colors, carpet, roofing material, and such. They will be same, though, with respect to the floor plan, the location of the windows, and with regard to all major structural elements. The contractor for an individual house knows how to instantiate the generic plan in light of the consumer's specific preferences and choices to yield a very cost-effective structure that nonetheless is somewhat personalized.

The extended example of software for consumer electronics presented in Chapter 1 serves as an illustration of a DSSA. (While this example was presented there as an illustration of product families, the two concepts are closely related; this relationship is carefully explored in Chapter 15.) Different consumer electronics applications can be created by parameterizing or specializing the core architecture. These specializations may represent adding new, unprecedented components into a television's architecture, for instance, but where those additions are performed on parts of the architecture are identified in advance as places for such extensions to occur.

The difficulty with DSSAs, of course, is that they are specialized for a particular domain and so are only of value if one exists for the domain wherein the engineer is charged with building a new application. While this may make it sound as though DSSAs are rare, the contrary is true. Companies tend to develop multiple applications within a particular area of expertise. This expertise manifests itself in strong similarities in structure between two products from the company and another. These similarities, and the rationale for them, is the basis of a DSSA. What is unfortunately true of such situations, however, is that frequently the common structure—the DSSA—is never written down, but remains latent in the minds of the company's engineers.

DSSAs and product families are explored in Chapter 15 in substantial detail, thus further discussion of these concepts is deferred. The reader should remember, however, that DSSAs are the preeminent means for maximal reuse of knowledge and prior development and are thus critical for developing a new product's design in an established domain.

4.3.2 Architectural Patterns

Architectural patterns are akin to DSSAs, but applied within a much narrower scope. They represent significant reuse of experience, but help you less fully. We repeat here the definition from Chapter 3:

> *Definition.* **An architectural pattern is a named collection of architectural design decisions that are applicable to a recurring design problem, parameterized to account for different software development contexts in which that problem appears.**

In the sections below, we sketch three very simple examples: state-logic-display, model-view-controller, and sense-compute-control.

State-Logic-Display (aka. Three-Tier)

The example used in Chapter 3 to illustrate this definition is the familiar three-tier architecture, which is commonly employed in business applications where there is a data store behind a set of business logic rules, and that business logic is accessed by user interface components. This pattern, also known as state-logic-display, has been popular since it maps nicely to a distributed implementation in which communication between the components

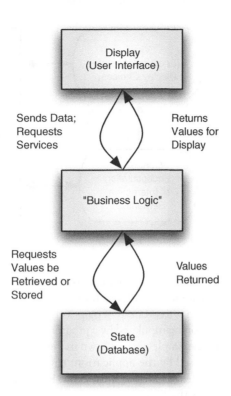

Figure 4-3.
*Canonical form
of state-logic-
display
architectures.*

is by remote procedure call. Figure 4-3 shows the pattern, redrawn in an orientation different from that used in Chapter 3.

In business applications, the data store is usually a large database server; the business logic component may implement, for instance, some banking transaction rules, and the display component be a relatively simple component for managing interaction with a user on a desktop PC. Multiplayer games also map nicely to this architecture, wherein the business logic component implements the game rules and the data store maintains the game state. Multiple players can simultaneously play the game wherein each user has his or her own display component. Many Web-based applications can be approximately characterized as three-tier architectures, where the display component is the user's Web browser, the business logic component is the software on the Web site (Web server plus application-specific logic), and the data store is a database accessed by the Web server on a local host. This characterization of Web applications is not entirely fair, however, as communication between the display component (browser) and the business logic component (Web server) is not by means of a remote procedure call, but rather by the HTTP protocol, which does not necessarily maintain a connection between the two components in between interactions.

Model-View-Controller (for Graphical User Interfaces)

Since its invention in the 1980s, the model-view-controller (MVC) pattern has been a dominant influence in the design of graphical user interfaces. While MVC certainly is applied at the low levels of program design and thus could be classified in the design

Figure 4-4.
*Notional model-
view-controller
pattern.*

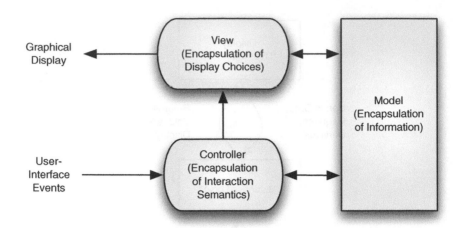

patterns category (and hence omitted from our discussion here), it can also be viewed as providing a structure for applications at a higher level.

The objective of the pattern is to promote separation, and thus independent development paths, between information manipulated by a program and depictions of user interactions with that information. The simple idea is shown in Figure 4-4. The model component encapsulates the information used by the application; the view component encapsulates the information chosen and necessary for graphical depiction of that information; the controller component encapsulates the logic necessary to maintain consistency between the model and the view, and to handle inputs from the user as they relate to the depiction.

The notional interactions between these components are as follows (variations exist in the practice). When the application changes a value in the model object, notification of that change is sent to the view so that any affected parts of the depiction can be updated and redrawn. Notification also typically goes to the controller as well, so that the controller can modify the view if its logic so requires. The view may query the model for additional data needed for the display. When handling input from the user (such as a mouse click on part of the view), the windowing system sends the user event to the controller; the controller may query the view for information to assist in determining what action to take. The controller then updates the model object in keeping with the desired semantics. Then, of course, if the model object changes values it must notify the view and controller so that the user interface can be updated, and so the cycle of interactions continues.

While Figure 4-4 shows three distinct components, from the description above of their interactions it is clear that there is often a very close coupling between the actions of the view component and the controller component. In many cases, therefore, the view and controller components are merged; such is the case with the architecture of Java's Swing framework.

At a much higher level of abstraction than programming, the MVC paradigm can be seen at work in the World Wide Web. Web resources correspond to the model objects; the HTML rendering agent within a browser corresponds to the viewer; the controller in the simplest case corresponds to the code that is part of the browser that responds to user input and which causes either interactions with a Web server or modifies the browser's display in some manner. In the more complicated situation, the controller would also encompass code uploaded from a server that governs user interaction with the display, such as JavaScript uploaded as part of a Web page or code on the server that determines the representation of the resource to transmit to the browser.

MVC has been the subject of much work, and a variety of references are available discussing the details of several different implementation approaches. MVC has also inspired the development of other related architectural patterns, such as presentation-abstraction-controller (PAC). Detailed citations are provided at the end of the chapter.

Sense-Compute-Control (aka. Sensor-Controller-Actuator)

The sense-compute-control (SCC) pattern is typically used in structuring embedded control applications. This may range from simple devices such as those found in kitchen appliances to sophisticated systems used in automotive applications or robotic control. The basic idea is illustrated in Figure 4-5. A computer is embedded in some application; sensors from various devices are connected to the computer and may be sampled to determine their value. Also attached to the computer are hardware actuators. By sending a signal to such devices the computer may, for example, open a value, lower flaps, or turn off a light, and hence control the system.

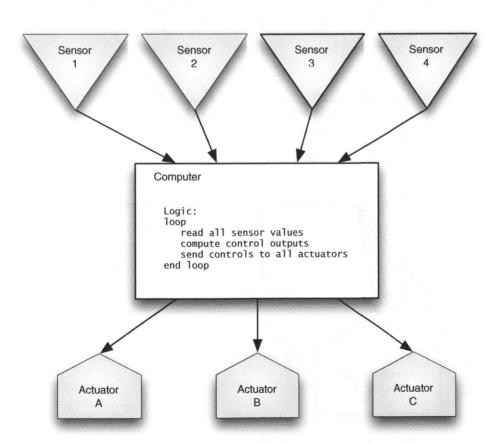

Figure 4-5.
Sense-compute-control: Different-shaped boxes are used to indicate the different types of devices present in the system.

The architectural pattern is simply one of cycling through the steps of reading all the sensor values, executing a set of control laws or functions, and then sending outputs to the various actuators. Typically, such a cycle is keyed to a clock, where the frequency of the clock ticks may be keyed to the maximum rate at which the sensors' values may change or to the sensitivity of the actuators to varying inputs on their input control lines. *Note that there is implicit feedback in such applications via the external environment.* That is, the typical situation is that by changing one of the actuators, something will change in the external environment that one of the sensors will ultimately detect, and hence cause a change in its value.

A simple flight control application can serve to make these ideas concrete. We will use the example of software controlling a notional lunar excursion module, or "lunar lander," to the surface of the moon, illustrated in Figure 4-6.

Figure 4-6.
Sense-compute-control applied to a lunar lander.

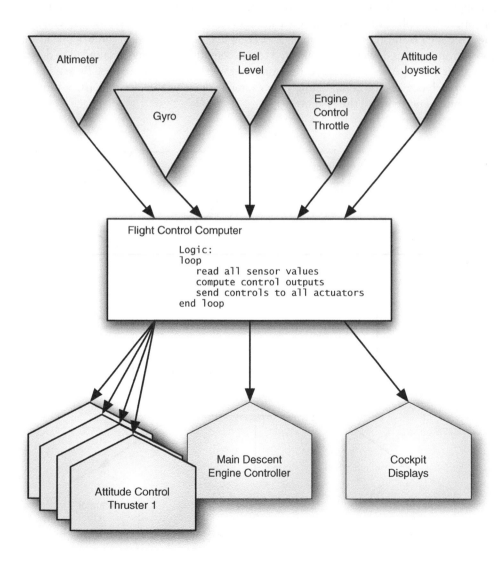

In this example there are five sensors on board the spacecraft: The altimeter (presumably radar) senses the altitude above the surface of the moon; the gyro provides information on the x-y-z axis orientation of the craft; the fuel level indicates the remaining fuel on board; the engine control throttle indicates to the computer the pilot's desired setting of the descent engine's thrust (for instance, 75 percent throttle); and the joystick indicates the pilot's inputs for orienting the spacecraft. (Keep in mind that this is an entirely fly-by-wire application, so there is no physical connection between the joystick, for instance, and any control surfaces. The computer is responsible for sensing all control device inputs.) The diagram shows six actuators: four attitude control thrusters, the main descent engine controller, and the cockpit displays.

As the craft approaches the surface, the sensors will provide to the computer information on the Lunar Lander's altitude, attitude, fuel remaining, and the pilot's control inputs. The flight control computer will process its control laws, computing values to be sent to the various actuators to control the descent engine, the attitude control thrusters, and update the cockpit displays. From changes in the altitude the computer could determine, for example, the descent rate, and display that to the pilot. Based upon the pilot's judgment, he or she could increase the throttle to slow the descent or decrease the throttle and allow the Lunar gravity to increase the descent rate.

Depending on the system designer's choices, a variety of control strategies could be programmed into the flight control computer. The scenario sketched above reflects the strategy applied in the Apollo landings. A fully automated landing sequence could also be programmed, in which the software would determine the optimal descent engine and attitude control thruster settings, based upon the altitude and attitude of the craft. From the standpoint of the software's architecture, these different strategies are all the same; at each cycle of the loop the software reads the current sensor values, computes the desired settings for the actuators, and sends those values to the actuators.

4.3.3 Introduction to Styles

Architectural styles are a primary way of characterizing lessons from experience in software system design. As such, they can be a key element in developing initial or detailed conceptions of a software system's architecture. As Figure 4-2 indicates, architectural styles are broadly applicable; they can be useful in determining everything from subroutine structure to top-level application structure. Styles, as used here and as seen in contrast with the architectural patterns of the preceding section, reflect less domain knowledge than architectural patterns, and hence are more broadly applicable. Keep in mind, however, that the boundaries between these concepts are not precise.

Chapter 3 introduced architectural styles in some detail, and presented the following definition:

> *Definition.* An architectural style is a named collection of architectural design decisions that (1) are applicable in a given development context, (2) constrain architectural design decisions that are specific to a particular system within that context, and (3) elicit beneficial qualities in each resulting system.

Accordingly, the discussion of styles will include the decisions and constraints comprising the style, as well as the beneficial qualities induced by these choices.

Styling with Perry and Wolf

Dewayne Perry and Alexander Wolf wrote early and persuasively on the importance of styles in software architecture. The influence of their work—widely cited in the literature—motivates inclusion of the following extended quote.

> The notion of architectural style is particularly useful from both descriptive and prescriptive points of view. Descriptively, architectural style defines a particular codification of design elements and formal arrangements. Prescriptively, style limits the kinds of design elements and their formal arrangements. That is, an architectural style constrains both the design elements and the formal relationships among the design elements. Analogously, we shall find this a most useful concept in software architecture.
>
> Of extreme importance is the relationship between engineering principles and architectural style (and, of course, architecture itself). For example, one does not get the light, airy feel of the perpendicular style as exemplified in the chapel at King's College, Cambridge, from Romanesque engineering. Different engineering principles are needed to move from the massiveness of the Romanesque to lightness of the perpendicular. It is not just a matter of aesthetics. This relationship between engineering principles and software architecture is also of fundamental importance.
>
> Finally, the relationship between architectural style and materials is of critical importance. The materials have certain properties that are exploited in providing a particular style. One may combine structural with aesthetic uses of materials, such as that found in the post and beam construction of Tudor-style houses. However, one does not build a skyscraper with wooden posts and beams. The material aspects of the design elements provide both aesthetic and engineering bases for an architecture. Again, this relationship is of critical importance in software architecture.
>
> Thus, we find in building architecture some fundamental insights about software architecture: multiple views are needed to emphasize and to understand different aspects of the architecture; styles are a cogent and important form of codification that can be used both descriptively and prescriptively; and, engineering principles and material properties are of fundamental importance in the development and support of a particular architecture and architectural style. . . .
>
> The important thing about an architectural style is that it encapsulates important decisions about the architectural elements and emphasizes important constraints on the elements and their relationships. The useful thing about style is that we can use it both to constrain the architecture and to coordinate cooperating architects. Moreover, style embodies those decisions that suffer erosion and drift. An emphasis on style as a constraint on the architecture provides a visibility to certain aspects of the architecture so that violations of those aspects and insensitivity to them will be more obvious.
>
> (Perry and Wolf 1992)

The architectural styles chosen for presentation here were selected on the basis of reflecting a diversity of approaches, common use, and being a part of the common vocabulary of software architects. Sufficient detail is presented so that the reader can appreciate the essence of each style and the situations for which it is appropriate. While this chapter does not present a comprehensive catalog of styles, many of the most popular and well known are discussed, showing the designer the kind of role that styles can play in solving design problems. (Chapter 11 will explore a few more advanced styles, such as REST, in some detail.)

There are a variety of potential ways of classifying and organizing styles. We have chosen to present the simple styles according to the following outline:

Traditional Language-Influenced Styles

- Main program and subroutines
- Object-oriented

Layered

- Virtual machines
- Client-server

Dataflow Styles

- Batch-sequential
- Pipe-and-filter

Shared Memory

- Blackboard
- Rule-based

Interpreter

- Interpreter
- Mobile code

Implicit Invocation

- Publish-subscribe
- Event-based

Peer-to-Peer

Later in the chapter, two slightly more complex styles are discussed: C2 and distributed objects, with specific consideration of CORBA.

Other organizations would highlight other similarities and relationships among the presented styles. The above categorization should thus only be taken as one coarse-grained perspective, useful primarily in the initial introduction of the styles. A summary/comparison of all the styles is included in Table 4-1 toward the end of the chapter.

Most of the styles presented will be illustrated by reference to a type of application for which the style is well suited and by sketching a game version of the lunar lander program that was used in illustrating the sense-compute-control (SCC) pattern. By using the same, or a similar, application with each style some sharp contrasts between the styles will be evident. The game version of lunar lander differs from the SCC version in one critical respect: The environment needs to be simulated. In a real flight control application, the actions of the physical universe affect the spacecraft. For instance, as the lander approaches the moon, the moon's gravitational field draws the spacecraft down. Each time the sensors are read different values will appear, not due to any action of the software, but simply because of the action of gravity. In the game version, the physics of the universe must be simulated. For example, upon each tick of a game clock the values of the sensors could be computed by an environment simulator, rather than read from genuine sensor devices. As you compare the various examples, please be aware that the various lunar lander games are not equivalent. The purpose of the examples is to help develop understanding of the various styles through reference to a common application context—not a common, precise, and complete requirements specification.

Some of the styles discussed have complex details associated with their use that have been omitted here. Our primary objective is to illustrate a wide range of diverse styles that represent the capture of extensive experience. The material presented here can serve as an introduction to the styles; detailed instructions for their use must be sought elsewhere.

4.3.4 Simple Styles

Traditional Language-Influenced Styles

The two styles considered here reflect the program styles that result from the traditional use of programming languages such as C, C++, Java, and Pascal. These languages, of course, can be used to implement architectures in very different styles; discussed here are architectures that primarily reflect the basic organizational and control-flow relationships between components provided by these imperative languages.

Main Program and Subroutines. The main program and subroutine style should be instantly familiar to anyone who has programmed in a language such as C, Fortran, Pascal, or Basic. The components are the main program and the various subroutines (aka. procedures); the connectors between the components are procedure calls. For purposes of this discussion we specifically exclude programs that use shared memory (such as global variables) as a means of communication from being a part of this style.

Style: Main Program and Subroutines (no shared memory)	**Summary:** Decomposition based upon separation of functional processing steps. **Components:** Main program and subroutines. **Connectors:** Function/procedure calls. **Data elements:** Values passed in/out of subroutines. **Topology:** Static organization of components is hierarchical; full structure is a directed graph. **Additional constraints imposed:** None. **Qualities yielded:** Modularity: Subroutines may be replaced with different implementations as long as interface semantics are unaffected. **Typical uses:** Small programs; pedagogical purposes. **Cautions:** Typically fails to scale to large applications; inadequate attention to data structures. Unpredictable effort required to accommodate new requirements. **Relations to programming languages or environments:** Traditional imperative programming languages, such as BASIC, Pascal, or C.

A simple version of the lunar lander game program is shown in Figure 4-7. Its design is based on the functional decomposition of the processing into repeated user interface steps

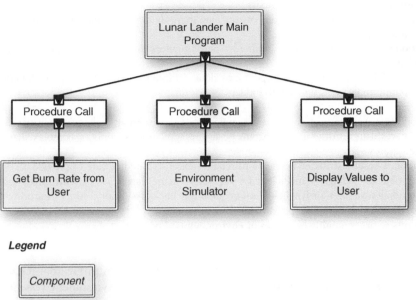

Figure 4-7.
*Lunar Lander:
Main program
and subroutines.*

(input and output) and all the processing that corresponds to simulating the environment and the actions of the spacecraft. Specifically, the main program displays greetings and instructions, then enters a loop wherein it calls the three subroutine components in turn. The first obtains the pilot's throttle-setting input. The second component primarily serves as the environment simulator, determining how much fuel is left and what the altitude and descent rate are. The only flight control law in this simple game is the translation of a pilot-specified throttle percentage into a volume/second fuel-flow setting (the burn rate) to control the descent engine. The third component displays the updated state. In this game there is no clock, so one cycle through the functional processing corresponds to one clock tick.

Object-Oriented. The object-oriented style should be similarly familiar. The only structuring provided is that of a world of objects whose lifetimes vary according to use. Comprehending a program structured in this manner requires understanding the numerous static and dynamic relationships among the objects.

Summary: State strongly encapsulated with functions that operate on that state as objects. Objects must be instantiated before the objects' methods can be called.
Components: Objects (aka. instance of a class).
Connector: Method invocation (procedure calls to manipulate state).

**Style:
Object-
Oriented**

Data elements: Arguments to methods.
Topology: Can vary arbitrarily; components may share data and interface functions through inheritance hierarchies.
Additional constraints imposed: Commonly: shared memory (to support use of pointers), single-threaded.
Qualities yielded: Integrity of data operations: data manipulated only by appropriate functions. Abstraction: implementation details hidden.

Typical uses: Applications where the designer wants a close correlation between entities in the physical world and entities in the program; pedagogy; applications involving complex, dynamic data structures.
Cautions: Use in distributed applications requires extensive middleware to provide access to remote objects. Relatively inefficient for high-performance applications with large, regular numeric data structures, such as in scientific computing. Lack of additional structuring principles can result in highly complex applications.
Relations to programming languages or environments: Java, C++.

The object-oriented design of the lunar lander game shown in Figure 4-8 has three encapsulations: the spacecraft, the user's interface, and the environment (essentially a physics model that allows calculation of the descent rate). Note a contrast with the main program and subroutine's (MPS) design: Interactions here with the user are handled by a single object, which performs both input and output functions. The functional decomposition of the MPS design resulted in those functions being performed by separate subroutines. Some details of the object-oriented design are apparent in Figure 4-9, which is a Unified Modeling Language characterization of the objects.

Layered

Layered styles are as simple and familiar as those above that reflect the traditional use of programming languages such as C or Java. The essence of a layered style is that an

Figure 4-8.
Lunar Lander in the object-oriented style.

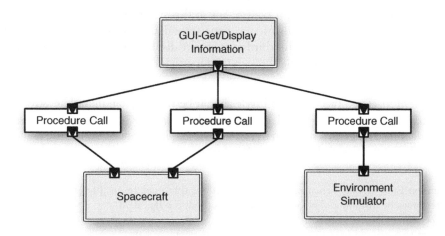

architecture is separated into ordered layers, wherein a program within one layer may obtain services from a layer below it. The virtual machines style is familiar to anyone who has studied computer and operating systems architectures; the client-server layered style is ubiquitous in business applications. Both are discussed below.

Virtual Machines. In the virtual machines style, a *layer* offers a set of services ("a machine with a bunch of buttons and knobs") that may be accessed by, at least, programs residing within the layer above it. The services that a layer offers can be termed the "provides interface" of the layer. The services may be implemented by various programs within the layer, but, when designing an architecture, from the perspective of the entities that *use* the layer's services such distinctions are not apparent. In Figure 4-10, for instance, program A in layer 1 can access the services provided by layer 2; those services may in fact be implemented by programs B and C, but such details are not of concern to program A.

In a strict virtual machines style, programs at a given level may only access the services provided by the layer immediately below it. Thus, again referring to Figure 4-10, program A can only access services provided by layer 2, and not layer 3. A nonstrict virtual machines style would allow A to access the services of layer 3 as well.

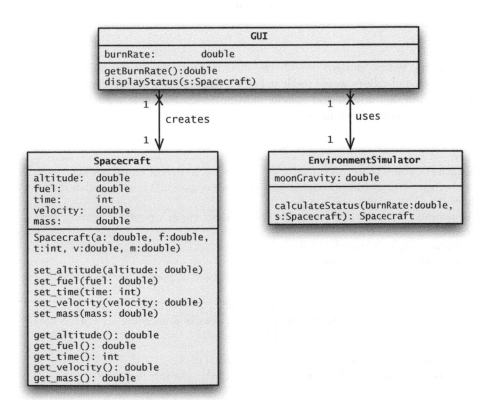

Figure 4-9. *UML representation of the classes used in Figure 4-8.*

Figure 4-10.
*Notional virtual
machines
architecture.*

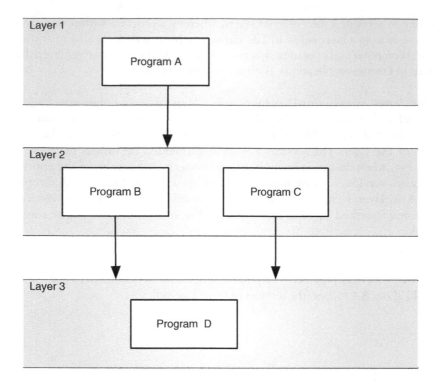

Operating systems designs provide the most common use of the layered style. For instance, user applications would reside in layer 1, directory and file manipulation services on level 2, and disk drivers and volume management software at level 3. Networking protocols are also often implemented in a layered style.

Style: Virtual Machines	**Summary:** Consists of an ordered sequence of layers; each *layer*, or virtual machine, offers a set of services that may be accessed by programs (subcomponents) residing within the layer above it.
	Components: Layers offering a set of services to other layers, typically comprising several programs (subcomponents).
	Connectors: Typically procedure calls.
	Data elements: Parameters passed between layers.
	Topology: Linear, for strict virtual machines; a directed acyclic graph in looser interpretations.
	Additional constraints imposed: None.
	Qualities yielded: Clear dependence structure; software at upper levels immune to changes of implementation within lower levels as long as the service specifications are invariant. Software at lower levels fully independent of upper levels.
	Typical uses: Operating system design; network protocol stacks.
	Cautions: Strict virtual machines with many levels can be relatively inefficient.

A five-level version of the lunar lander game is shown in Figure 4-11. The top layer handles inputs received from the user through the keyboard; it calls the second layer to service those inputs. The second layer includes all the details of the lunar lander that pertain to the game logic and the environment simulator. It calls the third layer to begin the process of displaying the updated Lander state to the user. The third layer is a generic, two-dimensional game engine. Such a layer is capable of supporting any of a wide variety of games that only require two-dimensional graphics. The fourth layer is the operating system, which provides, among other things, platform-specific user interface (UI) support, such as window management. The bottom layer is provided by firmware or hardware, and

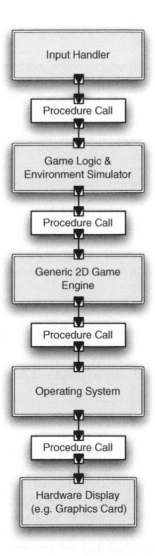

Figure 4-11.
Lunar Lander in the virtual machines style.

drives the physical user interface display. Each layer is independent of the layers above it, and only requires access to the services of the layer immediately below it. Note that the focus of this architecture is different from the preceding examples. The explicit inclusion here of a game engine, the operating system, and hardware is intended to help illustrate the layered style.

Client-Server. The client-server style can be simply understood as a two-layer virtual machine with network connections. That is, the server is the virtual machine below the clients, each of which accesses the virtual machine's interfaces via remote procedure calls or equivalent network access methods. Typically, there are multiple clients that access the same server; the clients are mutually independent. The obligation of the server is to provide the specific services requested by each client. Clients are sometimes referred to as "thin" or "thick," reflecting whether they include any significant processing beyond user interface functions.

Grossly simplified, a bank's automated teller machine (ATM) system is a client-server application. The clients are the ATMs and the server is the bank, which keeps track of all accounts and controls all of the transactions requested by users at the ATMs.

Style: Client-Server	**Summary:** Clients send service requests to the server, which performs the required functions and replies as needed with the requested information. Communication is initiated by the clients. **Components:** Clients and server. **Connectors:** Remote procedure call, network protocols. **Data elements:** Parameters and return values as sent by the connectors. **Topology:** Two-level, with multiple clients making requests to the server. **Additional constraints imposed:** Client-to-client communication prohibited. **Qualities yielded:** Centralization of computation and data at the server, with the information made available to remote clients. A single powerful server can service many clients. **Typical uses:** Applications where centralization of data is required, or where processing and data storage benefit from a high-capacity machine, and where clients primarily perform simple user interface tasks, such as many business applications. **Cautions:** When the network bandwidth is limited and there are a large number of client requests.

A multiplayer version of the lunar lander game is shown in Figure 4-12. In the system shown, three players simultaneously and independently play the game. All game state, game logic, and environment simulation is performed on the server. The clients perform the user interface functions. The connectors in this example are remote procedure calls, which are procedure call connectors combined with a distributor. A distributor identifies network interaction paths and subsequently routes communication along those paths. (The intricacies of connector types and their substructures will be explained in detail in Chapter 5.)

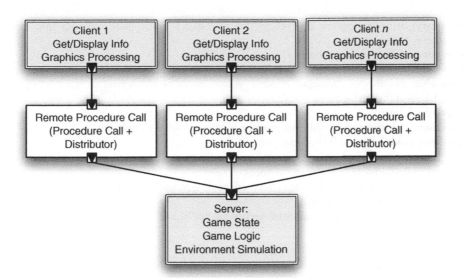

Figure 4-12.
A multiplayer version of Lunar Lander, in a client-server style.

Dataflow Styles

The two styles presented here can be characterized as dataflow styles. Their essence concerns the movement of data between independent processing elements.

Batch-sequential. The batch-sequential style is one of the oldest in the design of computer systems. It arose in the early days of data processing when the limitations of computing equipment required that large problems be subdivided into severable components that could communicate by the transfer of magnetic tapes.

A classic example of this style is shown in Figure 4-13. The application is one of updating a bank's record of all its accounts, based upon the overnight processing of the day's transactions (such as deposits or withdrawals from an account). The process starts with a master tape that has all of the bank's accounts on it, sorted by account number, and a daily tape that has the day's transactions on it.

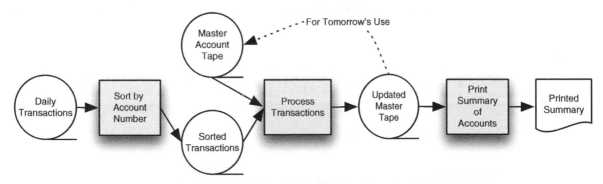

Figure 4-13. *Financial records processed in batch-sequential style.*

Style: Batch-Sequential.

Summary: Separate programs are executed in order; data is passed as an aggregate from one program to the next.
Components: Independent programs.
Connectors: The human hand carrying tapes between the programs, aka "sneaker-net."[5]
Data elements: Explicit, aggregate elements passed from one component to the next upon completion of the producing program's execution.
Topology: Linear.
Additional constraints imposed: One program runs at a time, to completion.
Qualities yielded: Severable execution; simplicity.

Typical uses: Transaction processing in financial systems.
Cautions: When interaction between the components is required; when concurrency between components is possible or required.
Relations to programming languages or environments: None.

Attempting to build a lunar lander game in the batch sequential style reveals how mismatched the style is to the application. The outline of such a (bizarre) design is presented in Figure 4-14. Here the game state is maintained on magnetic tapes.

Each functional processing step of the game is performed by a separate program. Upon performing the step's function, the program produces an updated version of the game state, which is then handed off to the next program in the process. After the final step of displaying the game state is performed, the produced tape is carried back to the first program for another pass. This is obviously not a highly interactive, real-time game!

Pipe-and-Filter. Though radically different in detail from batch-sequential, the pipe-and-filter style introduced in Chapter 1 is also a dataflow style. Recall that the essence of the style is that streams of character data are passed from one filter program to another. The filters can operate concurrently, with no requirement for a producing component to finish before a component that consumes the producer's output begins. Chapter 1 included a natural application of the pipe-and-filter style to the problem of producing a sorted list of selected file names.

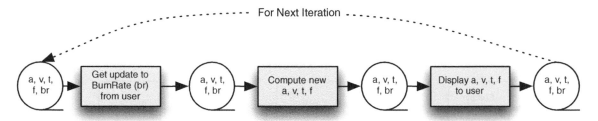

Figure 4-14. *Lunar Lander: Batch-sequential.*

---

[5]Savvy computer operators often wear athletic shoes, also known as "sneakers."

Summary: Separate programs are executed, potentially concurrently; data is passed as a stream from one program to the next.
Components: Independent programs, known as filters.
Connectors: Explicit routers of data streams; service provided by operating system.
Data elements: Not explicit; must be (linear) data streams. In the typical Unix/Linux/DOS implementation the streams must be text.
Topology: Pipeline, though T fittings are possible.
Qualities yielded: Filters are mutually independent. Simple structure of incoming and outgoing data streams facilitates novel combinations of filters for new, composed applications.

Typical uses: Ubiquitous in operating system application programming.
Cautions: When complex data structures must be exchanged between filters; when interactivity between the programs is required.
Relations to programming languages or environments: Prevalent in Unix shells.

Style: Uniform Pipe-and-Filter.

A design for the lunar lander game in the pipe-and-filter style appears in Figure 4-15. Get Burn Rate runs looping on its own, always polling the user for a value. When a value is generated it is sent off through the stream connector to the second filter. The second filter runs looping on its own as well, updating time as it chooses. It serves as the environment simulator and calculates the descent rate of the spacecraft. The third filter likewise loops, updating the display whenever new values become available on its input port. This design follows from a rather functional understanding of the game, similar to the main program and subroutines design. Functioning of a stream connector, and pipe-and-filter in general, is explored in much more depth in Chapter 5.

Shared State
The essence of shared state styles (sometimes colloquially referred to as "shared memory" styles) is that multiple components have access to the same data store, and communicate through that data store. This corresponds roughly to the ill-advised practice of using global data in C or Pascal programming. The difference is that with shared state styles the center of design attention is explicitly on these structured, shared repositories, and that consequently they are well-ordered and carefully managed. The use of global data in programming is usually only one of several means of communication between subprograms, and is done as an expedience.

Figure 4-15. *Lunar Lander in pipe-and-filter style.*

Blackboard. The blackboard style arose in artificial intelligence applications. The intuitive sense of the style is one of many diverse experts sitting around a blackboard, all attempting to cooperate in the solution of a large, complex problem. As any given expert recognizes some part of the problem on the blackboard for which he feels competent to solve, he grabs that subproblem, goes away and works on it, and when finished, returns and posts the solution on the blackboard. Posting that solution may enable another expert to identify a problem which he can solve, and so the process continues until the whole problem is solved. Thus the state of information on the blackboard determines the order of execution of the various "expert" programs.

Style: Blackboard	**Summary:** Independent programs access and communicate exclusively through a global data repository, known as a blackboard. **Components:** Independent programs, sometimes referred to as "knowledge sources," blackboard. **Connectors:** Access to the blackboard may be by direct memory reference, or can be through a procedure call or a database query. **Data elements:** Data stored in the blackboard. **Topology:** Star topology, with the blackboard at the center. **Variants:** In one version of the style, programs poll the blackboard to determine if any values of interest have changed; in another version, a blackboard manager notifies interested components of an update to the blackboard. **Qualities yielded:** Complete solution strategies to complex problems do not have to be preplanned. Evolving views of the data/problem determine the strategies that are adopted. **Typical uses:** Heuristic problem solving in artificial intelligence applications. **Cautions:** When a well-structured solution strategy is available; when interactions between the independent programs require complex regulation; when representation of the data on the blackboard is subject to frequent change (requiring propagating changes to all the participating components). **Relations to programming languages or environments:** Versions of the blackboard style that allow concurrency between the constituent programs require concurrency primitives for managing the shared blackboard.

Figure 4-16 shows the lunar lander program solved in a blackboard style. Here, a single connector regulates access from the various experts in manipulating the information on the blackboard. The blackboard maintains the game state; the experts perform the independent tasks of (1) updating the descent engine burn rate based upon input from the user, (2) displaying to the user the current state of the spacecraft and any other aspect of the game state, and (3) updating the game state based upon a time and physics model. That is, the third component determines how fast time passes and updates the game state in accordance with the passage of time and the physics model of the moon and the Lander.

Rule-Based/Expert System. A rule-based architecture is a highly specialized type of shared memory architecture. The shared memory is a so-called knowledge base, that is, a database that contains facts (statements of values of variables) and production rules which consist

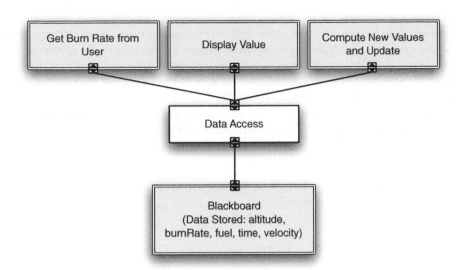

Figure 4-16.
*Lunar Lander in
blackboard style.*

of "if . . . then" clauses over the set of variables. A user interface component provides two modes: one for entering facts and production rules and another for entering queries, known as goals. Operating on the knowledge base, in response to user input, is an inference engine. Facts and production rules are added to the knowledge base; goals are compared against existing facts in the database. If an exact match is found, it returns *true* to the user interface. Otherwise, it evaluates the rules as necessary to determine the validity of the goal.

Style: Rule-Based/Expert System

Summary: Inference engine parses user input and determines whether it is a fact/rule or a query. If it is a fact/rule, it adds this entry to the knowledge base. Otherwise, it queries the knowledge base for applicable rules and attempts to resolve the query.

Components: User interface, inference engine, knowledge base.

Connectors: Components are tightly interconnected, with direct procedure calls and/or shared data access.

Data Elements: Facts and queries.

Topology: Tightly coupled three-tier (direct connection of user interface, inference engine, and knowledge base).

Qualities yielded: Behavior of the application can be easily modified through dynamic addition or deletion of rules from the knowledge base. Small systems can be quickly prototyped. Thus useful for iteratively exploring problems whose general solution approach is unclear.

Typical uses: When the problem can be understood as matter of repeatedly resolving a set of predicates.

Cautions: When a large number of rules are involved, understanding the interactions between multiple rules affected by the same facts can become very difficult. Understanding the logical basis for a computed result can be as important as the result itself.

Relations to programming languages or environments: Prolog is a common language for building rule-based systems.

Designing a solution for the lunar lander problem in the rule-based style requires thinking of the problem as one of maintaining a set of consistent facts about the spacecraft. This is fairly natural, as the physics model that determines the state of the spacecraft can be so understood. For instance, the passage of one second of time demands that the facts regarding the amount of fuel remaining, the velocity of the spacecraft, and the height of the spacecraft be brought up to date, consistently.

With regard to the user interaction model, in the example solution shown in Figure 4-17, the user enters the value of burn rate as a fact:

```
burnrate(25)
```

To see what the status of the spacecraft is, the user can switch to the goal mode and asks whether the spacecraft has landed safely:

```
landed(spacecraft)
```

Figure 4-17.
*Lunar Lander in
a rule-based
style.*

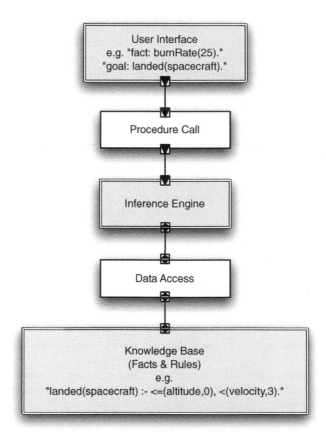

To handle this query, the inference engine queries the database. If the existing facts and other production rules satisfy the conditions "altitude <= 0" and "velocity < 3 ft/s," then the engine returns true to the user interface. Otherwise, it returns false.[6]

Interpreter

The distinctive characteristic of interpreter styles is dynamic, on-the-fly interpretation of commands. Commands are explicit statements, possibly created moments before they are executed, possibly encoded in human-readable and editable text. Commands are phrased in terms of predefined primitive commands. Interpretation proceeds by starting with an initial execution state, obtaining the first command to execute (possibly by reading some user input), executing the command over the current execution state, thereby modifying that state, then proceeding to execute the next command. Identification of the next command may be affected by the result of executing the previous command; indeed, in the general case the next command may be the product of the execution of the previous command.

The *basic interpreter* architectural style involves the execution of commands one at a time. Similarly, though typically at a larger granularity, the *mobile code* style involves the execution of one chunk of code at a time. The difference with mobile code is that the place where the commands are executed may vary over time.

Basic Interpreter. Execution of commands in the basic interpreter style is similar to the rule-based style described above, where the inference engine parses a command input and performs variable resolution based on the knowledge repository. In the case of the basic interpreter style, the command interpreter is more general (capable of more generic operations than performing inferences over a set of rules). The interpretation of a single command may involve numerous primitive operations. The knowledge repository is similarly more general since arbitrary data structures may be involved.

While perhaps sounding complicated, the interpreter style is quite familiar to what might be the world's largest cohort of programmers: the users of Microsoft Excel. Excel's formulas are in fact commands interpreted by the Excel execution engine—the interpreter. Similarly Excel's macros are interpreted by the Visual Basic interpreter. Many graphical editing programs are similarly interpreter based: a structure of commands describing the drawing is maintained by the drawing program. The drawing on the screen seen by the user is created by an internal interpreter running over the text, interpreting it, issuing drawing commands to the graphics engine.

---

[6]For a realistic model, the set of rules in the database will be extensive to perform the computation of a, v, t, f. A simple one-dimensional physics equation calculates altitude as follows:

$$\frac{1}{2} * (\text{accelerationThrust} - \text{accelerationGravity}) * t^2 + v * t + \text{altitudeOld}$$

However, a more realistic calculation of thrust is quite complicated (see notes at the end of the chapter for references).

Style: Interpreter

Summary: Interpreter parses and executes input commands, updating the state maintained by the interpreter.
Components: Command interpreter, program/interpreter state, user interface.
Connectors: Typically the command interpreter, user interface, and state are very closely bound with direct procedure calls and shared state.
Data elements: Commands.
Topology: Tightly coupled three-tier; state can be separated from the interpreter.
Qualities yielded: Highly dynamic behavior possible, where the set of commands is dynamically modified. System architecture may remain constant while new capabilities are created based upon existing primitives.

Typical uses: Superb for end-user programmability; supports dynamically changing set of capabilities.
Cautions: When fast processing is needed (it takes longer to execute interpreted code than executable code); memory management may be an issue, especially when multiple interpreters are invoked simultaneously.
Relations to programming languages or environments: Lisp and Scheme are interpretive languages, and sometimes used when building other interpreters; Word/Excel macros.

In the version of the lunar lander game shown in Figure 4-18, for each command entered, the interpreter engine processes the code and updates the interpreter state as necessary. The commands in this case are specific directives regarding how the spacecraft should be manipulated—most importantly, how the descent engine should be throttled. The interpreter, thus, has been programmed specifically to interpret such commands. It may return values to the user, depending on the command. Thus, when the user enters "BurnRate(50)," the interpreter takes BurnRate as the command and the parameter as the amount of fuel to burn. It then calculates the necessary updates to the altitude, fuel level, and velocity. Time is simulated by having t incremented each occasion the user enters a BurnRate command. When the user enters the CheckStatus command, the user receives the current state of altitude, fuel, time, and velocity.

Mobile Code. As the name suggests, mobile code styles enable code to be transmitted to a remote host for interpretation. This may be due to a lack of local computing power, lack of resources, or due to large data sets remotely located. Mobile code may be classified as code on demand, remote evaluation, or mobile agent depending on where the code is being transmitted, who requested the transmission, and where the program state resides. Code on demand is when the initiator has resources and state but downloads code from another site to be executed locally. Remote evaluation is when the initiator has the code but lacks the resources (such as the interpreter) to execute the code. Thus, it transmits code to be processed at a remote host, such as in grid computing. Results are returned to the initiator. Mobile agent is when the initiator has the code and the state but some of resources are located elsewhere. Thus the initiator moves to a remote host with the code, the state, and some of the resources. Processing need not return to the initiator.

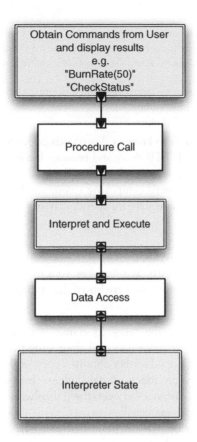

Figure 4-18.
*Lunar Lander in
interpreter style.*

In all of the mobile code styles, a data element (some representation of a program) is dynamically transformed into a data processing component (when those commands are interpreted or otherwise executed).

Summary: Code moves to be interpreted on another host; depending on the variant, state does also.

Components: Execution dock, which handles receipt and deployment of code and state; code compiler/interpreter.

Connectors: Network protocols and elements for packaging code and data for transmission.

Data elements: Representations of code as data; program state; data.

Topology: Network.

Variants: Code-on-demand, remote evaluation, and mobile agent.

Qualities yielded: Dynamic adaptability. Takes advantage of the aggregate computing power of available hosts; increased dependability through provision of migration to new hosts.

Typical uses: When processing large data sets in distributed locations, it becomes more efficient to have the code move to the location of these large data sets; when it is desirous to dynamically customize a local processing node through inclusion of external code.

**Style:
Mobile Code**

> **Cautions:** Security issues—execution of imported code may expose the host machine to malware. Other cautions—when it is necessary to tightly control the different software versions deployed; when costs of transmission exceed the cost of computation; when network connections are unreliable.
> **Relations to programming languages or environments:** Scripting languages (such as JavaScript, VBScript), ActiveX controls. Grid computing.

In Figure 4-19, one client Web browser downloads code-on-demand in the form of a Lunar Lander game applet via HTTP. A second browser loads a JavaScript Lunar Lander; a third uses some other form that is not detailed. Thus, all the game logic moves to the client machines, freeing the server's computing resources. In the figure as shown, each client machine maintains the game state independently of other clients.

Implicit Invocation

Unlike the previously discussed styles, the two styles below are characterized by calls that are invoked indirectly and implicitly as a response to a notification or an event. Ease of adaptation and enhanced scalability are benefits of the indirect interaction between very loosely coupled components.

Publish-Subscribe. Publish-subscribe takes its name from the analogous relationship between magazine or newspaper publishers and their subscribers. The publisher periodically creates information and the subscriber obtains a copy of the information or at least is informed of its availability. The architectural style reflects this kind of relationship. Several variants exist, differing in the distance between the publisher and the subscribers, and the way in which the relationship is managed.

In a simple publish-subscribe style the publisher maintains a list of subscribers to each of which a procedure call is issued when new information is available. Subscribers register their interest with publishers, providing them with the procedure interface to be used (the call-back) when information is published. Subscribers can also deregister their interest, having the call-back removed from the publisher's subscription list.

The simple publish-subscribe style works well within the context of a simple program. For large-scale, network-based applications, a more sophisticated set of services is needed. Publishers need to advertise the existence of information resources to which others may subscribe, either at system start-up, periodically, or on demand. Subscriptions can no longer take the form of call-back procedures, but involve the use of network protocols. Efficiency concerns argue against point-to-point relationships between publishers and subscribers; intermediate proxies or caches can help performance—just as with physical newspapers, where a paper carrier serves as proxy for the newspaper company, being responsible for delivery of the papers within a small geographic region.

The publish-subscribe style caters to applications where there is a clear delineation between producers and consumers of information. A familiar network-based application of the publish-subscribe style is an online job posting service. Hiring managers post, or publish, the job openings. Meanwhile, job seekers subscribe to the online service to receive notifications of new job postings. While this application works with perhaps only a few notifications per day, other network publish-subscribe applications operate with many notifications per second.

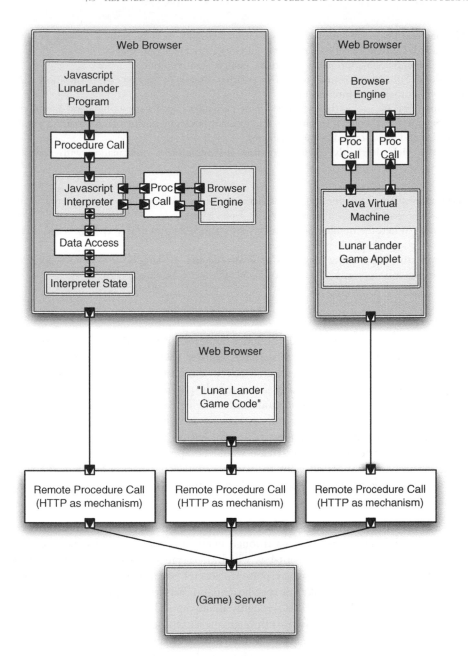

Figure 4-19.
Mobile code:
Lunar Lander as
code-on-demand.

Summary: Subscribers register/deregister to receive specific messages or specific content. Publishers maintain a subscription list and broadcast messages to subscribers either synchronously or asynchronously.
Components: Publishers, subscribers, proxies for managing distribution.

Style:
Publish-
Subscribe

Connectors: Procedure calls may be used within programs, more typically a network protocol is required. Content-based subscription requires sophisticated connectors.
Data elements: Subscriptions, notifications, published information.
Topology: Subscribers connect to publishers either directly or may receive notifications via a network protocol from intermediaries.
Variants: Specific uses of the style may require particular steps for subscribing and unsubscribing. Support for complex matching of subscription interests and available information may be provided and be performed by intermediaries.
Qualities yielded: Highly efficient one-way dissemination of information with very low coupling of components.

Typical uses: News dissemination—whether in the real world or online events. Graphical user interface programming. Multiplayer-network–based games.
Cautions: When the number of subscribers for a single data item is very large a specialized broadcast protocol will likely be necessary.
Relations to programming languages or environments: In large-scale systems support for publish-subscribe is provided by commercial middleware technology.

In the example of Figure 4-20, the lunar lander software is deployed to various network hosts. Players, who are the subscribers, register their hosts to a game server that publishes information, such as new Lunar terrain data, new spacecraft, and the (Lunar) locations of all the registered spacecraft currently playing the game. Once registered, the subscribed hosts receive notifications when any of the information they have registered for has been updated. The notifications may actually contain the information the subscriber is interested in, or obtaining the information via an explicit download could proceed as a separate step. The first case would be appropriate for a multiplayer game in which the Lander pilots all want to monitor each other during landing; the second case would be appropriate, for example, when an update to the game software is made available.

Event-Based. The event-based style is characterized by independent components communicating solely by sending events through event-bus connectors. In its purest form, components emit events to the event-bus, which then transmits them to every other component. Components may react in response to receipt of an event or may ignore it; the architectural style does not make any specific demand. While seeming to perhaps be rather chaotic and unpredictable, this style is roughly analogous to how we, as humans, behave in society. We are continually receiving—through our senses—events from the outside world: Some we react to and some we ignore. Similarly, we are continually emitting events into the world, such as by speaking. Again, sometimes they elicit a response from others and sometimes not—such as when you are talking to your teenage son.

For efficiency reasons, the pure form of event-based architectures is seldom used; it is more efficient to only distribute events to those components that express an interest in them. With this optimization, the style becomes similar to publish-subscribe. The distinctive character of the event-based style, however, is that there is no classification of components into publishers and subscribers; all components potentially both emit and

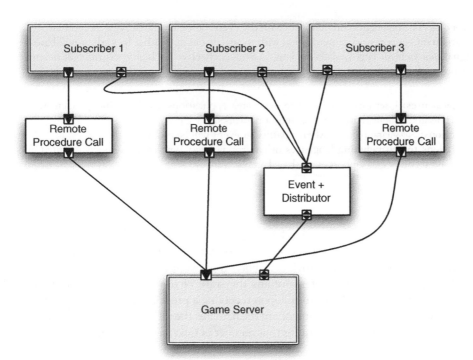

Figure 4-20.
*Lunar Lander in
publish-subscribe.*

receive events. With the event-based style, the optimization of event distribution is the responsibility of the connectors; registration of interest in particular events is only handled by the connectors. Similarly, replication of events for delivery to multiple recipients may take place late in the transmission process and would be transparent to both the event emitter and the event receiver. Finally, event distribution may be handled either on a push or pull basis. In the case of pull, or polling, event recipients can query the connector to see if a new event is available. Such a query could either be blocking (the component waits until an event is available) or nonblocking (the component returns immediately, either with a new value—if available—or not).

The event-based style is highly suited to strongly decoupled concurrent components, where at any given moment a component either may be creating information of potential interest to others or may be consuming information. A classic example usage is in financial markets: Independent companies (traders) may want to know the latest price of a commodity being sold in London; similarly, when that trader completes a deal, the results of that trade represent information of interest to others around the world.

Summary: Independent components asynchronously emit and receive events communicated over event buses.
Components: Independent, concurrent event generators and/or consumers.
Connectors: Event bus. In variants, more than one may be used.
Data elements: Events—data sent as a first-class entity over the event bus.

**Style:
Event-Based**

Topology: Components communicate with the event-buses, not directly to each other.
Variants: Component communication with the event-bus may either be push or pull based.
Qualities yielded: Highly scalable, easy to evolve, effective for highly distributed, heterogeneous applications.

Typical uses: User interface software, wide-area applications involving independent parties (such as financial markets, logistics, sensor networks).
Cautions: No guarantee if or when a particular event will be processed.
Relations to programming languages or environments: Commercial message–oriented middleware technologies support event-based architectures.

Figure 4-21 shows the lunar lander designed in an event-based style. The clock component drives the game. Every fraction of a second, the clock component sends out a tick notification to the event bus, which distributes that event to the other components.

The spacecraft component maintains the state of the spacecraft (its altitude, fuel level, velocity, and throttle setting). Upon receiving a predefined number of notifications from the clock, the spacecraft component recalculates the altitude, fuel level, and velocity (corresponding to simulated flight for that number of ticks) and then emits those values to the event bus.

The graphical user interface (GUI) component drives the game player's display. Receipt of events providing the spacecraft's altitude, fuel, and velocity causes the GUI component to update its display based on those values. The GUI component also obtains new burn rate settings from the user; when this happens the component emits a notification of this new value onto the event bus. Upon receipt of this notification the Spacecraft component updates its internal model of the spacecraft and, as always, emits the updated state back to the bus.

The game logic component, receiving both information about the state of the spacecraft and the amount of time that has passed (by counting clock ticks), determines whether the game is over, and if so, what the final condition of the spacecraft was when the game ended and hence the player's score.

Figure 4-21.
Lunar Lander in the event-based style.

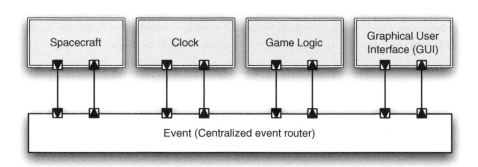

Implicit
Invocation

"Implicit invocation" describes the execution model of both the publish-subscribe and event-based styles. An action, such as invocation of a procedure, may be taken as the result of some activity occurring elsewhere in the system, but the two activities are distant from one another. Though there is a causal relationship, the invocation is indirect, since there is no direct coupling between the components involved. The invocation is implicit, since the causing component has no awareness that its action ultimately causes an invocation elsewhere in the system.

Peer-to-Peer

The peer-to-peer (P2P) architectural style consists of a network of loosely coupled autonomous peers, each peer acting both as a client and a server. Peers communicate using a network protocol, sometimes specialized for P2P communication—such was the case for the original Napster and Gnutella file-sharing applications. Unlike the client-server style where state and logic are centralized on the server, P2P decentralizes both information and control.

Absence of centralization makes resource discovery an important issue for P2P applications. In a pure P2P application, queries for information are issued to the network of peers at large; requests propagate until the information is discovered or some propagation threshold is passed. If the desired information is located, the peer obtains the direct address of that peer and contacts it directly. This style is limited by the network algorithm used to query the system and the network bandwidth available. Hybrid applications optimize this process by having certain peers play special roles, either for locating other peers or for providing directories locating information. The original Napster, for example, was not a true *peer-to-peer* application because it used a centralized server for indexing music and locating other peers. Although the term peer-to-peer has been popularized by file-sharing applications, it enables a host of applications such as business to business commerce, chat, remote collaboration, and sensor networks.

**Style:
Peer-to-Peer**

Summary: State and behavior are distributed among peers that can act as either clients or servers.
Components: Peers—independent components, having their own state and control thread.
Connectors: Network protocols, often custom.
Data elements: Network messages.
Topology: Network (may have redundant connections between peers); can vary arbitrarily and dynamically.
Qualities yielded: Decentralized computing with flow of control and resources distributed among peers. Highly robust in the face of failure of any given node. Scalable in terms of access to resources and computing power.

Typical uses: Where sources of information and operations are distributed and network is ad hoc.
Cautions: When information retrieval is time critical and cannot afford the latency imposed by the protocol. Security—P2P networks must make provision for detecting malicious peers and managing trust in an open environment.

In the example of Figure 4-22, a group of lunar lander spacecraft are on their way to land in different parts of the moon. Multiple Landers are used in this example to highlight that the P2P architectural style is designed to support interaction between highly autonomous components, and especially application contexts where the number of participating components may vary over time. Lunar Lander 1 (LL1) wants to find out if another spacecraft has already landed in a specific area, so that collisions can be avoided. Each of the spacecraft is configured to communicate with the others using a P2P protocol over a network. A spacecraft will only be able to communicate with others that are within a specified, limited distance.

Lunar Lander 1 will go through the following steps to obtain the information:

1. At time T_0, LL1 queries for available spacecraft, that is, spacecraft within communication range.

2. Only LL2 responds.

3. LL1 queries if LL2 has the requisite information.

4. Since LL2 does not have the information, it passes the query on to its adjacent communicating node, LL3 (that is, assume that LL2 and LL3 already have been communicating and do not have to discover each other).

5. Since LL3 does not have the information, it passes the query on to its communicating nodes, LL4, LL6, and LL7.

6. LL7 responds to LL3 that it has the desired information and passes the information requested to LL3.

7. LL3 passes the response back to LL2 and subsequently to LL1.

If at some later time T_n, LL7 comes within communication range, LL1 could directly contact it and query it for additional information, as shown at the bottom of the figure.

4.3.5 More Complex Styles

More complex styles than those discussed above have arisen from efforts to exploit design knowledge gained from substantial experience. The complexity reflects (a) provision of greater benefits, and (b) specialization to certain application contexts. As examples, the C2 and distributed objects styles discussed below combine elements of several of the preceding styles to yield powerful design tools capable of handling challenging problems. They both have resulted from an extended period of engineering experimentation, in which numerous design trade-offs were made.

The C2 (components and connectors) style grew out of a desire to obtain the benefits of the model-view-controller pattern in a distributed, heterogeneous platform setting. Concepts from layered and event-based architectures were added. The resulting style, though originally developed to support graphical user interface applications, was found to be beneficial in a wide variety of applications—indeed more so outside the domain of GUIs than within. C2's primary role in this presentation is showing how elements of many styles may be judiciously combined to meet a variety of needs.

The distributed objects style has its roots in the object-oriented style. As with C2, its developers sought to extend the benefits of a core style to a distributed heterogeneous world.

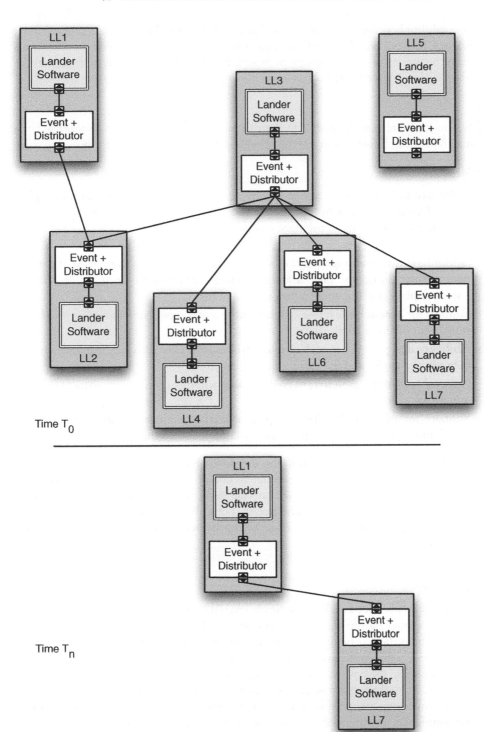

Figure 4-22.
*Lunar Lander as
a P2P
application.*

Interoperability between components or objects implemented in different programming languages is achieved via the use of connectors and adapters. The most obvious differences between the two styles are that several networking concerns are explicitly addressed in the distributed objects style while C2 has lower conceptual coupling between components.

C2

C2 is a much more complicated style than those considered earlier, so to motivate the complexity we start by listing some of the benefits achieved through application of the style.

C2 Benefits

- *Substrate independence:* ease in modifying the application to work with new platforms. This is in contrast to the typical case, where calls to platform services, such as operating systems and user interface toolkits, are coded into the body of components that need those services.
- *Accommodating heterogeneity:* enabling an application to be composed of components written in diverse programming languages and running on multiple, varying hardware platforms, communicating across a network.
- *Support for product lines:* ease of substituting one component for another to achieve similar but different applications.
- *Ability to design in the model-view-controller style:* but with very strong separation between the model and the user interface elements.
- *Natural support for concurrent components:* whether running on a shared processor or multiple machines.
- *Support for network-distributed applications:* wherein communication protocol details are kept out of the components and confined to connectors.

Each of these benefits has been seen in the simple styles above; the contribution of C2 is combining selected simple styles into a coherent comprehensive approach. The following paragraphs lay out C2's constraints. We provide more detail on the constraints here to enable understanding of the style. The reader should be aware, however, that even the simple styles described above have more detailed interface constraints in practice than we have presented.

C2 Constraints

Topology: Applications in the C2 style are layered networks of concurrent components hooked together by message-routing connectors. C2 depends entirely upon implicit invocation, as there is no direct component-to-component communication. All components and connectors have a defined top and bottom. The top of a component may be connected to the bottom of a single connector and the bottom of a component may be connected to the top of a single connector. No other connections are allowed. Arbitrarily many components and connectors may be attached to a single connector. When two connectors are attached to each other, it must be from the bottom of one to the top of the other. These rules induce layering, which promotes substrate independence and component substitutability.

Message-based communication: All communication between components is achieved by exchanging messages. Messages are classified either as requests (a specific request for a service to be performed) or notifications (statements of facts about the system, such as the change in value of some object). This requirement is suggested by the asynchronous nature of applications wherein users and the application perform actions concurrently and at arbitrary times, and where various components in the architecture must be notified of those actions. This constraint also promotes mutual independence of the components.

Message flow and substrate independence: Requests may only flow upward in an architecture; notifications flow downward. This rule induces limited visibility or "substrate independence"—a component within the hierarchy can only be aware of components above it and is completely unaware of components that reside beneath it. Since downward communication is limited to the emitting of notifications, a component cannot know which components, if any, below it will react to receipt of a notification.

Interfaces: Each component has a top and bottom domain. The top domain specifies the set of notifications to which a component may react, and the set of requests that the component emits up an architecture. The bottom domain specifies the set of notifications that this component emits down an architecture, and the set of requests to which it responds.

One important note concerns the apparent dependence of a given component on its superstrate, that is, the components above it, since a component can issue a specific request upward in an architecture. If each component is built so that its top domain closely corresponds to the bottom domains of those components with which it is specifically intended to interact in the given architecture, its reusability value is greatly diminished; it can only be substituted by components with similarly constrained top domains. To avoid this, C2 introduces the notion of domain translation. Domain translation is a transformation of the requests issued by a component into the specific form understood by the recipient of the request, as well as the transformation of notifications received by a component into a form it understands.

C2 supports compositionality, or hierarchical composition, whereby an entire architecture becomes a single component in another, larger architecture.

Each component may have its own thread(s) of control. This simplifies modeling and programming of multicomponent, multiuser, and concurrent applications, and enables exploitation of distributed platforms.

Finally, there can be no assumption of a shared address space among components. Any premise of a shared address space would be unreasonable in an architectural style that allows composition of heterogeneous, highly distributed components, developed in different languages, with their own threads of control, internal structures, and domains of discourse.

A simple C2 architecture for the lunar lander application is shown in Figure 4-23. With respect to the use of events, it operates largely like the solution shown in Figure 4-21, the event-based style. Here, however, both the spacecraft and clock components are *guaranteed by the architecture* to be completely unaware of the presence of the game logic and GUI components.

Figure 4-23.
*Lunar Lander in
the C2 style.*

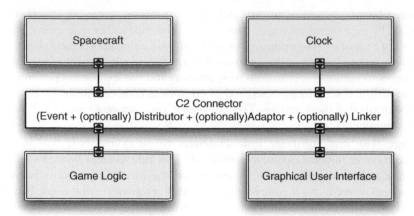

Style: C2

Summary: An indirect invocation style in which independent components communicate exclusively through message routing connectors. Strict rules on connections between components and connectors induce layering.
Components: Independent, potentially concurrent message generators and/or consumers.
Connectors: Message routers that may filter, translate, and broadcast messages of two kinds—notifications and requests.
Data elements: Messages—data sent as first-class entities over the connectors. Notification messages announce changes of state. Request messages request performance of an action.
Topology: Layers of components and connectors, with a defined top and bottom, wherein notifications flow downward and requests upward.

Additional constraints imposed:

- All components and connectors have a defined top and bottom. The top of a component may be attached to the bottom of a single connector and the bottom of a component may be attached to the top of a single connector. No direct component-to-component links are allowed; there is, however, no bound on the number of components or connectors that may be attached to a single connector. When two connectors are attached to each other, it must be from the bottom of one to the top of the other.

- Each component has a top and bottom *domain*. The top domain specifies the set of notifications to which a component may react and the set of requests that the component emits up an architecture. The bottom domain specifies the set of notifications that this component emits down an architecture and the set of requests to which it responds.

- Components may be hierarchically composed, where an entire architecture becomes a single component in another, larger architecture.

- Each component may have its own thread(s) of control.

- There can be no assumption of a shared address space among components.

Qualities yielded:

- Substrate independence: Ease in moving the application to new platforms.
- Applications composable from heterogeneous components running on diverse platforms.

- Support for product lines.
- Ability to program in the model-view-controller style, but with very strong separation between the model and the user interface elements.
- Support for concurrent components.
- Support for network-distributed applications.

Typical uses: Reactive, heterogeneous applications. Applications demanding low-cost adaptability.
Cautions: Event-routing across multiple layers can be inefficient. Overhead high for some simple kinds of component interaction.
Relations to programming languages or environments: Programming frameworks are used to facilitate creation of implementations faithful to architectures in the style. Support for Java, C, Ada.

A more instructive application of C2 is presented in Figure 4-25, in which a KLAX-like game[7] is supported. A screenshot from the game is shown in Figure 4-24. The essence of the game is that colored tiles fall from the chutes at the top of the user's screen. A palette is used to move horizontally across the screen; it can catch the tiles as they fall from the chutes. By inverting the palette, the tiles can be dropped into the wells below. By matching three or more tiles of the same color, horizontally, vertically, or diagonally across the wells, points are scored and the tiles subsequently removed from the game board. If tiles are not caught by the palette, lives are lost. Lives are also lost if the wells are allowed to overflow.

The components that make up the KLAX-like game can be divided into three logical groups. At the top of the architecture are the components that encapsulate the game's state plus the clock. These components are placed at the top because the game state is vital for the functioning of the other two groups of components. The game state components receive no notifications, but respond to requests and emit notifications of internal state changes. In a sense, these components play the role of servers, or perhaps of blackboards. Notifications are directed to the next level, where they are received by both the game logic components and the artist components.

The game logic components request changes of game state in accordance with game rules, and interpret game state change notifications to determine the state of the game in progress. For example, if a tile is dropped from a chute, Relative Position Logic determines if the palette is in a position to catch the tile. If so, a request is sent to Palette, adding the tile to the palette. Otherwise, a notification is sent that a tile has been dropped. This notification is detected by Status Logic, causing the number of lives to be decremented. The logic components perform their functions in keeping with receipt of a particular number of notifications from the clock.

The artist components receive notifications of game-state changes, causing them to update their depictions. Each artist maintains the state of a set of abstract graphical

---

[7]KLAX was a video game developed by Atari Games Corporation in 1990. KLAX is now a trademark of Midway Games West Inc.

Figure 4-24.
*Screenshot of
example
KLAX-like
game.*

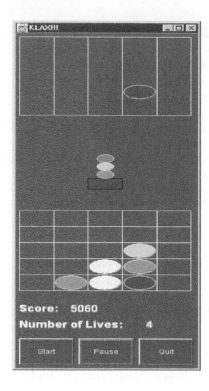

objects that, when modified, send state change notifications in the hope that a lower-level graphics component will render them on the screen. Tile Artist, for instance, provides a flexible presentation for tiles. Tile Artist intercepts any notifications about tile objects and issues notifications about more concrete drawable objects. For example, a Tile Created–notification received might result in issuance of a Rectangle Created–notification. The Layout Manager component receives all notifications from the artists and determines coordinates to ensure that the game elements are drawn in the correct two-dimensional juxtaposition. The Graphics Binding component receives all notifications about the state of the artists' graphical objects and translates them into calls to a window system. User events, such as a key press, are translated into requests that are sent upward to the artist components.

The application of the C2 style to this design yields several benefits. One is the easy creation of related, but different, games. By substitution of three components the game can be transformed into one where letters instead of tiles fall down the chutes, and the game logic is based upon spelling words in the wells. The components involved are the tile artist, tile match logic, and next tile placing logic, which become, respectively, the letter artist, word match logic, and next letter placing logic components. Similarly confined and easy substitutions or additions of components result in network-based multiplayer games, a high-score version, and so on. The application can run over network boundaries, the user interface toolkit can be swapped out without modification to the various artists, and components can execute concurrently.

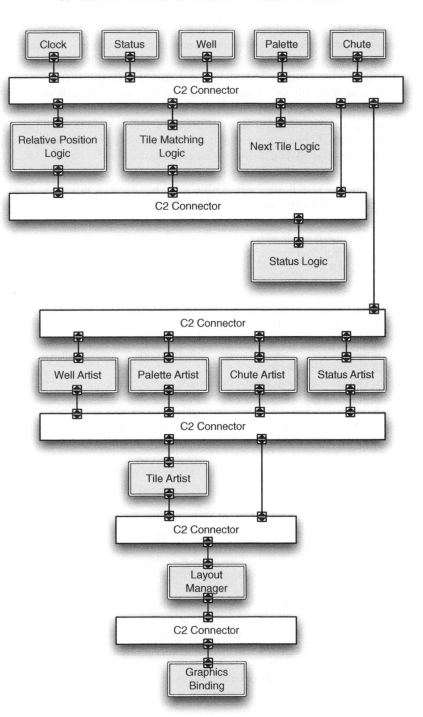

Figure 4-25.
A *KLAX-like*
video game in the
C2 style.

Distributed Objects

The distributed objects style represents a combination and adaptation of several simpler styles. The fundamental vocabulary comes, of course, from the simple object-oriented style considered earlier in the chapter. This style is augmented with the client-server style to provide the notion of distributed objects, with access to those objects from, potentially, different processes executing on different computers. The posited need for cross-machine and cross-language communication puts a constraint on the communication between the processes, however, and hence to some extent the influence of pipe-and-filter is seen, with serialization of parameters (data marshaling) for communication.

In this style, therefore, objects, in the standard object-oriented terminology sense, are instantiated on different hosts, each of which exposes a public interface. The objects can be anything from data structures to million-line legacy systems. The interfaces are special in that all the parameters and return values must be serializable so they can go over the network. The default mode of interaction between objects is synchronous procedure call, although asynchronous extensions are found in some particular versions of distributed objects, such as CORBA.

Style: Distributed Objects	**Summary:** Application functionality broken up into objects (coarse- or fine-grained) that can run on heterogeneous hosts and can be written in heterogeneous programming languages. Objects provide services to other objects through well-defined provided interfaces. Objects invoke methods across host, process, and language boundaries via remote procedure calls (RPCs), generally facilitated by middleware. **Components:** Objects (software components exposing services through well-defined provided interfaces). **Connector:** Remote procedure calls (remote method invocations). **Data elements:** Arguments to methods, return values, and exceptions. **Topology:** General graph of objects from callers to callees; in general, required services are not explicitly represented. **Additional constraints imposed:** Data passed in remote procedure calls must be serializable. Callers must deal with exceptions that can arise due to network or process faults. **Qualities yielded:** Strict separation of interfaces from implementations as well as other qualities of object-oriented systems in general, plus mostly-transparent interoperability across location, platform, and language boundaries. **Typical uses:** Creation of distributed software systems composed of components running on different hosts. Integration of software components written in different programming languages or for different platforms. **Cautions:** Interactions tend to be mostly synchronous and do not take advantage of the concurrency present in distributed systems. Users wanting services provided by middleware (network, location, and/or language transparency) often find that the middleware induces the distributed objects style on their applications, whether or not it is the best style. Difficulty dealing with streams and high-volume data flows. **Relations to programming languages or environments:** Implementations in almost every programming language and environment.

CORBA. CORBA is a standard for implementing middleware that supports development of applications composed of distributed objects. Many software development practitioners will have experience with, or at least heard of, CORBA technology. However, CORBA's relationship to software architecture and architectural styles is not always clear. While CORBA is no longer as popular a technology as it once was, it is emblematic of a collection of technologies (such as DCOM and RMI) that seek to support distributed objects, and hence worthy of study.

The basic idea behind CORBA is that an application is broken up into objects, which are effectively software components that expose one or more provided interfaces. In CORBA, these provided interfaces are specified in terms of a programming-language- and platform-neutral notation called the Interface Definition Language (IDL). IDL closely resembles the way class interfaces are specified in an object-oriented programming language. An IDL description of the interface for the data store component of a lunar lander system might look like the following.

```
interface IDataStore{
   double getAltitude();
   void setAltitude(in double newAltitude);

   double getBurnRate();
   void setBurnRate(in double newBurnRate);

   void getStatus(out double altitude,
                  out double burnRate,
                  out double velocity,
                  out double fuel,
                  out double time);
}
```

All access to an object occurs through calls to one of its IDL-specified interfaces. IDL is strongly typed, meaning that calls and parameters can be type-checked at compile time.

Figure 4-26 illustrates how CORBA connects objects across machine, language, and process boundaries. The top portion of the diagram shows the conceptual, or logical view, which should be familiar to anyone who has written an object-oriented program. A client program obtains a pointer to an object that can perform a service for it, here labeled the Object Instance. After obtaining this pointer, it makes calls on the object instance through one of its interface methods.

Within the context of a single programming language, in a single process running on a single machine, making an object call like this is straightforward. The pointer in this case is a direct memory reference, and the call represents a simple synchronous procedure call. When language, process, and machine boundaries are involved, things become more complicated, and this is the problem that CORBA attempts to overcome. Implementations of CORBA are accompanied by tools called IDL compilers that can target specific platform and programming language combinations (such as C++ on Windows). When an IDL interface is run through an IDL compiler, two code artifacts are created, known as an *object stub* and an *object skeleton*.

An object skeleton is an object in the target programming language/platform that provides empty implementations for each method defined in the IDL interface. IDL types are translated into local programming language types. The developer is then responsible for

Figure 4-26.
*Notional
CORBA
diagram.*

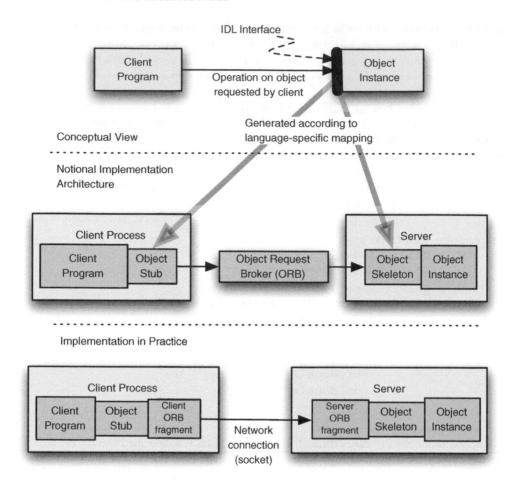

implementing these methods in the target programming language. These implementations make up the object instance, also known as the *true object*.

The object stub is the complement of the object skeleton. It is an object that provides implementations for each method in the IDL interface, again in the target programming language. These method implementations do not actually perform the services provided by the true object, however. Instead, when a method on the stub is called, the calling parameters are encoded into a block of binary data in a process called *serialization* or *marshaling*. The stub then sends this block of data across machine or process boundaries, using a network or another interprocess communication (IPC) mechanism, to the object skeleton. The software that facilitates this is known in CORBA as the *object request broker*, or ORB. Depending on the CORBA implementation, this may be a separate piece of software, or it may be part of the stub and skeleton. The skeleton receives the call data, makes the corresponding invocation on the object instance, and then marshals the return value or exception for return to the stub. The stub then returns this data to the caller, which in the figure is the client program.

In this way, a client program can invoke a remote object without explicit knowledge that it is remote. From the client program's perspective, the object stub is providing the service it needs. The object stub, however, is not really providing the service. Instead, it is sending the call data over the network to the skeleton, which calls the object instance—the true object—to perform the actual service. Data is returned by the same path in reverse.

The last part of the puzzle is how the client program/object stub pair obtain a pointer or reference to the object skeleton/object instance pair in the first place. This can be done in a number of ways, most commonly by a lookup or naming service known as an object request broker (ORB) that maintains a directory of objects running on hosts and allows clients to look them up by name. The conceptual placement of the ORB is shown in the middle of Figure 4-26. In practice, the ORB is distributed among the client and server processes, as illustrated in the bottom of the figure.

CORBA does the best it can to ensure that client and server object implementations are not aware that the call between them is traversing a language, process, or machine boundary. However, these boundaries never can be masked completely. There are two main differences between a local and a remote procedure call. First, all data that traverses a remote procedure call must be serializable. That is, the stub and skeleton must be able to transform the data into a block of binary data for transmission over a network. Parameters that contain pointers to arbitrary blocks of memory on the local machine or control objects like threads cannot be serialized, and thus cannot be passed or returned in a remote procedure call. Second, remote procedure calls suffer from a much wider variety of potential failures than local procedure calls. In a local procedure call, it is assumed that the call itself—the transfer of control and data from caller to callee—cannot fail. In a remote procedure call, network problems and dead processes can cause the call itself to fail. In these cases, a run-time exception is raised by the call, but such exceptions would not have been expected in the context of a local procedure call. (Additional problems with network-based applications are discussed in Chapter 11.)

Although remote procedure calls are in some ways more limited and fragile than local ones, they can be more flexible as well. Calls can be redirected or logged by the object request broker without any changes to the client or server objects. New server objects and even new hosts can be dynamically created and come online during application run-time, and then be looked up by later clients. This imparts a measure of dynamism to applications built using CORBA.

Figure 4-27 shows a simple application of CORBA in the design of a two-pilot trainer version of Lunar Lander. In this version, two independent user clients, Trainer and Trainee, can view the state of the Lander during its descent and both clients can adjust the fuel consumption rate, r. In addition, a third client, Houston, monitors the state of the Lander and the two pilots. The state of the Lander is maintained as a CORBA object on a remote server, the Lander Simulation System. The clients manipulate the burn rate by making calls through the CORBA services. Each pilot client also maintains the state of its pilot. Thus, when Houston views the altitude of the Lander, the request is routed to the server. However, when Client Houston views the heart rate of the pilots, the call is routed to both pilot clients.

The description here of CORBA has been quite brief, and the example simplistic. In practice, CORBA offers a rich set of services for managing distributed objects and constructing sophisticated distributed architectures. Most CORBA implementations are

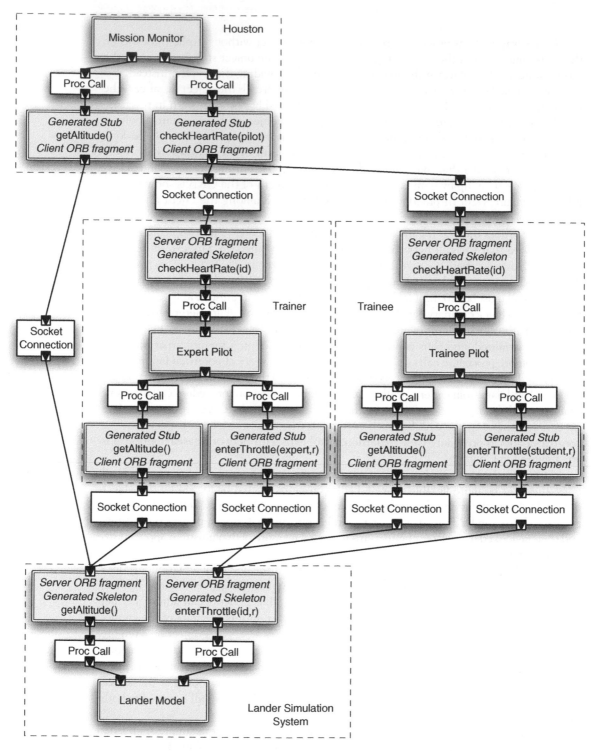

Figure 4-27. *Training version of Lunar Lander, in* CORBA. *Two pilots can have their hands on the controls.*

accompanied by CORBAservices, objects and interfaces that can be called to deal with object life cycles, relationships, persistence, externalization, naming, trading, events, transactions, concurrency, properties, queries, security, licensing, versioning, notification, and so on.

Selecting CORBA as the basis for a software development project is a double-edged sword. On one hand, using CORBA allows systems to be implemented using components written in different languages on different platforms, and the CORBA middleware automatically masks most of the differences. For developers faced with integrating modern technologies with legacy systems, the allure is almost too good to pass up. However, using CORBA comes with a price. The use of CORBA provides these interoperability benefits, but it also induces applications to be built in the distributed objects style.

Distributed objects is not an ideal style for every application. Drawbacks include for example, that components in a distributed objects style are required to explicitly specify provided interfaces, but not to specify required interfaces. Dependencies between objects may thus be deeply ingrained. Objects in the CORBA world are constantly created, linked, unlinked, and destroyed. This makes it difficult to understand the configuration of a CORBA application at any given time. Distributed object interactions tend to be synchronous call-return, and many such systems have difficulty with asynchronous invocations or data that travels in streams.

| The Big Ball of Mud architectural style has been described by Brian Foote and Joseph Yoder as the most common architectural style of all (Foote and Yoder 1997). The style imposes no constraints, other than "get the job done." It offers the benefits of, "We didn't have to think too much", and "It'll work for now. I hope." Software in the BBoM style is haphazard and thrown together. Such systems often grow by accretion: New bits of code are stuck onto preexisting code to meet new demands, without discipline, plan, or care. The BBoM style is an important style for designers to keep in mind for one simple but critical reason: "If you can't articulate why your application is *not* a big ball of mud, then it is." | **The Big Ball of Mud Style** |

4.3.6 Discussion: Patterns and Styles

Taking a step back from the myriad details associated with the styles and patterns discussed above, common characteristics are evident. Fundamentally, styles and patterns reflect experience and codify knowledge gained from that experience. Creating a good style entails reflection on experience, abstraction of the knowledge from the details, and possibly generalization. Thus styles are "refined experience in action."

Despite the fact that styles represent hard-won wisdom in system development, their use is sometimes resisted. Why? Because the very nature of styles, the adherence to a style during design, demands that the designer work within the set of constraints that comprise the style. Somehow the very notion of constraining the designer seems counterproductive and limiting. The curious, nonintuitive character of styles and designing, however, is that through the adherence to constraints, great freedom and effectiveness in design is achieved.

The Freedom of Constraints

When viewed as a set of constraints, styles limit the designer in several ways:

- The amount of detail or the number of concepts that the designer is allowed to deal with at any one time may be limited (for example, in three-tier architectures).
- The way elements of the design are allowed to interact may be restricted (for example, in event-based architectures, or in CORBA-based systems).
- There may be specific obligations on what particular elements must do—and not do (for example, requiring inter-component communication to be strictly mediated by first-class connectors).
- The style may constrain the solution of some subproblems to be addressed in a less than optimal way (for example, pipe-and-filter always requires character stream communication, even when complex data structures are communicated). In such a case, the benefits of consistent style, with its understandability and ability to be reused in standard, expected ways, outweighs any other limited benefit.

Where then does the freedom and effectiveness of styles come from? Numerous sources are apparent:

- Styles restrict one's focus, and thus create a space of issues that the design does not have to be concerned about. The styles free up thought space and direct attention to the essentials.
- Styles guarantee the applicability of particular analysis techniques.
- The constraints enable the use of code generation and framework implementation strategies—since patterns of interaction are regularized they can be automatically and/or efficiently supported in standard ways.
- Styles provide invariants—assertions that the designer can always count on ("As long as I follow the rules then I know the following must be true.").
- Styles make communication more efficient: Once project members know the rules, they form a baseline for communicating the added-value details.
- Similarly, styles promote understanding of design decisions after the fact, such as when the software is taken over by a new development team.

Combination, Modification, and Creation of Styles and Patterns

While studying the long list of architectural styles in the preceding pages may have been exhausting, the list is certainly not exhaustive. A point we have stressed is that styles capture experience and distill it to an essence that is useable in new development situations. Seen this way, each application domain may have a specific style associated with it. More commonly, however, styles appropriate for a particular domain will be aggregations or combinations of simpler styles.

The combination of styles is motivated by the desire to obtain multiple benefits in design. A good example of a composite, and specialized style, is the C2 style discussed in Section 1.3.5. C2 is a combination of model-view-controller, layered systems, and event-based styles. REST, an even more complicated example, will be discussed in Chapter 11. REST was introduced at the beginning of Chapter 1, but was discussed there without reference to how it was developed.

Knowing that styles can be combined, specialized, or developed from scratch leads to the danger of creating new styles unnecessarily or unwisely. Any designer could claim, with some justification, that his experience is what matters most to him, and hence codification of a style that represents that experience is important. Keep in mind, however, that one's own experience needs to be traded off against the aggregate experience of other designers within a company or application domain. Moreover formulation of yet-another-architectural-style (YAAS, indeed) negates one of the advantages of styles: the promotion of effective communication between designers. The lures of expediency and "good enough" seldom outweigh the genuine benefits of carefully applying established, well-known styles.

If, after consideration of substantial experience, a group decides to formulate a new style to capture that experience and their insights, it should be done with an eye to capturing only what is truly central, and avoiding incidental matters. "Less is more" should prevail until adequate validation is obtained for the newly formulated approach. An important goal for such an exercise should be a clear articulation of what invariants are gained as the result of adding constraints.

A brief summary of the styles considered in this chapter appears in Table 4-1. Each of the styles is listed in the left column. A capsule summary of the style is then presented, followed by advice on when to use it, and when to avoid it. Though this table is long, the advice and summaries are extremely brief, and hence omit the nuance and detail that are needed to fully guide their use. Hence this table should only be used as a first cut in determining what styles might be appropriate for a given design challenge. The more detailed tables and discussions which have appeared earlier in this chapter should then be referenced to assess the candidate styles.

4.3.7 Design Recovery

So far we have discussed situations in which an architect has, or has access to, prior experience in designing a particular kind of system for an understood domain. If this is not the case, the problem faced by the architect falls in the province of unprecedented design. However, before we consider approaches for dealing with unprecedented design, we will consider one more source of experience—design recovery.

Different software design methods clearly differ in the details of how developers arrive at a software system. However, to one extent or another, they all rely on the assumption that a software project starts with some form of requirements gathering and specification, reaches its major milestone with system implementation and delivery, and then continues, possibly indefinitely, into an operation and maintenance phase. The software system's architecture is in many ways the linchpin of this process: It is supposed to be an effective reification of the system's technical conception and to be faithfully reflected in the system's implementation. Furthermore, the architecture is meant to guide system evolution, while also being updated in the process.

Sadly, for many systems this turns out to be an idealized picture. Some systems are hacked without careful consideration or documentation of architectural concerns. Other systems are designed carefully and those initial designs are documented, but repeated modifications are subsequently made with little concern for maintaining intellectual coherence, resulting in substantial architectural erosion. Software evolution certainly requires in-depth understanding of an application, its complexity, its overall architecture, its major components, and their interactions and dependencies. Unfortunately, many of these requirements

Table 4-1
*A Comparison
Table of
Architectural
Styles*

Style Category & Name	*Summary*	*Use It When . . .*	*Avoid It When . . .*
Language-influenced styles			
Main program and subroutines	Main program controls program execution, calling multiple subroutines.	. . . application is small and simple.	. . . complex data structures needed (because of lack of encapsulation). . . . future modifications likely.
Object-oriented	Objects encapsulate state and accessing functions.	. . . close mapping between external entities and internal objects is sensible. . . . many complex and interrelated data structures.	. . . application is distributed in a heterogeneous network. . . . strong independence between components necessary. . . . very high performance required.
Layered			
Virtual machines	Virtual machine, or a layer, offers services to layers above it.	. . . many applications can be based upon a single, common layer of services. . . . interface service specification resilient when implementation of a layer must change.	. . . many levels are required (causes inefficiency). . . . data structures must be accessed from multiple layers.
Client-server	Clients request service from a server.	. . . centralization of computation and data at a single location (the server) promotes manageability and scalability. . . . end-user processing limited to data entry and presentation.	. . . centrality presents a single-point-of-failure risk. . . . network bandwidth limited. . . . client machine capabilities rival or exceed the server's.
Dataflow Styles			
Batch-sequential	Separate programs executed sequentially, with batched input.	. . . problem easily formulated as a set of sequential, severable steps.	. . . interactivity or concurrency between components necessary or desirable. . . . random-access to data required.
Pipe-and-filter	Separate programs, aka filters, executed, potentially concurrently. Pipes route data streams between filters.	[as with batch-sequential] . . . filters are useful in more than one application. . . . data structures easily serializable.	. . . interaction between components required.

			Table 4-1 (Continued)
Style Category & Name	*Summary*	*Use It When . . .*	*Avoid It When . . .*
Shared Memory			
Blackboard	Independent programs, access and communicate exclusively through a global repository known as blackboard.	. . . all calculation centers on a common, changing data structure. . . . order of processing dynamically determined and data-driven.	. . . programs deal with independent parts of the common data. . . . interface to common data susceptible to change. . . . interactions between the independent programs require complex regulation.
Rule-based	Use facts or rules entered into the knowledge base to resolve a query.	. . . problem data and queries expressible as simple rules over which inference may be performed.	. . . number of rules is large. . . . interaction between rules present. . . . high-performance required.
Interpreter			
Interpreter	Interpreter parses and executes the input stream, updating the state maintained by the interpreter.	. . . highly dynamic behavior required. High degree of end-user customizability.	. . . high performance required.
Mobile code	Code is mobile, that is, it is executed in a remote host.	. . . it is more efficient to move processing to a data set than the data set to processing. . . . it is desirous to dynamically customize a local processing node through inclusion of external code.	. . . security of mobile code cannot be assured, or sandboxed. . . . tight control of versions of deployed software is required.
Implicit Invocation			
Publish-subscribe	Publishers broadcast messages to subscribers.	. . . components are very loosely coupled. . . . subscription data is small and efficiently transported.	. . . middleware to support high-volume data is unavailable.
Event-based	Independent components asynchronously emit and receive events communicated over event buses.	. . . components are concurrent and independent. . . . components heterogeneous and network-distributed.	. . . guarantees on real-time processing of events is required.

(Continued)

Table 4-1
(*Continued*)

Style Category & Name	Summary	Use It When . . .	Avoid It When . . .
Peer-to-Peer	Peers hold state and behavior and can act as both clients and servers.	. . . peers are distributed in a network, can be heterogeneous, and mutually independent. . . . robustness in face of independent failures and high scalability required.	. . . trustworthiness of independent peers cannot be assured or managed. . . . designated nodes to support resource discovery unavailable.
More Complex Styles			
C2	Layered network of concurrent components communicating by events.	. . . independence from substrate technologies required. . . . heterogeneous applications. . . . support for product-lines desired.	. . . high-performance across many layers required. . . . multiple threads are inefficient.
Distributed objects	Objects instantiated on different hosts.	. . . objective is to preserve illusion of location-transparency.	. . . high overhead of supporting middleware is excessive. . . . network properties are unmaskable, in practical terms.

are often ignored, with a frequent willingness to compromise the quality and longevity of a system in order to, for example, decrease a new version's time to market. This attitude, coupled with the complexity of the involved systems and the sloppiness with which the changes to them are often documented, directly contributes to numerous recorded cases of architectural erosion.

Evolving a system with an undocumented, or documented but degraded, architecture poses tremendous challenges to engineers. It results in a real danger that the modifications intended to provide new functionality will be implemented incorrectly and those intended to remove a particular problem in the existing system will cause other, unforeseen problems. To deal with this issue, researchers and practitioners typically have engaged in architectural recovery, a process whereby the system's architectural design is extracted from its other artifacts, which are likely to be updated more reliably than the design itself. These artifacts may include requirements, formal specifications, test plans, and so on. However, most frequently, design recovery uses a system's implementation as the starting point.

Simply put, then, the task of design recovery is one of examining the existing code base—both source code and possibly binary files for any externally developed functionality that is reused off-the-shelf—and determining the system's components, connectors, and overall topology. As with other architectural tasks, the goals of recovery will be viewpoint-specific.

A common approach to architectural recovery is *clustering* of the implementation-level entities into architectural elements. Based on the approach used for grouping source code entities, such as classes, procedures, or variables, software clustering techniques can be divided into two major categories: *syntactic* and *semantic* clustering.

Syntactic clustering focuses exclusively on the static relationships among code-level entities. This means that the design recovery activity can be performed without executing the system. The functional characteristics or meaning of the code-level entities are not taken into consideration. Instead, the entities are grouped together based on naming conventions or the existence of particular relationships between them. For example, if source code analysis shows that one class is encapsulated inside another, the two classes can be grouped together to represent (a part of) a single system component. More examples of relationships of this kind include variable and class references, procedure calls, use of packages, association and inheritance relationships among classes, and so on. In addition, syntactic clustering approaches can embody intercomponent (aka coupling) and intracomponent (aka cohesion) connectivity measures.

The major drawback of syntactic clustering is that it may ignore or misinterpret many subtle relationships and interactions among the implemented system's entities. This is particularly the case with *dynamic* information, such as the interaction frequency between two classes or the actual method invoked in the case of polymorphism. This problem is remedied by semantic clustering, which includes all aspects of a system's domain knowledge and information about the behavioral similarity of its entities. This means that all implementation constructs with similar functionality can be grouped together to form a software component. For example, all classes that provide support for checking the users' authenticity can be clustered into a single component. Although this approach may provide more meaningful components, it requires interpreting the system entities' meaning, and possibly executing the system on a representative set of inputs. In order to infer the necessary information, semantic clustering may also require that the system be instrumented and monitored during execution. Another potential difficulty is that semantic clustering techniques tend to be domain- or application-specific, so that their rules cannot be easily applied to an arbitrary system.

Note that, even if correct and complete structural and behavioral information about the system were available to a clustering technique, a key challenge that remains is recovering design intent and rationale. For example, it may not be obvious which of the recovered architectural elements were meant by the system's designers to play a central role in the system. This information may be obscured by the implementation. It may also depend on the architectural style(s) used to guide the system's initial design; at the same time, it may not be clear from the implementation what those styles were and whether they are still appropriate. Without this information, it may be difficult to separate principal characteristics of the system from the less critical and even accidental ones.

An excellent example of fine work in performing architectural recovery is given by the Apache Modeling Project at the Hasso-Plattner-Institute for Software Systems Engineering in Potsdam, Germany. The recovery effort focused on the Apache HTTP server, which is the most widely used HTTP server worldwide. The project used the Fundamental Modeling concepts (FMC) approach. The high quality of the work done and the documentation produced is attested by praise given to the project by the Apache developers—who were not involved in the recovery project. Details can be found at (Gröne et al. 2004).

A similarly excellent recovery project focused on the Linux operating system and compared its recovered architecture with its prescriptive architecture (Bowman, Holt, and Brewster 1999).

The Apache Architecture Recovery Project

4.4 ARCHITECTURAL CONCEPTION IN ABSENCE OF EXPERIENCE: UNPRECEDENTED DESIGN

The primary focus of this chapter has been to indicate how to identify a feasible set of "alternative arrangements for the design as a whole" through the application of experience. Refined experience as codified in architectural patterns and styles has been a major focus, since they are so broadly and commonly useful. Even when experience has not been codified, it may still be found in preexisting systems, hence the discussion of design recovery. Novel design challenges do exist, however. As designer J. Christopher Jones (Jones 1970, pg. 24) said, " . . . the principle of deciding the form of the whole before the details have been explored outside the mind of the chief designer does not work in novel situations for which the necessary experience cannot be contained within the mind of one person." At a minimum, if a designer is ignorant of relevant experience, for that designer the new problem is indeed a novel one.

It should be obvious that the first effort a designer should make in addressing a novel design challenge is to attempt to assure himself that it *is* genuinely a novel problem. The cost differences are the reason: If experience can be applied, a much quicker and cheaper route to a solution is available. One risk is the "siren song of novelty." Tackling novel problems is fun; the added challenge and the opportunity to display creativity is a winsome combination. So, be careful to assess a problem carefully—the sheer delight of a new problem can be enjoyed most delectably if the novelty is indeed genuine.

Assuming that the designer has made a good-faith effort to map a new problem to existing solution strategies and has concluded that the problem presents sufficient differences to demand a greenfield effort, a variety of techniques are available to assist the designer. The essence is to adopt a design strategy and to control that strategy.

Basic Strategy

Failure to meet the needs of a new design challenge with approaches based upon past experience demands a rethinking of the problem and approaches to its solution. The multitude of authors who have discussed this situation—which exists in all fields of design, whether software-focused or not—essentially recommend the following process:

1. Divergence
2. Transformation
3. Convergence

Divergence is a step taken to shake off the confines of inadequate prior approaches and discover, or admit, a variety of new ideas, conceptions, and approaches that offer the promise of a workable solution.

Transformation is a combination of analysis and selection: based upon the information from the divergence step, solution possibilities and new understandings of or changes to the problem statement are examined and formulated.

Convergence is the step of selecting and further refining ideas until a single approach is selected for further detailed development.

As Jones said:

... the aim of divergent search is to de-structure, or to destroy, the original brief while identifying these features of the design situation that will permit a valuable and feasible degree of change. To search divergently is also to provide, as cheaply and quickly as possible, sufficient new experience to counteract any false assumptions that the design team members, and the sponsors, held at the start.

(Jones, p. 66)

There are both difficulties and risks in the critical first step. One difficulty is simply breaking free from prior understandings and approaches to the problem area. The desire to cling to the old tried and true approaches is common both in individuals and in organizations. The old approaches were the basis for whatever success the person or company has achieved to date, so moving into new territory likely will be viewed skeptically. Examples abound in ordinary life; whether the topic is new transportation systems, medical treatments, or communication technologies, new approaches often have difficult entry into practice.

The flip side of not adequately stepping away from better-understood approaches and techniques is not anchoring wide exploration in assessments of costs and benefits. Suppose one hundred new solution possibilities emerge from the divergence step. Should all be explored fully, to determine which one is best? Supposing one thousand possibilities emerge? The key is that the designer must make realistic judgments of the magnitude of the perceived penalties for *not* exploring a given alternative. The cost of analyzing a given approach must not exceed the value obtained by performing the analysis.

Yet another risk is tunnel vision. This occurs when an approach is explored that breaks sharply from previous practice, but enthusiasm for that one approach stifles any attempt to explore other novel alternatives. It is a difficult balance.

While much has been written about the activity of design and creative processes, most of that literature has come from the industrial design community or from academics. It is interesting to see how individuals who come from entirely different backgrounds come to very similar conclusions. John Boyd, a fighter pilot in the U.S. Air Force in the 1950s, went on to designing combat tactics, then combat aircraft, and ultimately to widescale military strategy. Toward the end of his long career he wrote the essay, "Destruction and Creation," which addresses the issue of designing solutions for novel problems. He formulated his approach as a two-step process:

1. Destruction/unstructuring/destructive deduction

2. Synthesis/restructuring/creative induction

He summarized these as follows:

Also, remember, in order to perform these dialectic mental operations we must first shatter the rigid conceptual pattern, or patterns, firmly established in our mind. (This should not be too difficult since the rising confusion and disorder is already helping us to undermine any patterns.) Next, we must find some common qualities, attributes, or operations to link isolated facts, perceptions, ideas, impressions, interactions, observations, etc., together as

A Fighter Pilot on Design

> possible concepts to represent the real world. Finally, we must repeat this unstructuring and restructuring until we develop a concept that begins to match-up with reality.
>
> [John Boyd, "Destruction and Creation," reprinted in (Coram 2002)]
>
> The additional insight shown here, as compared to the three-step process in the main text, is the focus on repeatedly cycling through the activities of destruction and synthesis, until a feasible solution emerges. Note as well the implied focus on understanding and formulating the problem in new terms and in new ways.

Detailed Strategies

Numerous detailed strategies for helping a designer tackle a novel problem have been articulated in books and articles over a long period of time. Most strategies are general and are appropriately focused on the divergence step. They are not specific to software development. This does not diminish their utility, however, as cookie-cutter solutions are by their very nature insufficient for novel situations. The need for creative, deep thought will be uncomfortable and unpleasant for some, but delightful for others. Jones (Jones 1970) catalogs thirty-five techniques; we have selected and adapted below a few of the most relevant for use in the software engineering context.

Analogy Searching. The idea of analogy searching is to examine other fields and disciplines unrelated to the target problem for approaches and ideas that are analogous to the problem at hand, and formulate a solution strategy based upon that analogy.

A common unrelated domain that has yielded a variety of solutions is nature, in particular the biological sciences. One arguable success from this approach has been neural nets: From understanding of how neural networks work in "wetware," that is, the neural systems of animals, ideas are offered for structuring software systems to parallel process certain types of data. Other domains have offered solution ideas such as flow architectures. Whether the inspiration was sewage systems, circulatory systems, or postal mail systems, a variety of software systems have flow structures and characteristics that reflect our common understanding of these physical systems.

Jones's discussion of analogy searching identifies four types of analogies: direct, personal, symbolic, and fantasy. The examples in the preceding paragraph are direct analogies: a concept in the domain of the analogy has a correspondent in the design domain.

Personal analogies are rather different; to quote Jones, "The designer imagines what it would be like to use one's body to produce the effect that is being sought, e.g., what would it feel like to be a helicopter blade, what forces would act on me from the air and the hub, . . ." (Jones 1970). While this type of analogy initially may seem to have limited usefulness in the domain of software architecture, one might consider its use in the development of intelligent systems that interact frequently and via various modes with a human user.

Symbolic analogies focus on metaphors and similes "in which aspects of one thing are identified with aspects of another" (Jones 1970). Perhaps the most obvious example of this in the World Wide Web, and especially with the notion there of broken links—the image of a damaged spider's web is very evocative.

Fantasy analogies are analogies to things which are wishes. A good, and useful, example is a sky hook—a device for lifting that attaches to the object to be carried on one end and to the air on the other end. Fantasy analogies can help to temporarily simplify a problem such that the remaining parts can be more directly addressed. Naturally one does have to return eventually to the real world but perhaps by then some feasible strategy will be identified.

When talking about the architecture of buildings, every analogy has limitations and it is important to recognize when those limits have been reached. The utility of analogies is in providing rich sets of initial concepts for developing a solution to a design problem. Development of the details can proceed in absence of further consideration of the analogy.

Brainstorming. Brainstorming is the technique of rapidly generating a wide set of ideas and thoughts pertaining to a design problem without (initially) assessing the feasibility, desirability, or qualities of those ideas. After the ideas are generated, a period of categorization and analysis of the results begins. Brainstorming can be done by an individual or, more commonly, by a group. The primary association of groups with brainstorming is based on the belief that expression of an idea by one individual in a group will trigger a creative response from another. As a strategy it is well known.

As many people who have participated in brainstorming sessions have observed, however, potential problems with the technique are numerous. A brainstorming session can generate a large number of ideas—all of which are low-quality. Sessions can degenerate into "coblabberation" or "blamestorming," to quote Harvard's David Perkins.

Successful brainstorming appears to require advance planning and careful management. Having people come to the session with a set of ideas already prepared and written can speed the process, remove awkwardness, and provide some egoless participation. The use of external facilitators (meeting supervisors) can help keep the discussion focused and avoid personality-based clashes. Jones's view is that the chief value of brainstorming is in identifying *categories* of possible designs, not any specific design solution suggested during a session. After a group brainstorming session is over, individuals may continue the process on their own, or the design process may proceed to the transformation and convergence steps.

Literature Searching. The classic design disciplines have used literature searching—the process of examining published information to identify material that can be used to guide or inspire designers—for decades. The advent of the Web, the ability to search electronically, and the availability of free or open-source software has breathed new life into this approach, however, making it especially useful.

Not only are all the historically useful ways of searching literature available, but digital library collections make searching extraordinarily faster and more effective. For software designers, the availability of the ACM Digital Library and IEEE Xplore offer a world of insightful, deep literature. More generally Google, Google Scholar, and other search engines offer the ability to examine a phenomenal base of information.

The importance of these digital resources is all the more important because, all too often, practitioners live in a small world with limited ability to interact with practitioners from other companies or with researchers—those people whose careers are devoted to investigating novel problems. There's always enough time for yet another group meeting or sensitivity-training seminar, but never enough time to read a technical magazine, attend a conference, or take a professional development seminar. Digital library resources offer some respite from this isolation.

The availability of free and open-source software adds special value to this technique. Even if a direct solution to the problem at hand is not freely available, the designer may be able to devise a solution composed of large pieces of preexisting software, perhaps composed in a manner totally unanticipated by the original developers.

Last, developers should not overlook the use of the patent database as a source of ideas, approaches, and inspiration. While learning to read a patent takes a bit of time, the astounding wealth of ideas in the world's patent databases makes them valuable electronic resources.

Morphological Charts. The essential idea of morphological charts is to (1) identify all the primary functions to be performed by the desired system, (2) for each function identify a means of performing that function, and (3) attempt to choose one means for each function such that the collection of means performs all the required functions in a compatible manner. Put another way, the problem is subdivided into parts, a solution for each subpart is devised, then (it is hoped) a solution for the whole is created by combining the subsolutions to the various parts. The trick, of course, is that the functions and subsolutions need to be independent and compatible with each other. If the functions, or their subsolutions, are not independent then the designer is bound to consider the functions together. If the chosen subsolutions are not mutually compatible, then another combination of subsolutions must be examined.

At first glance, this technique seems to be nothing more than a fancy name for the old, and somewhat discredited, top-down design. Its value, however, derives from the fact that the technique does not demand that the functions be shown to be independent when starting out; similarly, there is no a priori requirement for the subsolutions to a given problem be developed under the constraint of being compatible with all the subsolutions to other functions. Recall the overall aim: divergence. The technique offers help in constructing a variety of approaches to parts of the overall problem. During the transformation step, the functions and their subsolutions may be reshaped such that ultimately, during the convergence phase, a compatible solution is devised.

Removing Mental Blocks. Getting stuck on a problem is nothing new. It is no surprise, then, to hear that many mental strategies have been promulgated to help designers. Perhaps chief among these is transformation. For instance, if you can't solve the problem, change the problem to one you can solve. If the new problem is close enough to what is needed, then closure is reached. If it is not close enough, the solution to the revised problem may suggest new avenues for attacking the original.

A variety of transformation strategies are available, many of which can be seen and applied in software architecture. Elements of a solution may be adapted, modified, substituted, reordered, or combined to offer new structures.

Jones advocates a strategy of reassessing the design situation. This gets somewhat to the issue of tunnel-vision as mentioned above, but has broad utility. "Matchett's insistence . . . upon continually returning to the 'Primary Functional need' (that which *must* be satisfied if the design is to be accepted) is probably the most reliable way of side-stepping a difficulty. In most cases the designer will be reminded that the sub-problems are of his own choosing and that he can satisfy the Primary Functional Need with an entirely different set of sub-needs if he changes his view of the problem." (Jones, 1970). Or indeed, if the problem itself is changed.

Additional strategies are detailed in Stephen Albin's book, *The Art of Software Architecture* (Albin 2003) and other references provided at the end of the chapter.

Controlling the Design Strategies

The potentially chaotic nature of exploring diverse approaches to the problem demands that some care be used in managing the activity. If the search for novel solutions is unconstrained, a great deal of time and money can be wasted. This suggests the following four guidelines (two of which are adapted from Jones):

1. Identify and review critical decisions (that is, perform risk analysis). By identifying the critical issues, and the consequences of choices regarding those issues, the designer's focus can be kept on track.

2. Relate the costs of research and design to the penalty for making wrong decisions; "the penalty for not knowing must exceed the cost of finding out." Making a wrong decision may not be the end of the world; if the issue is not of great consequence, then a suboptimal approach may be acceptable. To keep making progress it can be necessary to make a decision, even a potentially poor one, to enable all issues to be surfaced and addressed.

3. Insulate uncertain decisions. Decisions for which the design is unsure, or for which the circumstances dictating the issue may change, argue for carefully insulating that decision from the rest of the design. This is the standard dictum of software engineering due to David Parnas: Matters likely to change should be encapsulated inside boundaries (such as a component with resilient interfaces) so that when change eventually does come, the rest of the system is unaffected. (This is analogous to the concept of shearing layers in building architecture, a topic discussed later, in Chapter 14.)

4. Continually reevaluate system requirements in light of what the design exploration yields. It is the rare system whose requirements are genuinely firm and which cannot be improved, or changed, as the result of divergent design explorations. Costs for meeting requirements must be reexamined, and opportunities for novel, unanticipated functionalities should be pursued.

4.5 PUTTING IT ALL TOGETHER: DESIGN PROCESSES REVISITED

The concepts and techniques for use in the design of software architectures presented here have ranged from the very basic—reminders to use abstraction and separation of concerns—to extensive treatment of architectures, styles, and patterns that encapsulate knowledge gained from experience with many prior systems. The chapter also presented approaches for designing in situations where there is little or no experience upon which to draw.

Faced with a new development task, system architects must sort through all the issues confronting them, choose a design approach, and see it through. As we have noted, the central task is choosing a feasible set of concepts upon which to build the design, then progressively refining and revising the concepts and the ensuing details until a satisfactory architecture is developed.

Perhaps the hardest part of the whole process is knowing whether to attempt to base the new design on some existing design—use the "Grand Tool of Experience"—or to approach the design task as one that is unprecedented. Whether an application presents novel challenges or not, significant insight can come from iteratively working with requirements for the system. Hence we call to mind a few thoughts that were introduced in Chapter 2 and expand upon them briefly. Implementation concerns can also further shape and guide the design process, hence we include below a short section dealing with that topic.

A comprehensive methodology for applying all these concepts such that any arbitrary problem can be tackled in a straightforward manner is beyond the scope of this text—indeed, beyond what anyone has yet credibly set forth. The design process—a good design process—will take many twists and turns after the initial attempt at concept formation. But that's part of the fun. You get to be creative.

4.5.1 Insights from Requirements

Chapter 2 pointed out the intimate relationship between requirements engineering and software architectures. Preexisting architectures provide a frame of reference for developing new requirements statements. Architectures provide:

- A *vocabulary*, not just of basic concepts, but of means, approaches, and possibilities.
- A *framework* for describing properties, such as by describing relationships between structural elements, or by categorization of types of design decisions.
- A *basis for analysis*, for example, through knowledge of previous design decisions and their consequences one can assess possible consequences of new requirements.

In many cases—perhaps most—new architectures can be created based upon experience with preexisting architectures and improvement to them.

Restated, the organic interaction between past design and new requirements means that many critical decisions for a new design can be identified or made:

- Experience can show what the most critical issues are, or what the most difficult problems are likely to be.
- Experience can suggest what the key levels of discourse are, and what vocabularies to use in each.
- Experience can show successful patterns of product specialization.
- Experience can show what architectural patterns and styles have been effective in the domain.
- Experience can show areas in which novel development has typically been required.

One aspect of this iterative conceptualization of the new application is in the identification of architectural tipping points—decisions that have profound consequences for the rest of the design and implementation. An important example is deciding whether part or all of the new application should be created as a modification of an existing system. This can be a very difficult choice: Modifying an existing system offers the potential of achieving substantial software reuse, with attendant cost and schedule benefits. Yet a time comes in the evolution of every system when achieving new requirements demands more of the preexisting architecture than it can bear, and hence an entirely new design is called for. Core algorithms, for example, may not be capable of scaling to new performance requirements, thus requiring a new approach. All of these are important aids in getting started with the design of a new application; they derive from the symbiosis of articulating new requirements using a vocabulary of known architectural choices.

In those rare cases where a requirements specification is used that does not make any reference to existing architectures, careful analysis is required to identify the critical factors, to distinguish between the incidental and the essential. A highly dynamic approach to the first critical steps of identifying "a set of alternative arrangements for the design as a whole" is required in such cases. Several such approaches were identified at the end of Section 4.1. You may need to attempt to design a solution using several different structures, applying various styles from the discussion in Section 4.3, then compare the results and the properties obtained, in order to determine the best course to take.

Design by Simulation: "Danger, Will Robinson!"

Many touted design strategies are simply transformations of requirements into, in effect, simulations of some part of the real world. As such, the architecture is determined simply by the domain and particular manner of stating the requirements, and not by thoughtful, creative design or the use of sound software design principles.

One example is the "underline the nouns, underline the verbs" approach to design first promulgated by Russell J. Abbot (Abbott 1983). The essence is that the identified nouns determine a program's data types (objects); the verbs become the names of the methods defined on those noun-objects. This approach to object-oriented design was popularized widely by Grady Booch. In (Booch 1986) he said, "Since we are dealing with a philosophy of design, we should first recognize the fundamental criteria [sic] for decomposing a system using object-oriented techniques: *Each module in the system denotes an object or class of objects from the problem space.*"

A similar tack was taken in the Jackson System Design (JSD) method: "From the late 1970s to the second half of the 1980s I worked with John Cameron and others on the JSD method of analysis and design for information systems. The method is based on separating the construction of a model (for example, in a database) of the real world from the construction of the information functions that extract and display the necessary information from the model. The model focuses chiefly on the behaviours of real-world entities over their lifetimes, representing each entity as one or more sequential processes: the local variables of these processes form the data part of the model of the entity. The method is described in my book *System Development.*" (Jackson 2007)

4.5.2 Insights from Implementation

A detailed discussion of techniques and approaches to use when moving from an architecture to an implementation is found in Chapter 9. Here we look at the feedback situation: how information and insights from the implementation domain, or from constraints on that activity, can or must be used in development of a detailed architecture.

First, constraints on the implementation activity may help shape the design. Externally motivated decisions may be principal, and hence be a part of the architecture. For example, external constraints may dictate the use of a particular type or brand of middleware (connector technology). A large project focused on software-defined radios, for instance, mandated the use of CORBA, even before any detailed designs for the radios had been completed. Accommodating such mandates can dramatically affect the system's architecture—and not always for the better.

Similarly, externally motivated constraints may dictate the use of particular programming languages, development environments, or implementation platforms. The skill set of the staff devoted to the implementation may be limited. These, and other similar constraints, can shape the architecture, perhaps restricting the set of architectural styles that may be used.

A more interesting impact on design may come from considerations of software reuse. The potential cost savings from reusing software—whether internal to the development organization or from free/open source sites—are substantial. But imperfect correspondence between the available software with the prescriptive design can require design modifications. Mismatches possible include functionality (the desired function is not there, but a similar one is), interface (the desired functionality is present, but the manner of invoking it is different from the current design), and nonfunctional properties (for example, the desired functionality and the desired interface are present, but the software runs too slowly or requires too much memory, or has inadequate security features).

Presence of such a situation invites an iteration between the design process and the implementation activity. The most effective course of action may in fact be to change the design to enable easier reuse. The decision of whether to reuse code and the manner in which it should be used (such as encapsulated or modified) is a principal design decision grounded in implementation issues, and hence must be considered during the design process.

Just as development of requirements and development of design must proceed cooperatively and contemporaneously, so too may design and implementation. Initial implementation activities may yield critical performance or feasibility information, allowing the designer to proceed with confidence in other aspects of the system's design. At all costs, architectural erosion must be prevented.

4.6 END MATTER

Designing architectures is the occasion when the designer can most obviously employ and exhibit all his or her innate creativity and talent. Designing well is a skill to be learned and practiced. It requires being willing to take risks, explore dark alleys, and occasionally backtrack. Timid, staid approaches may yield software that satisfies most requirements, but seldom will yield applications that give satisfaction to the user and enable the designer's organization to dominate the marketplace.

The most effective approaches to design will be those that have been refined and seasoned within the domain of the new application. Knowledge of effective design techniques and trade-offs is an important corporate asset; ensuring that such knowledge is shared among projects and between designers should be an important managerial goal.

All the major conceptual elements of architecture-centric software engineering now have been introduced. What remains is placing techniques and tools in the designer's hands to enable productive exploitation of these conceptual elements. The following chapter begins this process by exploring in depth the concept of architectural connectors. As we have noted earlier, the use of components is familiar, but connectors are unfamiliar to many software engineers, and their depth and richness is surprising to most. This topic is then followed by the lynchpin technology: explicit modeling of architectural decisions. With an architecture description language in hand the designer can proceed to design and document key decisions in a manner that supports the many development goals we have covered.

The Business Case

The essential business case for design is, "What's the alternative?" Creating products that are successful in the marketplace, effective to maintain, and that lead to future successful products demands a thoughtful approach to product design. Design of product families—such as the consumer electronics example discussed several places—is a key means for ensuring corporate growth through an expanding range of economically achieved products.

In addition to designing the software's structure, a company must equally deliberately design a product's user interface, interaction behavior, and "feel." Design of these domain-specific characteristics must proceed cooperatively with design of the software structures that implement them, a theme first emphasized in Chapter 2.

A company's design processes represent a central asset of an organization. The successful and efficient production of new products is at the heart of a company. Design carries corporate value, and processes and traditions outlive most products. Given inevitable turnover of personnel, maintenance of good design processes depends upon production of explicit designs and articulation of the rationale behind the design decisions underlying them.

Since designing is a central asset it should be no surprise that it is an activity that cannot be contracted offshore. Good design demands interaction with marketing, customers, domain experts, and business analysts. Once a design has been fully elaborated to crisp, low-level specifications, their implementation becomes a candidate for outsourcing, but even then caution is in order. The designers must be able to assure themselves that no principal design decisions will be made during implementation—and that can be a very difficult assurance to achieve.

Given the importance of designing to an organization, the training and development of designers throughout the organization should be a continual priority. If an organization sinks to a state where one or two master designers are allowed to dominate development, the organization becomes at risk. Design is teachable and is not the exclusive province of an elite few.

4.7 REVIEW QUESTIONS

1. How can experience be used as a design technique? What must be true about experience in order for it to be useful in the design of a new system?

2. Refined experience, in the form of architectural styles, for example, can appear and be applied at different levels of abstraction and at different degrees of domain specificity. What are some examples of different styles at different points in this space of abstraction and domain-specificity?

3. What types of applications are appropriate for the following styles? Alternatively, describe an example

application for each of the following styles: event-based, pipe-and-filter, layered, mobile code.

4. Describe a good process for designing an application for which the development team has no prior experience in the domain of the application and no prior architecture or code from which to work.

5. How can coding-related decisions, such as choosing a user-interface toolkit, affect an architecture?

4.8 EXERCISES

1. For many years design by stepwise refinement was viewed as an appropriate, effective strategy for program development. Today, it is viewed as quaint and inadequate. Explain what's wrong with the concept of stepwise refinement in the context of modern complex systems development.

2. Suppose an application has been in use by an organization for twenty years. It has been modified and expanded over that period to meet a steady stream of new demands. Now a new set of demands arise, requiring further changes. The software engineers in charge of the application are apprehensive about attempting to further modify the system to meet the new needs. How should the team decide whether to continue to try to modify the existing system or build a new application from the ground up?

3. Top-down or bottom-up? Under what circumstances would it make the most sense to attack the design problem for a large project by working initially on subparts of the problem—without being sure that any subassembly so designed would end up as part of the final design solution?

4. The numerous examples of designs for the lunar lander in the chapter are all sketches in that they do not include the details of how the various components communicate. Elaborate the lunar lander designs to the next level of detail, such that the designs could be handed over to a coder for final implementation. Assume a very simple textual user interface. State the assumptions made by the game in each example with regard to the use (or not) of a clock.

   a. Layered architecture

   b. Sense-compute-control pattern programmed as main-program-and-subroutines

   c. 4-Object-oriented

5. Describe the architecture of a compiler in terms of architectural styles. Is it a single style as found in this chapter? Multiple styles composed together?

6. This chapter uses a lunar lander to illustrate how many different architectural styles may be applied to the same problem. Choose another application (such as a desktop calendar application, a cell phone–based contact and phone number manager, an automated teller machine system, or a controller to be used to control a set of elevators in a building), and present sketches of three different solution architectures, where each architecture exhibits a different style drawn from the set discussed in this chapter.

7. What's the architecture of Microsoft Word? How can you tell? What would you need to see in order to know?

8. Examine the architecture of the Apache HTTP server as characterized by the Apache recovery project (Gröne et al. 2004). Which styles are involved, and how are they combined?

9. Examine the architecture of Linux, as characterized by Bowman (Bowman, Holt, and Brewster 1999). Which styles are involved, and how are they combined?

10. Some designers have argued that "PowerPoint architectures" promote good design, in particular, that the discipline of working within a confined frame (for instance, the amount of space you have on a single PowerPoint slide) force the designer to apply abstraction and hierarchy. Discuss the pros and cons of PowerPoint architectures.

4.9 FURTHER READING

Design has been a topic of study outside of computer science and software engineering for many years. The book by Jones (Jones 1970) cited several times in this chapter is an excellent example of insight about the design process as seen from the industrial design perspective. A revised version was issued in 1992 (Jones 1992). A more recent book, focusing on group and corporate process, comes from the founders of the IDEO design firm, (Kelley, Littman, and Peters 2001).

As mentioned at the end of Chapter 1, many excellent books on architectural design have been written, of course, but few provide substantive insights for software developers. Relative to this chapter, however, an important exception is Christopher Alexander's *The Timeless*

Way of Building (Alexander 1979) and a companion book, *A Pattern Language: Towns, Buildings, Construction* (Alexander, Ishikawa, and Silverstein 1977). As mentioned earlier, his work has influenced thinking on patterns for object-oriented programming, and more generally, software architecture styles. Another key classic in the study of design is *The Reflective Practitioner* (Schön 1983), by Schön, who characterizes design as an on-going conversation between the designer, the materials, and the context for the design.

A broad overview of *software* design as a research field—where it has been and where it is going—is found in "Software Design and Architecture: The Once and Future Focus of Software Engineering" (Taylor and van der Hoek 2007). This paper includes a large bibliography of software design books and papers, and constitutes an important reference and starting point for detailed investigations.

The model-view-controller pattern was developed in the late 1970s; an original paper plus a retrospective can be found in (Reenskaug, 1979, 2003). Numerous resources are available on the Web to further demon-strate its application. The mobile code styles are explored nicely in a paper by Fuggetta, Pico, and Vigna (Fuggetta, Picco, and Vigna 1998). The C2 architectural style has been described and illustrated in the literature in several places, including (Dashofy, Medvidović, and Taylor 1999; Medvidović, Oreizy, and Taylor 1997; Robbins et al. 1998; Taylor et al. 1996). CORBA references abound. Perhaps the best introduction to the concepts is found in Emmerich's book, *Engineering Distributed Objects* (Emmerich 2000). Abundant source materials can be found on the Object Management Group's Web site (www.omg.org).

Numerous resources are available in print and online, documenting and explaining the U.S. Apollo missions to the moon. Many of these resources are available directly from NASA as well as secondary republishers, and includes "Apollo 11 The NASA Mission Reports" (*Apollo 11: The NASA Mission Reports* 1999). An excellent introduction to the onboard software and a recounting of the errors that occurred and were overcome during the Apollo 11 Lunar descent can be found in (Eyles 2004).

5

Connectors

Designing and implementing the *functionality* and managing the *data* of modern large, complex, distributed, multilingual software systems is undoubtedly very difficult. As discussed in the preceding chapters, early software architectural models of system components, their key services, their abstract behaviors, and their nonfunctional properties are indispensable in this endeavor. However, experience has shown time and again that making architectural design decisions that pertain to *integrating* those components effectively and ensuring the components' proper *interaction* in a system is just as important. Moreover, arriving at such design decisions can be even more challenging than those restricted to the development of functionality. The particular importance in modern systems of mechanisms for assembling functional components and supporting their interaction, that is, software *connectors*, mandates that they be treated and studied separately. We will do just that in this chapter, and will return to this subject repeatedly throughout the remainder of the book.

Simply put, software connectors perform transfer of control and data among components. Connectors can also provide services, such as persistence, invocation, messaging, and transactions, that are largely independent of the interacting components' functionalities. These services are usually considered to be "facilities components" in widely used middleware standards such as CORBA, DCOM, and RMI. However, recognizing these facilities as connectors helps to clarify an architecture and keep the components' focus on application- and domain-specific concerns. Treating these services as connectors rather than components can also foster their reuse across applications and domains. Perhaps most importantly, connectors allow architects and engineers to compose heterogeneous functionality, developed at different times, in different locations, by different organizations. As such, connectors can be thought of quite appropriately as the guards at the gate of separation of concerns.

A common misconception about software connectors is that they are just calls between two components, in the manner of, say, a Java method invocation. A slightly more advanced view, inspired by middleware-based system development, is that component interactions take place via message passing and remote procedure calls (RPC). While it is frequently the case that two components will eventually be implemented to communicate using, say, a Java method call, it is important to realize that as a software system's architect you are not restricted to assuming and relying on only such primitive interaction mechanisms.

Traditional software engineering approaches embrace a rather narrow view of connectors that is unlikely to be successfully applicable across all development situations. This problem is further exacerbated by the increased emphasis on development using large, off-the-shelf components originating from multiple sources. As components become more complex and heterogeneous, the interactions among them become more critical determinants of system properties. Experience has shown that integrating components with mismatched assumptions about their environment is hard to do and can lead to many problems. It is the task of connectors to mitigate such mismatches.

An architect has a wide range of connector options that are applicable, and often tailorable, to different development needs and scenarios. For example, an architect can choose to use a connector that distributes a service request to specifically named recipient components or a connector that broadcasts a notification of a locally occurring event to any (unnamed and even unknown) component that may be interested and listening. The connector may require the sender component to suspend its processing until an acknowledgment of its request is received, or it may allow the sender component to continue with its processing; the connector can route each request in the order it received it, or it can try to order, filter out, or combine requests according to some prespecified rule; and so on. Therefore, a very important dimension of a software architect's job is to:

- Understand the component interaction needs.
- Carefully identify all of the relevant attributes of that interaction.
- Select the candidate connectors.
- Assess any trade-offs associated with each candidate.
- Analyze the key properties of the resulting component-connector assemblies.

The goal of this chapter is to provide insights, guidelines, and specific techniques to support accomplishment of these tasks. The remainder of the chapter will introduce:

1. The different roles connectors play in a software system.
2. Different connector types a software architect has at his or her disposal and the roles each type can fulfill.
3. A panoply of variation points for each connector type.

4. A set of general hints and guidelines about a connector's applicability, strengths, and drawbacks.

Throughout the chapter, we will provide examples of specific software connectors to illustrate the discussion. The reader will probably be familiar with many of these connectors, although sometimes under a different name. The chapter starts off with a simple concrete example, to set the stage for the subsequent discussion.

This chapter provides a detailed treatment of connectors. The type and amount of information provided is necessary for their thorough study. At the same time, some of the content may be unsuitable for an inexperienced reader. We recommend that everyone read at least Sections 5.1 through 5.4 as well as Sections 5.7 through 5.10. Section 5.5 contains a set of examples from the domain of large-scale data distribution systems, which can be followed by most readers, but their full appreciation may require prior experience with these types of systems. Section 5.6 is appropriate for all readers, but is targeted, in particular, at the experienced professionals and readers interested in practical guidelines for constructing advanced connectors.

5.1 CONNECTORS IN ACTION: A MOTIVATING EXAMPLE

One useful property of connectors is that they are for the most part application-independent architectural elements. That means that they enable us to understand a lot about *how* a software system accomplishes its tasks without necessarily having to know exactly *what* the system does. In other words, connectors directly support two key principles of software

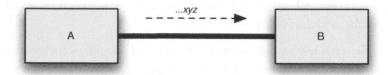

Figure 5-1. *A simple pipe-and-filter architecture consisting of two filters, A and B, communicating via untyped data streams through the unidirectional pipe connector P.*

engineering: abstraction and separation of concerns. Explicitly focusing on connectors also enables development and use of a specific vocabulary of software interaction. In turn, agreeing on appropriate terminology allows us to communicate easily and reason precisely about a number of software system properties that derive from the system components' interactions. To illustrate this, we use a very simple example involving two different types of connectors. We intentionally use the terminology associated with those connectors without defining it, to draw attention to this new "language." The appropriate definitions and explanations will be given in the subsequent sections. Nonetheless, you will probably find that you are familiar with some, if not most, of this terminology.

Different views of a software connector are useful for different tasks. In order to model a system and communicate its properties, a high-level view is suitable. For example, an architect may make the following concise, but meaningful statement about the configuration shown in Figure 5-1: "Components A and B communicate via a Unix pipe." That statement may be accompanied by a formal specification of the pipe's overall behavior. However, such a high-level description does not help us understand all the properties of the pipe, how it can be adapted, or under what conditions it can be replaced with another type of connector. A more detailed, lower-level view is needed to accomplish that.

In particular, the pipe in Figure 5-1 allows interaction via unformatted streams of data. It is a simple connector: It consists of a single interaction channel, or duct, and facilitates only unidirectional data transfer. Thus, the cardinality of the pipe is a single sender and a single receiver. You will recall from the preceding chapters that a pipe allows components (that is, filters) A and B to exhibit very low coupling: The components do not possess any knowledge about one another. For example, A's task is only to successfully hand off its data to the pipe; the actual recipient (if any) is unimportant to A. In turn, the particular pipe depicted in Figure 5-1 does not buffer the data. It attempts to deliver the data at most once; if the recipient is unable to receive the data for some reason, the data will be lost.

Let us now assume that we need to alter the manner in which A and B interact, such that B can also send information (for example, acknowledgement of data receipt) back to A. Furthermore, we want to ensure the delivery of data: If the recipient is not available, the pipe retries to send until the data is successfully transferred. Both these modifications can be potentially accommodated by pipes. The first modification would require introducing another pipe from B to A, and the second, data buffering in a pipe. Addition of any other components into the system would require further addition and/or replacement of pipes. The penalty we would pay is that these modifications may require substantial system downtime. Pipes can, therefore, accommodate these new

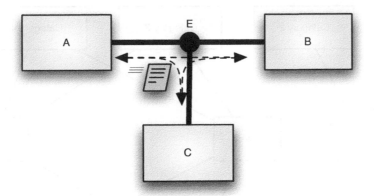

Figure 5-2. *An event-based architecture consisting of two components, A and B, communicating via typed discrete data packets (events) through the event bus connector E. The connector allows on-the-fly system modifications, such as adding a new component C.*

requirements, even though constantly adding and replacing them may not be the most effective solution.

If, however, we want to change the nature of the data from an unformatted byte stream to discrete, typed packets that can be processed more efficiently by the interacting components, pipes will not suffice. In such a case, an event bus connector will be a more suitable alternative. Although clearly different types of connectors, pipes and event buses exhibit a number of similar properties, such as loose component coupling, asynchronous communication, and possible data buffering. At the same time, event buses are better suited to support system adaptation: an event bus connector is capable of establishing ducts between interacting components on the fly; its cardinality is a single event sender (similarly to the pipe), but multiple observers. Thus, in principle, event buses allow components to be added or removed, and to subscribe to receive certain events, at any time during a system's execution. Figure 5-2 abstractly depicts the use of an event bus to accommodate the above changes.

5.2 CONNECTOR FOUNDATIONS

The underlying, elementary building blocks of every connector are the primitives for managing the *flow of control* (that is, changing the processor program counter) and *flow of data* (that is, performing memory access) in a system. These primitives give enough conceptual power to build sophisticated and complex connectors. In addition to these primitives, every connector maintains one or more *channels*, also referred to as *ducts*, which are used to link the interacting components and support the flow of data and control between them. A duct is necessary for realizing a connector, but by itself, it does not provide any additional interaction services. Very simple connectors, such as module linkers, provide their service simply by forming ducts between components. Other connectors augment ducts with some combination of data and control flow to provide richer interaction services. Very complex

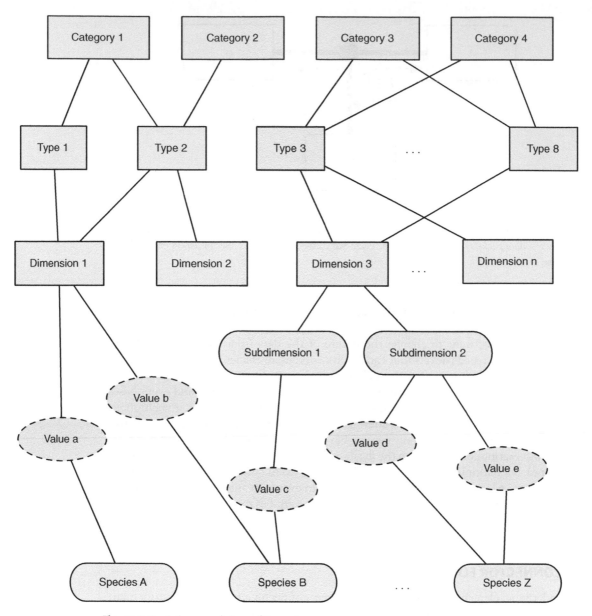

Figure 5-3. *A framework for studying software connectors.*

connectors can also have an internal architecture that includes computation and information storage. For example, a load balancing connector would execute an algorithm for switching incoming traffic among a set of components based on the knowledge about the current and past load state of components.

Simple connectors are typically implemented in programming languages. On the other hand, composite connectors are achieved through composition of several connectors (and possibly components), and usually are provided as libraries and frameworks. Simple connectors only provide one type of interaction service, whereas composite connectors may combine many kinds of interactions. Complex connectors can help overcome the limitations of modern programming languages. However, when creating such connectors it is important to be able to reason about their underlying, low-level interaction mechanisms, identify the appropriate design choices, and detect potential mismatches among the interaction mechanisms used to compose a connector.

To this end, we will use the connector classification framework shown in Figure 5-3: Each connector is identified by its primary service category and further refined based on the choices made to realize these services. The characteristics most commonly observed among connectors are positioned toward the top of the framework, whereas the variations are located in the lower layers. The framework comprises service categories, connector types, dimensions (and possibly their subdimensions), and values for the dimensions. A service category represents the broad interaction role the connector fulfills. Connector types discriminate among connectors based on the way in which the interaction services are realized. The architecturally relevant details of each connector type are captured through dimensions, and, possibly, further subdimensions. Finally, the lowest layer in the framework is formed by the set of values a dimension (or subdimension) can take. Note that a particular connector instance (that is, *species*) can take a number of values from different types. In other words, this classification does not result in a strict hierarchy, but rather in a directed acyclic graph.

The remainder of this chapter describes in more detail the classification framework and a comprehensive taxonomy that can be used as the foundation for studying, classifying, and using software connectors.

5.3 CONNECTOR ROLES

A software connector can provide one or more of four general classes of services: communication, coordination, conversion, and facilitation. Put another way, a connector can play one or more of these four roles. Since these services, or roles, fully describe the range of possible software component interactions, the topmost layer in our classification framework from Figure 5-3 is the service category. Discussions and simple examples of the four service classes follow.

Communication
Connectors providing communication services support transmission of data among components. Data transfer services are a primary building block of component interaction. Components routinely pass messages, exchange data to be processed, and communicate results of computations.

Coordination
Connectors providing coordination services support transfer of control among components. Components interact by passing the thread of execution to each other. Function calls and method invocations are examples of coordination connectors. Higher-order connectors, such as signals and load balancing connectors, provide richer, more complex interactions built around coordination services.

Conversion

Connectors providing conversion services transform the interaction required by one component to that provided by another. Enabling heterogeneous components to interact with each other is not a trivial task. Interaction mismatches are a major hindrance in composing large systems. The mismatches are caused by incompatible assumptions made by components about the type, number, frequency, and order of interactions in which they are to engage with other components. Conversion services allow components that have not been specifically tailored for each other to establish and conduct interactions. Conversion of data formats and wrappers for legacy components are examples of connectors providing this interaction service.

Facilitation

Connectors providing facilitation services mediate and streamline component interaction. Even when components have been designed to interoperate with each other, there may be a need to provide mechanisms for further facilitating and optimizing their interactions. Mechanisms such as load balancing, scheduling services, and concurrency control may be required to meet certain nonfunctional system requirements and to reduce interdependencies among interacting components.

Every connector provides services that belong to at least one of these four categories. Commonly though, connectors provide multiple services in order to satisfy the need for a richer set of interaction capabilities. For example, procedure call, one of the most widely used software connector types, provides both communication and coordination services.

5.4 CONNECTOR TYPES AND THEIR VARIATION DIMENSIONS

Interaction services broadly categorize connectors, but leave many details unexplained. This level of abstraction cannot help us build new connectors, and it cannot be used to model and analyze them in an architecture. Hence, we further classify connectors into eight different types, based on the way in which they realize interaction services:

- Procedure call
- Event
- Data access
- Linkage
- Stream
- Arbitrator
- Adaptor
- Distributor

Connector types are the level at which architects typically consider interactions when modeling systems.

Simple connectors can be modeled at the level of connector types; their details can often be left to low-level design and implementation. On the other hand, more complex connectors often require that many of their details be decided at the architectural level so that the impact of these decisions can be studied early and on a systemwide scale. Those details represent variations in connector instances and are treated as connector dimensions in the below classification. In turn, each dimension has a set of possible values. The selection of a single value from each dimension results in a concrete connector species. Instantiating dimensions of a single connector type forms simple connectors; using dimensions from different connector types leads to a composite (higher-order) connector species.

The remainder of this section will describe the key characteristics of each connector type as well as their variation points. Additionally, we will highlight the interaction role(s) played by each connector type. The discussion draws extensively from the connector taxonomy set forth by Nikunj Mehta, Nenad Medvidović, and Sandeep Phadke (Mehta, Medvidović, and Phadke 2000). It should be noted that the characteristics of different connectors introduced are meant to cover the entire space of connectors. However, it is possible that an individual connector of a given type may not possess each of that type's dimensions. The detailed connector characteristics presented below can be thought of as design templates that software architects can use to select the exact connectors needed in a given system. As will be discussed further in Chapter 6, several software architecture modeling notations support different variations of this selection process.

5.4.1 Procedure Call Connectors

Procedure call connectors model the flow of control among components through various invocation techniques. They are thus coordination connectors. Additionally, procedure calls perform transfer of data among the interacting components through the use of parameters and return values. They are thus also communication connectors. These connectors are among the most widely used and best understood connectors, and have been likened to the assembly language of software interaction. Examples of procedure call connectors include object-oriented methods, `fork` and `exec` in Unix-like environments, call-back invocation in event-based systems, and operating system calls. Procedure calls are frequently used as the basis for composite connectors, such as remote procedure calls or RPC, which also perform facilitation services.

The space of options available to a software engineer for constructing procedure call connectors is shown in Figure 5-4. Note that the values for certain dimensions and subdimensions are not shown: multiple versus single entry point, as well as fan in and fan out cardinality. These are numerical subdimensions that either take an obvious value (1 in the case of single entry point) or can take many values (in the case of the remaining three subdimensions). They are hence elided for simplicity; we likewise omit the values of all such dimensions and subdimensions in the case of the other seven connector types.

A typical programming language-level procedure call connector takes on a specific set of values from the choices depicted in the figure. For example, as most Java users will readily know, a procedure (that is, method) call provides the data transfer of its parameters by reference; it may have a return value unless the invoked method is declared as a `void`; it will have a single entry point, at the start of the invoked method; it will be a result of explicit invocation; its synchronicity will be blocking; its fan in and fan out cardinality will both be 1—that is, a Java method call always has a single source and a single destination; finally, its accessibility may be public or private.

Figure 5-4.
*Procedure call
connector type
and its variations.*

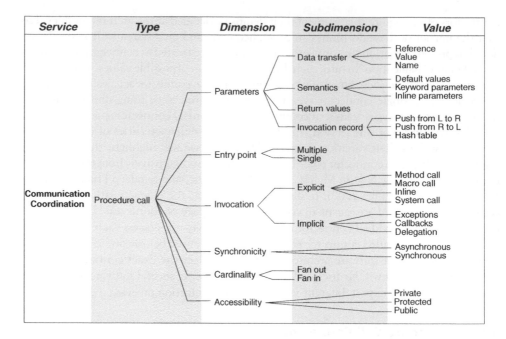

At this point, the reader is not necessarily expected to understand all of this connector type's various dimensions, subdimensions, and values, or all of the variation points of the remaining seven connector types discussed below and depicted in Figure 5-5 through Figure 5-11. One objective of this chapter is to sensitize the reader to the richness and potential complexity of the space of software connectors. The remainder of the chapter will continue to highlight only the representative or particularly interesting facets of each connector type.

5.4.2 Event Connectors

David Rosenblum and Alexander Wolf define an event as the instantaneous effect of the (normal or abnormal) termination of the invocation of an operation on an object, which occurs at that object's location (Rosenblum and Wolf 1997). Event connectors are similar to procedure call connectors in that they affect the flow of control among components, and thus provide coordination services. In this case, the flow is precipitated by an event. Once the event connector learns about the occurrence of an event, it generates messages (that is, event notifications) for all interested parties and yields control to the components for processing those messages. Messages can be generated upon the occurrence of a single event or a specific pattern of events. The contents of an event can be structured to contain more information about the event, such as the time and place of occurrence, and other application-specific data. Event connectors therefore also provide communication services.

Event connectors are also different from procedure calls in that virtual connectors are formed between components interested in the same event topics, and those connectors may appear and disappear dynamically depending on the components' changing interests. Event-based distributed systems rely on the notion of time and ordering of actions.

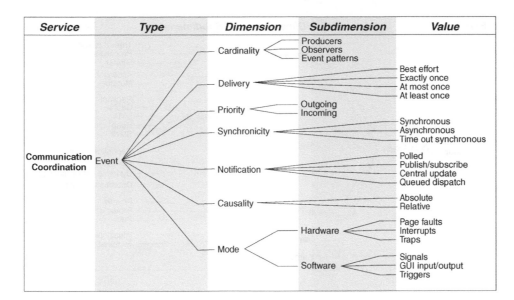

Figure 5-5.
Event connector type and its variations.

Therefore, dimensions such as causality, atomicity, and synchronicity play a critical role in event connector mechanisms. Event connectors are found in distributed applications that require asynchronous communication. An example is a windowing application (such as X Windows in Unix), where GUI inputs serve as the events that activate the system. Finally, some events, such as interrupts, page faults, and traps, are triggered by hardware and then processed by software. These events may affect global system properties, making it important to capture them in software architectures.

The space of options available to a software engineer for constructing event connectors is shown in Figure 5-5. For example, the cardinality of a multicasting event connector (recall the discussion of the C2 architectural style in Chapter 4) will be a single producer and multiple observer components; ideally the connector will support delivery of data exactly once (whatever is sent by the source component is delivered to the recipient components); its synchronicity may be asynchronous (that is, nonblocking); it could use the publish/subscribe notification mechanism; and so on.

5.4.3 Data Access Connectors

Data access connectors allow components to access data maintained by a data store component. Therefore, they provide communication services. Data access often requires preparation of the data store before and cleanup after access has been completed. In case there is a difference in the format of the required data and the format in which data is stored and provided, data access connectors may perform translation of the information being accessed, that is, conversion. The data can be stored either persistently or temporarily, in which case the data access mechanisms will vary. Examples of persistent data access include query mechanisms, such as SQL for database access, and accessing information in repositories, such as a software component repository. Examples of transient data access include heap and stack memory access and information caching.

Figure 5-6.
*Data access
connector type
and its variations.*

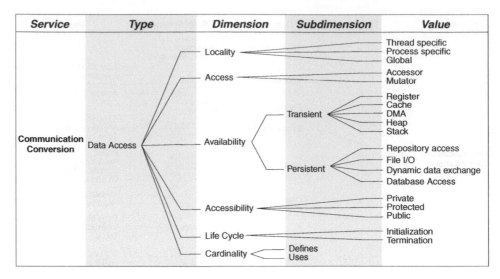

The space of options available to a software engineer for constructing data access connectors is shown in Figure 5-6. A data access connector could enable global access; allow mutating (that is, changing) the data; it could provide persistent access through file I/O; its cardinality would typically be a single entity that defines the data, but multiple entities that use the data; and so on.

5.4.4   Linkage Connectors

Linkage connectors are used to tie the system components together and hold them in such a state during their operation. Linkage connectors enable the establishment of ducts—the channels for communication and coordination—that are then used by higher-order connectors to enforce interaction semantics. In other words, linkage connectors provide facilitation services.

Once ducts are established, a linkage connector may disappear from the system or remain in place to assist in the system's evolution. Examples of linkage connectors are the links between components and buses in a C2-style architecture (recall Chapter 4) and dependency relationships among software modules described by module interconnection languages (MIL) (DeRemer and Kron 1976).

The space of options available to a software engineer for constructing linkage connectors is shown in Figure 5-7. Compared to the preceding dimensions, this is not a particularly rich connector dimension. The reference to linked components can be implicit, possibly even parameterized and mutable, or explicit. The granularity dimension refers to the size of components and level of detail required to establish a linkage. The subdimensions of granularity (unit, syntactic, and semantic) were directly influenced by Dewayne Perry's foundational study of software interconnection models (Perry 1987):

- *Unit* interconnection specifies only that one component—which can be a module, an object, or a file—depends on another. Examples of unit interconnection are configuration management and system building facilities such as *Make*.

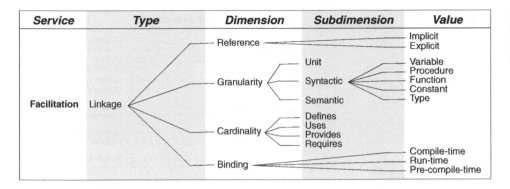

Figure 5-7.
Linkage connector type and its variations.

- *Syntactic* interconnection refines this relationship and establishes links between variables, procedures, functions, constants, and types within the linked components. This information can be used in static analysis (For example, locating unreachable code within a module) and smart compilation, where only the changed portions of a system are recompiled.
- *Semantic* interconnection specifies *how* the linked components are supposed to interact. Semantic interconnection ensures that the interaction requirements and constraints are explicitly stated and satisfied. This typically takes the form of an interaction protocol, such as those discussed in the context of architectural modeling and analysis in Chapter 6 and Chapter 8 respectively.

The cardinality of a linkage connector refers to the number of places in which a system resource—such as a component, procedure, or variable—is defined, used, provided, or required. Typically, a resource is defined and/or provided in a single location and used or required from multiple locations. Finally, a linkage connector can establish the binding between components very early (that is, prior to system compilation), early (that is, during compilation), or late (that is, during the system's execution).

5.4.5 Stream Connectors

Streams are used to perform transfers of large amounts of data between autonomous processes. Stream connectors therefore provide communication services in a system. Streams are also used in client-server systems with data transfer protocols to deliver results of computation. Streams can be combined with other connector types, such as data access connectors, to provide composite connectors for performing database and file storage access, and event connectors, to multiplex the delivery of a large number of events. Examples of stream connectors are Unix pipes, TCP/UDP communication sockets, and proprietary client-server protocols.

The space of options available to a software engineer for constructing stream connectors is shown in Figure 5-8. For example, a stream-based connector may be unnamed, as in Unix pipes; it may provide synchronous, remote interaction via structured data; it may guarantee at least one delivery; its cardinality may be binary, that is, a single sender and a single receiver; finally, its state value could be determined by a bounded buffer.

Figure 5-8.
Stream connector type and its variations.

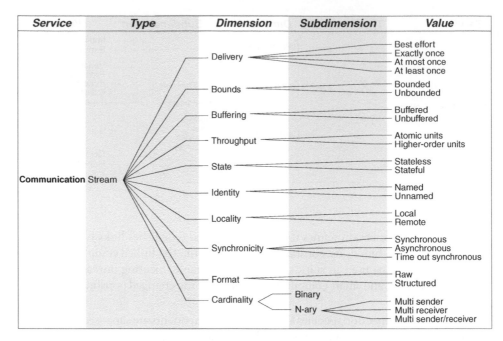

5.4.6   Arbitrator Connectors

When components are aware of the presence of other components but cannot make assumptions about their needs and state, arbitrators streamline system operation and resolve any conflicts (thereby providing facilitation services), and redirect the flow of control (providing coordination services). For example, multithreaded systems that require shared memory access use synchronization and concurrency control to guarantee consistency and atomicity of operations. Arbitrators can also provide facilities to negotiate service levels and mediate interactions requiring guarantees for reliability and atomicity. They also provide scheduling and load balancing services. Arbitrators can ensure system trustworthiness by providing crucial support for dependability in the form of reliability, safety, and security.

The space of options available to a software engineer for constructing arbitrator connectors is shown in Figure 5-9. Arbitrator connectors can aid with system fault handling, by determining and trapping component faults before they propagate. They can also ensure the appropriate concurrency semantics among the interacting components. For example, arbitrators can employ mechanisms, such as semaphores or monitors, to control access to the interacting components' resources. Arbitrator connectors may also support transactions and guarantee different levels of security (see Chapter 13). Finally, they can control the interacting components' execution scheduling. A specific example of arbitrator connectors is discussed in Section 5.5.

5.4.7   Adaptor Connectors

Adaptor connectors provide facilities to support interaction between components that have not been designed to interoperate. Adaptors involve matching communication policies and interaction protocols among components, thereby providing conversion services. These

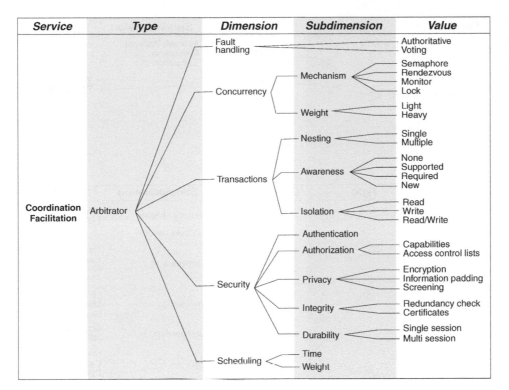

Figure 5-9.
*Arbitrator
connector type
and its variations.*

connectors are necessary for interoperation of components in heterogeneous environments, such as different programming languages or computing platforms. Conversion can also be performed to optimize component interactions for a given execution environment. For example, a distributed system may rely on remote procedure calls (RPC) for all interactions across process boundaries; if two interacting components are co–located within the same process for a given time period, a remote procedure call may be seamlessly converted to a local procedure call during that time. Adaptors may also employ transformations (for instance, table look-ups) to match required services to the available facilities.

The space of options available to a software engineer for constructing adaptor connectors is shown in Figure 5-10. Examples of adaptors include virtual memory translation; Daniel Yellin and Robert Strom's adaptors (Yellin and Strom 1994), which match incompatible component interaction protocols; virtual function tables used for dynamic dispatch of polymorphic method calls; and Robert DeLine's packagers, which separate a component's internal functionality, referred to as essence, from the manner in which it is accessed (DeLine 2001). XML meta–data interchange (XMI) is a relatively recent approach that supports interchange of models between applications and performs data presentation conversion.

5.4.8 Distributor Connectors

Distributor connectors perform the identification of interaction paths and subsequent routing of communication and coordination information among components along these paths. Therefore, they provide facilitation services. Distributor connectors never exist by

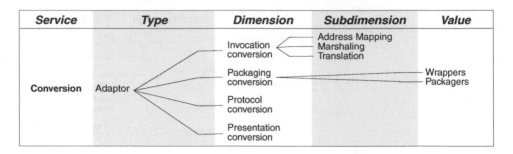

Figure 5-10.
*Adaptor
connector type
and its variations.*

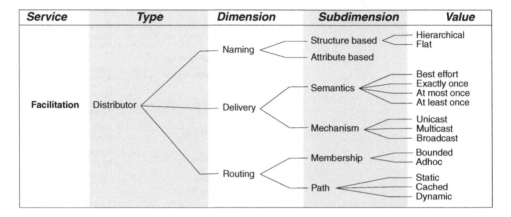

Figure 5-11.
*Distributor
connector type
and its variations.*

themselves, but provide assistance to other connectors, such as streams or procedure calls. Distributed systems exchange information using distributor connectors to direct the data flow. Distributed systems require identification of component locations and paths to them based on symbolic names. Domain name service (DNS), routing, switching, and many other network services belong to this connector type. Distributors have an important effect on system scalability and survivability.

The space of options available to a software engineer for constructing distributor connectors is shown in Figure 5-11. Issues that are particularly important in distributed systems are resource naming, semantics and mechanisms of data delivery, and characteristics of routing.

5.5 EXAMPLE CONNECTORS

The reader should be familiar at least with the frequently used procedure call and shared data connector types. It likely that the reader has seen or used several of the other connector types, such as distributors or adaptors, and has also been exposed to composite connectors. Furthermore, Chapter 4 introduced a number of connectors in the different Lunar Lander examples.

In this section, we illustrate the connector classification discussed above with four composite distribution connectors that are in wide use today: event-based, grid-based,

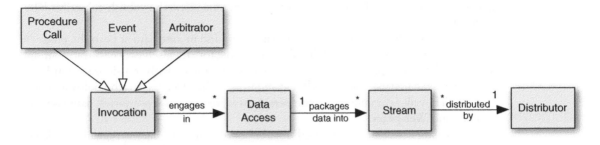

Figure 5-12. *Data distribution connectors involve a type of invocation (via arbitrator, event, or procedure call connectors), data access, stream, and distribution. Cardinality is indicated accordingly on the relationship arrows, where * refers to the cardinality of "many."*

client-server–based, and peer-to-peer–based (or P2P-based) connectors. These connectors distribute large amounts of content over a wide area network, such as the Internet. Such connectors are used in disseminating music, movies, scientific data, and so on. Several implementations of these connectors are in wide use by a number of research, industry, and government projects, as well as a large number of individuals around the world.

Distribution connectors can be described as different combinations of six of the connector types defined in the classification of Section 5.4. The exact combination of the six types' dimensions varies across the different distribution connectors, but in general, each distribution connector performs some form of data access, involving a stream-based reading (and packaging) of data, and distribution of the data to end users. Some connector classes are invoked via procedure calls (for example, client-server–based) while others are invoked via events (for example, event-based), or arbitration (for example, P2P-based). Figure 5-12 illustrates the choices and the relationships.

The remainder of this section describes each of the four data distribution connectors using the connector classification from Section 5.4. The seemingly verbose description of the connectors is necessary: it reflects the number of concerns an architect has to consider when selecting and composing connectors for a specific system, as well as the number of decisions that will be made in the process.

5.5.1 Event-Based Data Distribution Connectors

The event-based data distribution connectors are compositions of four of the connector types from Section 5.4: event, data access, stream, and distributor. These connectors send and receive data through asynchronous notifications called *events*. Events may arrive according to some fixed periodic schedule or at discrete aperiodic intervals. Typically, there are many producers and consumers of data in event-based distribution connectors. For example, science data servers (producers) may alert scientists (consumers) of the availability of new data sets. Event-based distribution connectors often employ an asynchronous best-effort delivery method for data, making no guarantees as to the completion or time of data deliveries. Data delivery events sent through the connectors can be prioritized, tailored to different use cases or deployment environments, and specified by system users. Events can be delivered using prioritized threaded queues, be locally or remotely managed, or be delivered using user registered preferences and the publish-subscribe delivery mechanism.

Event-based distribution connectors can access and mutate data at both the producer and consumer ends. Event-based distribution connectors themselves access transient and persistent data, both public and private. They communicate with transient session-based stores such as shared memory stores [for example, Apache's Derby (Apache Software Foundation)]. They also communicate with persistent stores such as repositories, databases, file systems, and Web pages.

After data access by event-based distribution connectors, data is typically packaged into streams, both structured and raw, using a best effort approach, with bounded packet size and data buffering. Streams can be identified via named uniform resource identifiers (URIs), and constructed using the asynchronous mode of operation. Streams may be constructed either locally or remotely, depending upon how the data was accessed.

Stream-based data is distributed from data producers to data consumers using a naming registry, via either a hierarchical or flat naming model. Data streams are delivered as events using best effort delivery and any combination of the unicast, broadcast, and multicast delivery mechanisms. Routing of events is typically determined by the specific network layer of the connector's deployment environment.

Example instances of event-based data distribution connectors include the Siena publish-subscribe middleware (Carzaniga, Rosenblum, and Wolf 2001), the Prism-MW middleware (Malek, Mikic-Rakic, and Medvidović 2005), and its subsequent extension allowing grid resource location and discovery, called GLIDE (Mattmann et al. 2005).

5.5.2 Grid-Based Data Distribution Connectors

The grid-based data distribution connectors are compositions of four of the connector types from Section 5.4: procedure call, data access, stream, and distributor. These connectors move and deliver large amounts of data between software components deployed in the grid environment—a virtual network of shared computing and data resources. Although the grid is further discussed in Chapter 11, this section will outline the architecture of the corresponding connectors. The reader may find it useful to return to this section again after reading Chapter 11.

Grid-based distribution connectors are invoked via a named, synchronous procedure call, often as a Web service call sent using the Simple Object Access Protocol (SOAP) (Mitra 2003). User authentication credentials are provided to the connector for integration with the Grid Security Infrastructure (GSI), a highly secure toolkit based on key pairs and certificate authorities. URLs sent via the connector invocation describe where the data is and where it is to be sent (that is, who the consumers are). Parameters are passed by value using "keyword equals value" semantics, with control messages being logged to the Grid API log layer.

Grid-based distribution connectors access and mutate transient and persistent data, both private and public, as long as there is some type of standard API (for instance, dynamic data exchange over XML, a repository access, or file I/O) for accessing it.

Data access through a grid connector is typically packaged as a stream of bytes (or blocks, configured via a parameter) with exactly-once delivery and (configurable) bounded buffering provided by the network's TCP/IP level. Data can be structured or raw. Buffering and throughput of data are parallelized via multiple concurrent time-out synchronous TCP/IP streams. Streams are named stateful URLs and URIs, and can exist both locally and remotely, depending upon where the data was accessed. A stream can be delivered to many consumers.

Grid-based distribution connectors distribute data using the grid environment for naming and location, including the Grid Meta–data Catalog Service (MCS) and Replica Location Service (RLS) components, and named URLs and URIs. Naming can be hierarchical, with resources and locations sharing parent-child relationships via the MCS. Alternatively, naming and discovery can be flat, structure-based. Data is delivered via parallelized unicast exactly once using TCP/IP concurrent streams, flooding the underlying network to its saturation, thus making the most efficient use of the available bandwidth possible. Reliability measures allow redelivery of lost packets if necessary, as well as partial data transfers, both sequential and out of order. Routing of data is handled by the underlying TCP/IP network layer.

Example instances of grid-based distribution connectors include the GridFTP software, bundled along with the Globus Grid Toolkit (The Globus Alliance), and the large files transfer protocol, or bbFTP (Farrache 2005).

5.5.3 Client-Server–Based Data Distribution Connectors

The client-server–based distribution connectors allow seamless distribution of data between distributed systems using RPC. They are compositions of four of the connector types from Section 5.4: procedure call, data access, stream, and distributor. These connectors are invoked via a synchronous remote procedure call that appears (to the consumers of data) as if it were a local method call. Keyword (named) parameters are passed to the method call to specify the distribution constraints, with parameters being passed by value or reference, depending upon the underlying remote procedure call implementation. Methods can have return values, which typically must conform to a standard set of primitive data types that are supported on all machines involved in the data distribution. Methods are interactions between one sender and one receiver, typically the producer of the data and its consumer, respectively.

Upon invocation, the client-server-based distribution connector engages in a data access, grabbing and mutating persistent and transient data. After data is accessed, it is packaged into streams that are delivered using exactly-once delivery and bounded packet size managed by the underlying TCP/IP protocol. Data can be raw or structured in the stream. Stream throughput is measured in atomic units (bits per second), and streams are identified using stateful Uniform Resource Names (URNs). Streams can be local or remote, depending on where the data was accessed or packaged.

Data is distributed from client-server–based connectors using a naming registry to locate the requesting consumer of data. Data is delivered through method (or interface) parameters and return values. It is sent exactly once, using the unicast delivery mechanism. Routing is performed by the underlying TCP/IP network using static membership identified via a naming registry.

Example instances of client-server–based data distribution connectors include HTTP/REST (recall Chapter 1), Java RMI, CORBA (recall Chapter 4), FTP, SOAP, and many commercial UDP technologies.

5.5.4 P2P-Based Data Distribution Connectors

The P2P-based data distribution connectors are compositions of four of the connector types from Section 5.4: arbitrator, data access, stream, and distributor. These connectors are unlike the other three categories. Rather than providing some sort of initial procedural or event-based invocation, these connectors typically rely on arbitration as a means of synchronization and invocation. Arbitration involves control flow redirection between distributed resources, or peers, operating in a networked environment. Arbitrators can negotiate protocols, scheduling, and timing issues. Fault handling and parameter passing is handled in an egalitarian fashion via voting and point-to-point or point-to-many communication between peers or groups of peers. P2P-based distribution connectors use rendezvous as a mechanism to achieve concurrency and scheduling. Transaction support is often available, and invocation can be rolled back if necessary.

Upon invocation, peers in a P2P-based distribution connector engage in data access, accessing transient (both process- and thread-specific) and persistent (for instance, repository, file I/O, and so on) data. Since peers can come and go in a P2P-based scenario, for the most part data access is transient in nature: A peer need not stick around for the entire distribution.

Data is accessed and packaged via streams, using a best effort bounded mechanism. Data can be structured or raw, as long as it can be organized into identifiable chunks that can be retransmitted and shared between peers handled by the connector. Streams are named URNs, typically identified using some hashing algorithm (such as SHA-1 or MD5), and are available both locally and remotely depending upon where the data was accessed or packaged.

Data is distributed in the P2P-based distribution connectors by locating other peers that have pieces of data a user wants to obtain or distribute. Location of other peers is based upon attributes such as resource type, SHA-1, and other domain-specific attribute meta–data (for instance, for movie files "production company" might be used or for music "artist name"). Delivery occurs in the form of chunks, sent to and from remote peers using best effort or at least once semantics over unicast and multicast transmission channels. Routing, while influenced by the underlying network layer, is handled by some sort of tracking mechanism, sometimes called trackers or super peers. Tracking mechanisms allow location of chunks of data streams that need to be distributed or obtained in a P2P-based connector.

Example instances of the P2P-based distribution connector class include BitTorrent (Cohen 2003) and JXTA-based data distributors, such as the Peerdata project at NASA's Jet Propulsion Laboratory. P2P systems employing such connectors are discussed in Chapter 11.

5.6 USING THE CONNECTOR FRAMEWORK

This section provides general guidelines for software architects in selecting connectors that meet their needs. The section discusses the issue of connector compatibility: Understanding which connectors, or connector dimensions, are and are not compatible is particularly important in cases where composite connectors are needed.

5.6.1 Selecting Appropriate Connectors

In selecting a software connector that meets the particular needs of a given (sub)system, a software architect must perform at least the following steps. Note that the descriptions of the steps are relatively general, meaning that this process places significant responsibility on the software architects and requires a great deal of familiarity with the technical details of connectors that are at their disposal.

1. Select the specific set of interacting components. Different sets of components, even in the same system, may have different interaction needs. This is why it is important for the architect to focus only on those components for which the desired connector is needed. This and the subsequent steps are repeated for each such component set, that is, for as many distinct connectors as are needed in the system.

2. Determine the interaction services the components need. It is critical to identify the precise characteristics of the components' interaction. This will likely involve studying the components' architectural descriptions, and may also require considering the implementation language and/or framework.

3. Based on the identified interaction services, determine a subset of the eight connector types that comprise the initial candidate set for providing those services. It is sufficient to establish that the connector types chosen in this step *may* be good candidates for supplying the needed services.

4. Evaluate each connector type from the chosen subset based on the details of the interaction requirements. Study these in light of the connector types' dimensions, subdimensions, and values. Eliminate any connector types whose usage is deemed to result in a suboptimal interaction solution for the specific set of components under consideration.

5. For each of the remaining candidate connector types, set the values for the necessary dimensions and subdimensions as appropriate. Identify the best (most natural) candidate connectors. This will require performing a trade-off analysis among multiple possible solutions. It may also result in selecting a composite connector, which combines features of multiple types, as further discussed below.

The classification of connectors described in Section 5.4 thus serves as the foundation for synthesizing new connectors as well as analyzing the compatibility of connector dimensions. Instantiating dimensions of a single connector type by choosing one or more values forms a simple connector species. On the other hand, using values of dimensions from different connector types leads to a composite (higher-order) connector species. Many real-world scenarios will force an architect to compose such higher-order connectors to satisfy all application requirements.

The reader should note that creating unprecedented, composite connectors is not a trivial task. At the least, this requires developing a deep understanding of the connectors' complementary, orthogonal, and incompatible characteristics. Without such an understanding, the resulting integration process may be misguided and the developed solutions suboptimal, or worse, completely ineffective. Examples of this have been documented in the literature [for example, in the well known case of the interactions among the large components used in the Aesop system (Garlan, Allen, and Ockerbloom 1995)].

Figure 5-13.
Connector compatibility matrix.

LEGEND:
& - requires
! - cautions
ø - restricts
x - prohibits

Connector compatibility matrix. Columns and rows are grouped into **Procedure Call** (Parameters, Entry Point, Invocation, Synchronicity, Cardinality, Accessibility), **Event** (Cardinality, Delivery, Priority, Synchronicity, Notification, Causality, Mode), and **Data Access** (Locality, Mode, Availability, Accessibility, Cardinality).

Group	Attribute	PC Parameters	PC Entry Point	PC Invocation	PC Synchronicity	PC Cardinality	PC Accessibility	Ev Cardinality	Ev Delivery	Ev Priority	Ev Synchronicity	Ev Notification	Ev Causality	Ev Mode	DA Locality	DA Mode	DA Availability	DA Accessibility	DA Cardinality
Procedure Call	Parameters	■	&	&	!		!							ø	ø	ø			
	Entry Point	&	■	&	!	!	ø	&		ø	&	&			!	ø			
	Invocation		!	■	&	!	ø				!	&			ø	!			
	Synchronicity		&	&	■	!			&	ø	ø	!			!	!			
	Cardinality		&	&	!	■		!	ø					!	ø				
	Accessibility	&	&	&	&	&	■								!	!		ø	
Event	**Cardinality**			!		!	ø	■					!		ø				!
	Delivery	ø	!	ø	ø		ø	&	■		ø	!	!		&	&	!		
	Priority									■		&	&						
	Synchronicity	!	!	ø	!	ø			!	ø	■	!			!	!	!		
	Notification		ø	ø	!	&	!		&		&	■	&			ø		x	!
	Causality	!		ø	ø								■	&	&				&
	Mode	!					ø		!		ø		&	■	&	&			&
Data Access	**Locality**		!		!	!	ø	!	ø		ø	ø		ø	■				
	Mode	ø	ø		ø	ø	ø		&	ø	ø	ø	ø	ø	&	■	!		
	Availability	ø	!		!		ø			ø			!	!	!		■		
	Accessibility	ø	ø	ø	ø	ø	!	ø	ø		ø	ø	ø	ø	&			■	
	Cardinality	ø	ø			!	!					!			&				■
Stream	Delivery	&			ø	ø	!								!	&			
	Format	ø		ø															
	Directionality	&	&	&	ø		!									!			
	Cardinality	&	ø	!	ø	ø	!	ø							&				
	State	&	ø	ø	ø	ø												&	
Linkage	**Granularity**	!	!	ø			!	&	!		!	!	&	!	&	!		&	
	Cardinality			!	ø	&	!	ø	!			!							ø
	Reference		!	ø	!	&	!								!	&	!		
	Binding	&	&	ø	!	ø	!								!	&			
Arbitrator	Fault handling	&	&	&	&	&	ø	&	!	&	&	&	&		&				
	Concurrency	&	&	&	!	&	&	&	!		!	&	&	&	!	ø			
	Transactions	&	!	&	!	&		&	!		!	&		&	&		&		
	Logging	&	&	&	&	&	ø	&			&	&	&	&	&	&	&		
	Security	&	&	&	!	&	&	&	!		!	&	&	&	&	&			
	Scheduling	&	&	&	!	&		&	!	ø	&	&	&	&	&	&			
	Pooling	&	&	ø	!	&	ø	&			&	&	&	&	&				
Adaptor	Invocation	&	&	&	&	ø	x	!	&	ø	&	&		&	&	&	&		&
	Presentation	&		&		ø	ø	&	ø	&				&	&	&	&		
	Packaging	&	&	&	!		x				&				&				
	Protocol		ø	ø	ø		&				&	!		&	&	&			
Distrib.	Naming	&		&	!		ø	&				&		&	ø			!	&
	Delivery	&	!	&	&	!	!	&	!	&	!	&	&		&	!	&	ø	!
	Routing	&		&		&		&	&		&		&	&	&	&	&		&

	Stream					Linkage				Arbitrator							Adaptor				Distrib.		
	Delivery	Format	Directionality	Cardinality	State	Granularity	Cardinality	Reference	Binding	Fault handling	Concurrency	Transactions	Logging	Security	Scheduling	Pooling	Invocation	Presentation	Packaging	Protocol	Naming	Delivery	Routing
	!		ø			!	!	&		&		&						&		&	&		
	&		&	&		!	!			&													
			&		&		!		&	&	ø	&			&		&	&					
			ø							&													
	!		&	&	&				&	&					&								
								!	!	&													
			ø			ø	&			&	&				&		&	&					&
	ø		!							&	&	ø		&		&	&					&	
			&							&						ø	&						
		ø								&	&		ø										
	&		&			!				&	!				&			&				&	
										&						ø							
	&	ø			&					&	&			ø	&								
								!		&	ø											ø	
						!				&	ø	&											
								!		&	ø	&						&					
						!							&						ø	&			
								!		&	&						&	&					
■									&			x			&		&	&				ø	
	■						ø		&		&										&	&	
		■			&					&									&	&	&	
			■			!				&									&	&	&	
				■		&				&	ø									&	&	
					■	&		&	&	&				&		&			&	!	
						■	&	&	&	&				&		&			&		
					■	&			&	&	&	&	!		&	&					
						&		■	&				!									
									■	&	&	!	!		&							
						&		&	&	■	&	&	&	&	&	&		&			
						&			&	&	■	&	&		&	&		&			
						&	!		&	&		■	&	!							
									&	&		■	&							&	
	&		&		&		&	ø			x	■	&			&	&	&	
	&		&		&		&		&			■				&	&	
					!		&						■					
					&		&						■				
				&	&	&		&	&	&		&		■	&	&
&		&		&	!	&			&				&		■	&
&		&	&	&	&	&		&		&			&	&	■

In the absence of a set of concrete, well-understood, and widely adopted rules for defining composite connectors, it becomes difficult to guide this process. Recent research by, for example, Bridget Spitznagel and David Garlan (Spitznagel and Garlan 2003) suggests some specific formalisms and strategies that can be adopted to address connector composition. However, ultimately a comprehensive classification of connectors, such as the one presented in this chapter, is necessary (though not sufficient) to create a general set of guidelines that specify the conditions under which two or more connectors can be composed. We discuss this issue in more depth next.

5.6.2   Detecting Mismatches

The connector taxonomy introduced in Section 5.4 can be leveraged to identify potential mismatches between incompatible connector dimensions, and to avoid such combinations. Figure 5-13 shows a compatibility matrix for the connector dimensions identified in the classification from Figure 5-4 through Figure 5-11. The matrix provides guidance regarding which combinations of dimensions are necessary and which should be avoided; the empty cells in the matrix denote combinations that are possible, but not required. The sparseness of the matrix suggests that the allowed design space of connectors is very large based on their current understanding. At the same time, some pitfalls are known to exist. Four kinds of rules for combining connector dimensions can be identified: requires, cautions, restricts, and prohibits.

The *requires* rule indicates that the choice of one dimension in one connector species mandates that another dimension be selected in another connector species; it also allows all possible combinations of the values of the given dimension and its required co-dimension. For example, if a distributor and an adaptor connector are composed, distributor's delivery requires that the adaptor support presentation conversion, that is, that it allow data to be marshaled for transport across address spaces.

Requires is a chaining rule and is used as the starting point for constructing the base connector species. For example, an event connector that requires delivery semantics also needs a notification dimension, which in turn requires cardinality, synchronicity, and mode. This chaining rule results in identification of dimensions that are mandatory in all species of a connector type, and those that are optional. In Figure 5-13, the mandatory dimensions are in **boldface**, whereas the optional dimensions are in regular font.

The *cautions* rule indicates that certain combinations of values for two connector dimensions that are required to be used in tandem, while valid, may result in an unstable or unreliable connector. For example, a component being invoked implicitly should not have multiple entry points since an implicit invocation mechanism cannot choose among the entry points. Another example is the relationship between arbitrator connector's concurrency dimension and data access connector's locality dimension: the granularity level at which concurrency is supported by the former (heavy-weight versus light-weight) should match the level at which locality is supported by the latter (process-specific versus thread-specific).

The *restricts* rule is used to indicate that the two dimensions are not required to be used together at all times, and that there are certain combinations of their values that are invalid. For example, thread-specific data access cannot use heavy-weight concurrency (see the intersection of data access-locality with arbitrator-concurrency). Likewise, passing parameters by name when those parameters have only transient availability can cause the parameters' values to disappear, be changed, or be affected by some read-modify-write condition; the problem is exacerbated when these parameters are passed by reference and the procedure has no place to store their new values or to access the old ones (see the intersection of procedure call-parameters with data access-availability).

Finally, the *prohibits* rule is used to exclude any combination of two dimensions from being used and indicates total incompatibility of the dimensions. For example, stream delivery cannot be built on transactional atomicity (see the intersection of stream-delivery with arbitrator-transactions). As can be seen in Figure 5-13, there are relatively few instances of the prohibits relationship. This is a positive indicator, as it shows that most connector combinations are legal at least under some circumstances. At the same time, the large numbers of restricts and cautions relationships in Figure 5-13 also indicate that software architects must be careful when composing connectors.

While the above discussion was restricted to the binary combinations of connector dimensions, the compatibility relations between dimensions are transitive. In other words, the compatibility rules can be successively applied to determine the n-ary compatibility between dimensions. The binary relations outlined in this section would serve as a necessary starting point for analyzing the n-ary relations.

Explicit, targeted study of software connectors is a relatively recent occurrence. There still are many details that need to be uncovered and understandings improved. Figure 5-13 is indicative of this: The sparser sections of the compatibility matrix argue for the need for greater understanding of certain combinations of connector types (such as data access and stream). It is reasonable to expect that, as our understanding of connectors improves over time, the compatibility matrix, as well as the rationale behind it, will also evolve.

5.7 END MATTER

Every software system employs connectors, frequently many of them. In complex distributed systems in particular, connectors can be the key determinants of whether the desired system properties will be met. This observation is often made, yet connectors are not always given first-class status in software systems, and have certainly not been studied to the same extent as components.

This chapter has presented a detailed study of software connectors. At the most basic level, each connector establishes a conduit (which can be thought of, and referred to, as a virtual channel or duct) for two or more components to interact by exchanging control and data in a software system. The actual manner in which data and/or control are exchanged, however, and the specific characteristics of that exchange, can vary widely. This is what makes the space of software connectors quite large and complex.

As this chapter has argued, the space of connectors can be better understood by considering the role (or roles) played by a given connector and the type (or types) of interaction supported by the connector. At the same time, the large number of variation points for each connector type (the dimensions, subdimensions, and values introduced in Section 5.4) require that the (in)compatibilities among connectors be considered carefully. While this area clearly requires further study, the existing body of knowledge, if applied judiciously, can be a great aid to software architects and developers.

The following several chapters will use this as well as the preceding chapters as the foundation for introducing the reader to a number of key activities in architecture-driven software development. Chapter 6 focuses on the principles of architecture modeling and presents the details of a number of software architecture description languages. Chapter 7 introduces the reader to the approaches for visualizing software architectures. Chapter 8 provides an overview of architectural analysis. Chapter 9 discusses the challenges and solutions for architecture-based system implementation. Finally, Chapter 10 focuses on the postimplementation concerns of system deployment and run-time mobility.

The Business Case	The engineering of complex software systems is difficult and expensive. In particular, composing large components, many of which may not have been developed to "play" together, can cause bloated systems with unacceptable performance, project schedule slippages, and budget overruns. Examples of software projects that fit this general description abound.
	If connectors in such scenarios are not considered explicitly, then every pair of components that needs to be integrated may need to be dealt with separately. While past experience may prove useful to architects and developers of such systems, the usually applied techniques (for instance, building wrappers and "glue code") will need to be reapplied in each individual case. Furthermore, this integration code will often be tightly coupled with one or more of the interacting components, rendering its reuse difficult or impossible. Perhaps most importantly, by constantly going back to the same integration toolbox, software engineers are likely to miss more appropriate, and perhaps less costly, component integration and interaction solutions.
	Having an intimate understanding of connectors, and treating them separately from the components, can potentially address all of the above concerns. One useful property of connectors, which is not shared by many components, is that they are largely application-independent. This means that there is actually a finite (although very large) number of component interaction and integration challenges. Many such challenges may be similar across like products (for instance, in a product family) or within a particular application domain.
	A given software development organization could thus develop and grow a large, reusable arsenal of explicit connectors, which would, in turn, help to curb the costs of future projects.

5.8 REVIEW QUESTIONS

1. Define a software connector.
2. How are connectors different from components?
3. What is a duct? What purpose does it serve?
4. What is the difference between the transfer of control and the transfer of data?
5. Name and describe the four possible roles played by a connector.
6. How is facilitation different from conversion?
7. Name and briefly describe the eight different connector types.
8. Why is connector composition challenging?
9. Are there connector types that can always be composed?
10. Are there types that can never be composed?
11. What are data-intensive connectors?
12. What characteristics do all data-intensive connectors share?

5.9 EXERCISES

1. For each connector type discussed in this chapter, try to identify a specific connector species that belongs to that type.

2. For the connectors identified in the previous question, enumerate the dimension and subdimension values that each of the connector species takes.

3. Analyze the connectors used in the different Lunar Lander examples in Chapter 4 to determine the connector types to which they belong. Specify the values they take for different dimensions and subdimensions.

4. Consider the Aesop system developed by Garlan et al. and described in (Garlan, Allen, and Ockerbloom 1995). Develop a detailed strategy for integrating Aesop's four major components by explicitly treating its connectors. Would your strategy have helped Aesop's developers to deal with the architectural mismatches among the components more effectively than their adopted strategy?

5. Select a software system with which you are intimately familiar. Isolate one of the connectors in the system (for example, a procedure call connector). Replace that connector with a connector of a different type (for example, an event connector). What were the required steps in doing so? Discuss the lessons learned.

6. Select a software system with which you are intimately familiar and which uses mostly procedure call connectors. Replace all procedure call connectors in the application with explicit, named connectors, thereby completely decoupling the interacting components. Discuss the relative merits of the two applications' architectures.

7. Repeat the above exercise by changing one or more connectors that support synchronous interaction between components with connectors that support asynchronous interaction. What challenges did you face in accomplishing this task? Does the modified application exhibit the same behavior as the original application? Why or why not?

8. Several open-source systems, available from Source Forge.net and similar online repositories, are accompanied by thorough design documentation. Select at least two open-source systems and study their architectures. Identify their connectors. Classify the connectors according to their types. Can you spot any trends in the systems' connector usage?

9. Mehta et al. (Mehta, Medvidović, and Phadke 2000) have argued that the Linux Process Scheduler subsystem identified in the study by Bowman et al. (Bowman, Holt, and Brewster 1999) is, in fact, a connector. Investigate the implications of this decision. In order to do so, you may want to consider treating Process Scheduler as a component, or as a subarchitecture comprising a composition of finer-grained components and connectors. Were Mehta et al. correct in their decision? Does their decision fundamentally alter the architecture of Linux, or one's understanding of it?

10. This chapter has suggested that, architecturally, the different classes of data-intensive connectors are similar to a certain extent. Select two such widely used connectors from different categories—for instance, client-server and peer-to-peer. Based on their architectures discussed in Section 5.5, outline a strategy for converting one connector into the other.

11. Study the Question 10's two connectors' architectures and implementations in more detail. Was your conversion strategy viable? If so, proceed with the conversion. If not, discuss the reasons why, adjust your strategy as appropriate, and proceed with the conversion.

5.10 FURTHER READING

Software connectors have been an important facet in developing large, complex software intensive systems for a long time. While they may not have been the primary focus of study, and may not have been identified explicitly, connectors figured prominently in the operating systems, programming languages, distributed systems, computer networks, and middleware literature [for instance (Reiss 1990), (Colouris, Dollimore, and Kindberg 1994), (Yellin and Strom 1994), (Orfali, Harkey, and Edwards 1996)].

The explicit focus on software connectors is more recent and has emerged from the body of work dealing with software architecture. Perry (Perry 1987) provided the needed foundation in his study of software interconnection models. Perry and Wolf (Perry and Wolf 1992) were the first to suggest connectors as first-class entities in a software architecture, and Shaw and Garlan (Shaw 1994; Shaw, DeLine, and Zelesnik 1996; Shaw and Garlan 1996) soon followed suit. Allen, Garlan, and Ockerbloom (Garlan, Allen, and Ockerbloom 1995) demonstrated that explicit connectors can provide a substantial aid in system specification, and can carry significant, inherent analytical power.

Several researchers have tried to classify connectors as an aid to software architects in making the most appropriate design choices. An early such effort by Hirsch, Uchitel, and Yankelevich (Hirsch, Uchitel, and Yankelevich 1999) was limited in scope, but it directly inspired the more detailed study by Mehta, Medvidović, and Phadke (Mehta, Medvidović, and Phadke 2000), which has been referenced extensively in this chapter. Bálek and Plášil (Balek and Plasil 2001) have proposed a formal connector model for dealing with software deployment (recall Chapter 3). In particular, they posit that the basic set of dynamic services that a connector should provide to aid deployment maps directly to the key service categories in Mehta et al.'s taxonomy: control and data transfer, interface adaptation and data conversion, access coordination and synchronization, communication intercepting, and dynamic component linking. Bálek and Plášil additionally demonstrate that their connectors can be composed to provide more advanced interaction services, in a similar vein to Spitznagel and Garlan's later work (Spitznagel and Garlan 2003).

6

Modeling

As we have stated, every software system has an architecture, whether it is a "good" architecture or not. We have previously defined architecture as the set of principal design decisions about a system. Once design decisions have been made, they can be recorded. Design decisions are captured in *models*; the process of creating models is called *modeling*. From Chapter 3 we have:

> **Definitions.** An architectural *model* is an artifact that captures some or all of the design decisions that comprise a system's architecture. Architectural *modeling* is the reification and documentation of those design decisions.

Models can capture architectural design decisions with varying levels of rigor and formality. They enable users to communicate about, visualize, evaluate, and evolve an architecture. Without models, architectures are inscrutable.

Throughout the chapter, we also discuss how architecture modeling *notations* are used to capture design decisions.

> **Definition.** An architectural modeling *notation* is a language or means of capturing design decisions.

Available architecture modeling notations range from the rich and ambiguous (such as natural language) to the semantically narrow and highly formal (such as the Rapide architecture description language). While some models conform to a single notation, a model may also use a mix of different notations. For example, a single model may use the Unified Modeling Language (UML) class diagram notation to describe the classes in a system, but annotate them with natural language descriptions of their functions.

This chapter introduces a broad variety of modeling concepts that are captured in architectural models, from basic architectural elements (for instance, components and connectors) to more complex properties of systems such as behavioral models. It then covers some of the many available options for capturing different aspects of an architecture, from the semantically weak (such as PowerPoint modeling) to those with formal semantics. Finally, it discusses the strengths and weaknesses of some of these notations as applied to some of the systems we've discussed already, such as Lunar Lander and the World Wide Web.

6.1 MODELING CONCEPTS

In this chapter, we discuss a broad spectrum of *kinds* of things that can be modeled in an architecture, and then discuss how various notations can be selected and used to facilitate this modeling. Specifically, for each concept we identify, we will identify what it takes to effectively model that concept—which notational features, and so on.

6.1.1 Stakeholder-Driven Modeling

One of the most critical decisions that architects and others stakeholders will make in developing an architecture is to choose:

1. The architectural decisions and concepts that should be modeled.
2. The level of detail.
3. The amount of rigor or formality.

These decisions should be based on *costs* and *benefits*. Architects should balance the benefits of having certain models in certain forms or notations with the costs of creating and maintaining those models. Thus, the choice of what to model, and at what level of detail, will be *stakeholder driven*. A good rule of thumb is that the most important or critical aspects of a system should be the ones that are modeled in the greatest detail with the highest degrees of rigor/formality.

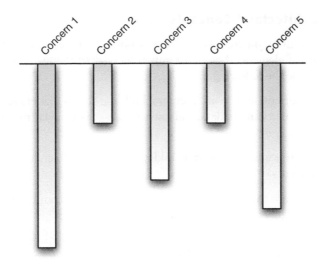

Figure 6-1.
*Modeling
different concerns
with different
depths (from
Maier and
Rechtin).*

Figure 6-1, borrowed from Mark Maier and Eberhardt Rechtin's book, *The Art of Systems Architecting* (Maier and Rechtin 2000), graphically depicts this concept. It shows five concerns about the system identified by stakeholders. In this particular case, Concern 1 is of great importance, and will be considered and modeled deeply—in great detail. Concerns 2 and 4 are less important and will be modeled shallowly. Because the concerns and their relative levels of importance will vary from project to project, each project will have somewhat different modeling needs.

Modeling is an activity, and as such it is often governed by a process. It will undoubtedly be part of the larger process of architecture-centric software development that we have been discussing in this book. However, modeling itself is a subprocess, and the process of modeling can vary widely from project to project.

The basic activities behind stakeholder-driven modeling are to:

1. Identify relevant aspects of the software to model.
2. Roughly categorize them in terms of importance.
3. Identify the goals of modeling for each aspect (communication, bug finding, quality analysis, generation of other artifacts, and so on).
4. Select modeling notations that will model the selected aspects at appropriate levels of depth to achieve the modeling goals.
5. Create the models.
6. Use the models in a manner consistent with the modeling goals.

Although the steps outlined above are in rough chronological order, they can be incorporated into an iterative process. It is almost never clear from the outset of a project what all the important aspects of a software system are, what the goals of modeling are, and whether those goals are achievable using available notations, technology, time, and money. As such, these estimations must be reevaluated and refined multiple times through a system's development and the models and modeling efforts adjusted accordingly.

6.1.2   Basic Architectural Concepts

While each architecture is different, we have previously identified (particularly in Chapter 4) certain kinds of elements that are of importance when talking about architectural designs. These include the following.

Components. Components are the architectural building blocks that encapsulate a subset of the system's functionality and/or data, and restrict access to them via an explicitly defined interface.

Connectors. Connectors are architectural building blocks that effect and regulate interactions among components.

Interfaces. Interfaces are the points at which components and connectors interact with the outside world—in general, other components and connectors.

Configurations. Configurations are a set of specific associations between the components and connectors of a software system's architecture. Such associations may be captured via graphs whose nodes represent components and connectors, and whose edges represent their interconnectivity.

Rationale. Rationale is the information that explains why particular architectural decisions were made, and what purpose various elements serve.

These concepts form a starting point for architectural modeling. At the most basic level, modeling these concepts requires a notation that can express a graph of components and connectors, preferably with well-defined connection points (interfaces). These languages can be relatively simple—basic box and arrow diagrams or lists with appropriate internal references will suffice. Rationale is somewhat different because it is more amorphous. Rationale is primarily used for communicating information and intent among stakeholders, and is generally not represented explicitly in the actual, built software system. As such, languages for expressing rationale need to be more expressive and less constrained—rationale is most often expressed using natural language for this reason.

Modeling at only the most basic level (that is, enumerating the existence and interconnections of the various components and connectors) provides a small amount of value, but these models will not suffice for most complex projects. Rather, these models must be extended and annotated with a host of other concepts: How are the functions partitioned among the components? What are the nature and types of the interfaces? What does it mean for a component and a connector to be linked? How do all these properties of a system change over time? These questions are at the heart of architectural modeling.

Depending on the nature of the system being developed and the domain, it may or may not be straightforward to represent these basic elements. For example, in a desktop application such as a word processor or spreadsheet, the software components and connectors will be relatively static and few in number. Even with a very complex desktop application containing, say, 500 to 1000 components and connectors, it is feasible to enumerate and describe each of these elements as well as the interconnections among them.

Applications that are large, dynamic, and distributed may be harder to model. For example, it is basically impossible to enumerate all the software components that are part of the World Wide Web or their configuration: There are too many of them and they are constantly coming and going. For these applications, it is probably more reasonable to model only parts of the system, or specific configurations that represent expected use cases. Alternatively, it may be more effective to model the architectural style that governs what kinds of elements may be included in the architecture and how they may be configured.

6.1.3 Elements of the Architectural Style

Recall that an architectural style is a collection of architectural design decisions that are applicable in a given development context, constrain architectural design decisions that are specific to a particular system within that context, and elicit beneficial qualities in each resulting system. In addition to modeling basic architectural elements, it is often useful to model the style that governs how these elements have been (and may be) used.

Note that architectural styles, like architectures, are made up of design decisions. These design decisions can also be modeled. Explicitly modeling the architectural style can be helpful for a number of reasons. It reduces confusion about what is and is not allowed in the architecture. It can help to reduce architectural drift and erosion. It makes it easier to distinguish whether a specific design decision in an architecture was made to conform to a stylistic constraint or for some other reason. It can help to guide the evolution of the architecture. It can be more feasible and useful than structural modeling (component and connector graphs) for large or dynamic systems. Because styles are generally applicable to many projects, style models can be reused from project to project. Styles represent a single place to capture cross-cutting concerns and rationale for an architecture.

The kinds of design decisions found in an architectural style are generally more abstract or general than those found in an architecture. Some kinds of design decisions that might be captured in a style model include:

Specific Elements. A style may prescribe that particular components, connectors, or interfaces be included in architectures or used in specific situations. This can be facilitated by a modeling approach that supports templates or base models that are then elaborated.

Component, Connector, and Interface Types. Specific *kinds* of elements may be permitted, required, or prohibited in the architecture. Many modeling approaches are accompanied by a type system, although they often have different semantics.

Interaction Constraints. Constraints on interactions between components and connectors may exist. These constraints can take many forms. They may be temporal ("calling components must call `init()` before any other method"). They may be topological ("only components in the *client* layer are allowed to invoke components in the *server* layer"). They may specify particular interaction protocols, either by name (FTP, HTTP) or specification (formal protocol specifications in a language such as CSP or sequence charts). Modeling approaches that support constraints generally leverage some sort of logic—first-order logic, temporal logic, and so on.

Behavioral Constraints. Constraints on the behavior of architectural elements, or kinds of elements, may be included. Constraints can run the gamut from simple rules to full-blown complete behavioral specifications for components expressed in a notation such as finite state automata. Here again, modeling approaches that support behavioral constraints use either logic or other formal models (such as automata diagrams).

Concurrency Constraints. Constraints on which elements perform their functions concurrently and how they synchronize access to shared resources can also be included in an architectural style. Approaches that support concurrency modeling often employ formal behavioral models of various architectural elements; many also include temporal modeling techniques, such as sequence charts and statecharts.

6.1.4 Static and Dynamic Aspects

Architectural design decisions may address both static and dynamic aspects of a system. Static aspects of a system are those that do not involve the system's behavior while it is executing. Dynamic aspects of a system involve the system's runtime behavior.

Static aspects are generally easier to model simply because they do not involve changes over time. Typical models of static system aspects might include component/connector topologies, assignments of components and connectors to processing elements or hosts, host and network configurations, or mappings of architectural elements to code or binary artifacts.

Dynamic aspects of a system can be harder to model because they must deal with how a system behaves or changes over time. Typical models of dynamic aspects may be behavioral models (describing the behavior of a component or connector over time), interaction models (describing the interactions between a set of components and connectors over time), or data flow models (describing how data flows through an architecture over time).

The static/dynamic distinction is often not a clear line. For example, a system's structure may be relatively stable, but may change occasionally due to component failure, the use of flexible connectors, or architectural dynamism (see Chapter 14). In these cases, models that capture both static and dynamic system aspects may be employed: For example, a (static) base topology may be accompanied by a set of transitions that describe a limited set of changes that may occur to that topology during execution.

There is an important distinction between modeling static and dynamic *aspects* of a system and using static or dynamic *models*. The former refer to properties of the system being modeled. The latter refer to changes to the models themselves. A *model of a dynamic aspect* of a system describes how the *system* (often, its internal state) changes as it executes. A *dynamic model* actually changes itself.

Dynamic models are not necessary to capture dynamic aspects of a system. Consider a statechart. A statechart can capture the behavior of a component over time (a dynamic aspect), but the statechart itself does not generally change (for example, acquire new nodes or transitions) as the component executes. If the statechart were connected to a running system such that the current state of the system was always highlighted in the statechart, then the statechart would become a dynamic model. Such a statechart would be useful for visualizing the behavior of an application, perhaps for debugging purposes.

Supporting dynamic models is more difficult than supporting static models. Once developed, static models can be incorporated into a system in "read-only" mode—they are static resources that can be used as a basis for implementation, comparison, and analysis. Dynamic models must be incorporated in "read-write" mode—the system's execution can change the model itself. This requires tool support to keep the model and the system synchronized and consistent. For these mechanisms to operate automatically, the model must be stored in a machine-readable and writable form, and the model must be appropriately mapped to the implemented system. Visualizations of the model must also be suitably dynamic, reflecting changes to the model on-the-fly if possible.

6.1.5 Functional and Non-Functional Aspects

Architecture can capture both functional and non-functional aspects of a system. Functional aspects relate to *what* a system does. Non-functional aspects relate to *how* a system performs its functions. A good rule of thumb for thinking about this distinction is that functional aspects of a system can be described using declarative, subject-verb sentences: *The system prints medical records*. Non-functional aspects of a system can be described by adding adverbs to these sentences: *The system prints medical records **quickly and confidentially***. An extensive survey of non-functional properties from an architectural perspective is contained in Chapter 12.

Because functional aspects are generally more concrete, they are easier to model and can often be modeled rigorously and formally. Typical functional models of a system might capture the services that are provided by different components and connectors and the interconnections that achieve the overall system functions. They may capture the behavior of components, connectors, or subsystems, describing what functions those elements perform. Functional aspects of a system can be static or dynamic.

Most modeling notations focus on capturing functional aspects of systems. Notations and approaches differ in the aspects of a system that can be described, and how. Any selected notation or modeling approach must employ a sufficient number of concepts to express the aspect; the underlying semantics of the approach will determine the kinds of reasoning and analysis that can be applied.

Non-functional aspects of systems tend to be qualitative and subjective. Models of non-functional aspects of systems may be more informal and less rigorous than functional models, but this does not mean they should not be captured. Often, functional aspects of systems are developed specifically to correspond with or achieve non-functional objectives. For example, a non-functional model might simply prescribe that the paycheck-processing component be fast. The functional model of the paycheck component may describe how the paycheck-processing component uses caches and local processing—two functional strategies that help to achieve the modeled non-functional aspect.

Much like design rationale, non-functional aspects of systems are difficult to model with rigor. Expressive, free-form notations such as natural language are often used for capturing non-functional aspects. It is useful, however, to employ approaches with support for traceability, which allow modelers to explicitly map non-functional properties to functional design decisions.

6.2 AMBIGUITY, ACCURACY, AND PRECISION

Architectures are abstractions of systems. They capture information about some aspects of the system and leave out other aspects. Ideally, the principal, most important aspects of a system will be well defined by the architecture. The parts that are specified may describe the nominal state of the system and leave out unusual states. This is, to some extent, normal: Architectures are not meant to be complete implementations of a system. Consequently, the notations used to capture architectures do not have to be completely unambiguous, accurate, and precise.

Three key concepts can be used to characterize architectural models: ambiguity, accuracy, and precision.

6.2.1 Ambiguity

Definition. A model is *ambiguous* if it is open to more than one interpretation.

Because conflicting interpretations of a model may lead to misunderstandings, bugs, and errors, it is generally desirable to eliminate ambiguity in design. Incompleteness is a primary reason for ambiguity in models: When some aspect of a system is left unspecified, different stakeholders may make different assumptions about how the gap should be filled in. Architectures are necessarily incomplete: They address *principal* design decisions about a system, not *every* design decision.

For this reason, it is generally impossible to completely eliminate ambiguity in architectural models. Additionally, the costs of attempting to do so will nearly always outweigh the benefits. Therefore, a balance must be struck. A good guideline is to allow aspects of the system to be ambiguous with the consent of appropriate stakeholders, proceeding when they agree that the architecture is "complete enough" and remaining decisions can be made in a future development activity. While this evaluation proceeds, it is useful to specifically identify and document ambiguous aspects of the architecture as a kind of design rationale.

6.2.2 Accuracy and Precision

Many conceptions of accuracy and precision, including dictionary definitions, conflate the two terms. Here, we will adopt an interpretation that more clearly delineates them.

Definition. A model is *accurate* if it is correct, conforms to fact, or deviates from correctness within acceptable limits.

Definition. A model is *precise* if it is specific, detailed, and exact.

Accuracy deals with correctness, while precision deals with exactness. In architectural terms, a model is accurate if it conveys correct information about the modeled system. A model is precise if it conveys a lot of detailed information about the modeled system. It may seem as if these concepts go hand in hand, but in fact they are somewhat orthogonal.

Figure 6-2 graphically depicts the distinction between accuracy and precision as a set of targets that have been shot. Consider each shot to be an assertion about a system being designed. Figure 6-2(a) shows a set of shots (assertions) that are neither accurate nor precise: they are not close together and are not near the target. Architecturally, this represents design decisions that are both incorrect (that is, inaccurate) and vague or general (that is, imprecise). Figure 6-2(b) shows shots that are accurate, but not precise: They are clustered around the target, but are not close together. These assertions are accurate (correct) but vague and lacking detail. Architecturally, this might be a result of ambiguity or correct descriptions of only a few aspects of the system. Figure 6-2(c) shows shots that are precise, but not accurate: They are clustered close together, but they are not near the

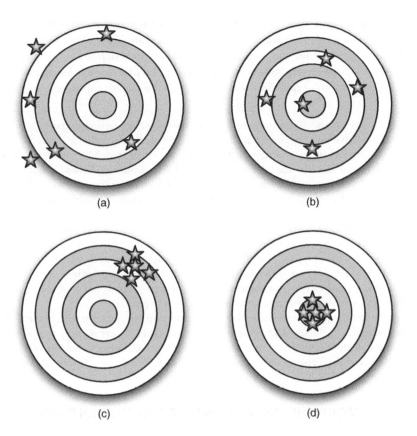

Figure 6-2.
*A graphical
depiction
distinguishing
accuracy and
precision.*

(a)   (b)

(c)   (d)

target. This could be interpreted as assertions about the system that are highly detailed, but wrong. Figure 6-2(d) shows shots that are both precise and accurate: The assertions are both detailed and correct.

In developing an architecture, accuracy should generally be favored over precision. Precision and completeness are, of course, desirable, but later phases of detailed design and implementation will necessarily flesh out the missing detail. However, inaccurate architectural models that mislead stakeholders in these later phases will generally lead to costly errors in later development activities.

Notations and modeling approaches can have a significant effect on the ambiguity, accuracy, and precision of models. Some notations include elements that are purposefully ambiguous—they allow stakeholders to interpret their meaning in the manner most useful to their project. Other notations are based on formal semantics, and encourage less ambiguous and more precise specifications. In these approaches, the designers specify what each element means and how it should be interpreted. Often, these interpretations are built directly into visualization and analysis tools.

Stakeholders can find utility in all kinds of modeling approaches, from the ambiguous and imprecise to those with formal semantics. Approaches that promote reduced ambiguity and increased accuracy and precision are often more costly to use because they have higher learning curves and require more detailed modeling. For these reasons, stakeholders should generally choose notations that allow unambiguous, accurate, and precise modeling of the aspects of the system *that are the most important*. Other approaches can be used for less important aspects of the system. Since no notation will be ideal for modeling every aspect of a system, combinations of notations should generally be used to capture an architecture.

The Illusion of Quality

Ultimately, we use architecture to ensure that the system we are developing attains specific desired qualities: reliability, robustness, maintainability, evolvability, and many others.

Often, stakeholders assume that using a particular notation or modeling approach will (substantially) guarantee that the modeled system will achieve some set of these qualities. This sentiment is embodied in familiar statements such as, "We know we have a good architecture because we designed it using UML," or "Of course our architecture is reliable—it conforms to DoDAF."

The reality is that, in many notations, it is just as easy to model bad design decisions as good ones. For this reason, it is important to understand the limitations of the notations and approaches selected for a project. Not all are created equal; in some notations, for example, it may be possible to formally verify (with the help of tools) that a system is free of deadlock, or that a real-time system will never miss its deadlines. However, compared to more permissive approaches such as UML's, these notations are rarely used in practice.

It is easy to be fooled. Consider a model of a system written in a notation with low ambiguity and high precision. As discussed in Section 6.2.2, it is possible to create very precise system specifications that are nonetheless wrong or simply describe a bad design. Good software is often modeled precisely, but precise models do not necessarily imply that the software is good.

6.3 COMPLEX MODELING: MIXED CONTENT AND MULTIPLE VIEWS

Architecture models are complex artifacts. They attempt to capture all the design decisions about a system that are important to a wide variety of stakeholders. Additionally, different aspects of the same concept will be captured simultaneously, for example, a component's interconnections to other components, its behavior, and its version history. There is simply too much information to deal with all at once, and attempting to do so is not productive: Stakeholders generally want to interact with the parts of the architecture that are most important from their own perspective.

In general, no single approach will be able to capture all the aspects of an architecture for a project. This means that various parts of the architecture may have to be modeled using different approaches. For example, non-functional aspects of a system may be captured using natural language, structure with a component-connector graph, and various component behaviors with statecharts.

6.3.1 Views and Viewpoints

This situation induces the notion of *views* and *viewpoints*.

> *Definition.* A *view* is a set of design decisions related by a common concern (or set of concerns).

> *Definition.* A *viewpoint* defines the perspective from which a view is taken.

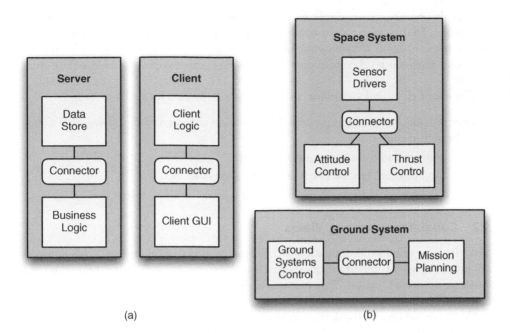

Figure 6-3.
The deployment views of the architectures of two different systems.

(a)   (b)

A view is an instance of a viewpoint for a specific system. Put another way, a viewpoint is a filter for information, and a view is what you see when you look at a system through that filter. For example, consider the domain of systems in which software components are distributed across multiple hosts. The *deployment viewpoint* is a perspective on such systems that captures design decisions related to how components are assigned to hosts. The *deployment view* of a particular system captures how components are assigned to hosts for that particular system.

Figure 6-3 shows the deployment views of two different systems. Figure 6-3(a) shows the deployment view of a client-server system. Figure 6-3(b) shows the deployment view of a distributed space-ground system like Lunar Lander. However, both of these views are taken from the deployment viewpoint; that is, they both capture design decisions dealing with the deployment of components onto hosts.

In general, viewpoints are associated with one concern. Examples of viewpoints that are commonly captured include:

- *Logical Viewpoint:* Captures the logical (often software) entities in a system and how they are interconnected.
- *Physical Viewpoint:* Captures the physical (often hardware) entities in a system and how they are interconnected.
- *Deployment Viewpoint:* Captures how logical entities are mapped onto physical entities.
- *Concurrency Viewpoint:* Captures how concurrency and threading will be managed in a system.
- *Behavioral Viewpoint:* Captures the expected behavior of (parts of) a system.

It is also possible for multiple views to be taken from the same viewpoint for the same system. That is, there might be multiple deployment views for a single system, with different levels of detail. One view might show only top-level components, while another might show both top-level components as well as subcomponents and additional internal structure.

The use of views and viewpoints in modeling is important for several reasons:

- They provide a way to limit presented information to a cognitively manageable subset of the architecture.
- They display related concepts simultaneously.
- They can be tailored to the needs of specific stakeholders.
- They can be used to display the same data at various levels of abstraction.

6.3.2 Consistency among Views

Often, the same or related information will be present in two or more views. This immediately gives rise to an important question: How does one know whether two views are consistent with each other? This requires a definition of consistency with respect to architectural views.

Views are *consistent* if the design decisions that they contain are compatible. Alternatively, consistency can be seen as the absence of inconsistency. An *inconsistency* occurs when two views assert design decisions that cannot both be simultaneously true. Many kinds of inconsistency can arise. Some kinds of inconsistency that might occur in a multiple-view architecture description include the following.

Direct Inconsistencies. These inconsistencies occur when two views assert directly contradictory propositions such as "the system runs on two hosts" and "the system runs on three hosts." These inconsistencies can often be detected by automatic mechanisms that employ appropriate constraints and rules.

Refinement Inconsistencies. These inconsistencies occur when two views of the same system at different levels of detail assert contradictory propositions. For example, a "top level" structural view contains a component that is absent from a structural view that includes subarchitectures. These inconsistencies can also be automatically detected with appropriate consistency rules, provided both the top-level and refined views contain enough information to understand the relationship between the two.

Static Aspects versus Dynamic Aspects. In this inconsistency, a view of a static aspect of a system conflicts with a view of a dynamic aspect. For example, a message sequence chart view might depict the handling of messages by a component that is not contained in the structural view. These inconsistencies can be somewhat harder to automatically detect, depending on how explicit the dynamic aspect's specification is.

Dynamic Aspects. In this inconsistency, two views of dynamic aspects of the system conflict. For example, a message sequence chart depicts a specific interaction between components that is not allowed by the behavioral specifications contained in those components' statecharts. These inconsistencies are often extremely difficult to detect automatically because it would require extensive state exploration or simulations.

Functional versus Non-Functional Aspects. These inconsistencies occur when a non-functional property of a system prescribed by a non-functional view is not met by the design expressed in functional views. For example, a non-functional view of a client-server system may express that the system should be robust, but the physical view of the system may show only a single server with no evidence of failure-handling machinery. These inconsistencies are the most difficult to detect because of the general and abstract nature of non-functional properties.

Figure 6-4 shows two hypothetical views of a distributed Lunar Lander system. The physical view (a) depicts three hosts, a Ground System, a Command Module Computer, and a Lander Computer. However, the deployment view (b) shows components assigned to only two hosts, a Ground System and a Lunar Lander. It is fairly easy to see that something is not right here—there is an inconsistency between the physical and deployment view. The inconsistency fits our above definition—the physical view asserts the design decision that Lunar Lander runs on two hosts, while the deployment view asserts the decision that Lunar Lander runs on three.

This inconsistency is relatively easy to spot just by looking. However, other, more subtle inconsistencies (such as inconsistencies between different behavioral specifications of an architecture) are harder to detect and more costly to fix.

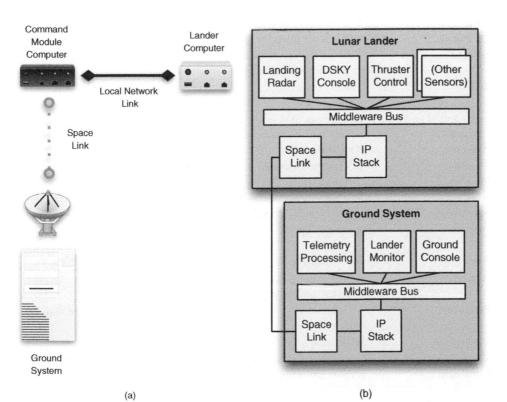

(a)

(b)

Figure 6-4.
A *Lunar Lander system's physical view (a) and logical view (b).*

Detecting, identifying, and resolving inconsistencies among views is a difficult problem. First, stakeholders must agree on what "consistency" means for their particular choice of views and modeling notations. Then, strategies must be employed to locate and deal with inconsistencies. These can range from manual approaches such as inspections and checklists to automated approaches such as model checking and simulation. Chapter 8, which covers architectural analysis, discusses in detail specific approaches for dealing with inconsistency.

Inconsistency is generally, but not always, undesirable. Inconsistencies will arise as a natural part of doing exploratory design—as you design an architecture, parts of it may be temporarily inconsistent as the design evolves. Sometimes, inconsistencies are left in an architecture deliberately upon agreement of the stakeholders to deal with a special case, or because repairing the inconsistency would be too costly.

6.4 EVALUATING MODELING TECHNIQUES

In the past sections, we have explored a number of dimensions that can be used to characterize different modeling techniques. These dimensions can be turned into a rubric for critically thinking about and evaluating different modeling techniques. This rubric will be applied to several techniques in the remainder of this chapter.

Modeling Techniques Rubric		
	Scope and Purpose	What is the scope of the technique? What is it intended to model and what is it *not* intended to model?
	Basic Elements	What are the basic elements or concepts (for example, the "atoms") in the technique? How are these modeled?
	Style	To what extent does the technique support modeling of stylistic constraints, and for what kinds of styles?
	Static and Dynamic Aspects	To what extent does the technique support modeling static aspects of architecture? To what extent does it support modeling dynamic aspects of architecture?
	Dynamic Modeling	To what extent can the model be changed to reflect changes as a system executes?
	Non-Functional Aspects	To what extent does the technique support modeling non-functional aspects of architecture? (Here, we leave out functional aspects because we assume that those will be adequately covered by other parts of the rubric).
	Ambiguity	What measures does the approach take to limit (or allow) ambiguity?
	Accuracy	To what extent does the approach provide support for determining the correctness of models?
	Precision	At what level of detail can the various aspects of architecture be modeled?
	Viewpoints	What viewpoints does the model support?
	View Consistency	To what extent does the approach provide support for determining the consistency of different views expressed in a model?

6.5 SPECIFIC MODELING TECHNIQUES

Architects have at their disposal a panoply of notations and techniques for modeling different aspects of architectures. These techniques vary along many dimensions: what they can model, how precisely they can capture architectural semantics, how good their tool support is, and so on. Which methods are used, and for what purposes, will be largely up to a system's architects and stakeholders. While many approaches for modeling architectures are broadly scoped and applicable to many systems in many domains, it is important not to become dogmatically attached to any one approach.

The next sections discuss and evaluate various approaches that can be used for modeling software architectures. A simple version of the Lunar Lander system is used as a running example to illustrate and compare modeling techniques.

6.5.1 Generic Techniques

These techniques are often used to describe a software architecture in whole or in part, although they were not specifically developed or adapted for this purpose. As such, they tend to be flexible but have few semantics.

Natural Language

Natural languages, such as English, are an obvious way to document architectural design decisions. Natural languages are expressive, but tend to be ambiguous, nonrigorous, and nonformal. Natural language cannot be effectively processed and understood by machines, and thus can only be checked and inspected by humans.

Despite these drawbacks, natural-language modeling can be the best way to capture some aspects of an architecture. For example, non-functional requirements are often captured using natural language since they are abstract and qualitative. Natural language is easily accessible to stakeholders and can be manipulated with common tools such as word processors.

An alternative to using pure natural language is to use a restricted form of it. Users can create and consistently employ a dictionary of terms in order to limit certain kinds of problems (for instance, ambiguity that can arise from using different terms for the same concept, or lack of clarity). Statement templates, which are natural language statements or paragraphs with fill-in-the-blanks parameters can be another way to increase rigor in natural language. However, overusing this strategy has a negative effect—essentially, it creates a domain-specific language without any of the flexibility benefits of natural language.[1]

---

[1]In the early days of computing, some programming language designers believed that programming languages could be improved by making them more like natural language with added syntactic rigor. Thus, languages like COBOL included statements such as, "MULTIPLY X BY 5 GIVING Z," instead of the terser "z = x * 5." Such techniques have fallen out of favor, as they only served to make programs more verbose.

Scope and Purpose	Describing arbitrary concepts with an extensive vocabulary, but in an informal way.
Basic Elements	Any concepts required, no special support for any particular concept.
Style	Stylistic concepts can be described by simply using more general language.
Static and Dynamic Aspects	Both static and dynamic aspects of systems can be modeled.
Dynamic Modeling	Models must be changed by humans and can be rewritten with a tool such as a word processor, but there is no feasible way to tie these models to implementation.
Non-Functional Aspects	Expressive vocabulary available for describing non-functional aspects of systems (although there is no support for verifying them).
Ambiguity	Plain natural language is perhaps the most ambiguous notation available for expressing architectures; techniques such as statement templates and well-defined dictionaries of terms can be used to reduce ambiguity.
Accuracy	Correctness must be evaluated through manual reviews and inspections, and cannot be automated.
Precision	Additional text can be used to describe any aspect of architecture in greater detail.
Viewpoints	All viewpoints (but no specific support for any viewpoint).
View Consistency	Correctness must be evaluated through manual reviews and inspections, and cannot be checked automatically.

Lunar Lander in Natural Language

Here, we introduce a simple three-component version of the Lunar Lander application that will be used throughout the remainder of this chapter to illustrate the use of different modeling approaches.

The Lunar Lander application might be described in natural language as shown in Figure 6-5, which provides a fairly significant amount of information about the Lunar Lander system. For example, the structure of the components and their dependencies is explicitly stated, as well as a description of their behaviors, inputs, outputs, and general responsibilities. The description stops short of specifying certain details that are required for implementing the system. For example, it does not explain the algorithm the *calculation* component uses for its computations, the particular formats of the different data values, anything about the connectors between the components, or what the user interface should look like.

Many different implementations could satisfy this architectural description, and they may not all function identically. This is partially due to the nature of architectural models in general—they document *principal* design decisions, not *all* design decisions. It is also partially due to the ambiguity inherent in natural language specifications. This specification is not the tersest or most understandable way of expressing aspects of this system such as its structure—readers of the specification are likely to build up a mental graph of the system's constituent components as they read, since one is not provided.

The Lunar Lander application consists of three components: a **data store** *component, a* **calculation** *component, and a* **user interface** *component.*

The job of the **data store** *component is to store and allow other components access to the height, velocity, and fuel of the lander, as well as the current simulator time.*

The job of the **calculation** *component is to, upon receipt of a burn rate quantity, retrieve current values of height, velocity, and fuel from the* **data store** *component, update them with respect to the input burn rate, and store the new values back. It also retrieves, increments, and stores back the simulator time. It is also responsible for notifying the calling component of whether the simulator has terminated, and with what state (landed safely, crashed, and so on).*

The job of the **user interface** *component is to display the current status of the lander using information from both the* **calculation** *and the* **data store** *components. While the simulator is running, it retrieves the new burn rate value from the user, and invokes the* **calculation** *component.*

Figure 6-5.
Lunar Lander model in natural language (American English).

Takeaways. Natural language should be used as an adjunct to more rigorous and formal languages, for aspects of architecture where formalism is infeasible or unnecessary. It is particularly good for specifying non-functional properties in a way that almost no other language can match.

Informal Graphical PowerPoint-style Modeling

Tools such as Microsoft PowerPoint (Microsoft Corporation 2007) and OmniGraffle (The Omni Group 2007) provide users with the ability to create decorative diagrams of interconnected shapes through a point-and-click graphical interface. These are ubiquitous and it is easy to use them to create aesthetically pleasing diagrams. The size limitations of such diagrams (one slide, one sheet of paper) help to ensure that they remain suitably abstract.

Informal graphical notations have a lot in common with natural languages—they provide informal, unconstrained ways of expressing ideas (although they primarily use symbols rather than words). Informal graphical diagrams often capture few (if any) semantics. This makes it difficult to reliably interpret the meaning of the diagrams, undermining the key advantages of using an architecture in the first place (communication, analysis, and so on). These diagrams are good for early prototyping and exploration, capturing ideas at an abstract, conceptual level. However, they lack the rigor required for more concrete models.

Scope and Purpose	Arbitrary diagrams composed of graphical and textual elements, with few restrictions on them.
Basic Elements	Geometric shapes, splines, text strings, clip art.
Style	In general, no support.
Static and Dynamic Aspects	Because these models lack architectural semantics, there is no notion of modeling static or dynamic aspects of systems.
Dynamic Modeling	Model formats are generally proprietary and difficult to change outside of their native environment. However, some environments expose externally callable interfaces that allow models to be manipulated programmatically (for example, PowerPoint exposes its models through a COM interface).

Evaluation
Rubric for
Informal
Graphical
Modeling

Non-Functional Aspects	Non-functional aspects can be modeled using natural-language decorations on diagrams.
Ambiguity	As with natural language, ambiguity can be controlled through the use of a controlled symbolic vocabulary or dictionary.
Accuracy	In general, correctness is determined through manual inspection and cannot be checked automatically.
Precision	Modelers can choose an appropriate level of detail; however, they are generally limited by the amount of information that can fit on one diagram or slide.
Viewpoints	Because these models lack architectural semantics, there is no direct support for multiple viewpoints. In theory, a model can show any viewpoint.
View Consistency	In general, consistency is determined through manual inspection and cannot be checked automatically.

Lunar Lander in PowerPoint. There are many ways to express the Lunar Lander architecture in a tool like Microsoft PowerPoint, limited only by the symbol palette available in the tool.

A Lunar Lander architectural model in PowerPoint is shown in Figure 6-6. As with most PowerPoint architecture diagrams, the particular symbology used is not directly explained—there is no underlying semantic model (other than the reader's expectations)

Figure 6-6.
Lunar Lander architectural model in PowerPoint.

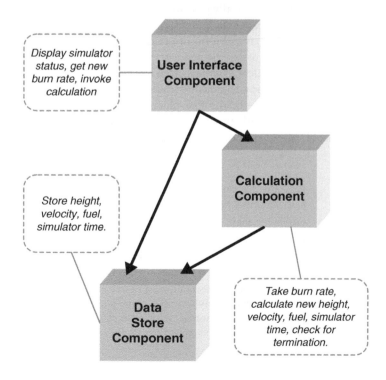

through which to interpret this diagram. The meanings of the three-dimensional boxes, the arrows, and the rounded rectangles are not provided. More serious modeling efforts might provide a symbolic dictionary to accompany such a diagram. However, this can be dangerous: Even when users employ consistent or well-understood symbols, informal diagramming tools cannot provide automated consistency checks or analysis.

The intended interpretation of this particular diagram is that the three-dimensional boxes are software components, the arrows indicate invocation dependencies, and the rounded rectangles are commentary on the intended behavior and responsibilities of the components. Assuming that the reader correctly interprets the meanings of the symbols, this model is in certain ways easier to understand than the natural language model. For example, the componentization of the system and the component dependencies are immediately obvious, and the behaviors are visually connected to the components.

Takeaways. PowerPoint and similar tools are seductive because they make it very easy to create graphical diagrams. However, great care should be taken in using informal graphical diagrams as part of any official architecture description—they can be valuable for early back-of-the-napkin architecture descriptions, but as soon as basic decisions are made, more rigorous notations should be employed for real architecture capture.

The Unified Modeling Language (and Its Cousins)

UML, the Unified Modeling Language (Booch, Rumbaugh, and Jacobson 2005), is the most popular notation for writing down software designs. It is unified in that it combines concepts from earlier notations such as Booch diagrams (Booch, 1986), James Rumbaugh's OMT (Rumbaugh et al. 1990), Ivar Jacobson's OOSE (Jacobson 1992), and David Harel's Statecharts (Harel 1987). UML's main strengths are its large variety of modeling constructs and viewpoints, extensive tool support, and widespread adoption.

UML is a massive notation about which entire books can be and have been written. We summarize its role as an architectural modeling language here. Further information about UML as a standard for software and system modeling is presented in Chapter 16.

UML is an inherently graphical notation, with views consisting of textually annotated graphical symbols. It provides its users with an extremely wide variety of modeling constructs and concepts. UML 2.0 includes thirteen different viewpoints, called "diagrams" in UML parlance. These viewpoints cover many of the dimensions identified earlier in this chapter, including basic architectural elements, stylistic constraints, and static and dynamic aspects of systems.

Much debate has ensued over the years as to UML's suitability for modeling software systems at the architecture level. Early versions of UML (1.0 and 1.1) (Booch, Rumbaugh, and Jacobson 1998) had a strong focus on detailed design—below the level of common architectural constructs such as components and connectors. They were biased toward the design of object-oriented systems that communicate primarily through procedure calls. UML 2.0 significantly expanded UML to provide much better support for higher-level architectural constructs. Existing viewpoints were extended with new elements and entirely new viewpoints were added.

UML's broad range of diagrams makes it an attractive option for modeling all kinds of software systems. However, it is vitally important for architects not to get locked in to

Figure 6-7. *A UML component diagram showing a dependency between two components.*

UML as their one and only modeling solution for architectures, or to overestimate the benefits conferred by using UML.

UML's viewpoints remain mostly focused on design. In many ways, these viewpoints still retain an inherent bias toward object-oriented systems. Some of the viewpoints extend into other life cycle activities, capturing some requirements- and implementation-related aspects. Explicit support is minimal for activities such as testing and maintenance and meta-activities such as management. Architectural decisions can affect any of these aspects of development; this is why additional notations should be used to capture a complete architecture.

Understanding the semantics of UML diagrams is key to making them useful in describing architectural design decisions. UML is more precise than arbitrary diagrams that would be produced in, say, PowerPoint. However, it has been designed to be purposefully ambiguous in many respects so as to increase its generality.

For example, the dashed open-headed arrow is a "dependency" arrow. It indicates that the element at the tail of the arrow has some dependency on the element at the head of the arrow. Figure 6-7 shows a simple UML component diagram with two components. The dashed arrow indicates that the Calculation component is dependent on the Data Store component. However, this could mean any number of things, including:

- Some element of Calculation calls Data Store.
- Instances of Calculation contain a pointer or reference to an instance of Data Store.
- Calculation requires Data Store to compile.
- Calculation's implementation has a method that takes an instance of Data Store's implementation as a parameter.
- Calculation can send messages to Data Store.

And so on, and so on. Most constructs in UML are similarly semantically ambiguous. (It is even unclear what the components in Figure 6-7 refer to: They could be classes in an object-oriented programming language, C modules, Web services, or something else.)

This approach gives UML great flexibility but limits its semantic precision. Fortunately, UML includes facilities that allow its users to define new attributes (called *stereotypes* and *tagged values*) and constraints that can be applied to existing elements to specialize them. Constraints in UML can be specified in any language (including natural language), but a companion language called the Object Constraint Language (OCL) provides a convenient way to write rigorous constraints for UML. A collection of these additional attributes and constraints is known as a UML *profile*. Profiles are generally designed for specific applications, product lines, or domains, and serve to increase the semantic precision of UML diagrams within that scope.

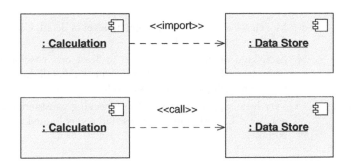

Figure 6-8.
*UML component
diagrams with
more specific
semantics
provided by using
stereotypes.*

Figure 6-8 shows two variants of the component diagram in Figure 6-7. Each of these uses a UML *stereotype* to provide additional detail about the meaning of the dependency arrow. This does not make the dependency arrow completely unambiguous, however—understanding it still relies on the reader's interpretation of "import" or "call." The top diagram indicates that Calculation imports Data Store. The bottom diagram indicates that Calculation calls Data Store. The available selection of stereotypes and their specific meanings are defined by the UML profile in use.

UML diagrams alone do not carry enough information to completely interpret them. Stakeholders may make agreements among themselves about how to interpret particular aspects of UML diagrams on a project and document these agreements in external natural-language documents. Stakeholders should also strongly consider defining or selecting a profile with documented interpretations for the included stereotypes, tagged values, and constraints.

Scope and Purpose	Capture design decisions for a software system using up to thirteen different diagram types.	**Evaluation Rubric for UML**
Basic Elements	A multitude—classes, associations, states, activities, composite nodes, constraints (in OCL) and so on.	
Style	Stylistic constraints can be expressed in the form of OCL constraints or by providing (partial) models in one of the many viewpoints.	
Static and Dynamic Aspects	Includes a number of diagrams for modeling both static (for example, class diagram, object diagram, package diagram) and dynamic aspects (for example, state diagram, activity diagram) of systems.	
Dynamic Modeling	Depends on the modeling environment; in practice very few systems are tied directly to a UML model such that the UML model can be updated as they run.	
Non-Functional Aspects	No direct support, except perhaps in textual annotations.	
Ambiguity	In general, UML elements can mean different things in different contexts. Ambiguity can be reduced through the principled use of UML profiles, including stereotypes, tagged values, and constraints.	
Accuracy	Aside from OCL constraint checking and basic well-formedness checks (that is, no broken links, every element has a name, and so forth), there is no standard for assessing the accuracy of a UML model.	

Precision	Modelers can choose an appropriate level of detail; UML offers wide flexibility in this regard.
Viewpoints	Each kind of diagram represents at least one possible viewpoint; through overloading or partitioning, one kind of diagram can be used to capture multiple viewpoints as well.
View Consistency	Very little support is provided for checking consistency among diagrams; OCL constraints can be used in a very limited fashion for this purpose.

Figure 6-9.
Lunar Lander component diagram in UML.

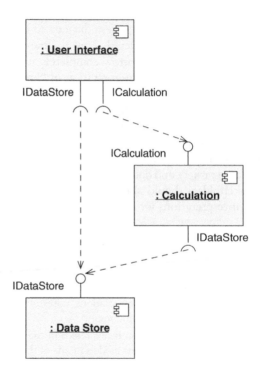

Lunar Lander in UML. UML provides many possible viewpoints from which to model the Lunar Lander architecture. Stakeholders are responsible for choosing which viewpoints are used and how precise each view will be. Here, we will use the component, statechart, and sequence viewpoints to describe the Lunar Lander at roughly the same level of detail as has been shown in the natural language and informal graphical examples.

The component diagram for Lunar Lander might look like Figure 6-9.[2] This diagram looks very similar to the informal graphical diagram, because it largely depicts the same

---

[2]This diagram uses the UML 2 ball-and-socket icons to represent provided and required interfaces, respectively. In earlier versions of UML 2, the socket and ball could be directly graphically joined (without an intervening dependency arrow) to indicate connection, but this diagrammatic style has been deprecated by the UML committee except in composite structure diagrams.

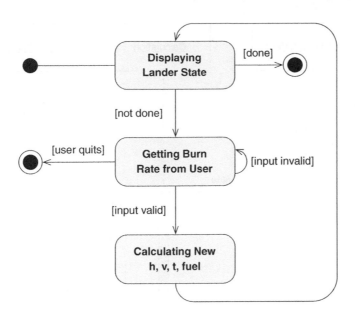

Figure 6-10.
*Lunar Lander
statechart
diagram in
UML.*

aspect of the architecture. Unlike the informal graphical diagram, though, this diagram has a rigorous syntax and some underlying semantics. The symbols used are documented in the UML specification, and have specific meanings. Unlike the unadorned three-dimensional boxes intended to represent components in the PowerPoint view of Lunar Lander, the well-defined UML "component" symbol is used here. This is not to say that the diagram is completely unambiguous—for example, the diagram says nothing about what a component is in this context, or when and how the calls among components are made. Some of these details can be specified in other UML diagrams.

The behavior of the system might be specified in a UML statechart diagram, as shown in Figure 6-10. The start state is indicated by the plain dark circle, and the end state is indicated by the outlined dark circle. Each rounded rectangle represents a state of the system, and arrows represent transitions between the states. The conditions in square brackets indicate guards that constrain when state transitions may occur.

This statechart indicates that the Lunar Lander system begins by displaying the lander state. If the simulation is done, the simulator will stop. Otherwise, the system will request a burn rate from the user. Here, the user may choose to end the program early. Otherwise, if the burn rate is valid, the program will then calculate the new simulator state and display it. This control loop will repeat until the simulation is done.

While this statechart diagram provides a more rigorous and formal description of the system behavior than either the natural language or informal graphical architecture description, it leaves out some important details contained in both those descriptions—namely, which components perform the specified actions. This information can be captured in another UML diagram, such as a UML sequence diagram.

A sequence diagram for the Lunar Lander application might look like Figure 6-11. This diagram depicts a particular sequence of operations that can be performed by the three Lunar Lander components. Sequence diagrams such as this one are not intended to

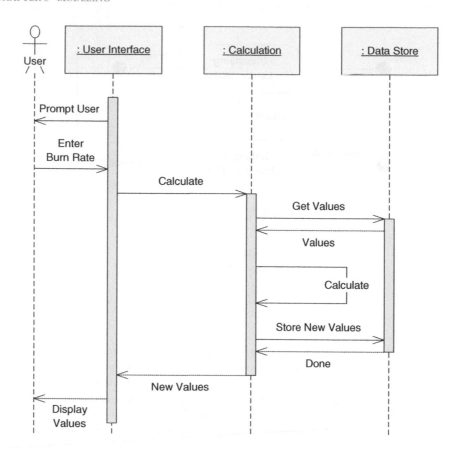

capture all the behavior of a system; rather, they are used to document particular scenarios or use cases. The above diagram depicts one nominal scenario—User Interface gets a burn rate from the user, Calculation retrieves the state of the lander from the Data Store and updates it, and then returns the termination state of the lander to User Interface.

Figure 6-9, Figure 6-10, and Figure 6-11 represent three different views of the Lunar Lander architecture. These views capture both static (structural) and dynamic (behavioral) aspects of the system. A natural question to ask is whether these views are consistent with one another. There is no standard way to answer this question, as there is no universal notion of consistency in UML. Instead, we have to establish our own criteria for consistency and check the views against these criteria. For example, we could check whether each component in the component diagram is represented in the sequence diagram, and whether the calls in the sequence diagram are allowed by the dependency arrows in the component diagram.

Checking the consistency of the statechart and sequence diagrams is a more difficult task. These two diagrams model behavioral aspects of the architecture at substantially different levels. The statechart describes the overall functioning of the system without regard to its structure, while the sequence diagram shows a particular scenario in a different context: the interactions between components. In this case, inspections and stakeholder agreement are probably the best way to determine the consistency of the diagrams.

Takeaways. UML is a syntactically rich notation with extensive tool support. As a way of expressing architectural design decisions, it is superior to a symbols-only notation such as PowerPoint's. However, UML's purposeful ambiguity about the meaning of most of its symbols leaves it open for abuse. Even well-intentioned development groups can interpret the same UML diagrams in different ways, especially when stakeholders are geographically separated and do not have face-to-face opportunities to come to a mutual understanding. When UML is employed, profiles must be developed and used to ensure consistent modeling, although this does not necessarily guarantee unambiguous interpretations. Profiles are not a panacea.

6.5.2 Early Architecture Description Languages

The 1990s spawned nearly a decade of research on how to best capture software architectures. The result of this research was a proliferation of architecture description languages (ADLs), notations developed specifically for software architecture modeling.

During this period, there was substantial debate over what does and does not constitute software architecture. This debate continues today. A parallel debate naturally emerged: Which notations or modeling approaches can be called "architecture description languages?" There is no established litmus test to determine whether a particular notation can or cannot be called an ADL, and there is significant variability in the spectrum of languages that are identified by their creators as ADLs. Nenad Medvidović and Richard Taylor (Medvidović and Taylor 2000) surveyed a wide variety of early ADLs and found that the common denominator among them was explicit support for modeling:

- Components.
- Connectors.
- Interfaces.
- Configurations.

Additionally, they found that languages identified as ADLs tended to be semantically precise but lacked breadth and flexibility. This largely mirrored the prevailing sentiment about software architecture; namely, that it was a high-level structural view of a system extended with rich semantics.

This book takes a much broader view on software architecture. While high-level component-and-connector views are still important when describing a software system's architecture, our definition of architecture as the set of principal design decisions about a system encompasses a much broader range of concepts.

During the 1990s, there was significant debate about whether design notations like UML could be called "architecture description languages." Early versions of UML lacked explicit support for component-and-connector style modeling as well as precise semantics, leading many researchers to conclude that UML was not, in fact, an architecture description language. In our broader conception of architecture, any language used to capture principal design decisions is effectively an architecture description language, including UML.

The early "first-generation" architecture description languages described in this chapter are, for the most part, research projects. None of these is still used actively in practice. We present them here because of their unique contributions to the field of architecture modeling, but their use in practice may prove difficult for extrinsic reasons, such as lack of current tool support.

Darwin

Darwin (Magee et al. 1995) is a general-purpose architecture description language for specifying the structure of systems composed from components that communicate through explicit interfaces. Darwin has a canonical textual representation in which components and their interconnections are described. There is an associated graphical visualization that depicts Darwin configurations in a more accessible but less precise way.

In Darwin, systems are modeled as a set of interconnected components. There is no notion of explicit software connectors in Darwin, but a component that facilitates interactions could be interpreted as a connector. Darwin components expose a set of provided and required services, sometimes called *ports*. Services in Darwin correspond to our notion of provided and required architectural interfaces. Configurations are specified by a set of bindings between interfaces. Darwin also has support for hierarchical composition—that is, components that have internal structures also consisting of components, services, and bindings.

Evaluation Rubric for Darwin	**Scope and Purpose**	Structures of distributed systems that communicate through well-defined interfaces.
	Basic Elements	Components, interfaces (required and provided), links (called bindings), hierarchical composition.
	Style	Limited support through the use of parameterizable constructs.
	Static and Dynamic Aspects	Support for static structural views, additional support for dynamic architectures (for example, those that change at run time) through lazy and direct dynamic instantiation and binding.
	Dynamic Modeling	Not available.
	Non-Functional Aspects	Not available.
	Ambiguity	How Darwin's constructs (for instance, components, interfaces) can be composed and used within a Darwin model is well defined. Their external meaning (for instance, what it means to be a component or an interface) is subject to stakeholder interpretation.
	Accuracy	Darwin can be modeled in the formalism known as the *pi*-calculus, which allows the models to be checked for internal consistency.
	Precision	Detail limited to structural elements and their interconnections.
	Viewpoints	Structural viewpoints, deployment viewpoints through the use of hierarchical composition.
	View Consistency	Not available.

Lunar Lander in Darwin. Darwin is primarily a structural description notation, and we can use it to describe the three-component Lunar Lander's structure. The textual visualization of

```
component DataStore{
    provide landerValues;
}

component Calculation{
    require landerValues;
    provide calculationService;
}

component UserInterface{
    require calculationService;
    require landerValues;
}

component LunarLander{
inst
    U: UserInterface;
    C: Calculation;
    D: DataStore;
bind
    C.landerValues -- D.landerValues;
    U.landerValues -- D.landerValues;
    U.calculationService -- C.calculationService;
}
```

Figure 6-12.
*Lunar Lander
architecture in
Darwin's textual
visualization.*

Lunar Lander in Darwin might be expressed as shown in Figure 6-12. Here, each component is described with explicit provided and required interfaces. The overall application structure is defined using a top-level component with an internal structure; that is, the Lunar Lander application itself is a component containing the `UserInterface`, `Calculation`, and `DataStore` components.

As stated above, Darwin also has a canonical graphical visualization; the model expressed in that visualization might look like Figure 6-13. The use of multiple visualizations to depict the same architectural model will be discussed extensively in the next chapter.

One of the most interesting aspects of Darwin is the set of constructs with which configurations of components can be specified. Many declarative ADLs simply enumerate all the components and bindings in an architecture one by one (and Darwin supports this—the above model of Lunar Lander uses Darwin in this way). However, Darwin also supports the creation of configurations using programming-language-like constructs such as loops. For example, consider a Web application where a number of identical clients are all connecting to the same Web server. We might model this architecture in Darwin shown in Figure 6-14.

Graphically, this model might look like Figure 6-15. In this Darwin model, the actual number of clients is parameterizable. Using these facilities, relatively terse models can be constructed that describe a wide variety of architectures without a great deal of redundancy in the model.

Takeaways. Darwin represents a more rigorous and formal way of capturing an architecture's structure than any notation we have seen thus far in the chapter. It provides

Figure 6-13.
*Lunar Lander
architecture in
Darwin's
graphical
representation.*

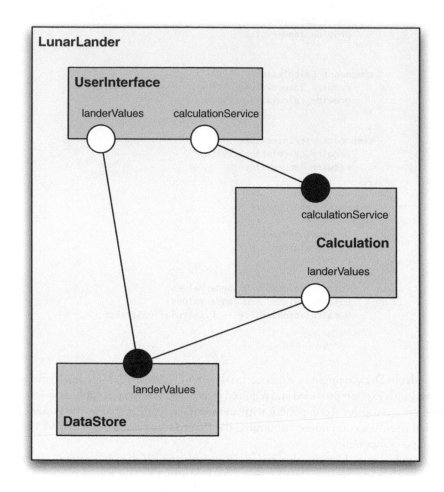

Figure 6-14.
*Model of a
multiclient Web
application in
Darwin's textual
visualization.*

```
component WebServer{
    provide httpService;
}

component WebClient{
    require httpService;
}

component WebApplication(int numClients){
    inst S: WebServer;
    array C[numClients]: WebClient;
    forall k:0..numClients-1{
        inst C[k] @ k;
        bind C[k].httpService -- S.httpService;
    }
}
```

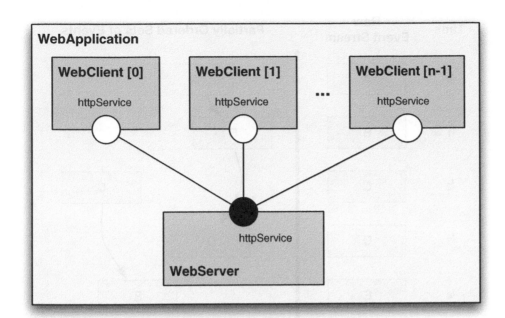

Figure 6-15.
*Model of a
multiclient Web
application in
Darwin's
graphical
visualization.*

a well-defined textual syntax with an associated graphical visualization, along with specific, well-defined semantics. It is not overly complex and can be understood by straightforward reading. For structural modeling, Darwin is an excellent choice. For modeling other aspects of architecture, however, other notations should be used.

Rapide

Rapide (Luckham et al. 1995) is an architecture description language developed to specify and explore dynamic properties of systems composed of components that communicate using events. In Rapide, events are simply the result of an activity occurring in the architecture. Traditional procedure calls are expressed as a pair of events: one for the call and one for the return value.

The power of Rapide comes from its organization of events into partially ordered sets, called POSETs (Luckham 2002). Rapide components work concurrently, emitting and responding to events. There are causal relationships between some events: for example, if a component receives event A and responds by emitting event B, then there is a causal relationship from A → B. Causal relationships between events A and B in Rapide exist when any of the following are true (from the Rapide documentation):

- A and B are generated by the same process.
- A process is triggered by A and then generates B.
- A process generated A and then assigns to a variable v, another process reads v and then generates B.
- A triggers a connection that generates B.
- A precedes C which precedes B (transitive closure).

Figure 6-16.
*Partially ordered
sets of events.*

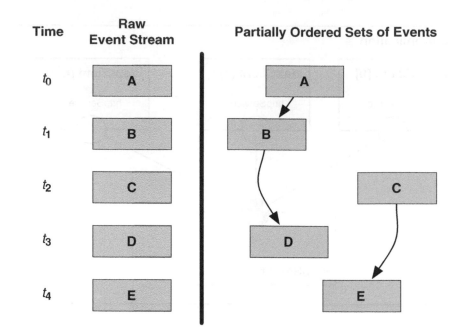

As a program runs, its various components will generate a stream of events over time. Some of these events will be causally related (by one of the above relationships). Some of them may occur around the same time as other events, but be causally unrelated.

Figure 6-16 depicts this situation. The left portion of the figure shows a raw event stream over time: Components in the architecture send events A, B, C, D, and E at times t_0 through t_4, respectively. These events are temporally ordered, but not causally ordered. The right portion of the figure shows the causal ordering of the events. Here, there are two partial order sequences: one consisting of events A, B, and D, and one consisting of events C and E. This is called a *partial* order because not all the events are causally ordered with respect to one another. The fact that B occurred earlier in time than C is only a coincidence—an accident of the scheduler: C could just as easily have occurred before B.

Rapide focuses on capturing dynamic aspects of software architectures. Architecture specifications in Rapide are interesting because they are *executable*. Rapide is accompanied by a tool that allows users to execute the architecture description, in effect simulating the operation of the described system. The result is a graph of events similar to the one depicted above in Figure 6-16, showing events as nodes and causal orderings as directed edges.

Evaluation Rubric for Rapide	Scope and Purpose	Interactions between components in terms of partially ordered sets of events.
	Basic Elements	Architectures (structures), interfaces (components), actions (messages/events), and operations describing how the actions are related to one another.
	Style	Not available.

Static and Dynamic Aspects	Interconnections among components capture static structure of the architecture, actions and behaviors capture dynamic aspects of the architecture.
Dynamic Modeling	Architectural models do not change during run time, although some tools provided limited animation capabilities.
Non-Functional Aspects	Not available.
Ambiguity	The semantics of the behaviors are well defined.
Accuracy	An automatic simulator produces results that can be examined to determine if the architecture's behavior matches expectations. Rapide constraints can also be checked automatically for violations.
Precision	Interconnections and behaviors in terms of event exchanges can be modeled in detail.
Viewpoints	A single structural/behavioral viewpoint.
View Consistency	There is no way to automatically check view consistency (for example, between multiple models describing the same architecture). Inspections can be used to check for consistency across simulator outputs.

Lunar Lander in Rapide. The description of Lunar Lander in Rapide looks, on the surface, similar to a Darwin description: A textual notation resembling a programming language is used to define the components and their interface operations. However, the Rapide description also includes behavioral information. This information is used, along with the application structure, to generate event graphs. Since Rapide is optimized for operating on concurrent applications where multiple threads of control interact, we will use it to evaluate a cooperative two-player version of Lunar Lander.

Such an architecture might be specified as shown in Figure 6-17. This specification begins by defining the types of available components primarily in terms of their interfaces. Each interface has a number of events it can receive and send out ("in" and "out" actions, respectively). Each component has a behavioral specification as well, defining how it reacts to different events. This simple example takes advantage of only a small number of Rapide language features; it has support for defining and manipulating the data that makes up the events as well. A more complex Lunar Lander specification might actually be able to simulate the entire Lunar Lander game, including data, new state calculations, and so on.

At the end of the specification, the system's structure is defined: first components that implement the various interface types, and then links between the component interfaces. This Rapide architecture is relatively straightforward: The players start off by sending an updated burn rate, making their first move of the game. Then, they wait for the display to be updated with new status before making another move. Players are limited to three moves in this system so the game does not go into an infinite loop (as there is no other end-game condition). The `Calculation` component waits for a `SetBurnRate` event. When it receives one, it will fire an internal event, `CalcNewState`, and then fire a `DoSetValues` message to the `DataStore` component to update the game state. When the game state is updated, the `DataStore` fires a `NotifyNewValues` event,

Figure 6-17.
*Cooperative
two-player Lunar
Lander
architecture in
Rapide.*

```
type DataStore is interface
  action in  SetValues();
         out NotifyNewValues();
  behavior
  begin
         SetValues => NotifyNewValues();;
end DataStore;

type Calculation is interface
  action in  SetBurnRate();
         out DoSetValues();
  behavior
         action CalcNewState();
  begin
         SetBurnRate => CalcNewState(); DoSetValues();;
end Calculation;

type Player is interface
  action out DoSetBurnRate();
         in  NotifyNewValues();
  behavior
         TurnsRemaining : var integer := 1;
         action UpdateStatusDisplay();
         action Done();
  begin
         (start or UpdateStatusDisplay) where \
            ($TurnsRemaining > 0) => \
            if ( $TurnsRemaining > 0 ) then \
               TurnsRemaining := $TurnsRemaining - 1; \
               DoSetBurnRate(); \
            end if;;
         NotifyNewValues => UpdateStatusDisplay();;
         UpdateStatusDisplay where $TurnsRemaining == 0 \
            => Done();;
end UserInterface;

architecture lander() is
  P1, P2 : Player;
  C : Calculation;
  D : DataStore;
connect
  P1.DoSetBurnRate to C.SetBurnRate;
  P2.DoSetBurnRate to C.SetBurnRate;
  C.DoSetValues to D.SetValues;
  D.NotifyNewValues to P1.NotifyNewValues();
  D.NotifyNewValues to P2.NotifyNewValues();
end LunarLander;
```

which causes the players' displays to be updated, thus prompting them to make their next moves.

In prose, as described here, this implementation strategy might sound perfectly reasonable. But is it? Rapide's analysis and simulation capabilities can help to make that determination. If we remove the second player from the specification to create only a

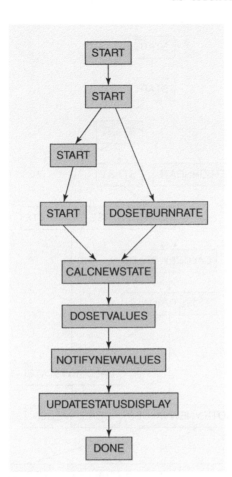

Figure 6-18.
*Event graph of a
one-player Lunar
Lander
architecture.*

one-player game and run the Rapide simulator, a graph like the one in Figure 6-18 is generated. The only counterintuitive aspect of this graph is the group of "start" events that are fired initially. As one of Rapide's primary focus areas is concurrent architectures, it attempts to trigger simultaneous processing by loading the simulation with a number of "start" events at the beginning. For one player, this trace of Lunar Lander looks reasonable.

The two-player version of the graph, shown in Figure 6-19, is more complex. This is to be expected. However, by examining the causality arrows, we can see that something is not quite right. The two pathways are intertwined. Requests are getting intermingled, since there is no locking or transaction support in this design. Furthermore, we can see a fan-out of display updates at the bottom. Each user's display is getting updated twice—once for their own move and once for their partner's. For one turn, this is fine, but recall that the specification calls for the player to make a move each time the display is updated. With more players and more moves come more display updates, and each one will cause a player to try to move, compounding the effect of the interleaving. This is a non–obvious bug in the specification: All players should not reactively move after each screen update. Without

Figure 6-19.
*Event graph of a
two-player Lunar
Lander
architecture.*

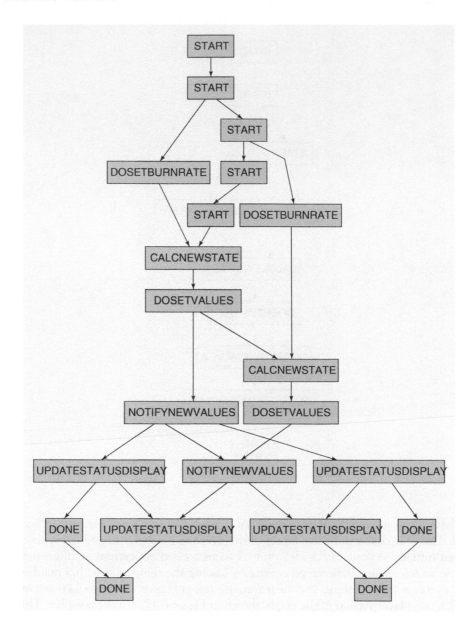

Rapide's graphs, however, it is not easy to see this. This is the kind of bug that can remain undetected until it is discovered late in development during implementation or testing, when it is costly to fix.

Takeaways. Rapide addresses dynamic aspects of architecture directly, and provides tool support for the simulation of those aspects. Stakeholders can directly see how the components in a software system are intended to interact and are dependent upon each other by looking at the results of these simulations. Rapide has several significant drawbacks, however: The notation is arcane, with a steep learning curve, and it lacks support for implementing architectures in a way that is consistent with their specifications.

Wright

Wright (Allen and Garlan 1997) is focused on checking component interactions through their interfaces. Interfaces in Wright are specified using a notation derived from the Communicating Sequential Processes (CSP) formalism (Hoare 1978). Wright specifications can be translated into CSP, and then analyzed with a CSP analysis tool like FDR [Formal Systems (Europe) Ltd. 2005]. These analyses can determine, for example, if connected interfaces are compatible, and whether the system will deadlock. Additionally, Wright has the ability to specify stylistic constraints as predicates over instances.

Scope and Purpose	Structures, behaviors, and styles of systems that are composed of communicating components and connectors.	**Evaluation Rubric for Wright**
Basic Elements	Components, connectors, ports and roles (equivalent to interfaces), attachments, styles.	
Style	Supported through predicates over instance models.	
Static and Dynamic Aspects	Static structural models are annotated with behavioral specifications that describe how components and connectors should both behave and interact.	
Dynamic Modeling	Not available.	
Non-Functional Aspects	Not available.	
Ambiguity	Wright specifications can be translated into the CSP formalism and thus have a formal semantic basis. However, external meaning (for example, specifically what it means to be a component or a connector) is not specified.	
Accuracy	Wright can be modeled in the formalism known as CSP, which allows the models to be automatically checked for, for example, structural consistency and deadlock freedom.	
Precision	Can describe architecture structures and their behavior in great detail (in fact, formal behavioral specifications are required for analysis).	
Viewpoints	Structural viewpoints, behavioral viewpoints, style viewpoints.	
View Consistency	Structural and behavioral aspects are intertwined because behavior is specified as a decoration on structural elements. Consistency between style and instances can be automatically determined with a CSP evaluator.	

Lunar Lander in Wright. The structural aspects of Lunar Lander, modeled in Wright, look similar to depictions we have seen earlier (for example, in a UML component diagram or Darwin). Wright's distinguishing feature is the CSP-based formal specifications of component/connector interfaces and behavior. These specifications can be specified in a notation that resembles mathematical equations, or an equivalent (if less decorative) ASCII notation. Lunar Lander, specified in Wright, might look like that in Figure 6-20.

Figure 6-20.
Lunar Lander modeled in Wright. Some behavioral specifications are omitted for simplicity but the Call connector is fully specified.

```
Component DataStore
    Port getValues (behavior specification)
    Port storeValues (behavior specification)
    Computation (behavior specification)

Component Calculation
    Port getValues (behavior specification)
    Port storeValues (behavior specification)
    Port calculate (behavior specification)
    Computation (behavior specification)

Component UserInterface
    Port getValues (behavior specification)
    Port calculate (behavior specification)
    Computation (behavior specification)

Connector Call
    Role Caller = call‾ → return → Caller[] §
    Role Callee = call → return‾ → Callee[] §
        Caller.call → Callee.call‾ → Glue
    Glue = []Callee.return → Caller.return‾ → Glue
        [] §

Configuration LunarLander
    Instances
        DS : DataStore
        C : Calculation
        UI : UserInterface
        CtoUIgetValues, CtoUIstoreValues, UItoC, UItoDS : Call

    Attachments
        C.getValues as CtoUIgetValues.Caller
        DS.getValues as CtoUIgetValues.Callee

        C.storeValues as CtoUIstoreValues.Caller
        DS.storeValues as CtoUIstoreValues.Callee

        UI.calculate as UItoC.Caller
        C.calulate as UItoC.Callee

        UI.getValues as UItoDS.Caller
        DS.getValues as UItoDS.Callee
End LunarLander.
```

The main thing to notice about this specification is the detailed set of formal specifications of behavior. The CSP formalism, while semantically sound and well-documented, is somewhat arcane and has a steep learning curve that is quite different from learning, for example, a new programming language. The value of these specifications is that properties such as freedom from deadlock can be analyzed, which are difficult or impossible to detect in systems implemented in traditional programming languages.

Takeaways. Wright's formal specifications have an extremely high learning curve and cognitive overhead even for the simplest of systems. The analysis capabilities are powerful, but limited to a small set of properties (such as freedom from deadlock). However, the extensive formal modeling might be worth the effort in, for example, safety-critical systems. Support for refining architectural specifications into implementations is lacking. Like other early ADLs, Wright is not actively used and supported today.

6.5.3 Domain- and Style-Specific ADLs

The ADLs surveyed above are suitable for describing a wide variety of software systems in many domains and architectural styles. However, some ADLs are domain-specific or style-specific, or at least optimized for describing architectures in a particular domain or style.

Domain- and style-specific ADLs are important for several reasons. First, their scope is better tailored to stakeholder needs since they target a particular group of stakeholders, rather than software and systems developers in general. Second, they are able to leave out unnecessary details and excessively verbose constructs because there is little need for genericity. Assumptions about the domain or style can be directly encoded into the ADL's semantics instead of being repeated in every model. For example, if a particular style mandates the use of a single kind of connector between each pair of linked components, there is no need to include the notion of a connector in the ADL—the ADL's users and tool set can just assume that such connectors exist on each link implicitly.

Examples of domain- and style-specific ADLs include Koala, Weaves, and AADL. We have discussed Koala previously; it is an ADL used to model families of consumer electronics devices. Weaves is both an architectural style and an associated ADL for modeling systems composed of components that interact through streams of objects. AADL is an industrial ADL tailored for modeling embedded, real-time systems (both hardware and software).

Koala

Koala (van Ommering et al. 2000) was developed by Philips Electronics to capture the architecture of consumer electronics devices such as televisions, VCRs, and DVD players. It is, to a large extent, a domain-specific ADL—it was developed for the specific use of one company for modeling software in a single domain to address specific issues within that domain. The software systems that Koala models are composed of interconnected software components that communicate via explicit provided and required interfaces.

Semantically and syntactically, Koala is a descendant of Darwin. It uses Darwin's structural concepts of input and output ports, but expands on them through the addition of constructs to support product-line architectures. Product lines were introduced earlier, in Chapter 1. Product lines are prevalent in the consumer electronics domain, where a single product like a television may have a host of feature variations: diagonal size, audio/video inputs and outputs, and optional components such as integrated VCRs, DVD players, or both. Separately documenting the software architectures of each of these products would be redundant and error-prone, since substantially the same elements would be repeated over and over again in each product. Koala addresses this by having specific constructs in the language for explicitly defining points of variation. In this way, multiple products can be described with a single model, with differences between the products encoded as variation points.

The product-line concepts in Koala will be discussed in detail later in this book, specifically in Chapter 15. We defer the discussion of the specifics of the notation until then; interested readers should skip ahead. The evaluation rubric for Koala is presented here for completeness.

Evaluation Rubric for Koala		
Scope and Purpose	Capturing the structure, configuration, and interfaces of components in the domain of embedded consumer electronics devices.	
Basic Elements	Components, interfaces, and constructs for specifying explicit points of variation: diversity interfaces, switches, and multiplexers.	
Style	Koala descriptions capture the architectures of related, variant products simultaneously, and this might be seen as defining a narrow architectural style.	
Static and Dynamic Aspects	Only static structure and interfaces are modeled.	
Dynamic Modeling	Although points of variation are defined statically in the architecture, the selection of variants could change at run time.	
Non-Functional Aspects	Not explicitly modeled.	
Ambiguity	Koala elements are concrete and closely mapped to implementations.	
Accuracy	Koala models have well-defined rules and patterns of interconnection. Koala elements are also closely mapped to implementations. Errors in models should be relatively easy to identify by looking for pattern violations or implementation problems such as compiler errors.	
Precision	The configuration of a system is well defined in a Koala model, but other aspects of a system are not specified.	
Viewpoints	Structural viewpoint with explicit points of variation.	
View Consistency	In general, Koala specifications do not include multiple views.	

Weaves

Weaves (Gorlick and Razouk 1991) is both an architectural style and an accompanying notation. Weaves is used to model systems of communicating small-grain "tool fragments" that process objects of data. Weaves can be seen as a variant of the pipe-and-filter style with three significant differences. First, Weaves tool fragments process object streams instead of pipe-and-filter's byte streams. Second, Weaves connectors are explicitly sized object queues, whereas pipe-and-filter connectors are implicit pipes. Weaves connectors serve to facilitate the transfer of both data and control among components. They receive objects from input ports, return control to the calling tool fragment, and then pass the object to tool fragments on output ports in a separate thread of control. Third, Weaves tools can have multiple inputs and outputs, whereas pipe-and-filter components have one input and one output.

Figure 6-21 shows a basic architecture expressed in the Weaves notation. The component Tool Fragment 1 outputs a stream of objects to an explicit queue connector Q1, which forks the stream and forwards the objects to both Tool Fragment 2 and Tool Fragment 3. As is obvious from this diagram, the Weaves notation is graphical and minimalist: Components are represented by shadowed boxes and queue connectors are represented by plain boxes; configurations are expressed using directed arrows connecting components and connectors.

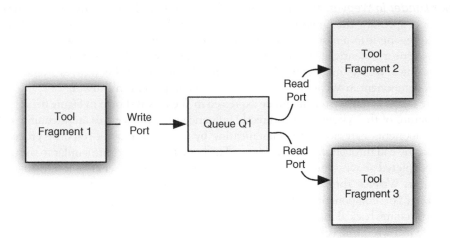

Figure 6-21.
*A basic weave in
the Weaves
notation.*

Although the Weaves notation is minimal, it is adequate to serve as a description nota-tion for the Weaves style. Here, additional complexity is unnecessary: Weaves' extreme simplicity and straightforwardness makes it easy to understand and interpret, and the semantic interpretations of the few elements are provided by the style itself.

Scope and Purpose	The structure and configuration of components in architectures that conform to the Weaves architectural style.	**Evaluation Rubric for Weaves**
Basic Elements	Components, connectors (queues), and directed interconnections.	
Style	Weaves models conform to the Weaves architectural style; the con-straints of that particular style are implicit in the model.	
Static and Dynamic Aspects	Only static structure is modeled.	
Dynamic Modeling	Although there is no direct support for dynamic modeling, the Weaves style establishes a close correspondence between components in the architectural model and components in the implementation; changes tracked in one can be straightforwardly applied to the other.	
Non-Functional Aspects	The Weaves style induces certain non-functional properties on systems but these are not explicitly modeled.	
Ambiguity	The meaning of Weaves elements is well defined and not ambiguous.	
Accuracy	Errors in models are limited to broken links and interconnection prob-lems, which are easy to identify. It should be easily possible to determine whether implementations correspond to Weaves models since there is a close correspondence established by the style.	
Precision	The configuration of components and connectors in a system is well defined in a Weaves model, but other aspects of a system are not specified.	
Viewpoints	Structural viewpoint.	
View Consistency	In general, Weaves specifications do not include multiple views.	

Lunar Lander in Weaves. Because Weaves is both a style and an architecture description notation, expressing the Lunar Lander architecture in Weaves means something different from expressing it in a more style-neutral notation such as UML or Darwin. The actual models are nearly identical, but even though the models are similar, their meanings are not. Interpreting a Weaves model must be done through the lens of the Weaves architectural style: A component in Weaves is not the same as a component in Darwin.

The Lunar Lander system might be expressed in Weaves as shown in Figure 6-22. Here, the structure of the system itself is directly influenced by the Weaves architectural style. The components here are not communicating by means of request-response procedure calls, but instead through streams of objects. The basic flows of data are similar to the other models depicted above. One notable difference is the explicit presence of return channels for data: in Weaves, the fact that a request travels from the `User Interface` to the `Calculation` component (in the above model, through queue Q1) does not imply that a response comes back along the same path. This response's path must be explicitly specified and have its own queue (Q2 in the model).

Figure 6-22.
*Model of the
Lunar Lander
application in
Weaves.*

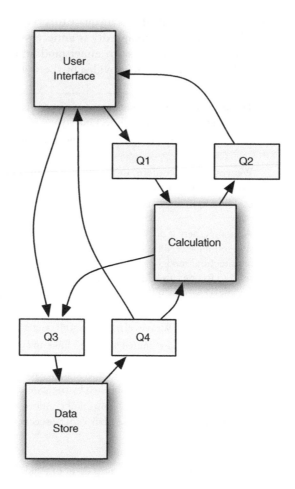

Another interesting characteristic of the Weaves model is that it provides information about structural connections, but does not capture aspects of how those connections are used (for example, the sequences or protocols of objects that are passed through them). These details could be specified in an additional model, in natural language or a more formal notation. To elaborate the model above, we might include the following natural language specification:

> The connection from *User Interface* to *Calculation* (via Q1) carries objects that include a burn rate and instruct the calculation component to calculate a new lander state. The connection from *Calculation* to *User Interface* (via Q2) indicates when the calculation is complete and also includes the termination state of the application. The connections from *User Interface* and *Calculation* to Data Store (via Q3) carry objects that either update or query the state of the lander. The connections back to *User Interface* and *Calculation* from *Data Store* (via Q4) carry objects that contain the lander state, and are sent out whenever the state of the lander is updated.

Takeaways. Weaves shows how binding a notation to a particular style can greatly simplify that notation. Syntactically, Weaves diagrams are extraordinarily simple (even simpler than Darwin diagrams). Unlike Darwin or other general-purpose ADLs, however, the constructs in Weaves diagrams have more specific meanings. The connection from a read port to a write port does not mean just any kind of data or control flow. Rather, it implies a very specific notion of control and data flow involving object streams passed by components running in independent threads of control. When a style is being used, tailored style-specific notations can significantly reduce the cognitive overhead of specifying and interpreting architecture models.

The Architecture Analysis and Design Language (AADL)

The Architecture Analysis and Design Language (AADL, formerly the Avionics Architecture Description Language) (Feiler, Lewis, and Vestal 2003) is an architecture description language for specifying system architectures. While its historical name indicates that its initial purpose was for modeling avionics systems, the notation itself is not specifically bound to that domain—instead, it contains useful constructs and capabilities for modeling a wide variety of embedded and real-time systems such as automotive and medical systems. It is an outgrowth of the earlier MetaH architecture description language (Binns et al. 1996) developed by Honeywell.

Like many of the other ADLs we have surveyed, AADL can describe the structure of a system as an assembly of components, though AADL has special provisions for describing both hardware and software elements, and the allocation of software components to hardware. It can describe interfaces to those components for both the flow of control and data. It can also capture non-functional aspects of components (such as timing, safety, and reliability attributes).

Syntactically, AADL is primarily a textual language, accompanied by a graphical visualization and a UML profile for capturing AADL information in different ways. The syntax of the textual language is defined using Backus-Naur Form (BNF) production rules.

The basic structural element in AADL is the component. AADL components are defined in two parts: a component *type* and a component *implementation*. A component type defines the interfaces to a component—how it will interact with the outside world. A component implementation is an instance of a particular component type. There may be many instances of the same component type. The component implementation defines the component's interior—its internal structure and construction, and so on. One additional element that affects components is a component's *category*. AADL defines a number of categories (or kinds) of components; these can be hardware (for example, memory, device, processor, bus), software (for example, data, subprogram, thread, thread group, process), or composite (for example, system). The category of a component prescribes what kinds of *properties* can be specified about a component or component type. For example, a thread may have a period and a deadline, whereas memory may have a read time, a write time, and a word size.

AADL is supported by a growing base of tools, including a set of open-source plug-ins for the Eclipse software development environment that provide editing support and import/export capabilities through the Extensible Markup Language (XML) (Bray, Paoli, and Sperberg-McQueen 1998). An additional set of plug-ins is available for analyzing various aspects of AADL specifications—for example, whether all the elements are connected appropriately, whether resource usage by the various components exceeds available resources, and whether end-to-end flow latencies exceed available time parameters.

Evaluation Rubric for AADL		
	Scope and Purpose	Multilevel models of interconnected hardware and software elements.
	Basic Elements	Myriad hardware and software elements: networks, buses, ports, processes, threads, and many others.
	Style	No explicit support.
	Static and Dynamic Aspects	Captures primarily static aspects of a system, although properties can capture some dynamic aspects.
	Dynamic Modeling	No explicit support.
	Non-Functional Aspects	User-defined properties can capture non-functional aspects, but these cannot be automatically analyzed.
	Ambiguity	Elements such as processes and buses have real-world or physical analogs with well-understood semantics. Properties add detail about behavior to reduce ambiguity.
	Accuracy	Structural and other properties can be automatically analyzed with sufficiently annotated models.
	Precision	Properties on elements specify characteristics of each element with detail sufficient for analysis.
	Viewpoints	A number of interconnected hardware and software viewpoints: system, processor, process, thread, network, and so on.
	View Consistency	The Open Source AADL Tool Environment (OSATE) includes several plug-ins for various consistency checks.

Lunar Lander in AADL. AADL captures the hardware and software elements of a system in great detail, and relates them all to one another. As such, AADL specifications that capture all these elements can become large. Because of this, here we model only a part of the Lunar Lander system: the Calculation component and its connection to the Data Store component. In this version of Lunar Lander, the two components are connected by a physical Ethernet bus. Also, this is a real-time version of Lunar Lander—instead of operating only when the user inputs a burn rate, the calculation component periodically queries and updates the Data Store component at regular intervals. Here, perhaps the burn rate is not input from the user at the keyboard, but read at periodic intervals from a sensor connected to a burn-rate knob. This is more consistent with a sense-compute-control architectural style.

This part of the Lunar Lander system expressed in AADL might look like Figure 6-23. The first thing to note about this model is the level of detail at which the architecture is described. A component (`calculation_type.calculation`) runs on a physical processor (`the_calculation_processor`), which runs a process (`calculation_process_type.one_thread`), which in turn contains a single thread of control (`calculation_thread`), all of which can make two kinds of request-

```
data lander_state_data
end lander_state_data;

bus lan_bus_type
end lan_bus_type;

bus implementation lan_bus_type.ethernet
properties
  Transmission_Time => 1 ms .. 5 ms;
  Allowed_Message_Size => 1 b .. 1 kb;
end lan_bus_type.ethernet;

system calculation_type
features
  network        : requires bus access lan_bus.calculation_to_datastore;
  request_get    : out event port;
  response_get   : in event data port lander_state_data;
  request_store  : out event port lander_state_data;
  response_store : in event port;
end calculation_type;

system implementation calculation_type.calculation
subcomponents
  the_calculation_processor : processor calculation_processor_type;
  the_calculation_process : process calculation_process_type.one_thread;
connections
  bus access network -> the_calculation_processor.network;
  event data port response_get -> the_calculation_process.response_get;
  event port the_calculation_process.request_get -> request_get;
  event data port response_store -> the_calculation_process.response_store;
properties
  Actual_Processor_Binding => reference
              the_calculation_processor applies to the_calculation_process;
end calculation_type.calculation;

processor calculation_processor_type
features
  network : requires bus access lan_bus.calculation_to_datastore;
end calculation_processor_type;
```

Figure 6-23.
Partial Lunar Lander model in AADL.

(Continued)

Figure 6-23.
(*Continued*)

```
process calculation_process_type
features
   request_get    : out event port;
   response_get   : in event data port lander_state_data;
   request_store  : out event data port lander_state_data;
   response_store : in event port;
end calculation_process_type;

thread calculation_thread_type
features
   request_get    : out event port;
   response_get   : in event data port lander_state_data;
   request_store  : out event data port lander_state_data;
   response_store : in event port;
properties
   Dispatch_Protocol => periodic;
end calculation_thread_type;

process implementation calculation_process_type.one_thread
subcomponents
   calculation_thread : thread client_thread_type;
connections
   event data port response_get -> calculation_thread.response_get;
   event port calculation_thread.request_get -> request_get;
   event port response_store -> calculation_thread.response_store;
   event data port request_store -> request_store;
properties
   Dispatch_Protocol => Periodic;
   Period => 20 ms;
end calculation_process_type.one_thread;
```

response calls through ports (`request_get/response_get, request_store/ response_store`) over an Ethernet bus (`lan_bus_type.ethernet`). Each of these different modeling levels is connected through composition, mapping of ports, and so on. This level of detail emphasizes the importance of tools, such as graphical editors, for modeling this information in a more understandable fashion.

The second thing to note about this specification is the use of properties to define specific characteristics of some of the elements (for example, the calculation process runs periodically, every 20ms). In a complete system specification, these properties would be even more detailed and elaborate, and could be used by tools to answer questions about availability and timing that are critical in a real-time context.

Takeaways. AADL is a high-cost, high-value notation. The syntax and capabilities of AADL are the product of a significant amount of thought and development effort, and the kinds of analyses that can be done on AADL specifications are nontrivial. However, while users leverage the effort of the AADL developers, they also incur their own costs: AADL specifications are complex and extensive, even for small systems. This, in itself, entails significant risks and costs for users. For the specific domain in which AADL is positioned (embedded real-time systems), these costs may be worth it: These systems are often safety-critical and expensive or impossible to redeploy.

6.5.4 Extensible ADLs

There is a natural tension between the expressiveness of general-purpose modeling languages such as UML and the semantic power of more specialized ADLs such as Wright, Weaves, and Rapide. On one hand, architects need the ability to model a wide variety of architectural concerns. On the other hand, they need semantically precise languages to reduce ambiguity and increase analyzability. Furthermore, as we have discussed, architectural concerns and product needs can vary widely from project to project. One solution is to use multiple notations, each addressing a different set of architectural concerns. However, this creates difficulty in keeping the different models consistent and establishing traceability between models. Additionally, even using multiple notations, there may be certain concerns that cannot be adequately captured in any existing notation. Extensible architecture description languages can be used to combine the flexibility of generic languages with the analyzability and precision of semantically rich languages.

Extensible ADLs generally provide a basic set of constructs for describing certain common architectural concerns (for example, components and connectors). Additionally, they also include support (through the notation and associated tools) for extending the notation's syntax to support new, user-defined constructs. In some cases, the extensions may only modify the existing base constructs. Other notations allow users to create entirely new constructs and concepts.

The basic approach to employing an extensible ADL is as follows:

1. Determine which concerns can be modeled using the existing (baseline) capabilities of the ADL.

2. For those concerns that cannot be modeled using the baseline capabilities, choose how to extend the ADL to support their modeling (or reuse an extension developed by another user).

3. Extend the ADL and its supporting tools as necessary to support the modeling of the unique features.

Effectively, extensible ADLs can be seen as "domain-specific ADL factories." Through extension mechanisms, users can tailor these ADLs to meet the needs of their particular domain or project. Examples of extensible ADLs include Acme, ADML, and xADL.

Acme

Acme (Garlan, Monroe, and Wile 1997) is perhaps the earliest example of an ADL that emphasized extensibility. Acme has a base set of seven constructs: *components* and *connectors*, *ports* and *roles* (roughly equivalent to this book's notion of interfaces on components and connectors, respectively), *attachments* (equivalent to this book's notions of links), *systems* (configurations of components, connectors, ports, roles, and attachments), and *representations* (inner architectures for components and connectors). These constructs provide a vocabulary for expressing structural design decisions about a system: basically, the system's component and connector makeup in a box-and-arrow form.

Extensibility in Acme is derived through the use of *properties*. Properties are decorations that can be applied to any of the basic seven kinds of elements. Properties are optionally typed name-value pairs. Names are simple strings, and the values should conform to the property's type, if it has one. Acme includes a number of simple property types (integers,

Booleans, and so on), as well as the ability to define custom types. Either way, from Acme's point of view, properties and their values are uninterpreted. It is up to user-written tools to parse these properties (and any internal structure they contain) and do something useful with the contents (for example, provide analysis or visualization capabilities).

Originally, it was anticipated that Acme's primary use would be as an architecture *interchange* language, rather than an ADL or even an extensible ADL. That is, developers of other ADLs such as Wright and Rapide would develop translators that mapped their languages to and from Acme: In this way, models could be interchanged among many different tools for, say, analysis. This strategy was never applied on a wide scale, however, possibly because of substantial semantic differences and conflicts among target ADLs.

Evaluation Rubric for Acme		
	Scope and Purpose	Modeling the structural aspects of a software architecture, with the addition of properties to define other aspects.
	Basic Elements	Components, connectors, ports and roles (interfaces), attachments (links), representations (internal structure), and properties.
	Style	Stylistic similarities can be modeled through the use of Acme's type system.
	Static and Dynamic Aspects	Static structure is modeled natively, dynamic properties can be captured by decorating the static elements with formatted properties.
	Dynamic Modeling	A software library, AcmeLib, allows Acme models to be manipulated programmatically.
	Non-Functional Aspects	Properties can capture non-functional aspects, but these cannot be automatically analyzed.
	Ambiguity	The use of various elements (for example, components and connectors) is well defined, but what they mean externally (for example, what it means to be a component) is not defined. In general, Acme properties are not interpreted and can introduce ambiguity if not accompanied by tools or documentation.
	Accuracy	The use of various elements (for example, components and connectors) is well defined. Typing can be used to check whether elements have particular properties, but external tools are required to check the contents of properties.
	Precision	Properties can annotate the existing element types with whatever detail is required, but it is not generally possible to define new kinds of architectural elements.
	Viewpoints	Natively, structural viewpoints are supported; properties can be used to provide additional viewpoints.
	View Consistency	External tools must be developed to check the consistency of views.

Lunar Lander in Acme. The basic specification of Lunar Lander in Acme is similar to models shown above. It is largely structural and includes components, connectors, ports, roles, and attachments. Lunar Lander, specified in Acme, might look like Figure 6-24.

```
//Global Types
Property Type returnsValueType = bool;

Connector Type CallType = {
  Roles { callerRole; calleeRole; };
  Property returnsValue : returnsValueType;
};

System LunarLander = {
  //Components
  Component DataStore = {
    Ports { getValues; storeValues; }
  };
  Component Calculation = {
    Ports { calculate; getValues; storeValues; }
  };
  Component UserInterface = {
    Ports { getValues; calculate; }
  };

  // Connectors
  Connector UserInterfaceToCalculation : CallType {
    Roles { callerRole; calleeRole; };
    Property returnsValue : returnsValueType = true;
  };
  Connector UserInterfaceToDataStore : CallType {
    Roles { callerRole; calleeRole; };
    Property returnsValue : returnsValueType = true;
  };
  Connector CalculationToDataStoreS : CallType {
    Roles { callerRole; calleeRole; };
    Property returnsValue : returnsValueType = false;
  };
  Connector CalculationToDataStoreG : CallType {
    Roles { callerRole; calleeRole; };
    Property returnsValue : returnsValueType = true;
  };

  Attachments {
    UserInterface.getValues to UserInterfaceToDataStore.callerRole;
    UserInterfaceToDataStore.calleeRole to DataStore.getValues;

    UserInterface.getValues to UserInterfaceToDataStore.callerRole;
    UserInterfaceToDataStore.calleeRole to DataStore.getValues;

    UserInterface.calculate to UserInterfaceToCalculation.callerRole;
    UserInterfaceToCalculation.calleeRole to Calculation.calculate;

    Calculation.storeValues to  CalculationToDataStoreS.callerRole;
    CalculationToDataStoreS.calleeRole to DataStore.storeValues;

    Calculation.getValues to CalculationToDataStoreG.callerRole;
    CalculationToDataStoreG.calleeRole to DataStore.getValues;
  };
};
```

Figure 6-24.
*Structural Acme
model of the
Lunar Lander
application.*

One interesting thing to note about this model is its verbosity, especially compared to some earlier models. This is a result of two key decisions made by the Acme designers. First, the Acme language is domain-neutral: little can be abbreviated out of the model, because the underlying Acme semantics make few assumptions that allow information to be conveyed implicitly. Second, the Acme designers intended Acme models to be edited through graphical tools and developed an environment called AcmeStudio that allows users to design Acme structures using a GUI interface rather than writing the complete textual description of the model in a text editor. This limits the amount of additional effort Acme users must expend to deal with Acme's verbosity.

A second thing to notice about the model is the use of properties. In this basic model, only one kind of property is used: Each procedure call connector is annotated with a property indicating whether or not the operation has a return value. This might be useful to designers looking to make a partially asynchronous version of Lunar Lander: Calls without return values may be able to return control to the caller without waiting for their completion. Acme's type system is used to declare a connector and a property type, such that regularity can be imposed over connectors and properties that are similar (for example, all connectors in the above Lunar Lander model are of the same type: CallType). Types in Acme work in a manner similar to stereotypes in a UML profile: They allow the user to set expectations on instance elements that can be checked later.

Compared to the other Lunar Lander models above, this basic Acme model is not very innovative. However, additional properties can add detail to this model in a number of ways, depending on the stakeholder's needs. For example, we might say more about how the DataStore component stores its data, as shown in Figure 6-25. This extended description of the component is intended to indicate that the DataStore component should store its data in a non-replicated table called "LanderTable" in a relational database. However, the fact that the model uses these particular property names and values is not a standard: Tools and stakeholders must be informed about which properties to expect and how to process their values.

Takeaways. Notwithstanding the relative failure of architectural interchange, the notion that extensibility should be a primary concern in ADL development is a good one—it is an explicit recognition that there cannot be a one-size-fits-all ADL. Property-based decorations as an extensibility mechanism provide a degree of flexibility, but the breadth of architectural concerns that stakeholders want to capture requires the ability to define new first-class constructs.

The Architecture Description Markup Language (ADML)

The Architecture Description Markup Language (ADML) (Spencer 2000) is an XML-based architecture description language whose syntax is derived from Acme. It was originally developed by the MicroElectronics and Computer Technology Consortium (MCC) and is maintained as a standard by the Open Group. Semantically, the two are nearly identical, with ADML's primary addition being support for meta-properties. In ADML, meta-properties provide a mechanism by which users can specify the properties (and property types) that should be present on particular elements.

```
Property Type StoreType = enum { file, relationalDatabase, objectDatabase };

Component DataStore = {
  Ports {
    getValues; storeValues;
  };

  Property storeType : StoreType = relationalDatabase;
  Property tableName : String = "LanderTable";
  Property numReplicas: int = 0;
};
```

Figure 6-25.
*Extended
definition of the
Lunar Lander*
`DataStore`
*component in
Acme.*

Using the Extensible Markup Language (XML) as the basis for an architecture modeling notation confers several benefits. XML provides a standard framework for expressing the syntax of notations. It is well suited to describing hierarchical organizations of concepts, and internal references can be used to create "pointers" from one element to another. A significant practical benefit of the use of XML is the panoply of off-the-shelf commercial and open-source tools that are available for parsing, manipulating, and visualizing XML documents. Using these tools can significantly reduce the amount of time and effort needed to construct architecture-centric tools such as analyzers, editors, and so on.

XML can be used to create languages with extensible syntax. However, early XML standards provided limited support for this. ADML's syntax is defined using an XML document type definition (DTD), one of the earliest XML meta-languages, which uses production rules to define syntax. XML DTDs have been used to create extensible languages, but the mechanisms are somewhat cumbersome. Instead, ADML provides its extensibility through the same mechanism as Acme—name-value pair properties applied to a core set of elements.

Lunar Lander in ADML. Because ADML is so similar to Acme, we will not provide a complete ADML description for the Lunar Lander application. The description of the `DataStore` component in ADML might look like Figure 6-26. Although the semantic content of this ADML snippet is virtually identical to its Acme counterpart, the use of XML as a standard syntactic framework opens this specification up to a much wider array of tools such as parsers and editors that would not necessarily be otherwise available (or as ubiquitous). One obvious drawback is that by employing XML, the already verbose Acme description becomes even denser. This reflects the overall attitude of XML in general—computing resources and data storage have become inexpensive and plentiful,

```
<Component ID="datastore" name="Data Store">
  <ComponentDescription>
    <ComponentBody>
      <Port ID="getValues"   name="getValues"/>
      <Port ID="storeValues" name="storeValues"/>
    </ComponentBody>
  </ComponentDescription>
</Component>
```

Figure 6-26.
*Description of
one Lunar
Lander
component in
ADML.*

and editing tools have become ubiquitous. Conservation of data bytes is no longer a driving force in language design.

Takeaways. XML provides many extrinsic benefits for architecture modeling, and nearly all architecture description notations still under development at least have the option to import from and export to XML. ADML does not take advantage of XML's own extensibility mechanisms, and instead provides extensibility by simply encoding Acme's name-value pair properties into XML.

xADL: An Extensible XML-based Architecture Description Language

xADL (Dashofy, van der Hoek, and Taylor 2005) is an attempt to provide a platform upon which common modeling features can be reused from domain to domain and new features can be created and added to the language as first-class entities (not just extensions to other entities as with Acme and ADML). Like ADML, xADL is an XML-based language. That is, every xADL model is a well-formed and valid XML document. The main difference is that unlike ADML, xADL fully leverages XML's extensibility mechanisms for its language extensions.

The syntax of the xADL language is defined in a set of XML schemas. XML schemas are similar to DTDs in that they provide a format in which to define the syntax of a language. Whereas DTDs define document syntax through production rules, XML schemas define syntax through a set of data types, similar to the way data structures are defined in an object-oriented programming language. Like classes in an object-oriented programming language, XML schema data types can be extended through inheritance. Derived data types can be declared in separate schemas. Through this mechanism, data types declared in one schema can be extended in a different schema to add new modeling features.

Syntactically, the xADL language is the composition of all the xADL schemas. Each xADL schema adds a set of features to the language. The constructs in each schema may be new top-level constructs or they may be extensions of constructs in other schemas. Breaking up the feature set in this way has several advantages. First, it allows for *incremental adoption*—users can use as few or as many features as makes sense for their domain. Second, it allows for *divergent extension*—users can extend the language in novel, even contradictory ways to tailor the language for their own purposes. Third, it allows for *feature reuse*—because feature sets are defined in XML schema modules, schemas can be shared among projects that need common features without each group having to develop its own (probably incompatible) representations for common concepts.

From time to time, new schemas are added to xADL as they are developed, by both its creators and outside contributors. Current xADL schemas are shown in the box.

Current xADL Schemas	*Schema*	*Features*
	Structure and Types	Defines basic structural modeling of prescriptive architectures: components, connectors, interfaces, links, general groups, as well as types for components, connectors, and interfaces.
	Instances	Basic structural modeling of descriptive architectures: components, connectors, interfaces, links, general groups.

Abstract Implementation	Mappings from structural element types (component types, connector types) to implementations.
Java Implementation	Mappings from structural element types to Java implementations.
Options	Allows structural elements to be declared optional—included or excluded from an architecture depending on specified conditions.
Variants	Allows structural element types to be declared variant—taking on different concrete types depending on specified conditions.
Versions	Defines version graphs; allows structural element types to be versioned through association with versions in version graphs.

Because xADL can be extended with unforeseen constructs and structures in nearly arbitrary ways, it induces challenges that do not exist in languages with unchanging syntaxes and semantics (most of the other ADLs we have covered). Specifically, parsers, editors, analyzers, and other tools must be developed to cope with a notation whose syntax may change from project to project.

xADL addresses these challenges with an associated set of tools that make it easier for users to implement their own tools (for example, analyzers, editors) that can handle the language's extensible syntax. These include the following.

The xADL Data Binding Library. A data binding library is a software library that provides an API for parsing, reading, writing, and serializing (writing back out to disk or other storage) documents in a particular language. In xADL's case, the data binding library consists of a set of Java classes that correspond to xADL data types. A program can query and manipulate instances of these classes to explore and change an xADL document. Although xADL documents can also be read, written, and manipulated with any XML-aware tool, the data binding library provides a much simpler interface and is the basis for most of the other xADL tools developed to date.

Apigen. The data binding library would be of limited use if it had to be manually rewritten each time schemas were added to xADL. Apigen (Dashofy 2001) is xADL's data binding library generator: Given a set of XML schemas, it can generate the complete data binding library with support for those schemas. If a user changes or adds a schema, a new data binding library can be generated by rerunning Apigen; this library will contain classes for querying and manipulating the new or changed data types defined in the user's schema.

---

xADL and xADLite

The native storage format of xADL is in an XML format. Although XML is designed to be readable by both humans and software tools, certain factors can impede the human-readability of XML documents. Specifically, xADL's extensive use of XML namespaces and multiple schemas adds a significant amount of "housekeeping" data to xADL documents. This data is not without use—it is used by tools such as the data binding library and XML validators—but it makes it more difficult to comprehend a xADL document for humans attempting to read it for content.

For example, a simple component in xADL's XML format might look like this:

```
<types:component xsi:type="types:Component"
                 types:id="myComp">
  <types:description xsi:type="instance:Description">
```

```
      MyComponent
    </types:description>
    <types:interface xsi:type="types: Interface"
                     types:id="iface1">
    <types:description xsi:type="instance:Description">
      Interface1
    </types:description>
    <types:direction xsi:type="instance:Direction">
      inout
    </types:direction>
    </types:interface>
</types:component>
```

Even with namespace and XML typing information removed, the result is still verbose:

```
<component id="myComp">
  <description>
    MyComponent
  </description>
  <interface id="iface1">
    <description>
      Interface1
    </description>
    <direction>
      inout
    </direction>
  <interface>
</component>
```

From time to time in this book, we will use an alternate, more readable representation of xADL documents called xADLite. xADLite is a more syntactically terse format than xADL's native XML representation, but the transformation from xADLite to XML and back again is lossless—no information is lost when translating a document from xADLite to xADL or back again. The same component in xADLite looks like this:

```
component{
  id ="myComp";
  description ="MyComponent";
  interface{
    id ="iface1";
    description ="interface1";
    direction ="inout";
  }
}
```

Scope and Purpose	Modeling architecture structure, product lines, and implementations, with support for extensibility
Basic Elements	Components, connectors, interfaces, links, options, variants, versions, plus any basic elements defined in extensions.
Style	Stylistic aspects of an architecture can be modeled through the use of types and type libraries.
Static and Dynamic Aspects	Static structure is modeled natively, dynamic properties can be captured through extensions. The MTAT project (Hendrickson, Dashofy, and Taylor 2005) extends xADL to describe the external behavior of components and connectors that communicate through messages.
Dynamic Modeling	The xADL data binding library allows xADL specifications to be manipulated programmatically.
Non-Functional Aspects	Extensions can be written to capture non-functional aspects.
Ambiguity	The xADL language is purposefully permissive in how its elements may be used, although documentation indicates their intended use. Tools are available to automatically check constraints on xADL documents and allow users to define their own constraints.
Accuracy	Tools are provided to check the correctness of xADL documents; additional constraints can be written into these tools to handle extensions.
Precision	Extensions can be used to annotate existing element types with whatever detail is required or create entirely new first-class constructs.
Viewpoints	Natively, structural viewpoints (both run time and design time) are supported as well as product-line views; extensions can be used to provide additional viewpoints.
View Consistency	External tools can check the consistency of views; frameworks for developing such tools are provided.

Evaluation Rubric for xADL

Lunar Lander in xADL. For basic structural specifications, xADL has a great deal in common with Acme and ADML. The basic structure of the Lunar Lander application, expressed in xADL's xADLite textual visualization might look like Figure 6-27. Like Darwin and other ADLs, xADL also has an associated graphical visualization. This visualization is provided by an editor called Archipelago, which is part of the xADL tool set.

The model of Lunar Lander rendered by Archipelago is shown in Figure 6-28. As with Acme, the key notational contribution of xADL lies in its extensibility. xADL's extensibility goes beyond adding properties to the core constructs. In fact, xADL has no fundamental separation between core concepts and extensions. xADL allows the addition of completely new syntactic elements in addition to structured extensions to existing elements.

Reusing the example of the improved data source component specification above for Acme, let's look at how more detail about the data store component might be added to xADL (and the xADL specification of Lunar Lander). The XML schema specification for a "plain" xADL component (as used above) is shown in Figure 6-29. Simply put, this specification says that a component has the following.

- One identifier (a string attribute).
- One description (a string element).

Figure 6-27.
*Lunar Lander
architecture
described in
xADLite.*

```
xArch{
   archStructure{
      id = "lunarlander";
      description = "Lunar Lander";
      component{
         id = "datastore";
         description = "Data Store";
         interface{
            id = "datastore.getValues";
            description = "Data Store Get Values Interface";
            direction = "in";
         }
         interface{
            id = "datastore.storeValues";
            description = "Data Store Store Values Interface";
            direction = "in";
         }
      }
      component{
         id = "calculation";
         description = "Calculation";
         interface{
            id = "calculation.getValues";
            description = "Calculation Get Values Interface";
            direction = "out";
         }
         interface{
            id = "calculation.storeValues";
            description = "Calculation Store Values Interface";
            direction = "out";
         }
         interface{
            id = "calculation.calculate";
            description = "Calculation Calculate Interface";
            direction = "in";
         }
      }
      component{
         id = "userinterface";
         description = "UserInterface";
         interface{
            id = "userinterface.getValues";
            description = "User Interface Get Values
                              Interface";
            direction = "out";
         }
         interface{
            id = "userinterface.calculate";
            description = "User Interface Calculate Interface";
            direction = "out";
         }
      }
   }
```

Figure 6-27.
(*Continued*)

```
link{
  id = "calculation-to-datastore-getvalues";
  description = "Calculation to Data Store Get Values"
  point{
    anchorOnInterface{
      type = "simple";
      href  = "#calculation.getValues";
    }
  }
  point{
    anchorOnInterface{
      type = "simple";
      href  = "#datastore.getValues";
    }
  }
}
link{
  id = "calculation-to-datastore-storevalues";
  description = "Calculation to Data Store Store
                 Values"
  point{
    anchorOnInterface{
      type = "simple";
      href  = "#calculation.storeValues";
    }
  }
  point{
    anchorOnInterface{
      type = "simple";
      href  = "#datastore.storeValues";
    }
  }
}
link{
  id = "ui-to-calculation-calculate";
  description = "UI to Calculation Calculate"
  point{
    anchorOnInterface{
      type = "simple";
      href  = "#userinterface.calculate";
    }
  }
  point{
    anchorOnInterface{
      type = "simple";
      href  = "#calculation.calculate";
    }
  }
}
```

(*Continued*)

Figure 6-27.
(*Continued*)

```
link{
  id = "ui-to-datastore-getvalues";
  description = "UI toto Data Store Get Values"
  point{
    anchorOnInterface{
      type = "simple";
      href = "#userinterface.getValues";
    }
  }
  point{
    anchorOnInterface{
      type = "simple";
      href = "#datastore.getValues";
    }
  }
}
}
}
```

Figure 6-28.
*Lunar Lander in
xADL, as
visualized by the
Archipelago
graphical editor.*

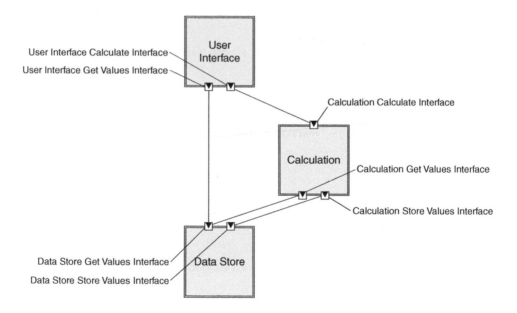

- Zero or more interfaces.
- An optional link to its type.

By adding another schema, we can create an extended form of a component that can be used to capture more information about where the component will store data. An example extension is shown in Figure 6-30. This extension to the xADL language adds several new capabilities. First, it defines a new abstract data type called `Database`. This is like declaring an abstract class in an object-oriented programming language: It indicates we are going to define many different subtypes of `Database` that will be

```
<complexType name="Component">
  <sequence>
    <element name="description"
             type="Description"/>
    <element name="interface" type="Interface"
             minOccurs="0" maxOccurs="unbounded"/>
    <element name="type"
             type="XMLLink"
             minOccurs="0" maxOccurs="1"/>
  </sequence>
  <attribute name="id" type="Identifier"/>
</complexType>
```

Figure 6-29.
*XML schema
description of an
xADL
component.*

```
<complexType name="Database" abstract="true"/>

<complexType name="RelationalDatabase">
  <complexContent>
    <extension base="Database">
      <sequence>
        <element name="tableName" type="string"/>
        <element name="numReplicas" type="int"/>
      </sequence>
    </extension>
  </complexContent>
</complexType>

<complexType name="FileDatabase">
  <complexContent>
    <extension base="Database">
      <sequence>
        <element name="fileName" type="string"/>
        <element name="hostName" type="string"
                 minOccurs="0" maxOccurs="1"/>
      </sequence>
    </extension>
  </complexContent>
</complexType>

<complexType name="DatabaseComponent">
  <complexContent>
    <extension base="Component">
      <xsd:sequence>
        <xsd:element name="database"
                     type="Database"/>
      </xsd:sequence>
    </xsd:extension>
  </xsd:complexContent>
</xsd:complexType>
```

Figure 6-30.
*XML schema
extension adding
database
component
capabilities to
xADL.*

Figure 6-31.
*Extended Lunar
Lander* Data
Store
*component in
xADL.*

```
component type="DatabaseComponent" {
  id = "datastore";
  description = "Data Store";
  interface{
    id = "datastore.getValues";
    description = "Data Store Get Values Interface";
    direction = "in";
  }
  interface{
    id = "datastore.storeValues";
    description = "Data Store Store Values Interface";
    direction = "in";
  }
  database type="RelationalDatabase" {
    tableName = "landerData";
    numReplicas = "1";
  }
}
```

substitutable whenever a Database is needed. Then, it defines two concrete subtypes of Database: RelationalDatabase and FileDatabase. These have different characteristics: a RelationalDatabase has a table name and a number of replicas, while a FileDatabase has a file name and an optional host name on which the file resides.

Finally, it defines an extension to the plain xADL Component datatype. A DatabaseComponent has everything that a component does, plus a Database element. Because both RelationalDatabase and FileDatabase are Databases, either one can be used here (as well as other user-defined database types in other schemas).

We can now extend the original xADL description of the Data Store component in the Lunar Lander application, as shown in Figure 6-31. Using these mechanisms, stakeholders can define their modeling needs very precisely. When the new "DatabaseComponent" schema is ready, Apigen can generate a new data binding library that supports the new constructs. Furthermore, sharing of schemas is possible (and encouraged)—the above "DatabaseComponent" schema could be reused from project to project, as well as any tools that provide advanced processing (editing, analysis, and so on) on elements from this schema.

Takeaways. While xADL's basic modeling capabilities rival those of other ADLs we have covered, xADL's primary contribution is in its extensibility. xADL heavily leverages XML's (and XML Schema's) extensibility mechanisms to create a domain-specific ADL factory, where domain-specific ADLs (and supporting tools) can be created at a much lower cost than developing them from scratch. xADL is supported by a variety of visualization, analysis, and utility tools in the ArchStudio environment. These various tools will be discussed throughout the remainder of the book.

6.6 WHEN SYSTEMS BECOME TOO COMPLEX TO MODEL

In this chapter, we have shown how various notations can express a simple application like Lunar Lander. The Lunar Lander architecture has certain properties that simplify modeling:

It has a finite number of well-known components that run on a single host. Even large distributed systems can be modeled in similar ways, although the effort required to model these systems increases with their size. However, certain applications (especially Internet-scale applications) cannot be modeled using these same techniques. For example, it would be virtually impossible to model the Web, or Gnutella (Kan, 2001) using some of the modeling techniques above. These are gigantic and diverse applications. The configuration of components and connectors on the Internet is constantly changing. In fact, they are so big and so volatile that it is *impossible* to know the configuration of components and connectors at any given time. Thus, it is not possible to generate a model of these systems in the traditional components-connectors-and-configurations sense. There are far too many components, and the structure of the application is changing too fast.

Modeling applications with this kind of complexity is possible, using some of the techniques we have already discussed. All of them involve abstracting away aspects of the complexity to get to a point where modeling is feasible but still useful. This is the essence of modeling. Strategies to consider in this case include the following.

- *Model limited aspects of the architecture:* Many times, the largest or most complex part of an architecture is limited to one particular perspective. For example, trying to model the structure of the Web would be impossible. However, use cases or interaction patterns are more limited, and might be modeled more easily.

- *Model an instance:* The first thing to consider is whether a complete model of such a system is actually needed. In general, nobody needs to model the entire Web or Gnutella P2P network at any given time. Instead, consider modeling only the portion of the system that is relevant, which will almost certainly be a (relatively) small subset of the total system.

- *Exploit regularity:* Often, extremely large systems have low heterogeneity. Large portions of the system will, for modeling purposes, look almost exactly like other portions of the system. These portions can be modeled once and repeated automatically, or decorated with a property indicating how many of them there are. Recall Darwin's ability to specify multiple homogenous clients using a "for loop" construct.

- *Model the style:* As discussed earlier in the book, the Web is based on the REST architectural style. Instead of modeling the Web as an application, consider modeling the REST style instead. We have discussed several notations that allow modeling of different kinds of architectural style constraints; these can be used for this purpose.

- *Model the protocol:* The "contract" that large distributed systems adhere to is often captured in the interaction protocol between components. For example, the Web is, in large measure, characterized by adherence to the HTTP protocol (Fielding et al. 1999). A number of the notations discussed in this chapter can be used to model protocol details, such as natural language (albeit informally) and Wright.

6.7 END MATTER

In this chapter, we have introduced architecture modeling and identified many of the issues that occur in the modeling process. We have also introduced and provided examples of many architecture description notations.

It is impossible to provide deep coverage of the variety of architecture description notations in this text—indeed, books, theses, and academic papers abound discussing each notation in great detail. Instead, we have attempted to highlight the distinguishing aspects of each notation. We encourage interested readers to leverage the Web and the resources indicated at the end of the chapter to investigate these ADLs more thoroughly from primary sources.

The goal of this chapter is to give readers a sense of the breadth of the modeling activity, as well as the notations, tools, and techniques that are available to support it. What should be obvious is that no single notation—even an extensible notation—is sufficient to capture all the aspects of architecture that will be important for a complex project. Stakeholders must make informed choices of techniques, based on the needs of the project at hand. The following table recaps the modeling approaches we have discussed in this chapter and attempts to group them into categories that share characteristics. Note that some approaches fall in more than one category. One example is Darwin. It is grouped with the syntactically rigorous ADLs such as UML and OMT because of its usefulness as a straightforward way of rigorously capturing and communicating architectural structure. It is also in the formal category because of its formal foundations in the *pi* calculus, although these formal foundations are rarely exploited.

Ideally, stakeholders and architects would simply be able to select a mature notation that would cover their modeling and analysis needs. However, the reality is that there are not enough mature notations currently available to make this possible. Even if one were prepared to use several notations simultaneously (and deal with the costs of managing consistency among them), there will likely still be gaps between what can be modeled and what stakeholders need. This means that architects will not only have to invest in modeling, but invest in developing the technologies they use to model. Modeling would be substantially more effective if a portion of the total design budget of a system were devoted to enhancing the fundamental technologies used to do the design. Nevertheless, selecting and using at least one architecture modeling notation—preferably an extensible

Category	Category Characteristics	Examples
Informal/Free-form	High expressiveness, ambiguity, lack of rigor, no formal semantics	Natural language, informal graphical diagrams.
Syntactically rigorous	Rigorous syntax but few semantics, primarily useful for communication.	UML, OMT, Darwin.
Formal	Rigorous syntax and underlying formal semantics, automated analyses possible, steeper learning curves.	Darwin, Rapide, Wright.
Domain- or style-specific	Optimization for a particular domain or style, has strong mapping to domain or style-specific concepts.	Weaves, Koala, AADL.
Extensible	Support for a core set of constructs and the ability for users to define their own.	ACME, ADML, xADL, UML.

notation—is worlds better than not doing modeling at all, and significantly better than using a semantically impoverished notation such as PowerPoint or UML.

Selecting notations for use on a project is a subtle and complex activity. This chapter focused on what aspects of architecture are modeled by different notations, and how those notations model those aspects. These are only two factors in selecting a notation. Other important questions must also be answered: What kinds of visualizations are available with the notation? What kinds of analyses can be performed on models in the notation? How can models in this notation be tied to other life cycle phases? All these aspects of designing will be addressed in subsequent chapters. The next chapter focuses specifically on visualizations, where we separate the abstract concept of a notation (a way of organizing the information in design decisions) from the different ways that the information can be interacted with and depicted.

The Business Case

Deciding what to model and what approaches to use is very much a choice driven by costs and benefits. Modeling takes time and effort, as does maintaining models that have already been created. The more complex, precise, and unambiguous the models, the more cognitive effort, time, and money will be invested in creating them.

Different kinds of models produce different kinds of benefits. These benefits generally come in the form of cost mitigation: The models themselves do not produce revenue (except perhaps in the case when they are part of documentation or training that can be sold to customers). Typical benefits of modeling include:

- *As documentation:* Models can serve as points of reference and vehicles for communicating ideas about the system among diverse stakeholders. This increases understanding and reduces confusion, which can lead to fewer problems in later development stages such as integration and acceptance testing; it can also help to determine whether the system is consistent with its requirements and whether the requirements are themselves appropriate.

- *Earlier fault detection:* Good models can help stakeholders detect problems earlier (through inspection and analysis) and fix them before they become costly.

- *Lower change costs:* By giving developers a specific sense of the current architecture (and architectural style), changes can be made following established guidelines with more insight about the effect of a given change on the system.

- *Generation of other artifacts:* Some models can be used to generate specific types of documentation or even (partial) implementations automatically, thus saving the costs of generating these artifacts manually. Generation has the added benefit that it costs less to maintain the connection between models and other development activities, since models can simply be used to regenerate other artifacts when they change.

As part of project inception and business planning, it is a good idea to develop a modeling strategy, which is simply an agreement between stakeholders on what kinds of models will be constructed, what notations or tools will be used, what consistency criteria will be applied, how those models will be used in the overall development activity, and so on. It is also advisable to develop and document cost/benefit arguments for each model or type of model, capturing the rationale for each model's creation and use. Additionally, just as project scheduling can be used to estimate the time and cost of implementing various aspects of the system, scheduling can also be applied to the development and maintenance of models.

6.8 REVIEW QUESTIONS

1. What is an architectural model? What is its relationship to an architecture? To design decisions?

2. What is the difference between accuracy and precision in general? In the context of architectural modeling?

3. What is the difference between a view and a viewpoint?

4. Enumerate some common architectural viewpoints. What kind of data is captured in each viewpoint?

5. What does it mean for two views to be consistent? What kinds of inconsistencies can arise in multiview models?

6. What kinds of dimensions can you use to evaluate a modeling notation?

7. Enumerate some modeling notations and describe what kinds of design decisions they can capture.

8. What are the distinctive modeling features of Darwin? Of Wright? Of Rapide? Of Weaves?

9. What are the advantages of using an extensible ADL? What are some disadvantages?

10. What are some modeling strategies that can be used when a system is too big or complex to create a complete architectural model?

6.9 EXERCISES

1. Research in more depth the syntax and semantics of one of the ADLs in this chapter and model a system of your choosing in that ADL.

2. Download a tool set for one of the modeling notations described in this chapter and model a simple application like Lunar Lander in that tool set. Reflect on your experiences and the strengths and weaknesses of the tool set.

3. Map the syntax of an earlier ADL (for example, Darwin, Wright, Rapide) to an extensible ADL. What services are provided by the extensible ADL? What extensions are needed to fill in the gaps? Define these extensions using the mechanisms provided by the extensible ADL.

4. Choose a software-intensive system and research how this system's developers employed modeling. What kind of models were created and how are they used? How are they maintained?

5. Research how other disciplines (for example, computer engineering or building architecture) approach the modeling task. What do they model? What notations do they use? Do similar issues (such as view consistency) occur in those disciplines? How are they handled there?

6. Do you agree that UML is an architecture description language? Argue for or against.

7. Model a simple system like Lunar Lander in two different notations, or in two different viewpoints in the same notation (for example, two UML diagrams). Ensure that the models are consistent, and explain why and how you established that consistency.

8. Choose a concern or view not supported by one of the extensible ADLs and develop an extension to support that concern or view.

6.10 FURTHER READING

The chapter opens with an insight about modeling from Maier and Rechtin's *The Art of Systems Architecting* (Maier and Rechtin 2000). While not solely about modeling, this book addresses architecture from the perspective of a systems engineer, which is, in general, broader and less concrete than the perspective of a software engineer. As with much of the content of this book, Maier and Rechtin's advice is often equally applicable to both systems and software development.

The bulk of this chapter introduces and surveys a broad variety of modeling notations. Although we have endeavored to distill each notation down to its essence and comment on the aspects of the notations that we believe are distinctive, the few pages dedicated to each notation often cannot adequately capture its scope and subtlety. Interested readers should investigate source documents and specifications related to these notations for more in-depth treatments. Tools for working with unconstrained graphical notations such as PowerPoint (Microsoft Corporation 2007), Visio (Microsoft Corporation 2007), and OmniGraffle (The Omni Group 2007) are widely available. Many books have been written about UML, but the canonical reference is from the developers themselves (Booch, Rumbaugh, and Jacobson 2005). Medvidović and Taylor surveyed early ADLs (Medvidović, and Taylor 2000). These included Darwin (Magee et al., 1995), Wright (Allen and Garlan, 1997) [treated even more extensively in Allen's Ph.D. thesis (Allen 1997)], and Rapide (Luckham et al. 1995), which inspired

Luckham et al.'s later work in complex event processing (Luckham 2002). UML's takeover of modeling most of the generic architectural views resulted in second-generation ADLs like Koala (van Ommering et al. 2000) and AADL (Feiler, Lewis, and Vestal 2003) [itself based on an earlier ADL, MetaH (Binns et al. 1996)], that addressed more domain-specific concerns. An exciting direction in ADL development remains the creation and growth of extensible ADLs, from early examples like Acme (Garlan, Monroe, and Wile 1997) and ADML (Spencer 2000) to later, more flexible examples such as xADL 2.0 (Dashofy, van der Hoek, and Taylor 2005).

Clements et al. (2002) have dedicated an entire book to the issue of documenting software architectures, which focuses primarily on modeling. Their book takes a viewpoint-centric approach, surveying a wide variety of viewpoints and providing guidance as to what should be captured in each. Their book also surveys salient notations and standards.

7

Visualization

The previous chapter covered modeling: how we capture the design decisions that make up a software system's architecture. In practice, there are often different ways to display and interact with the information contained in those models. This is the domain of architectural *visualization*.

> **Definition.** An architectural *visualization* defines how architectural models are depicted, and how stakeholders interact with those depictions.

This is an intentionally broad definition of visualization. Here, visualization consists of two key aspects: *depiction* and *interaction*. Put simply, a depiction is a picture or visual representation of architectural design decisions in a particular format. Visualization tools can provide one or more interaction mechanisms through which users can interact with those decisions in terms of the depiction. These mechanisms may include keyboard commands, point-and-click operations, and so on.

This chapter discusses the relationship between architecture modeling notations and visualizations, and how various modeling languages are visualized. It then covers various strategies for designing and evaluating visualizations to maximize their effectiveness. The chapter ends with a survey of various visualization techniques and evaluations of the strengths and weaknesses of each technique.

This chapter is not intended to be a treatment of techniques for usability design or information visualization in general; these subjects are too broad for the scope of this book. Instead, the chapter focuses on identifying the kinds of visualizations that can be used for architectural models and discusses issues specifically related to visualization of architectures.

7.1 VISUALIZATION CONCEPTS

Visualization plays a critical role in software architecture. The most important message of this chapter is that the way architectures are *visualized* can be, to an extent, separate from the way they are *modeled*. The two are closely related; in fact, each modeling notation is associated with one or more canonical or native visualizations. (This will be discussed in more detail below.) Fundamentally, however, *a model is just organized information*. In the case of architectural models, the information consists of design decisions. Visualizations are the means by which the information in a model is given form: how it is depicted and how users interact with it.

A single architectural model can be visualized in any number of ways, and multiple diverse models can be visualized in similar ways. Thus, visualization can be used to hide (or at least smooth over) differences in back-end modeling notations. Second, visualizations can vary widely—many are graphical, but most ADLs have textual visualizations as well. Research has even been done in the area of esoteric visualizations, such as three-dimensional virtual realities (Feijs and De Jong 1998).

The goal of this section is to distinguish visualizations from their underlying modeling notations, introduce the kinds of visualizations that can be used to model architectures (textual, graphical, and hybrid), and then discuss the issues that arise when multiple visualizations (of all these kinds) are simultaneously applied to an architecture.

7.1.1   Canonical Visualizations

It is difficult to separate the abstract information in a model from the concrete ways in which that information is visualized. No information is completely divorced from visualization. However, we mentally make this separation often in our daily lives. A sign that depicts a stick figure pedestrian with a bar across it and a nearby sign that says "Do Not Cross" are simply two different ways of visualizing the same information: one graphical and one textual.

From this perspective, architectural modeling notations are simply ways of organizing information. Every notation has at least one visualization that is directly and specifically associated with it. We call this visualization the notation's *canonical visualization*. Models with multiple views are often associated with multiple canonical visualizations—one per view; views will be covered in the next section.

Text-based ADLs (including XML-based ADLs) are natively expressed using text-based visualizations. Not all modeling notations are textual, however. PowerPoint and OmniGraffle models are manipulated entirely in graphical visualizations, and there is no easy way to extract a text-based depiction of the model. Natively, UML diagrams are primarily graphical. Some parts of UML, such as the Object Constraint Language (OCL) constraints that are used to constrain relationships between model elements, are textual, having a well-defined syntax and semantics all their own.

A common pitfall is for users to associate an architecture modeling notation *only* with its canonical visualization, or to view a notation and its canonical visualization as the same thing. They are not: The notation is a way of organizing (abstract) information and the visualization dictates how the information is depicted and interacted with. For example, most tools that deal with architectural models store the model in data structures in memory, associated with no specific visualization; it is not until an editor is invoked that this information is visualized. Canonical visualizations present the information in a way that is closely related to its organization, but remember that this is almost always not the only way to present the information.

Not all visualizations are optimal for all uses, so notations for which there exist multiple visualizations are generally preferable to those that have only a single canonical visualization. In complex projects, desired architectural goals may be easier to achieve by developing a new visualization for an existing notation than by developing or selecting an entirely new notation.

7.1.2 Textual Visualizations

Textual visualizations depict architectures using ordinary text files. These text files generally conform to a particular syntactic format, much like a .c or .java file conforms to the syntax of the C or Java language. (As we have discussed, architectural decisions can also be documented using natural language, in which case the textual visualization would only be constrained by the grammar and spelling rules of that language.)

Figure 7-1 shows two textual depictions of the architecture of a Web client consisting of only one component: a Web browser. The first depiction depicts an architecture in xADL's native XML format, and the second depicts the same exact architecture in xADLite. This is an example of different visualizations being applied to the same model. The XML visualization of the architecture is easily read, manipulated, and syntactically validated by XML tools. The xADLite visualization describes the same architecture (and is, in fact, directly derived from the same model), but is better optimized for human readability.

Textual visualizations have several advantages. They generally depict the entirety of an architecture in a particular notation in a single file. Hundreds of text editors are readily available that allow the user to interact with text files. Years of research have gone into technologies for parsing, processing, and editing structured text. When a textual syntax is

Figure 7-1.
*Textual
depictions for an
architecture in
xADL and
xADLite.*

```
<instance:xArch xsi:type="instance:XArch">
  <types:archStructure xsi:type="types:ArchStructure"
                       types:id="ClientArch">
    <types:description xsi:type="instance:Description">
      Client Architecture
    </types:description>
    <types:component xsi:type="types:Component"
                     types:id="WebBrowser">
      <types:description xsi:type="instance:Description">
        Web Browser
      </types:description>
      <types:interface xsi:type="types:Interface"
                       types:id="WebBrowserInterface">
        <types:description xsi:type="instance:Description">
          Web Browser Interface
        </types:description>
        <types:direction xsi:type="instance:Direction">
          inout
        </types:direction>
      </types:interface>
    </types:component>
  </types:archStructure>
</instance:xArch>
```

```
xArch{
  archStructure{
    id = "ClientArch"
    description = "Client Architecture"
    component{
      id = "WebBrowser"
      description = "Web Browser"
      interface{
        id = "WebBrowserInterface"
        description = "Web Browser Interface"
        direction = "inout"
      }
    }
  }
}
```

defined using a meta-language such as Backus-Naur Form (BNF), many tools are available to generate program libraries that can parse and check the syntax of text documents written in that language. Many text editors provide additional developer support for particular notations with features such as autocomplete and syntax checking as you type.

Textual notations have disadvantages, as well. Textual notations are good at depicting data linearly and hierarchically. (Think of a program in a language like C or Java: Linear ordering is done using lines from top-to-bottom, and hierarchical structure is captured using braces and indentation.) However, graphlike structures are not easily understood (by people) through a textual visualization. Additionally, text editors are generally limited to showing a contiguous screenful of text, with few options to organize the text differently (although some advanced environments may include features such as code folding that allow users to collapse a block of text into a single line).

7.1.3 Graphical Visualizations

Graphical visualizations depict architectures (primarily) using graphical symbols instead of text. Like textual visualizations, graphical visualizations generally conform to a syntax (this time of symbols instead of text elements), but they may also be free-form (high-level or overview diagrams of architectures are often free-form and stylistic).

Figure 7-2 shows two graphical depictions of the Lunar Lander architecture. The top depiction is a high-level overview of the lander and its mission. While this depiction lacks rigor or formality, it does convey useful information to stakeholders that are encountering the application for the first time. Such depictions are often used as conceptual overviews of complex applications, especially those consisting of many interconnected systems. Standards such as the Department of Defense Architecture Framework (DoDAF, discussed more extensively in Chapter 16) include such depictions—this depiction would satisfy the DoDAF "OV-1" view of the Lunar Lander architecture (DoD Architecture Framework Working Group 2004). Note, however, that it is ambiguous or misleading in several important ways. For example, the lander is tilted somewhat with respect to the moon's surface, which may imply a two- or three-dimensional aspect to the game that does not exist in the final application. It also depicts Earth in the background, which may lead one to believe that communications from Earth play a role in the lander simulation.

The bottom depiction is a logical view of the Lunar Lander architecture, depicting its structure in terms of a component and connector graph. This view is more rigorous,

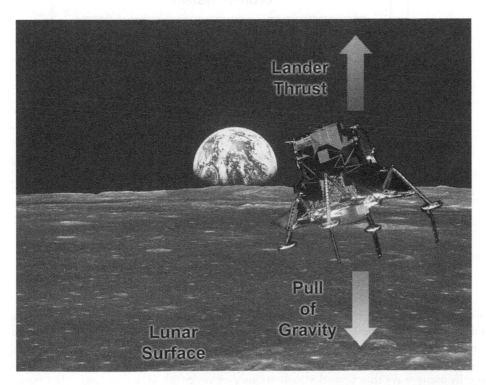

Figure 7-2.
Two graphical visualizations of the same architecture.

(Continued)

Figure 7-2.
(Continued)

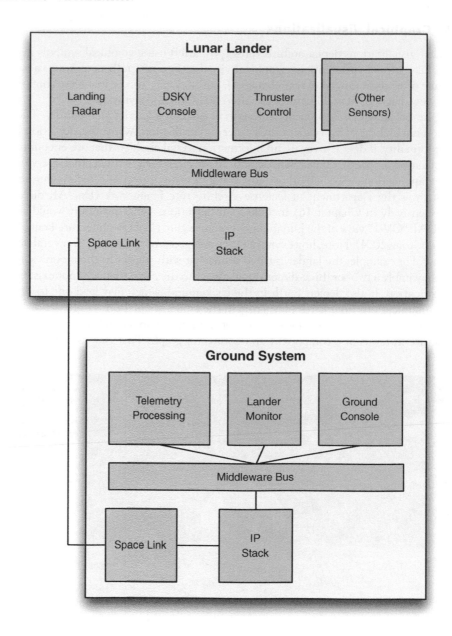

less ambiguous, and depicts more information at the cost of being less accessible to outside stakeholders. The overall mission and purpose of the system is lost in the detail of the components and their interconnections.

Graphical visualizations give stakeholders access to information about an architecture in many ways that textual visualizations cannot. Symbols, colors, and other visual decorations generally can be distinguished more easily than elements of structured text.

Nonhierarchical relationships between elements can be seen much more easily in a graph than a text file. Graphical visualizations can use spatial relationships to express relationships among elements. Advanced graphical visualizations may also employ animation or other visual effects to highlight or demonstrate different aspects of architecture. Options for interacting with graphical visualizations are generally superior to text visualizations, as well: Scrolling, zooming, drilling down, showing and hiding different levels of detail, and direct manipulation of objects with the mouse are all commonplace in graphical visualization tools. For example, a graphical environment might allow a user to connect components by simply drawing a line between their interfaces with the mouse.

A major disadvantage of graphical visualizations is the cost of building tools to support them. Many tools exist for creating graphical diagrams—PowerPoint, Visio, OmniGraffle, Photoshop, and Illustrator are a few of the more popular ones. However, these tools lack understanding of architectural semantics, and it is difficult or impossible to add appropriate semantics and interaction operations to these tools so they can be integrated into a wider software engineering environment. Furthermore, these tools generally have their own (usually proprietary) file formats and in-memory models that are difficult to connect to a more architecture-centric representation [(Goldman and Balzer 1999) (Ren and Taylor 2003)].

7.1.4 Hybrid Visualizations

Graphical and textual are rough ways of categorizing visualizations. Many visualizations blur the line between these categories. Few graphical visualizations use only symbols—generally, text is used to decorate, label, or explain the meaning of various elements. Some visualizations go even further, expressing some kinds of design decisions using graphics and others using text. For example, a UML class diagram is primarily composed of interconnected symbols, but constraints on relationships between the symbols are depicted in the Object Constraint Language (OCL) with an exclusively textual visualization.

Figure 7-3 depicts UML as a hybrid visualization. The class diagram is primarily graphical, capturing the three primary Lunar Lander elements—user interface, calculation, and data store. Alongside the class diagram, textual OCL is employed to depict the constraint that the new burn rate must be nonnegative.

Some visualizations can be composites of many different visualizations, both graphical and textual. For example, the UML composite structure diagram is a primarily graphical visualization used to contain other UML diagrams. Such composite visualizations can be good for displaying relationships between different aspects of the same architecture. Composite visualizations can become complex and confusing quickly as different depiction and interaction mechanisms are combined. Strategies such as drill-down interaction mechanisms, where users can navigate to subvisualizations from a higher-level composite visualization, can mitigate this complexity.

7.1.5 The Relationship between Visualizations and Views

Some visualizations may depict the whole architectural model at once, but more often different visualizations are used to depict different views of the architecture. Chapter 6 presented the concept of views: subsets of the architecture, usually organized around a

Figure 7-3.
*UML with
constraints as a
hybrid
visualization.*

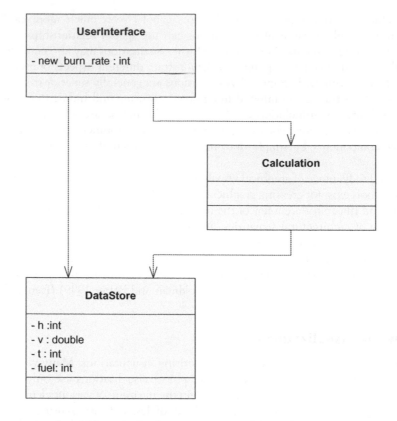

context UserInterface
inv: new_burn_rate >= 0

single concern or set of concerns. Recall the definitions presented:

Definition. **A *view* is a set of design decisions related by a common concern (or set of concerns).**

Definition. **A *viewpoint* defines the perspective from which a view is taken.**

Effectively, views and viewpoints let us consider different subsets of the design decisions in an architecture. We can apply the same concept of a subset to visualizations: A visualization for a viewpoint defines depiction and interaction mechanisms only for the kinds of design decisions included in that viewpoint. We associate visualizations with viewpoints rather than views because the same visualization can be used to visualize many different architectures; we do not create a new visualization for every architecture. For example, the UML class diagram is a visualization that can be used to visualize the class structure of many different applications. Two different class diagrams are not two separate visualizations; they are simply two instances of the UML class diagram visualization.

When a notation is associated with a set of viewpoints, it is often the case that each viewpoint has its own canonical visualization. UML is a good example of this: Each kind of UML diagram can be seen as a separate visualization. Although UML's canonical

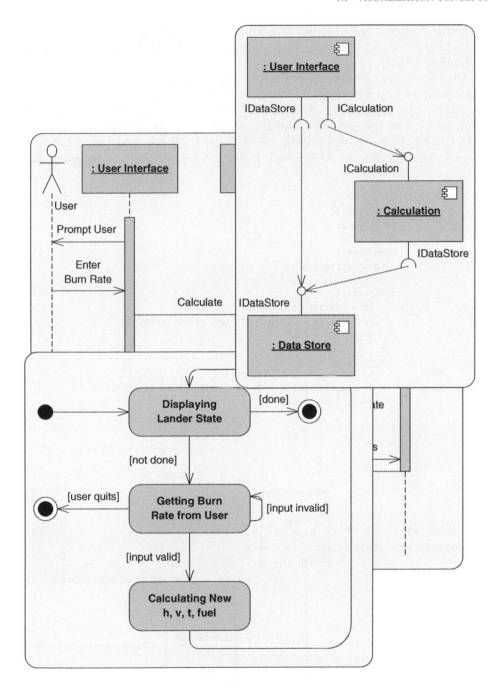

Figure 7-4.
*Various UML
diagram types.*

visualizations are all graphical, they differ widely. The box-and-arrow–style diagram used to depict components and their relationships bears little resemblance to the automata-like statechart or timeline-like sequence diagrams, as seen in Figure 7-4. This is a natural consequence of the fact that architectural models capture a wide variety of information about a system. What constitutes a useful visualization for one concern may be useless for another concern. Just as system stakeholders should identify the viewpoints they will use to examine and work with an architecture, they should also identify appropriate visualizations for each viewpoint.

All of our earlier comments about the relationship between visualizations and models apply equally to partial models—that is, views. If the same set of architectural design decisions is simply depicted in two different ways, these are *not* two different views of the architecture, but are two different visualizations applied to the same view.

In Chapter 6, we showed a depiction of Lunar Lander in xADLite, followed by the equivalent depiction in Archipelago. Figure 7-5 repeats the two depictions from

Figure 7-5.
Lunar Lander in
two different
visualizations: an
xADLite textual
visualization
(abbreviated for
space) and an
Archipelago
visualization.

```
xArch{
  archStructure{
    id = "lunarlander";
    description = "Lunar Lander";
    component{
      id = "datastore";
      description = "Data Store";
      interface{
        id = "datastore.getValues";
        description = "Data Store Get Values Interface";
        direction = "in";
      }
      interface{
        id = "datastore.storeValues";
        description = "Data Store Store Values Interface";
        direction = "in";
      }
    }
    . . .
  }
}
```

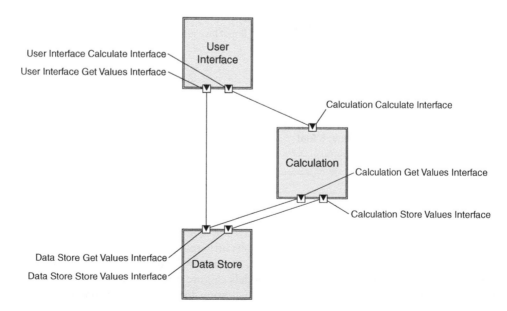

Chapter 6 (although the extensive xADLite visualization has been abbreviated). This is an example of two different visualizations for the structural viewpoint being applied to the same subset of design decisions (that is, view) of the Lunar Lander architecture. Thus, we would not say that these are the xADLite view and Archipelago view of the Lunar Lander architecture; these are the xADLite and Archipelago *depictions* of the *structural view* of the Lunar Lander system.

7.2 EVALUATING VISUALIZATIONS

The above sections outlined what visualizations are, what kinds of visualizations exist, and the relationships between visualizations, models, views, and viewpoints. However, a key question now emerges: What makes a visualization "good?" How can one distinguish visualizations from one another and choose the best one? Ultimately, the worth of a visualization is dependent upon how well it fits the needs of a project's stakeholders. As we have seen, stakeholder needs and priorities vary from project to project, so a visualization that is perfect for one project may be useless in another. Nonetheless, it is possible to identify some desirable qualities for visualizations, which can be prioritized by stakeholders to fit their specific situations. These qualities include:

Fidelity
Fidelity is a measure of how faithfully a visualization represents the underlying model. In general, the minimum acceptable fidelity for a visualization requires that information presented in the visualization be consistent with the underlying model. It would be extremely confusing, for example, if a structural visualization showed components that were not actually in the architecture, and so on. However, visualizations do not have to address *all* the information in an underlying model. Leaving some detail out can often make visualizations more effective by focusing attention on the parts of the model that matter in a given situation. Such is the case for visualizations that are associated with particular viewpoints, for example.

Fidelity affects both depiction and interaction. An interaction mechanism is faithful if it respects the underlying syntax and semantics of the visualized notation. For example, an interface that allows stakeholders to change the model in invalid ways may be confusing. A balance must be struck between fidelity and usability; preventing users from making mistakes entirely limits exploratory design.

Consistency
Consistency is a measure of how well a visualization uses similar depictions and interaction mechanisms for similar concepts. This sense is one of internal consistency (whether a visualization is consistent with itself) rather than consistency with the underlying model (which we call fidelity). In terms of depiction, consistent visualizations display similar concepts in similar ways. For example, in UML, an object is always depicted as a rectangle with an underlined name regardless of the context in which it appears. UML is not perfectly visually consistent, however: In most diagrams, a dashed open-headed arrow represents a dependency, but in a sequence diagram, it represents an asynchronous invocation or message. In terms of interaction, consistent visualizations permit the user to do similar things in similar ways. If double-clicking on one element allows the user to assign a name

to that element, requiring the user to right-click and select a menu option to assign a name to another kind of element would be inconsistent.

In general, more consistent visualizations are preferable to less consistent ones. The exception once again occurs at the extremes: Being too consistent might cause a visualization to have a huge and confusing variety of symbols (to make sure no two concepts share a symbol) or limit the conciseness of a visualization.

Comprehensibility

Comprehensibility is a measure of how easy it is for stakeholders to understand and use a visualization. This makes comprehensibility a function of both the visualization and the stakeholders who use it. Many factors contribute to comprehensibility, including the complexity of the visualization and how information is presented, the complexity of the interaction interface, and the skill sets and prior experiences of the stakeholders.

One way to improve comprehensibility is to narrow the scope of a visualization, limiting the number of concepts it tries to present and optimizing the visualization for only these concepts. Trying to display too much information at once—or many unrelated concepts simultaneously—complicates a visualization and increases its complexity. Alternatively, the comprehensibility of a visualization can be improved by leveraging stakeholder knowledge. For example, using a UML component symbol to represent components in non-UML diagrams can make a visualization more comprehensible to stakeholders that already have experience with UML. (Of course, this can backfire if stakeholders bring along assumptions about UML components that are not being implied by the use of the symbol.)

Dynamism

Dynamism is a measure of how well a visualization supports models that change over time; in Chapter 6 these are referred to as *dynamic models*. Information about changes flows two ways: changes to the model (from whatever source) can be reflected in the visualization, and changes to the visualization (through one of the interaction mechanisms) can be reflected in the model.

A range of possibilities exists here. An ideal dynamic visualization will be immediately updated when the underlying model changes from any source. Additionally, changes to the visualization through interaction mechanisms should cause the model to be updated accordingly.

In general, the depiction of a dynamic model will involve some kind of asynchronous animation; otherwise, the visualization will become inconsistent as the model changes. A less desirable alternative is to allow the user to manually refresh the visualization, optionally notifying the user when the underlying model has changed so that they can perform a refresh operation. With respect to interaction, any visualization that allows editing must be, to some extent, dynamic. Visualizations that update the underlying model in real-time, as the user works, are generally preferable to those that only synchronize changes periodically or at the user's request through, for example, a Save operation.

View Coordination

View coordination is how well one visualization is (or can be) coordinated with others. In general, environments that allow multiple visualizations to be presented and used simultaneously give users more insight and capability when designing or reviewing an architecture. However, coordinating multiple visualizations is not always straightforward or easy. Strategies for coordinating visualizations are discussed in their own section below.

Aesthetics

Aesthetics is a measure of how pleasing a visualization is to its users. Aesthetics is not limited to depiction; user interfaces have aesthetic qualities as well. Here, depiction is the look and interaction is the feel of the visualization. Compared to other qualities, aesthetic qualities are extremely subjective. However, there is an enormous amount of literature available on evaluating and designing aesthetically pleasing displays of information. This comes from both the computer science community (for example, user interface design) and from other communities (art, advertising, marketing, and so forth). For example, color theory is instructive in choosing attractive and complementary colors for graphical visualizations. Determining which colors are complementary is easy with a color wheel and some basic knowledge of how color schemes are constructed, but difficult using intuition alone.

Technologists have a tendency to ignore or deprioritize aesthetic aspects of visualizations because they generally add little functional value. However, aesthetic qualities can often make the difference between a visualization being accepted or rejected by potential users.

Extensibility

Extensibility is a measure of how easy it is to modify a visualization to take on new capabilities, for either depiction or interaction. Just as underlying models and notations are often extended to support domain- and project-specific goals, visualizations of those models must be extended as well. A visualization that is difficult or impossible to extend will become less and less useful as underlying models expand to take on new concepts.

Mechanisms to support extensible visualizations include plug-in APIs, scripting support, and even simply open-sourcing the code that implements the visualization so others can modify it.

7.2.2 Constructing a Visualization

By now, it should be clear that the kinds of concepts that can be captured in an architecture are diverse and complex. They range from structural components and connectors to their interfaces to the schedules according to which they will be developed. Stakeholders choosing to include these elements in their architectures will also have to choose how they are depicted and manipulated in various visualizations.

If a preexisting or off-the-shelf notation is used to capture the architecture, its canonical visualizations will be available. For example, UML captures the notion of a class and has a specific symbol used to depict that class.

When decisions are captured that do not have a canonical visualization, or the canonical visualization is insufficient or inadequate, stakeholders have the option of constructing new visualizations. Creating good visualizations is somewhat of an art form, but there are a few things that can help.

Borrow Elements from Similar Visualizations. Even if you choose not to use UML to capture your architecture, it may be valuable to borrow certain symbols or conventions from UML, such as the shape of a package symbol to depict one of your packages or the closed white-headed arrow to depict a generalization relationship. This has the advantage that many users already will be familiar with the depiction and its meaning. However, there are also drawbacks: Users may assume that your diagrams *are* UML (when they are not) or they may assume specific semantics that you did not mean to import when you used the symbol. A good visualization will strike a balance. One good source for generic symbols that do not carry extensive semantic implications is flowcharting. Although flowcharts have fallen further and further into disuse as programs have become more complex, they are still well understood by a wide variety of users. Common flowcharting symbols useful outside the context of flowcharts include the diamond (decision point), the vertical drum (disk storage), the sideways drum (memory storage), and so on.

Be Consistent among Visualizations. If you are depicting the same concept in many visualizations, use similar symbology. Likewise, try to avoid using the same symbology to depict different concepts in different visualizations.

Give Meaning to Each Visual Aspect of Elements. In a diagram depicting many components, it is tempting to assign different colors to components just so the diagram will not look too monochromatic. While this may be aesthetically pleasant, it is confusing from a semantic perspective since the visual aspect of color has no relationship with the underlying architectural model. It is a good idea to use visual decorations, but each decoration should have precise meaning.

On a related note, users have a tendency to (often subconsciously) embed real semantic information in visual decorations without making that information explicit in the architectural model. For example, in a box-and-arrow graph depiction, a user might place components close to one another to indicate that they share functionality or arrange the components in a layered fashion to reflect an implicit understanding that there are layer-like dependencies in the architecture. When this occurs (and the relationships are not formally documented), valuable information becomes embedded and lost in the visualization. Here, stakeholders should consider whether these visual relationships have semantic importance and, if so, find a way to include them explicitly in the system's models.

Document the Meaning of Visualizations. While we would all like to think that our diagrams and other visualizations are self-explanatory, this is generally not the case. Documenting what each aspect of the diagram means, using a legend, design document, or organizational standard is key to reducing confusion among stakeholders. At best, each aspect of the visualization should correspond to a piece of information in the model.

Balance Traditional and Innovative Interfaces. It is fair to assume that most stakeholders involved in software design will have used a significant amount of software themselves. As we have pointed out, borrowing well-known depiction and interaction techniques allows users to leverage their previous experience. However, adhering too closely to this guideline will result in stagnant visualization design. From time to time, consider borrowing useful nontraditional and innovative visualization features as well, or even developing one's own.

For example, most users will assume that a box-and-arrow graph visualization for an architecture's structure will look and work like that of PowerPoint or Visio. However, it is almost certainly not the case that PowerPoint and Visio have perfected box-and-arrow graph editing. Here, one could consider advanced layout paradigms such as fish-eye layouts, where information is displayed at large sizes in the center of the display and at smaller sizes at the edges, or drill-down paradigms, where zooming in is used as a visual metaphor for looking at more detailed information. A good source of inspiration in visualization design is other software packages that are outside the realm of software design, such as CAD applications, video games, and so on. Aspiring visualization designers should take note of unusual but useful user interfaces that they encounter and determine how to apply those design ideas to architecture visualization.

Edward Tufte, professor emeritus of statistics, information design, interface design, and political economy at Yale University, is best known for a series of influential books, including *The Visual Display of Quantitative Information* (Tufte 2001) and *Envisioning Information* (Tufte 1990), that offer practical advice on how to visualize complex data sets to maximize impact and effectiveness. While Tufte's work focuses primarily on static depictions of statistical and quantitative data, many of his lessons can be useful in the design and evaluation of software architecture visualizations as well.

Tufte's approach can be summarized as one of parsimony. A core concept in Tufte's work is maximizing the *data-ink ratio*—designing depictions that focus on depicting the target data and interpretation aids with as few distractions, decorations, or embellishments as possible. He coined the term "chartjunk" to refer to such elements that detract from the display of data. Chartjunk may be obvious—the use of meaningless colors, shadows, photographic or textured fills, and so on. Chartjunk can also be subtle—excessively bold grid lines in a background, thick borders around data elements that diminish the perceived importance of the data, and so on. For Tufte, graphical depictions are not always ideal: Simple textual organizations of data (primarily tables) can often convey the same information with far less "ink" and far fewer distractions.

Tufte's advocacy of parsimony does not necessarily equate to minimalism, however. Many of Tufte's examples, particularly where complex data sets are used, are extraordinarily dense and display multiple properties of the data simultaneously. Nonetheless, these depictions still focus strongly on the data itself. *Envisioning Information* in particular delves into issues related to the display of such data sets.

In *Envisioning Information*, Tufte generally advocates increasing the dimensionality of representations as a way to deal with complex data. Tufte opens by lamenting the limitations of "flatland"—the two-dimensional space provided by pieces of paper and computer screens. He presents several different strategies for breaking out of flatland, primarily through integrating additional spatial or temporal dimensions into depictions. In a two-dimensional medium, perspective can be used to create three-dimensional spatial pictures. At the time of the book's publication in 1990, three-dimensional rendering technologies were still somewhat inaccessible, and many examples in the book show three-dimensional depictions hand-drawn by artists, although a few simple computer-generated examples appear as well. Another way to add spatial dimensions to flatland is through layering: breaking up the data into multiple depictions that are combined or overlaid on one another. Temporal dimensions can also be taken into account by showing the same data several times in different states, representing different snapshots in time. Spatial and temporal dimensions can be added through a concept Tufte calls "small multiples"—showing many small, simple depictions of related data (or the same data at different times) next to each other in succession, making it easy for readers to compare at a glance.

These techniques (three-dimensional depictions, layering, time variation, and small multiples) can all be applied to the construction of software architecture visualizations, although it is certainly the case that few visualizations take advantage of them today. This also represents an area of ongoing research; for example, the EASEL project (Hendrickson and van der Hoek 2007) is focused on bringing interactive layering concepts to an xADL-based architecture development environment.

Applying Edward Tufte's Lessons to Software Architecture Visualization

Tufte's work focuses primarily on static depictions of information, but a new set of possibilities opens up when the interactivity of a computer is brought to bear. Computers, particularly modern PCs with fast processors, high-resolution color displays, and specialized graphics hardware, can be used to create interactive visualizations that provide an even more immersive escape from flatland. Although still confined to a fundamentally two-dimensional screen, three-dimensional rendering technology is now available to everyone, and three-dimensional depictions no longer have to remain fixed on a page. A user can easily take a three-dimensional model and rotate, examine, and manipulate it in virtual space from any angle using a computer. Three-dimensional views of software architectures have not yet made a mainstream impact. This may be because they are not mature enough, or it may be that they are simply not useful for depicting the kind of data that comprises an architectural model. Projects like EASEL, cited above, not only break down architectures into layers, but allow live interaction with those layers, turning them on and off, using them to express alternatives, and so on. Animation has been used in limited ways to provide a temporal dimension to architectural visualizations (usually effect visualizations that result from some sort of simulation) but far more work needs to be done here as well.

Tufte and the designers of architecture visualizations have much to learn from each other. Tufte's work provides valuable insights on depicting information far more complex than the average architectural model in a very limited medium (static two-dimensional paper). Even with these restrictions—and perhaps because of them—he advocates exploiting dimensions that are still not well utilized by modern architecture visualizations. On the other hand, architectural visualizations, especially those implemented in an editor or other tool, can exploit the resources of fast computers with high-resolution displays to create much more dynamic visualizations than are possible on paper. Those wishing to design new visualizations (or evaluate existing ones) would do well to absorb Tufte's lessons and contextualize them in terms of an interactive computer-based medium.

7.2.3 Coordinating Visualizations

When multiple visualizations of the same information are available, it is key to coordinate these visualizations with each other, so that changes to the information via one visualization are accurately reflected in other visualizations. If the visualizations are not coordinated, they can become out of sync and cause confusion.

It is important to distinguish the *coordination of multiple visualizations* from *maintaining architectural consistency*. Here, we are only dealing with ensuring that multiple visualizations of the same (parts of the) architectural model are up to date with respect to the model. Inconsistencies and conflicts between design decisions stored in the model are a separate issue.

Stakeholders must decide how and how much to allow multiple visualizations to display the same architectural information at the same time. If users are only allowed to view information through one visualization at a time, visualizations can be synchronized with the architectural model when they are called up. They can also assume that the model will not change due to some external influence while they are active—any changes to the model will be made through this single visualization.

However, if the same information can be visualized in many ways simultaneously, it is generally a good idea to synchronize the visualizations in real-time so that they accurately depict the underlying model. This situation is much more complicated, since any visualization can change the model, and the other visualizations must respond appropriately to

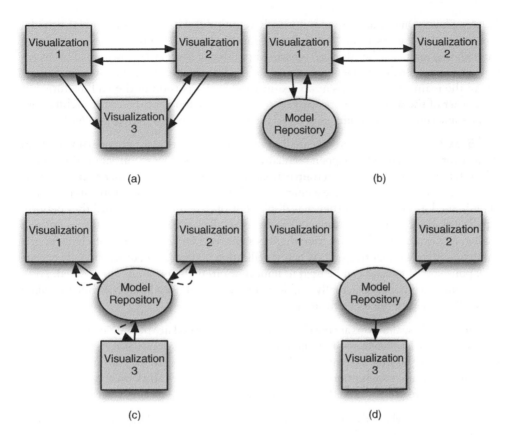

Figure 7-6.
*Multiple
strategies for
coordinating
visualizations of
the same
information:
(a) peer-to-peer,
(b) master-slave,
(c) pull, and
(d) push.*

that change. If the visualizations include both depiction *and* interaction, then both the depiction and the interaction state of the visualizations must be updated. This might mean changing editing modes, updating menu options, and so on.

Coordinating multiple visualizations can be accomplished through many well-known methods, depending on the situation. For situations where information may be visualized through only one visualization at a time, a simple import-export method usually works best: Initial depictions are created when the visualization is called up and stored (if necessary) when the visualization is dismissed.

Situations where multiple simultaneous visualizations are allowed are harder to deal with. In these cases, four general synchronization strategies are available (see Figure 7-6):

Peer-to-Peer. The visualizations maintain their own copies of information from the model, know about each other and explicitly notify one another about changes. These strategies can be brittle because they tend to tightly couple visualizations. They require many point-to-point dependencies. The number of dependencies is $\frac{v(v-1)}{2}$ where v is the number of visualizations. This grows exponentially as the number of visualizations increases. Because of this, the peer-to-peer strategy is most suitable for a small, fixed number of visualizations chosen in advance.

Master-Slave. One visualization is primarily responsible for interacting with the model repository, and it serves as the "master" visualization. Other slave visualizations coordinate through this master, either through a push- or pull-based strategy (see below). This works well when one visualization is auxiliary to another; for example, imagine a graphical editor where the main window shows a zoomed-in version of a portion of the architecture, but the corner of the window is portioned off to show a thumbnail of the entire architecture at the same time (for providing context to the user or serving as a navigation aid).

Pull-Based. Each visualization repeatedly queries a shared model for changes and updates itself accordingly. This may happen manually—at the user's request, automatically at periodic intervals, or in response to certain actions (for example, when the user clicks on a new visualization or attempts to make a change to a different visualization). One disadvantage of pull-based strategies is that they may display out-of-date information until they perform a pull operation. Pull-based strategies can be used when the model repository is entirely passive (for example, a data structure that does not send out events when it changes, or a database system without triggers). When visualization updates are computationally expensive, pull-based strategies can be used to limit how often visualizations are updated. Also, if only one visualization is actually visible at a time, it might not be worthwhile to update a visualization until the user calls it up.

Push-Based. Visualizations are notified and consequently update themselves whenever the model changes. Notifications are usually multicast to visualizations through asynchronous events. This is the strategy employed by the model-view-controller pattern. Push-based strategies keep all visualizations up to date. These strategies work well when multiple visualizations are presented to the user simultaneously.

In situations where the architecture is organized into multiple (partial) models, it is sometimes possible to coordinate access to these models through a single visualization, thus masking some of the differences between notations or combining the strength of multiple visualizations. Figure 7-7 shows an architecture whose component-and-connector structure is expressed in xADL 2.0, but the detailed design of each component is expressed in UML.

7.2.4 Beyond Design: Using Visualization Dynamically

As discussed above, architecture visualizations are primarily used to depict and allow interaction with the design decisions that comprise an architecture. However, more advanced and dynamic visualizations can be used to gain an even deeper understanding of the architecture.

We now introduce the concept of effect visualizations.

> ***Definition.*** An *effect visualization* is a visualization that does not represent architectural design decisions directly, but instead represents the *effects* of architectural design decisions.

For example, imagine an architectural model that contains enough information that it can be used as the basis for a behavioral simulation. The output or results of this simulation are not strictly an architectural model, since they are the results of the design decisions made in the architecture rather than the decisions themselves. Thus, visualizations of such results are not strictly architectural visualizations. These results, however, can be

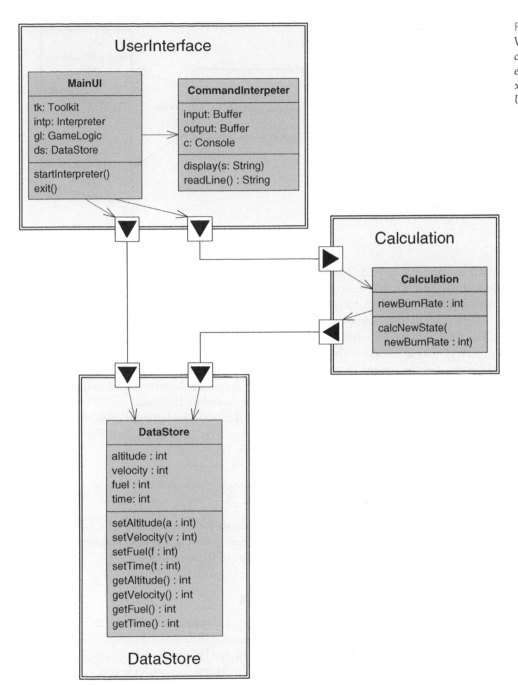

Figure 7-7.
*Visualization
combining
elements from
xADL and
UML.*

Figure 7-8.
*Generating effect
visualizations.*

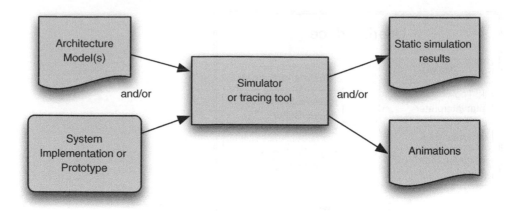

extremely effective in helping stakeholders to better comprehend, implement, or debug the architecture. Therefore, it is useful to consider these effect visualizations in tandem with more traditional architecture visualizations.

Figure 7-8 shows common strategies for generating effect visualizations. In general, a rich architectural model serves as one input, and an implemented version of the system or a prototype may serve as another. These are fed into a tool that can analyze or simulate the behavior of the system, or perhaps record and trace the operation of the system implementation or prototype. The output of this tool may include static simulation results or animations that demonstrate the operation of the (simulated) system.

Several architecture tools provide effect visualizations, including Rapide, the Labeled Transition State Analyzer (LTSA), and the Message Tracing and Analysis Tool (MTAT). These tools are discussed in more detail in Section 7.5.

7.3 COMMON ISSUES IN VISUALIZATION

While this chapter has focused mainly on techniques for constructing a broad variety of effective visualizations, we can also learn from common mistakes people make in designing visualizations. The following sections present some of these mistakes.

7.3.1   Same Symbol, Different Meaning

When the same symbol is used multiple times in the same visualization, or even across related visualizations, it becomes confusing for users if different meanings are applied to the symbol. This is extremely common for generic symbols such as basic shapes (rectangles, ovals, arrows with default heads). Graphical visualizations provide users with a wide variety of ways of creating distinctive symbols—shapes, decorations, icons, borders, arrowheads, fills, and so on. All of these can be used to make visualizations richer and more precise.

Figure 7-9 shows a simple but deceptive diagram of a client-server system. Here, both the clients and the server are represented by the same symbol (a rectangle), even though

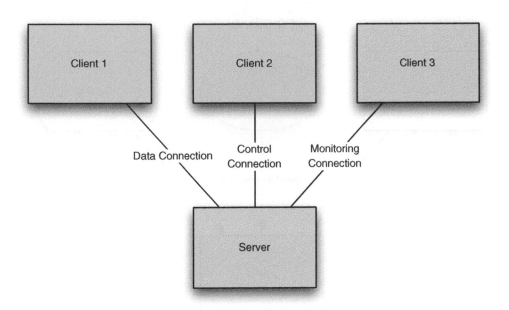

Figure 7-9.
*Example of same
symbol, different
meaning.*

they are distinct. The clients and server are all connected with the same type of plain line, although labels clearly indicate that these are different kinds of connections. Additionally, given the duties of the clients indicated by these connections—data, control, monitoring—it is possible that the clients are not even like one another, even though they appear to be.

7.3.2 Differences without Meaning

Graphical visualizations in which similar elements are repeated over and over (such as the same kinds of components or the same kinds of links) can often appear uninteresting or aesthetically flat. It is common to try to spice up such diagrams by adding decorations and other changes to symbols, primarily for their aesthetic value.

Figure 7-10 shows an example of this situation. Here, the otherwise uniform PC clients each are depicted with a different symbol. Different connection styles (including a random assortment of line styles and arrowheads) connect these uniform clients to the server, all for the same purpose. While this diagram does indeed look more interesting than the one in Figure 7-9, it only serves to confuse. It implies that there is heterogeneity among the clients, and that the connections between the clients and the server are substantially different.

7.3.3 Decorations without Meaning

Differences without meaning are not the only problem some graphical visualizations suffer. A related mistake is the consistent inclusion of visual decorations that indicate meaning but are not intended to convey it. A classic example of this is the use of double-headed arrows to indicate a simple connection between two symbols. The arrowheads imply directionality:

Figure 7-10.
*Example of
"differences
without
meaning."*

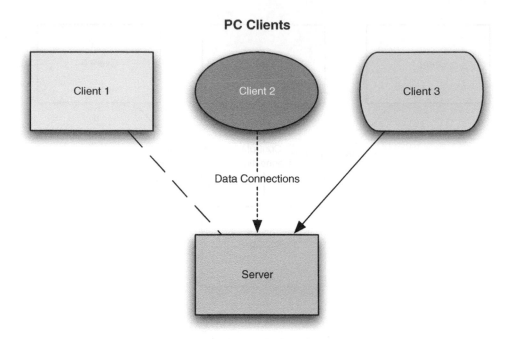

that information or control is flowing in both directions across the connection. Often, the intended meaning is simply an association; in this case, the arrowheads only serve to confuse the issue by indicating flows where there are none.

Figure 7-11 shows a seemingly innocuous entity-relationship (ER) diagram. These diagrams are used to indicate various elements of a system and their quantity relationships to each other. For example, there is one business logic element in the system, associated with one ordinary server and many backup servers. However, the connections on the diagram are all two-headed arrows. Traditionally, ER diagrams do not include directional associations, since they are not meant to imply dependency, data flow, or any other meaning commonly associated with arrows. These additional decorations may imply things about the relationships between these elements that are simply not true.

7.3.4   Borrowed Symbol, Different Meaning

Visualizations are never truly interpreted anew; they are always seen through the lens of the user's previous experience and knowledge. Experienced users are familiar with a catalog of other visualizations and the symbols and meanings associated with those visualizations. Using symbols that are strongly associated with a different visualization is a good idea if the (rough) meaning of the symbol is brought along as well. Using the same symbol to mean something completely different is a recipe for disaster. For example, using the closed white-headed arrow in a diagram to mean "calls" will likely confuse UML users who will interpret that arrow as meaning "generalization."

Figure 7-12 shows a simple logical layout for an application. In terms of the issues above, it fares well: three different kinds of symbols are used for three different kinds of

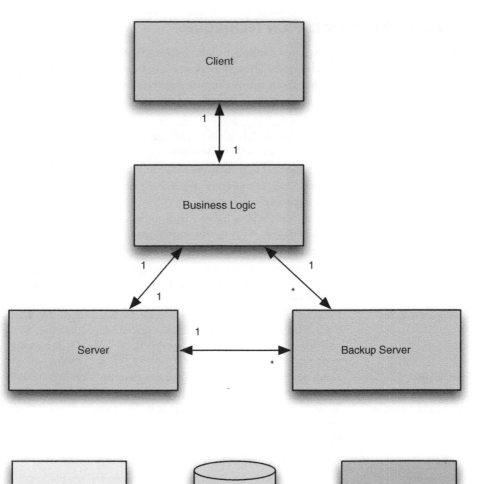

Figure 7-11.
*Example of
decorations
without meaning.*

Figure 7-12.
*Example of
borrowed
symbol, different
meaning.*

components, only one kind of arrow is used and it indicates a calling dependency, and
so on. The problem with this diagram lies in the choice of symbols. All these symbols are
used in classic flowchart diagrams. The vertical cylinder, used in this diagram to represent
the business logic component, is generally used in flowcharting to indicate a data store or
disk. The box with a wavy bottom, used here to represent the data store component, is
usually used to represent a document or data file. Users familiar with these interpretations
might incorrectly infer that the data store was not a component, but simply a file, and that
the business logic also acted as some sort of data store.

7.4 EVALUATING VISUALIZATION TECHNIQUES

In the past sections, we have explored a number of dimensions that can be used to characterize different visualization techniques. These dimensions can be straightforwardly turned into a rubric for critically thinking about and evaluating different visualizations. This rubric will be applied to several techniques in the remainder of this chapter.

Visualization Techniques Rubric		
	Scope and Purpose	What kinds of models can the technique visualize? Is it an architectural visualization or an effect visualization?
	Basic Type	What is the basic type of the visualization: Graphical? Textual? Hybrid?
	Depiction	How does the visualization depict the model? What are the basic constituents of the depiction?
	Interaction	How can stakeholders interact with the visualization? What kind of interface is used? What are the capabilities of the interface?
	Fidelity	How faithful is the visualization to the underlying model?
	Consistency	How consistent is the use of symbols in depicting information, especially across viewpoints? How consistent are the interaction mechanisms?
	Comprehensibility	How easy is it to comprehend the information being visualized? What kinds of information is the visualization optimized for conveying? How well does the visualization leverage existing stakeholder understandings to increase comprehensibility?
	Dynamism	How does the visualization use dynamic elements such as animation to depict changes over time?
	View Coordination	To what extent is the visualization of multiple views allowed? What strategies are used to coordinate the visualization of multiple views? How effective are these strategies?
	Aesthetics	How aesthetically pleasing is the visualization to its users?
	Extensibility	How easy is it to tailor or adapt the visualization for new purposes?

7.5 TECHNIQUES

This section surveys representative examples of a variety of architecture visualizations that are used in research and practice, from traditional textual and graphical visualizations to more exotic tools that use animation and effect visualizations.

7.5.1 Textual Visualizations

There are literally as many textual visualizations as there are text editors. Many models' canonical visualizations are text-based. The most rudimentary text-based visualizations are provided by editors such as Windows Notepad, or "pico" and "joe" on UNIX systems. These editors display architectural models in a structured text format, in a single font and color. Interactions in these basic text editors is limited—users can edit through rudimentary commands such as inserting and deleting characters, and copying-and-pasting blocks of text.

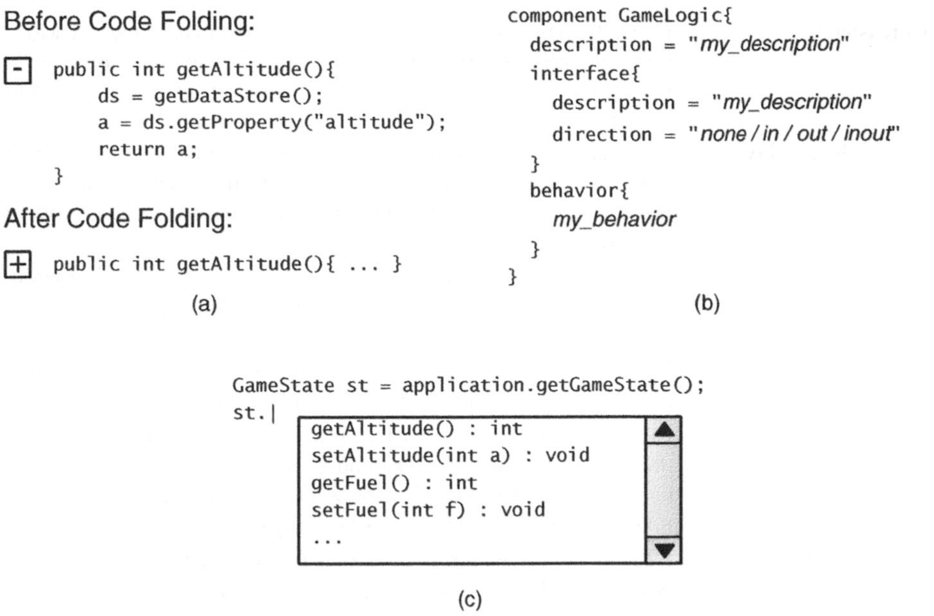

Before Code Folding:

```
[-]  public int getAltitude(){
         ds = getDataStore();
         a = ds.getProperty("altitude");
         return a;
     }
```

After Code Folding:

```
[+]  public int getAltitude(){ ... }
```

(a)

```
component GameLogic{
    description = "my_description"
    interface{
        description = "my_description"
        direction = "none / in / out / inout"
    }
    behavior{
        my_behavior
    }
}
```

(b)

```
GameState st = application.getGameState();
st.|
```

```
getAltitude() : int             ▲
setAltitude(int a) : void
getFuel() : int
setFuel(int f) : void
...                             ▼
```

(c)

Figure 7-13. *Various advanced techniques used in text visualizations: (a) code folding, (b) templates, and (c) autocomplete.*

Enhanced text editors, such as those found in many integrated software development environments, support a similar base-feature set, but offer many improvements as well. These improvements are mostly available through the text editor having some internal knowledge of the syntax or semantics of the underlying notation. Common depiction enhancements include syntax coloring and code folding. Editors with syntax coloring support identify segments of text as tokens and color them to represent the type of token (keyword, character string, number, variable, and so on). Code folding is a technique whereby the editor can identify blocks of text and "fold" those blocks into a single line to reduce the amount of detail shown. Both these techniques require that the editor have an understanding of the syntax of the underlying notation. Common interaction enhancements include code completion and templates. Interfaces with code completion allow the user to type some or all of a token, and have the editor present options for completing the token to save typing. Templates allow the user to insert a block of text with placeholders and then enter data for each placeholder. Some of these depiction and interaction techniques are shown in Figure 7-13.

		Evaluation Rubric for Textual Visualizations
Scope and Purpose	Depicting and editing models that can be expressed as (structured) text.	
Basic Type	Textual.	
Depiction	Lines of text composed of characters; depending on the syntax characters will be grouped into ordered tokens.	
Interaction	For basic text editors, insert/delete/copy/paste. Enhanced editors may provide syntax/semantic-aware features such as syntax coloring, code folding, code completion and templates.	
Fidelity	In general, textual visualizations depict the entire model including all detail.	

Consistency	Depends on how well the language syntax is defined; a language with a poorly designed syntax might use the same token for different purposes in different contexts. Interaction mechanisms are generally consistent because they do not vary.
Comprehensibility	In general, textual visualizations are best for visualizing information that can be organized linearly or hierarchically. They have low comprehensibility for complex models with many interrelated elements, or elements organized in graph structures.
Dynamism	Depends on the editor in use; there are some integrated environments where model changes will cause immediate updates to textual visualizations.
View Coordination	In some integrated environments, textual visualizations can be coordinated with other visualizations of other views via a shared model.
Aesthetics	Depends on the syntax of the language, as well as how the visualization organizes and presents the text. Long, continuous blocks of text tend to be perceived as aesthetically poor; well-organized, attractively colored text tends to be perceived as aesthetically pleasing.
Extensibility	Depends on the editor; some editors provide well-defined extension points for adding in new language syntax and supporting features such as syntax coloring and autocompletion for new languages.

7.5.2   Informal Graphical Editors

PowerPoint and similar graphical editors [(Microsoft Corporation 2007) (Microsoft Corporation 2007) (The Omni Group 2007)] are commonly used to capture architectural design decisions despite the fact that these tools have no support for architectural semantics—they are simply diagram editors. With no real graphical syntax or semantics, the power and allure of informal graphical modeling is not derived from the model or the notation, but from its visualization. From a depiction standpoint, informal graphical diagrams are generally straightforward and aesthetically pleasing. Text, symbols, and bitmap graphics coexist in depictions as needed. Nothing is hidden; everything in the depiction is visible on a single page or slide. The page provides a natural limitation on how much detail can be presented at a time; by having finite boundaries, it limits the complexity of the visualized information. By building up a slide deck or using tools such as PowerPoint's animation capabilities, it is even possible to depict the evolution of an architecture over time.

The most attractive aspect of informal graphical editors, however, is their user interfaces. These editors are characterized by point-and-click interfaces that allow users to create and manipulate diagrams with great ease and flexibility. Symbols can be created and moved simply by dragging and dropping. PowerPoint's connector lines will even maintain their connections as the shapes they connect are moved around the canvas. Users can easily add media from outside sources as well: Bitmap graphics, vector graphics, screenshots, and even video and audio clips in nearly any format can be added to these diagrams with only a few mouse clicks.

Figure 7-14 shows PowerPoint being used to draw a Koala-style architecture. Although the visualization is attractive, certain problems are already apparent. The various elements shown are just independent shapes and text. For example, the interfaces on the components

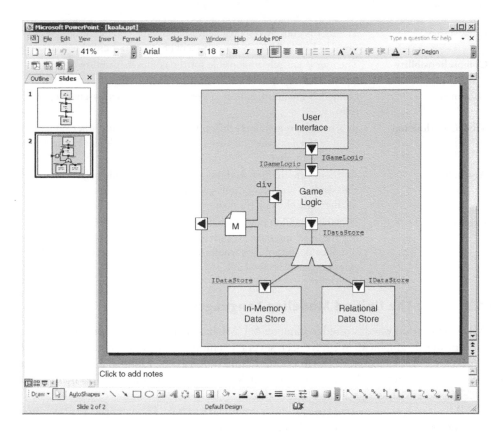

Figure 7-14.
Screenshot of PowerPoint being used to draw a Koala-style architecture.

are simply white boxes with black triangles on top; PowerPoint has no concept of an architectural interface. They are not even attached to the rectangles representing components; they simply overlap the edges. Because the diagram is not bound to any semantic representation, keeping it consistent with other models must be done manually. The graphical shapes and decorations available cannot be easily extended. There are no facilities in the user interface for establishing repeated patterns or for extending the interface to take into account architectural concepts.

		Evaluation Rubric for Informal Graphical Visualizations
Scope and Purpose	Visualization of arbitrary collections of symbols, text elements, clip art, and so on.	
Basic Type	Hybrid: primarily graphical with some textual annotations and elements.	
Depiction	As a canvas containing floating graphical and textual elements, positioned arbitrarily by the user. Elements occupying the same space are drawn one on top of the other, with the top-to-bottom ordering determined by the user.	
Interaction	Primarily a point-and-click user interface, with options for dragging, dropping, and manipulating elements with the mouse and keyboard.	
Fidelity	In general, the underlying model is coupled directly to the visualization and nothing is hidden so the visualization is completely faithful.	

Consistency	The user is entirely responsible for developing consistent representations; lack of consistency is a persistent problem in these visualizations.
Comprehensibility	The user is entirely responsible for the comprehensibility of the presented information.
Dynamism	Limited animation facilities are provided for depicting changes over time.
View Coordination	In general, it is extremely difficult to coordinate with other visualizations, or even connect elements on multiple pages/slides in the same file to one another.
Aesthetics	Aesthetics are the responsibility of the user; the wide palette of available symbols and decorations gives users enormous freedom to create aesthetically pleasing (or poor) visualizations.
Extensibility	In general, adding new symbols is straightforward; however, extending the user interface to provide new interaction options is more complicated. Scripting capabilities or published interfaces that allow extensions may be available.

7.5.3 UML: The Unified Modeling Language

UML as a notation was discussed in Chapter 6. UML has an associated canonical depiction that is primarily graphical. We have seen several examples of UML diagrams already, such as in Figure 7-4. Compared to the free-form nature of informal graphical editors that deal in boxes and arrows, UML diagrams are visualizations of more semantically meaningful elements such as classes and statechart nodes.

UML concepts are mapped to particular graphical symbols. For example, the "generalizes" relationship between elements is mapped to an arrow with a closed, white, triangular head. While certain concepts (and, as such, their associated symbols) are only present in certain diagrams, diagrams that incorporate common concepts use the same symbol in each diagram. For example, the "generalizes" relationship is present in both the class and object diagrams, and the same symbol (the closed white arrow) is used to represent the concept in both diagrams. Interestingly, although UML's syntax is defined in a graphical meta-model, the UML meta-model does not actually map UML concepts to symbols; this mapping is described in other documentation.

Even when taking into account this additional documentation, UML is only associated with a canonical depiction and not a canonical user interface. That is, UML's designers prescribe how UML diagrams should look, but not how the user should interact with them in tools or editing environments. These decisions are left up to individual tool vendors, and tools such as Rational Rose (Rational Software Corporation 2003) and ArgoUML (*Argo/UML*) have different mechanisms for manipulating and otherwise interacting with UML diagrams. Figure 7-15 shows a screenshot from ArgoUML editing a UML model. Note that the canonical graphical visualization is only one part of the environment. Another visualization of the model as a tree is present on the left side. Tools accessible from the menu and from the tabbed area below allow the model to be manipulated in different ways.

Tools such as Rose and ArgoUML provide compelling user interfaces, but often can blur the distinction between what is provided by the tool and what is provided by a modeling

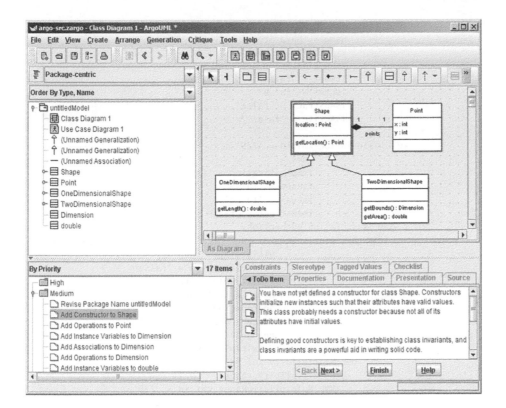

Figure 7-15.
Screenshot of ArgoUML.

notation. For example, the screenshot in Figure 7-15 includes an editor for a to-do list. UML itself has no concept of a to-do list; this is a feature of ArgoUML. Users must be cognizant of these distinctions, as they can make it more difficult to integrate multiple tools operating on the same model, or to switch from one environment to another.

The canonical graphical visualization is not the only visualization available to UML users. Although it is not part of the core UML standard, it is possible to visualize UML data using text through the use of XMI (Object Management Group 2002). XMI is an XML-based format devised to facilitate interchange of models between tools. It is an interchange format in which a UML model can be encoded in XML. XMI helps to draw out the distinction between UML and its canonical graphical visualization. Plain XMI encodes only the information in a UML model, but not information about diagram layout from graphical visualizations. An extension to XMI that includes this information is provided in a separate standard. Figure 7-16 shows an excerpt of an XMI document generated by ArgoUML. Note the amount of text used to depict a simple point-to-point association, as well as the lack of information about graphical depiction, layout, or positioning.

One of the main advantages of UML's canonical graphical visualization is the (mostly) consistent use of symbols across diagrams and projects. The rationale behind this decision is that it increases the ability of stakeholders who are familiar with UML to quickly understand the meaning of diagrams in different contexts. In this regard, UML's popularity creates a network effect: The more people who use UML, the more valuable the consistent use of these symbols becomes.

Figure 7-16.
*Excerpt of an
XMI document
showing the
representation of
a UML class and
association.*

```
<UML:Class xmi.id = '723'
          name = 'Data Store'
          visibility = 'public'
          isSpecification = 'false'
          isRoot = 'false'
          isLeaf = 'false'
          isAbstract = 'false'
          isActive = 'false'/>

<UML:Association xmi.id = '725'
          name = ''
          isSpecification = 'false'
          isRoot = 'false'
          isLeaf = 'false'
          isAbstract = 'false'>
  <UML:Association.connection>
    <UML:AssociationEnd xmi.id = '726'
                        visibility = 'public'
                        isSpecification = 'false'
                        isNavigable = 'true'
                        ordering = 'unordered'
                        aggregation = 'none'
                        targetScope = 'instance'
                        changeability = 'changeable'>
      <UML:AssociationEnd.multiplicity>
        <UML:Multiplicity xmi.id = '727'>
          <UML:Multiplicity.range>
            <UML:MultiplicityRange xmi.id = '728'
                                   lower = '1'
                                   upper = '1'/>
          </UML:Multiplicity.range>
        </UML:Multiplicity>
      </UML:AssociationEnd.multiplicity>
      <UML:AssociationEnd.participant>
        <UML:Class xmi.idref = '71F'/>
      </UML:AssociationEnd.participant>
    </UML:AssociationEnd>

    <UML:AssociationEnd xmi.id = '729'
                        visibility = 'public'
                        isSpecification = 'false'
                        isNavigable = 'true'
                        ordering = 'unordered'
                        aggregation = 'none'
                        targetScope = 'instance'
                        changeability = 'changeable'>
      <UML:AssociationEnd.multiplicity>
        <UML:Multiplicity xmi.id = '72A'>
          <UML:Multiplicity.range>
            <UML:MultiplicityRange xmi.id = '72B'
                                   lower = '1'
                                   upper = '1'/>
          </UML:Multiplicity.range>
        </UML:Multiplicity>
      </UML:AssociationEnd.multiplicity>
```

```
       <UML:AssociationEnd.participant>
          <UML:Class xmi.idref = '721'/>
       </UML:AssociationEnd.participant>
     </UML:AssociationEnd>
   </UML:Association.connection>
</UML:Association>
```

Figure 7-16.
(*Continued*)

UML's consistent use of symbols has limitations and disadvantages, however. Symbolic consistency in visualization cannot create semantic precision at the notational level. That is, if the concept of generalization is semantically ambiguous, the consistent use of the same arrow shape to depict the concept cannot repair this ambiguity. Additionally, the use of the same set of symbols across project and domain boundaries limits how much UML can be specialized for a particular domain. UML tools and standards do not generally support a lot of customization in UML visualizations for individual projects or domains. For example, Rational Rose allows users to associate stereotypes with graphical icons, but will not fundamentally change the symbol of the element to which the stereotype is being applied.

Scope and Purpose	Canonical visualization of UML models via (currently) thirteen diagram types.	**Evaluation Rubric for UML Visualizations**
Basic Type	Hybrid: primarily graphical with some textual annotations and elements (such as OCL constraints)	
Depiction	Each UML diagram type has a canonical depiction. Each diagram type is composed of a handful of basic elements—the class diagram, for example, includes distinctive elements for classes, methods, different kinds of associations, and so on.	
Interaction	Depends on the tool in use; different UML tools have different interaction interfaces. Most allow point-and-click editing in the style of PowerPoint, and available editing options are generally guided by UML's syntax and semantics.	
Fidelity	As a canonical visualization, these depictions are generally completely faithful.	
Consistency	UML attempts to use consistent symbols, even across diagram types; there are small exceptions. (An open-headed dashed arrow might indicate a dependency in a class diagram or a message in a sequence diagram.)	
Comprehensibility	Most diagrams can be interpreted at a very general level with no prior knowledge. However, properly interpreting each diagram requires specific knowledge of the meaning of each of UML's symbols. Most diagrams have roots in earlier notations (for example, OMT and statecharts) that may be familiar to stakeholders outside the context of UML.	
Dynamism	Few UML tools use animation to depict changes in the underlying model.	
View Coordination	Multiple UML diagrams can be used to represent multiple views of a system, but there is no agreed-upon standard for linking common information in multiple views. Some editors allow multiple instances of the same element to be present in multiple diagrams simultaneously and will make changes to this element simultaneously in all diagrams.	

Aesthetics	UML diagrams use a limited set of relatively basic shapes to reduce complexity, although this can make diagrams seem overly simplistic and uniform. Some editors enhance this by allowing UML elements to be colored or enhanced with decorative icons to more clearly indicate element properties, for example.
Extensibility	Depends on the tool/editor in use; most support UML's basic extension mechanisms: stereotypes, tagged values, and constraints. Adding a new diagram type or extending UML's syntax would require major work, however.

7.5.4 Rapide

Effect visualizations, which depict the effects of architectural decisions rather than the decisions themselves, can be seen in the Rapide project (Luckham and Vera 1995). Chapter 6 shows several architectural models in Rapide's canonical textual visualization. However, the real power of Rapide comes from tools that allow users to run simulations of these architectural models. The Rapide simulator takes architecture models in the Rapide notation as input, and then simulates the interaction of the various components as defined by the behaviors specified in the model. Simulation runs generate a stream of events, some of which are causally related to one another. Because Rapide components run in parallel, the results of simulations are not strictly deterministic: Repeated simulations of the same architecture can generate different event streams depending on how the simulator's scheduler allocates time to the various components.

The result of a Rapide simulation is a directed graph of nodes, with each node representing an event and each edge representing a causal relationship between events. An example, originally presented in Chapter 6, is shown again in Figure 7-17. This can be seen as a kind of visualization of the system and its architecture. Even though it does not necessarily depict specific design decisions, it depicts the direct result of architectural design decisions and can equally serve to provide stakeholders with insights about the workings of the architecture.

Evaluation Rubric for Rapide	Scope and Purpose	Specification of architectural structure and component behavior in a textual format; display of simulation results in a graphical format.
	Basic Type	Architectural models are specified in a textual visualization; effect depictions are graphical.
	Depiction	Models in rigorous text format; effect visualizations are directed graphs containing nodes representing events and edges representing causal dependencies.
	Interaction	Models are edited in an ordinary text editor; effect visualizations are not editable.
	Fidelity	Textual visualization of the model is canonical; effect visualizations show one possible simulation run. Multiple simulations may produce different results in a nondeterministic system.
	Consistency	Limited vocabulary of symbols ensures consistency.
	Comprehensibility	Architectural models can be difficult to write and understand, although this is largely due to the complexity of the underlying notation. Effect

	visualizations are straightforward to understand, although complex systems may generate very large intertwined graphs that are difficult to interpret.
Dynamism	No support.
View Coordination	Effect visualizations are generated automatically from architectural models.
Aesthetics	Models are in a familiar programming-language style although the vocabulary of operators is fairly large. Effect visualization graphs are simple and unadorned.
Extensibility	Difficult to extend; Rapide and its tool set are a relative black box.

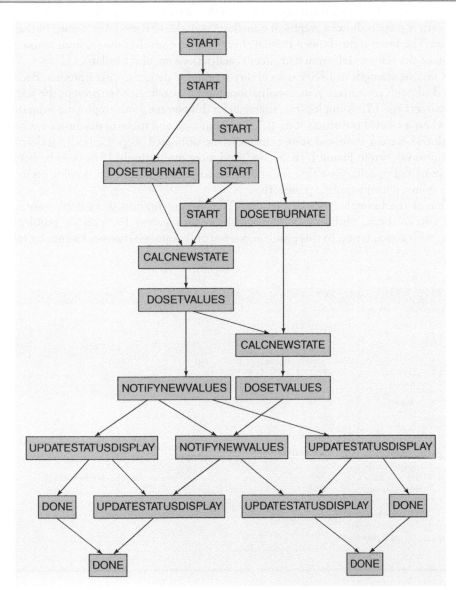

Figure 7-17.
*Rapide effect
visualization of
the Lunar Lander
application.*

7.5.5 The Labeled Transition System Analyzer (LTSA)

The Labeled Transition System Analyzer (LTSA) project from Imperial College in London, UK, is a way of analyzing and simultaneously visualizing concurrent systems (Magee and Kramer 2006). A system in LTSA is modeled as a set of interacting finite state machines. Users specify component behaviors in a compact process algebra called finite state processes (FSP); FSP is then compiled into state machines with labeled transitions. The LTSA tools can visualize these state machines graphically using a traditional nodes-and-arrows visualization.

Figure 7-18 shows a screenshot of the LTSA tool. Multiple concurrently maintained visualizations are shown. The upper-right area shows the canonical textual visualization of the model: raw FSP. To its left is a tree-based visualization of the project's organization. The lower-center section shows a graphical visualization of the FSP model as a state-transition diagram. The lower-right shows a textual effect visualization that results from automated analysis of the FSP model; animated effect visualizations are also available.

A unique strength of LTSA is its ability to employ dynamic visualizations. Because LTSA deals with concurrency, its visualizations have a specific need to present the state of systems over time. LTSA employs two strategies for this purpose, both employing animation. First, when a labeled transition state (LTS) is simulated and its state machines are being viewed, the current state and state transitions are animated atop the nodes-and-arrows visualization shown in Figure 7-18. Second, and more interestingly, LTSes can be hooked up to animated visualizations that use animation to directly show what is going on in the system from a domain-specific perspective.

One of the examples included in the LTSA documentation is an implementation of the famous dining philosophers problem shown in Figure 7-19, a classic problem in dealing with concurrency. In this problem, a set of philosophers sit around a circular table.

Figure 7-18.
Screenshot of the LTSA tool.

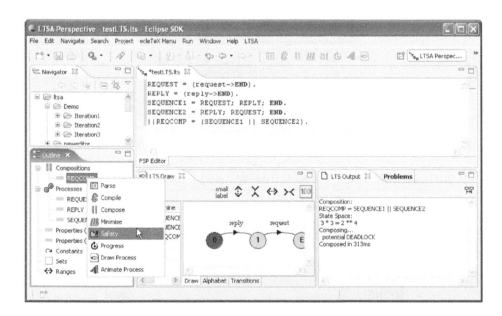

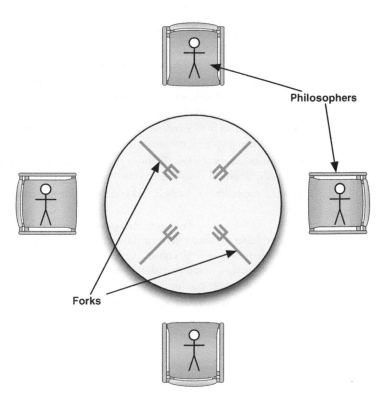

Figure 7-19.
*Four dining
philosophers.*

In between each pair of philosophers is a fork. Philosophers need to pick up both their adjacent forks to eat, but are also constrained by a set of rules as to when they can pick up and put down forks. The challenge in the problem is coming up with a set of rules such that all philosophers get to eat periodically and the system does not enter a locked state (for example, in which each philosopher picks up one fork and none will put one down).

The LTSA tools model the philosophers as communicating state machines, but can also visualize the models as a diagram of a table surrounded by philosophers, similar to what is shown in Figure 7-19. State changes, like a philosopher acquiring a fork, are visualized as an actual picture of a philosopher picking up fork. Simulations of other applications, such as air traffic control, use similar domain-specific visualizations hooked up directly to the component behavior simulators (such as pictures of airplanes circling and landing). Unlike Rapide, which only allows users to visualize event traffic in a graph after the fact, LTSA allows users to visualize the system being simulated in real-time, using animations and symbols that are directly drawn from the real domain. Although users of LTSA have to spend time and effort to construct these domain-specific visualizations for each application, their value comes from the fact that they go a long way to communicate the real meaning of abstract state machines. It may be difficult to understand the meaning of a particular state transition in a nodes-and-arrows diagram, but it is much easier to understand a picture of a philosopher actually picking up a fork.

Scope and Purpose	Coordinated visualization of FSP models and different effect visualizations.
Basic Type	Multiple textual and graphical model views and effect visualizations.
Depiction	FSP models are visualized both in text and in graphical state-transition diagrams. Effect visualizations may be textual, animated on the state-transition diagrams, or custom and domain-specific.
Interaction	An integrated set of tools allow the user to manipulate FSP models in both text and graphical visualizations.
Fidelity	Coordination between visualizations and models are maintained automatically; graphical visualizations may elide some information.
Consistency	Limited vocabulary of symbols and concepts helps to ensure consistency.
Comprehensibility	FSP is a complex textual notation but is somewhat easier to understand than other formalisms. State-transition diagrams are straightforward and their format is well known. Custom domain-specific visualizations can increase comprehension substantially by tying models back to domain concepts graphically.
Dynamism	Animation on state-transition diagrams and custom domain-specific visualizations.
View Coordination	Views are coordinated automatically.
Aesthetics	Well-known state-transition diagrams are easy to interpret; domain-specific visualizations tie abstract models to concrete real-world concepts.
Extensibility	New custom domain-specific visualizations can be added as plug-ins.

7.5.6 xADL 2.0

The syntax of the xADL 2.0 language is defined in a set of XML schemas. As such, the canonical visualization for xADL 2.0 files is textual, in XML that conforms to the syntax prescribed by the schemas. One of the most interesting aspects of xADL 2.0, however, is that its canonical visualization is rarely (if ever) used or even seen by its users. Tools that support xADL 2.0 modeling provide a variety of alternative visualizations, both graphical and textual (Dashofy 2007). Some of these visualizations include the following.

xADLite

The xADLite visualization has been used throughout this book to describe various architectures. xADLite is a textual visualization that captures xADL 2.0 models using textual tokens organized in a manner similar to C-like programming languages: Hierarchical blocks are surrounded by curly braces, the "=" operator is used to denote assignment, double-quotes surround string values, and so on. This visualization was specifically crafted to capture all the data in a xADL 2.0 model in a compact format, using few extraneous characters. The programming-language-like symbology was chosen due to the popularity of this organization: Experienced software developers are comfortable with these symbols and organization and can read it easily without additional training. From a user-interface perspective, xADLite files are written and manipulated using standard text editors.

ArchEdit

ArchEdit, shown in Figure 7-20, is a tool that provides a semigraphical visualization of xADL 2.0 models. The document structure is depicted in a tree format with selectable nodes. When a node is selected, text attributes of that node are displayed for editing. Although the information in this view is organized hierarchically (much like the XML or xADLite visualizations), the user interface of ArchEdit is far more interactive. ArchEdit has a point-and-click interface that not only allows users to expand and collapse subtrees of the document, but also provides context-sensitive menus that provide the user specific options to add, remove, or manipulate elements. ArchEdit provides a *syntax-directed* visualization: the user interface and what is displayed on the screen are both derived, at least partially, from the syntax of xADL 2.0 itself. For example, when you right-click on an element in ArchEdit, it brings up a menu of children that can be added to that element. The list of available children is generated based on the definition of the xADL 2.0 language, and is not hardcoded in the tool itself. For a language with malleable syntax like xADL 2.0, syntax-directed visualizations and other tools become even more valuable. The primary disadvantage of (even the best) syntax-directed visualizations is that the syntax of the underlying notation drives how the information is visually presented. If the notation is treelike and hierarchical, it is likely that a syntax-directed visualization of the notation will also employ trees and hierarchy.

Archipelago

Archipelago, shown in Figure 7-21, is a tool that provides graphical visualizations of xADL 2.0 models. Archipelago's visualizations are semantically aware, meaning that specific

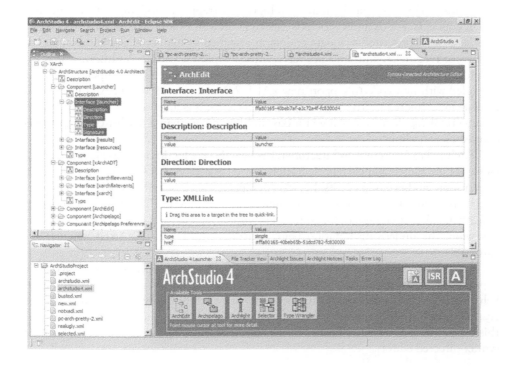

Figure 7-20.
*ArchEdit
screenshot.*

Figure 7-21.
*Archipelago
screenshot.*

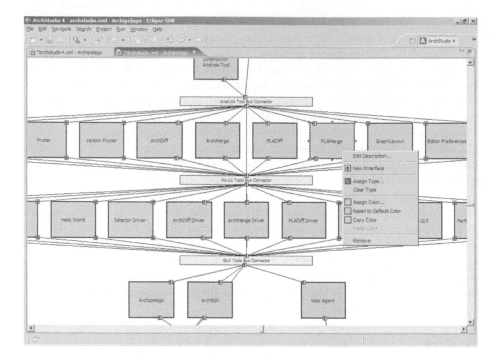

depictions and behaviors are built into Archipelago to represent and interact with different xADL concepts. For example, components and connectors are represented as rectangles, interfaces are represented as square endpoints attached to the borders of component and connector rectangles, and links are represented as splines. Unlike ArchEdit, which can adapt its user interface automatically to new syntactic elements, Archipelago must be extended with new code to support new xADL 2.0 concepts. However, Archipelago can provide much more intuitive visualizations to its users; it is much easier to understand an architectural topology by looking at a box-and-line graph than a flat list of components, connectors, and links.

Archipelago's internal architecture relies heavily on plug-ins for implementing visual elements and their graphical representations as well as behaviors—how Archipelago reacts to user input and external events. In fact, Archipelago itself is really a small core of extension points; almost all of its behavior is implemented by plug-ins. This makes Archipelago a highly flexible environment for adding new visual elements and behaviors, a real necessity when the underlying notation being visualized (xADL 2.0) is itself modular and extensible.

The primary disadvantage of fully semantics-aware editors such as Archipelago is the expense of creating and maintaining them. Users expect intuitive, comprehensive, custom behavior tailored to individual notations, and for more extensive notations this can be quite costly to build. Archipelago attempts to limit this cost by using a modular architecture, but this cannot reduce the complexity of such editors to anywhere near the level of simpler syntax-directed editors.

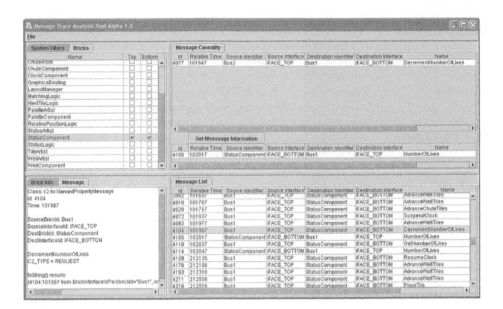

Figure 7-22.
*MTAT
screenshot.*

MTAT

The Message Tracing and Analysis Tool (MTAT) (Hendrickson, Dashofy, and Taylor 2005), shown in Figure 7-22, provides additional visualization support for xADL 2.0 architectures that are mapped to implementations composed of components that interact using asynchronous events. Like Rapide and LTSA, MTAT's visualizations capture a dynamic aspect of a system's architecture, namely the sending and receiving of events. However, unlike Rapide and LTSA that work only on simulated architectures, MTAT provides a unified visualization of two life cycle activities: architecture design and implementation. Events visualized in MTAT are real events sent among components in a real system. Animation can overlay these events on structural diagrams of the architecture visualized in Archipelago, and the user can follow a string of events from component to component, watching how the running application works at the same time.

		Evaluation Rubric for xADL 2.0 Visualizations
Scope and Purpose	Multiple coordinated textual, graphical, and effect visualizations of xADL 2.0 models.	
Basic Type	Coordinated textual, graphical, and effect.	
Depiction	Textual visualizations as XML or xADLite; graphical visualizations as trees and text (in ArchEdit) or symbol graphs (in Archipelago); hybrid effect visualizations in MTAT.	
Interaction	Multiple coordinated editors each with its own interaction paradigm that resembles comparable editors for other notations.	
Fidelity	Textual visualizations and ArchEdit display entire model without leaving out detail; various graphical visualizations elide some detail.	
Consistency	Each visualization has its own method of depicting concepts, although features such as common icons unify them. Interaction mechanisms are also optimized for the particular visualization, although they tend to be consistent with similar tools for other notations.	

Comprehensibility	Different visualizations have different levels of comprehensibility. Graphical visualizations tend to be easier to understand than textual notations, but they leave some information out. Different visualizations are optimized for displaying different kinds of information.
Dynamism	Visualizations such as MTAT use animation to depict the behavior of running systems; other visualizations are coordinated live so that changes in one visualization appear immediately in others.
View Coordination	Different visualizations are coordinated through a common model repository that maintains an in-memory representation of the underlying xADL model.
Aesthetics	Different visualizations attempt to increase aesthetic appeal by being specialized for depicting a particular kind of information.
Extensibility	New visualizations can be added by hooking into the common model repository; visualizations such as Archipelago are also extensible through their own internal plug-in mechanisms.

7.6 END MATTER

We have focused here on the role of visualization in software architecture-based development. Visualizations comprise depiction (how a set of design decisions is visually presented) and interaction (how stakeholders interact with, explore, and manipulate those depictions).

Perhaps the most important lesson from this chapter is that visualizations are not the same things as their underlying modeling notations. Every modeling notation has at least one canonical visualization, which may be textual, graphical, or a combination of both. It is difficult and sometimes counterintuitive to try to mentally separate the information content of a model from its canonical visualization, but making this distinction is useful. Once this distinction is made, it is possible to think about alternative or coordinated visualizations for the same model. It is also possible to separate the strengths and weaknesses of a modeling notation from the strengths and weaknesses of how that notation is visualized. This distinction also helps to explain phenomena such as the use of PowerPoint-like tools for architecture modeling. Here, the visualization is extremely mature and versatile, but the underlying model is devoid of semantics. This makes these tools attractive but dangerous to use in the long run.

When selecting visualizations for a project, do not neglect effect visualizations. Recall that effect visualizations do not visualize architectural design decisions directly, but the results of applying some process to those design decisions—analysis, simulation, and so on. Often, so much focus is put onto model visualization that these effect visualizations get short shrift. Remember that analysis and simulation results are critical and must be interpreted correctly; this can be made substantially easier with the use of appropriate effect visualizations.

Used appropriately, visualizations can make working with, understanding, exchanging, and communicating about architectural design decisions much easier. To maximize this effect, select visualizations with high degrees of fidelity, consistency (both internal and external), comprehensibility, dynamism, and so on. These decisions should be considered in the context of the target stakeholders and their own needs, skills, and prior experiences.

In this chapter and Chapter 6, we discussed how architectural design decisions can be captured in models, and how those models can be visualized. We have reiterated that semantically rich models are more valuable than semantically poor ones. The next chapter explains why. There, we discuss how architectural analysis leverages semantic information in models to help stakeholders discover important system properties early, before they propagate into later design phases where they are expensive to change.

The Business Case

Visualizations can be seen as the user interfaces to architectural models. In many ways, they fulfill the same role as a user interface in a software system. They define the look and feel of the underlying model to stakeholders. They can make it easier to work with the underlying concepts and semantics, but do not modify them. Because of this, even the best visualizations cannot rectify semantic problems in their target notations, but they can add substantial value to already-adequate notations, and have a tremendous effect on the practical usability of those notations.

For these reasons, it is important to consider visualizations—not just notations—up front in a software development effort. One key factor to keep in mind while selecting visualizations is the set of stakeholders that will be using them. Visualizations can take complex models and present them (or a subset of them) in a way that makes intuitive sense to stakeholders. The kinds of visualizations that are most useful for a project manager, for example, are not the same as those that are useful for a software engineer. While canonical visualizations are always available, remember that alternatives are often available as well.

The decision to develop a new visualization should be made with great care. As noted in the chapter, new visualizations can be very costly to develop and maintain. If possible, leverage extensibility mechanisms available in existing visualizations rather than developing one from scratch. Developing a new visualization can be a viable strategy in certain circumstances. Some notations, particularly esoteric or research-based notations, may have valuable semantics or analysis capabilities but lack good visualization support. When developing a family of systems in a particular domain (see Chapter 15), creating new domain-specific visualizations may also be valuable, and the cost is amortized over all projects that use the visualization.

7.7 REVIEW QUESTIONS

1. What is a visualization? What two key elements comprise a visualization?

2. What is the difference between a visualization and a modeling notation? What is a canonical visualization?

3. Identify and describe the two primary categories of visualizations.

4. What are hybrid visualizations? Identify a hybrid visualization and describe why it is a hybrid.

5. What is the relationship between visualizations, viewpoints, and views?

6. Enumerate and describe some criteria that can be used to evaluate visualizations.

7. When should you consider creating a new visualization? Enumerate and describe some strategies for creating an effective new visualization.

8. What does the work of Edward Tufte have to say about software architecture visualizations? What are his key insights?

9. Enumerate and describe some strategies for coordinating multiple visualizations.

10. What are effect visualizations? Where do they come from? How are they different from ordinary architecture visualizations?

11. Enumerate and describe some common problems that arise in architecture visualization.

12. What kinds of visualizations are associated with UML? How do these complement and differ from each other?

13. How do Rapide and LTSA utilize effect visualizations?

14. What kinds of visualizations are associated with xADL 2.0? What are the strengths and weaknesses of these visualizations?

7.8 EXERCISES

1. Identify a notation that is supported by two different visualizations (for example, a graphical and textual visualization). Model a system of your choosing, such as Lunar Lander, in both visualizations. Compare and contrast the experiences, and note especially what kinds of information were easy, hard, or impossible to capture in either.

2. Acquire and install a system that uses effect visualizations, such as Rapide, LTSA, or MTAT. Find a partner and have each of you model a small system using these tools. Trade systems and see how the effect visualizations can be used to help understand each other's models.

3. Choose one or more architectural visualizations not described here and evaluate it using the evaluation rubric presented in the chapter. What are their strengths and weaknesses?

4. Choose an architecture modeling notation and construct a simple novel visualization for it. For example, develop a simplified graphical editor that focuses only on a few kinds of elements, or use a translation technology such as XSLT to transform a complex textual depiction into something more readable.

5. Identify an unusual user interface feature (depiction, interaction, or both) that you have seen outside the context of architecture visualizations—perhaps in another application, a Web interface, or a video game. How might you apply this to architecture visualization? Would it be an improvement or a hindrance?

6. Choose an architecture visualization (or set of visualizations) not presented here. Does it follow the guidelines in this chapter for effective visualizations? Does it exhibit any of the common problems associated with visualizations? Develop a constructive critique of the visualization along these lines.

7.9 FURTHER READING

Most of the visualizations you will encounter are canonical visualizations, and so are documented in the same places as their associated tools or underlying notations. Such is the case for PowerPoint-like tools [(Microsoft Corporation 2007) (Microsoft Corporation 2007) (The Omni Group 2007)] and UML (Booch, Rumbaugh, and Jacobson 2005), as well as several others. It is also interesting to investigate related visualizations that are not canonical, such as XMI (Object Management Group 2002). Systems like Rapide (Luckham and Vera 1995) and LTSA (Magee and Kramer 2006) are interesting for their use of effect visualizations.

The work of Edward Tufte (Tufte 2001; Tufte 1990), cited in a sidebar in this chapter, is excellent reading for anyone who wants to present complex information in a clear, coherent way. Although he focuses mainly on the display of scientific, quantitative data, many of his ideas are easily translated to other domains and applications.

8

Analysis

Rigorous models of software architectures present a number of advantages over informal boxes-and-lines diagrams. They force the software architect to address issues that might otherwise be missed or ignored. They allow more precise communication among the system's various stakeholders and form a solid blueprint for the system's construction, deployment, execution, and evolution. And they typically present more detail about the architecture than do informal models, so that more questions can be asked and answered more precisely—although there are certainly times where sufficient understanding about certain aspects of a system can be obtained even from informal models.

> **Definition. Architectural analysis** is the activity of discovering important system properties using the system's architectural models.

Getting early, useful answers about relevant aspects of the system's architecture can help identify inappropriate or incorrect design decisions before they are propagated into the system, thus reducing the risk of system and project failures. It is important for a software architect, as well as other system stakeholders, to know which questions to ask about the architecture and why, how to ask them, and how best to ensure that they can be answered by extrapolating and interpreting the necessary information captured in the architecture's model.

All models will not be equally effective in helping to determine whether a given architecture satisfies a certain requirement. For example, consider the diagram representing the Lunar Lander architecture in Figure 8-1, initially introduced in Chapter 6. This diagram might help the architect get clarifications from the system's customers and vice versa; it may also be (informally) analyzed by a manager to ensure that the project's scope is appropriate. At the same time, such an early, informal model will not always be useful for communicating with, and within, the system development teams. The model, for example, does not help answer questions such as how exactly

Figure 8-1.
*A diagram
informally
representing the
Lunar Lander
architecture using
Microsoft
PowerPoint.*

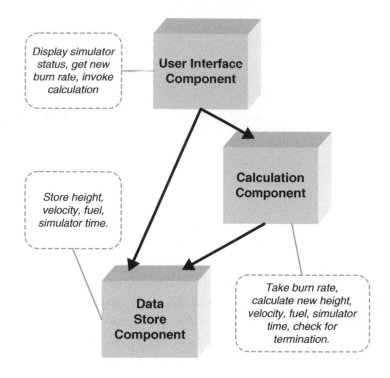

the components (that is, the model's boxes) interact, where they are deployed with respect to each other, and what the nature of their interactions (that is, the model's lines) is.

On the other hand, a more formal architectural model of the given system may precisely define component interfaces, the conditions under which invoking a given interface is legal, a component's internal behavior, its legal external interactions, and so on. Such a model of the Lunar Lander architecture was given in Chapter 6; it is shown again in Figure 8-2. This model can be analyzed for a number of properties. For example, the model can help to ensure component composability into the system in the manner specified by the architectural configuration. After that analysis is successfully completed, the individual components may be assigned to developers for implementation. In some cases, individual component models instead may be used in further analysis to discover closely matching existing components to be grabbed off the shelf and reused in the new system. Yet another alternative would be to analyze the component model by an automated code generation tool whose output would be the component's implementation in a given programming language.

At the same time, such a rich model may not be the most effective means for answering questions about the given project's scope or about the resulting system's satisfaction of key requirements. Such questions may be more effectively answered by the system's

```
type DataStore is interface
  action in  SetValues();
         out NotifyNewValues();
  behavior
  begin
         SetValues => NotifyNewValues();;
end DataStore;

type Calculation is interface
  action in  SetBurnRate();
         out DoSetValues();
  behavior
         action CalcNewState();
  begin
         SetBurnRate => CalcNewState(); DoSetValues();;
end Calculation;

type Player is interface
  action out DoSetBurnRate();
         in  NotifyNewValues();
  behavior
         TurnsRemaining : var integer := 1;
         action UpdateStatusDisplay();
         action Done();
  begin
         (start or UpdateStatusDisplay) where \
             ($TurnsRemaining > 0) => \
             if ( $TurnsRemaining > 0 ) then \
                 TurnsRemaining := $TurnsRemaining - 1; \
                 DoSetBurnRate(); \
             end if;;
         NotifyNewValues => UpdateStatusDisplay();;
         UpdateStatusDisplay where $TurnsRemaining == 0 \
             => Done();;
end UserInterface;

architecture lander() is
  P1, P2 : Player;
  C : Calculation;
  D : DataStore;
connect
  P1.DoSetBurnRate to C.SetBurnRate;
  P2.DoSetBurnRate to C.SetBurnRate;
  C.DoSetValues to D.SetValues;
  D.NotifyNewValues to P1.NotifyNewValues();
  D.NotifyNewValues to P2.NotifyNewValues();
end LunarLander;
```

Figure 8-2.
A partial, formal model of the Lunar Lander architecture corresponding to the diagram from Figure 8-1. The architecture is modeled using the Rapide ADL.

less technical stakeholders, such as managers and customers, through informal, perhaps manual analysis of less rigorous and detailed models.

It is also crucial to recognize that analyzing a software architecture does not have the same objectives, and is not dealing with the same issues, as analyzing software programs.

Architects will have to determine which problems identified in their architectures are critical, and which are not. Some problems uncovered by analysis may be acceptable if the system is still undergoing architectural design, for example, if certain parts of the architecture are still missing.

Another dimension to this issue is induced by off-the-shelf reuse of existing functionality. In naïve theory, software developers should strive to achieve perfect matches among their system's components: Each service provided by a given component will be needed by one or more components in the system, and each service required by a given component will be provided by another component in the system. In other words, there is neither any unneeded functionality provided in the system nor is there any needed functionality missing from the system. Systems developed in this manner are simpler and conceptually cleaner. However, this does not work in most large software systems, for which architecture-based development is geared. Most such systems involve the reuse of off-the-shelf functionality, and design and implementation of extensible components that will be usable in multiple systems. Therefore, certain mismatches among the components in a given architecture may be not only acceptable, but also desirable in this larger context.

The objective of this chapter is to present and relate different facets of architectural analysis. To this end, this chapter organizes the discussion around eight dimensions of concern relevant to architectural analysis:

1. The goals of analysis.
2. The scope of analysis.
3. The primary architectural concern being analyzed.
4. The level of formality of the associated architectural models.
5. The type of analysis.
6. The level of automation.
7. The system stakeholders to whom the results of analysis may be relevant.
8. The applicable analysis techniques.

The chapter expounds upon each of the seven dimensions, and discusses how they relate to and sometimes constrain each other.

8.1 ANALYSIS GOALS

As with analysis of any software artifact, the analysis of architectural models can have varying goals. Those goals may include early estimation of system size, complexity, and cost; adherence of the architectural model to design guidelines and constraints; satisfaction of system requirements, both functional and non-functional (see Chapter 12); assessment of the implemented system's correctness with respect to its documented architecture; evaluation of opportunities for reusing existing functionality when implementing parts of the modeled system; and so forth. We categorize such architectural analysis goals into four categories, as discussed below. We refer to these as the four Cs of architectural analysis.

8.1.1 Completeness

Completeness is both an external and an internal analysis goal. It is *external* with respect to system requirements. The main goal of assessing an architecture's completeness in this context is to establish whether it adequately captures all of a system's key functional and non-functional requirements. Analyzing an architectural model for external completeness is nontrivial. Software systems for which an architecture-centric development perspective is most useful are often large, complex, long lived, and dynamic. In such settings, both the captured requirements and the modeled architecture may be very large and complex, and may be captured using a multitude of notations of various levels of rigor and formality. Furthermore, both likely will be specified incrementally and will change over time, so that the system's engineers need to carefully select points at which external completeness of the architecture can and should be assessed meaningfully.

Analyzing an architecture for *internal* completeness establishes whether all of the system's elements have been fully captured, both with respect to the modeling notation and with respect to the system undergoing architectural design.

Establishing the completeness of the model with respect to the modeling notation (recall Chapter 6) ensures that the model includes all the information demanded by the notation's syntactic and semantic rules. For example, the architectural model depicted in Figure 8-2 is captured in the Rapide architecture description language and thus must adhere to Rapide's syntax and semantics. Given this choice of modeling notation, the component instances in the `architecture` portion of the model must be attached to one another (see the `connect` statement Figure 8-2) according to the rules of Rapide: A component's `out action` must be connected to another component's `in action`; furthermore, connectors are not declared explicitly in Rapide.

Note, however, that fulfilling the modeling requirements of a language such as Rapide does not ensure that the architecture is, in fact, captured completely. Rapide is agnostic as to whether the architect accidentally omitted a major system component or whether a specified component's interface is missing critical services. Establishing the completeness of the architectural model with respect to the system being designed requires checking— often manually, as will be further discussed later in the chapter—whether there are missing components and connectors in the architecture; whether the specified components' and connectors' interfaces and protocols of interaction are fully specified; whether all of the dependencies and interaction paths are captured by the system's architectural configuration; and so on.

In principle, internal completeness is easier to assess than external completeness, and is amenable to automation. A number of software architecture analysis techniques have focused on this very analysis category, as will be elaborated later in this chapter.

8.1.2 Consistency

Consistency is an internal property of an architectural model, which is intended to ensure that different elements of that model do not contradict one another. The need for consistency derives from the fact that software systems, and thus their architectural models, are complex and multifaceted. As a result, even if no architectural design decisions are invalidated during the architectural design process, capturing the details of those decisions during architecture modeling may result in many inadvertently introduced inconsistencies. Examples of inconsistencies in a model include the following.

- Name inconsistencies.
- Interface inconsistencies.
- Behavioral inconsistencies.
- Interaction inconsistencies.
- Refinement inconsistencies.

Name Inconsistency

Name inconsistencies can occur at the level of components and connectors or at the level of their constituent elements, such as the names of the services exported by a component. The experience from using programming languages may suggest that name inconsistencies are trivial and easy to catch, but this is not always the case, especially at the architectural level. First, multiple system elements and/or services may have similar names. For example, a large system may have two or more similarly named GUI-rendering components; likewise, a large GUI component may provide two or more similarly named widget-rendering services. Determining that the wrong component or service is accessed may be difficult.

The second problem with possible name inconsistencies concerns the richness of design choices available to the software architect. In a programming language such as Java, attempting to access a nonexistent class or method will most often result in compile-time errors which the engineer must correct before moving on. This is a by-product of relatively tight coupling of different program elements: early binding, type checking, and synchronous point-to-point procedure call semantics. On the other hand, a software architect may rely on highly decoupled architectures characterized by publish-subscribe or asynchronous event broadcast component interactions. Furthermore, the architecture may be highly adaptable and dynamic, such that tracking all name mismatches at a given time may be meaningless: A component or service referred to in the architecture initially may be unavailable but will be added to the system by the time it is actually needed.

Interface Inconsistency

Interface inconsistencies encompass the issues present in name inconsistencies. Specifically, all name inconsistencies are also interface inconsistencies, but not the other way around. A component's required service may have the same name as another component's provided service, but their parameter lists, as well as parameter and return types, may differ.

For illustration, consider the following. The interface of a required service in a simple QueueClient component, specified using an architecture description language, may be as follows:

```
ReqInt: getSubQ(Natural first, Natural last, Boolean remove)
        returns FIFOQueue;
```

This interface is intended to access a service that returns the subset of a `FIFOQueue` between the specified `first` and `last` indices. The original queue may remain intact, or the specified subqueue may be extracted from it, depending on the value of the `remove` parameter.

On the other hand, the QueueServer component providing the service may export two `getSubQ` interfaces as follows:

```
ProvInt1: getSubQ(Index first, Index last)
          returns FIFOQueue;

ProvInt2: getSubQ(Natural first, Natural last, Boolean remove)
          returns Queue;
```

All three interfaces have identical names, so it can be immediately observed that there is no name inconsistency. However, the three interfaces' parameter lists and return types are not identical. Specifically:

1. The types of the `first` and `last` parameters in the required interface `ReqInt` and the provided interface `ProvInt1` are different.

2. The required interface `ReqInt` introduces a Boolean `remove` parameter, which does not exist in `ProvInt1`.

3. Finally, the return types of the provided interface `ProvInt2` and required interface `ReqInt` are different.

Whether these differences result in actual interface inconsistencies will depend on several factors. If the QueueClient and QueueServer were objects implemented in a programming language such as Java, and their respective provided and required interfaces denoted method invocations, the system might not even compile. However, as has been demonstrated repeatedly throughout this book, software architecture provides a much richer set of choices to an engineer. Consider all three differences between the provided and required interfaces, and their impact on potential interface inconsistency.

1. If the data type `Natural` is defined to be a subtype of `Index`, then requesting the `getSubQ` service will not cause a type mismatch between `ReqInt` and `ProvInt1`. Instead, a simple type cast will occur and the request will be serviced normally.

2. If the connector between QueueClient and QueueServer components is a direct procedure call, then an interface inconsistency will occur between `ReqInt` and `ProvInt1` because of the additional parameter in the required interface. No such inconsistencies will occur between `ReqInt` and `ProvInt2`, which have identical parameter lists. On the other hand, if the two components interact via an implicit invocation mechanism, such as an event connector, the connector may simply package the request such that the QueueServer component can still service it via the `ProvInt1` interface, by ignoring the `remove` parameter: QueueServer will access only the two parameters it needs, and will not need to be concerned with any additional parameters that may have been delivered via the event. In this case, the default implementation of the `getSubQ` service will simply be executed. For example, the default implementation may be that the specified subqueue is extracted from the queue. It is, of course, possible that this will not match the QueueClient's expectation of `getSubQ`'s behavior, if the value of `remove` is set to false. This issue is further discussed below in the context of behavioral inconsistency.

3. Unless this system's architectural description explicitly specifies that Queue is a subtype of FIFOQueue, or that they are identical types, `ProvInt2` will not be able to service the `ReqInt` request.

Determining whether there exists an interface inconsistency in a system thus depends on several factors. At the same time, this is an architecture analysis task that can be accomplished relatively easily and should be readily automatable.

Behavioral Inconsistency

Behavioral inconsistencies occur between components that request and provide services whose names and interfaces match, but whose behaviors do not. As a very simple example, consider the service exported by the following interface:

```
subtract(Integer x, Integer y) returns Integer;
```

This service takes two integers as its input and returns their difference. It is natural to assume that the subtraction is arithmetic, and many math libraries will support this as well as much more complex operations. However, the component providing this service need not calculate the two numbers' arithmetic difference, but instead may provide a calendar subtraction operation. Thus, for example, the requesting component may expect that the difference between 427 and 27 will be 400, while the component providing the service may treat it as the subtraction of 27 days from April 27, and return 331 (March 31).

An architectural model may provide a behavioral specification for the given system's components and their services. The behavioral specifications may take different forms, as illustrated in Chapter 6. For example, each required and provided interface can be accompanied with preconditions, which must hold true before the functionality exported via the interface is accessed, and postconditions, which must hold true after the functionality is exercised.

For example, let us assume that the above discussed QueueClient component requires a `front` operation, whose purpose is to return the first element of the queue. Furthermore, let us assume that QueueServer provides this operation, and that the two corresponding interfaces match. QueueClient's required service behavior is specified as follows:

```
precondition q.size ≥ 0;
postcondition ~q.size = q.size;
```

where $\sim$ denotes the value of the variable q after the operation has been executed. Therefore, the QueueClient component assumes that the queue may be empty and that the `front` operation will not alter the queue.

Let us assume that the QueueServer component's provided `front` operation has the following pre- and postconditions:

```
precondition q.size ≥ 1;
postcondition ~q.size = q.size - 1;
```

The precondition asserts that the queue will be nonempty, while the postcondition specifies that the operation will alter the size of the queue (that is, that the front element will be dequeued).

A casual analysis of the two specifications indicates that the behavior of the `front` operation required by QueueClient does not match that provided by QueueServer. The postconditions clearly are different; moreover, the provided operation assumes that `front` will not be invoked before the existence of at least one element in the queue is ascertained.

A component's behavior may be specified in several different ways. Chapter 6 discussed several examples, including state-transition diagrams, communicating sequential processes, and partially ordered events sets. The exact manner in which the behavioral consistency between services is ensured will vary across these notations, and hence is outside the scope of this text. On the other hand, the overall analysis process will follow the general pattern outlined above, regardless of the behavior modeling notation.

Interaction Inconsistency

Interaction inconsistencies can occur even if two components' respective provided and required operations have consistent names, interfaces, and behaviors. An interaction inconsistency occurs when a component's provided operations are accessed in a manner that violates certain interaction constraints, such as the order in which the component's operations are to be accessed. Such constraints comprise the component's interaction *protocol*.

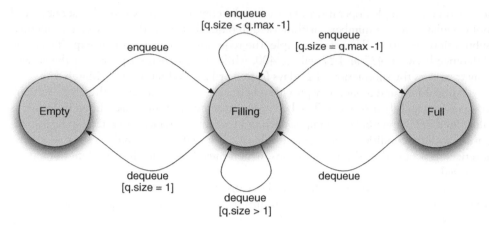

Figure 8-3. *Interaction protocol for the* QueueServer *component. Transitions corresponding to operations such as* **front** *and* **is_empty**, *typically provided by a queue component, have been elided for clarity. Transition guards are enclosed within brackets. The assumption is that the queue can contain at least two elements.*

A component's interaction protocol can be specified using different notations. Frequently, it is modeled via state-transition diagrams (Yellin and Strom 1994). Analyzing the system for interaction consistency in that case consists of ensuring that a given sequence of operation requests matches some sequence of legal state transitions specified by each component's protocol.

An example of such interaction protocol is provided in Figure 8-3. In the figure, the QueueServer component requires that at least one element always be enqueued before an attempt to dequeue an element can be made; furthermore, it assumes that no attempts to enqueue elements onto a full queue will be made. A QueueClient component that does not adhere to these constraints—that is, whose sequence of invocations cannot be executed by the state machine from Figure 8-3—will cause an interaction inconsistency with the QueueServer.

Refinement Inconsistency

Refinement inconsistencies stem from the fact that a system's architecture is frequently captured at multiple levels of abstraction. For example, a very high-level model of the architecture may only represent the major subsystems and their dependencies, while a lower-level model may elaborate on many details of those subsystems and dependencies. As an illustrative example, Figure 8-4 shows the high-level architecture of the Linux operating system, provided by Ivan Bowman and colleagues. (Bowman, Holt, and Brewster 1999), and its Process Scheduler subsystem modeled as a composite connector, provided by Mehta et al. (Mehta, Medvidović, and Phadke 2000). Analyzing Linux's architecture for consistency would require establishing the following three conditions:

1. The elements of the higher-level architectural model have been carried over to the lower-level model—that is, no existing architectural elements have been lost in the course of the refinement.

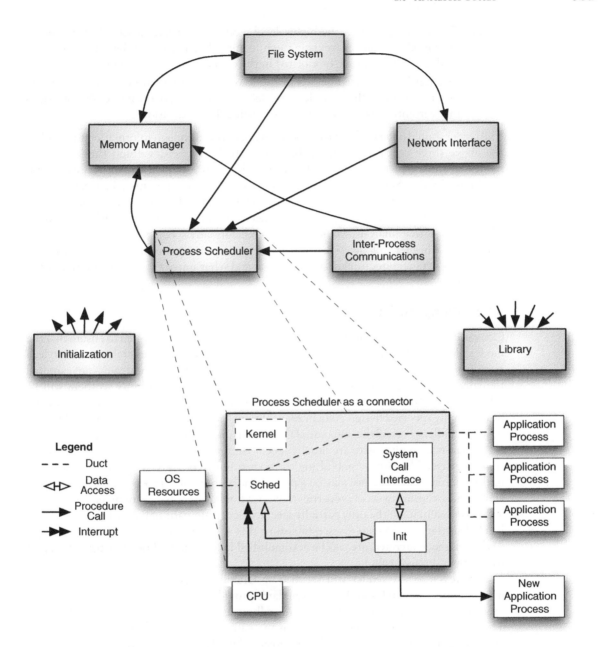

Figure 8-4. *A very high-level model of the Linux operating system [adopted from Bowman et al. (Bowman, Holt, and Brewster 1999) © 1999 ACM, Inc. Reprinted by permission.] and a detailed model of the Linux Process Scheduler connector.*

2. The key properties of the higher-level model have been preserved in the lower-level model—that is, no existing architectural design decisions have been omitted, inadvertently changed, or violated in the course of the refinement.

3. The newly introduced details in the lower-level model are consistent with the existing details of the lower-level model—that is, none of the new design decisions inadvertently change or violate the existing design decisions.

The reader should observe that Figure 8-4 does not contain enough information to establish the above three conditions. This is because both the higher-level and the lower-level models are incomplete. The one observation that can be made with certainty is that the Linux Process Scheduler has been maintained as a separate entity between the two refinement levels. However, at the lower level it is modeled as a connector, while at the higher level it was a component. Further analysis, and additional information on which to base that analysis, would be required before any specific determination can be made as to whether this decision—to change a component into a connector—violated any higher-level architectural design decisions and what impact it had on the rest of the architecture.

8.1.3 Compatibility

Compatibility is an external property of an architectural model, intended to ensure that the model adheres to the design guidelines and constraints imposed by an architectural style, a reference architecture, or an architectural standard. If the design constraints are captured formally, or at least rigorously, ensuring an architecture's compatibility to them will be relatively straightforward. If an architecture must be compatible with a set of semiformally or informally specified design guidelines, analyzing the architecture for compatibility may be more challenging and the outcome of the analysis process also may be ambiguous at times.

Reference architectures are usually specified formally, using an architecture description language. Therefore, establishing the compatibility of a given system's architecture to the reference architecture may be a precise and automatable process. Since a reference architecture captures a set of properties that must hold true across any number of systems in a given domain, it may be only partially specified or certain parts of it may be at a very high level of abstraction. In such cases, establishing that a product-specific architecture adheres to the reference architecture can be accomplished by ensuring refinement consistency, in the manner discussed above.

However, as the reader will recall from Chapter 4 and will see in later chapters, most architectural styles and many standards provide general, high-level design guidelines, so that establishing an architecture's adherence to them may be more challenging. The difficulty may arise from fuzziness on the part of the style definition or imprecision or incompleteness on the part of the architectural model. For example, Figure 8-5 depicts the Lunar Lander architecture according to the event-based style. This diagram was first shown in Chapter 4, with a slightly different component layout, as were the relatively similar diagrams for the Lunar Lander architectures in the C2 (Figure 4-23) and blackboard (Figure 4-16) styles. Determining the style to which this architecture adheres is a nontrivial task: The depicted configuration of components may, in fact, also adhere to C2's principles, such as substrate independence. Likewise, this particular visual layout of the architecture's topology may be misleading, for the Spacecraft component may in fact play the role of a blackboard in this system. In cases such as this, the architect may need to

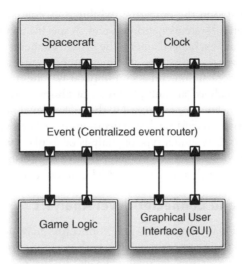

Figure 8-5.
*A depiction of the
Lunar Lander
architecture
according to the
event-based style.*

obtain additional information, rely on tacit knowledge, and use one or more architectural analysis techniques presented later in this chapter.

8.1.4 Correctness

Correctness is an external property of an architectural model. A system's architecture is said to be correct with respect to an external system specification if the architectural design decisions fully realize those specifications. Furthermore, the system's implementation is correct with respect to the system's architecture if the implementation fully captures and realizes all the principal design decisions comprising the architecture. Correctness is therefore *relative*: It is the result of architecture to some other artifact, where the artifact is either intended to elaborate and fulfill the architecture or the architecture is intended to elaborate and fulfill the artifact.

An interesting observation arises in the implementation of many large, modern software systems that reuse off-the-shelf functionality, or off-the-shelf architectural solutions such as reference architectures. In such cases, it is very likely that, through the off-the-shelf components, the implemented system will include structural elements or functionality, as well as non-functional properties, that are not specified in the requirements and/or not modeled in the architecture. With a 1970's notion of *refinement-based correctness*, such systems would not be considered to be correct with respect to the architecture. However, with the notion of correctness built upon fulfillment, as described above, such systems are not only correct, but they are likely efficiently created and form a suitable basis for efficiently fulfilling new system requirements.

8.2 SCOPE OF ANALYSIS

A software system's architecture can be analyzed from different perspectives and at different levels. Architects may be interested in assessing the properties of individual components or connectors, or even their constituent elements, such as interfaces or ports. More frequently, architects may be interested in the properties exhibited by compositions of components and connectors in a given subsystem or entire system. A specific focus of (sub)system-level analysis may be on the data exchanged among the system elements.

In addition to assessing the properties of a single architecture, architects may at times need to consider two or more architectures simultaneously. One such case is when a given system's architecture is analyzed at multiple levels of abstraction. For example, a more detailed architectural model may be compared to the higher-level model from which it has been derived, to ensure that no existing design decisions have been violated or unintended design decisions introduced. A similar type of analysis takes place when two architectural models at similar levels of abstraction are compared to establish design similarities or conformance to constraints such as those embodied in a reference architecture.

8.2.1   Component- and Connector-Level Analysis

In a large system, individual components and connectors may not always be as interesting to an architect as their compositions, but both components and connectors need to provide specific services at specific quality levels. In the case of components, this typically means application-specific functionality; in the case of connectors, this means application-independent interaction services.

The simplest type of component- and connector-level analysis ensures that the given component or connector provides the services expected of it. For example, a component's or connector's interface can be inspected to make sure that no expected services are missing. As an illustration, Figure 8-6 shows Lunar Lander's Data Store component modeled in xADLite. It is trivial to analyze this component, either manually or automatically, to establish that it provides both `getValues` and `storeValues` services; furthermore, if a system stakeholder expects or requires the Data Store component to provide further services, it can easily be ascertained that no such services currently exist. Even if the component were much larger and provided many more services, this task would not be significantly harder.

Of course, "checking off" the services a component or connector provides does not ensure that those services are modeled correctly. The described analysis can be thought of as equivalent to establishing only name consistency. A component or connector may provide services with the expected names, but with incorrect interfaces. For example, `getValues` in the above example may be modeled to expect the values in a wrong format, such as untyped versus typed or string versus integer. Therefore, it is not sufficient to establish that

Figure 8-6.
Lunar
Lander's Data
Store component
modeled
in xADLite. This
model is extracted
from that provided
in Chapter 6,
in Figure 6-27.

```
component{
    id = "datastore";
    description = "Data Store";
    interface{
        id = "datastore.getValues";
        description = "Data Store Get Values Interface";
        direction = "in";
    }
    interface{
        id = "datastore.storeValues";
        description = "Data Store Store Values Interface";
        direction = "in";
    }
}
```

```
connector Pipe =
  role Writer = write —→ Writer ⊓
                  close —→ √
  role Reader =
    let ExitOnly = close —→ √
    in let DoRead = (read —→ Reader ⊓
                       read-eof —→ ExitOnly)
    in DoRead ⊓ ExitOnly
  glue = let ReadOnly = Reader.read —→ ReadOnly ⊓
             Reader.read-eof —→ Reader.close —→ √ ⊓
             Reader.close —→ √
  in let WriteOnly = Writer.write —→ WriteOnly ⊓
         Writer.close —→ √
  in Writer.write —→ glue ⊓
     Reader.read —→ glue ⊓
     Writer.close —→ ReadOnly ⊓
     Reader.close —→ WriteOnly
```

Figure 8-7.
*Pipe connector
modeled in
Wright.*

the component or connector provides appropriately named services; the complete interface of the component or connector has to be analyzed. The information provided in Figure 8-6 will thus have to be supplemented with additional details, possibly from other models.

Taking this argument a step further, it is not sufficient to ensure that the component's or connector's services are exported via an appropriate interface. The semantics of those services as modeled (and, eventually, as implemented) may be different from the desired semantics. Thus, for example, the `getValues` service from Figure 8-6 may not be modeled such that it accesses the Data Store to obtain the needed values, but instead may request those values from a system user. Since the intended usage of the component, implied in its name, is to access a repository, this implementation of `getValues`, while legitimate in principle, would be wrong for this context.

Similarly, a connector may provide interaction services with semantics that are different from the expected semantics. For example, a connector may be expected to support asynchronous invocation semantics, but is actually modeled for synchronous invocation. Establishing this type of semantic consistency is not trivial. Consider as an illustration a model of a *Pipe* connector in the Wright ADL discussed in Chapter 6; the model is depicted in Figure 8-7. The *Pipe* connector plays two roles; that is, it provides two services: `Reader` and `Writer`. Their interplay, that is, the connector's overall behavior, is captured by the connector's `glue`. Even though a pipe is a relatively simple connector, establishing manually that it adheres to its expected behavior is significantly more challenging than with name or interface conformance. For example, is the intended semantics to allow unimpeded writing to the pipe, as in the current specification of the `Writer` role, or does the pipe have a bounded buffer so that writing a certain amount of data would require that at least some of that data be read before additional data can be written? Assessing more complex connectors for these types interaction properties will be much more difficult and may be especially error-prone.

8.2.2 Subsystem- and System-Level Analysis

Even if individual components and connectors have desired properties, no guarantees can be made that their compositions in a given system will behave as expected, or even be legal. The interplay among complex components can itself be very complex. Architects may assess the properties of their compositions at the level of the entire system or incrementally, by focusing on particular subsystems.

The most manageable increment is pair-wise conformance, where only two interacting components are considered at a time, and name, interface, behavior, and interaction conformance are established as discussed above. The next step up is to take a set of components possibly interacting through a single connector, such as those shown in Figure 8-5. Most analysis techniques can easily support both these cases. Ensuring desirable properties at the level of large subsystems and entire systems can be quite challenging, and many analysis techniques have tried to get a handle on this problem.

In certain scenarios it may be obvious that compositions of two or more components that respectively possess properties α, β, γ, and so forth will have some combination of those properties. For example, combining a data encryption component—intended to provide communication security—with a data compression component—intended to provide communication efficiency—can be expected to provide both security and efficiency.

Much more frequent in practice is the situation where the interplay among the components will result in their interference and either enhancement or diminishment of each other's properties. This will be acceptable, and even desirable, in certain cases. For example, a component that provides a critical service very efficiently may be vulnerable to malicious attacks. The system architects may decide that sacrificing some of the efficiency is acceptable in order to enhance the system's security, and may compose this component with one or more components that provide services such as encryption, authentication, or authorization. Likewise, in many real-time systems, a component that computes its results or provides data more quickly and/or frequently than the system requires will be composed with a (simple) component that introduces the necessary delays. Such compositions will be synergistic: The system will ultimately be greater than the sum of its parts.

Such interference among system components will not be desirable in all situations. More importantly, such interference will often not be as obvious as in the above scenarios and will result in unintended composite properties. Examples abound. One such well-known example from software engineering literature involved integrating two components that both assumed that they owned the system's main thread of control, ultimately resulting in an unusable system (Garlan, Allen, and Ockerbloom 1995). Another similar example involved integrating concurrent components implemented in two different programming languages. The resulting system's performance was unacceptable, and a long and painstaking analysis of the system uncovered that the individual components' threading models were incompatible (Maybee, Heimbinger, and Osterweil 1996). The reader can easily envision many other such scenarios, such as when a system comprises interacting memory-efficient components (which use computationally intensive data compression algorithms) and CPU-efficient components (which use techniques such as data caching and prefetching) or, further, when a component introducing a fault-tolerance service (for example, via continuous state replication) is introduced into such a system.

Architectural Analysis and Honey-Baked Ham

Scenarios such as those discussed in this section are a direct reason why many modern software systems suffer from poor performance, security, and scalability; unnecessarily large size; high complexity; limited adaptability; and so on. For example, a concurrent system in which any component or subsystem considered in isolation is deadlock free, livelock free, and starvation-free may in fact suffer from deadlock, livelock, or starvation because of the unforeseen interplay of multiple components and/or subsystems.

This is what Dewayne Perry has colloquially referred to as the *honey-baked ham syndrome*: Honey is fat free, while ham is sugar free; honey-baked ham, therefore, must be both fat free and sugar free. Clearly, this is not true, and drawing such conclusions based on the evidence available from a system's individual components may be wrong and perilous. The honey-baked ham syndrome is a primary reason why subsystem- and system-level architectural analysis is critically important.

8.2.3 Data Exchanged in the System or Subsystem

In many large, distributed software systems large amounts of data are processed, exchanged, and stored. Examples of data-intensive systems are numerous and appear in such wide ranging domains as scientific computing, many Web-based applications, e-commerce, and multimedia. In such systems, in addition to the properties of the individual structural architectural elements—components and connectors—and the entire architectural configuration, it is important to ensure that the system's data is properly modeled, implemented, and exchanged among the structural elements. This involves assessing the data elements, including the following.

- *The structure of the data*, such as typed versus untyped or discrete versus streamed.
- *The flow of the data through the system*, such as point-to-point versus broadcast.
- *The properties of data exchange*, such as consistency, security, and latency.

As a simple example, consider a system consisting of a data-producer component and two data-consumer components, whose architectural configuration is depicted in Figure 8-8. The figure also shows the respective frequencies at which they are able to exchange data. The Producer component sends one megabit per second, and Consumer 1 is able to receive and process that data in a timely manner. In fact, Consumer 1 may wait idly up to 50 percent of the time to receive additional data from the Producer. However, Consumer 2 is able to receive and process the data at a rate that is only one-half of the production rate. This means that Consumer 2 may lose up to one-half of the produced data.

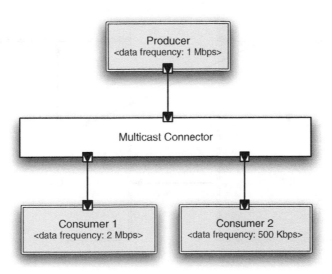

Figure 8-8.
A simple system with one data producer and two consumers, with the frequencies at which they are able to send and receive data, respectively.

This problem may be mitigated if the Multicast Connector servicing the three components is able to buffer data, but clearly, if the system is long running, the connector's buffer will eventually overflow. The connector will also have to include additional processing logic to store the data temporarily and also route it to the two components in the order received, which will introduce additional overhead in the system. If the two Consumer components require the data to be in different formats from that generated by the Producer, the connector will also have to act as an adapter, introducing further overhead. Likewise, the connector may have to perform additional tasks based on the architectural requirements, such as encrypting the data for security, ensuring that the data is delivered according to the specified routing policy (for example, best-effort or exactly-once), or compressing the data if necessary.

8.2.4   Architectures at Different Abstraction Levels

During the architectural design process, architects frequently address the critical system requirements first, and then both introduce additional elements into the architecture and refine the architecture to include additional details that are necessary for the architecture's realization into the final system. This may involve the addition and further breakdown of architectural elements, as well as the introduction and refinement of existing design decisions.

Consider a simple example. A high-level architectural breakdown of a system may look like the diagram shown in Figure 8-9. For simplicity, the connectors are depicted only as arrows indicating the interacting components as well as the direction of interaction. For example, component C1 initiates the interactions with components C3 and C4. As is the

Figure 8-9.
*A high-level
architectural
configuration.*

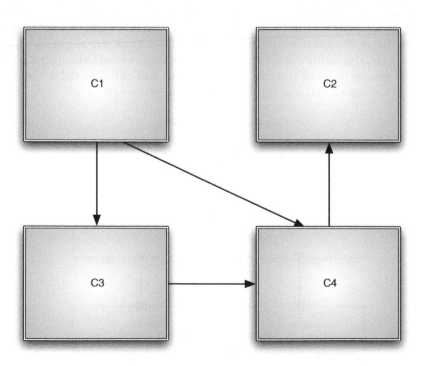

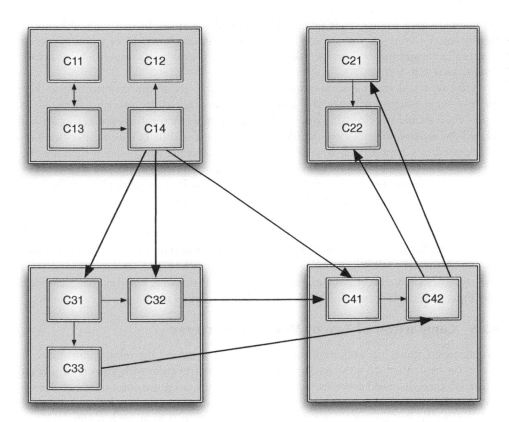

Figure 8-10.
A *refined, more
detailed
architectural
configuration*.

case with all boxes-and-arrows architectural descriptions, many details of this architecture are missing, including the components' interfaces, details of their behaviors and of the data exchanged, as well as the semantics of their interactions, such as that involving components C1, C2, and C3. While important, such information is not critical to this discussion.

Figure 8-10 depicts another architectural configuration, which is intended to be a refinement of that shown in Figure 8-9. For convenience, groups of components in the refined architecture which are presumed to comprise the original components are highlighted. For example, components C11, C12, C13, and C14 along with their interconnections in Figure 8-10 comprise the component C1 from Figure 8-9. Furthermore, the connectors are refined, such that it is clear that only C1's subcomponent C14 is engaged in interactions with the subcomponents of C3 and C4.

In the process of refinement, several problems can be introduced, as discussed above in the context of refinement incompatibility. The easiest cases to address are those where an architectural design decision has been clearly invalidated. However, even the addition or modification of architectural decisions may cause a refinement inconsistency depending on the context and on the range of architectural changes that are allowed. For example, the architecture depicted in Figure 8-9 and Figure 8-10 may need to abide by an architectural constraint stating that interactions crossing the boundaries of the system's original four components must have a single target and a single destination. In that case, elaborating the interactions among the architecture's components as shown in Figure 8-10 would violate the constraints, both in the case of component C1's interactions with C3 and C4's interactions with C2.

Clearly, based on the scant information provided about the architecture in Figure 8-9, it is unclear whether the changes to the original architecture depicted in Figure 8-10 should be allowed. This will depend on many factors, and some, though not all, will be apparent from a more detailed and rigorous modeling of the architecture such as discussed in Chapter 6. This will also depend on a refinement policy, which may be explicitly stated. Thus, for example, Mark Moriconi and colleagues define a refinement policy called *conservative extension* (Moriconi, Qian, and Riemenschneider 1995). Conservative extension essentially precludes an architect from introducing any new features into a system's architecture, and instead restricts him or her to either elaborating or possibly eliminating those features already existing in the more abstract, that is, higher-level, architecture. While a property such as conservative extension may not always be useful in practice, Moriconi and colleagues have shown it to be amenable to formal specification and analysis. Other refinement policies may be much less restrictive, but that very flexibility may make it difficult to establish that they are being adhered to in a concrete situation.

8.2.5   Comparison of Two or More Architectures

In certain situations it is important for architects to understand the relationship between the architecture they are interested in and a baseline architecture with known properties. One such case, discussed previously in this chapter, is ensuring the compliance of a given system's architecture with a reference architecture. Other cases may include ensuring the architecture's compliance with the design guidelines captured in an architectural style or with a particular architectural pattern. It is, of course, also possible that the baseline architecture is simply one that the architect knows and understands. The architect may have encountered the architecture in literature, it may be the architecture of a related product he or she and colleagues had developed previously, or it could even be an architecture that has been recovered from a system (possibly even competitor's system) that exhibits desired properties.

Such comparisons of two or more architectures involve comparing the processing and data storage capabilities provided by the components, the interactions as embodied in the connectors, the characteristics of the data exchange, the components' and connectors' compositions into the system's configuration, and the sources of the non-functional properties exhibited by the system. It is possible for the architectures in question to be at different levels of abstraction, in which case the techniques discussed in the previous subsection can be employed.

8.3 ARCHITECTURAL CONCERN BEING ANALYZED

Architectural analysis techniques are directed at different facets of a given architecture. Some techniques strive to ensure primarily the architecture's *structural* properties; others focus on the *behaviors* provided by the architectural elements and their composition; yet others may analyze whether the *interactions* among the architectural elements adhere to certain requirements and constraints; finally, the *non-functional properties* exhibited by the architecture are frequently considered to be very important and are thus studied carefully.

In practice, a given analysis technique, or suite of techniques, will address more than one architectural concern at a time. In this section, we focus on each concern individually for ease of exposition and also discuss the relevant characteristics of each.

Structural Characteristics

The structural characteristics of a software architecture include concerns such as the connectivity among an architecture's components and connectors, containment of lower-level architectural elements into composite higher-level elements, possible points of network distribution, and a given system's potential deployment architectures. These concerns can help to determine whether the architecture is well formed. Examples include components or subsystems that are disconnected from the rest of the architecture, missing pathways between components and connectors that are intended to interact, existing pathways between components and connectors that are not wanted, encapsulation of components or connectors that must be visible and accessible at a higher level of hierarchical composition, and so on. Structural analysis can also establish adherence to architectural constraints, patterns, and styles. Structural concerns can also help in the analysis of different aspects of system concurrency and distribution, as they tie the system's software elements and their properties with the hardware platforms on which they will execute.

Behavioral Characteristics

A well-structured architecture is of limited utility if the individual components do not provide the behaviors that are expected of them and, further, if they do not combine to provide the expected system-level behaviors. Therefore, analyzing an architecture's behavioral characteristics has two related facets:

1. Considering the internal behaviors of individual components.
2. Considering the architectural structure to assess composite behaviors.

It is possible, especially in systems composed with third-party components obtained off the shelf, that an architect's insight into the internal workings of different system components will be restricted to the components' public interfaces. As indicated earlier, particularly in Section 8.1, the types of behavioral properties that can be inferred at the level of interfaces are quite limited, and many potential problems with the architecture may remain undetected.

Interaction Characteristics

The relevant characteristics of interactions in a given architecture may include the numbers and types of distinct software connectors, and their values for different connector dimensions (recall Chapter 5). Interaction characteristics can help to establish whether the architecture will actually be able to fulfill some of its requirements. For instance, a non-buffering connector in the example from Figure 8-8 would result in a system in which one of the components received at most one-half of all the data.

Analysis of interaction characteristics may also encompass the interaction protocols for different system components (for example, recall Figure 8-3) and internal behaviors specified for different system connectors (for example, recall Figure 8-7). Such details would aid in the analysis of finer-grain interaction characteristics, such as whether a component interacting through an otherwise appropriate connector will be legally accessed or whether a set of interacting components may deadlock.

Non-Functional Characteristics

Non-functional characteristics form a critical dimension of almost all software systems. These characteristics typically cut across multiple components and connectors, which makes them particularly difficult to assess. Furthermore, non-functional characteristics are often not properly understood, they are qualitative in nature, and their definitions are partial or informal. Therefore, while the non-functional characteristics present an important and formidable challenge to software architects, architectural analysis techniques focusing on these characteristics are scarce.

8.4 LEVEL OF FORMALITY OF ARCHITECTURAL MODELS

The relationship between architectural models and analysis is symbiotic: What the system's stakeholders want to be able to analyze will influence what software architects capture in their architectural models. Conversely, what architects capture in the architectural models directly determines what they will be able to analyze and what analysis methods they will use to do so.

Architectural models have been discussed in detail in the preceding chapters, and particularly in Chapter 6. Here, we will look specifically at the role they play in the context of architectural analysis. For that purpose, architectural models can be classified as informal, semiformal, and formal.

Informal Models

Informal models are typically captured in boxes-and-lines diagrams such as shown in Figure 8-1. Informal models can provide a useful high-level picture of the system. They are amenable to informal and manual analyses, typically by a broad section of stakeholders, including nontechnical stakeholders such as managers and system customers. For example, system managers can use them to determine a project's overall staffing needs. At the same time, informal models should be approached cautiously because of their inherent ambiguity and lack of detail.

Semiformal Models

Most architectural models used in practice are semiformal. A notation that strives to be useful to a large number of system stakeholders, both technical and nontechnical, will typically try to strike a balance between a high degree of precision and formality on the one hand, and expressiveness and understandability on the other. One widely used example is the Unified Modeling Language (UML). Semiformal languages such as the UML are amenable both to manual and automated analysis. Their partial imprecision makes it difficult to perform some more sophisticated analyses, for which formal models are needed.

Formal Models

While semiformal modeling notations typically only have a formally defined syntax, formal notations also have formally defined semantics. An example formal notation is Wright, which was used to specify the Pipe connector in Figure 8-7. Formal models are inherently amenable to formal, automated analysis and are typically intended for the system's technical stakeholders. At the same time, producing complete architectural models using a formal notation can be painstaking. Furthermore, formal models have been frequently shown in practice to suffer from scalability problems.

8.5 TYPE OF ANALYSIS

One useful categorization of architectural analysis techniques is into static, dynamic, or scenario-based techniques. We discuss the three categories and the role architectural models play in each.

Static Analysis

Static analysis involves inferring the properties of a software system from one or more of its models, without actually executing those models. A simple example of static analysis is syntactic analysis: Determining if the system model adheres to the syntactic rules of the modeling notation, whether it be an architectural description language, design diagramming notation, or programming language. Static analysis can be automated (for example, compilation) or manual (for example, inspection). All architectural modeling notations, including the informal boxes-and-lines diagrams, are amenable to static analysis, although the more formal and expressive notations can be harnessed to provide more precise and sophisticated answers. Formal notations used in modeling software systems include:

- *Axiomatic notations*, which model systems via logical assertions; an example is Anna (Luckham and Henke 1985).
- *Algebraic notations*, which model systems via collections of equivalence relations; an example is LARCH (Guttag, Horning, and Wing 1985).
- *Temporal logic notations*, which model systems in terms of order of execution and timing; an example is GIL (Dillon et al. 1992).

It should be noted that the above example notations cannot be considered as architecture description languages, or ADLs, since by themselves they do not provide any explicit architecture modeling constructs. However, it is possible to use them as a basis of an ADL, much in the same way that Wright leverages communicating sequential processes (CSP) as discussed in Chapter 6.

Dynamic Analysis

Dynamic analysis involves actually executing or simulating the execution of a model of the software system. In order to perform dynamic analysis on an architectural model, its semantic underpinning must be executable or amenable to simulation. State-transition diagrams are an example executable formalism with which the reader should be familiar.

Other executable formalisms include discrete events, queuing networks (Lazowska et al. 1984), and Petri nets.

Scenario-Based Analysis

For large and complex software systems, it is often infeasible to assert a given property for the entire system over the entire space of its possible states or executions. For such systems, specific-use cases are identified that represent the most important or most frequently occurring system usage scenarios, and the analysis is focused on those. Scenario-based analysis can be an instance of both static analysis—as a tool for reducing a modeled system's state space, as discussed later in this chapter—and dynamic analysis—as a tool for reducing the system's execution space. At the same time, scenario-based analysis requires that architects be very careful about the inferences they make from their inherently limited evidence.

8.6 LEVEL OF AUTOMATION

Different architectural analysis techniques are amenable to different levels of automation. The level of automation depends on several factors, including the formality and completeness of the architectural model and the property being assessed. In general, an architectural model provided in a more formal notation will be more amenable to automated analysis than a model provided in a more informal notation. Likewise, a model that captures a greater number of the architectural design decisions for the given system will be more amenable to rigorous, automated analysis than a model that is missing many such design decisions. Finally, a well-understood property that is quantifiable and can itself be defined formally will be easier to assess automatically than a qualitative property that may not be as well understood. This last point is particularly important in software engineering: As will be demonstrated in Chapter 12, many non-functional properties, which are critical to the success of most all software systems, are understood at the level of intuition, anecdote, and informal guideline.

Manual

Manual analysis of software architectures requires significant human involvement, and is thus expensive. However, manual analysis can be performed on models of varying levels of detail, rigor, formality, and completeness. It has the added advantage that architectural rationale, which is often tacit, can be taken into account. This type of analysis may also be required when multiple, potentially clashing properties must be ensured in tandem.

A number of architectural analysis techniques fall in this category. These are inspection-based techniques and will be further elaborated upon later in this chapter. One well-known example is the architecture trade-off analysis method, or ATAM (Clements, Kazman, and Klein 2002). The analysis results emerging from manual analysis are typically qualitative. Since it is not always possible to quantify important properties of a software system—such as scalability, adaptability, or heterogeneity—any analysis of the extent to which the system exhibits those properties will not be quantifiable. The analysis results are also frequently qualified by a particular context in which a system may exhibit a given property. Scenario-based techniques fall in this category.

Given the human-intensive nature of this category of architecture analysis techniques, a critical concern must be to make the analysis reliable and repeatable. Since the architectural models as well as the properties of interest may be less than formally captured, the focus of many manual analysis techniques has been on specifying a detailed process that must be followed by the system architects and other stakeholders participating in the analysis.

Partially Automated

Growing levels of rigor in architectural models, and in understanding of the software systems' key properties, present opportunities for automating different facets of architectural analysis. In fact, most architectural analyses can be at least partially automated, involving both software tools and human intervention. In that sense, architectural analysis techniques can be thought of as covering a spectrum of automation, with manual and fully automated analysis being the ends of that spectrum.

Most architecture modeling notations presented in Chapter 6 are amenable to ensuring a given architectural description's syntactic correctness, as well as different degrees of semantic correctness. For example, an xADL model can be analyzed for style-specific component interconnectivity rules, while Wright allows one to analyze a given composition of components communicating through a connector for deadlocks. At the same time, neither model can be analyzed automatically for other properties, such as reliability, availability, dependability, or latency. This is at least in part because system parameters that are relevant to assessing these properties are not captured—to the necessary degree, or at all—by these architectural modeling notations.

Fully Automated

It can be argued that the specific analyses mentioned above, such as ensuring the syntactic correctness or deadlock freedom in an architectural description, can be considered fully automatable since it is possible to complete them without human involvement. At the same time, the results of automated analyses are typically partial: The fact that an architectural description provided in a given ADL fully adheres to that ADL's syntax, or that a partial system description is deadlock free, still leaves a large number of questions about the respective models unanswered. This means that, in practice, fully automated architectural analysis techniques must be combined with other techniques, which themselves may need human intervention, in order to get more comprehensive answers.

8.7 SYSTEM STAKEHOLDERS

The stakeholders in a software project will often have different objectives. For example, customers may be interested in getting the most functionality as quickly as possible, for the lowest amount of money possible. A project manager may be interested in ensuring that the project is staffed appropriately and that the rate of expenditure does not exceed some target. The architects' primary objective may be to deliver a technically sound system that will be easily adaptable in the future. Finally, a developer may be interested primarily in ensuring that the modules he or she is responsible for are implemented on time and bug-free. Therefore, the different stakeholders will not necessarily have identical architecture analysis needs. The remainder of this section highlights the role architectural analysis plays in the case of each stakeholder type.

Architects

Software architects must take a global view of the architecture and are interested in establishing all four Cs in the architecture: completeness, consistency, compatibility, and correctness. Depending on the project's context and objectives, architects may need to rely on all types of architectural models at all levels of scope and formality. While they may prefer to use automated analysis techniques, architects will frequently have to rely on manual and semi-automated techniques.

Developers

Software developers often take a more limited view of the architecture—namely, the modules or subsystems for which they are directly responsible. As such, developers are interested primarily in establishing the consistency of their modules with other parts of the system with which these modules will interact, as well as compatibility with the required architectural styles, reference architectures, and standards. They need not worry about the architecture's completeness, and can at best assess its partial correctness. The models that developers will likely find most useful are formal, with all necessary details specified and ready for implementation. However, these likely would be models of individual elements for which a given developer is directly responsible, rather than models of the entire architecture.

Managers

Project managers are typically primarily interested in an architecture's completeness— Are all the requirements satisfied?—and correctness—Are the requirements appropriately realized in the architecture and thus eventually will be realized in the implementation? Managers may also be interested in the architecture's compatibility if the architecture and eventually the implemented system must adhere to a reference architecture or a set of standards.

Consistency is a system's internal property, and managers typically do not concern themselves with it, that is, they naturally delegate such responsibilities to architects and developers. There are exceptions, however. For example, architectural defects may become a major issue that begins affecting the project's schedule or budget. Alternatively, customers or project contracts may explicitly mandate certain consistency properties, in which case managers would need to explicitly consider them.

The types of architectural models that are useful to managers are usually less formal models of the entire system. A manager's focus will frequently be on cross-cutting non-functional system properties, as well as the system's structural and dynamic characteristics.

Customers

Customers are interested primarily in the commissioned system's completeness and correctness. Their concerns can be summarized with two key questions:

1. Is the development organization building the right system?
2. Is the development organization building the system right?

A customer may also be interested in the system's compatibility with certain standards, and possibly reference architectures in which the customer has a vested interest. Consistency is not of critical importance unless it is reflected in externally visible system defects.

In terms of architectural models, customers typically favor understandability over formality of models. They are interested in overall models (the "big picture") and the system's key properties. They are often interested in scenario-driven assessment of a system's structural, behavioral, and dynamic characteristics.

Vendors

Software vendors typically sell technology, such as individual components and connectors, rather than architecture. As such they are interested primarily in composability of those components and connectors as well as their compatibility with certain standards and widely used reference architectures. Like a given system's customers, vendors may value the understandability of architectural models, but their customers are software developers who may demand formal models of the software they purchase from the vendor. The vendors' primary focus is on the analysis of the individual elements and their properties. The structural characteristics of the overall architecture are not as important, although dynamic characteristics may be since they may have implications on the composability of the individual elements in future systems.

8.8 ANALYSIS TECHNIQUES

A large number of analysis techniques are available to software architects. Some of them are variations on techniques applied to other software development artifacts—primarily formal specifications and code—while others have been developed specifically with software architectures in mind. In this section we discuss a cross-section of architectural analysis techniques. Although it is not intended to provide a complete overview of existing techniques, the cross-section is broadly representative.

We divide architectural analysis techniques into three categories:

- Inspection- and review-based.
- Model-based.
- Simulation-based.

The discussion of the techniques within these categories will focus on the architectural analysis dimensions outlined above and summarized in Figure 8-11.

8.8.1 Inspections and Reviews

Software inspections and reviews are widely used code-analysis techniques. If unfamiliar with these techniques, the reader is encouraged to consult an introductory software engineering text. *Architectural* inspections and reviews are conducted by different stakeholders to ensure a variety of properties in an architecture. They involve a set of activities conducted by system stakeholders in which different architectural models are studied for specific properties. These activities often take place in architecture review boards, where several stakeholders define the objective of the analysis—such as ensuring that the architecture

Figure 8-11.
*Architectural
analysis
dimensions
discussed in this
chapter.*

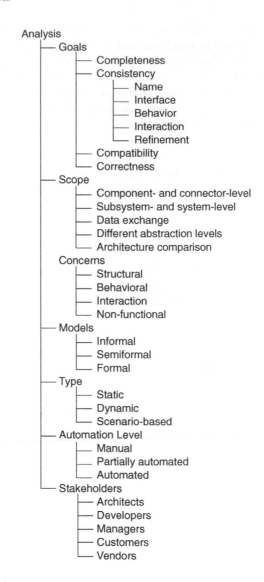

Figure 8-11.
Architectural analysis dimensions discussed in this chapter.

satisfies a given non-functional property—and then, as a group, carefully study and critique the architecture or some of its parts.

Inspections and reviews are manual analysis techniques, and as such can be expensive. On the other hand, they have the advantage of being useful in the case of informal or partial architectural descriptions. They can also be employed effectively in the case of "soft" architectural properties, such as scalability or adaptability, which are not precisely understood and amenable to formal definition. Another advantage of inspections and reviews is that they can simultaneously take into account the objectives of multiple system stakeholders and consider multiple desired architectural properties.

Depending on the context, inspections and reviews can have any of the four architectural analysis *goals*: consistency, correctness, completeness, and compatibility. In terms of consistency, they will typically be well suited to name and interface consistency analysis. Behavior, interaction, and refinement consistency analysis may be conducted by the technical stakeholders—architects and developers—although doing so manually may be a difficult and error-prone task. For example, recall the interaction characteristics embodied in the single Wright Pipe connector from Figure 8-7, and even the comparatively simpler single state-transition interaction protocol of the QueueServer component from Figure 8-3. Dealing with a large number of such models manually would cognitively overload even the most capable architects. Thus, if analyzing for any of the three latter types of consistency is undertaken during an architectural inspection or review, it may be advisable to restrict the analysis to carefully confined subsets of the architecture.

The *scope* of inspections and reviews can vary. The stakeholders may be interested in individual components and connectors, or their compositions in a specific subsystem or the entire system. The stakeholders may also center on the data exchanged among the specific components and connectors or, globally, across the entire architecture. They may try to assess the compliance of the architecture to a higher-level architecture that served as its starting point. They may also try to assess the architecture's similarity to an existing architecture with known properties.

Similarly, the specific *concern* of the analysis can vary. The stakeholders may focus on the structural, behavioral, or interaction properties, although as mentioned above, the latter two may be difficult to assess manually. Inspections and reviews may be particularly well suited to establishing certain non-functional properties, especially those that require some interpretation and consensus reaching by the human stakeholders.

In terms of the types of *models* particularly amenable to inspections and reviews, any level of formality may be suitable in principle. However, highly formal models will not be useful to the nontechnical stakeholders, and even the technical stakeholders may find them difficult to read and understand. At the other end of the spectrum, informal models may be useful if, for example, the objective of the inspection is to develop a common understanding of the architecture's general characteristics. On the other hand, it may not be very meaningful to rely on informal models when inspecting the architecture for concrete properties of interest.

By their nature, the *types* of analysis for which inspections and reviews are geared are static and scenario-based. Since the stakeholders manually assess the architectural models, they have to focus on the architecture's static properties, such as proper connectivity, interface conformance between interacting components, adherence to desired architectural patterns, and so on. Furthermore, as discussed below in the case of the ATAM analysis technique, the stakeholders may manually run through some critical scenarios to ensure that the architecture will behave as expected.

As already mentioned, in terms of *automation level* inspections and reviews are manual and very human intensive.

Finally, all system *stakeholders*, save for perhaps component vendors, may participate in inspections and reviews. Architects and developers will conduct inspections and reviews most frequently, and will periodically be joined by project managers and possibly by customers.

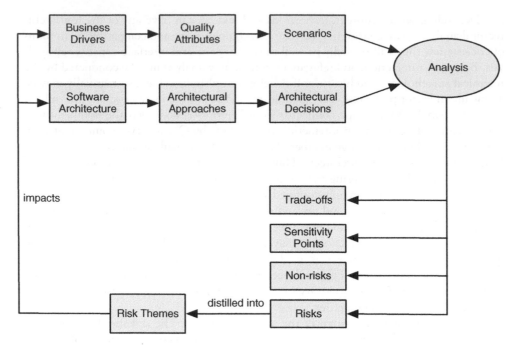

ATAM

The Architectural Trade-Off Analysis Method (Clements, Kazman, and Klein 2002), or ATAM, developed at Carnegie Melon's Software Engineering Institute, is a human-centric process for identifying risks in a software design early in the development life cycle. ATAM specifically focuses on the quality attributes, or non-functional properties (NFPs), of modifiability, security, performance, and reliability. Its objective is to reveal not only how well an architecture satisfies given quality goals, but also how those goals trade off against each other.

The ATAM process requires the gathering of the software architects designing the system, other important stakeholders of that system, and a separate independent architecture evaluation team. An evaluation using ATAM typically takes three to four days. The set of activities followed are depicted in Figure 8-12.

Two key inputs into the ATAM process are the *business drivers* and the system's *software architecture*. A project's decision maker, who is usually the project's manager or customer, first presents the system's major business drivers. These include:

- The system's critical functionality.
- Any technical, managerial, economic, or political constraints.
- The project's business goals and context.
- The major stakeholders.
- The principal *quality attribute* (NFP) goals that impact and shape the architecture.

The quality attributes become a basis of eliciting a set of representative scenarios that will help ensure the system's satisfaction of those attributes. There are three scenario categories in ATAM.

- *Use-case scenarios*, which describe how the system is envisioned by the stakeholders to be used.
- *Growth scenarios*, which describe planned and envisioned modifications to the architecture.
- *Exploratory scenarios*, which try to establish the limits of architecture's adaptability by postulating major changes to the system's functionality, operational profiles, and underlying execution platforms.

Once the scenarios are identified, they are prioritized in terms of importance by the system's stakeholders.

Another thread of activity in ATAM involves the project's architects presenting the key facets of the architecture. This includes:

- *Technical constraints*, such as the required hardware platforms, operating systems, middleware, programming languages, and off-the-shelf functionality.
- *Any other systems* with which the system under development must interact.
- *Architectural approaches* that have been used to meet the quality requirements.

An architectural approach in ATAM refers to any set of architectural design decisions made to solve the problem at hand. Architectural approaches are typically architectural patterns and styles. The architectural approaches are used to elaborate the architectural design decisions made for the system.

The key step in ATAM is the *analysis* of the architectural approaches in the context of the identified scenarios, with the primary goal of establishing the relationship between the approaches—that is, architectural design decisions—and quality attributes. The analysis is not rigorous, but rather is intended to observe general, coarse-grained characteristics of the architecture. To this end, for each architectural approach a set of analysis questions are formulated that are specific to the quality attributes and architectural approach under consideration. The system's architects engage with the ATAM evaluation team in answering these questions. The answers particularly focus on the architectural approach's known *risks* (weaknesses), *non-risks* (strengths), *sensitivity points*, and quality *trade-off points*.

Depending on the architects' responses, any of the answers may be used as a starting point for further analysis. For example, let us assume that an architect is unable to answer questions about a given subsystem's event processing priorities or about the overall system's deployment—that is, the allocation of software components to hardware nodes, further discussed in Chapter 10. In that case, there will be no point in investing further resources to perform rigorous model-based or simulation-based analyses such as the construction of queueing networks or rate-monotonic performance analysis.

Finally, the risks identified in the given iteration of ATAM are distilled into *risk themes* and are fed back to the ATAM inputs of software architecture and business driver. The objective is to repeat the above process until all major architectural risks are properly mitigated.

Regardless of its actual effectiveness, any inspection- and review-based architectural analysis process such as ATAM will sensitize a system's stakeholders to the important facets of their architecture. In ATAM's case, because of its focus and objectives, as well as the prolonged participation of system stakeholders, it has a high potential of resulting in clarified quality attribute requirements for the system, a better documented basis for architectural decisions, identification of risks early in the life cycle, and increased communication among stakeholders.

ATAM: Analysis Summary		
Goals	Completeness	
	Consistency	
	Compatibility	
	Correctness	
Scope	Subsystem- and system-level	
	Data exchange	
Concern	Non-functional	
Models	Informal	
	Semiformal	
Type	Scenario-driven	
Automation Level	Manual	
Stakeholders	Architects	
	Developers	
	Managers	
	Customers	

8.8.2 Model-Based Analysis

Model-based architectural analysis techniques rely solely on a system's architectural description and manipulate that description to discover properties of the architecture. Model-based techniques involve analysis tools of different levels of sophistication. These tools are frequently guided by architects, who may have to interpret the intermediate analysis results and guide the tool in further analysis.

Because of their tool-driven nature, model-based techniques are much less human intensive, and hence usually less costly, than inspections and reviews. On the other hand, they can only be used to establish "hard" properties of a system's architecture, that is, those properties that can be encoded in the architectural model. They cannot easily account for implicit properties—those that a human might readily infer from the existing information and thus chooses not to model explicitly. Additionally, model-driven analysis techniques cannot typically assess "soft," but very important, aspects of an architecture, such as design intent and rationale. Model-based techniques usually also focus on a single, specific facet of a system's architecture, such as syntactic correctness, deadlock freedom, adherence to a given style, and so forth.

Another concern with model-driven analysis techniques is their scalability: More sophisticated techniques are required to keep track of a very large number of the modeled system's elements and properties. The usual trade-off encountered in many static analysis tools, of which model-based architectural analysis tools are an instance, is between scalability on the one hand and precision or confidence on the other. In other words, architects may be able to arrive at highly precise analysis results with a high degree of confidence in those results for smaller systems, but would have to sacrifice that precision and confidence for larger systems. Because of all these reasons, the results of model-driven analyses are usually partial, and multiple such techniques are used in tandem in any given architecture-driven software development project. Even then, model-based analysis usually does not provide all the needed answers to an architect, and is coupled with techniques from the other two categories—inspections and reviews and simulation-based analysis.

The *goals* of model-based architectural analysis techniques are usually consistency, compatibility, and internal completeness. The goals can also include certain aspects of external completeness and correctness. Recall that both external completeness and correctness assess the adherence of a system's architectural model to the requirements, and of the system's implementation to the architectural model. Certain facets of external completeness and correctness, such as structural completeness or correctness, can be established from the architectural model. Furthermore, the output of the analysis technique may be automatic generation of (partial) system implementation from the architectural model, which would ensure external completeness and correctness by construction. If the analysis involves system requirements, then to some extent the requirements will need to be formalized.

The *scope* of model-based architectural analysis can span individual components and connectors, their compositions in a specific subsystem or the entire system, as well as the data exchanged among the specific components and connectors or, globally, across the entire architecture. Model-based techniques may also try to assess the compliance of the model to a higher-level model from which it has been derived. Analysis techniques in this category may also try to assess the architecture's similarity to an existing architecture with known properties. This presumes that both architectures are modeled in one of the notations supported by the analysis technique.

Similarly, the specific *concern* of model-based analysis can vary. The techniques may focus on the structural, behavioral, or interaction properties. Behavioral and interaction properties may be difficult to assess completely using model-based techniques alone, and these techniques are usually coupled with simulation-based approaches. Model-based techniques can be used to analyze an architecture's non-functional properties, but usually require the use of specific formalisms.

In terms of the types of *models* particularly amenable to this type of analysis, the general rule of thumb is that more formality yields more meaningful and precise results. Thus, for example, a Rapide specification, such as that shown in Figure 8-2, will be much more amenable to manipulation by an analysis tool than an informal diagram such as that shown in Figure 8-1. Usually the architectural models to which sophisticated analysis tools are applied have formally specified syntax as well as semantics.

By their nature, the *type* of analysis for which model-based techniques are well suited is static analysis. These techniques are well suited to assessing properties such as proper connectivity, type conformance, definition-use analysis of architectural services, interface and behavioral conformance between interacting components, structural adherence to desired architectural patterns, deadlock freedom, and so on.

As already mentioned, with regard to *automation level* model-based techniques are typically at least partially automated, and are often fully automated, requiring no human intervention.

Finally, model-driven architecture analysis techniques are usually targeted at the technical *stakeholders*, namely architects and developers. Other stakeholders may be interested in summaries of analysis results, but typically these techniques require a certain degree of mastery and provide low-level insights into the architecture.

The remainder of this section will survey the spectrum of model-based analysis techniques developed for different architecture description languages and discuss how architectural models can be leveraged to enable analysis of a representative non-functional property—reliability.

Model Checking

A particular, widely used model-based analysis technique in computer-based systems (software as well as hardware) is model checking. Model checking is a method for algorithmically verifying formal systems. This is achieved by verifying whether the model derived from a hardware or software design satisfies a formal specification expressed as a set of logic formulas. Several software model-checking techniques have emerged over the past decade; interested readers should consult a recent survey of this area by Dwyer and colleagues (Dwyer et al. 2007).

The model of a system is usually expressed as a finite state machine, in other words, a directed graph consisting of vertices and edges. A set of atomic propositions is associated with each vertex, that is, state. The edges represent possible executions that alter the system's state. Finally, the atomic propositions represent the properties that hold at the given point of execution.

The model-checking problem can be stated as follows: Given a desired property, expressed as a temporal logic formula p, and a model M with initial state s, decide if the model satisfies the logic formula, or formally

$$M, s \models p$$

If model M is finite, model checking is reduced to a graph search. Unfortunately, this is rarely the case with software systems, and the critical challenge faced by model-checking tools is *state explosion*, an exponential growth in the state space. Each model-checking technique must address state explosion in order to be able to solve real-world problems.

Researchers have developed several techniques that can help alleviate state explosion, including symbolic algorithms, partial-order reduction, binary decision diagrams, and abstraction of uninteresting or noncritical system characteristics. Another strategy for combating the exponential growth in the state space, successfully adopted by the Alloy technique (Jackson 2002), is to explicitly bound the size of the state space, thus ensuring the technique's feasibility. Of course, doing so introduces optimistic inaccuracy into the analysis process: While no defects may have been found during analysis, there is no guarantee that the model is in fact defect-free.

When using analysis tools such as model checkers, a software system's architects will have to trade off the risks of undiscovered critical defects against the practical limitations of applying a model checker on a very large architectural model.

Model-Based Analysis Enabled by ADLs

The types of analyses for which an ADL is well suited depend on its underlying semantic model and, to a lesser extent, its specification features. For example,

- Wright (Allen and Garlan 1997) uses communicating sequential processes, or CSP, to analyze a system's connectors and the components attached to them for deadlocks. The objective of the analysis is to identify any conditions under which a component requires access to a currently unavailable system resource in order to continue its processing, but the system is unable to make that resource available. For example, if component C_i needs to access a record in a database, but that record is locked by another component C_j, and C_j is unable to release the lock until some chain of conditions ending with component C_i is met (for example, C_i may need to free up some other system resource so that C_j can complete its current task), then the system will deadlock.

- Aesop (Garlan, Allen, and Ockerbloom 1994) ensures style-specific topological constraints and type conformance among architectural elements. For example, Aesop will disallow a server to make requests in a client-server architecture.
- MetaH (Honeywell 1998) and UniCon (Shaw et al. 1995) support schedulability analysis by specifying non-functional properties, such as the criticality and priority of components. Then techniques such as rate-monotonic analysis (Liu and Layland 1973) are applied to ensure that the architecture as-modeled can, in fact, accomplish its required functionality. This is particularly important in the case of systems with stringent performance requirements, such as real-time requirements.

Language parsers and compilers are another kind of analysis tools. Parsers analyze architectures for syntactic correctness, while compilers establish semantic correctness. All architecture modeling notations used in practice have parsers. Several—for example, Darwin (Magee and Kramer 1996), MetaH, and UniCon—also have compilers of sorts, which enable them to generate executable systems from architectural descriptions, provided that component implementations already exist. Rapide's compiler generates executable simulations of Rapide architectures (Luckham et al. 1995).

Another aspect of analysis is enforcement of constraints. Parsers and compilers enforce constraints implicit in type information, non-functional attributes, component and connector interfaces, and semantic models. Rapide also supports explicit specification of other types of constraints, and provides means for their checking and enforcement. Its Constraint Checker analyzes the conformance of a Rapide simulation to the formal constraints defined in the architecture. An architecture constraint checking tool, Armani (Monroe 1998), which is based on the ACME ADL (Garlan, Monroe, and Wile 2000), allows specification and enforcement of arbitrary architectural constraints. UML allows the specification of architectural constraints in its Object Constraint Language, or OCL, but does not natively enforce those constraints; additional tool support must be obtained or built to do so.

Languages such as SADL (Moriconi, Qian, and Riemenschneider 1995) and Rapide provide support for refining an architecture across multiple levels of detail. SADL requires manual proofs of the correctness of mappings of constructs between an abstract and a more concrete architectural style. For example, an abstract architectural style can be the dataflow style, a more concrete style would be the pipe-and-filter style, and an even more concrete style would be the pipeline style. The proof in SADL is performed only once; thereafter, SADL provides a tool that automatically checks whether any two architectures described in the two styles adhere to the mapping. Rapide, on the other hand, supports event maps between individual architectures. The maps are compiled by Rapide's Simulator, so that its Constraint Checker can verify that the events generated during simulation of the concrete architecture satisfy the constraints in the abstract architecture.

A summary of the different ADLs' combined analysis foci is given in the table below.

ADLs: Analysis Summary		
Goals	Consistency	
	Compatibility	
	Completeness (internal)	
Scope	Component- and connector-level	
	Subsystem- and system-level	
	Data exchange	
	Different abstraction levels	
	Architecture comparison	
Concern	Structural	
	Behavioral	
	Interaction	
	Non-functional	
Models	Semiformal	
	Formal	
Type	Static	
Automation Level	Partially automated	
	Automated	
Stakeholders	Architects	
	Developers	
	Managers	
	Customers	

Reliability Analysis

A software system's reliability is the probability that the system will perform its intended functionality under specified design limits, without failure. A *failure* is the occurrence of an incorrect output as a result of an input value that is received, with respect to the specification. An *error* is a mental mistake made by the designer or programmer. A *fault* or a *defect* is the manifestation of that error in the system. In other words, a defect is an abnormal condition that may cause a reduction in, or loss of, the capability of a component to perform a required function; it is a requirements, design, or implementation flaw or deviation from a desired or intended state.

Failure in the above definition denotes that a particular system component is not operational. Reliability can be assessed using several metrics, such as:

- *Time to failure*, for example, mean time until a system fails after its last restoration.
- *Time to repair*, for example, mean time until a system is repaired after its last failure.
- *Time between failures*, for example, mean time between two system failures.

Modeling, estimating, and analyzing software reliability has been an active discipline for several decades. During most of that time, techniques for reliability analysis have been developed and applied at the level of system implementation artifacts. The reason is that several key system parameters are known during or after implementation, including the system's operational profile and possibly its failure and recovery history. Those parameters typically are used in the creation of a state-based model of the system, in which the probabilities of transitions between the states are derived from the system's operational profile and failure data. Then, this model is fed into a stochastic model such as a discrete-time Markov chain, or DTMC (Stewart 1994), which is solved using standard techniques to determine the reliability of the system in question.

Engineers need not, and should not, wait to estimate the reliability of a system until the system has been implemented. A software architectural model can be analyzed for reliability in a manner similar to that described above. At the same time, there are several sources of uncertainty inherent in an architectural model that must be addressed:

1. Software developers may work within different development scenarios. Examples of development scenarios may include implementing entirely new systems, reusing components and/or architectures from previous projects, purchasing software from a vendor, and so forth. Each scenario introduces different reliability challenges.

2. The granularity of the architectural models may vary significantly. A system may be accompanied by coarse-grained models for very large components, partial models for commercial off-the-shelf components, very detailed models for safety-critical components, and so forth.

3. Finally, different sources of information about the system's likely usage may be available. Developers may have at their disposal little or no information about an unprecedented system, a functionally similar system whose usage will also likely be similar, access to experts or extensive domain knowledge, and so forth.

These types of variation must be accounted for in architecture-level reliability modeling and analysis. As in the case of implemented systems, a state-based model corresponding to the architecture can be constructed. However, certain information such as the operational profile and system failure frequencies cannot be obtained, but must be estimated. For this reason, the reliability values obtained at the level of architecture should not be treated as absolute values, but should instead be qualified by the assumptions, such as the presumed operational profile, made about the system. Furthermore, the uncertainties inherent in the architecture-level reliability model suggest that it may be more meaningful to leverage stochastic models other than DTMCs. One such model, specifically intended to deal with modeling uncertainties, is the hidden Markov model, or HMM (Rabiner 1989).

		Facets of Reliability Analysis
Goals	Consistency	
	Compatibility	
	Correctness	
Scope	Component- and connector-level	
	Subsystem- and system-level	
Concern	Non-functional	
Models	Formal	
Type	Static	
	Scenario-based	
Automation Level	Partially automated	
Stakeholders	Architects	
	Managers	
	Customers	
	Vendors	

8.8.3 Simulation-Based Analysis

Simulation requires producing a dynamic, executable model of a given system, or of a part of the system that is of particular interest, possibly from a source model that is otherwise not executable. For example, the model of QueueServer component's behavior from Section 8.1, specified in terms of its operations' pre-and post-conditions, is not executable. On the other hand, its interaction protocol from Figure 8-3 can be simulated by selecting a possible sequence of component invocations, which can also be referred to as a sequence of system events. This event sequence would be used to execute QueueServer's interaction protocol state machine. For instance, if we assume that the `Empty` state is the start state in the state machine, the following will be valid sequences of events

```
<enqueue, enqueue>
<enqueue, dequeue, enqueue>
<enqueue, enqueue, dequeue, enqueue, dequeue>
```

while the single-event sequence

```
<dequeue>
```

is invalid, as is any sequence that starts with the `dequeue` event or has more `dequeue` than `enqueue` events. Note that the validity of a sequence such as

```
<enqueue, enqueue, enqueue>
```

cannot be established without introducing additional information about the system, namely, the size of the queue.

Simulation need not produce identical results to the system's execution: The source model, such as an architectural model, may elide many details of the system. For example, the QueueServer component's model says nothing about the frequency with which the component will be invoked, the sizes of elements that will be placed on the queue, the processing time required to store or access and return the queue elements, and so on. Because of this, the output of simulation might be observed only for event sequences, general trends, or ranges of values rather than specific results. Note that a system's implementation can be thought of as a very faithful executable model. Likewise, running that implementation model can be thought of as a highly precise simulation.

Clearly not all architectural models will be amenable to simulation—recall as a simple example the informal model from Figure 8-1. Even those architectural models that are amenable to simulation may need to be augmented with an external formalism in order to enable their execution. For example, models of event-based architectures may not provide event generation, processing, and response frequencies. To include that information, the architectural model may be mapped, for example, to a discrete event system simulation formalism or a queueing network, with possible ranges of such frequencies specified, and then simulated.

Of course, every time additional information such as event frequency is introduced, architects run the risk of injecting imprecision into the architectural model, and hence into the analysis results. On the other hand, since simulation is tool supported, architects can supply many different values for the model parameters, representing different possible system usage scenarios. They would thereby obtain more precise results than would

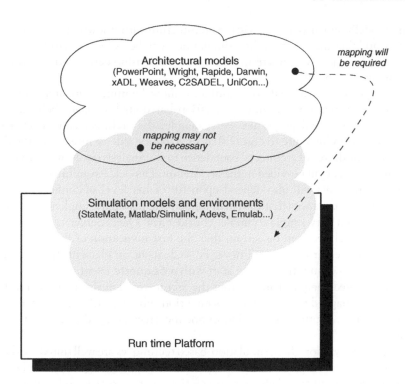

Figure 8-13.
*The conceptual
relationship
between
architectural and
simulation
models.*

be possible with one-size-fits-all model-based analysis, and do so much more easily and inexpensively than via inspections and reviews.

Several software simulation platforms exist, and different ADLs discussed in Chapter 6 and in the previous section have made use of them. The conceptual relationship between ADLs and simulation models and platforms is depicted in Figure 8-13: Certain architectural models (such as UML's state-transition–based models or Rapide's partially ordered event-based models) can be simulated directly; other models may require a mapping to the simulation substrate. The required mapping from an architectural model to a simulation model may be partial or complete and of various degrees of complexity, depending on the semantic closeness between the ADL and the simulation platform. In turn, the simulation platform can be executed on top of a specific run time platform.

The *goals* of simulation-based architectural analysis techniques can be any of the four Cs: completeness, consistency, compatibility, and correctness. However, similarly to software testing, because of the nature of simulation these properties can be established only with a limited degree of confidence and possibly only for a particular subsystem or system property.

The *scope* of simulation-based architectural analysis usually is the entire system or a particular subsystem, as well as the dataflow in the system. However, it is possible to isolate individual components and connectors and simulate their behaviors as well. Simulation-based techniques can be particularly effective in assessing the compliance of the given architectural model to a higher-level model from which it has been derived, as well as the model's similarity to an existing architecture with known properties. Because such models, and thus the results of their simulations, can be expected to differ, additional know-how may be required to determine the exact relationship between the architectural models under consideration.

Since simulation-based analysis techniques allow "running" an architecture and observing the outcome, the *concern* of simulation-based analysis spans behavior, interaction, and non-functional properties. For example, the architect can target a set of components in the architecture to ensure that they will be able to interact in the desired manner. Again, the degree of architects' confidence in the analysis results will vary depending on the amount of detail provided in the architectural model. An architect's confidence in the simulation results will also depend upon his or her level of confidence that the selected operational scenarios (that is, system inputs) will match the implemented system's eventual usage. As a very simple example, consider the QueueServer component from Figure 8-3: If the architect can be certain that the first invocation of the component in its actual execution environment will never be to dequeue an element, he can trust the results of simulations even if they do not start with a `dequeue` event.

Simulation-based analysis demands that the architectural *models* be formal. Informal models cannot be mapped to the necessary simulation substrate unless the system's architects make many impromptu, possibly arbitrary and incorrect, design decisions in the course of the mapping.

The *types* of analysis for which simulation-based techniques are well suited are dynamic and, in particular, scenario-based analysis. Simulation-based techniques are well suited to assessing the system's run time behavior, interaction characteristics, and non-functional qualities. If known system usage scenarios are postulated, the architects no longer need to be concerned with the completeness of the analysis results and whether the results will be representative of the system's actual use.

As already discussed, with regard to *automation level* simulation-based techniques are typically fully automated, requiring no human intervention other than supplying system inputs. However, the process of mapping an architectural model to a simulation model may require significant human involvement. This, in turn, can render the process error-prone.

Finally, simulation-driven architecture analysis techniques can be useful to all system *stakeholders*. Setting up and running simulations may require a high degree of technical expertise and familiarity with the architectural model, the architecture modeling notation, as well as the simulation substrate.

XTEAM

The eXtensible Tool-chain for Evaluation of Architectural Models (XTEAM) is a model-driven architectural description and simulation environment for mobile and resource-constrained software systems (Edwards, Malek, and Medvidović 2007). XTEAM composes two existing, general-purpose ADLs, enhancing them to capture important features of mobile systems. It implements model generators that take advantage of the ADL extensions to produce simulation models.

For modeling architectural concerns, XTEAM builds an architectural meta-model. This meta-model leverages xADL's Core, which, as the reader will recall from Chapter 6, defines architectural structures and types common to most other ADLs. This meta-model is augmented with finite state processes, or FSP, which allows the specification of

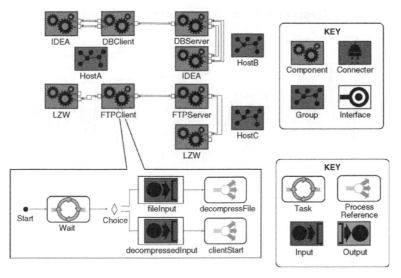

Figure 8-14. *An example* XTEAM *model of a system comprising three hardware hosts and eight software components. The behavior of one of the components has been highlighted. This behavior represents* XTEAM's *syntactic overlay on top of FSP.* XTEAM *allows behaviors to be abstracted in the form of the* ProcessReference *construct.*

component behaviors (Magee and Kramer 2006). The combination of xADL and FSP allows the creation of architectural representations that can be simulated. XTEAM masks many of the details of the two notations via a visual language depicted in Figure 8-14.

Models conformant to the composed ADL contain sufficient information to implement a semantic mapping into low-level simulation constructs, which can be executed by an off-the-shelf discrete event simulation engine, such as adevs (Nutaro). This semantic mapping is implemented by XTEAM's model interpreter framework. When invoked by an architect, the XTEAM interpreter framework traverses the architectural model, building up a discrete event simulation model in the process. The interpreter framework maps components and connectors to discrete event constructs, such as atomic models and static digraphs. The FSP-based behavioral specifications encoded in XTEAM, such as the model shown in the bottom diagram of Figure 8-14, are translated into the state-transition functions employed by the discrete event simulation engine. The interpreter framework also creates discrete event entities that represent various system resources, such as threads. Hook methods provided by the framework allow an architect to generate the code needed to realize a wide variety of dynamic analyses.

XTEAM implements simulation-based analysis capabilities for end-to-end latency, memory utilization, component reliability, and energy consumption. Each analysis type requires the implementation of the needed XTEAM ADL extensions and a model interpreter. For example, XTEAM implements the component reliability modeling extension and analysis technique using the HMM-based approach discussed in Section 8.8.2. This reliability estimation approach relies on the definition of component failure types, the probabilities of those failures at different times during component execution, and the probability of, and time required for, recovery from failure. In order to support this type of analysis,

Figure 8-15.
*End-to-end
latency, energy
consumption,
and reliability
profiles of
different elements
of the architecture
from Figure
8-14, obtained
from adevs
simulations. The
simulations were
generated
automatically
from the
XTEAM model.*

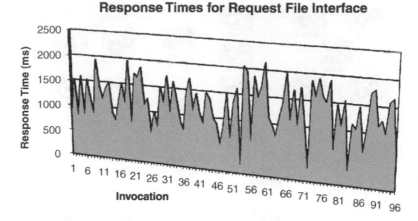

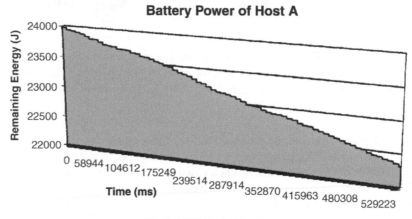

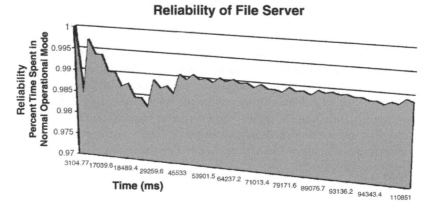

XTEAM's FSP-based behavior language had to be extended to include failure and recovery events and probabilities. XTEAM was then augmented with an analysis technique that determines if and when failures occur as the components in the system progress through different tasks and states.

Another analysis supported by XTEAM is that of the modeled mobile system's energy consumption rate. The selected energy consumption model by Seo (Seo, Malek, and Medvidović 2007) was implemented as another XTEAM ADL extension and model interpreter, which incorporated the necessary elements of the energy cost model. Then, another adevs simulation was generated by XTEAM to show the system's likely energy consumption over time, under certain usage assumptions. The results of three different simulations for the architecture depicted in Figure 8-14 are shown in Figure 8-15.

		XTEAM: Analysis Summary
Goals	Consistency	
	Compatibility	
	Correctness	
Scope	Component- and connector-level	
	Subsystem- and system-level	
	Data exchange	
Concern	Structural	
	Behavioral	
	Interaction	
	Non-functional	
Models	Formal	
Type	Dynamic	
	Scenario-based	
Automation Level	Automated	
Stakeholders	Architects	
	Developers	
	Managers	
	Customers	
	Vendors	

8.9 END MATTER

A major part of what makes good architectural practice is deciding what one wants out of the architecture. An individual or organization cannot and should not focus on architecture just because it is widely accepted that doing so is the right thing to do. Instead, system stakeholders should first decide on the specific benefits they want to gain from the explicit architectural focus. One clear benefit of this is the establishment of a system's properties of interest before the system has been implemented and deployed. It is critical to make sure that the system possesses the key required properties and does not have or is reasonably unlikely to have any undesirable characteristics. Architectural analysis provides system stakeholders with a powerful suite of techniques and tools for doing that.

However, architectural analysis is neither easy nor cheap (see "The Business Case" sidebar). It should be planned for and applied carefully. The system's stakeholders must be clear about their project objectives and must map those objectives to specific architectural analyses. This chapter has provided a structure that can be used to determine the architectural analysis techniques that are best suited for specific system development scenarios. In many cases, multiple analysis techniques may need to be used in concert. Again, deciding which techniques to use is a critical part of an architect's job: using too many will expend the project's resources unnecessarily; using too few will run the risk of propagating defects into the final system; using wrong analyses will have both of these drawbacks.

Once a system's architecture is properly designed and modeled, and it is established through analysis that it possesses the desired properties, the architecture is ready to be implemented. Chapter 9 presents a detailed overview of architectural implementation challenges, techniques, and tools. Chapter 10 then discusses the software architectural implications in an implemented system's deployment and run time mobility. Chapter 14 will return to these issues in the context of architectural adaptation.

The Business Case	The up-front costs in an architecture-driven software development project can be significant. Even if we consider architectural analysis alone,

1. Techniques for architectural inspections and reviews typically involve the participation of many stakeholders over several days. Recall ATAM for example.

2. Model-based analysis requires the development or acquisition of multiple tools as well as the possible introduction of formalisms, each with its own learning curve, required by those tools. For example, recall the adoption of Markov models for reliability analysis or Wright's incorporation of CSP to ensure deadlock freedom.

3. Finally, simulation-based analysis most often requires augmenting the architectural model or recasting it into the form required by the simulation substrate. Recall XTEAM's reliance on xADL, FSP, and adevs.

Clearly, architectural analysis can be costly. These are the very costs of which many managers and organizations are leery since the planned revenue from the system under development is still very far off. Therefore, the costs must be offset by the benefits gained from architectural analysis. The benefits of detecting and removing software system defects early on are well known: Many sources, starting with Barry Boehm's seminal work *Software Engineering Economics* (Boehm 1981), have documented that discovering defects earlier rather than later can reduce the cost of mitigating those defects by an order of magnitude or more.

This does not mean that all costs of architectural analysis are automatically justified. There is no particular need to do analysis for the sake of demonstrating that one can do it or to show off a technique or tool. Analysis must have a clear objective and take place within a particular, well-defined context. Put another way, the undertaken analysis activity must recoup its own costs via the benefits it yields. Nobody should pay more for something than the value it gives back. For example, a system's architects should not spend more to perform deadlock analysis than the projected risk and associated cost of deadlock for the system in question. The bottom line for any project with a tight budget—which, in practice, means for the great majority of projects—is that under no circumstances should the cost of architectural analysis impinge upon the organization's ability to actually implement the system.

8.10 REVIEW QUESTIONS

1. What are the architectural analysis criteria?
2. What are the four Cs of architectural analysis?
3. What is the difference between internal and external consistency?
4. What is interface inconsistency? Provide an example.
5. What is interaction inconsistency? Provide an example.
6. What are the advantages and disadvantages of informal architectural models as pertaining to analysis?

7. What are the advantages and disadvantages of formal architectural models as pertaining to analysis?

8. Why is system-level analysis important if you have already completed component- and connector-level analysis?

9. Why is the analysis of the data exchanged in an architecture important?

10. Why is it important to analyze an architecture for non-functional concerns?

11. Who are the possible stakeholders in architectural analysis?

12. Is scenario-driven analysis a special case of static analysis or dynamic analysis? Justify your answer.

13. Name some advantages and disadvantages of architectural inspections and reviews.

14. What is model checking? How does it pertain to architectural analysis?

15. How does one analyze an architecture for deadlocks?

16. What are discrete-time Markov chains used for?

17. What is simulation?

18. If an architectural model is expressed in a notation that does not have executable semantics, can it still be simulated? Justify your answer.

8.11 EXERCISES

1. Select one of the models of Lunar Lander from Chapter 4 or Chapter 6. Determine its components. For each individual component, model the services it provides and requires in terms of their names and interfaces. After you have completed the model, analyze the model manually for name and interface inconsistencies.

2. Model the behaviors of the Lunar Lander components used in the previous exercise, by specifying each component operation's pre- and post-conditions, as discussed in this chapter. After you have completed the model, analyze the model manually for behavioral inconsistencies.

3. As an alternative, or in addition to the pre- and post-condition based behavior model from the preceding exercise, model the Lunar Lander component behaviors with state-transition diagrams, such as those used by UML. Discuss the specific advantages and difficulties in using this model in ensuring behavioral consistency. Research whether any available techniques can be adopted or adapted for ensuring the consistency of two state-transition diagrams.

4. Select one of the models of Lunar Lander from Chapter 4 or Chapter 6. Determine its components. Construct each component's interaction model. Analyze these models for interaction inconsistencies. What, if any, are the differences between this task and the task described in the preceding exercise?

5. Download and study the Alloy modeling language and analysis tool suite (alloy.mit.edu). Discuss the possible ways in which Alloy can be used to aid architecture modeling and analysis. Demonstrate your arguments with specific examples of simple architectures, architectural properties, architectural styles, and so on.

6. Select an existing application with a documented architecture. This can be an application you have worked on or an open-source system. Study the architecture if you are unfamiliar with it. Follow the ATAM process to determine the quality attributes important to the system, as well as the architectural decisions employed. Develop a set of scenarios and key decisions underlying the architecture. Use the scenarios to determine whether the architectural decisions result in the required quality attributes.

7. Discuss the potential shortcomings of applying the ATAM process without all the prescribed stakeholders and a separate architecture evaluation team.

8. Select one of the models of Lunar Lander from Chapter 4 or Chapter 6. Provide its state-based reliability model as discussed in this chapter. Study an existing off-the-shelf technique for reliability estimation (such as DTMC or HMM). Apply this technique on your reliability model. Devise strategies for improving your system's reliability.

9. Select an important property of a software system, such as reliability, availability, or fault tolerance. State the assumptions required in order to be able to assess this property at the architectural level. Discuss the missing knowledge about the system that necessitates the assumptions. Then discuss the implications and reasonableness of each assumption.

10. Select two existing ADLs of your choice. Use each ADL to model the Lunar Lander architecture. Use the two ADLs' respective analysis tools to analyze each model for the properties on which the given ADL focuses. Discuss the extent to which the two ADLs' modeling features impact the available analyses versus the extent to which the selected analyses appear to impact the available modeling features.

11. Download and study an available simulation engine such as adevs (www.ornl.gov/~1qn/adevs/index.html). Provide a mapping from an ADL of your choice to the simulation engine. Discuss the challenges in doing so and the range of architectural properties for which the simulations can be used. Practically demonstrate the use of simulation for at least one such property.

8.12 FURTHER READING

A significant amount of literature on software architecture has focused on architecture-based analysis. The early work on ADLs, such as Wright and Rapide, focused as much on the enabled analysis techniques as it did on the modeling features. Likewise, when UML first came onto the software development scene in the mid- to late-1990s as a de facto modeling standard, it was almost immediately accompanied by a continuing stream of publications on how UML models can be effectively analyzed for many different types of properties of interest. A widely cited overview of ADLs and their associated analysis capabilities was provided by Medvidović and Taylor in 2000 (Medvidović and Taylor 2000). That work has been recently revisited and the perspective expanded by Medvidović, Dashofy, and Taylor (Medvidović, Dashofy, and Taylor 2007).

Carnegie Mellon University's Software Engineering Institute has, over time, proposed a number of architectural analysis approaches that entail inspections and reviews. Examples are ATAM, studied in this chapter;

its precursor, Software Architecture Analysis Method, (SAAM); and an evaluation method for partial architectures, called ARID. These techniques are described in a book by Paul Clements, Rick Kazman, and Mark Klein (Clements, Kazman, and Klein 2002). Recently, Liliana Dobrica and Eila Niemelä provided a broader survey of inspection and review-based architectural analysis approaches (Dobrica and Niemelä 2002).

Leveraging explicit architectural models for determining a system's key non-functional properties has gained a lot of interest over time. This has resulted in a cross-pollination of ideas from established disciplines such as reliability, dependability, and fault-tolerant computing on the one hand, and software architecture on the other hand. In 2007 alone, Anne Immonen and Niemelä (Immonen and Niemelä 2007) have provided a survey of architecture-based methods for availability and reliability estimation, while Swapna Gokhale conducted a separate survey of architecture-based reliability analysis approaches (Gokhale 2007).

9

Implementation

Implementation is the one phase of software development that is not optional. Regardless of how well the requirements have been captured or how carefully the architecture has been designed and reviewed, software systems must be implemented in code to achieve their ends. Architecture is used to capture important design decisions about a system, using sound engineering principles and knowledge to increase confidence that the target system's qualities match the expectations of its stakeholders. To imbue these qualities in the target system, the implementation *must* be derived from its architecture.

In terms of implementation, architecture is both prescriptive and restrictive. It is prescriptive in the sense that it gives implementers direction on what to produce—how to structure code modules, how they should be interconnected, and how they should behave. It is restrictive in the sense that its guidelines—particularly those specified in the architectural style—tell developers what they may *not* do: the forms of communication that are prohibited, the kinds of behaviors or system states that are not allowed, and so on.

The problem of relating architecture to implementation is one of *mapping*. Concepts defined at the architecture level should be directly connected to artifacts at the implementation level. This correspondence is not necessarily one-to-one. For example, in general, a software component or connector will be implemented using many code and resource artifacts. Likewise, a single software library may be shared among several component implementations (as long as its manner of use does not violate style rules). When this mapping is not maintained, architectural degradation can occur—specifically, the gradual deviation of a system's implementation from its architecture. This generally makes software harder to understand and maintain, and makes it difficult to achieve or retain the qualities embodied by the architecture.

Properly implementing a system so that the architecture survives in the implementation requires a well-formed understanding of how concepts in the architecture (and the architectural style) map onto implementation technologies such as programming

337

languages, development environments, reusable libraries and components, middleware, and component models. Implementation technologies such as middleware and component libraries can help, but they can also hinder: They nearly always come with their own assumptions that can influence or get in the way of architectural decisions made earlier. Even concepts we take for granted, such as object-oriented programming, can have architectural influences. In this chapter, we discuss techniques and technologies for creating and maintaining mappings between architecture and implementation.

We also introduce and focus on a concept known as an *architecture implementation framework*, which is software that bridges the gap between architectures and implementation technologies. We discuss how to identify, evaluate, and create new frameworks. We also relate frameworks to other, similar technologies such as middleware and component frameworks.

9.1 CONCEPTS

Here, we will discuss concepts and issues related to architecture-based implementation.

9.1.1 The Mapping Problem

Implementing an architecture is a problem of mapping—specifically, mapping design decisions to specific implementation constructs that realize those decisions. From a software-quality perspective, this mapping is a form of *traceability*. In general, the term traceability can refer to any mechanism for connecting different software artifacts; in this context we specifically mean traceability from architecture to implementation. Choosing how to create and maintain this mapping is critical in architecture-based development. Here, we discuss implementation mappings for several kinds of design decisions discussed in Chapter 6.

Components and Connectors. Design decisions about components and connectors partition the application's functionality into discrete elements of computation and communication. In general, programming environments provide mechanisms such as packages, libraries, or classes that are used to partition functionality in implementations. Here, the challenge is to maintain a mapping between the partitions established by the architecture-level components and connectors and the partitions established by the implementation-level packages, libraries, classes, and so on. If implementations are not partitioned according to the component and connector boundaries specified in the architecture, then component boundaries may break down and cause architectural drift and erosion.

Interfaces. At the architectural level, interfaces can be specified in many different ways. If interfaces are specified in terms of method or function signatures similar to those in the target programming language, mapping is a straightforward process of translating the method signatures into code. However, if the architecture-level interface definition is more complex—specifying a protocol or set of state transitions, then greater effort will be required to create an appropriate implementation.

Configurations. At the architectural level, configurations are often specified as linked graphs of components and connectors. These graphs specify and constrain how the components and connectors interact through their interfaces. The same interactions and topologies must be preserved in the implementation. Many programming languages include features that allow one module to refer to another module by way of its interface, rather than its implementation (for example, though explicitly defined interfaces as in Java, or function pointer tables in C). Additionally, some programming languages and middleware systems allow the use of reflection or dynamic discovery to connect and disconnect components at runtime. When these constructs are available, it is often possible for the implementation-level links between components and connectors to be specified independent of the components and connectors themselves, or even generated from the architecture description.

Design Rationale. Design rationale is a construct that often has no specific mapping to implementation, since it is not something that directly influences the functionality of the application. Often, the best way to retain design rationale during implementation is by writing it down in source-code comments or external documentation.

Dynamic Properties (Behavior). Depending on how they are modeled, architecture-level behavioral specifications can ease or facilitate implementation. Some behavioral specifications can be translated directly into implementation skeletons or even complete implementations. However, this is not always the case; formal behavioral specifications often lack bindings to programming-language–level constructs and therefore it is difficult to determine whether a behavioral specification is actually implemented correctly. Some behavioral specifications are more useful for generating analysis or testing plans than for implementations.

Non-Functional Properties. Implementing non-functional properties is perhaps one of the most difficult propositions in software engineering. The best way to accomplish this is through a combination of techniques—documenting rationale, inspections, testing, user studies, and so on. This difficulty is why refining non-functional properties into functional design decisions (when possible) is so important.

One-Way and Round-Trip Mapping

Architectures and implementations must inevitably co-evolve. Architectures can evolve because of changing requirements or increased understanding, and these changes must be propagated to the implementation. Likewise, discoveries and changes made during implementation will affect the architecture. Keeping architecture and implementation in sync is a challenging problem, involving issues of process, tool support, and organizational culture. Aspects of the mapping that lack strong traceability are often the first to diverge.

Maintaining the architecture-implementation mapping in the face of change depends on the process of change. One option is to mandate that all changes begin from the architecture—the architecture is changed first, the mappings to implementation are used, and then the implementation is updated through the use of automated tools or manual processes. This is effectively a one-way mapping. Another option is to allow changes to be initiated in either the architecture or the implementation. In this case, automated tools or manual processes are still used to update the other artifact. This is a two-way mapping.

Two-way mappings are better for detecting and resolving architectural drift and erosion, but they are also more complex and expensive to create and maintain. This is sometimes known as a round-tripping problem because changes have to be mapped from architecture to implementation and back again. Various strategies for maintaining both one-way and round-trip mappings are discussed in this chapter.

9.1.2 Architecture Implementation Frameworks

When developing a system, an ideal approach would be to define the architecture first and then select implementation technologies (programming languages, software libraries, operating systems, and so on) that most closely match its needs. This ideal is difficult to achieve—programming languages rarely have explicit support for architecture-level constructs. Moreover, selection of implementation technologies will often be driven by extrinsic or accidental factors such as cost, maturity, platform support, organizational culture, and even externally imposed or wrongheaded requirements specifications or standards.

An important strategy for bridging the gap between concepts in an architecture and a system's implementation technologies is to use (or develop) an architecture implementation framework (Malek, Mikic-Rakic, and Medvidović 2005).

> **Definition.** An *architecture implementation framework* is a piece of software that acts as a bridge between a particular architectural style and a set of implementation technologies. It provides key elements of the architectural style *in code*, in a way that assists developers in implementing systems that conform to the prescriptions and constraints of the style.

By far, the most common example of an architecture framework in use today is the Standard I/O library in UNIX (University of California 1986) and similar operating systems. Although few developers may recognize it as such, it is actually a bridge between the pipe-and-filter style (which is character-stream oriented and concurrent) and procedural, nonconcurrent programming languages such as C. It provides architectural concepts such as access to interfaces via readable and writable character streams in a way that fits the target environment (for example, procedure calls). A fuller discussion of how the Standard I/O library serves as an architectural framework appears later in this chapter.

Architecture frameworks are effectively technologies that assist developers in conforming to a particular architectural style. However, most frameworks will not prevent developers from wandering outside the constraints of the style. For example, just because a UNIX program imports the Standard I/O library does not mean that the program will work in a pipe-and-filter style; it may read and write all its data from named disk files and ignore the standard input and output streams completely.

It is possible to develop applications in almost any architectural style without the use of an architecture framework. However, this usually means weaving the architectural concepts throughout the implementation and makes it difficult to develop and maintain them. In the cases where no framework exists for a particular programming language/operating system combination, developers will usually end up implementing a set of software libraries and tools that amount to an architecture framework anyway.

A natural question to ask is: How are frameworks represented in architectural models? From an architectural perspective, frameworks are often considered to be a substrate underlying all components and connectors. Therefore, it is unusual to see a framework modeled as a component or connector in the architecture itself. However, frameworks often include implementations for common components and connectors (such as those defined by the style—a pipe connector or an event-bus, for example) that serve as implementations for components and connectors that are specified in the architecture.

Same Style, Different Frameworks

A single architectural style can be supported by a number of different, alternative frameworks. This can happen for a number of reasons. First, different programming languages and implementation platforms usually require different frameworks. For example, Java applications use classes in the java.io package (Harold 2006) to perform stream input and output; these classes are how Java implements functions similar to the C standard I/O library. C++ programmers can either use the object-oriented iostream library or the procedural stdio library for the same purpose. Each of these architecture frameworks bridges the same architectural style (pipe-and-filter) to different implementation technologies (Java, C++, or C).

Sometimes, multiple frameworks for the same combination of style, programming language, and operating system will be developed. Usually, these frameworks distinguish themselves based on different qualities or capabilities. A good example is the New I/O (java.nio) package in Java (Hitchens 2002). Like the older java.io package, java.nio allows programs to read and write data streams from various sources. However, the New I/O package provides enhanced capabilities such as native support for buffering, better control over synchronization, and the ability to use fast data transfer techniques such as memory mapping. Users can choose the appropriate framework for their application based on the quality needs of those applications.

9.1.3 Evaluating Frameworks

Frameworks, like any software system, can vary widely along nearly any quality dimension. This is why many frameworks are often developed to support the same architectural style in the same environment. Evaluating a framework, then, is similar to evaluating any important software component.

Platform Support

An architecture framework brings together three key elements: an architectural style, a programming language, and an operating system. One of the most basic criteria for evaluating a framework, then, is platform support. Once an architectural style has been identified, the availability of architecture frameworks for a target programming language/operating system combination can be determined. If the project has the freedom to select the implementation platform based on the architecture (which is becoming increasingly rare as software systems are more and more likely to run on existing platforms already in the field) then the availability of suitable architecture frameworks should be a criterion for platform selection.

Fidelity

One quality that is particularly important in architecture implementation frameworks is fidelity, specifically fidelity to the target architectural style. To be useful, a framework need not provide direct implementation support for every single design decision in its target style; for example, it may provide communication mechanisms but leave the concurrency of the architecture up to the individual component implementers. Furthermore, frameworks often provide support for following stylistic constraints, but not enforcement; that is, the framework will make it easy for implementers to follow the constraints of the style, but will not explicitly prevent them from breaking the constraints. More faithful frameworks are generally better at preventing or avoiding architectural drift and erosion. However, this generally comes at a cost because the frameworks are more complicated, bigger, or less efficient.

Matching Assumptions

Architectural styles induce certain design decisions and constraints on applications. Frameworks can do the same thing—ideally, the decisions and constraints induced by the framework are the same as those induced by the target style. However, styles often leave many aspects of a system unconstrained, and frameworks have the additional responsibility of supporting the concrete implementation activity. For these reasons, frameworks may induce additional constraints on applications. For example, a framework might assume that the system will be instantiated and configured only by the framework, or that individual components and connectors will not start their own threads of control, or that each software component in the architecture can be associated with a module in the target programming language.

Problems can occur when the assumptions of a framework conflict with the assumptions of other implementation technologies used on a project. Consider an architecture framework for an object-oriented programming language. This framework might require that every component have a main class that is derived from a base class provided by the framework. However, the project might include several GUI elements, and the GUI toolkit may require that GUI element classes extend base classes provided by the toolkit.

If the programming language is one that does not support multiple inheritance (like Java) there is a serious mismatch between the GUI toolkit and the implementation framework. This situation may not even be an architectural mismatch; it is a mismatch of particular implementation decisions. Nonetheless, strategies must be identified to alleviate this situation.

Thus, when evaluating an architecture framework, it is important to enumerate the assumptions it makes and compare those with the assumptions made by other components, toolkits, libraries, and environments with which the application will interact. Sometimes, workarounds can be developed, especially if the mismatch is a low-level implementation detail. However, if the mismatch is architectural, this might call into question the compatibility of the architectural style itself with the choice of implementation technologies for the implemented application.

Efficiency

In general, architecture frameworks add a layer of functionality between the application and the hardware it runs on. One of the primary dangers of introducing new layers is a decrease in application efficiency. This concern is especially important when dealing with architecture frameworks, since they tend to pervade the application. An architecture framework may mediate all communication between components in a system, for example, or dictate the concurrency policy for the entire application. When this is the case, efficiency should be a primary selection criterion for a framework.

Before committing to a framework, it is a useful exercise to run benchmarks on the framework with parameters derived from the target application to get a feel for the upper bound of application performance using the framework. For example, if a framework can exchange 10,000 messages per minute in a dummy application whose sole purpose is to exchange messages as quickly as possible, it is not realistic to build an application with that framework that will exchange 20,000 messages per minute.

Other Considerations

As noted above, the issues involved in selecting an architecture framework are very similar to those involved in selecting any software component. It could be argued that because frameworks have such a pervasive effect on applications, they are the most critical element of all to select. Qualities such as size, cost, ease of use, availability of source code, reliability, robustness, portability, and many others are all important when choosing a framework.

9.1.4 Middleware, Component Models, and Application Frameworks

A spectrum of technologies exists to integrate software components and provide services above and beyond those provided by a given programming language/operating system combination. These technologies go by a number of different names: middleware, component models (or component frameworks), and application frameworks. We will refer to these systems collectively as "middleware." Popular examples include CORBA (Object Management Group 2001), JavaBeans (JavaSoft 1996), COM/DCOM/COM+ (Sessions 1997), .NET, Java Message Service (JavaSoft 2001), various Web Services technologies, and so on.

There are many similarities between architecture frameworks and middleware. Both of them provide developers with implementation services that are not natively available in the underlying programming language or operating system. For example, CORBA middleware provides services such as remote procedure calls (RPCs) and the ability to dynamically discover the interfaces of objects. The JavaBeans component model introduces a new concept to Java: the bean, an object that follows certain interface guidelines that make it possible to compose beans more easily.

Architecture implementation frameworks are a form of middleware. The difference between traditional middleware and architecture frameworks is the focus on architectural style. Architecture implementation frameworks are implemented specifically to support development in one or more architectural styles. Here, the *style* is the primary artifact driving the implementation technology. Middleware is created based on the services that are provided, generally without regard to the style of the application being developed.

How Middleware and Component Frameworks May Induce a Style

Middleware often constrains applications in ways that are similar to architecture frameworks. Middleware often influences how an application's functionality is broken up into components, how those components interact (often through middleware-provided services akin to connectors) and also the application's topology. These are generally architectural concerns. In this sense, middleware can induce an architecture or architectural style on an application (Di Nitto and Rosenblum 1999).

CORBA [and CORBA-like technologies such as COM and RMI (Grosso 2001)] are a good example of how middleware can influence application architectures. CORBA breaks up an application into objects that may reside on different hosts. Objects that participate in the application expose their own services through provided interfaces whose method signatures are specified in an interface definition language (IDL). Objects look up other objects through services such as naming services or trading services, and then call each other using a request-response pattern, passing only serializable parameters across the interface boundaries. Together, these constraints comprise an architectural style that might be referred to as the "distributed objects" style.

If system stakeholders have chosen the distributed objects style for their application, then CORBA-like middleware might serve as an ideal architecture framework. However, things are rarely this simple. Presented with an application to design, software architects have to make hundreds of design decisions. Choosing the application's architectural style is one of the most important decisions they will make. However, experienced architects are also familiar with many different middleware technologies and the advantages of those technologies. The services provided by many middleware technologies can be seductive, and often the capabilities of a particular middleware system will influence an architect's decision-making process. Architects must be especially careful to avoid having a middleware technology overly influence their designs.

Resolving Mismatches between Architectural Styles and Middleware

Two major conflicts can arise between architectural styles and middleware:

1. The architectural style chosen for the application does not match that induced by the middleware chosen.
2. The application's designers chose a middleware first based on services provided and let this have an undue influence over the architectural style of the application.

When selecting implementation technologies, it is critical to understand that the quality benefits provided by that technology often come with architectural implications, which may not be compatible with your architecture's design. For example, CORBA provides the benefits of distribution and reflection, but in a form that induces systems that are based on objects that communicate by request-response procedure calls. This may cause certain architectural drawbacks, such as increased latency and synchronization. Allowing the choice of middleware to influence the architecture is backward: It is the tail wagging the dog. Architecture should influence your choice of middleware.

When there is an architectural mismatch between middleware and the target architectural style, several options are available:

Change the Style. The architectural style can be changed to better fit the middleware. This should be done only when the benefits of using the middleware outweigh the costs of adapting it to work with the target style.

Change the Middleware. The middleware can be adapted to better fit the architectural style. This strategy can be difficult because middleware packages are often large, complex, or proprietary.

Develop Glue Code. Architecture frameworks can be built on top of middleware, leveraging the parts of middleware that match, and working around the parts that do not. This way, neither the style nor the middleware itself has to be adapted.

Ignore Unneeded Middleware Services. Some middleware packages or component frameworks might provide a host of services that cut across many aspects of application development. However, it may be possible to use a subset of these services selectively, and ignore the services that are not compatible with (or relevant to) the target architectural style.

Hide the Middleware. Developers use middleware because it provides certain services. If those services are not necessarily cross-cutting, and can be applied at specific points in the architecture, then it may be possible to hide the middleware inside individual components or connectors. For example, if CORBA is being used only to facilitate communication between heterogeneous components running on different hosts, all CORBA-related code can be isolated within individual connectors that need cross-host communication. Other CORBA services such as lookup and dynamic interface discovery might be used entirely within the context of the connectors or simply ignored.

Using Middleware to Implement Connectors

Many middleware packages provide services that are effectively communication-centric: They provide different mechanisms for heterogeneous components to communicate. If improving communication in an architecture is a goal, then using middleware as the basis for implementing connectors, rather than the whole application, can allow a system to avoid having the middleware's assumptions bleed into and corrupt the architecture's design decisions.

In this scenario, architects first should define and identify the capabilities required for a connector, ideally without regard to how that connector will be implemented. Then, middleware should be selected that can provide all (or most) of those capabilities and also fit with the other project goals. If capabilities are not provided directly by the middleware, they should be implemented as part of the connector's implementation. The result is a connector that fulfills the architectural need, rather than one that bows to assumptions made by middleware developers.

For example, a connector might be needed that provides message-passing support between a C++ component running on Linux and a Java component running on Windows. Two message-oriented middleware packages may be available: a commercial package that has C++ and Java support for both platforms, but is proprietary and expensive, and an open-source solution that supports both platforms but only C++ components. If budgets are tight, the open-source solution can be selected, and a Java Native Interface (JNI) adapter (Liang 1999) can be written to allow the Java component to communicate with the middleware.

9.1.5 Building a New Framework

Occasionally, circumstances motivate the development of a new architecture implementation framework. Good reasons to develop a new framework include:

- The architectural style in use is novel.
- The architectural style is not novel but it is being implemented on a platform for which no framework exists.
- The architectural style is not novel and frameworks exist for the target platform, but the existing frameworks are inadequate.

Developing an architecture framework is a task that should not be approached lightly. These frameworks will impact almost every part of the applications built atop them and can be a make-or-break factor for the success of those applications, so great care should be undertaken in their design. Developing an architecture framework is, in many respects, like developing any other application—it requires the development of requirements, a design, input from many stakeholders, quality evaluation, and so on. As such, almost everything we have said in this book about developing applications in general can be applied to architecture frameworks. There are, however, some additional guidelines that can be applied specifically to framework development:

Have a Good Understanding of the Style First. Developing an architecture framework with an incomplete understanding of the target architectural style is a recipe for disaster. There will be no standard by which to measure the framework for fidelity or completeness. A clear, concise set of the rules and constraints of the architectural style should be developed before framework design begins.

Limit the Framework to Issues Addressed in the Architectural Style. To the greatest extent possible, an architecture implementation framework should be independent from any specific target application. Including application-specific features (that are not part of the style) in a framework limits the reusability of the framework and blurs the line between what is part of the application and what is part of its framework.

Choose the Scope of the Framework. Well-implemented architecture frameworks are valuable reusable assets for the organizations that develop them. Developers of a new framework must decide how the framework will be reused in the future to properly scope its capabilities. For example, a particular architectural style may be amenable to dynamic architectures—those that change their structure on the fly. However, the initial target applications built in the style may not take advantage of this. Whether or not to implement dynamism in the framework depends on how likely it is that dynamism will be needed in a future project (or a future version of the current project). This leads to the following related piece of advice.

Avoid Over-engineering. When building new frameworks, it is tempting to include all sorts of clever or useful capabilities, regardless of whether the target applications will actually use them. This is especially true because frameworks are often (and should be) developed separately from specific applications. These additional capabilities can involve additional layers and levels of abstraction and have significant effects on the framework, particularly on its usability and performance.

Limit Overhead for Application Developers. Every framework puts some additional burden on application implementers—to include boilerplate code in components, to implement a standard set of behaviors that the framework can call upon, and so on. As burdens on application developers increase, frameworks become more cumbersome and less palatable. Limiting their additional obligations (either through framework design or tool support) can mitigate this.

Develop a Strategy for Legacy and Off-the-Shelf Resources. Almost any application is bound to include elements (components, connectors, middleware, and so on) that were not developed with the framework in mind. Without a documented or tool-supported strategy for integrating these external resources, developers will be forced to come up with their own mechanisms on an ad hoc basis. This can cause problems as developers reinvent the wheel (or worse, reinvent different wheels). Framework developers should strongly consider the kinds of external resources that might be incorporated in applications and establish strategies for integrating these resources to distribute with the framework.

9.1.6 Concurrency

In the past, many software-intensive systems could be designed to run on a single computer with a single processor. Today, even individual computers have multicore or multithreaded processors that can perform multiple tasks simultaneously. Furthermore, many modern applications include some form of distribution over a network, where each network host will have one or more processors. In the very near future, systems will have to be designed for concurrency: multiple tasks in the system executing simultaneously (Magee and Kramer 2006). Concurrency is generally implemented with a variety of strategies; on a single host, multiple threads or operating system processes are generally employed. On a network, different hosts necessarily run independent processes that must work together and implement the behavior of the system as a whole.

Most architectural styles have some notion of concurrency, whether it is simple synchronization or complex multiprocessing. Pipe-and-filter, one of the simplest styles, was developed to take advantage of concurrency to process partial results in parallel; it was an improvement over batch processing systems that were unable to do so. Many of the architectural styles identified in Chapter 4 have specific provisions for which elements can (or should) run concurrently.

Many architecture implementation frameworks and middleware packages have concurrency management as one of their primary features. Later in this chapter, two example implementations of Lunar Lander in both the pipe-and-filter and C2 architectural styles are presented. In both cases, concurrency is handled entirely by the underlying framework or operating system. In the case of the pipe-and-filter system, each filter runs in a concurrent operating system process; in the case of the C2 system, each component and connector runs in its own thread of control.

An increasing amount of research is going into new programming models to support concurrency. However, concurrent programs are still difficult to write. If the architectural style has a concurrency policy that is well-matched to the target application, support for concurrency can be implemented primarily in the architecture framework. Concurrency bugs can lead to race conditions and deadlock—two of the most difficult faults to reproduce and track down. Encapsulating the implementation of concurrency in well-tested framework or middleware code can help to mitigate the risks of deadlock and race conditions (although it cannot eliminate them).

9.1.7 Generative Technologies

One proposed "silver bullet" that has received quite a bit of attention over the years is the idea that software system implementations can be made much more efficient and effective by generating (parts of) those implementations directly from their designs. Indeed, this is the focus of the Object Management Group's (OMG) Model Driven Architecture initiative (Mukerji and Miller 2003), described in Chapter 16, as well as many generative technologies that have been developed over the years.

Because generation can derive (partial) implementations directly from designs, generation is an attractive strategy for maintaining the mapping from architecture to code. However, it is generally not a comprehensive (or easy) solution to implement properly. Some generative strategies that can be employed in architecture-centric development are described in the following text.

Generation of Complete Implementations of Systems or Elements. Given a sufficient architectural specification, including structural, interface, and complete behavioral specifications, it is possible to generate a complete implementation for a component, connector, or even an entire system. When this strategy is employed, architectural drift and erosion can be effectively eliminated, since implementations are simply transformations of the architecture. In practice, however, this is extremely difficult, due to the extensive amount of detail needed to generate implementations—the behavioral specifications for a component, for example, are usually of equal complexity to code implementing the component.

Generation of Skeletons or Interfaces. It is also possible to generate partial implementations of elements or systems from architectural models. For example, if interfaces are well described, it is possible to generate code skeletons for each service or method in the interface, and allow implementers to fill in the behavior. Likewise, if partial behavioral specifications are available (in the form of statecharts, for example), finite-state automata can be generated in code with the behavior for each state left up to coders.

Generation of Compositions. In situations where a library of reusable component and connector implementations is already available and systems are simply composed from this library, architectural models can be used to generate the configurations and glue code needed to connect the elements into a complete system. This strategy is generally most effective in the context of domain-specific software engineering (see Chapter 15).

In any generative effort, the round-tripping problem becomes paramount. In the context of generation, one-way approaches allow one artifact to be generated from another—for example, for code to be generated from architectural models. Round-trip approaches allow changes in the target artifact to be reflected back in the source artifact automatically. For example, in a one-way approach, a component in an architectural model might result in the creation of a new Java package containing class files. In a round-trip approach, the creation of a new Java package might result in the generation of a new component in the architectural model, as well. In general, this requires maintaining some meta-data in the generated code—usually in specially formatted comments. While round-trip approaches are preferable to one-way approaches, they are generally tricky to implement correctly, especially when architectural modeling and code development tools are not well integrated (as is often the case).

9.1.8 Ensuring Architecture-to-Implementation Consistency

Even with the use of an architectural framework, it is rarely obvious whether an implementation actually conforms to its prescribed architecture. Determining whether this is the case will generally require a combination of techniques, including manual inspection and review. There are several strategies that can make this task easier.

Create and Maintain Traceability Links. The existence of links, or explicit mappings, from architectural elements to implementation elements can assist developers in determining whether each architectural element has a corresponding implementation and vice versa. Having these links makes it easier to determine whether something has been inadvertently ignored. If these links are to concrete parts of an architecture model and/or concrete implementation artifacts, then automated link checking can be used to determine whether any links have broken due to changes in either the model or the implementation. This strategy works well for concrete artifacts, but mapping across different levels of abstraction or elements that do not have a direct architecture-to-implementation link can be tricky.

Include the Architectural Model. An architectural model may contain information that can be used directly in a system's implementation. For example, a description of a system's structure in a model (indicating how components are to be instantiated and connected) can be used as an implementation artifact. A tool can be used to extract information about components, connectors, and their topology directly from the architecture description and wire the system up in this way automatically. This can be done at build time or during system startup. In either case, one form of architecture-implementation-correspondence is guaranteed, because the structure of the implemented application is derived directly from the architectural model.

Generate Implementation from the Architecture. Depending on the form and contents of an architectural model, it may be possible to generate portions of an implementation directly from the model using automated tools. If the set of components in a system is specified and the architectural style of the application is known, it is possible to generate component skeletons for a target architecture implementation framework. If behavioral information is also available in the model, it may be possible to generate some or all of the implementations of those components from the model.

9.2 EXISTING FRAMEWORKS

This section presents examples of architecture implementation frameworks that have been implemented for various architectural styles, shows how they satisfy our definition of a framework, and evaluates their strengths and weaknesses.

9.2.1 Frameworks for the Pipe-and-Filter Architectural Style

Many programmers have used an architecture framework without necessarily being aware of it, specifically an architecture framework for the pipe-and-filter style. Nearly every programming language implemented on every major operating system is bundled with a library or module that serves as an architecture framework for the pipe-and-filter style.

The Standard I/O Framework

The C programming language is single-threaded, uses call-return control flow for procedures and functions, and generally stores and retrieves all data from memory by address. How, then, is the C language made compatible with the pipe-and-filter style, where filters can run in parallel, are generally activated when data becomes available, and where filters retrieve and send data through byte streams? The answer is an architecture framework called the standard input-output (I/O) library, also known by its abbreviated name, `stdio`.

Recall that an architecture framework serves as a bridge between the needs of an architectural style and the services provided by the programming language and the operating system. Here, the C programming language provides generic services: control constructs, the ability to read from and write to memory, and so on. The operating system, on the other hand, provides a number of useful services: concurrency at the process level[1] as well as at least two distinguished data streams for each process ("standard input" and "standard output").

The `stdio` library provides C programs access to the operating system's provided standard input/output streams through a procedural API that treats the streams in the same way as files on a sequential-access storage device like a hard drive. Low-level routines such as `getchar(...)` and `putchar(...)` allow programs to read and write a single byte at a time; more complex routines such as `scanf(...)` and `printf(...)` allow the reading and writing of larger quantities of formatted data. Depending on how streams are implemented in the underlying operating system, different `stdio` implementations may employ techniques such as buffering to improve performance. Different implementations may also have different abilities with respect to blocking: If bytes are written to an output

---

[1] When implementations of C are available on an operating system that supports process concurrency such as UNIX or Windows, the operating system's process scheduler will generally be used to assign CPU time to each filter. However, pipe-and-filter has also been supported on single-process operating systems like DOS: In this case, the filters run entirely in sequence and the output of each filter is stored in a temporary file on the hard disk. This effectively turns all pipe-and-filter applications into batch-sequential applications.

stream, and the next filter in the pipeline is not ready to consume those bytes, then `stdio` may cause the write operation to block (make the caller wait) until the receiver is ready, or it may buffer the data and allow the caller to continue.

This is certainly not the only way that such a framework could be implemented. For example, one could imagine a framework where bytes arriving on the standard input triggered the program to begin execution, rather than the operating system invoking the program's `main(...)` method. With this understanding, we can now evaluate the `stdio` framework in terms of the qualities we discussed earlier.

Platform Support. The `stdio` interface is constructed specifically for the C programming language, and its implementation ships with every implementation of the language. Similar libraries may exist in other languages. Implementations of the framework on platforms with little or no operating system support for streams as an interprocess communication mechanism may be more complicated, or may not support pipe-and-filter applications at all.

Fidelity. The `stdio` library's support for streams is good, but a program that uses it is not constrained to working as a filter. Programs are free to ignore both the standard input and output streams, and do input/output through other mechanisms (for example, interfacing directly with the keyboard or using GUI libraries for data output).

Matching Assumptions. The default assumptions of the `stdio` library with respect to pipe-and-filter systems is that each filter will be a separate operating system process and the operating-system–provided streams (standard input and standard output) will be used for communication. If the application wants to use pipe-and-filter differently (for instance, with filters as portions of a C application running in a single process, or perhaps using a disk file as intermediate storage), then the application has to be modified somewhat. Because the `stdio` library provides practically identical interfaces for reading and writing to different kinds of streams (file streams, in-memory streams, interprocess streams and so on) this widens the kinds of pipe-and-filter applications that can be built with it.

Efficiency. Whether filters run concurrently (one of the key efficiency benefits of pipe-and-filter over batch-sequential architectures) is largely dependent on how the underlying operating system schedules processes. For single-process operating systems, output has to be stored in shared memory or secondary storage as each filter runs sequentially. Largely, the `stdio` library itself has no control over how this is handled.

The java.io Framework

The Java programming language is multithreaded, object-oriented, uses call-return method calls for transfer of control, and bundles code and data within objects. The object classes that are used for constructing pipe-and-filter applications in Java are found in the package `java.io`. Although these classes share a purpose with C's `stdio` library, their design is different. The `java.io` class library defines two primary base classes: `InputStream`, which allows callers to read a sequence of bytes, and `OutputStream`, which allows callers to write a sequence of bytes. Each of these provides a small set of methods for reading and writing single bytes or groups of bytes, as well as a few auxiliary methods for rewinding within a stream during reading and flushing writes.

These low-level base classes define minimal functionality for readable and writable byte streams. These classes are not used directly; instead, subclasses are used. In `java.io`, two kinds of subclasses are provided. One set provides access to concrete data sources and sinks: files, network sockets, in-memory byte arrays, and so on. In addition, three distinguished objects are provided by the runtime environment: `System.in`, `System.out`, and `System.err`, which are used for reading from and writing to the standard input, output, and error streams of the operating system process and are used for creating multiprocess pipe-and-filter applications. Another set of subclasses adds functionality to the basic input and output streams by wrapping these low-level streams. For example, `BufferedInputStream` and `BufferedOutputStream` add buffers to improve performance. `DataInputStream` and `DataOutputStream` add additional interface methods to wrapped streams that allow the reading and writing of basic Java data types (integers, floats, and so on). With this in mind, we can now evaluate `java.io` and contrast it with the `stdio` library.

Platform Support. The `java.io` library is part of the standard set of Java packages, and so is available on any platform that can run Java. Platform-specific features such as how the operating system's standard input and output streams are accessed are abstracted away.

Fidelity. The library's support for streams is comprehensive, but as with `stdio`, programs that use this library do not have to work as a filter. On the other hand, pipe-and-filter architectures running within a single program are easier to construct with `java.io` due to the existence of streams that read from and write to memory, and in-process pipe classes that allow in-process streams to be connected.

Matching Assumptions. The `java.io` library matches the assumptions of the pipe-and-filter style well. In-process pipe-and-filter structures can be constructed with relative ease due to Java's innate support for threading, and the ability to run multiple internal filters concurrently.

Efficiency. Java gives programmers fine-grained control over efficiency mechanisms: Buffers can be used by wrapping a stream in a buffered stream, and threads can be explicitly allocated to separate I/O operations from computationally intensive operations (which can increase performance on multiprocessor machines). However, with increased cooperation from the operating system, it is often possible to achieve even higher efficiency. This motivated the construction of the later `java.nio` (New I/O) package, which can take advantage of faster mechanisms.

9.2.2 Frameworks for the C2 Architectural Style

Constructing applications in the C2 architectural style [(Taylor et al. 1996) (see Chapter 4)] differs markedly from traditional procedure-call and object-oriented programming. It imposes strict rules on how applications are constructed internally and how components within an application communicate. It governs both transfers of control and data within an application, and makes assumptions about concurrency and threading. Because of these differences, frameworks are essential for effective C2 development.

Services provided by a C2 framework arise from the various C2 architectural style constraints. For example, C2 requires that application functionality be partitioned into discrete components (for computation) and connectors (for communication). Therefore,

C2 frameworks provide support, at the programming-language level, for application developers to partition their functionality into modules. C2 components and connectors communicate via asynchronous messages and should operate as if they run in separate threads of control. Frameworks supporting this constraint must provide a concept of an asynchronous message, and must allocate (from the operating system) or simulate (via a technique such as round-robin scheduling of a single thread's activities) multiple threads of control.

C2 frameworks have been developed for many platform/language combinations. C2 frameworks have been developed for C++, Ada, Java, and other languages running on Windows, UNIX, the Java Virtual Machine, and so on. Several different Java C2 frameworks have been developed, each with different characteristics. We will compare and contrast a basic framework called the Lightweight C2 Framework and a larger but more configurable framework called the Flexible C2 Framework.

The Lightweight C2 Framework

The first C2 framework implemented in Java is known as the Lightweight C2 framework, implemented in only sixteen classes (about 3000 lines) of Java code.

Figure 9-1 shows a selected set of classes from the Lightweight C2 Framework, as well as their relationships, as a UML class diagram. To implement an application using this framework, developers create component and connector implementations as subclasses of the `Component` or `Connector` abstract base classes. Developers may also create additional classes as needed that are called by these component and connector classes. The component and connector classes communicate with each other using only messages, which are instances of the `Request` and `Notification` classes. The developer then creates a main program that uses the interface of the `Architecture` class to instantiate and hook up the various components and connectors.

Figure 9-1 shows some of the key design choices made by the framework authors. C2 components and connectors are implemented as Java classes that extend abstract base classes (`Component` and `Connector`) provided by the framework. Messages are encoded as objects with a string name and a string-to-object property map containing the message contents.

Certain aspects of the framework—such as threading and message queuing—are left up to individual components and connectors. Two threading policies are available to implementers: If application developers extend the base classes `Component` and `Connector`, a single application thread will service the entire application. Developers using this strategy must be careful that they do not block this thread and inadvertently hang their applications. If developers extend the base classes `ComponentThread` and `ConnectorThread`, then each component or connector gets an independent thread of control. This takes up more resources, but also reduces the possibility of inadvertent deadlock. Message queuing is handled through `Port` objects, which are objects that are capable of receiving incoming messages for a component or connector. Note that ports are a concept introduced entirely by this framework—they are not part of the C2 style itself. The framework provides only one kind of port: a first-in-first-out (FIFO) queue. With FIFO ports, messages are processed in the order received; no message is given priority over any other. Developers are free to implement their own non-FIFO ports as long as those ports extend the abstract `Port` class.

It is also interesting to note that not every constraint of the C2 style is reflected in the framework. For example, nothing in the framework enforces the rule that components

Figure 9-1.
*Selected classes
and relationships
from the
Lightweight C2
Framework.*

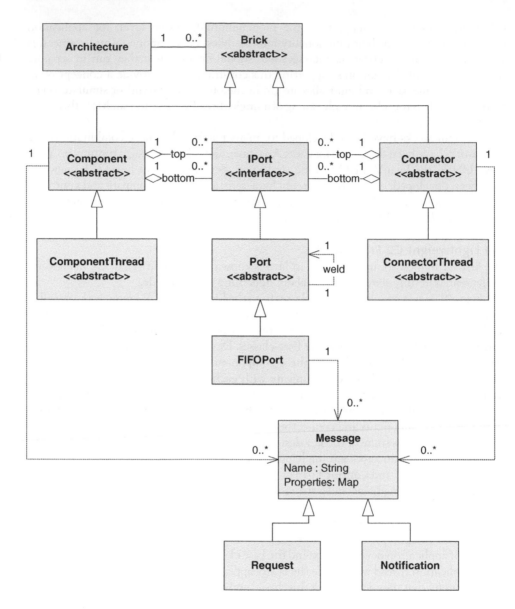

and connectors must act as if they run in separate memory spaces. In a single-process application, if a component or connector inserts a Java object reference into a message object, other components or connectors could modify this object directly without sending any messages. This would constitute illegal communication in the C2 style. However, Java does not have any support for the concept of separate in-process memory spaces, so enforcing this constraint in a framework would be prohibitively expensive. This represents a situation in which fidelity is traded for efficiency and where a framework is used to aid, but not enforce, implementations that conform to the target style.

The Flexible C2 Framework

The Flexible C2 Framework was developed later, and incorporates more aspects of the architectural style directly into the framework. As such, it is larger with seventy-three classes (approximately 8500 lines of code). Figure 9-2 shows a similar set of selected

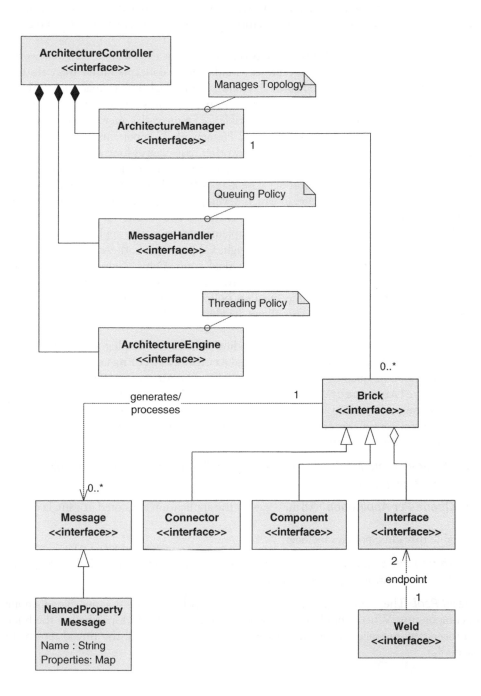

Figure 9-2.
Selected Flexible C2 Framework classes and their relationships.

classes in the Flexible C2 framework. Application developers using this framework follow a similar course of action as those using the Lightweight C2 Framework. They first implement application components and connectors as classes that implement the `Component` and `Connector` interfaces. These classes exchange data through objects that implement the `Message` interface. They then write a main class that instantiates, connects, and starts these components and connectors using the `ArchitectureController` interface.

One obvious difference between the two frameworks is the Flexible C2 Framework's pervasive use of Java interfaces to represent fundamental concepts rather than abstract base classes. As a programming language, Java allows only single inheritance among object classes. However, a single class can implement multiple interfaces. The use of Java interfaces rather than abstract base classes makes the Flexible C2 Framework somewhat easier to adapt to different contexts than the Lightweight C2 Framework. Components, connectors, and messages created by developers can extend any other base class as long as they implement the appropriate interface. Some boilerplate code is required to implement each interface, and so the framework provides abstract base classes (not shown in Figure 9-2) for each interface for the common situation in which developer classes are not required to extend an external base class.

Another obvious difference is in the implementation of the application threading and message queuing policies. In the Lightweight C2 Framework, these policies were distributed throughout the application in individual components, connectors, and ports. In the Flexible C2 Framework, these concerns are centralized through classes called `MessageHandlers`, which define queuing policies, and `ArchitectureEngines`, which define threading policies. This allows developers to define and select these policies on an application-wide basis.

Figure 9-3 shows how queuing and threading policies can be plugged in to an application. The interfaces, `MessageHandler` and `ArchitectureEngine`, define internal APIs common to all queuing and threading policies. The `AbstractMessageHandler` and `AbstractArchitectureEngine` abstract base classes implement boilerplate functions common to all queuing and threading policies. Finally, the framework provides several alternative concrete queuing and threading policies that can be selected for an application. Available queuing policies include:

One-Queue-Per-Interface. Each interface (in the C2 style, top or bottom interfaces) gets its own message queue.

One-Queue-Per-Application. All messages for the application are stored in a single queue.

Available threading policies include:

One-Thread-Per-Brick. Each brick (component or connector) in the architecture gets its own thread of control for processing its messages.

Thread Pool. The application gets a constant-sized pool of threads that are shared among all components. When a brick has a message waiting, a thread is dispatched to the brick to process the message. When the message processing completes, the thread returns to the pool.

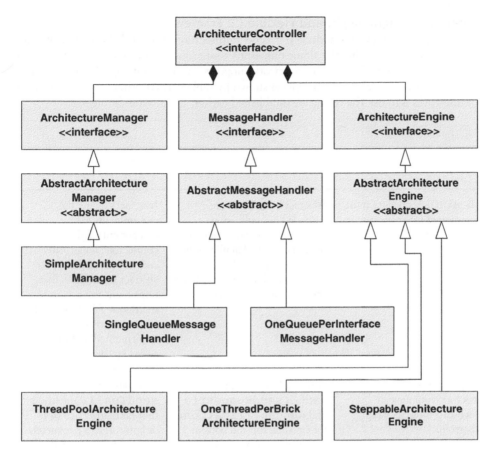

Figure 9-3.
The implementation of pluggable message queuing and threading policies in the Flexible C2 Framework.

Steppable Engine. A special case of the thread pool policy, the application gets one thread that is controlled by a GUI. When the user presses a 'step' button, the thread is dispatched to process a single message. In this way, applications can be more easily debugged.

All of these policies are allowable within the C2 style, but dramatically affect how applications are developed and how much component developers have to consider when writing code. For example, it would be relatively difficult to change a Lightweight C2 Framework application from a one-thread-per-brick to a steppable threading policy, since this would require changes to each component's and connector's code. In the Flexible C2 Framework, this change can be made in one line of code in the application's main class. Still, centralized, uniform policies can make it more difficult to implement applications in which different individual components and connectors behave differently with respect to queuing and threading.

Both C2 frameworks address similar subsets of the C2-style constraints—for example, neither explicitly addresses the requirement that components and connectors are not allowed to communicate through shared memory. As explained above, this requirement is simply too expensive to implement in Java.

Comparing the Lightweight and Flexible C2 Frameworks

Because both C2 frameworks address the same architectural style and the same platform, they can be compared directly along numerous dimensions. The first is the technical dimension—examining how each framework supports (or does not support) each of the constraints of the C2 architectural style, as shown in Table 9-1. Another way of comparing the frameworks is to use the rubric we established earlier, as shown in Table 9-2.

Table 9-1
Technical Support of C2 Architectural Style.

C2 Style Constraint	Lightweight Framework Support	Flexible Framework Support
Application functionality must be partitioned into components and connectors.	Abstract base classes are extended by application developers to create components or connectors; all application functionality must be implemented within or called by these extended base classes.	Interfaces define the requirements for components and connectors; boilerplate code is provided in abstract base classes that implement these interfaces. All application functionality must be implemented within or called by these extended base classes.
All components and connectors communicate through two interfaces: top and bottom.	Abstract base class provides methods `sendRequest()` and `sendNotification()` for emitting top and bottom messages, respectively, and `handleNotification()` and `handleRequest()` for receiving top and bottom messages.	Base class provides a `sendToAll()` method that takes interface (top or bottom) as a parameter, and `handle()` method that is called when a message is received on any interface. Messages are tagged with the interface they arrived on.
Components and connectors should operate as if they run in their own threads of control.	Threads are created by component and connector base classes.	Threads are controlled by a central threading policy object called an `ArchitectureEngine`. Different engines can provide alternative threading policies.
Messages sent to the top interface of a component or connector should be received on the attached component or connector bottom(s) and vice versa.	Methods `sendRequest()` and `sendNotification()` look up connected components and connectors and directly enqueue messages in queues belonging to those elements.	Message queuing policy is centralized in an object called a `MessageHandler`. `MessageHandlers` ensure that messages get deposited in appropriate queues for processing.

Table 9-1
(*Continued*)

C2 Style Constraint	Lightweight Framework Support	Flexible Framework Support
Components and connectors should operate as though they do not share memory; all messages exchanged must be serializable.	Message objects are structured as sets of name-value pair properties, where both names and values are strings.	All messages must implement the java.io.Serializable interface, but are not constrained to any particular format. An implementation of name-value pair set messages is also provided.
Components may be connected to at most one connector on each side; connectors may be connected to zero or more components or connectors on each side.	Connecting a component to more than one connector on any side will result in the previous connection being undone before the new one is created.	No explicit support; developers are assumed to check this constraint.
Components may make assumptions about services provided above, but no assumptions about services provided below.	No explicit support; developers are assumed to build components in a way that obeys this constraint.	No explicit support; developers are assumed to build components in a way that obeys this constraint.

Table 9-2
Comparison Rubric for Frameworks.

Concern	Lightweight Framework	Flexible Framework
Platform support	Java Virtual Machine on multiple platforms.	Java Virtual Machine on multiple platforms.
Fidelity	Assists developers in dealing with many C2-style constraints, but does not actively enforce them.	Assists developers in dealing with many C2-style constraints, but does not actively enforce them.
Matching assumptions	Component and connector main classes must inherit from provided abstract base classes; all communication must be through messages that consist of string names and name-value pair properties.	Component and connector main classes must implement from provided Java interfaces; all communication must be through messages which can be in any serializable fomat.
Efficiency	Framework is small and lightweight; can use only a single thread of control if desired, but this risks application deadlock.	Framework is larger but more flexible; can select from many queuing and threading policies to tune efficiency on an application-by-application basis.

9.3 EXAMPLES

We have introduced many architectural alternatives for the Lunar Lander application; Chapter 4 presents a catalog of architectural styles, with Lunar Lander designed to fit the constraints of each style. Here, we will examine how architecture frameworks can be used to assist in the construction of working Lunar Lander implementations in two of those styles: pipe-and-filter and C2.

Note that the following sections will include code samples showing actual implementations of Lunar Lander. Certain good coding practices, such as the use of externalized string constants, comprehensive exception and null-value checking, and so on will be left out for simplicity's sake. Real implementations should take these practices into account as they apply equally when doing architecture-based software development.

9.3.1 Implementing Lunar Lander in the Pipe-and-Filter Style Using the java.io Framework

Recall the introduction of a pipe-and-filter-style Lunar Lander architecture from Chapter 4, as shown in Figure 9-4. Here, Lunar Lander is broken up into three components: the first gets the burn rate from the user, the second computes new values, and the third outputs those values back to the user. Communication among the components is one-way and is done through character streams as mandated by the style.

Assuming we want to implement this application in Java, we have two obvious choices for architecture frameworks: the java.io package and the java.nio package. Because the amount of data being transferred is small and we want a simple implementation, we will implement the system using `java.io`. The next choice we must make is whether to implement the system as an in-process or multiprocess system.

In-Process. In an in-process system, each component will be implemented by one or more Java classes. These will communicate by way of internal streams, leveraging internal stream classes provided by the `java.io` framework. The application configuration will need to be created in an application `main` method that we write.

Multiprocess. In a multiprocess system, each component will be implemented by one or more Java classes comprising a small application. They will communicate by way of the operating-system–provided streams `System.in` and `System.out`, and the operating system will also provide the pipe connectors. The application configuration will be done on the command line.

For simplicity, we will implement the application as a multiprocess system, which saves us from having to write additional code creating our own pipes and doing tasks such as

Figure 9-4.
Lunar Lander in the pipe-and-filter architectural style.

data buffering and threading. The operating system's internal services will provide buffers among the filters as well as process-level concurrency.

The first task in implementing the Lunar Lander application is to implement the three filters depicted in the proposed architecture. Because the filters are independently composable, this can be done in any order, although the order of implementation does have practical consequences. For example, in a large application, you may want to implement stubs and skeletons for testing purposes, and whether you implement the application from left-to-right or right-to-left has implications on the sorts of stubs and skeletons you must implement. For our implementation, we will work from left-to-right, starting with the GetBurnRate filter.

Recall that, in a pipe-and-filter application, all data travels from left-to-right in character streams. If applications need to communicate structured data, that structure must be encoded in the character streams. Additionally, in a strict pipe-and-filter application, all user input comes from the system input stream on the left-most filter, and all output to the user console comes from the system output stream on the right-most filter.

In this application, we need to send structured data down the pipeline. We will use a simple encoding scheme: Messages will be separated by newline characters, and each message will be preceded by a control character indicating the type of message. We will preface user-output messages with a pound sign (#) and data messages with a percent sign (%). There is nothing particularly special about these characters; they are chosen arbitrarily for this example.

Figure 9-5 shows the GetBurnRate filter implementation for Lunar Lander. This component effectively represents the user interface of the application. First, it opens a BufferedReader on the system-provided class System.in, which the Java virtual machine connects to the operating system's input stream. BufferedReader is a class provided by the java.io package for reading structured data such as lines and integers from a character stream. Next, it enters a loop, continually prompting the user for a new burn rate, reading the value, and sending it on to the next filter.

Figure 9-6 shows the implementation of the CalcNewValues filter for Lunar Lander. This is the most complex of the three filters; it must read the new burn rate from the GetBurnRate filter, store and update the application's state, and then send output values to the final filter, which formats those values for display. The basic structure of the filter is similar to that of GetBurnRate—the program opens a reader on the system input stream, processes the input, and writes data to the system output stream. Here, the filter reads two kinds of data from GetBurnRate: user messages and burn rates. User messages are passed unchanged to the next filter; burn rates trigger a computation. When a new burn rate is read, the filter updates its internal state values—the current altitude, velocity, fuel, and time—and sends those new values to the next filter. It continues until the altitude reaches zero (or less), at which point it determines whether the lander crashed or landed successfully—either way, the game is over.

The same control character scheme is used in this filter: User messages are prefaced with pound signs and data messages are prefaced with percent signs. The data messages are further coded with a second character indicating the type of data: altitude, fuel, velocity, or time. As should be obvious by this point, ensuring that the various filters have matching assumptions about the encoding scheme is critical in constructing a working application. The encoding scheme is, in effect, the interface contract for the pipe-and-filter application.

Figure 9-5.
The
`GetBurnRate`
filter for Lunar
Lander.

```java
//Import the java.io framework
import java.io.*;

public class GetBurnRate{
  public static void main(String[] args){

    //Send welcome message
    System.out.println("#Welcome to Lunar Lander");

    try{
      //Begin reading from System input
      BufferedReader inputReader =
        new BufferedReader(new
        InputStreamReader(System.in));

      //Set initial burn rate to 0
      int burnRate = 0;
      do{
        //Prompt user
        System.out.println(
          "#Enter burn rate or <0 to quit:");

        //Read user response
        try{
          String burnRateString = inputReader.readLine();
          burnRate = Integer.parseInt(burnRateString);

          //Send user-supplied burn rate to next filter
          System.out.println("%" + burnRate);
        }
        catch(NumberFormatException nfe){
          System.out.println("#Invalid burn rate.");
        }
      }while(burnRate >= 0);
      inputReader.close();
    }
    catch(IOException ioe){
      ioe.printStackTrace();
    }
  }
}
```

Figure 9-7 shows the implementation of the `DisplayValues` filter for Lunar Lander. The structural similarities to the other two filters are again evident here—the filter reads lines from system input and writes them to system output. The purpose of this filter is simply to format data for output to the console. Unformatted user messages from previous filters are output directly, while data values are annotated with descriptions for output. Here, control characters are parsed on input, but no control characters are written to the output stream; the application assumes that it is the final filter in the application and that the output data is intended for display on a console rather than as input to another application filter.

```
import java.io.*;

public class CalcNewValues{

  public static void main(String[] args){
    //Initialize values
    final int GRAVITY = 2;
    int altitude = 1000;
    int fuel = 500;
    int velocity = 70;
    int time = 0;

    try{
      BufferedReader inputReader = new
        BufferedReader(new InputStreamReader(System.in));

      //Print initial values
      System.out.println("%a" + altitude);
      System.out.println("%f" + fuel);
      System.out.println("%v" + velocity);
      System.out.println("%t" + time);

      String inputLine = null;
      do{
        inputLine = inputReader.readLine();
        if((inputLine != null) &&
          (inputLine.length() > 0)){

          if(inputLine.startsWith("#")){
            //This is a status line of text, and
            //should be passed down the pipeline
            System.out.println(inputLine);
          }
          else if(inputLine.startsWith("%")){
            //This is an input burn rate
            try{
              int burnRate =
                Integer.parseInt(inputLine.substring(1));
              if(altitude <= 0){
                System.out.println("#The game is over.");
              }
              else if(burnRate > fuel){
                System.out.println("#Sorry, you don't" +
                  "have that much fuel.");
              }
              else{
                //Calculate new application state
                time = time + 1;
                altitude = altitude - velocity;
                velocity = ((velocity + GRAVITY) * 10 -
                  burnRate * 2) / 10;
                fuel = fuel - burnRate;
                if(altitude <= 0){
                  altitude = 0;
```

Figure 9-6.
*The Calc-
NewValues*
*filter for Lunar
Lander.*

Figure 9-6.
(Continued)

```java
            if(velocity <= 5){
              System.out.println("#You have " +
                "landed safely.");
            }
            else{
              System.out.println("#You have " +
                "crashed.");
            }
          }
        }
        //Print new values
        System.out.println("%a" + altitude);
        System.out.println("%f" + fuel);
        System.out.println("%v" + velocity);
        System.out.println("%t" + time);
      }
      catch(NumberFormatException nfe){
      }
    }
  }
  }while((inputLine != null) && (altitude > 0));
  inputReader.close();
}
catch(IOException ioe){
  ioe.printStackTrace();
}
}
}
```

Together, these three filters make up the Lunar Lander application. One task remains, which is to determine how to instantiate and connect the application. This is done easily on the command line:

```
java GetBurnRate | java CalcNewValues | java DisplayValues
```

This command line invokes all three filters as separate processes. (The need for the invocation of java in each process is an artifact of how the Java Virtual Machine works: Each process is an instance of the virtual machine running the class passed as the first parameter to the java command.) Input from the console is fed to the system input stream of the left-most filter (GetBurnRate). The output of GetBurnRate is piped to the input of CalcNewValues. The output of CalcNewValues is likewise piped to the input of DisplayValues, and output to the console comes from the system output stream of that filter.

Reflections on the Pipe-and-Filter Lunar Lander Implementation

The architecture framework (java.io) in this implementation of Lunar Lander provides several useful services to the application. It includes a number of classes for reading and writing to the system input and output streams (such as BufferedReader). These classes allow data to be read from and written to character streams such as the system input and output streams in different ways: as individual characters, lines, integers, and so on. This allows the implementation to focus more on application functionality and less on the constraints of the architectural style.

```
import java.io.*;

public class DisplayValues{

  public static void main(String[] args){
    try{
      BufferedReader inputReader = new
        BufferedReader(new InputStreamReader(System.in));

      String inputLine = null;
      do{
        inputLine = inputReader.readLine();
        if((inputLine != null) &&
          (inputLine.length() > 0)){

          if(inputLine.startsWith("#")){
            //This is a status line of text, and
            //should be passed down the pipeline with
            //the pound-sign stripped off
            System.out.println(inputLine.substring(1));
          }
          else if(inputLine.startsWith("%")){
            //This is a value to display
            if(inputLine.length() > 1){
              try{
                char valueType = inputLine.charAt(1);
                int value =
                  Integer.parseInt(inputLine.substring(2));

                switch(valueType){
                  case 'a':
                    System.out.println("Altitude: " +
                      value);
                  break;
                  case 'f':
                    System.out.println("Fuel remaining: " +
                      value);
                    break;
                  case 'v':
                    System.out.println("Current Velocity: "
                      + value);
                    break;
                  case 't':
                    System.out.println("Time elapsed: " +
                      value);
                    break;
                }
              }
              catch(NumberFormatException nfe){
              }
            }
          }
        }
      }while(inputLine != null);
```

(Continued)

Figure 9-7.
*The Dis-
playValues
filter for Lunar
Lander.*

Figure 9-7.
(*Continued*)

```
                        inputReader.close();
                      }
                      catch(IOException ioe){
                        ioe.printStackTrace();
                      }
                    }
                }
```

The operating system itself provides the pipe connectors, as well as the concurrency policy for the architecture. The filter implementations in this system are closely aligned with the properties of the underlying framework and operating system, although this is not necessarily obvious from reading the code. For example, the filters assume that they are going to be running concurrently. In a few operating systems, such as MS-DOS, pipe-and-filter applications actually run in batch mode, collecting all the output from each filter before sending it to the next filter. If this version of Lunar Lander were to operate in batch mode, user messages sent out by the first two filters would not be output by the third filter until all the input to the first filter was completed. The application would not work properly in this circumstance. Additionally, the filters assume that lines written to the system output stream will be flushed automatically to the next filter. If this were not true, output messages would appear late and the application would operate in a broken or confusing way. These potential mismatching assumptions are subtle, but developers must be aware of them to determine whether an application will or will not operate as desired.

The implementation activity is often the time where underspecified or deficient architectures become evident. For example, the (admittedly simple) architecture for pipe-and-filter Lunar Lander specifies what data should pass from filter to filter, but not the format of that data. A component that communicated using XML-based data encoding, while being conformant with the architecture, would not interoperate with the filter components implemented above. Clearly, this architecture has not been elaborated to a point where component interoperability can be inferred from the architecture alone. A mismatch between XML and line-oriented data formats would be easily caught during system integration, but more subtle bugs can be even more dangerous. For example, in the case of the Mars Climate Orbiter, an interface mismatch between metric and imperial units of measure was a substantial cause for the loss of the orbiter.

9.3.2 Implementing Lunar Lander in the C2 Style Using the Lightweight C2 Framework

A C2-style Lunar Lander architecture shown in Figure 9-8 is different from the pipe-and-filter Lunar Lander version. First, the application functionality is broken up differently. Here, a game state component retains all game state and broadcasts updates to other components. A game logic component reads the game state, calculates a new state, and updates the game state component with that state. The GUI component is responsible for reading new burn rate values from the user and keeping the user informed as to the current game state. The most significant departure from the pipe-and-filter version is the addition of a clock component, which emits "tick" events, or messages, at periodic intervals. This changes the character of the game substantially; instead of waiting indefinitely for a new

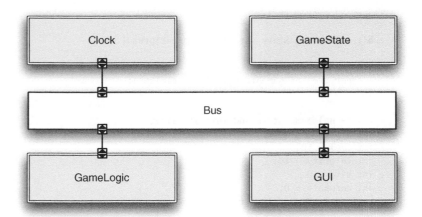

Figure 9-8.
*Lunar Lander in
the C2
architectural
style.*

burn rate value from the user as in the pipe-and-filter version, this version of Lunar Lander is played in real-time. In this version, the game state changes whenever the clock ticks, and not when new burn rate values are entered. Here, the user may update the current burn rate as often as desired between ticks. When the clock ticks, the current burn rate value is used to calculate the new game state.

Many C2 frameworks exist for different programming languages and platforms. Assuming we want to implement the system in Java, we still must choose between frameworks such as the Lightweight C2 Framework and the Flexible C2 Framework. Because it results in slightly simpler component code, we will use the Lightweight C2 Framework for this implementation.

As with the pipe-and-filter example, we can implement these components in any order, but the order we choose has practical consequences. Because of the substrate independence (that is, layering) rules in C2, lower components may make assumptions about the services provided by upper components, but upper components may not make assumptions about lower components. (Note that this is reversed from traditional layered or virtual-machine depictions where upper layers depend on lower layers.) This means that the topmost components have no dependencies, and that lower components are progressively more dependent. We will take a least-dependent-first implementation strategy,[2] which means that the topmost components get implemented first.

The code for the GameState component is shown in Figure 9-9. The first line of code imports the `c2.framework` package, which belongs to the Lightweight C2 Framework. The class declaration shows that the `GameState` class extends the `ComponentThread` base class. This base class is extended by all component classes that run in their own thread of control (as is the norm in C2-style systems). This base class provides the code required for the component to receive and send requests and notifications, as well as the threading and synchronization code required to coordinate with the other components and connectors.

---

[2]This is ordinarily called a bottom-up implementation strategy, but this terminology can be confusing in C2 architectures, where the least-dependent components are represented at the top in the canonical graphical visualization.

Figure 9-9.
The
GameState
component in
C2.

```java
import c2.framework.*;

public class GameState extends ComponentThread{

  public GameState(){
    super.create("gameState", FIFOPort.class);
  }

  //Internal game state and initial values
  int altitude = 1000;
  int fuel = 500;
  int velocity = 70;
  int time = 0;
  int burnRate = 0;
  boolean landedSafely = false;

  protected void handle(Request r){
    if(r.name().equals("updateGameState")){
      //Update the internal game state
      if(r.hasParameter("altitude")){
        this.altitude =
          ((Integer)r.getParameter("altitude")).intValue();
      }
      if(r.hasParameter("fuel")){
        this.fuel =
          ((Integer)r.getParameter("fuel")).intValue();
      }
      if(r.hasParameter("velocity")){
        this.velocity =
          ((Integer)r.getParameter("velocity")).intValue();
      }
      if(r.hasParameter("time")){
        this.time =
          ((Integer)r.getParameter("time")).intValue();
      }
      if(r.hasParameter("burnRate")){
        this.burnRate =
          ((Integer)r.getParameter("burnRate")).intValue();
      }
      if(r.hasParameter("landedSafely")){
        this.landedSafely =
          ((Boolean)r.getParameter("landedSafely"))
          .booleanValue();
      }

      //Send out the updated game state
      Notification n = createStateNotification();
      send(n);
    }
    else if(r.name().equals("getGameState")){
      //If a component requests the game state
      //without updating it, send out the state

      Notification n = createStateNotification();
      send(n);
```

Figure 9-9.
(*Continued*)

```
        }
    }

    protected Notification createStateNotification(){
        //Create a new notification comprising the
        //current game state

        Notification n = new Notification("gameState");
        n.addParameter("altitude", altitude);
        n.addParameter("fuel", fuel);
        n.addParameter("velocity", velocity);
        n.addParameter("time", time);
        n.addParameter("burnRate", burnRate);
        n.addParameter("landedSafely", landedSafely);
        return n;
    }

    protected void handle(Notification n){
        //This component does not handle notifications
    }
}
```

The first method, GameState(), is a simple boilerplate constructor. This C2 framework requires that each component and connector be given a name (in this case, gameState), as well as the class that will implement the ports (that is, message queues) used to exchange messages with attached connectors. For simplicity, all components and connectors in this architecture will use FIFO (first-in, first-out) ports—that is, ordinary queues.

The next block of code declares a set of member variables that represent the game state, including velocity, altitude, fuel remaining, current burn rate, whether the lander has landed safely, and so on. These will be read and updated as the game is played.

Each component and connector in the Lightweight C2 Framework has two primary responsibilities: handling requests (messages traveling upward in the architecture and arriving on the bottom port) and handling notifications (messages traveling downward in the architecture and arriving on the top port).

The next method, handleRequest(), is called automatically by the framework when a request arrives for this component. Recall that in the Lightweight C2 Framework, all requests and notifications have the same structure: a character string name, plus a set of name-value pair properties. This method handles two requests: an updateGameState request and a getGameState request. Upon receiving an updateGameState request, the component reads from the property set various new state values corresponding to elements of the game state. After updating the game state with the new values, the component always creates and emits a new gameState notification containing all the updated state values. Upon receiving a getGameState request, the component simply creates a new game state notification with current state values and sends it out. Sending out a request or a notification in the Lightweight C2 Framework is simple. First, a new Request or Notification object is created, given a name, and populated with properties. This object can be passed to a send() method present in the abstract base class, in this case, ComponentThread. The framework routes the message appropriately.

The handleNotification() method for this component is empty; this component does not handle notifications. Because we are aware, from an architectural perspective, that no components will be connected above this one, we know that it will not receive any.

This component is entirely reactive. It is idle until a request arrives on its bottom port. If the request is of a recognized type (updateGameState or getGameState), then the component reacts, either updating its internal state and sending out a new state notification, or simply sending out the current game state. This is a relatively typical pattern of interaction for state components in C2-style systems. It is also worth noting that this component acts entirely as a data store—data validation and processing is done in other components (primarily the GameLogic component). Maintaining this separation allows architects to more easily swap out different data structures or game logic components.

The code for the Clock component is shown in Figure 9-10. The basic scaffolding for this component is similar to that for the GameState component—this component also

Figure 9-10.
The Clock
component in
C2.

```
import c2.framework.*;

public class Clock extends ComponentThread{
  public Clock(){
    super.create("clock", FIFOPort.class);
  }

  public void start(){
    super.start();

    Thread clockThread = new Thread(){
      public void run(){
        //Repeat while the application runs
        while(true){
          //Wait for five seconds
          try{
            Thread.sleep(5000);
          }
          catch(InterruptedException ie){}

          //Send out a tick notification
          Notification n = new Notification("clockTick");
          send(n);
        }
      }
    };
    clockThread.start();
  }

  protected void handle(Notification n){
    //This component does not handle notifications
  }

  protected void handle(Request r){
    //This component does not handle requests
  }
}
```

extends `ComponentThread` and includes the same boilerplate constructor. Unlike the `GameState` component, however, the `Clock` handles neither requests nor notifications. Its job is simply to emit tick notifications at a predefined interval. This is done through the creation of a new clock thread in the component's `start()` method. The `start()` method is another distinguished method in the Lightweight C2 Framework; it is called by the framework automatically when the application starts. In this implementation, the clock thread creates and emits a new tick notification every five seconds (5000 milliseconds). The use of a separate clock thread is needed because the component's internal thread (provided by the `ComponentThread` base class) is used only for handling notifications and requests—attempting to co-opt it for sending out ticks would interfere with the message-handling behavior of the component.

The code for the `GameLogic` component is shown in Figure 9-11. This component is the most complex of the C2 Lunar Lander components. Structurally, it is very similar to the `GameState` component. Instead of responding to requests from lower components, however, it reacts to notifications coming from upper components. `GameLogic` responds to two kinds of notifications. The first is a `gameState` notification from the `GameState` component. Whenever the `GameLogic` component is notified that the game's state has changed, it updates internal state values that are used for later calculation. For a simple game like Lunar Lander, where nearly all the game state is used by the single `GameLogic` component, keeping separate copies of the game state in the `GameState` and `GameLogic` components may seem redundant. In more complex applications, however, logic components rarely need all the game state; instead, they would retain only the parts of the state necessary to do their own computations. An additional question that might occur to developers familiar with procedural or object-oriented programming is why the `GameLogic` component does not simply query the `GameState` component for data when it is needed. The answer lies in the architectural style—in C2, such synchronous component-to-component queries are not allowed.

The second notification handled by the `GameLogic` component is a clock tick from the `Clock` component. Recall that this version of Lunar Lander is driven not by user input of new burn rates, but by the tick of the real-time clock. When a clock tick occurs, the latest game state stored in the `GameLogic` component is used to calculate the next state—burning some amount of fuel, descending (or ascending) a certain distance, and so on. This state is then sent to the `GameState` component in an `updateGameState` request, which we saw handled by that component, above.

One additional detail in the `GameLogic` implementation is the `start()` method. On startup, the `GameLogic` component sends an asynchronous request upward to the `GameState` component for the initial game state. Without doing so, the calculation that occurs on the first clock tick might be based on incorrect (that is, all-zero) values as initialized in the `GameLogic` component.

Effectively, the behavior of the `GameLogic` component can be summed up by the statechart in Figure 9-12. The component starts and sends a `getGameState` request upward. It then idles, waiting for notifications. When a `GameState` notification is received, the internal state of the component is updated. When a `clockTick` notification is received, a new game state is calculated and a request to update the game state is sent upward.

The code for the `GUI` component of the Lunar Lander is shown in Figure 9-13. This component handles all interaction with the user. This particular implementation uses

Figure 9-11.
The
GameLogic
component in
C2.

```java
import c2.framework.*;

public class GameLogic extends ComponentThread{
  public GameLogic(){
    super.create("gameLogic", FIFOPort.class);
  }

  //Game constants
  final int GRAVITY = 2;

  //Internal state values for computation
  int altitude = 0;
  int fuel = 0;
  int velocity = 0;
  int time = 0;
  int burnRate = 0;

  public void start(){
    super.start();
    Request r = new Request("getGameState");
    send(r);
  }

  protected void handle(Notification n){
    if(n.name().equals("gameState")){
      if(n.hasParameter("altitude")){
        this.altitude =
          ((Integer)n.getParameter("altitude")).intValue();
      }
      if(n.hasParameter("fuel")){
        this.fuel =
          ((Integer)n.getParameter("fuel")).intValue();
      }
      if(n.hasParameter("velocity")){
        this.velocity =
          ((Integer)n.getParameter("velocity")).intValue();
      }
      if(n.hasParameter("time")){
        this.time =
          ((Integer)n.getParameter("time")).intValue();
      }
      if(n.hasParameter("burnRate")){
        this.burnRate =
          ((Integer)n.getParameter("burnRate")).intValue();
      }
    }
    else if(n.name().equals("clockTick")){
      //Calculate new lander state values
      int actualBurnRate = burnRate;
      if(actualBurnRate > fuel){
        //Ensure we don't burn more fuel than we have
        actualBurnRate = fuel;
      }

      time = time + 1;
```

```
        altitude = altitude - velocity;
        velocity = ((velocity + GRAVITY) * 10 -
          actualBurnRate * 2) / 10;
        fuel = fuel - actualBurnRate;

        //Determine if we landed (safely)
        boolean landedSafely = false;
        if(altitude <= 0){
          altitude = 0;
          if(velocity <= 5){
            landedSafely = true;
          }
        }

        Request r = new Request("updateGameState");
        r.addParameter("time", time);
        r.addParameter("altitude", altitude);
        r.addParameter("velocity", velocity);
        r.addParameter("fuel", fuel);
        r.addParameter("landedSafely", landedSafely);
        send(r);
    }
  }

  protected void handle(Request r){
    //This component does not handle requests
  }
}
```

Figure 9-11.
(Continued)

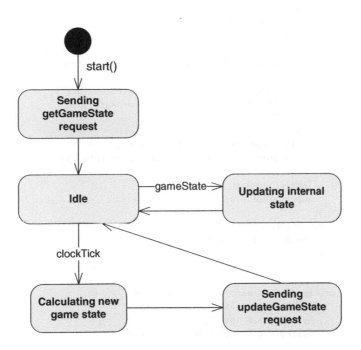

Figure 9-12.
Statechart describing the behavior of the `GameLogic` *component in C2.*

Figure 9-13.
The GUI
component in
C2.

```java
import java.io.BufferedReader;
import java.io.IOException;
import java.io.InputStreamReader;

import c2.framework.*;

public class GUI extends ComponentThread{
  public GUI(){
    super.create("gui", FIFOPort.class);
  }

  public void start(){
    super.start();
    Thread t = new Thread(){
      public void run(){
        processInput();
      }
    };
    t.start();
  }

  public void processInput(){
    System.out.println("Welcome to Lunar Lander");
    try{
      BufferedReader inputReader = new BufferedReader(
        new InputStreamReader(System.in));

      int burnRate = 0;
      do{
        System.out.println("Enter burn rate or <0" +
          "to quit:");
        try{
          String burnRateString = inputReader.readLine();
          burnRate = Integer.parseInt(burnRateString);

          Request r = new Request("updateGameState");
          r.addParameter("burnRate", burnRate);
          send(r);
        }
        catch(NumberFormatException nfe){
          System.out.println("Invalid burn rate.");
        }
      }while(burnRate >= 0);
      inputReader.close();
    }
    catch(IOException ioe){
      ioe.printStackTrace();
    }
  }

  protected void handle(Notification n){
    if(n.name().equals("gameState")){
      System.out.println();
      System.out.println("New game state:");
```

Figure 9-13.
(*Continued*)

```
      if(n.hasParameter("altitude")){
        System.out.println("  Altitude: " +
          n.getParameter("altitude"));
      }
      if(n.hasParameter("fuel")){
        System.out.println("  Fuel: " +
          n.getParameter("fuel"));
      }
      if(n.hasParameter("velocity")){
        System.out.println("  Velocity: " +
          n.getParameter("velocity"));
      }
      if(n.hasParameter("time")){
        System.out.println("  Time: " +
          n.getParameter("time"));
      }
      if(n.hasParameter("burnRate")){
        System.out.println("  Current burn rate: " +
          n.getParameter("burnRate"));
      }

      if(n.hasParameter("altitude")){
        int altitude =
          ((Integer)n.getParameter("altitude")).intValue();
        if(altitude <= 0){
          boolean landedSafely =
            ((Boolean)n.getParameter("landedSafely"))
            .booleanValue();
          if(landedSafely){
            System.out.println("You have landed safely.");
          }
          else{
            System.out.println("You have crashed.");
          }
          System.exit(0);
        }
      }
    }
  }

  protected void handle(Request r){
    //This component does not handle requests
  }
}
```

simple console (that is, text)-based input and output routines. The GUI component has two primary responsibilities. First, it creates an independent thread for reading user input—in this case, burn rates—from the console. Whenever a new burn rate is read, it is wrapped in an updateGameState request and sent upward. Again, a separate thread is needed here to avoid interference with the message processing thread that belongs to the component. Second, the GUI component listens for gameState notifications. Upon receiving an updated game state, the component formats and writes the state to the console.

Now that all the components have been coded, they must be instantiated and connected. This is done by way of a main bootstrapping program shown in Figure 9-14. In the pipe-and-filter example, we were able to use the command-line shell to instantiate and connect the components. For a C2 application, we must instead write this bootstrapping program ourselves, calling upon the services of the Lightweight C2 Framework to instantiate and connect the components. The bootstrapper itself is relatively straightforward. First, an `Architecture` is created, the C2 framework's object that represents an architectural structure. Then, instances of each of the components are created, along with a single connector called `bus`. The components and connectors are added to the `Architecture`, and then links among them (called `Welds` in C2 parlance) are created. With everything connected, the `Architecture`'s `start()` method is called, which creates internal threads, calls each component and connector's individual `start()` method, and performs other tasks needed to start the application.

Figure 9-14.
The Lunar Lander main program in C2.

```java
import c2.framework.*;

public class LunarLander{

    public static void main(String[] args){
        //Create the Lunar Lander architecture
        Architecture lunarLander = new
            SimpleArchitecture("LunarLander");

        //Create the components
        Component clock = new Clock();
        Component gameState = new GameState();
        Component gameLogic = new GameLogic();
        Component gui = new GUI();

        //Create the connectors
        Connector bus = new ConnectorThread("bus");

        //Add the components and connectors to the architecture
        lunarLander.addComponent(clock);
        lunarLander.addComponent(gameState);
        lunarLander.addComponent(gameLogic);
        lunarLander.addComponent(gui);

        lunarLander.addConnector(bus);

        //Create the welds (links) between components and
        //connectors
        lunarLander.weld(clock, bus);
        lunarLander.weld(gameState, bus);
        lunarLander.weld(bus, gameLogic);
        lunarLander.weld(bus, gui);

        //Start the application
        lunarLander.start();
    }
}
```

9.4 END MATTER

It is imperative that, to the extent possible, the design decisions in the architecture are reflected in the implemented system. Conflicts or mismatches are the hallmarks of architectural drift and erosion. Sometimes these divergences are obvious and known to the system's stakeholders, and additional documentation of these cases can help to mitigate the risks or provide plans for future work to bring the architecture and implementation back in sync. Sometimes, however, they are not, and stakeholders remain unaware of the problem. This is usually compounded in system maintenance phases, when it is expedient to update the implementation without going back and updating architectural models to match. In some ways, it is more harmful to have conflicting information in the architecture and the implementation than to have an underspecified architecture, since at least an underspecified architecture will not mislead stakeholders.

Maintaining a consistent architecture-to-implementation mapping is almost never easy, and various techniques can be used to do so. The strongest mappings are possible when architectural models become *part of* the system implementation and are closely connected to implementation artifacts by way of explicit mappings embedded in the models to elements implemented in architecture implementation frameworks. This strategy works well for concrete design decisions, such as structural design decisions, but is more difficult for more abstract design decisions concerning, for example, non-functional properties. In this case, stakeholders must negotiate and make decisions about how they will convince themselves that their architecture is reflected adequately in their implementation. Doubtlessly, this will involve a combined spectrum of strategies from peer review to traceability links between documents to the use of architecture implementation frameworks.

In the past set of chapters, we focused on design activities—architectural design, modeling, visualization, and analysis. In this chapter, we discussed how to move from design to implementation. Once the system is implemented, it must be deployed to its users. This is the focus of the next chapter. As we will see, maintaining architectural models with strong mappings to implementations are useful in post-implementation activities as well.

The Business Case

In general, a good design should result in a good system. The way to maximize your chances of getting a good system out of a good design is to use careful practices for mapping your architecture to your code. A small investment in a good, reusable architecture framework can instill consistency throughout a project and over its lifetime.

Generation technologies are especially powerful in reducing costs and minimizing architectural drift and erosion. While it may not be a silver bullet, generating even partial implementations from architecture is always vastly superior to making the connection manually, especially if round-trip software engineering is in place. Every line of code written by a *program* rather than a *programmer* is money in the bank.

Maintenance costs are the highest in any successful software engineering project (more than 50 percent). These costs are exacerbated by spaghetti-code, post hoc changes that (often unknowingly) violate design principles set out at the beginning of the project, and lack of clear understanding of the system. When design principles are violated, the software qualities anticipated and imbued by the design may not manifest themselves in the final, implemented system.

Good architecture-to-implementation mappings help to mitigate risks, especially those due to personnel turnover. Turnover is inevitable in any development effort, and a well-defined architecture with a corresponding implementation will dramatically improve the ability of new personnel to be effective on an old project.

9.5 REVIEW QUESTIONS

1. What are some architectural concerns that can be mapped to implemented systems? What strategies can be used to map these concerns?

2. What is the difference between one-way and round-trip mapping?

3. What is an architecture-implementation framework? How does an architecture-implementation framework differ from middleware?

4. What is the relationship between an architecture-implementation framework and an architectural style?

5. When might multiple frameworks be developed for a single architectural style?

6. What are some criteria that can be used to evaluate architecture implementation frameworks?

7. How do middleware and component frameworks induce architectural styles?

8. What are some strategies for resolving mismatches between architectural styles and middleware?

9. When should a new architecture-implementation framework be developed? What criteria or strategies should be used in developing the new framework?

10. What kinds of generative approaches can assist in moving from architecture to implementation?

11. Enumerate some existing architecture implementation frameworks.

12. How is the Standard I/O package an architecture framework for pipe-and-filter systems? How does it support the various rules and constraints of the pipe-and-filter style?

9.6 EXERCISES

1. Run the implemented Lunar Lander applications in this chapter through a debugger and examine how control and data are exchanged through the framework.

2. The chapter compares and contrasts the Lightweight C2 Framework and the Flexible C2 Framework in terms of both structure and how they support the rules of the C2 style. Perform the same comparison for the java.io and java.nio packages vis-à-vis the pipe-and-filter style.

3. Choose an architecture implementation framework and a simple application, and implement that application atop the framework. Reflect on how you maintained the constraints of the architectural style in your implementation, and how the framework assisted (or hindered) you in doing so.

4. Choose one of the simple architectural styles in Chapter 4 and construct an architecture-implementation framework for your preferred platform/operating system combination. Enumerate the rules of the style and how your framework does or does not support those rules.

5. Construct an architecture framework as suggested in Exercise 4, and then use your framework for Exercise 3.

6. Learn about one or more middleware technologies, such as CORBA, COM, RMI, JavaBeans, and so on. Identify the architectural style rules imposed by the middleware platform. Find an example application built atop the middleware and see whether or not it obeys the style rules.

9.7 FURTHER READING

This chapter looks toward architecture-implementation frameworks as a primary method of mapping architectural design decisions to implementation artifacts. Surprisingly little has been written on the subject of such frameworks characterized in this way; Sam Malek et al. (Malek, Mikic-Rakic, and Medvidović 2005) is a notable exception. However, many software systems exist that closely resemble architecture implementation frameworks without the explicit focus on styles. Some of these, such as the Standard I/O framework in C (Kernighan and Ritchie 1988) and the Java I/O (Harold 2006) and New I/O (Hitchens 2002) packages are architecture implementation frameworks in disguise, providing the services of a framework without explicitly being identified as such.

Middleware such as CORBA (Object Management Group 2001), COM and its variants (Sessions 1997), JavaBeans (JavaSoft 1996), Java RMI (Grosso 2001), Java Message Service implementations (JavaSoft 2001), and other message-passing systems such as MQSeries (IBM 2003) and MSMQ (Houston 1998) are often used as architecture-implementation frameworks. However, Elisabetta Di Nitto and David Rosenblum (Di Nitto and Rosenblum 1999) insightfully called out the fact that middleware *induces* an architectural style on applications that use it.

A recent trend growing in popularity is the extensive use of generative techniques, particularly under the banner of Model-Driven Architecture (Mukerji and Miller 2003), which can generate whole or partial implementations through models. Generative approaches have been identified as silver bullets before, and time will tell whether Model-Driven Architecture lives up to its initial promise.

10

Deployment and Mobility

After a software system has been designed, implemented, and validated, it is ready for operation. That usually requires that the system's components and connectors first be distributed to the "target" hardware processors. A software system cannot fulfill its purpose until it is deployed, that is, until its executable modules are physically placed on the hardware devices on which they are supposed to run. The outcome of the activity of placing a system's software components on its hardware hosts is the *deployment* of the system's architecture.

Once the system is in operation, it is possible, and often necessary, to change the physical location of its hardware hosts. For example, laptop computers, personal digital assistants (PDAs), cellular telephones, software-controlled radios, and computers embedded in a vehicle, all move regularly while staying connected. More challenging, more interesting to a software engineer (and even a user), and more pertinent to this book is the relocation or migration of a *software* component or connector from one hardware host to another. This may need to be done to improve the system's performance, perhaps by collocating a processing component with the data it needs, lessen the computational load on a given host, or to achieve some other property. Relocating software modules in this manner changes the deployment view of the software system's architecture during the system's run time, and is referred to as *migration* or *redeployment*. Run time system migration (or redeployment) is thus a type of a software system's *mobility*.

It should be noted that changing a system's deployment while it is running in many ways entails a superset of concerns that engineers face during initial deployment, including the following.

- During a component's migration, its run time state may need to be preserved and migrated. On the other hand, during initial deployment, prior to system start-up, components are typically stateless.

- Systems experience temporary downtimes, or at least degradations in provided capabilities and performance, during the migration process. These concerns do not affect the system during its initial deployment.

- The time at which a component is migrated during execution must be chosen very carefully, as the component must not be in the middle of computation or interaction with another component. Again, these concerns are not applicable during the system's initial deployment.

- The added complexity of run time redeployment, indicated in the above points, is coupled with the usually significantly reduced amount of time available to ensure that all critical system properties have been preserved. In contrast, engineers can carefully plan and analyze a system's initial deployment over a comparatively much longer period of time.

Fundamentally, the role of hardware in the context of deployment and mobility is to support a system's software architecture, including the functionality embodied in processing components, the information exchanged via data components, the interactions facilitated by connectors, and the overall structure defined by the configuration. The hardware configuration can, in turn, also present constraints that must be supported by the software architecture: The choice of distribution points will induce certain architectural decisions. The deployment view of a software system's architecture can be critical in assessing whether the system will be able to satisfy its requirements. For example, placing many large components on a small device with limited memory and CPU power, or transferring high volumes of data over a network link with low bandwidth will negatively impact the system, much like incorrectly implementing its functionality will.

To illustrate these issues, consider the configuration of hardware devices shown in Figure 10-1. This configuration is typical of those used in wireless sensor network systems those found in many commercial buildings, power plants, and transportation systems. The sensor devices host software that can help determine the conditions of their outside environment, such as motion, vibration, fire, and moisture. Sensors are typically highly resource-constrained and can only perform minimal amounts of computation and data storage. The gateway devices aggregate, process, and can possibly share this information. They pass it on to the hubs, which may run software that can make appropriate decisions in the case of certain events or changes in system status. For example, if a gateway fails, a hub may instruct another gateway to take over the management of the "orphaned" sensors; likewise, if multiple sensors report events of a given type (such as excess moisture), the hub may decide that it is appropriate to sound an alarm. Both the gateways and hubs have significantly higher capacities than

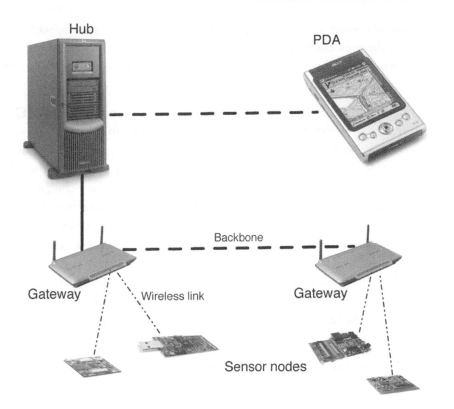

Figure 10-1.
*A wireless sensor
network system
comprising
hardware devices
of several types,
on which a
software system
is deployed.*

the sensors, and may be able to perform large amounts of computation and/or store large amounts of data. Finally, humans can observe the system's operation via PDAs, which communicate with the hubs. PDAs are usually more capacious than sensors, but not as capacious as the hubs or the gateways. The four types of devices may all run different operating systems and other system-level software, require different dialects of programming languages, and support different network protocols.

Software engineers must take into account information such as the above when deciding how to deploy the software system onto the requisite hardware hosts. Furthermore, this information will directly impact the options an engineer has for redeploying the system's components—and possibly connectors—during run time. The idiosyncrasies of a given platform will thus serve as software deployment and mobility constraints.

In addition to considering the characteristics of the involved hardware devices, certain application-level requirements may have a significant impact on the given software architecture's deployment and mobility. For example, the maximum allowed round-trip time between the reporting of an event by a sensor and the acknowledgment that the event has been received by an upstream processing component may affect where certain processing and data components are placed in the system, such as on the gateway or the hub. Such a requirement may also impact the flow of information, for instance whether and when human users need to be informed versus when the software system itself can make a decision.

As another illustrative example, consider an emergency response system (ERS), whose screenshot is shown in Figure 10-2. The devices in this system are somewhat more homogeneous than in the previous example: There is a small number of powerful laptop computers, which are overseeing the overall operation. The laptops interact primarily with a set of high-end PDAs that are in charge of specific segments of the operation; in turn, each of these PDAs interacts with a large number of lower-end PDAs, which are used by individuals who participate as first-line responders. Even though they run different operating systems, each device type is capable of displaying a user interface, running Java, and communicating via TCP/IP. Therefore, aside from the computational and storage capabilities of the different devices, the number of constraints that need to be considered during a software system's deployment, and redeployment, is smaller than in the case of the wireless sensor network system from Figure 10-1.

In this chapter, we study the impact of an explicit software architectural focus on system deployment and mobility. Conversely, we will also study the impact of deployment

Figure 10-2.
An instance of the family of emergency response systems (ERS), which help with deploying and organizing teams of humans in cases of natural disasters, search-and-rescue operations, and military crises (© IEEE 2005).

and mobility on software architecture. The reader should note that deployment can be viewed as a special case of mobility, that is, as the mobility of software modules *prior to* the system's run time. The two concepts are thus closely related and many of their resulting challenges, ramifications, techniques, and tools are similar.

The objective of this chapter is to define and, where necessary, clarify the role of software architecture in deployment and mobility, to discuss different approaches to software deployment and mobility, and to present a set of deployment and mobility techniques that are at an engineer's disposal. We illustrate the main points in the discussion via examples from existing solutions. While software deployment and mobility are two important and growing areas of study, our focus here is specifically on their architecturally relevant aspects. An annotated list of references will be given at the end of the chapter for a broader treatment of the two areas.

10.1 OVERVIEW OF DEPLOYMENT AND MOBILITY CHALLENGES

Modern software systems can present a number of deployment and mobility challenges. Several of these are outlined below.

1. The target processors may be geographically widely distributed, sometimes even throughout the solar system, as is the case with some of NASA's space missions. Physically deploying the software in such settings presents logistical problems, especially if the software has to be distributed and deployed during the system's execution. For example, it may take minutes, and even hours, for the software to reach the intended target host. An accompanying concern is the security of such systems, especially during the transfer of code.

2. The target processors may be embedded inside heterogeneous devices that have different operating environments and serve different purposes. For example, aircraft, mobile robots, consumer electronic devices, mobile phones, and desktop computers present very different characteristics. A software component running on one device may not be able to run on another. Therefore, transferring a component

from one such device to another may require use of sophisticated adaptor software connectors (recall Chapter 5), thus potentially affecting the system's overall performance. Such redeployments may often be impossible.

3. Different software components may require different hardware configurations for their successful execution, whether screen resolution, CPU speed, I/O devices, or memory. Again, this requires careful planning and analysis of the intended deployment profiles or run time software migrations.

4. Typical system life spans may stretch over decades and require periodic maintenance, meaning usually that parts of the system may need to be redeployed. For example, a "buggy" component may be replaced or a more reliable connector introduced. This means that redeployment is an unavoidable activity in most software systems. It also means that, as existing components exhibit problematic behaviors, engineers may resort to migrating software to improve system performance.

5. Similarly, the deployed system is likely to evolve over time, again requiring redeployment. New functionality may be introduced and individual components or even entire hosts may be replaced with newer versions. The danger in this, as well as in the previous case, is that the deployed system's architecture will degrade.

6. The emerging class of mobile code solutions, such as mobile agents (Fuggetta, Picco, and Vigna 1998), require that *running* components be redeployed from one host to another. This requires carefully assessing acceptable (partial) system downtimes and employing techniques for capturing and transferring the relevant portion of the system's *dynamic state* in addition to the code.

7. After a component has been relocated, it still must be able to discover and access, from its new location, the system services it needs at run time. Likewise, the rest of the system needs to be able to locate and access the services provided by that component. Selecting existing or developing new mechanisms for ensuring continuous access to system services is a major architectural consideration in mobile systems.

Traditionally the problem of mobility, and especially initial system deployment, is handled in a relatively uniform manner, and it does not always reflect the above scenarios. For example, if a Windows PC user wants to upgrade an operating system or application on his or her PC, or install a patch that will remove an existing problem, he either will obtain a CD-ROM with the needed software or go to a Web site and download the software; the user will then have to shut down all applications running on the PC in order to complete the procedure. While the PC user is controlling the deployment process, this human user-in-the-loop approach relies on certain assumptions, such as the fact that a computer's operating environment is one of a small handful of tightly controlled environments supported by the provider of new functionality. Regardless of a PC user's technical prowess, the user usually will have little insight into the changes done to the code running on the PC. In other words, the precondition for, say, installing a new spell-check component into a word processor is that its user place full trust in the component's developer, hope that the new software will work correctly, that it will eliminate any problems the user may have had with the previous spell-checker, and that it will not introduce any new bugs. As we all know from experience, sometimes these patches fix the problems, and sometimes they do not, but eventually most PC users reach the point where the performance of the computer has degraded so badly that the only true remedy is to "reinstall the PC" completely.[1]

The situation is even more extreme if a commodity device, such as an automobile, cellular telephone, or "smart" cable TV box, begins misbehaving. In such cases, chances are that the owner or user will have to rely on a trained professional for a remedy. That will often require relinquishing control of the device for a period of time, during which all software running on the device will be redeployed and reinstalled from scratch or simply will be replaced along with the processor on which it is running. In the process, any questions the owner or user may have about what is actually going on with the device will almost assuredly be given euphemistic nonanswers because even the trained professionals do not understand the underlying causes, other than the fact that over time something in the software went awry.

Whatever that "something" is, it probably has underlying architectural causes. Every time a new software system is deployed on its target hosts, its initial deployment architecture is established. When that initial system is changed—via a security patch, by deploying a new component, or by adding a new host—its architecture also changes. If the architectural implications of those changes are not carefully analyzed and clearly understood, the system's architecture is bound to degrade. Eventually, the architecture degrades to the point where the system is unable to function properly, requiring a complete overhaul, as in the above scenarios.

Even though the two are related, the remainder of the chapter addresses separately the role of software architecture in the deployment and in the mobility of software systems.

10.2 SOFTWARE ARCHITECTURE AND DEPLOYMENT

Deployment is the set of activities that result in placing a given software system's components and connectors on a set of physical hosts. This set of activities can take place both during the system's construction, that is, prior to run time, as well as during its execution. In the latter case, deployment entails the transfer and activation of components/connectors that are added to the system for the first time—in other words, either new elements or new versions of existing elements. If the elements deployed on a given host had previously been running on another host in the system, thus possibly having run time state, that is considered to be a case of code mobility and is discussed in the next section.

In the rest of this section, we first introduce the basic concepts underlying software deployment. We then elaborate the set of key deployment activities with a specific focus on the role software architecture plays in them. Finally, we discuss the tool support required of architecture-driven software deployment.

---

[1] This phrase is sometimes used by Windows PC owners and users to indicate that the hard drive must be formatted, and the operating system, device drivers, and application programs reinstalled from scratch. Unix and Macintosh users are typically unfamiliar with such behavior.

10.2.1 Basic Concepts

The overview of the key concepts that underlie software deployment, provided in this section, draws from a deployment technology characterization framework by Antonio Carzaniga, Alfonso Fuggetta, Richard Hall, Dennis Heimbigner, André van der Hoek, and Alexander Wolf (Carzaniga et al. 1998).

A software system is deployed on one or more hardware devices, referred to as *hosts* or *sites*. Each site provides a set of *resources* needed for hosting and executing the system or some of its subsystems. The resources include the different elements of the following.

- The hardware architecture (such as memory and CPU).
- The network architecture (such as available protocols and IP port numbers).
- The peripheral devices (such as hard disk and keyboard).
- The system software (such as operating system, device drivers, and middleware).
- Other application-level software (such as GUI builders and databases).
- The data resources (such as data files and Globally Unique Component Identifiers or GUIDs).

Resources can be either *exclusive* (such as IP port number, GUID) or *sharable* (such as CPU, data file).

A software system is composed from a specific set of components and connectors, with carefully prescribed interconnections and allowed interactions. Multiple versions of the components and connectors may exist, meaning that the system itself may have multiple versions as well. A *version* is defined to be a time-ordered revision, a platform-specific variant, or a functional variant.

Initial system deployment involves the transfer of system components or connectors from one or more *source* or *producer* hosts to one or more *destination* or *consumer* hosts. Subsequent deployment activity will typically involve introducing new functionality (that is, new components) to the system, or replacing existing components or connectors with different versions.

10.2.2 Deployment Activities

Architecture-driven software deployment comprises a process that must be carefully planned, modeled, analyzed, and finally effected or executed. We discuss these four activities in more detail below, and specifically focus on the relationship between each activity and software architecture.

Planning

It is critical that the deployment of a software system be carefully planned. Many important system properties, particularly in a distributed setting, will be affected by the system's deployment. For example, the system's latency in delivering a given service can be improved if the system is deployed such that the most frequent and voluminous interactions required for that service occur either locally or over reliable and capacious network links.

For any large, distributed system, many deployments—that is, mappings of software components and connectors onto hardware hosts—will be possible in principle. Some of those deployments will be more effective than others in ensuring the desired system properties, such as its dependability, availability, security, and fault-tolerance. A system that meets its requirements and possesses these properties is said to deliver a desired level of service quality, most often referred to as QoS for "quality of service," to its users. Of course, in order to be able to claim that the system delivers the required QoS, the different QoS dimensions must be measurable and quantifiable. We revisit this issue in the next section. In the remainder of this section, we assume that the QoS dimensions in question are, in fact, measurable and quantifiable.

It should be noted that there are cases in which the deployment decisions can be and are made with relative ease—regardless of whether they are actually a good fit for the given system or not. One example is a typical desktop environment, in which a human user decides the software that he wants installed on his personal computer. Another example would be a system deployed by a space agency, comprising an interplanetary probe and a ground station. In such systems, it is typically known a priori on which side (flight or ground) the system's different components will reside. Yet another example, to an extent, is the wireless sensor network system depicted in Figure 10-1: The GUI components implemented in Java will reside on the PDAs, while the computationally intensive components implemented in C++ will be deployed to either the hubs or gateways (Malek et al. 2007). While the potential presence of multiple hubs and gateways, and multiple types of PDAs, still will require that the system's architects and engineers consider the effects of their deployment decisions within each class of components (in this example, GUI components and computationally intensive components, respectively), the number of possible deployments is significantly reduced.

The deployment problem is substantially more challenging in a system such as the one depicted in Figure 10-2, in which the number of hardware hosts is significantly larger and all devices provide roughly similar execution environments (in this case, Java). The problem of determining an effective deployment becomes intractable for a human engineer if, in addition to this, multiple QoS dimensions such as latency, security, availability, and power usage must be considered simultaneously, while taking into account any additional constraints. For example, component X may not be deployed on hosts Y and Z because of the component's size, the hosts' inability to provide the resources necessary for its execution, security concerns, or something else. This is a particularly challenging problem because of the following issues.

- A very large number of system parameters influence the QoS dimensions of a software system. It may be possible to identify a subset of system parameters, such as network bandwidth, network reliability, and frequencies of component interactions, that influence the majority of QoS dimensions; however, it may not be possible to identify all of them.
- Many services provided by a system and their corresponding QoS influence the system users' satisfaction.
- Different service qualities may be conflicting; that is, improving one may degrade another. A simple example is security and efficiency: If the system's designers elect to use powerful encryption facilities for all network traffic, such a decision will very likely have a direct, negative impact on the system's performance.
- The space of possible deployment architectures for a given software system is exponentially large.

Figure 10-3.
*A small subset of
the ERS system's
architecture,
comprising two
software
components and
two hardware
hosts. The
components are
depicted in UML
for convenience.*

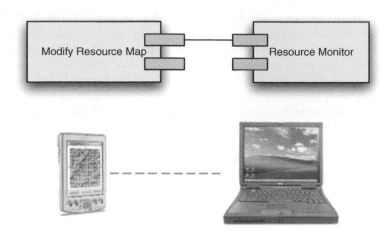

In general, for a system comprising c software components and connectors that need to be deployed onto h hardware hosts, there are h^c possible deployments. Clearly, some of those deployments may not be valid due to location constraints such as those mentioned above, memory restrictions on different devices, network bandwidth considerations, or availability of hardware and system software. This will reduce the space of possible deployments. On the other hand, the human user still must determine which deployment he prefers, why, and, in the process, may have to consider multiple invalid deployments.

As a simple example, consider the following scenario. A very small subset of the ERS system's architecture sketched in Figure 10-2 is depicted in Figure 10-3. This particular system contains only two software components and two hardware hosts; the connector enabling the interaction between the two components has been elided for simplicity. The two components interact to provide a `schedule resource` service, and the only property (that is, QoS dimension) of interest is latency. This small system has four possible deployments:

1. Both components are deployed on the PDA.
2. Both components are deployed on the laptop.
3. `ModifyResourceMap` is deployed on the PDA, while `ResourceMonitor` is deployed on the laptop.
4. `ResourceMonitor` is deployed on the PDA, while `ModifyResourceMap` is deployed on the laptop.

For such a small system, it is, in fact, possible to consider all of the possible deployments and to measure their actual latency. Let us assume that the measured latencies of the four deployments are as shown in Figure 10-4(a). These values are hypothetical, used here for illustration only. From this data, it is easy to determine that the first deployment exhibited the shortest latency and is thus the optimal deployment.

Let us now extend the example slightly and introduce another QoS dimension—durability. We define durability as the inverse of the system's rate of energy consumption. In many embedded and mobile settings, systems with higher energy consumption rates

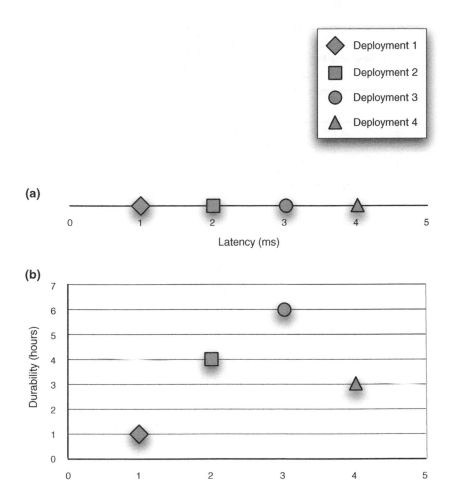

Figure 10-4.
*Evaluating deployments of the ERS subsystem from Figure 10-3.
(a) Latency is the only QoS dimension of interest.
(b) Latency and durability are the two QoS dimensions of interest.*

will run out of battery power sooner, that is, they will have lower durability. Therefore, deployments that reduce the energy consumption rate will increase the system's durability.

Figure 10-4(b) shows the (hypothetical) durability values plotted alongside the previously obtained latency values. The first deployment still exhibits the shortest latency, but the third deployment is most durable. This phenomenon is known as *Pareto optimal* in multicriteria problems such as this one: No single deployment can be considered optimal unless additional criteria are introduced that will allow an architect to reconcile the two competing deployment options. In this example, if the system's stakeholders deemed durability more important than latency, the third deployment would likely be selected over the first one. However, even if there is no such additional criterion, the architect still has all relevant data available and can make the decision(s) he deems most appropriate.

To illustrate how quickly this problem becomes intractable, let us consider a slightly expanded scenario, depicted in Figure 10-5: This subsystem of the ERS has three components and three hosts. Even though it does not directly impact the discussion below, for

Figure 10-5.
*A slightly larger
subset of the ERS
system's
architecture,
comprising three
software
components and
three hardware
hosts.*

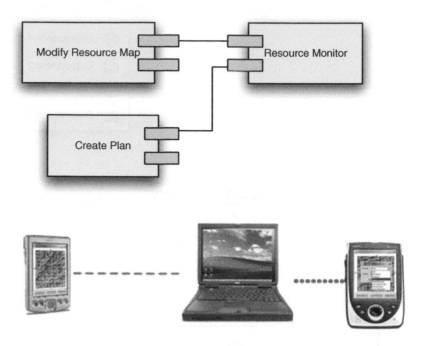

the sake of completeness it should be noted that this three-component system provides an `exchange plan` service as well as the `schedule resource` service. Furthermore, there are now three QoS dimensions of interest: In addition to minimizing latency and maximizing durability, the system must also minimize the total volume of data exchanged across the network.

This system has twenty-seven possible deployments (3^3). For each of those deployments, let us assume that the three QoS properties have been measured or estimated. Visualizing the twenty-seven data points in a single three-dimensional diagram would be possible, though difficult. Note that visualizing software deployment scenarios with greater numbers of components and hosts, and especially with four or more QoS dimensions, in a single diagram would be essentially impossible. Instead, architects would most likely plot separate two-dimensional diagrams to study the relationships between pairs of QoS dimensions. The three such diagrams for the scenario from Figure 10-5 are shown for illustration in Figure 10-6.

It should be obvious from this example that, even for a system that is as small as the one depicted in Figure 10-5, manually calculating the QoS values of individual deployments and then determining the best deployment from those values is infeasible. Therefore, a solution that meets the challenges identified above and allows a software system's architects to plan the system's deployment appropriately will need to (1) provide an extensible model that supports inclusion of arbitrary system parameters; (2) support the definition of new QoS dimensions using the system parameters; (3) allow users to specify their QoS preferences; and (4) provide efficient and generic algorithms that can be used to find a solution (that is, deployment architecture) which maximizes the users' satisfaction in a reasonable amount of time.

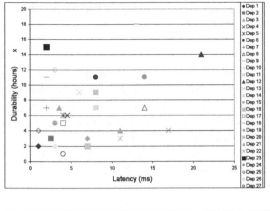

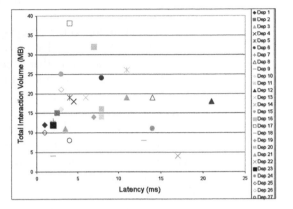

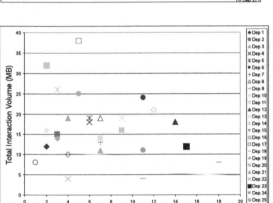

Figure 10-6. *The pair–wise trade-offs among the three QoS of interest (latency, durability, and interaction volume) for the ERS subsystem shown in Figure 10-5.*

This solution is amenable to implementation, alleviating at least some of the architect's responsibility. In turn, this allows architects to focus on tasks such as specifying concrete targets for QoS dimensions of interest, rather than on menial but critical tasks such as determining whether a given deployment satisfies all of the system constraints and, if so, calculating the values of its various QoS dimensions.

For example, in the case of the scenario from Figure 10-5 and Figure 10-6, the architect may be interested in a deployment with specific latency, durability, and interaction volume thresholds. Manually determining and analyzing each individual deployment that is possible, that is, that satisfies all system constraints, and choosing one that in fact meets the set thresholds, would be overly time consuming (it could take hours for this small scenario and years for even only slightly larger systems) and error-prone. Furthermore, the architect will likely elect to stop once he has found the first deployment that meets the desired criteria. In contrast, a software-based solution working on the same problem would likely be able to determine a number of valid deployments that meet the QoS criteria, and choose the best one.

Automated support for deployment modeling and analysis would also allow architects to study, and quantify, any changes in a system's run time behavior. In turn, this would allow them to formulate plans regarding whether and when to redeploy the system or some of its parts.

Modeling

In order to be able to make and effect a deployment plan for a large, long-lived, distributed software system, the system's architects first need to create a detailed model comprising all concerns pertaining to the system's deployment. This is an example of several concerns pertaining to the system's hardware and network infrastructure permeating the space of principal design decisions, that is, the system's software architecture.

Consider the two diagrams in Figure 10-7, corresponding to a subset of the ERS application depicted in Figure 10-2: The top diagram shows a high-level view of the ERS system's architectural configuration, while the bottom diagram shows the configuration of the hardware hosts on which the software is to be deployed. For simplicity, the top diagram does not show any software connectors. Instead, all interaction paths among the components are represented simply as lines. The reader can choose to interpret them as procedure calls for the purpose of the ensuing discussion. The dashed lines in the bottom diagram depict network connectivity.

A software architect would need a lot more information than is contained in the two diagrams in Figure 10-7 to determine what an effective deployment of ERS's software components to its hardware hosts would be. For example, the architect would need to know how computationally intensive the Deployment Advisor component is; how large the Repository is; how frequently the Clock component updates the remaining components in the system; what type of GUI facilities the five UI components in the system require; and so on. Furthermore, the architect would need to know many of the characteristics of the five hosts (such as their capacities, available peripheral devices, system-level software running on each, and so on) as well as the network links connecting them (such as the available bandwidth, protocol, link reliability, and so on). Only after all of this information is available can the architect make appropriate deployment decisions.

Therefore, an effective deployment model requires the following elements:

- Software system elements (components and connectors), their configuration, and their parameters.
- Hardware system elements (hardware hosts and network links), their configuration, and their parameters.
- Any constraints on the system elements and/or their parameters.
- Formal definitions of QoS dimensions of interest.

The architects may also need to represent system users or user types and their preferences in order to make appropriate decisions in situations in which multiple deployment options are acceptable.

For any moderately-sized software system, the above model can be very large, especially if architects decide to capture many parameters and constraints of the overall system and its individual hardware and software elements. Example parameters of a software component are the CPU and memory requirements for the component's execution, characteristics of the required execution substrate, such as the needed version of the Java Virtual Machine, and so on. Likewise, for a connector enabling the interaction of two or more components,

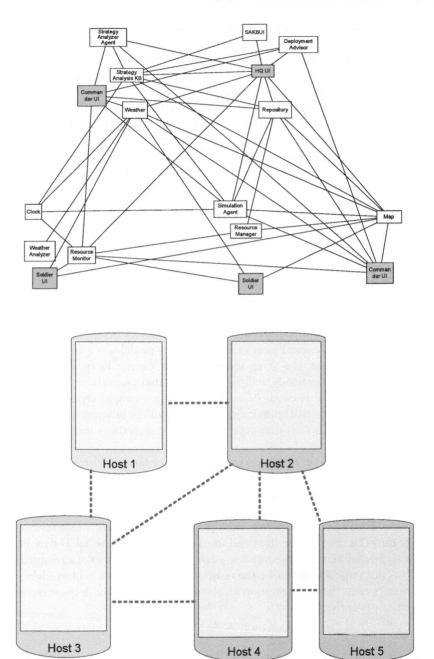

Figure 10-7.
The software architectural configuration of a subset of the ERS application (top) and the hardware configuration on which the software is to be deployed (bottom).

the system model would encompass many of the same parameters as in the case of components, but would also capture parameters such as the sizes and frequencies of the interaction between the components, security mechanisms available, and whether the connector assumes a particular distribution profile (such as single address space, interprocess, or network-based).

Even though the primary responsibility of a software architect is to focus on a system's software aspects, in the case of deployment modeling software architects must also consider the characteristics of the hardware platforms and the network. Extensible architecture descriptions languages such as xADL, AADL, and even UML, discussed in Chapter 6, are able to or already incorporate such modeling elements.

There may be many constraints specified on the software and hardware elements of a deployment model. For instance, location constraints may specify the relationship between software and hardware elements: requiring, allowing, or prohibiting that certain elements be deployed on certain hosts. In the example from Figure 10-7, it may be required that the Clock component reside on Host 2, while the Repository component may be prohibited from residing on that host.

Collocation constraints specify groups of components and connectors that need to be deployed, and redeployed, as a collection, as well as groups of components and connectors that may not be deployed on the same host. For example, another way of specifying the above two location constraints for Figure 10-7 would be to couple the Clock component's location constraint (that it must reside on Host 2) with a collocation constraint stating that the Clock and Repository components may not reside on the same host.

Beyond location and collocation, other constraints may restrict the versions of software connectors that may be used to enable the interactions of specific versions of components, the hardware configurations that are required or disallowed for deploying a given component, and so on. A final, critical facet of a deployment model is a quantification of the QoS dimensions of interest. If a given system property cannot be quantified, it cannot be estimated or measured precisely and the impact on that property of a system's particular deployment cannot be assessed objectively. Thus, for example, trying to determine a deployment of the ERS that will optimize its usability would be inherently difficult: Usability is a largely subjective notion that depends on many, sometimes implicit and possibly ill-understood, factors.

Fortunately, many important system properties can be quantified: reliability, availability, size, energy consumption rate, latency, and data volume are examples. Some of these properties may have multiple interpretations, which will differ across architects, projects, and organizations. Nonetheless, in principle it is possible to select a specific definition for a given property. Thus for example, one possible definition of availability for a system service (such as `schedule resource` discussed in the context of Figure 10-3) may be as the ratio of the successfully completed service requests to the total number of attempted service requests. It is not critical that this be the only, or the best, definition of availability. It is much more important that the definition fits the needs of the project in question, and that it is applied consistently.

Analysis

Developing a detailed deployment model will be a sizeable, human-intensive task for any large, distributed application: Many parameters of many system elements will have to be modeled; many constraints will have to be captured; QoS dimensions of interest will have to be formally defined; system users and their preferences will have to be modeled; and so on. Doing all that will be worthwhile only if the model is used effectively to make the necessary, complex deployment decisions. To that end, the system's deployment model will have to be analyzed for properties of interest.

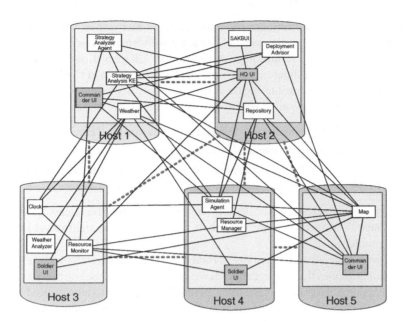

Figure 10-8.
*Two possible
deployments of
the subset of ERS
depicted in
Figure 10-7.*

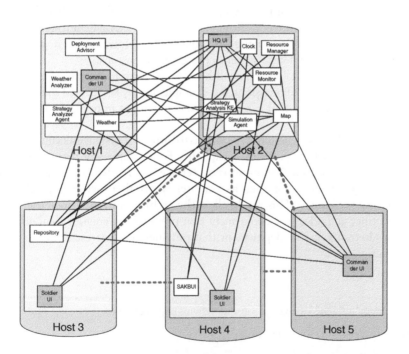

Consider for illustration the two diagrams in Figure 10-8. Both represent deployments of the ERS application's software elements onto its hardware nodes. The connectivities of both the software and the hardware configurations in the two Figure 10-8 diagrams are identical to those depicted in Figure 10-7. In other words, the applications corresponding to the two deployments are functionally equivalent to each other. The only difference between the two diagrams is that some of the software elements have been repositioned across the hosts. Using the terminology introduced in Chapter 3, we can then say that the two diagrams represent different candidate deployment views of the ERS application's architecture. An architect considering these two candidate deployments will have to make certain determinations, as detailed below.

1. First, are both deployments valid? That is, do they satisfy all ERS system constraints?
2. Secondly, which of the two deployments is better?
3. Finally, once the better deployment is selected, does that deployment exhibit acceptable properties, or must an even better deployment be found?

Answering the first question—Is a deployment valid?—is relatively easy. If the system constraints have been specified rigorously, then this becomes a straightforward constraint satisfaction problem.

The answer to the second question—Which deployment is better?—is more uncertain. To answer that question, the architect must have a clearly defined measure of goodness for a system's deployment. That means that the system's deployment model will need to provide definitions of all QoS dimensions of interest. In turn, these QoS dimensions will have to be measured, or at least estimated. If multiple QoS dimensions are under consideration, as will be the case with most all large systems, the architect will very likely have to deal with Pareto optimal situations (recall from Figure 10-4(b)): One deployment may prove superior with respect to one subset of the QoS dimensions, while another deployment may be better with respect to a different subset of the QoS dimensions.

For this reason, additional criteria will have to be introduced into the model. One possibility is to rank the QoS dimensions. For example, it may be decided that durability is more critical than latency. In that case, the third deployment from Figure 10-4(b) would be selected.

Another possibility, as suggested previously, is to introduce system users into the deployment model and capture their preferences explicitly. For example, one user could state that high durability of the `schedule resource` service in the ERS system is more important, by a given quantified factor, than its low latency; another user may specify another, possibly clashing preference. This would allow the architects to introduce the notion of the system's utility and select the deployment that provides the greatest total utility to all the users, or alternatively, the deployment that provides the greatest utility to the most important user or users.

Better-Cheaper-Faster—Pick Any Two!

One of the frequently used axioms of software systems engineering is:

> Better-cheaper-faster—pick any two!

This means that for any software system, only two of these three properties can be achieved at one time. For example, it is possible to construct a high-quality system (better) that delivers its functionality efficiently (faster), but that will be a costly enterprise (cheaper is sacrificed). Likewise, if we want an inexpensive system (cheaper) that is also highly performant (faster), we should expect the system's quality (better) to be compromised.

There are alternative ways of stating this principle. For example:

Functionality-scalability-performance—pick any two!

All of the various incarnations of this principle point to the inherent trade-offs among the properties in a software system.

Relating this to the deployment problem, it should not be surprising to a software engineer that all system users will not be able to have all of their preferences satisfied in a chosen system deployment. This will be the case for even those users who are deemed "very important." Large, distributed software systems such as the ones that are being discussed here are multifaceted and involve many trade-offs, such as those mentioned above. Thus, a system's user will not be able to expect realistically that the system will deliver its services in the optimal (for that user) fashion. Rather, the best a person can hope for when addressing the system deployment problem is that the suboptimality in the system's delivered QoS will be minimized.

Another way of looking at this is that, when making deployment decisions, some or even all of the system's users are likely to be unhappy with the system. This stems directly from the "better-cheaper-faster" axiom. The software architect's job is to use the concepts provided in this chapter to minimize that unhappiness.

Answering the third question—Is there a better deployment than the current one?—can be very challenging. It may require considering a very large number of deployment options and for each of them establishing the deployment's validity and comparing the new deployment to the existing one. This question is closely related to a more general question—What is the best deployment possible for a given system?—which is infeasible to answer in the general case because of the deployment problem's exponential nature.

There is a class of algorithms that can be applied to questions such as these. As stated above, the deployment problem is an instance of multidimensional optimization problems. Techniques such as mixed-integer linear programming (MIP) and mixed-integer nonlinear programming (MINLP) are frequently used to solve such problems (Nemhauser and Wolsey 1988). The main shortcoming of MIP is that it searches exhaustively for the best solution to a problem, and is thus inapplicable to even moderately large deployment scenarios. MINLP algorithms in turn provide approximate, rather than optimal, solutions. Furthermore, MINLP algorithms may not always converge on a solution.

There are other heuristic-based strategies that can be applied to solving complex problems such as this, including greedy, genetic, and decentralized strategies (Malek et al. 2007). However, none of those strategies can guarantee that the suggested deployment is the optimal one. In the case of the simpler formulation of the third question—Is there a better deployment than the current one?—this may result in failing to identify a better deployment even though many such deployments may exist. In the case of the question's more general formulation—What is the best deployment possible for a given system?—this may result in selecting a deployment that is actually suboptimal but is the best deployment the chosen algorithm can find.

Implementation

Once the deployment problem has been modeled and a specific software system's deployment suggested in the manner outlined above, that deployment needs to be effected. As noted by Richard Hall and colleagues (Hall et al. 1997; Hall, Heimbigner, and Wolf 1999)

Figure 10-9.
*Software
deployment
process:
deployment
activities and
their
relationships.
The diagram has
been adopted
from (Carzaniga
et al. 1998).*

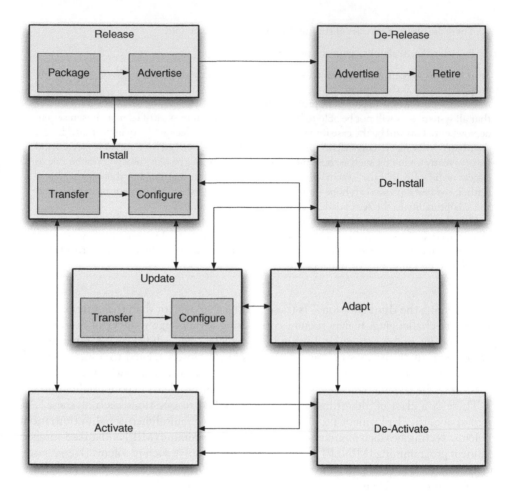

and Carzaniga and colleagues (Carzaniga et al. 1998), some of the activities in a software system's deployment process take place on the host that is the source of the deployed component, while other activities take place on the host that is the destination of the deployed component. Source hosts are also referred to as producers, while destination hosts are referred to as targets, or consumers. The overall relationship among these activities is shown in Figure 10-9. We will briefly discuss each of these activities below, with a particular focus on the role of software architecture in the deployment process.

Release. A software system's release is the initial activity in that system's deployment process. It takes place on the producer site, or sites, after the system's development has been completed. The system is packaged so that it can be transferred to the consumer sites. In certain settings (such as desktop computing) the system may need to be advertised to potential consumers. The packaged system will typically contain the following:

1. The system's description, including its software architectural configuration, dependencies on system-level facilities and any external components, and

requirements specific to individual software system elements and the entire system.

2. All of the necessary software modules—both the application and any helper components necessary for the released application's correct execution.

3. A deployment model indicating which components need to be deployed on which processes and/or hosts.

4. The deployment procedures that must be effected on the consumer sites in order to extract and deploy the software system from the release package.

5. Any additional information that is needed to manage the system at the consumer sites, such as the necessary periodic updates to the data used by the system and expected downtimes for specific system services.

Install. Once the system has been packaged at the producer sites and transferred to the consumer sites, it is ready to be configured and installed for operation. Installation is a complex activity that encompasses all of the steps necessary to enable the system to execute. In other words, installation deals with:

1. Extracting from the deployment package the system's description, including its software architecture and deployment models.

2. Based on those models, assembling all of the system's elements—both the application-level components as well as any accompanying utilities.

3. Ensuring that all the resources needed for the system's correct operation are available and properly configured.

4. Establishing any required conditions on the target hosts, such as setting any global system variables, establishing the needed directory structures, and setting up the appropriate classpaths.

Activate. Once the system is installed, it needs to be activated for use on the target hosts. Activation consists of providing a command, or sequence of commands, that will be required to start up the system.

Deactivate. Deactivation involves disabling and/or shutting down a system, or any of the system's facilities that are still active on the target hosts.

Update. Once a system has been installed and activated on the target hosts, over time it may need to be updated for different reasons. Updates are initiated by the system's producers, and involve the same activities as the system's original installation, with the caveat that only the necessary subset of the system is packaged and received from the producer hosts. The system may need to be deactivated before it is updated, and then reactivated thereafter. Alternatively, the system may support dynamic redeployment (recall the above discussion and also see Chapter 14). It is critical that the software system's update be properly reflected in its architectural models. If this is not ensured, the architecture will degrade, and any subsequent updates may result in system defects.

Adapt. Adaptation encompasses a wide range of activities that result in changing the system, possibly dynamically, in response to events in the system's execution environment. Adaptation is an important aspect of architecture-based software development, thus Chapter 14 is dedicated to it. With respect to software deployment, adaptation can result in the system's redeployment (that is, repositioning of its software components across execution processes and/or hardware hosts). Adaptation will be further discussed below in the context of mobility.

De-Install. If the system is no longer needed on the consumer sites, it will need to be removed. A simple view of de-installing a system is that it simply reverses the steps taken during the installation. However, any subsequent updates and adaptations must also be taken into account, as must any dependencies that other systems on the given consumer host have to the system being removed. This is why it is critical to maintain current architectural models for all deployed software systems. It should also be noted that, before the system is de-installed, it may need to be deactivated first.

De-Release. After some time, the producer of a given system may decide not to support the system any longer. In other words, the producer may decide to retire the system. This may be because one or more of the system's subsequent versions are superior, the market size for the product is too small, the producer has discontinued the product, or the producer has gone out of business. The withdrawal of the producer's support for the system is usually advertised. The system's consumers can then decide whether they still want to use the system, with the accompanying risks, or to de-install it.

10.2.3 Tool Support

To properly support the software architecture-based deployment modeling, analysis, and implementation activities discussed above, engineers must be supplied with appropriate software tools. Some of those tools, such as those for software installation, are widely used. For example, most all desktop software comes with an installation wizard. Tools for other activities are not as prevalent, and furthermore, they frequently fail to consider the system's software architecture. This carries the risk that important architectural concerns will be missed during deployment and re-deployment. It also carries the risk that key architectural design decisions will be violated. Ideally, a deployment tool set will enable architects to do the following.

1. *Model* in detail the software system's deployment concerns.
2. *Analyze* the deployment model for desired properties.
3. Effect or *implement* that deployment model.
4. Actively *monitor* the system for properties of interest.
5. *Update* or *adapt* the system as a result.

Tools exist that support many facets of the above activities [such as Software Dock (Hall, Heimbinger, and Wolf 1999)], but they frequently take an implementation–centric, rather than a software architecture–centric, view of the deployed system. Here we will briefly focus on a few examples of architecture-based deployment tools.

An example of an integrated tool set that allows several of these activities to take place seamlessly for the ERS application family is shown in Figure 10-10. The environment allows an architect to graphically model certain aspects of a system's deployment, including the following.

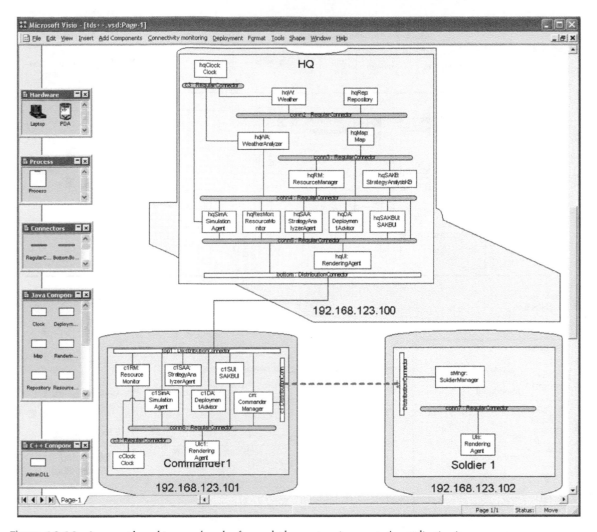

Figure 10-10. *An example architecture-based software deployment environment. An application is modeled as a collection of software components and connectors, as well as hardware hosts and network links. The network link between the two bottom hosts is temporarily down (denoted by the dashed line).*

- Software components and connectors, as well as the locations of their implementations in Java and/or C++.
- Their connectivity in the particular application's architectural configuration.
- Hardware nodes and their IP addresses.
- The physical network's connectivity.

Once the model of an application's deployment is completed, this tool is capable of releasing and installing the application, as well as monitoring it during run time. For example, the screenshot in Figure 10-10 shows that the network link between the two PDAs is down.

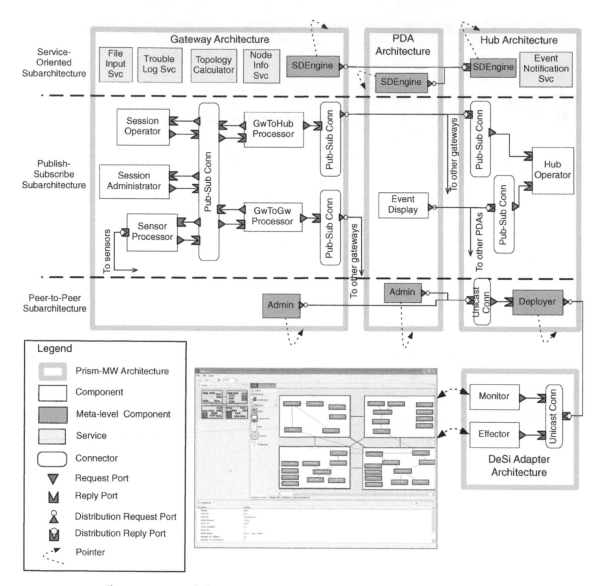

Figure 10-11. *A deployment view of a software system distributed across three types of devices (top). A deployment modeling and analysis tool interacts with the system at run time to ensure the preservation of its key properties (bottom).*

A more sophisticated distributed system deployment tool, called DeSi (Malek et al. 2005), is depicted in the bottom portion of Figure 10-11. DeSi allows an architect to provide a more extensive model of the system's deployment, such as that discussed earlier in this chapter. The tool also is able to analyze the model and suggest an effective deployment for a given system, which will ensure the system's key QoS dimensions. An example deployment for an application is shown in the top portion of Figure 10-11. Interested readers can refer to (Malek et al. 2007) for further details of this particular application. Finally, the tool is able to interact with the system's implementation platform, observe, and analyze any changes in the system's operating conditions. In response, DeSi reevaluates the deployment view of the system's current architecture, and may suggest and effect an improved one.

10.3 SOFTWARE ARCHITECTURE AND MOBILITY

Once a software system is in operation, parts of it may need to be redeployed, or migrated, in response to changes in the run time environment or the need to improve certain non-functional properties of the system. The redeployment of a software system's components is a type of software system *mobility*.

Mobility is an area that has received significant attention recently. This chapter focuses specifically on those aspects of mobility that are relevant to a software system's architecture. The reader should note that, in order for software mobility to be possible, certain low-level system implementation facilities, such as dynamically linked libraries and dynamic class loading, usually must also be available. We will not focus on such facilities here as they are outside the scope of this book.

10.3.1   Basic Concepts

Mobile computing involves the movement of human users together with their hosts across different physical locations, while still being able to access an information system unimpeded. This is also referred to as *physical mobility*. Such mobile computing need not necessarily involve the mobility of software systems, or portions of them, from one host to another. If a piece of software moves across hardware hosts during the system's execution, that action is referred to as *code mobility*, or *logical mobility*.

If a software module that needs to be migrated contains run time state, then the module's migration is known as *stateful mobility*. If only the code needs to be migrated, that is known as *stateless mobility*. Clearly, supporting stateful mobility is more challenging since the mobile component's state on the source host needs to be captured, migrated, and reconstituted on the destination host. Furthermore, the component may be moved only at certain times [such as when it is not operating on its internal state; that is, when it is quiescent (Kramer and Magee 1988), as discussed in Chapter 14]. Finally, the effect of the component's migration, and thus its temporary downtime, on the rest of the system and its dependence on the component's internal state must be considered. This is why Alfonso Fuggetta, Gian Petro Picco, and Giovanni Vigna (Fuggetta, Picco, and Vigna 1998) refer to stateful mobility as *strong* mobility, while they consider stateless mobility to be *weak* mobility.

10.3.2   Mobility Paradigms

It is widely accepted that there are three general classes of mobile code systems: remote evaluation, code-on-demand, and mobile agent (Fuggetta, Picco, and Vigna 1998). These are typically distinguished from "fixed" code paradigms such as client-server. In a client-server system, the server has both the logic and the resources needed for providing a given service, while the distribution of such know-how and resources varies across the mobile code paradigms.

Remote Evaluation

In remote evaluation, a component on the source host has the know-how but not the resources needed for performing a service. The component is transferred to the destination host, where it is executed using the available resources. The result of the execution is returned to the source host.

In the terminology used previously in this chapter (that is, from a software architectural perspective), this means that in remote evaluation a software component is:

1. Redeployed at run time from a source host to a destination host.
2. Installed on the destination host, ensuring that the software system's architectural configuration and any architectural constraints are preserved.
3. Activated.
4. Executed to provide the desired service.
5. Possibly de-activated and de-installed.

Code-on-Demand

In code-on-demand, the needed resources are available locally, but the know-how is not. The local subsystem thus requests the component(s) providing the know-how from the appropriate remote host(s).

From a software architectural perspective, code-on-demand requires the same steps as remote evaluation; the only difference is that the roles of the target and destination hosts are reversed.

Mobile Agent

If a component on a given host (1) has the know-how for providing some service, (2) has some execution state, and (3) has access to some, though not all, of the resources needed to provide that service, the component, along with its state and local resources, may migrate to the destination host, which may have the remaining resources needed for providing the service. The component, along with its state, will be installed on the destination host and will access all of the needed resources to provide the service.

As mentioned above, from a software architectural perspective, mobile agents are stateful software components. Therefore before the steps outlined above are taken, a mobile agent must first be safely de-activated and possibly de-installed from the source host. This may pose certain challenges.

10.3.3 Challenges in Migrating Code

Run time mobility of software depends on several factors that are not architectural in nature. For example, the run time platform must be able to support dynamic loading and linking of code modules. Likewise, both the source and target hosts must provide all of the software and hardware utilities necessary to execute the code.

At the same time, there are architectural concerns of which engineers must be aware. One such concern is quiescence. It may be unsafe to attempt to migrate a software component in the middle of processing, while it is waiting for a result from another component, or while other components are requesting its services. Therefore, the system must provide facilities that allow temporary suspension of all interactions originating from or targeted at the component in question, until the component is relocated to a new host.

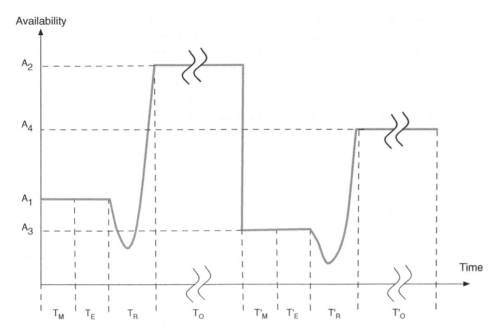

Availability

Figure 10-12.
Mobility of software components will negatively impact a system's quality of service (QoS): Certain services will be unavailable during the migration process, temporarily (but possibly significantly) decreasing the delivered QoS.

In general, quiescence requires at least two capabilities. The first one must be embodied in the component itself, allowing the system to instruct the component to cease any autonomous processing and to later restart it. The second capability may require that special-purpose elements, such as adaptor connectors, be inserted into the system temporarily, to insulate the component from outside requests. These modules may also log the received requests and route them for processing after the component has been migrated.

Another important issue concerns the system's provided quality of service as a result of code mobility. Consider the example of Figure 10-12. The postulated system provides a given level of availability for its services. The system is monitored for a time, T_M, and it is established that the provided availability is A_1. If the system's stakeholders want to improve the system's availability to a higher level A_2, for example, by migrating one or more of its components to different hosts, they will first evaluate, during time T_E, where those components should reside. This evaluation can be accomplished by using a deployment analysis capability such as those discussed previously in this chapter. Once the target hosts have been determined, the mobile components are rendered quiescent, packaged for redeployment, and migrated to their target hosts. Once they are installed on the target hosts and activated, the system indeed operates at availability level A_2 during the next time period T_o.

The system will operate at this availability level until some change occurs in the system itself—such as a software or hardware failure—or in the physical environment—such as the emergence of obstacles. Such changes may cause the availability level to decrease to some level, A_3, as shown in the right portion of Figure 10-12. The above process will then need to be repeated in order to improve once again the system's availability to an acceptable level, A_4. This pattern may occur many times during a mobile system's execution.

But what about the time period T_R needed to effect the redeployment? Since one or more system components were inaccessible, the system's quality of service may have gone down significantly. In fact, it is possible that the dip in availability, however temporary, may be unacceptable to the system's users. In that case, migrating the components in question will not be the best approach, and other dynamic adaptation techniques (such as component replication with continuous state synchronization) may need to be considered. Dynamic adaptability of software system architectures is treated in Chapter 14.

10.4 END MATTER

System deployment and mobility are critical needs in today's long-lived, distributed, decentralized, pervasive, and embedded software systems. Architectures of a number of such systems will be presented and discussed in Chapter 11, and will be revisited in the context of architectural change and adaptation in Chapter 14. The nature of these systems demands that the past assumptions and techniques, employed particularly in the domain of desktop computing, be reassessed. The complexity of these systems also mandates that deployment and mobility be considered from a software architectural perspective. While many facets of both deployment and mobility depend on implementation and low-level system issues, they are significantly impacted by—and significantly impact—a given system's software architecture. This chapter identified a number of pertinent concerns and suggested strategies for addressing them.

The perspective on software architecture we have adopted in this book—that it is a set of principal design decisions about a software system—directly and naturally enables an architect to embrace deployment and mobility and exert control over their relevant facets. The modeling and analysis of deployment and mobility at the architectural level helps to ensure the system's proper functionality and desired quality attributes. Moreover, maintaining the relationship between the system's architectural model and its implementation allows system monitoring to be reified into architectural (re-)deployment and mobility decisions, which are then effected on the running system. By broadening the notion of software architecture to encompass an area that has traditionally been considered outside its scope, software architects can gain significant added leverage in stemming architectural degradation.

In addition to the architecture-focused concerns discussed in this chapter, many nonarchitectural issues are pertinent to deployment and mobility as well. "Further Reading" provides pointers to some of the relevant literature.

| The Business Case | Dynamism in the form of deployment and mobility is a fact of life in modern systems. It is impractical, often unacceptable, for many of today's systems to have static configurations or to be brought down for upgrades. Moreover, deploying a system in a manner that ensures its key properties and satisfies all of the constraints placed on it is a difficult, perhaps even impossible, task for a human engineer. Modeling and analyzing the appropriate concerns at the architectural level provides at least some added leverage, and can help answer many questions before significant resources are invested into supporting the required low-level deployment and mobility facilities. |

At the same time, supporting deployment and mobility at the level of architecture requires a lot of careful preparation, as was indicated in this chapter in the case of deployment modeling. It also requires keeping a close watch on the architecture. Even more dangerous and costly than diving into low-level system details right away would be the architecture's degradation. The observation repeated throughout this book applies in this case as well: The benefits, monetary and otherwise, of an architecture-based software development philosophy can be reaped only if the architecture remains the linchpin of all development activities, including the deployment and postdeployment activities.

10.5 REVIEW QUESTIONS

1. What is deployment?
2. What is mobility?
3. How are deployment and mobility related to and different from one another?
4. Discuss the challenges in determining the optimal deployment for a software system.
5. How can software architecture aid in addressing those challenges?
6. Which facets of a system should be modeled in order to solve the deployment problem?
7. Which, if any, of those facets fall outside the realm of software architecture, and why?
8. What is Pareto optimal?
9. Name and describe the different deployment activities.
10. Which activities take place on the source hosts, and which ones on the target hosts?
11. What is the difference between physical and logical mobility?
12. What is the difference between stateful and stateless mobility? Which is more challenging to realize?
13. What is remote evaluation? What steps does it require?
14. How is remote evaluation different from code-on-demand?
15. How do mobile agents work?
16. Describe quiescence and the challenges it entails.
17. Discuss the impact of mobility on a system's provided quality of service.

10.6 EXERCISES

1. Select one of the implemented Lunar Lander applications from Chapter 9 and deploy it on (a) a single host and then (b) at least two hosts. Discuss the issues you encountered.
2. In what ways would the knowledge that an application, such as Lunar Lander, may need to be deployed on multiple hardware hosts impact its design? For example, would the design of Lunar Lander from Figure 9-8 in Chapter 9 be any different if the architects had known that the GUI component would need to run on a separate host from the remaining components?
3. Leverage the Lightweight C2 framework discussed in Chapter 9 in providing run time mobility support for the implemented Lunar Lander application. Develop and execute a mobility scenario. Discuss the challenges you encountered.
4. Develop a simple application scenario, or reuse an existing application, that must run on at least three hosts and satisfy at least three quality-of-service (QoS) dimensions. Model the application's architecture in xADLite. Define formally each QoS dimension. Your objective is to determine the optimal deployment of your architecture. What system parameters did you have to consider? Did you run into a Pareto optimal situation?
5. To help you deal with the preceding problem, select a set of system users and elicit utility functions from them. What issues did you encounter in this process? Are your users readily able to provide the information in the form you need? Why or why not?

6. A software system consisting of N components is distributed across M hardware hosts (N>M). Given

   - a particular deployment for the software system
   - the definition of system availability as the ratio of attempted intercomponent interactions to completed interactions
   - the reliability for each network link as the percentage of time the link is up
   - the bandwidth for each link
   - the frequency of component interactions
   - the size of exchanged data in each interaction, the available memory on each hardware device
   - the required memory for each component

   devise an algorithm that will find the system's deployment that will maximize the system's availability. Discuss the computational complexity of your algorithm. Suggest enhancements that may decrease the algorithm's complexity. Discuss the trade-offs you have to consider in order to effect those enhancements. You may assume that a central view of the system's deployment architecture is available.

7. A swarm of M mobile robots is collaborating to achieve a common task using N software components. Unlike the above problem, there is no single location from which the system's deployment architecture (that is, the view of the system such as that shown in Figure 10-10) may be retrieved. In addition, there are the following two constraints:

   - Each robot can be connected at most M-2 other robots.
   - Each robot can "see" only those robots to which it is directly connected.

   Devise a decentralized algorithm in which each robot autonomously decides the migration of its local components to improve the system's overall availability. You may not assume that any robot will be able to obtain a global view of the system. Each robot may acquire the relevant local deployment information from robots to which it is directly connected.

8. As discussed in this chapter, a component is typically rendered quiescent during migration. However, other, especially remote components will likely continue sending the migrating component service requests. Those requests will not be serviced immediately and cannot be simply ignored. Devise and describe at least three solutions for servicing the requests made of a component during migration. Compare and contrast your solutions and discuss their trade-offs.

10.7 FURTHER READING

The general problem of software deployment has been studied extensively. However, a comparatively smaller number of existing techniques have tried to address deployment from a software architecture-based perspective. The most relevant related work is overviewed here.

In the deployment modeling area, the Unified Modeling Language (UML) provides deployment diagrams, which enable a static visual representation of a system's deployment. SysML (SysML Partners 2005) is a modeling language standard for specifying systems engineering artifacts. SysML's allocation diagrams allow arbitrary modeling elements to reference one another (for example, allocation of behavioral elements to structural elements, or software elements to hardware elements). Neither UML nor SysML gives engineers feedback as they create or visualize (possibly inappropriate) deployment models of a system. Some promising approaches in deployment architecture modeling have been built on the previous research in architecture description languages. Two notable examples of ADLs that are capable of modeling a deployment view of a system's architecture are xADL (Dashofy 2003; Dashofy, van der Hoek, and Taylor 2005) and AADL (Feiler, Lewis, and Vestal 2003). In fact, the DeSi deployment modeling and analysis tool discussed in this chapter is built around xADL as its architecture modeling core.

Several existing techniques have attempted to analyze the impact of a system's deployment architecture on its provided quality of service. One (Bastarrica, Shvartsman, and Demurjian 1998) proposes the use of binary integer programming (BIP) for generating an optimal deployment of a software application over a given network, such that the overall remote communication is minimized. Solving the BIP model is exponentially complex in the number of software components, however, rendering it applicable only to small systems. Coign

(Hunt and Scott 1999) provides a framework for distributed partitioning of COM applications across the network in a manner that minimizes communication time. Coign only addresses scenarios involving two-host client-server applications. Component placement problem (CPP) (Kichkaylo, Ivan, and Karamcheti 2003) is a model for describing a distributed system in terms of network and application properties and constraints. This technique only searches for a single valid deployment that satisfies the specified constraints.

A wide variety of technologies exist to support various aspects of the deployment process. Carzaniga et al. (Carzaniga et al. 1998) provide an extensive comparison of existing software deployment techniques. They identify three classes of software deployment technologies: installers, package managers, and application management systems. Widely used examples of installers are Microsoft Windows Installer and Install-Shield (InstallShield Corporation 2000). Examples of package managers are Linux RedHat's RPM, and SUN Solaris's pkg commands. Finally, examples of application management systems are IBM Tivoli Composite Application Manager and OpenView from Hewlett Packard. An application management system must provide active system monitoring (both hardware and software) and various deployment activities that may need to be performed as a result.

Before it is possible to assess and improve a system's deployment architecture, one may need to study and understand the properties of a deployed system. Typically this is accomplished via system monitoring. Numerous techniques have focused on the problem of remote monitoring of a distributed system. They belong in two categories: (1) techniques that monitor an application at the granularity of software architectural constructs (such as components, connectors, their interfaces); and (2) techniques that monitor an application at the granularity of system architectural constructs (such as software applications, hardware hosts, network links). Prominent examples of the first category are MonDe (Cook and Orso 2005), GAMMA (Orso et al. 2002), and COMPAS (Mos and Murphy 2004), while some prominent examples from the second category are JAMM (Tierney 2000) and Remos (Dinda et al. 2001).

Redeployment—in other words, mobility—is a process of installing, updating, and/or relocating a distributed software system. In a software architecture-based system, these activities fall under the larger category of dynamic reconfiguration, which encompasses run time changes to a software system's architecture via addition and removal of components, connectors, or their interconnections. Oreizy et al. (Oreizy 1998; Oreizy, Medvidović, and Taylor 1998; Oreizy et al. 1999) describe several aspects of dynamic reconfiguration, which determine the degree to which change can be reasoned about, specified, implemented, and governed. This work is further discussed in Chapter 14. Garlan et al. (Garlan, Cheng, and Schmerl 2003) propose a general purpose architecture-based adaptation framework, which monitors the system and leverages ADLs in adapting and achieving architectural conformance. However, this approach models the software architectural aspects of a system, but not those of the hardware platforms. Haas et al. (Haas, Droz, and Stiller 2003) provide a framework for autonomic service deployment in networks. The authors of this technique consider the scalability of their autonomic algorithms, which divide the network into partitions and perform a hierarchical deployment of network services. However, their approach is not applicable to application-level deployment. Finally, Software Dock (Hall, Heimbigner, and Wolf 1999) is a system of loosely coupled, cooperating, distributed components. It supports software producers by providing a Release Dock and a Field Dock. The Release Dock acts as a repository of software system releases. The Field Dock supports a software consumer by providing an interface to the consumer's resources, configuration, and deployed software systems. The Software Dock employs agents that travel from a Release Dock to a Field Dock in order to perform specific software deployment tasks.

11

Applied Architectures and Styles

The preceding chapters have described the core of software architecture, providing the notations, tools, and techniques that enable the designer to specify an architecture, implement, and deploy it. On the basis of those chapters one should be able to approach any design problem and successfully proceed. Such a simple declaration, however, belies the difficulties that arise when dealing with complex problems. Some problems just do not lend themselves to obvious solutions, or simple, uniform structures. One theme that characterized the chapter on designing architectures was benefiting from the lessons of experience. We continue that theme in this chapter, discussing how a wide variety of important and challenging architectural problems have been solved, thereby enhancing the repertoire of insights and styles that a designer possesses to bring to bear on his own problem.

Our motivation is the recognition that most new applications are complex, and must deal with a range of issues. Notably, many applications must deal with issues that arise from the application being on a computer network, wherein the application interacts with other software systems located remotely. Network-based applications may involve the Web, be focused on parallel computation, or focus on business-to-business interaction. We describe architectural styles for these and other applications.

In this chapter we also use the lens of software architecture to explicate a variety of design notions that are at least in part fundamentally architectural, but which have largely been described in idiosyncratic terms, such as "grid computing" and peer-to-peer (P2P) applications—terminology belonging to other computer science subcommunities, rather than software engineering. Such description enables a more direct comparison of their merits with alternative approaches to similar problems.

The goals of this chapter are thus to:

- Describe how the concepts from the previous chapters can be used, sometimes in combination, to solve challenging design problems.

- Highlight key issues in emerging application domains that have architectural implications, or where an architectural perspective is essential for system development within that domain.
- Show how emerging architectures, such as P2P, can be characterized and understood through the lens of software architecture.

The sections of this chapter deal first with distribution and network-related issues; the increasingly important topic of decentralized architectures is then considered. The chapter concludes with a section on architectures from a few specific domains.

11.1 DISTRIBUTED AND NETWORKED ARCHITECTURES

The phrase "distributed application" is used to denote everything from an application that is simply distributed across multiple operating system processes all running on the same physical uniprocessor, to integrated applications that run on multiple computers connected by the Internet. Distributed applications have been in general use since at least the late 1970s when commercial networking technologies began to proliferate, and became increasingly common in the 1980s with the advent of efficient remote procedure calls and the availability of cheap computing power at the fringes of the network. Consequently we do not pretend to offer anything remotely close to a detailed treatment of such applications here. A variety of excellent texts are available that treat the subject in depth [see, for example, (Emmerich 2000; Tanenbaum and van Steen 2002)].

In Chapter 4 we discussed one popular approach to constructing distributed applications, CORBA, as representative of a variety of similar approaches, such as The Open Group's Distributed Computing Environment (DCE) (The Open Group 2005). That presentation omitted consideration of the broader issues associated with distributed applications, hence we begin with that discussion here.

11.1.1 Limitations of the Distributed Systems Viewpoint

One of the principal motivations for the development of the CORBA technology, and indeed of much distributed computing technology, was to enable use of the object-oriented development style in a distributed computing context. A particular design choice the designers made was to attempt to provide the illusion of "location transparency." That is, that a developer should not need to know where a particular object is located in order to interact with that object. (Several other forms of transparency are also supported, such as implementation transparency wherein the developer need not know or be concerned with the choice of programming language in which a particular object is implemented.) If such transparency is provided to the developer, all the concerns and issues associated with working across a network can be ignored, for those issues will be taken care of by the underlying CORBA support.

Unfortunately a quick look at the details of CORBA's API, that is, the interface that programmers have to work with, reveals that achieving such transparency has not proved to be fully possible. CORBA has a variety of special mechanisms, visible to the programmer, which reveal the presence of a network underneath, and the possibility of various networking issues impacting the programming model, such as network failure or response timeout.

The multiple difficulties of attempting to mask the presence of networks and their properties from application developers was recognized early and became canonized by Peter Deutsch in his short list "Fallacies of Distributed Computing" (Deutsch and Gosling 1994). As Deutsch and his colleague James Gosling say, "Essentially everyone, when they first build a distributed application, makes the following eight assumptions. All prove to be false in the long run and all cause big trouble and painful learning experiences." The fallacies are, as stated by Gosling:

1. The network is reliable.
2. Latency is zero.
3. Bandwidth is infinite.
4. The network is secure.
5. Topology doesn't change.
6. There is one administrator.
7. Transport cost is zero.
8. The network is homogeneous.

Directly addressing any one of these issues may lead to particular architectural choices and concerns. For instance, if the network is unreliable, then the architecture of a system may need to be dynamically adaptable. The presence of latency (delay in the receipt or delivery of a message) may require applications to be able to proceed based upon locally created estimated values of messages, based upon the value of previously received messages. Bandwidth limitations, and bandwidth variability, may require inclusion of adaptive strategies to accommodate local conditions. Existence of more than one administrative domain may demand that explicit trust mechanisms be incorporated. Accommodating network heterogeneity may involve imposition of abstraction layers or a focus on interchange standards.

Dealing *explicitly* with these issues that arise due to the presence of networking leads to our consideration of network-based and decentralized architectures. Rather than attempting to be comprehensive in our coverage, however, we select several deep examples that reveal how architectures can be designed to accommodate specific needs and goals.

11.2 ARCHITECTURES FOR NETWORK-BASED APPLICATIONS

We begin with an extended discussion of the REpresentational State Transfer (REST) style, which was first introduced in Chapter 1. REST was created as part of the effort to take the Web from its earliest form to the robust, pervasive system that we rely upon today. The derivation of REST is instructive, as the interplay between requirements from the application domain (namely, distributed decentralized hypertext) and the constituent parts of the style can be clearly shown.

User Visibility of the Network

"Tanenbaum and van Renesse . . . make a distinction between distributed systems and network-based systems: a distributed system is one that looks to its users like an ordinary centralized system, but runs on multiple, independent CPUs. In contrast, network-based systems are those capable of operation across a network, but not necessarily in a fashion that is transparent to the user. In some cases it is desirable for the user to be aware of the difference between an action that requires a network request and one that is satisfiable on their local system, particularly when network usage implies an extra transaction cost. . . ." —Roy T. Fielding (Fielding 2000)

11.2.1   The REpresentational State Transfer Style (REST)

Chapter 1 of this textbook began with a brief exposition of the REST architectural style, describing how it was used to design the post-1994 World Wide Web (which includes the HTTP/1.1 protocol, the Uniform Resource Identifier specification, and other elements). The goal of that presentation was to begin to indicate the power of software architecture, showing its impact on one of the world's most widespread technologies. That presentation also indicated how software architecture is not something you can necessarily derive by looking at a piece of source code (for example, the Apache Web server), for the Web's architecture represents a set of design decisions that transcends many independent programs. It is the way those programs must work together that the REST style dictates.

The presentation in Chapter 1 did not describe how the REST style was developed: what motivated its creation and what prior architectural influences were combined to yield this influential style. The presentation below addresses these topics. Beyond just understanding the "why" of the Web, the reader should see how selected simple styles can be combined in judicious ways to address a complex, and conflicting, set of needs.

Application Drivers

The need for a next-generation Web arose from the outstanding success of the first generation—and the inability of that first generation's architecture to function adequately in the face of enormous growth in the extent and use of the Web. The characteristics of the Web as an application and the properties of its deployment and use provide the critical context for the development of REST.

The WWW is fundamentally a *distributed hypermedia* application. The conceptual notion is of a vast space of interrelated pieces of information. The navigation of that space is under the control of the user; when presented with one piece of information the user may choose to view another piece, where the reference to that second piece is contained in the first. The information is distributed across the Internet, hence one aspect of the application is that the information selected for viewing—which may be quite large—must be brought across the network to the user's machine for presentation. (Note that some current uses of the Web, such as for business-to-business transactions, do not fit this model, and are discussed later under Web services.)

Since the information must be brought to the user across the network, all of the network issues listed in the preceding section are of concern. Latency, for example, may determine user satisfaction with the navigation experience: Actions at the client/user agent (that is, the browser) must be kept fast. As large data sets are transferred it is preferable if some of the information can be presented to the user while the remainder of the data transfer takes place, so that the user is not left waiting. Since the Web is not only a distributed hypermedia application, but a *multi-user* application, provision must also be made for circumstances in which many users request the same information at the same time. The latency intrinsic in the transfer of the information is compounded by potential contention for access to the resource at its source.

The Web is also a heterogeneous, multi-owner application. One goal for the Web was to enable many parties to contribute to the distributed information space by allowing locally administered information spaces to be linked to that of the broader community, and to do so easily. This implies that the information space is not under a single authority—it is a *decentralized* application. The openness of the Web implies that neither the uniformity of supporting implementations nor the qualities of those implementations can be assumed. Moreover, the information so linked may not be reliably available. Previously available information may become unavailable, necessitating provision for dealing with broken links.

The heterogeneity of the Web also has a prospective view: Various contributors to the information space may identify new types of information to link (such as a new type of media) or new types of processing to perform in response to an information retrieval request. Provision for extension must therefore be made.

Lastly, the matter of scale dominates the concerns. Any proposed architectural style must be capable of maintaining the Web's services in the face of continuing rapid growth in both users and information providers. Keep in mind that REST was developed during a period when the number of Web sites was doubling every three to six months! The scale of the application today—in terms of users and sites—is far beyond what was imagined in 1994: 50 million active Web sites/100 million hostnames.

Derivation of REST

The REST style was created to directly address these application needs and design challenges. REST, as a set of design choices, drew from a rich heritage of architectural principles and styles, such as those presented in Chapter 4. Figure 11-1 summarizes the

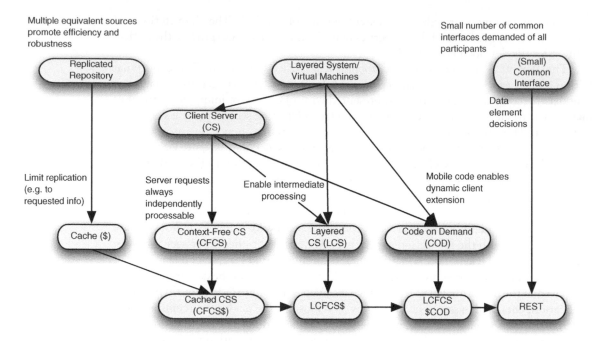

Figure 11-1. *Notional derivation of the REST style from simpler styles.*

architectural heritage of REST. Key choices in this derivation, explained in detail below, include:

- *Layered separation* (a theme in the middle portion of diagram), to increase efficiencies, enable independent evolution of elements of the system, and provide robustness.
- *Replication* (left side of the diagram), to address latency and contention by allowing the reuse of information.
- *Limited commonality* (right side) to address the competing needs for universally understood operations with extensibility.

Also critical in the derivation was the decision to require requests on the server to be independently serviceable or "context-free"; that is, the server can understand and process any request received based solely on the information in the request. This supports scalability and robustness. Finally, dynamic extension through mobile code addresses independent extensibility. The following paragraphs elaborate these issues and choices. More detailed expositions can be found in (Fielding 2000; Fielding and Taylor 2002).

Layered Separation. The core design decision for REST was the use of layered systems. As described in Chapter 4 layered systems can take many forms, including client-server and virtual machines. The separations based upon layering principles can be found several places in REST.

The use of a client-server (CS) architecture was intrinsic to the original Web. Browsers running on a user's machine have responsibility for presentation of information to the user and are the locus of determining the user's next interactions with the information space.

Servers have responsibility for maintaining the information that constitutes the Web, and delivering representations of that information to the clients. Software that addresses the user interface can hence evolve independently from the software that must manage large amounts of data and respond to requests from many sources. This separation of responsibilities simplifies both components and enables their optimization.

The client-server style is then further refined through imposition of the requirement that requests to a server be independently processable; that is, the server is able to understand and process any request based solely on the information in that one request. This design constraint is often referred to as a "stateless server," and the corresponding HTTP/1.1 protocol is often referred to as a "stateless protocol." This terminology is unfortunate, as it suggests that the server does not maintain *any* state. The server certainly may maintain state of various kinds: Previous client requests may have caused new information to be stored in a database maintained by the server, for instance. Rather, the focus here is that the server does not keep a record of any session of interactions with a client. With this requirement the server is free to deallocate any resources it used in responding to a client's request, including memory, after the request has been handled. In absence of this requirement the server could be obliged to maintain those resources until the client indicated that it would not be issuing any further requests in that session. In the diagram we have labeled this specialization of the CS style as "context-free" since a server request can be understood and processed independently of any surrounding context of requests.

Imposition of this requirement on interactions between clients and servers strongly supports scalability, as servers may efficiently manage their own resources—not leaving them tied up in expectation of a next request. Moreover, all servers with access to the same back-end databases become equal—any one of a number of servers may be used to handle a client request, allowing load sharing among the servers.

The possibility of cheap load balancing is a result of another application of layering in the design of REST. Intermediaries may be imposed in the path of processing a client request. An intermediary (such as a proxy) provides the required interface for a requested service. What happens behind that interface is hidden to the requestor. An intermediary, therefore, may determine which of several equivalent servers can be used to provide the best system performance, and direct calls accordingly. Intermediaries may also perform partial processing of requests, and can do so because all requests are self-contained. Finally, they may address some security concerns, such as enforcing boundaries past which specified information should not be allowed to flow.

Replication. The replication of information across a set of servers provides the opportunity for increased system performance and robustness. The existence of replication is hidden from clients, of course, as a result of intermediate layers.

One particular form of replication is caching information. Rather than duplicating information sources irrespective of the particular information actually requested of them, caches may maintain copies of information that has already been requested or that is anticipated to be requested. Caches may be located near clients (where they may be termed "proxies"), or near servers (where they may be termed "gateways"). The critical feature is that since requests are always self-contained, a single cache may be utilized by many different clients. If the cache determines, on the basis of inspecting the request message, that it has the required information, that information may be sent to the requestor without involving any processing on the part of a server. System performance is thus improved since the user obtains the desired information without incurring all the costs that would normally be expected. For this to work, responses from servers must be determined to be cacheable or not. For instance, if a request is for "the current temperature in Denver," the response is not cacheable since the temperature is continually varying. If the request, however, is for "the temperature in Denver at 24:00 on 01/01/2001," that value is cacheable since it is constant.

Limited Commonality. The parts of a distributed application can be made to work together either by demanding that a common body of code be used for managing all communications, or through imposition of standards governing that communication. In the latter case multiple, independent implementations are possible; communication is enabled because there is agreement upon how to talk. Clearly the use of standards to govern communication is superior to common code in an open, heterogeneous application. Innovation is fostered, local specializations may be supported, different hardware platforms used, and so on. The question, though, is what kind of communication standards should be imposed?

One option is the feature-rich style. In this approach, every possible type of interaction is anticipated and supported directly in the standard. This approach has the disadvantage that whenever any change to any part of the protocol is required, all implementations must be updated to conform. Another option, the one taken in REST, is essentially two-level: The first level (a) specifies how information is named and represented as meta-data, and (b) specifies a very few key services that every implementation must support. The second level focuses on the packaging of arbitrary data (including any type of request or operation encoded as data), in a standardized form for transmission. This is designed to be efficient for large-grain hypermedia data transfer, thus optimizing for the target application of the Web, but resulting in an interface that is not optimal for other forms of interaction.

Dynamic Extension. Allowing clients to receive arbitrary data, described by meta-data, in response to a request to a server allows client functionality to be extended dynamically. Data obtained by a client may be, for example, a script or an applet that the client could choose to execute. With such execution, the client is able to perform new functions and essentially be customized to that client's user's particular needs. REST thus incorporates the code-on-demand variant-style of mobile code.

Summary

REST is an exemplar of an architectural style driven by deep understanding of both the particular application domain supported (open network-distributed hypermedia) and the benefits that can be obtained from several simple architectural styles. Constraints from several styles are judiciously combined to yield a coherent architectural approach which is summarized in the box below. The success of the Web is due to this careful engineering.[1]

---

[1] The Web as it exists today in the form of the union of the HTTP/1.1, URI, and other standards, along with various server implementations, should not be equated with REST. Several elements of the Web in current use are at odds with REST; origins of this architectural drift are explored in Fielding's dissertation, as cited earlier.

Summary: Constrained client-server with focus on data elements communicated.

Components: Origin server (such as Apache httpd, Microsoft IIS); gateway (such as Squid, CGI); proxy; user agent (such as Safari, Internet Explorer, search bots)

Connectors: Client-side interface (such as libwww); server-side interface (such as Apache API); tunnel (such as SOCKS, SSL after HTTP CONNECT)

Data Elements: Resource (the intended conceptual target of a hypertext reference); resource identifier (URL); representation (such as HTML document, JPEG image); representation meta-data (such as media type, last-modified time); resource meta-data (such as source link, alternates); control data (such as if-modified-since, cache-control)

Topology: Multi-client/multi-server with intermediate proxies.

Constraints imposed: Six REST Principles, or RPs:

- *RP1:* The key abstraction of information is a resource, named by an URL. Any information that can be named can be a resource.

- *RP2:* The representation of a resource is a sequence of bytes, plus representation meta-data to describe those bytes. The particular form of the representation can be negotiated between REST components.

- *RP3:* All interactions are context-free—each interaction contains all of the information necessary to understand the request, independent of any requests that may have preceded it.

- *RP4:* Components perform only a small set of well-defined methods on a resource producing a representation to capture the current or intended state of that resource and transfer that representation between components. These methods are global to the specific architectural instantiation of REST; for instance, all resources exposed via HTTP are expected to support each operation identically.

- *RP5:* Idempotent operations and representation meta-data are encouraged in support of caching and representation reuse.

- *RP6:* The presence of intermediaries is promoted. Filtering or redirection intermediaries may also use both the meta-data and the representations within requests or responses to augment, restrict, or modify requests and responses in a manner that is transparent to both the user agent and the origin server.

Qualities yielded: Open, extensible, highly scalable network applications. Reduces network latency in distributed applications while facilitating component implementations that are independent and efficient.

Typical Uses: The World Wide Web (distributed hypermedia).

Cautions: Numerous Web sites and books purport to characterize or exemplify REST principles. The reader should be very cautious, as many sources misrepresent or mischaracterize REST.

Relations to Programming Languages or Environments: The code-on-demand and dynamic aspects of the Web favor languages such as JavaScript, Java, Scheme, Ruby, and Python.

Style: REpresentational State Transfer (REST)

The REST style is certainly a powerful tool to use in network-based applications where issues of latency and agency (authority boundaries)[2] are prominent. It is also instructive in guiding architects in the creation of other specialized styles. The trade-offs made in

---

[2] An agency boundary denotes the set of components operating on behalf of a common (human) authority, with the power to establish agreement within that set (Khare and Taylor 2004).

developing REST, such as how many operations to include in the limited interface specification, highlight that creation of such a style is not straightforward. Nonetheless combination of constraints from a variety of simpler styles can yield a powerful, customized tool.

11.2.2 Commercial Internet-Scale Applications

Akamai

The REST architecture has been successful in enabling the Web to scale through a time period when use of the Web was growing exponentially. One of the key features of REST that enabled that scaling was caching. While caching may potentially be performed by any component in a REST architecture, a key aspect of REST's support for caching is enabling the presence of intermediaries between a user agent and an origin server, in particular proxies. Proxies can store the results of HTTP GET requests; if the information so stored stays current for a time, further requests for that information that pass through that proxy may be satisfied by that proxy, without further routing the request on to the origin server. In dynamic, high-demand situations, however, proxies may not be able to prevent problems. Consider, for example, when a popular sporting event is being covered by a news company, maintaining a record of the event's progress on its Web site. As the event progresses many thousands of fans may attempt to access the information. Proxies throughout the Web will not be of much help because the information is being updated frequently—the contention will be for access to the origin server. These flash crowd demands for access to the origin server may induce it to fail or, at least, will induce unacceptable latency while each request is processed in turn.

Akamai's solution to the problem, in essence, is to replicate the origin server at many locations throughout the network, and direct a user agent's requests to the "replicant" origin server, called an edge server, closest to that user. This redirection, referred to as mapping, is performed when the Internet address (IP address) for the requested resource (such as www.example.com/bicycle-race/) is determined by the Internet Domain Name Server (DNS)—one of the first steps in processing an HTTP GET request. Akamai has located many thousands of its edge servers throughout the Internet, such as at the places where Internet Service Providers (ISPs) join their networks to the Internet. One of Akamai's strengths is in the way in which the closest edge server is identified. This calculation may involve the results of monitoring the status of parts of the Internet and computing locations whose access will be least impeded by demand elsewhere in the network. The edge servers, of course, will have to access the origin server to update their content, but by directing end user agent requests to the edge servers, demand on the origin server is kept manageable.

Viewed architecturally, Akamai further exploits the notion of replicated repositories. REST's separation of resources from representations enables many edge servers to provide representations of the resource located at the origin server. Further, REST's context-free interaction protocol enables many requests from a single user agent to be satisfied by several different edge servers. Akamai's redirection scheme succeeds because of the strong separations of concerns present in the Internet protocols.

Google

Google as a company has grown from offering one product—a search engine—to a wide range of applications. Since the search engine and so many of Google's products are so closely tied to the Web one might expect the system architecture(s) to be REST-based. They are not. Google's systems are architecturally interesting, however, because they address matters of scale similar to the Web, but the nature of the applications and the business strategy of the company demands a very different architecture. Google is interesting as well because of the number of different products that share common elements.

The fundamental characteristic of many of Google's applications is that they rest upon the ability to manipulate very large quantities of information. Terabytes of data from the Web and other sources are stored, studied, and manipulated in various ways to yield the company's information products. The company's business strategy has been to support this storage and manipulation using many tens of thousands of commodity hardware platforms. In short, inexpensive PCs running Linux. The key notion is that by supporting effective replication of processing and data storage, a fault-tolerant computing platform can be built that is capable of scaling to enormous size. The design choice is to buy cheap and plan that failure, of all types, will occur and must be effectively accommodated. The alternative design would be to buy, for example, a high-capacity, high-reliability database system, and replicate it as required. Whether this would be as cost-effective is debatable (it most probably would not), but another key insight from Google's design process is that their applications do not require all the features of a full relational database system. A simpler storage system, offering fewer features, but running atop a highly fault-tolerant platform meets the needs in a cost-effective manner. This system, know as the Google File System, or GFS, is the substrate that manages Google's highly distributed network of storage systems. It is optimized in several ways differently from prior distributed file systems: The files are typically very large (several gigabytes), failure of storage components is expected and handled, files are typically appended to (rather than randomly modified), and consistency rules for managing concurrent access are relaxed.

Running atop GFS are other applications, notable of which is MapReduce. It offers a programming model in which users focus their attention on specifying data selection and reduction operations. The supporting MapReduce implementation is responsible for executing these functions across the huge data sets in the GFS. Critically, the MapReduce library is responsible for all aspects of parallelizing the operation, so that the thousands of processors available can be effectively brought to bear on the problem without the developer having to deal explicitly with those matters. Once again, the system is designed to gracefully accommodate the expected failure of processors involved in the parallel execution.

The architectural lessons from Google are several:

- Abstraction layers abound: GFS hides details of data distribution and failure, for instance; MapReduce hides the intricacies of parallelizing operations.
- Designing, from the outset, for living with failure of processing, storage, and network elements, allows a highly robust system to be created.
- Scale is everything. Google's business demands that everything be built with scaling issues in mind.
- Specializing the design to the problem domain, rather than taking the generic "industry standard" approach, allows high-performance and very cost effective solutions to be developed.
- Developing a general approach (MapReduce) to the data extraction/reduction problem allowed a highly reusable service to be created.

The contrast between the last two points is instructive: On the one hand, a *less general* solution strategy was adopted (a specialized file system rather than a general database), and on the other hand, a *general* programming model and implementation was created (abstracting across the needs of many of Google's applications). Both decisions, while superficially at odds, arise from deep knowledge of what Google's applications are—what they demand and what key aspects of commonality are present.

11.3 DECENTRALIZED ARCHITECTURES

In the preceding discussion of REST we referred to the World Wide Web as being a distributed, *decentralized*, hypermedia application. Decentralization refers to the multiple authority, or *agency*, domains participating in an application. The sense is that the various parts of an application are owned and controlled by various parties, and those parts communicate over a network (hence decentralization essentially implies *distribution* as well) to achieve the goals of the application. The Web is a good example of this cooperation between independent agencies. The millions of Web sites around the world are owned and controlled by as many individuals and organizations. By agreeing to the basic standards of the Web, such as HTTP, any user may traverse the Web to obtain information, and in so doing may cross many agency boundaries.

Designing decentralized software architectures poses challenges beyond the design of distributed systems. Designing decentralized applications is not, however, a new idea: Everyday society is filled with designed decentralized applications. International postal mail is one large-scale example; individual countries issue their own postage stamps and control local collection and delivery of mail. International post, however, involves cooperation at several levels between the parties involved, including standards to govern how mail is addressed, how postage is marked, and the agreements that are in place to govern the physical routing and hand off of mail. International commerce is an even more extensive and rich example.

Decentralized architectures are created whenever the parties desiring to participate in an application want to retain autonomous control over aspects of their participation. Web site owners, for instance, typically want to retain the ability to take their sites offline at arbitrary times, to add new content, or to add new servers. Such autonomy can be the source of many design challenges. Since there is no single authority, there is no guarantee, for example, that a participant in a system will always be participating with the best of intentions. Decentralized systems are also distributed, so coping with the new challenges of multiple agencies comes on top of the challenges of dealing with latency and the other issues of distribution.

Computer application developers have worked so long in a world where applications were fundamentally centralized in terms of authority (even if under the banner of "distributed systems") that as we begin to build new applications we have to call those assumptions into question and adapt to new realities. This section explores several systems and approaches that have been designed to both exploit the advantages of open, decentralized systems, while mitigating some of the problems encountered. We begin the discussion by briefly discussing grid computing, then focus on several peer-to-peer systems, as they simply and clearly illustrate some of the challenges and design solutions possible. Discussion then turns to Web services, a design approach targeted to supporting business-to-business interactions.

11.3.1 Shared Resource Computation: The Grid World

Grid computing is coordinated resource sharing and computation in a decentralized environment. The notion is to allow, for example, a team of researchers to temporarily bring numerous diverse hardware and software resources to bear on a computational problem. The resources may be under the authority of various owners, but for the time when the grid is logically in place the system behaves as though it is a distributed application under a single authority.

The supporting grid technology is designed to make transparent all the details of managing the diverse and distributed resources. Included in this goal of transparency is management of the details of crossing authority boundaries. A *single sign-on* is thus a particular goal. Grid applications have been used to support visualization of earthquake simulation data, simulate the flow of blood, support physics simulations, and so on.

While many different grid systems have been built, a common architecture for them has been put forth (Foster, Kesselman, and Tuecke 2001), as shown in Figure 11-2. The architecture is layered, with the ability of components within any layer to build upon services provided by any lower layer. The Application layer contains the components that implement the user's particular system. The Collective layer is responsible for coordinating the use of multiple resources. The Resource layer is responsible for managing the sharing of a single resource. The Connectivity layer is responsible for communication and authentication. The Fabric layer manages the details of the low-level resources that ultimately comprise the grid; the upper layers provide a convenient set of abstractions to this set of resources. The diagram particularly calls out the notion of the application layer calling upon the first three layers below it, but not the Fabric layer. Presumably this is to indicate that management of the lowest-level resources is best left to the grid infrastructure.

Unfortunately the elegance and clean design of this architecture is not fully maintained by several popular and well-known grid technologies. By performing architectural recovery

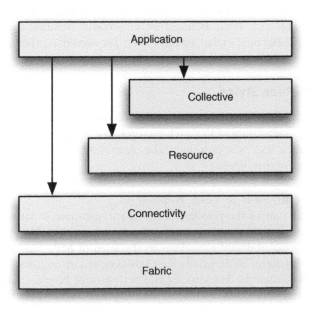

Figure 11-2. *Architecture of the Grid, according to Foster, Kesselman, and Tuecke. Adapted from (Foster, Kesselman, and Tuecke 2001).*

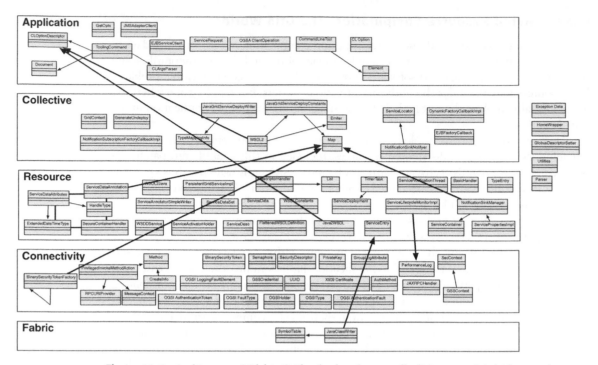

Figure 11-3. *Architecture of Globus Grid technology (recovered). (Mattmann, Medvidović et al. 2005).*

based upon the source code of grid systems, an as-built architecture can be compared to the prescriptive architecture of Figure 11-2. For example, Figure 11-3 portrays the recovered architecture of the Globus grid system (Mattmann, Medvidović et al. 2005). In this case, for example, several up-calls in the architecture are present, violating the layered systems principle. Similar architectural violations have been discovered in other grid technologies as well.

11.3.2 Peer-to-Peer Styles

Chapter 4 introduced the idea of peer-to-peer architectures. Discussion there centered on the fundamental characteristics of P2P architectures, but did not present many details or rationale for when the style is appropriate. The examples below, Napster, Gnutella, and Skype, provide some of this detail.

Hybrid Client-Server/Peer-to-Peer: Napster

P2P systems became part of the popular technical parlance due in large measure to the popularity of the original Napster system that appeared in 1999. Napster was designed to facilitate the sharing of digital recordings in the form of MP3 files. Napster was not, however, a true P2P system. Its design choices, however, are instructive.

Figure 11-4 illustrates the key entities and activities of Napster. Each of the peers shown is an independent program residing on the computers of end users. Operation begins

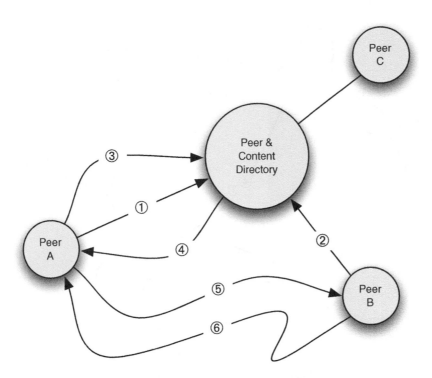

Figure 11-4.
Notional view of the operation of Napster. In steps 1 and 2, Peers A and B log in with the server. In step 3, Peer A queries the server where it can find Rondo Veneziano's "Masquerade." The location of Peer B is returned to A (step 4). In step 5, A asks B for the song, which is then transferred to A (step 6).

with the various peers registering themselves with the Napster central server, labeled in the figure as the Peer & Content Directory. When registering, or later logging in, a peer informs the server of the peer's Internet address and the music files resident at that peer that the peer is willing to "share." The server maintains a record of the music that is available, and on which peers. Later, a peer may query the server as to where on the Internet a given song can be obtained. The server responds with available locations; the peer then chooses one of those locations, makes a call directly to that peer, and downloads the music.

Architecturally, this system can be seen as a hybrid of client-server and pure P2P. The peers act as clients when registering with the Peer & Content Directory and querying it. Once a peer knows where to ask for a song, a P2P exchange is initiated; any peer may thus sometimes act as a client (asking others for a song) or as a server (delivering a song it has to another peer in response to a request). Napster chose to use a propriety protocol for interactions between the peers and the content directory; HTTP was used for fetching the content from a peer. (The decision to use a proprietary protocol offered dubious benefits, including limiting file sharing to MP3 files.)

The architectural cleanness of this design is also its downfall. If, for example, a highly desired song becomes available, the server will be swamped with requests seeking its location(s). And of course, should the server go down, or be taken down by court order, all peers lose the ability to find other peers.

Pure Decentralized P2P: Gnutella
Alleviating the design limitations of Napster was one of the design goals of Gnutella (Kan 2001). Gnutella's earliest version was a pure P2P system; there is no central server—all

Figure 11-5.
*Notional
interactions
between peers
using the original
Gnutella
protocol.*

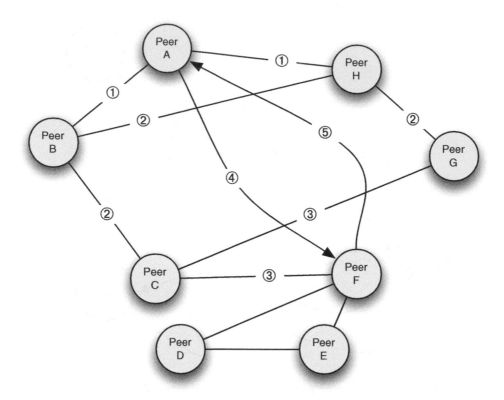

peers are equal in capability and responsibility. Figure 11-5 helps to illustrate the basic protocol. Similar to Napster, each of the peers is a user running software that implements the Gnutella protocol on an independent computer on the Internet. If Peer A, for instance, is seeking a particular song (or recipe) to download, he issues a query to the Gnutella peers on the network that he knows about, Peers B and H, in step 1. Assuming they do not have the song, they pass the query along further, to the peers they know about: each other, and Peers C and G, in step 2. Propagation of the query proceeds to spread throughout the network either until some retransmission threshold is exceeded (called the "hop count") or until a peer is reached that has the desired song. If we assume that Peer F has the song, it responds to the peer that asked it (Peer C in step 3), telling Peer C that it has the song. Peer C then relays that information, including the network address of Peer F, to the peers that requested the information from it.

Eventually, Peer A will obtain the address of Peer F and can then initiate a direct request to F in step 4 to download the song. The song is downloaded in step 5. As with Napster, the Gnutella protocol was custom designed, but the direct download of the music was accomplished using an HTTP GET request.

Several issues facing P2P systems are apparent in this example. When a new peer comes on to the network, how does it find any other peers to which its queries can be sent? When a query is issued, how many peers will end up being asked for the requested resource *after* some other peer has already responded and provided the information? Keep in mind that all the peers know only of the requests that they have received, and the requests that they have issued or passed along; they do not have global knowledge. How long should the requesting peer wait to obtain a response? How efficient is the whole process?

Perhaps most interesting, when a peer responds that it has the requested resource, and the requestor downloads it, what assurance does the requestor have that the information downloaded is that which was sought? Experience with Gnutella reveals what might be expected: Frequently the majority of responses to a resource request were viruses or other malware, packaged to superficially appear as the requested resource.

These significant weaknesses aside, a critical observation of Gnutella is that it is highly robust. Removal of any one peer from the network, or any set of peers, does not diminish the ability of the remaining peers to continue to perform. Removal of a peer may make a specific resource unavailable if that peer was the unique source for that resource, but if a resource was available from several sources it could conceivably still be found and obtained even if many peers were removed from the network. In this regard, Gnutella reflects the basic design of the Internet: Intermediate routers and subnetworks may come and go, yet the Internet protocol provides highly robust delivery of packets from sources to destinations.

Despite the benefit of being highly robust, the intrinsic limitations of the Gnutella approach have led to the search for improved mechanisms. Recent versions of Gnutella have adopted some of the Napsterish use of "special peers" for improvement of, for instance, the peer location process.

Napster and Gnutella are interesting mostly for their historical role and for ease in explaining the benefits and limitations of P2P architectures. A mature, commercial use of P2P is found in Skype, which we consider next.

Overlayed P2P: Skype

Skype is a popular Internet communication application built on a P2P architecture.[3] To use Skype, a user must download the Skype application from Skype (only). In contrast to Gnutella, there are no open-source implementations, and the Skype protocol is proprietary and secret. When the application is run, the user must first register with the Skype login server. Subsequent to that interaction the system operates in a P2P manner.

Figure 11-6 illustrates how the application functions in more detail. The figure shows Peer 1 logging into the Skype server. That server then tells the Skype peer the address of Supernode A which the peer then contacts. When Peer 1 wants to see if any of his buddies are online, the query is issued to the supernode. When the user makes a Skype call (that is, a voice call over the Internet), the interaction will proceed from the calling peer to the supernode, and then either to the receiving peer directly (such as to Peer 2) or to another supernode and then to the receiving peer. If both peers are on public networks, not behind firewalls, then the interaction between the peers may be set up directly, as is shown in the figure between Peer 2 and Peer 3.

Supernodes provide, at least, directory services and call routing. Their locations are chosen based upon network characteristics and the processing capacity of the machine they run on, as well as the load on that machine. While the login server is under the authority of Skype.com, the supernode machines are not. In particular, *any* Skype peer has the potential

---

[3]Skype is a trademark of Skype Limited or other related companies.

Figure 11-6.
*Notional instance
of the Skype
architecture.*

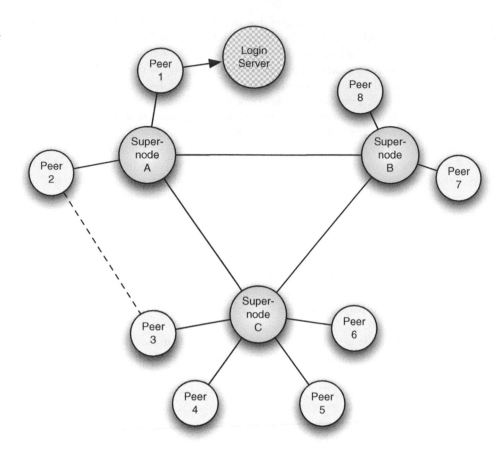

of becoming a supernode. Skype peers get "promoted" to supernode status based upon their history of network and machine performance. The user who downloaded and installed the peer does not have the ability to disallow the peer from becoming a supernode. Note the potential consequences of this for some users. Suppose a machine's owner installs a Skype peer, and that the owner pays for network connectivity based upon the amount of traffic that flows in and out of the machine on which the peer is installed. If that peer becomes a supernode, the owner then will bear the real cost of routing a potentially large number of calls—calls the owner does not participate in and does not even know are occurring.

Several aspects of this architecture are noteworthy:

- A mixed client-server and peer-to-peer architecture addresses the discovery problem. The network is not flooded with requests in attempts to locate a buddy, such as would happen with the original Gnutella.
- Replication and distribution of the directories, in the form of supernodes, addresses the scalability and robustness problems encountered in Napster.

- Promotion of ordinary peers to supernodes based upon network and processing capabilities addresses another aspect of system performance: "Not just any peer" is relied upon for important services. Moreover, as many nodes as are dynamically required can become supernodes.

- A proprietary protocol employing encryption provides privacy for calls that are relayed through supernode intermediaries.

- Restriction of participants to clients issued only by Skype, and making those clients highly resistant to inspection or modification, prevents malicious clients from entering the network, avoiding the Gnutella problem.

This last point prevents us from too strongly asserting how Skype works. The details provided here have resulted from extensive study of Skype by third-party scientists, citations for which are provided at the end of the chapter. The accompanying sidebar description of Skype is from material provided on the Skype.com Web site.

Skype on Skype from www.skype .com

"The following are some of the techniques that Skype employs to deliver state-of-the-art IP-based telephony.

Firewall and NAT (Network Address Translation) traversal: Non-firewalled clients and clients on publicly routable IP addresses are able to help NAT'ed nodes to communicate by routing calls. This allows two clients who otherwise would not be able to communicate to speak with each other. Because the calls are encrypted end-to-end, proxies limit the security or privacy risk.

Likewise, only proxies with available spare resources are chosen so that the performance for these users is not affected.

Several new techniques were also developed in order to avoid end-user configuration of gateways and firewalls, whose nonintuitive configuration settings typically prohibit the majority of users from communicating successfully. In short, Skype works behind the majority of firewalls and gateways with no special configuration.

Global decentralized user directory: Most instant message or communication software requires some form of centralized directory for the purposes of establishing a connection between end users in order to associate a static username and identity with an IP number that is likely to change. This change can occur when a user relocates or reconnects to a network with a dynamic IP address. Most Internet-based communication tools track users with a central directory which logs each username and IP number and keeps track of whether users are online or not. Central directories are extremely costly when the user base scales into the millions. By decentralizing this resource-hungry infrastructure, Skype is able to focus all of our resources on developing cutting-edge functionality.

. . . The Global Index technology is a multi-tiered network where supernodes communicate in such a way that every node in the network has full knowledge of all available users and resources with minimal latency.

Intelligent routing: By using every possible resource, Skype is able to intelligently route encrypted calls through the most effective path possible. Skype even keeps multiple connection paths open and dynamically chooses the one that is best suited at the time. This has the noticeable effect of reducing latency and increasing call quality throughout the network."
—2008 © "Skype Limited"

Resource Trading P2P: BitTorrent

BitTorrent is another peer-to-peer application whose architecture has been specialized to meet particular goals. The primary goal is to support the speedy replication of large files on individual peers, upon demand. The distinctive approach of BitTorrent is to attempt to maximize use of all available resources in the network of interested peers to minimize the burden on any one participant, thus promoting scalability.

The problem that BitTorrent solves can be seen by considering what happens in either Napster or Gnutella, as described above, when one peer in the network has a popular item. Any peer who announces availability of a resource (either by registering the resource with the Napster server, or responding to a network query in the case of Gnutella) can quickly become the recipient of a very large number of requests for that resource—possibly more than the machine can support. These flash crowds burden the peer-server possessing the resource and can hence dissuade the server's owner from participating further in the P2P network.

BitTorrent's approach is to distribute parts of a file to many peers and to hence distribute both the processing and networking loads over many parts of the peer network. A peer does not obtain the requested large file from a single resource; rather the pieces of the file are obtained from many peers and then reassembled. Moreover, the requesting peer does not only download the pieces, but is also responsible for uploading the portions of the file that it has to other interested peers—keep in mind the operating context is one in which many peers are simultaneously interested in obtaining a copy of the file.

Architecturally, BitTorrent has made the following key decisions:

- Responsibility for the discovery of content is outside the scope of BitTorrent. Potential users use other means, such as Web searches, to locate content on the Web.
- A designated (centralized) machine called the tracker is used to oversee the process by which a file is distributed to an interested set of peers, but the tracker does not perform any of the file transfer. Peers use interaction with this machine to identify the other peers with which they communicate to effect the download.
- Meta-data is associated with the file, and is used throughout the download process. The meta-data describes how the large file is "pieced," the attributes of those pieces, and the location of the tracker.
- Each peer participating in a file's replication runs a BitTorrent application that determines (a) what piece of the file to download next, and (b) which peer to obtain that piece from. All the participating peers maintain knowledge of which peers have which pieces. The algorithms are designed to achieve the goals of quick distribution through maximizing use of the resources available at all peers. (If a peer is manipulated so that it does not participate in uploading pieces, but only downloading, it is penalized by the other peers through deprioritization of access to the pieces that it needs.)

As with all well-designed P2P applications, BitTorrent accounts for the possibility of any given peer dropping out of the process at any time.

11.3.3   Summary Notes on Latency and Agency

The preceding sections have covered applications and architectures that have substantial complexity resulting from the need to deal with two primary issues in decentralized systems:

latency and agency. Latency has been understood as an issue for a long time, and strategies for dealing with it are well known. Caching of results, intelligent searching strategies, and judicious use of centralized servers can all play roles in reducing latency.

Agency is a richer issue, and of more recent concern. Agency implies concerns with heterogeneity (such as of programming language platforms), unreliability, uncertainty, trust, and security. Effectively coping with all the concerns induced by multiple agencies requires careful thought. The REST style, and styles derived from it, offer proven guidance for dealing with several aspects of both agency and latency. Other issues remain, though, such as trust and security, as discussed in Chapter 13.

11.4 SERVICE-ORIENTED ARCHITECTURES AND WEB SERVICES

Service-oriented architectures (SOA) are directed at supporting business enterprises on the Internet. The notion is that business A could obtain some processing service b from vendor B, service c from vendor C, service d from vendor C, and so on. The service that A obtains from C might be based upon the result obtained from B in a preceding interaction. As a more specific example, a company might obtain bids from multiple travel agencies for a requested travel itinerary, select one of the travel agencies, then have that agency interact directly with subcontractors to contract the various specific services. Such services might include ticketing airline flights, obtaining a credit check, and issuing electronic payments to a vendor. All these interactions would be supported by SOA mechanisms.

Independence of the various interacting organizations, or at least of the services comprising a SOA, is fundamental to the SOA vision. Accordingly service-oriented architectures are conceptually part of the decentralized design space. SOAs must deal with all the network issues of distributed systems, plus the trust, discovery, and dynamism issues present in open, decentralized systems. Indeed, service-oriented architectures are the computer-based equivalents of the decentralized systems we see active in ordinary person-to-person commerce: Businesses and customers interact with each other in myriad, complex ways. Customers have to find businesses that offer the services they require, must determine if a business proffering a service is trustworthy, engage subcontractors, handle defaults, and so on.

From an architectural perspective, participating organizations on the Internet present a virtual machine layer of services of which users (client programs) may avail themselves. This view is portrayed in Figure 11-7, where a client has an objective (such as obtaining all the reservations, tickets, and travel advances associated with an itinerary) and calls upon various services throughout the Internet to meet this objective. Various of these services may themselves call upon other services on the network to achieve their subgoals. The virtual machine of the service-network is rather unlike the virtual machine architectures discussed in Chapter 4, however. The various SOA services, corresponding to functions in a classical virtual machine architecture, are offered by different controlling agencies; they may be implemented in widely varying ways, pose varying risks (such as being impersonated by a malicious agency), may come and go over time, and so on. The challenge, thus, is to provide the necessary support to a client who wants to use the service-network to achieve its goals. *Web services*, a particular way of providing an SOA, responds to this challenge by offering up a plethora of approaches, standards, and technologies.

Figure 11-7.
*Web services as a
layered, virtual
machine.*

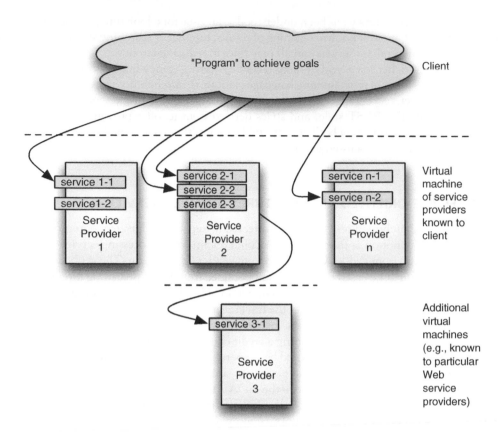

The core problem is, how, architecturally, should the notion of business applications created using the virtual machine of the service network be realized? The answer, not surprisingly, entails:

- Describing the components—that is, the services.
- Determining the types of connectors to use—how the services will communicate and interact.
- Describing the application as a whole—how the various services are orchestrated to achieve the business goals.

Additionally one might also consider how new services are discovered, since the context is one in which independent agencies may create new services that enterprises may want to weave into their current processes.

The services of SOAs are simply independent components, as we have discussed and illustrated throughout the text. They have an interface describing what operations they provide. They have their own thread of control. Services can be described in the Web services world using WSDL—the Web Services Description Language. WSDL describes services using XML as a collection of operations that may be performed on typed data sent to/from the service. In a more general SOA context, their interfaces may

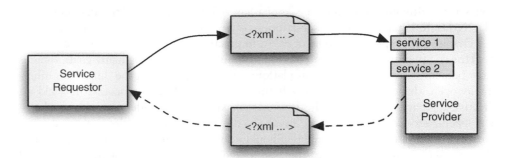

Figure 11-8.
*Two models of
Web service
interaction.*

be described by APIs written in some particular programming language, such as Java or Ruby.

Connectors are the more interesting part of SOAs. The simplest mechanism used by SOA is asynchronous event notification. The top half of Figure 11-8 illustrates this. The basic model in this example is that a service requestor sends an XML document to a service provider across the network by any of a variety of protocols, anything from e-mail to HTTP. The obligation on both parties is that the XML document be structured so that both understand it. In this simplest model, the service provider may take some action upon receiving and reading the document, but there is no obligation for the provider to return anything to the requestor. Naturally, there are many situations where the desired interaction is indeed for the provider to return information to the requestor; that is supported too, and is shown in the dotted lines in the bottom half of Figure 11-8. Note that in this second example, the connection model has shifted from one-way, asynchronous events to an asynchronous request-response model, resembling a remote procedure call or perhaps a distributed object method invocation.

One key point here, of course, is that such interactions do not have the same semantics as a remote procedure call or the semantics of a distributed object invocation. The presence of agency issues, interaction based upon XML document exchange, and absence of various programming semantics, such as object persistence, are the bases for the differences.

With regard to the application as a whole, in essence what is required is an architecture description language, such as considered at length in Chapter 6. SOAs demand, however, that the ADL used must be executable; formality and complete semantics are thus required. Essentially, an SOA application could be described in a generic scripting language, but so doing would likely obscure important relationships between the services. The more natural choice is to use a language that allows effective expression of business workflows/processes. One language used is WS-BPEL, the Web Services Business Process Execution Language. BPEL is a scripting language that is compositional; that is, a BPEL program can appear as a service (component) in another workflow. The language is statically typed and expressed in XML, though proprietary graphical editors are available.

Other architectural styles and concepts appear throughout SOAs. Notable is the use of publish-subscribe mechanisms for discovery of newly available services or service providers. Other developers have created declarative models for utilizing Web services, akin to the interpreter style discussed in Chapter 4. Most—if not all—of the styles discussed in Chapter 4 have been used somewhere in the Web services world. (Note however that though the

Web services literature sometimes speaks of a "layered set of protocols" this does not imply a layered architecture, as protocol descriptions often do not correspond to components.)

Despite the simple core model of SOA, in practice there is a great deal of complexity. This complexity arises from attempting to simultaneously satisfy many goals, such as interoperability across heterogeneous platforms, while coping with the difficulties inherent in open, decentralized systems. All this complexity does not necessarily yield an effective approach. For instance, the decision to make service providers announce and support specific services that others can "invoke"—the virtual machines decision—induces a particular kind of fragility and rigidity. Should a service provider ever change the interface to a service then all users of that service must become aware of the change and modify their requests accordingly. This is directly analogous to the problems of programming in a language such as Java and having a public method signature be modified—all of the code that is dependent on that interface must change. For this and other reasons, many decentralized enterprise application developers have chosen to base their designs on REST (thus focusing on the exchange of representations/data), rather than SOAP/Web services (thus focusing on the invocation of functions with arguments).[4] Amazon.com, for example, offers its Web services to developers either in REST form or as SOAP/Web Services interfaces. In practice, the REST-based interfaces have proven popular with developers.

This SOA design decision to focus on invocation of functional interfaces was not the only option. Just as not all programs depend on calls to public interfaces, an SOA could have been defined wherein service *requestors* pose descriptions of *computations* that they want performed, and leave it to service providers to determine if they are able to perform that computation and, if so, how.

Words about Words in Web Services

Popular literature regarding Web services is replete with acronyms and jargon; some reader caution is in order. The Web services standard that governs how the exchanged XML documents are to be structured and exchanged is SOAP. SOAP used to stand for "Simple Object Access Protocol," but of course "objects" are not being accessed, so SOAP is now just a name—but one where all the letters are always capitalized.

Similarly Web services are sometimes described as being "RPC over HTTP," when HTTP is used as the transport protocol for SOAP messages. Of course the actions are not the same as for a remote procedure call, so this is inaccurate as well.

Use of the term "Web services" would suggest that Web technology is necessarily involved in Web services—such as a Web server or browser. Web servers such as Apache are not necessary to respond to a SOAP message, so "Web services" is a misnomer too.

The fun starts when you get to the acronyms. They cover standards and approaches for building various "architectural" models on top of a service network, for governing exchange of information in the network, for dealing with the many complexities of a multi-agency, networked world, and so on. The aggregate of the Web service specifications (such as WS-Security, WS-MessageData, WS-Events, WS-Coordination, WS-Policy, WS-Reliability, and many others) is sometimes referred to as WS-*, otherwise known as "the Web services Death Star." *Caveat emptor.*

---

[4]See the feature, "Words about Words in Web Services," to learn about the term SOAP.

11.5 ARCHITECTURES FROM SPECIFIC DOMAINS

This section examines the architectures of applications from a few specific domains. Through this examination we show, by example, how various architectural styles and patterns have been refined and exploited to provide the foundational core of effective solutions. While the architectures are drawn from specific application domains, the techniques used in developing the solution architectures, the analyses that accompanied the design, and even the resulting styles themselves are widely useful, extending beyond the confines of these source domains.

11.5.1 Robotics

The field of robotics consists of a class of systems that reveals a great deal of diversity based on differences in the degree of autonomy and mobility the various robotic systems exhibit. Exemplars of this variety are:

- Mobile tele-operated systems, such as bomb disposal robots, where full or partial control of the robot system's movement and actions is in the hands of a human operator who may be located hundreds of miles away.
- Industrial automation systems, such as automotive assembly robotic arms, which autonomously perform predefined tasks without the need to move or adjust to their environment, as it is assumed that the environment, by design, conforms to the robot's task and movements.
- Mobile autonomous robots, such as DARPA Grand Challenge vehicles, which are not only responsible for their own autonomous control without human intervention but have to also traverse through and deal with unpredictable environments.

Challenges

From an architectural and general software engineering perspective, two factors are primarily responsible for making software development challenging in the robotics domain: the physical platforms and devices comprising the robots and the unpredictable nature of the environments in which they operate.

Robotic platforms are integrations of a large number of sensitive devices prone to malfunctions, such as wireless radio communications and vision sensors, complicating the need to coherently integrate the devices. The software systems operating robotic platforms must be capable of continued operation in the face of diminished hardware capacity and the loss of essential functions. The information provided by hardware devices such as sensors may also exhibit a high degree of unreliability and intermittent spikes of erroneous sensor readings, necessitating the capacity to not only continue operating but also to compensate seamlessly for such errors.

The second challenging element is the need to operate within environments that can be dynamic and unpredictable. Developing a mobile robot that can traverse unknown terrain through varying weather conditions and with potentially moving obstacles, for example, greatly increases the difficulty of designing its software control systems in a way that can account for and continue operating under conditions not fully predicted during the system's design and development.

Given these challenges and the nature of the domain, several software qualities are of special interest in robotic architectures: robustness, performance, reusability, and adaptability. The unreliability of many robotic environments motivates the need for robustness; the often stringent demands of working within a real-time environment (the world in which the robot operates) induces specific performance requirements. The need for reuse of developed software components across a variety of robotic systems is driven by the high cost of developing the high-performance and reliable modules necessary for the domain. Moreover, many robotic platforms use the same or very similar hardware components and therefore share a common need for drivers and interfaces for those devices. Finally, adaptability is particularly important given that the same hardware platform can be used with a modified software control system in order to perform a different task with unchanged devices.

Robotic Architectures

Robotic architectures have their origins in artificial intelligence techniques for knowledge representation and reasoning. They have been subsequently improved in response to shortcomings in the application of these concepts, as well as general advances in the field. The following sections present a brief overview of this progression, discussed in the context of specific architectural examples, the trends they embody, and their key architectural decisions and goals.

Sense-Plan-Act. Recognizing the inability of building robotic systems solely using artificial intelligence search algorithms over a world model, the *sense-plan-act* (SPA) architecture (Nilsson 1980) identifies the necessity of using continuous feedback from the environment of a robot as an explicit input to the planning of actions. SPA architectures contain three coarse-grained components with a unidirectional flow of communication between them, as illustrated in Figure 11-9: The *sense* component is responsible for gathering sensor information from the environment and is the primary interface and driver of a robot's sensors. This sensor information is provided as an input to the *plan* component, which uses this input to determine which actions the robot should perform, which are then communicated to the *act* component—the interface and driver for the robot's motors and actuators—for execution. To this level of detail the architecture resembles the sense-compute-control (SCC) pattern of Chapter 4. A closer look reveals an important distinction, however.

Figure 11-9.
An illustration of SPA architectures. The emphasis is on planning actions based on its internal world model subarchitecture.

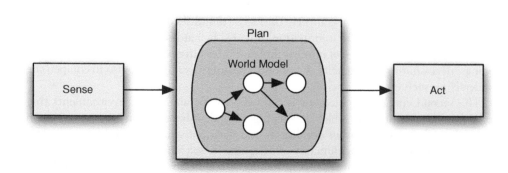

The *plan* component is the primary driver of robot behavior in SPA architectures. Borrowing from artificial intelligence techniques, planning involves the use of sensory data to reconcile the robot's actual state—as deduced by this sensory data—with an internal *model of the robot's state in the environment*. This internal model is then used in conjunction with a task specification to determine which actions should be performed next by the *act* component in order to complete the robot's intended activity. The internal model is repeatedly updated in response to newly acquired sensory inputs, indicating what progress the robot is making (if any), with the objective of keeping the model consistent with the actual environmental conditions. The SCC pattern, in contrast, does not maintain such a model or perform sophisticated planning.

From an architectural perspective, the SPA architecture captures an iterative unidirectional data flow between the three components, similar to a pipe-and-filter architecture, with a subarchitecture for the *plan* component varying and depending on the kind of planning and robot state model used by a specific SPA architecture.

Systems following the SPA architecture suffer from a number of issues primarily relating to performance and scalability. The main drawback is that sensor information must be integrated—referred to as sensor fusion—and incorporated into the robot's planning models in order for actions to be determined at *each step* of the architecture's iteration: These operations are quite time-consuming and usually cannot keep up with the rate of environmental change. The performance of this iterative model-update-and-evaluation does not scale well as robotic system capabilities and goals expand. This poor performance is a handicap when the environment changes quickly or unpredictably, and is the primary driver for the development of alternative robotic architectures.

Subsumption. Attempting to address the drawbacks of SPA architectures, the subsumption architecture (Brooks 1986) makes a fundamental architectural decision: the abandonment of complete world models and plans as the central element of robotic systems. While the flow of information originates at sensors and eventually terminates at actuators that effect action (as in SPA and SCC architectures), there is no explicit planning step interposed between this flow. Subsumption architectures—as can be seen in Figure 11-10—are

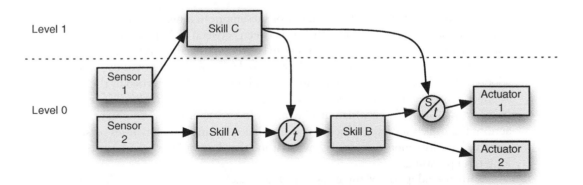

Figure 11-10. *An illustration of an example subsumption architecture, showing the inhibition and suppression operations between levels of components.*

composed of a number of independent components, each encapsulating a specific behavior or robot skill. These components are arranged into successively more complex layers that communicate through two operations: *inhibition* and *suppression*. These operations are used, respectively, to prevent input to a component and to replace the output of a component. In the figure, output from `Skill` C may cause the input from `Skill` A to `Skill` B to be delayed by time *t*; similarly output from `Skill` C may override the output of `Skill` B to `Actuator` 1 for time *t*.

The fundamental architectural feature of subsumption architectures is the modularization of robot behavior and functionality: Rather than behavior being represented in a single model, independent components arranged in layers each capture one facet of the overall behavior without a single, overarching representation. Each of these components independently relies on sensory inputs in order to trigger the actions it is supposed to perform, and overall robot behavior emerges from the execution of those actions without a central plan coordinating this behavior. Subsumption architectures, therefore, are more reactive in nature. This characteristic explicitly addresses the performance shortcomings of SPA architectures, and subsumption architectures garnered popularity for their fast and nimble performance.

Architecturally, subsumption adopts a component-based approach to the basic data flow between sensors and actuators allowing for data flow cycles, although the interfaces of these components are simple and capture the value of a single signal. In contrast to SPA, the overall behavior of a subsumption robot depends on the overall topology of the system and how components are connected rather than a single abstract model.

Subsumption architectures are not without drawbacks, despite their better performance characteristics compared to SPA robots. The fundamental drawback of subsumption in practice is the lack of a coherent architectural plan for layering and consequential support. While the conceptualization of the subsumption architecture describes the use of layers in order to organize components of different complexities, there is no explicit guidance or support for such layering in the architecture. Components are inserted into the data flow depending on their specific task, without their position necessarily being related to the layer within which they are positioned, and without components belonging to the same layer being inserted in similar manners and positions.

Three-Layer. Following the development of subsumption, a number of alternatives were developed that attempted to bridge the gap between between SPA's plans and subsumption's reactive nature; these hybrid architectures can be grouped together under the rubric of *three-layer* (3L) architectures. [One of the earliest examples is found in (Firby 1989).] The widely adopted 3L architectures—illustrated in Figure 11-11—are characterized by the separation of robot functionality into three layers (the names of which may differ from system to system): the *reactive* layer, which quickly reacts to events in the environment with quick action; the *sequencing* layer, which is responsible for linking functionalities present in the reactive layer into more complex behaviours; and the *planning* layer, which performs slower long-term planning.

With the adoption of three separate layers each concerned with a different aspect of a robot's operation, 3L architectures attempt to combine both reactive operation and long-term planning. The planning layer, then, performs tasks in a manner similar to SPA architectures by maintaining long-term state information and evaluating plans for action

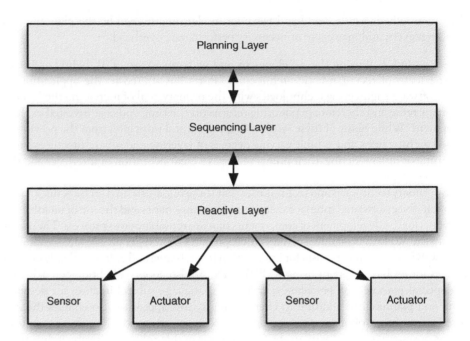

Figure 11-11.
An illustration of 3L architectures, showing the relationship between each layer and the basic sensors and actuators.

based on models of the robot's tasks and its environment. The reactive layer—in addition to containing the basic functions and skills of the robot such as grasping an object—captures reactive behavior that must execute quickly and immediately in response to environmental information. The sequencing layer that links the two is responsible for linking reactive layer behaviors together into chains of actions as well as translating high-level directions from the planning layer into these lower-level actions. The majority of 3L architectures adopt some kind of special-purpose scripting language for the implementation of the sequencing layer of the architecture. The sequencing layer, then, often is simply a virtual machine that executes programs written in these scripting languages.

From an architectural perspective, 3L is an example of a layered architecture with a bidirectional flow of information and action directives between the layers while using independent components to form each layer. The behavior of 3L architectures is dependent not only on the arrangement of their components, but also on the operation of the internal subarchitecture of the sequencing layer.

One challenge associated with the development of 3L architectures is understanding how to separate functionality into the three layers. This separation is dependent on the robot's specific tasks and goals and there is little architectural guidance to help in this task; the separation largely depends on the design expertise of the architect. Depending on the tasks the robot is intended to perform, there is also a tendency for one layer to drastically dominate others in importance and complexity, which clouds the hybrid nature of 3L architectures. The interposition of the sequencing layer in the middle of the architecture also results in difficulties when translating the higher-level planning directives into lower-level execution. This translation necessitates the maintenance and reconciliation of the potentially disparate world and behavior models maintained by the planning and sequencing layers, and may cause unnecessary performance overhead.

Reuse-Oriented. Following the development and widespread use of 3L hybrid architectures, the focus of recent robotic architecture efforts has shifted to the application of modern software engineering technologies with the primary goal of increasing the level of component reuse and therefore maximizing returns on the time and cost invested in their development. While many of these systems adopt ideas and principles from the previously discussed architectures and exhibit varying degrees of layering and subarchitectures based on planning or task modeling, their primary focus is a clear definition of interfaces and the promotion of reuse.

The primary techniques and technologies that these reuse-oriented architectures adopt are explicit object-oriented interface definitions for components and the use of middleware frameworks for the development of components that are reusable across projects. The architecture of the WITAS unmanned aerial vehicle project (Doherty et al. 2004), for example, adopts CORBA as the mechanism for information interchange and enforces clearly defined interfaces for each component using CORBA IDL. It also adopts a hybrid approach that uses a special-purpose *task procedure* specification language subarchitecture for decision making and planning. In addition to enabling reuse, this approach also enables the distributed operation of robot components for better resource utilization. Another example of this class of systems can be found in the CLARATy reusable robotic software architecture (Nesnas et al. 2006): This two-layer architecture adopts a goal-network approach for planning while focusing on defining generic device interfaces that clearly identify the primary functions of a class of devices in a way that is decoupled from the specific device used in any particular instance of a CLARATy architecture. By doing so, different devices of the same type (rangefinders, for example) can be seamlessly integrated into the architecture without the need to redefine this device's interface.

Development Frameworks for Robotic Systems	While many robotic systems are designed and built independently, a number of frameworks and tools have been developed to facilitate and speed the development process. Each of these frameworks is usually targeted toward a specific aspect of robotic development, and includes special support for that purpose. While certainly not a complete survey, the following briefly presents some of the more popular ones.

- Player (http://playerstage.sourceforge.net)—The Player open-source project is primarily targeted to Unix-based environments, and provides networked accessible interfaces to a large variety of devices with support for distributed operation of robotic components. The framework also supports integrations with the Stage and Gazebo three-dimensional systems for quickly accessible simulation capabilities.
- Orca (http://orca-robotics.sourceforge.net)—Orca is an open-source, cross-platform framework (only the core of the project is supported under Windows) focused on developing component-based robotic systems. The Orca project uses the Ice middleware framework for cross-component communication, and Orca provides libraries that ease the use of the middleware.
- Microsoft Robotics Studio (http://msdn.microsoft.com/robotics)—The Microsoft Robotics Studio (MRS) is a free integrated environment for robotic system development. MRS supports a .NET-based service-oriented architecture with primary support for the C# and

> VB.NET languages, and the environment includes simulation support through the PhysX simulation engine.
> - Lego Mindstorms (http://mindstorms.lego.com/)—This package combining both hardware and software has found great popularity, primarily because of its low cost and easy application to educational needs. The Mindstorms package combines a collection of servos and sensors along with a special-purpose operating system and the LabVIEW graphical development environment (developed by National Instruments).

11.5.2 Wireless Sensor Networks

Robotic systems represent a very active type of application: The software must make a physical system perform some set of tasks. Sensor nets are, in a manner of speaking, a largely reactive application: Their first task is to monitor the environment and report on its state. Wireless sensor network (WSN) systems are now used in a variety of domains, including medical systems, navigation, industrial automation, and civil engineering for tasks such as monitoring and tracking. These systems enjoy the benefits of low installation cost, inexpensive maintenance, easy reconfiguration, and so on. Nonetheless WSNs can be very challenging to implement, for they may need to be integrated with legacy wired networks, other embedded devices, and mobile networks that include PDAs and cell phones for user notification. The wireless devices themselves are typically highly constrained with respect to power consumption, communication bandwidth and range, and processing capacity. Wireless sensor *systems* impose further constraints with regard to fault-tolerance, performance, availability, and scalability.

The Bosch Research and Technology Center, in conjunction with researchers at the University of Southern California, have explored how WSNs should be designed to meet the multitude of challenges present (Malek et al. 2007). The architecture–centric design that has emerged for Bosch's applications is interesting for it explicitly combines three separate architectural styles to achieve all the system's goals. The design is sketched in Figure 11-12.

As depicted, MIDAS's reference architecture applies three different architectural styles. The peer-to-peer portion of the architecture is shown in the bottom portion of the diagram. It is responsible for deployment activities, including the exchange of application-level components. The publish-subscribe portion of MIDAS corresponds to the communication backbone responsible for the routing and processing of sensor data among the various platforms. The service-oriented portion of MIDAS is depicted at the top of the diagram. These services represent generic, but less frequently used system monitoring and adaptation facilities. These services are distributed among the platforms.

11.6 END MATTER

The central theme of this chapter has been that architectures for complex applications result from deep understanding of the application domain, careful choice of constituent elements and styles based upon experience and their known properties, and hybridization of these elements into a coherent solution. REST is the example par excellence of this. The Web would not be the success it is today without this careful architecture.

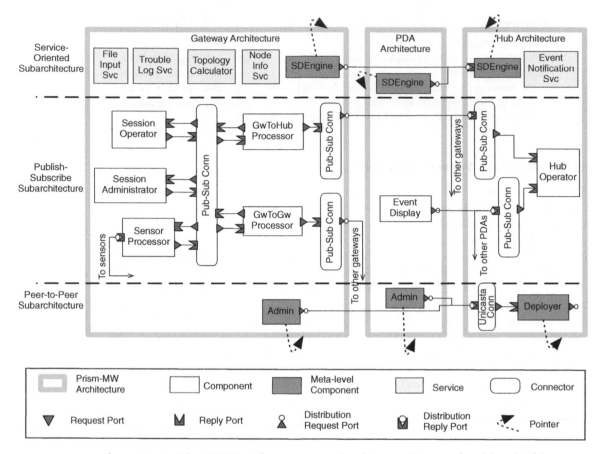

Figure 11-12. *The MIDAS wireless sensor network architecture. Diagram adapted from (Malek et al. 2007) © IEEE 2007.*

More than just exemplifying how a complex style arises from the combination of elements from simpler styles, REST illustrates important means for coping with issues that arise due to the presence of network issues, notably latency and agency. REST thus serves as a model from which solutions to related problems can be derived.

Networking issues—especially latency and agency—have been emphasized in the chapter since an increasingly large proportion of applications are now network based. The discussion of peer-to-peer systems highlighted concerns with discovery of other peers, search for resources, and risks due to potential performance problems and malicious entities. The particular issues of security and trust will be covered in detail in Chapter 13.

Note that just because an application grows in scope the solution architecture does not necessarily become more complex. Insight into the essence of a problem coupled with effective exploitation of a few simple ideas can yield a highly effective application. This is clearly the case with, for example, Google, Akamai, and Skype. Great solutions to tough, commercial problems do not just happen: They result from great architectures that reflect experience, choice, and discriminating taste.

Concern for non-functional properties such as scale, performance, and security has dominated the designs considered in this chapter. In the next three chapters we examine specifically how to design to achieve such properties. The design techniques presented in each of these three chapters have emerged from experience in creating applications such as those considered above. Chapter 12 considers such properties as efficiency and dependability, while Chapter 13 is devoted to designing applications to achieve certain security and trust properties. The non-functional property of *adaptability* seen in the preceding discussion of, for instance, peer-to-peer systems is given additional in-depth treatment in Chapter 14.

The Business Case

Development of a great software architecture is a critical step in ensuring the long-term financial success of a software product line. Product management and financial difficulties arise when an initial architecture fails to accommodate changes and new demands. Scaling a product to meet new demands in amount of processing is a simple and traditional example. The emergence of the network at the leitmotif of most new applications presents a greater and more subtle challenge than performance, however. In addition to the security risks raised, the network offers the challenges and opportunities of working in an open, dynamic world. The potential is for applications that more quickly adapt to changing circumstances, whether on the individual consumer's side, or in terms of business alliances.

This new landscape presents particular challenges for in-house development of systems. If an organization has traditionally worked only in a closed-shop, LAN-based context, moving to an open network (or even a globally distributed intranet) it is likely to find the transition rocky. New technologies, and notably new and distinctly different architectures, are required.

11.7 REVIEW QUESTIONS

1. The eight fallacies of distributed computing, as given in the chapter, are stated as lies. For instance, "The network is reliable." What are the consequences for a distributed application's architecture from realizing the network is *not* reliable?

2. What are the consequences for a distributed application's architecture from the other seven fallacies?

3. What are the three main stylistic elements from which REST was derived?

4. How do pure peer-to-peer systems, such as the original Gnutella, discover the presence of resources (such as an .mp3 file) in the network? How do hybrid P2P systems improve on that?

5. What are the main styles for robotics architectures, and what problems were observed with the early styles?

11.8 EXERCISES

1. Any two architectural styles can be combined simply by fully encapsulating the use of one style inside of a single component that is present in the usage of the other style. REST however, shows how some styles can be compatibly used together, at the same level of abstraction. For all six pair combinations of the following styles, describe how the styles can be used together at the same level of abstraction, or explain why they cannot.

   a. Layered/virtual machines
   b. Event-based
   c. Pipe-and-filter
   d. Rule-based

2. Develop an architecture for a lunar lander video game example that shows the result of (effectively) using two or more architectural styles in combination.

3. Create a diagram like that of Figure 11-1 that indicates the intellectual heritage of the C2 style, as described in Chapter 5.

4. Search on the Web and identify other applications (than the Web itself) to which REST has been applied.

5. What is the architecture of AOL's Instant Messenger? How does it compare to the architecture of ICQ's chat features? How do they compare to the architecture of IRC (Internet Relay Chat)?

6. What are the trust assumptions of the Napster architecture? Develop a modification to the Napster architecture that would decrease the risk of downloading malicious content from another peer.

7. Are service-oriented architectures peer-to-peer systems? Describe why this is and why this is not a valid description.

8. Several software architecture styles take inspiration, and sometimes their name, from interactions in real, physical life. Peer-to-peer interactions is one example. This relationship can go the other direction too: Software architectures can also be used to describe interactions in everyday society. Describe the service architecture of a fast-food restaurant (such as In-N-Out Burger or McDonald's) using the styles of Chapter 4, in combination as necessary.

9. The grid style described in the chapter is very high level, and described to be broadly descriptive of many grid applications. Identify one actual grid application and describe its architecture. How does that architecture compare to the nominal architecture of Figure 11-2?

10. Koala has been used to develop architectures for consumer electronics, such as televisions. If a distributed media system were to be developed (with media sources located one place in the network, and various processing and display devices and software located elsewhere in the network), would Koala still be a good choice for describing the architecture? Why or why not? What would be essential in such a situation?

11.9 FURTHER READING

References for further study of distributed architectures and the REST style were provided in the text. Central are Tanenbaum's text on distributed systems (Tanenbaum and van Steen 2002), Fielding's dissertation (Fielding 2000), and subsequent journal publication (Fielding and Taylor 2002).

Google's architecture is becoming increasingly public, with many of its technologies described in papers available at labs.google.com/papers.html. The Google File System, for example, is explained in (Ghemawat, Gobioff, and Leung 2003) and MapReduce is presented in (Dean and Ghernwat 2004). Further information on Akamai is available in (Dilley et al. 2002); other resources are available at the company's Web site.

As the main chapter text mentioned, knowing Skype's architecture exactly is somewhat difficult to determine because the client software has been obscured using several sophisticated techniques. The architecture described in the text reflects a forensic analysis. One key publication in this regard is (Baset and Schulzrinne 2004), which reflects observation of the Skype client in action. Another project worked at analyzing the obscured client code. Results can be found at recon.cx/en/f/vskype-part1.pdf and recon.cx/en/f/vskype-part2.pdf.

Good references for Web services are somewhat hard to come by. Many publications and Web sites are shallow in their technical presentation, imprecise, or else focused on only a narrow facet. A good introduction, however, is found in (Vogels 2003). A technically richer paper is (Manolescu et al. 2005). WS-BPEL is described in (OASIS 2007).

A high-performance computing architecture that forms an interesting contrast to grid architectures is MeDICi (Gorton 2008; Gorton et al. 2008).

The architecture of Linux has been recovered and described (Bowman, Holt, and Brewster 1999), showing the differences between the application's prescriptive and descriptive architectures. As elsewhere mentioned in this text, the architecture of the Apache Web server has also been recovered and described (Gröne, Knöpfel, and Kugel 2002; Gröne et al. 2004). Both projects are interesting studies in architectural recovery; they also are useful for retrospectively seeing how multiple styles are combined to solve challenging problems.

12

Designing for Non-Functional Properties

Engineering software systems so that they satisfy all their myriad functional require-ments is difficult. As we have seen so far, software architectures can help in that task through effective compositions of well-defined components and connectors, which have been verified to adhere to the necessary structural, behavioral, and interaction constraints. While satisfying functional requirements is essential, unfortunately it is not sufficient. Software developers must also provide for non-functional properties (NFPs) of software systems.

> **Definition.** A *non-functional property (NFP)* of a software system is a constraint on the manner in which the system implements and delivers its functionality.

Important NFPs of software systems include security, reliability, availability, efficiency, scalability, and fault-tolerance. For example, in the case of the Lunar Lander system discussed throughout this book, the efficiency NFP may be characterized as the con-straint that the system must respond to navigation commands within a specific, very short time span; the reliability NFP may be characterized as the constraint that the system may not be in a specified failure state longer than a specific time span.

Software engineering methodology lays stress on doing the correct things from the very beginning of the software development process in order to curb development and maintenance costs. In particular, the emergence of the study of software architec-ture has marked an important trend in software system design—one that in principle allows designers and developers to codify NFPs such as availability, security, and fault-tolerance early on in the architectural models and to maintain their traceability across the system's artifacts and throughout its lifespan.

There are, however, still many domains in which certain critical NFPs have not been explicitly identified or dealt with early in development. This is most frequently evidenced by experiences with Web-based systems and desktop operating systems. At least in part, developers of these systems have dealt with issues such as security and dependability as an afterthought. For example, many security patches for Microsoft Windows appear only after a security hole is exposed by a third party. Additionally, these existing systems frequently provide no explicit, active description of the system's architecture to be used as a basis for adding capabilities in support of their dependability. Even if they did, however, it is not always clear how those architectural models would be used. Existing literature is almost completely devoid of the relationship of key architectural elements (software components, connectors, and configurations) to a system's dependability.

An added difficulty is that many NFPs tend to be qualitative rather than quantitative and are often multidimensional. Thus, it is fundamentally hard to measure an NFP precisely and prove or disprove the extent to which it has been addressed in a given system. One such property is, in fact, dependability. Dependability has become an NFP of prime importance in modern distributed and decentralized systems. In an idealized scenario, a dependable system is one on which the users can completely rely. Clearly, this definition is inherently qualitative and can lend itself to subjective interpretations. Dependability can be described more precisely in terms of its different dimensions: A dependable system should be secure, reliable, available, and robust, and at the same time it should be able to deal with failures and malicious tampering such as denial-of-service attacks. However, even if there were well-defined measures for each of the dimensions, quantifying dependability would still present a challenge. For example, it may be difficult to decide in a general case which system is more dependable: one that is highly reliable but not as secure or one that is highly secure but less reliable.

Another source of pressures on software architects in ensuring NFPs has stemmed from nontechnical issues. Traditionally, NFPs such as security or reliability have taken a backseat to the more lucrative attractions of time-to-market, as well as the pressing concerns of functional requirements. In these scenarios, security has been shoehorned into a software system, sometimes as an afterthought, while reliability is addressed with often problematic implementation-level solutions. In the case of security, these practices are also complicated by the fact that security is hard to implement, so that malicious individuals have almost always had an advantage over software security practitioners.

While the picture painted may seem bleak, software architectures can significantly improve the prospects for achieving NFP goals. From the perspective of architectural design, employing good design practices can aid the achievement of these properties, just like poor design practices can harm a system. In this chapter, we provide a set of design guidelines that a software architect can follow in pursuing several common NFPs:

- Efficiency
- Complexity
- Scalability
- Adaptability
- Dependability

The guidelines are just that: guidelines. They are not infallible rules that can be mindlessly applied and yet yield good results. Various caveats and exceptions will be discussed. The job of the architect is to think through the multiple issues and determine an appropriate strategy to pursue.

For each of the above NFPs, we will provide a definition of the NFP, discuss its impact on a software system's architecture, and, conversely, discuss the role of different architectural elements—which embody the architectural design decisions—as well as architectural styles—the guidelines for arriving at and constraints on those design decisions—in satisfying the NFP. We will consider both the characteristics that make an architecture more likely to exhibit a given property and the characteristics that may hamper an architecture's support for an NFP. Whenever appropriate, we will illustrate the discussion with concrete examples from existing architectures and architectural styles.

Note that the above list omits security, an NFP of great, and growing, importance. Because of its importance and significant architectural implications, all of Chapter 13 is dedicated to that topic.

Non-Functional Properties and Quality of Service

A term that has entered software engineering literature relatively recently is *quality-of-service* (QoS). This term typically is associated with networking and distributed systems domains, and has been used somewhat imprecisely within software engineering. For example, it is frequently but incorrectly equated with NFPs. Even though we will not focus on QoS specifically in this book, the term warrants a brief discussion so that the reader can relate it properly to NFPs.

A system's QoS informally can be thought of as the degree to which the system delivers its services so that it satisfies its users' expectations—the users may be humans or other software. Therefore, QoS encompasses a system's functional as well as its non-functional properties. For example, a system that correctly implements its functionality, but is vulnerable to malicious attacks or fails frequently, would not provide NFPs such as security, reliability, or robustness; it also would not provide good QoS, for the same reasons. Conversely, a system that is "unbreakable" would provide the above NFPs (regardless of its functional properties), but may still suffer from poor QoS unless it also provides the functionality its users expect.

12.1 EFFICIENCY

Definition. **Efficiency is a quality that reflects a software system's ability to meet its performance requirements while minimizing its usage of the resources in its computing environment. In other words, efficiency is a measure of a system's resource usage *economy*.**

Note that this definition does not directly address the issue of system correctness. Instead, it implicitly assumes that the system will function as required. In other words, a system cannot be considered efficient if it implements the wrong functionality.

A common misconception is that software architecture has little to say about efficiency since architecture is a design-time entity while efficiency is a run time property. This is wrong. Selecting appropriate styles or patterns and instantiating them with appropriate components and connectors will have a direct and critical impact on the system's performance. While it is difficult to enumerate all of the possible performance requirements and related architectural decisions, we will outline certain general guidelines. The reader should be able to use these guidelines as a starting point for a more complete list that will be amassed over time in the reader's personal arsenal.

12.1.1 Software Components and Efficiency

Keep Components Small

For efficiency, ideally each component should satisfy a single need and serve a single purpose in the system. This helps avoid employing components when the majority of their services will not be used.

This guideline can directly impact a component's reusability: Many off-the-shelf components are very large and by design include significant functionality that may not be needed in a particular system. Put another way, constructing reusable components can be an impediment to constructing efficient systems.

As with all the guidelines introduced in this chapter, this one should be applied with appropriate caution. Clearly, there are off-the-shelf components whose memory footprint and/or run time performance have been optimized over time; such components will likely outperform one of a kind components built from scratch. Another, quite common exception is a direct by-product of caching: Caching data locally for later use can result in components with larger memory footprints, but it also can result in faster systems.

Keep Component Interfaces Simple and Compact

A software component is accessed only via its public interface. The interface should expose only those component services that are intended to be visible from the outside. Similarly, in general, a component should never expose its internal state other than via the operations intended to modify that state.

If a component's interface is cumbersome, generalized for a broad set of usage scenarios, or geared to a broad class of potential clients, the component's efficiency may be compromised. For example, the component may require different types of adaptors or wrappers to specialize it for use in specific contexts. Alternatively, the component may internally convert the parameters to or from a lowest common denominator form.

Conversely, an interface stripped to its bare bones can also negatively impact the efficiency of a component. An example is a Unix pipe-and-filter–based system, in which the components (filters) rely on untyped ASCII data streams to maximize their reusability. However, this may require constant conversion of such streams to typed data for more advanced processing, and for improving system reliability, as will be discussed further below.

Note that insisting on compact interfaces for the sake of efficiency may negatively impact other desirable properties of the component, such as its reusability, support for heterogeneity, and even scalability. This will be discussed in the context of the next guideline, and will be revisited later in the chapter.

Allow Multiple Interfaces to the Same Functionality

Software components are typically built to be usable in multiple run time contexts. Even within a single system, they may need to provide services to multiple client components executing on different platforms, implemented in different programming languages, or encoding their data using different standards. They may also need to enforce, for example, different protocols of interaction, transaction support, or persistency rules, as required by the different clients. In such situations, architects may choose to provide the needed services via multiple components that essentially replicate each other's functionality. Clearly, that would hurt the system's efficiency (unless the system is distributed in such a manner that a physically closer copy of the component in question is provided with the appropriate locally needed interface).

Another option is to wrap the component using an adaptor connector that performs all of the needed data conversions. Such a solution is more flexible as the component itself remains unchanged and maintains its memory footprint and run time performance properties. At the same time, the adaptor will likely introduce some amount of run time overhead.

Since the adaptor-based approach may result in a narrowly applicable component, a third option is to construct the component such that it *natively* exports multiple interfaces to its functionality. This solution will likely be more efficient than both of the above options. At the same time, this solution carries the danger that the component will be bloated in situations where only one of its interfaces may be used. The three options are illustrated in Figure 12-1.

Separate Processing Components from Data

Modeling data separately from processing has several potential efficiency benefits. First, it allows the data's internal representation to be fine-tuned or altered, based on local design objectives and without affecting the processing components. Similarly, this allows processing algorithms to be optimized without affecting the data representation, which may be used by multiple components in the system. Separating processing from data also allows architects to ensure, in the architecture, that the appropriate data is at the disposal of the appropriate processing components, thus aiding system correctness arguments.

Separate Data from Meta-Data

In many distributed, heterogeneous, data-intensive systems, system data is frequently separated from the meta-data. Meta-data is "the data about the data." In other words, in such systems it may be unclear a priori how the data is structured and intended to be used. The data may, for example, arrive at run time in unpredictable forms. Meta-data can be used as a way of describing the data so that the processing components can discover at run time how to process the data. Meta-data is heavily used to describe Web content elements and the content of e-mail messages.

Separating data from meta-data makes the data smaller, reducing the system's run time memory footprint; every time a data packet is sent from one processing component to another, it may not need to be accompanied with header information fully describing that data. Thus, if a component already is hardwired to process data of a particular type, it may do so directly. However, keeping the meta-data around and using it to interpret every data packet will, over time, induce a run time performance penalty in the general case.

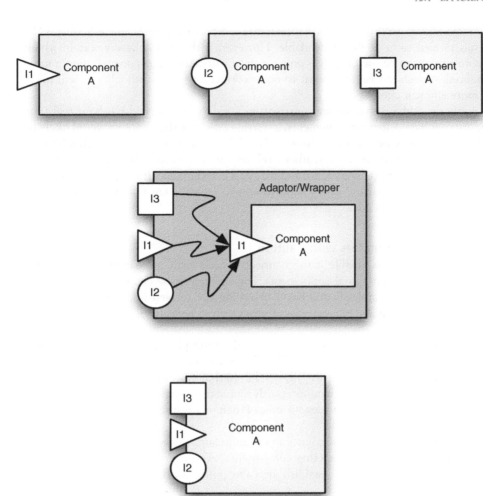

Figure 12-1.
Alternatives for allowing a component to export multiple interfaces to the same functionality. Multiple copies of the same component exporting different interfaces (top); a wrapper exporting the different interfaces (middle); the component itself exporting the three interfaces (bottom).

12.1.2 Software Connectors and Efficiency

Carefully Select Connectors

As argued in Chapter 5, software connectors are first-class entities in a software architecture. They encapsulate all of the interaction facilities in a system. Especially in large, complex, and distributed software systems, the interactions among the system components become the determinants of key system properties, including efficiency. Careful selection of connectors is thus critical.

While many different types of connectors may provide the minimum level of service required by a given set of components in a system, some connectors will be a better fit than others, and thus may improve system efficiency. For example, the architect may select a message broadcasting connector, such as the connectors in the C2-style Lunar Lander architecture from Chapter 4, because that connector has been used in a number of systems, can accommodate varying numbers of interacting components (that is, its cardinality is N), and has proven to be highly dependable. However, if the particular context in which the connector is to be used involves only a pair of interacting components, then a more specialized, though less flexible, point-to-point connector (with cardinality 2) will likely be a more efficient choice.

Similarly, if the system under construction is safety-critical and has hard real-time computing or data delivery requirements, a starting point for the architect would likely be synchronous connectors with exactly-once data delivery semantics. On the other hand, if the system being constructed is a weather satellite ground station, a data stream connector with at-most-once data delivery semantics may be a better choice. It is highly unlikely that a loss of weather data packets over a short time span—even a few minutes—will severely impact the system or its users.

Use Broadcast Connectors with Caution

A system may be more flexible if the connectors used in it are capable of broadcasting data to multiple interested components. For example, new components can attach to such a connector seamlessly and begin observing the relayed information. However, that flexibility can come at the expense of other system properties, such as security and efficiency.

It is possible that a single interaction may involve multiple components, and the temptation may thus be to rely on broadcast. The downside occurs if some of the components receiving the information do not actually need it. In that case, the system's performance is impacted, not only because data is unnecessarily routed through the system, but also because the recipient components have to devote some of their processing time to establish whether the data is relevant to them.

An alternative to broadcast connectors is multicast connectors, which maintain an explicit mapping between interacting components. Another possibility is to rely on a publish-subscribe mechanism to establish such a mapping during run time.

Make Use of Asynchronous Interaction Whenever Possible

In a highly distributed and possibly decentralized setting, it may be difficult for multiple components to synchronize their processing so that their interactions take place at times that are ideal for all of the involved components. If this does not happen and the connectors servicing the components only support synchronous interaction, then, in essence, the slowest component will drag down the performance of the entire system, and may result in multiple components having to wait idly until an interaction can be completed.

In such situations, asynchronous interaction is preferable, where a component is able to initiate the interaction via the connector and then continue with its processing until a later time when it receives a response. Likewise, each invoked component will respond to the incoming service requests as its availability and processing load allow; after it services the request, the component will send its reply to the connector and immediately be able to continue with its processing.

Note that this will not always be possible (single-threaded systems being the simplest example), and that it does not come without a performance cost. If the interaction among a set of components is asynchronous, it will be the connector's responsibility to ensure that the service requests and replies are properly associated with one another.[1] This means that the connector will have to do additional processing to maintain many such mappings and determine the ordering of requests and replies as well as their destinations. Furthermore, the nature of a given component, or of a given request, may be such that the component has to suspend its processing and wait for a response, in which case the benefit of employing an asynchronous connector will be lost.

Use Location Transparency Judiciously

Location transparency, also referred to as distribution transparency, shields a distributed system's components from the details of their deployment. In principle, this allows components to be designed as if all of their interactions are local, that is, as if they are co-located on one host with all of the components with which they need to interact. In turn, this allows easy system adaptation, enabling redeployment of some of the components across hosts without affecting the remaining components; it is the task of the systems' connectors to ensure this transparency. An illustration is provided in Figure 12-2.

In practice, however, complete location transparency is difficult to achieve. Remote interactions, for example, are many times slower than local interactions. By some measurements they may be slower by a factor of forty or more. Thus both the interacting components and their users may quickly notice the difference. This means that any distributed system with specific performance requirements *and* the goal of location transparency may have to assume the worst-case scenario—that each component is located on a separate host. A preferred alternative is to clearly distinguish remote from local connectors. This may impact the system's adaptability but ensure appropriate performance.

12.1.3 Architectural Configurations and Efficiency

Keep Frequently Interacting Components Close

The number of indirections through which two or more components communicate will hamper that interaction's efficiency. This is especially true for systems with real-time performance requirements. Architectural styles or configurations that place many points of indirection between such components will be a poor fit. For example, if a component A naturally fits two or more layers above component B in a layered architecture, yet the two components need to interact frequently in a short time frame, a strictly layered architecture is not a good choice for the system: Every interaction will need to be forwarded by the intermediate layers.

An example of a layered architecture in which the distance between interacting layers proves to be a problem is that of the mobile robot system discussed by Mary Shaw and David Garlan (Shaw and Garlan 1996), and depicted in Figure 12-3. The Robot Control component observes the environment and invokes the Sensor Interpretation component in response to events of interest. In turn, the Sensor Interpretation component may need to invoke the component (that is, layer) above it, Sensor Integration, for a more meaningful,

---

[1] In many systems, this may be accomplished by having the components themselves maintain the correspondence between requests and replies, for example, by associating and exchanging special identifiers ("tokens") with the request and reply messages. While such solutions may work in practice, this association is ultimately an interaction issue, and as such belongs in the connector.

Figure 12-2.
Distribution transparency. Conceptual view of the architecture (a) and deployment view of the same architecture (b). The system's components are unaware of the deployment profile. The connectors render that profile transparent. If the same connectors are used for local and distributed scenarios, the system's efficiency likely will be compromised.

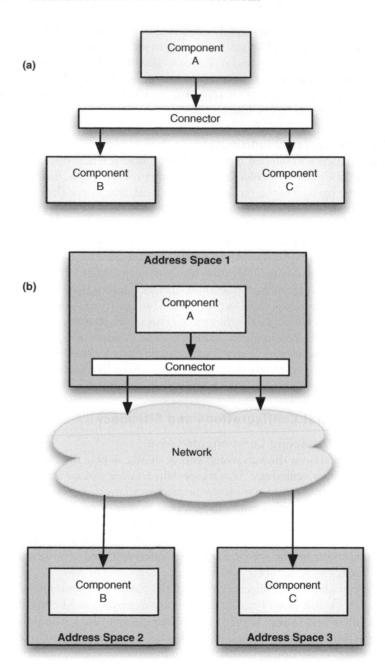

nonlocal interpretation of the sensed events. Likewise, the Sensor Integration component may require the help of the component above it, and so on, until eventually the highest-level component, Supervisor, is reached. Once a component in a given layer is capable of servicing the request it received, it returns the results to the component immediately

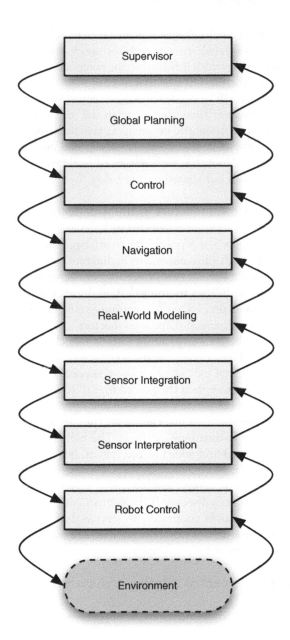

Figure 12-3.
*A layered
architecture for a
mobile robot
system in which
the strict layering
may induce
performance
penalties.*

below it; this sequence continues until the Robot Control component receives the necessary information to respond to the sensed event.

In this architecture, it is possible that a request from Robot Control must be propagated to as many as seven other components, and returned via them, before it is serviced. For example, if a given class of events from Robot Control pertains to the robot's Navigation, these events are still propagated, and the responses to them returned, via the three intermediate components. Clearly, this is not an efficient solution. Shaw and Garlan recognize this and discuss several alternative architectures for the system.

A common way of keeping frequently interacting components close is to cache, hoard, or prefetch data needed for their interaction. All three of these techniques try to anticipate the remote information that will be needed by a given component, and try to deliver that information during a convenient time, that is, when the impact on the system's overall performance will be minimal, *before* the information is actually needed. This is one way of mimicking location transparency. Caching, hoarding, and prefetching are a part of a software connector's duties. Note that such advanced facilities will invariably add to a connector's complexity, which is discussed further below.

Carefully Select and Place Connectors in the Architecture

Any large system is likely to comprise components with heterogeneous interaction requirements. As discussed in Chapter 5, it is possible to create large connectors that are capable of simultaneously servicing multiple components in different ways. Multiple such connectors could then be used in the system. However, each connector would support a superset of the needed interaction capabilities, meaning that, in the average case, many of the connector's features would remain unused, yet still consume resources. Furthermore, it will be difficult to optimize the larger, general-purpose connectors.

For this reason, it may be preferable for an architect to choose multiple connectors, each geared to the given subset of components' specific interaction needs, as opposed to fewer but larger connectors that can service more components in the system and their multiple needs. An obvious example is the procedure-call connector. Procedure calls are simple and efficient. By themselves, they may be unable to provide more advanced interaction facilities, such as asynchronous invocation, yet they are able to satisfy a majority of today's systems' needs, even in distributed settings. The higher-order connector facilities can, of course, still be selected and added to the system, but only if and when they are needed.

Likewise, if a given software component has multiple performance requirements, several options are at the architect's disposal. If the component exports multiple interfaces, the architect can employ multiple connectors to service the component, one per interface type. Alternatively, the architect can try to separate the multifaceted component into multiple separate components.

Consider the Efficiency Impact of Selected Architectural Styles and Patterns

Some styles are not a good match for certain types of problem. Examples abound; consider a few below.

- Asynchronous interactions, such as those in publish-subscribe systems, cannot be used effectively in systems with real-time requirements.
- Large repository-based systems, such as those adhering to the blackboard architectural style, may make it difficult to satisfy stringent memory constraints.
- Systems that are required to process continuous data streams can be designed using event-based architectures, but transforming a stream into discrete events and possibly recomposing the stream after the transfer carries a computational penalty.

- If data needs to be delivered to its user incrementally, a batch sequential system will be a poor fit. Similarly, a pipe-and-filter system may be a poor fit as well, unless the employed variant of the pipe-and-filter style supports incremental data delivery.

An analogous argument holds for architectural patterns. For example, the model-view-controller pattern may work well in a centralized setting, but it may not be a good fit for highly distributed and decentralized environments because of the frequent tight interaction between the components.

It also should be noted that, while adaptability in certain cases—such as supporting location transparency—may harm a system's efficiency, in other cases system adaptation can be used as a tool to address performance requirements. For example, a style that supports redeployment in a distributed architecture may be able to support certain performance requirements more effectively.

12.2 COMPLEXITY

Software complexity can be thought of from different perspectives, and thus defined in different ways. For example, the IEEE definition of complexity (IEEE 1991) is as follows.

> **Definition.** *Complexity* is the degree to which a software system or one of its components has a design or implementation that is difficult to understand and verify.

This definition implies that complexity is partial to the specific perspectives of system understanding and verification. The definition does not say how complexity may be manifested in a software system or how it would impact other objectives, such as satisfying performance requirements. Perhaps worst of all, the determination of the degree to which a system is complex depends on the particular individual who is asked how "difficult to understand" the system is.

In order to understand the impact of software architecture on complexity, the traits of the system itself must be taken into account. A different and somewhat more useful definition follows.

> **Definition.** *Complexity* is a software system's property that is proportional to the size of the system, the number of its constituent elements, the size and internal structure of each element, and the number and nature of the elements' interdependencies.

To make this definition more precise, we would also need to define "size," "internal structure," and "nature of interdependencies." Still, the reader should have an intuitive understanding of these terms from introductory programming classes. For example, size of a software system can be measured in terms of source lines of code, number of modules, or number of packages. The reader should also be familiar with an element's internal structure from the discussions of architectural models and with different types of module interdependencies from the discussion of software connectors in Chapter 5.

There are several observations that emerge from the second definition of complexity that also agree with our general intuitions about software systems. These observations help us discuss the architectural implications of complexity and formulate some guidelines to help reduce or mitigate its presence.

12.2.1   Software Components and Complexity

Separate Concerns into Different Components

Conventional software engineering wisdom suggests that each of the various types of tasks performed by a system should be supported by a different component or set of components. This guideline may be obvious to any software engineer, for it stems from the application of the fundamental software development principles of abstraction, modularity, separation of concerns, and isolation of change. At the same time, this guideline needs to be clarified with respect to a related, perhaps obvious, observation: All other things being equal, a software system with a greater number of components is more complex than a system with a smaller number of components.

At first blush, this would suggest that architects should strive to minimize the number of components in their system. In other words, architects should try to co-locate multiple concerns in a single component in order to reduce the number of components. In fact, the guideline (that different system concerns should be separated into different components) and the observation (that larger numbers of components result in added complexity) are not inconsistent. In an architecture, the sheer number of components may not be as relevant to the system's complexity as the number of component *types*. Components of the same type can be easier to understand and analyze, may be more naturally composable, and can help abstract away the details of their instances. Conversely, a system with relatively fewer instances of components but which are of many different types may, in fact, increase overall complexity.

The notion of types used here is broader than that typically employed in the areas of programming languages or formal methods. For the purpose of this discussion, a component type may refer, for instance, to a similar structure, behavior, application domain, organization that developed the components, or standardized API. In other words, a type in this context refers to any set of component features that may ultimately lessen the effort required for the encompassing system's construction, composition, integration, verification, or evolution. For example, a system developed entirely in CORBA may be easier to understand than the same system that is developed using a collection of heterogeneous technologies. The reason is that both systems may be composed of the same number of element instances, but the CORBA system is composed of a smaller number of element types.

Also of note is that reducing the number of components in a system does not guarantee lower complexity if it results in increasing the complexity of each individual component. In other words, a system with larger constituent components is typically more complex than a system with smaller components. Put a slightly different way, a system with more complex components is itself more complex. Again, this is a relative measure and it will depend on the number of components in question. For example, a small number of complex components, belonging to a small number of component types, need not necessarily result in a complex system.

One final observation, applicable both to components and to connectors, is that from the architectural perspective, individual components are often "black boxes." As long as they can be treated as such—that is, as long as the engineers can avoid examining the components' details when establishing a system's property of interest—their internal complexity does not matter. In other words, this is the very type of complexity that is abstracted away by good architectural design.

Of course, it is a fair question to ask how realistic it is that engineers will not have to consider a component's internal details. In fact, while component-based software development has aided engineers in some significant ways, experience to date suggests that the really insidious problems involve the interplay of multiple components and often require the consideration of both their interactions as well as their internal structure and behavior. This is why an architecture-based approach to software development allows the inclusion of many concerns, including intracomponent concerns, in the set of a system's principal design decisions.

Keep Only the Functionality Inside Components—Not Interaction

While components in a software system contain application-specific functionality and data, they must also interact with other parts of the system, often in intricate and heterogeneous ways. In most commercial software systems, a component is encumbered with at least some of its own interaction responsibilities. The most prevalent examples, of course, are the use of procedure calls and shared memory access. Components typically support one of these two mechanisms in order to integrate and interact with external components.

While there may be legitimate reasons for coupling computation or data with interaction (for example, in order to improve the component's efficiency in a given system), it ultimately violates the basic software engineering principle of separation of concerns and results in more complex components. Furthermore, a decision to place the interaction facilities inside a component may hamper the component's reusability: The interaction facilities will be integrated into the component, yet they may be a poor fit for future systems. For example, if a component incorporates elements enabling it to communicate synchronously via remote procedure calls, that component will be slated for use in certain distributed settings. On the other hand, such design actually will ultimately harm the efficiency of the component, as well as that of its encompassing systems, if the component needs to be used in an alternative setting in which its interactions need to be asynchronous or local, or both. In such cases, adaptor connectors will need to be used to integrate the component with the rest of the system.

Placing interaction facilities inside a component also violates the principle of separation of concerns from the point of view of the connector: The interaction facilities housed within the component will need to be isolated to make them reusable, optimize them, or improve their reliability over time. This will be discussed further below.

Keep Components Cohesive

This guideline is similar to the "Keep the components small" guideline from Section 12.1.1; refer back to that section for the essence of the argument. At the same time, one reality of software development cannot be avoided: Regardless of how principled or clever architectural design decisions are, complex problems frequently require complex solutions. Software architecture can play a role in controlling that complexity, but architecture cannot eliminate the complexity. Therefore, a component may in fact need to be complex if the functionality it provides is complex.

Nevertheless, that complexity will be easier to tackle if the component has a clear focus, that is, if it addresses a specific, well-defined need in the system and does not incorporate solutions for multiple, disparate system requirements. One example of components that are not cohesive was discussed in the previous guideline: Coupling functionality with interaction inside a component will ultimately increase the component's complexity, and may result in several other undesirable characteristics. Another potential such class of components will be discussed next.

Be Aware of the Impact of Off-the-Shelf Components on Complexity

In general, off-the-shelf reuse has many well-documented benefits. Among them are the potential to reduce development effort, time, and cost, and to improve system dependability. At the same time, off-the-shelf components are often very large and complex systems in their own right. They may demand a great deal of careful study to understand them, and intricate techniques for integration with other components.

Therefore, off-the-shelf components may impact a system's complexity in two ways: (1) as a by-product of their own internal complexity, and (2) by requiring that complex connectors be used in the system. The first source of complexity can be avoided as long as the component can be treated as a black box. However, as soon as the engineer has to "peek inside" the component, the complexity of the system in question may increase significantly.

The second source of complexity arises from a common misconception in off-the-shelf reuse-based development. That misconception is that clean, well-documented APIs will necessarily simplify the integration of a component into a new system. While such APIs are certainly needed to effectively use the component, they can still mask many idiosyncrasies in the way the component is actually intended to be used. For example:

- The API typically will not provide guidance on how the component should be configured in a given environment and initialized for use.
- The API may not give any hints about the assumptions made by the component. For instance, does the component assume that it will control the system's main thread of execution?
- The API may not clearly indicate which operations are synchronous, and which ones asynchronous.
- The order in which operations can be legally invoked may be unclear in the API.
- The component state or mode of operation assumed for invoking a given element of the API may be unclear.
- Any side-effects of operations may be unstated.

The connectors required to integrate off-the-shelf components have to account for such details. They will therefore be a very real source of complexity, and one of which a software architect must be keenly aware.

Insulate Processing Components from Changes in Data Format

Processing components that need access to system data will likely rely on that data being presented in a particular format. Should the data format change—which is possible, even likely, in long-lived, distributed, and decentralized systems—the components themselves may need to change. Indeed, it is conceivable that a simple change in the data may affect a large portion of a system. Furthermore, the impact of data changes may not be easily foreseen as many architecture modeling notations do not take into account data access dependencies.

To avoid such undesirable situations, architects should employ techniques to control the complexity of processing-to-data and data-to-data dependencies. One such solution is to use dedicated meta-level components to address data resource discovery and location tracking. Another solution is to make use of explicit adaptor connectors that enable the processing components to rely on the same data "interface." Finally, as discussed in the case of efficiency above, data should be separated from meta-data, allowing components to dynamically interpret the data they are accessing.

12.2.2 Software Connectors and Complexity

Treat Connectors Explicitly

The impact of coupling functionality, data, and interaction on a system's complexity has been discussed above, in the guidelines for designing, constructing, and selecting components. One of the key contributions of software development from an explicit architectural perspective is that application-specific functionality and data should be separated from the application-independent interaction. That interaction should be housed in explicit software connectors. Chapter 5 discusses the many arguments in favor of treating connectors explicitly.

Keep Only Interaction Facilities Inside Connectors

Connectors are in charge of the application-independent interaction facilities in a given software system. The task of a connector is to support the communication and coordination needs of two or more components, and to provide the needed conversion and facilitation capabilities to improve that communication and coordination.

Nonetheless, just as the temptation may exist to place advanced interaction facilities inside components, it may be similarly tempting to place application-specific functionality or data inside a connector. There are seldom any good reasons to do this—it will always be possible to add a new component to house any such functionality—and there are many reasons not to do it. Therefore, as a general guideline, making a connector responsible for providing application-specific functionality or data should always be avoided.

Separate Interaction Concerns into Different Connectors

Interaction concerns in a given system could be simply the general connector roles discussed in Chapter 5, such as separating communication from facilitation. Those concerns could also be more application-specific, such as decoupling the exchange of data between two specific distributed components from the compression of that data to enable more efficient transmission across the network.

The basic argument underlying this guideline is analogous to the one applied to software components in Section 12.2.1. In principle, each connector should have a single, specific, well-defined responsibility. This allows for connectors to be updated, even at system run time. It also allows the architect to clearly assess the components interacting through those connectors, as well as the impact of any modifications of those components. Any issues with the system will be easier to isolate and address as well.

Restrict Interactions Facilitated by Each Connector

In distributed software systems, interaction will often surpass computation as the dominant factor for determining a given system's key characteristics. For example, the study of battery power consumption in some distributed systems has shown that communication costs typically dwarf computational costs; because of this, a system's computational energy costs are, in some cases, considered to be little more than noise, and thus are ignored in the system's overall energy cost assessment.

Similar arguments can be made about other properties, including efficiency, adaptability, and, in particular, complexity. If a connector unnecessarily involves components in interactions in which they are not interested (for example, by sending them data), the system's overall complexity will increase. In the best-case scenario, the interaction attempt will be ignored. In certain situations, components may be forced to make an explicit effort to ignore the unwanted interaction overtures by the connector, that is, some processing will be expended unnecessarily, in addition to the unneeded data traffic. In the worst case, the components may accidentally engage in the interaction and erroneously affect the system's functionality and state. In such situations, discovering which interaction paths—intended or accidental—caused the system defect may be very difficult.

The simplest rule of thumb is to use direct point-to-point interaction whenever possible. Indirect interaction mechanisms, such as event-based or publish-subscribe, are very elegant means for ensuring many properties in distributed systems, such as adaptability, heterogeneity, or decentralization. However, the specific interactions that take place in the system and that may be causing run time defects can be difficult to track down when such mechanisms are used. Likewise, synchronous interaction lends itself better than asynchronous interaction to determining precisely the interaction paths among the system's components.

Put another way, while certain styles of interaction and system composition have become prevalent in large, distributed, and decentralized software systems, and are direct enablers of several desirable system properties, they tend to negatively impact the system's complexity. It is an engineering trade-off.

Be Aware of the Impact of Off-the-Shelf Connectors on Complexity

Connectors provide application-independent services, so they would appear to be a natural target for attempting reuse. However, there are a number of pitfalls that an engineer should avoid. Most of these are similar to the pitfalls discussed in the analogous guideline applied to components in Section 12.2.1. A simple example is reusing a connector that possesses far more features and capabilities than a given situation requires.

One additional observation, specific to off-the-shelf connectors, is that it typically will be more difficult to ensure the proper communication paths in the given system since the engineer will likely have a lower degree of control as compared to custom-built connectors.

12.2.3   Architectural Configurations and Complexity

Eliminate Unnecessary Dependencies

Large software systems are typically more complex than small ones. This means, by extension, that systems with larger software architectures also tend to be more complex. The size of an architecture in this sense can be measured in terms of the size of the architectural model as indicated, for example, by the number of statements or diagram elements in the modeling notation. It can also be measured in terms of the number of constituent components, connectors, and, perhaps most significantly, interaction paths in the architectural configuration.

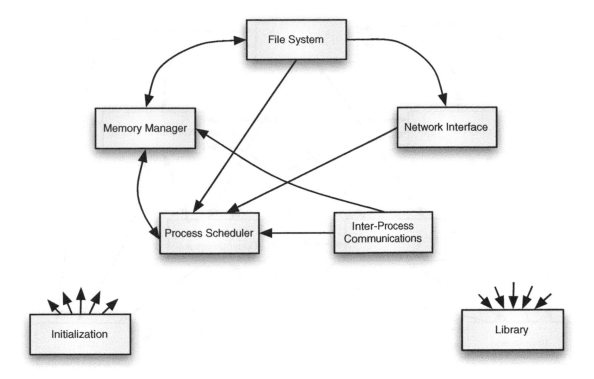

Figure 12-4. *The architecture of the Linux operating system as documented. Adapted from Bowman et al. (Bowman, Holt, and Brewster 1999) © 1999 ACM, Inc. Reprinted by permission.*

Most frequently, a system with more interdependencies among its modules is more complex than a system with fewer interdependencies. The reasons are at least two-fold. First, there is a greater number of possible interaction paths in such a system. Second, it is more difficult to control the behavior and predict the properties of such a system, precisely because of the added interaction paths.

Consider, for example, the architecture of the Linux operating system, as studied by Ivan Bowman and colleagues and shown in Figure 12-4 and Figure 12-5. Figure 12-4 shows the "as-documented" architecture of Linux, which the authors extracted from the available Linux literature. Figure 12-5 shows the "as-implemented" architecture, which the authors extracted from the Linux source code. For the purpose of this discussion, we will treat each identified subsystem as a single component in the architecture.

The two diagrams are quite dissimilar: The as-documented architecture is very clean, with a small number of unidirectional dependencies. On the other hand, the as-implemented architecture depicted in Figure 12-5 is a fully connected graph in which almost all of the dependencies are bidirectional. Any modifications to this architecture will be significantly more difficult to effect correctly because of this added complexity.

For example, the Network Interface component in Figure 12-4 depends only on Process Scheduler, and is depended upon by File System. On the other hand, in Figure 12-5 the same component both depends on and is depended upon by nearly every other component in

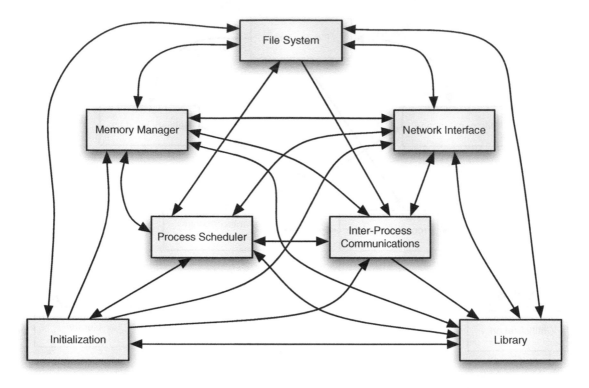

Figure 12-5. *The architecture of the Linux operating system as implemented. Adapted from Bowman et al. (Bowman, Holt, and Brewster 1999) © 1999 ACM, Inc. Reprinted by permission.*

the system; the only exception is the Initialization module, with which Network Interface has a unidirectional dependency.

   The main questions in this situation are why are there so many component interdependencies, and are they all necessary? Even if they are indeed necessary, an architectural configuration that is revealed via a fully connected graph of components and connectors very likely indicates a poor design.

   In such a case, the architect needs to carefully reconsider his design decisions. He may also need to reconsider the selected architectural styles and patterns. While a style or pattern will be unable to eliminate the inherent complexity in a system, a given style or pattern will be appropriate for some classes of problems, but may be inappropriate for others.

Manage All Dependencies Explicitly

For illustration, we will continue referring to the example of Figure 12-4 and Figure 12-5. However, the reader should note that this example is by no means atypical. Cases in which an architecture degrades badly over time abound. The Linux developers clearly had chosen to call out, and likely rely on, the documented architecture (Figure 12-4) as the correct one. This decision may have been accidental, that is, a product of a long succession of small, undocumented violations to the architecture of which most Linux developers were unaware. On the other hand, the decision may also have been deliberate, as the number of dependencies that an engineer would have to consider—in case a new component had to be added, an existing one modified, or a defect in the system remedied—was much smaller and the architecture easier to justify than would be the case with the architecture in Figure 12-5.

At the same time, the documented architecture clearly omitted a majority of the dependencies. Just because those were hidden from the engineers, their modification tasks would not be made easier. Quite the contrary, engineers may have had to discover these missing dependencies on their own, after they discovered that system adaptations that should have behaved a given way in fact did not work properly. The engineers would in such situations ultimately be forced to study the source code, after realizing that the documentation is not only incomplete, but also misleading.

It is because of these pitfalls that the real complexity of a system should not, and cannot, be hidden, and that all dependencies should be managed explicitly in the architecture.

Use Hierarchical (De)Composition

Hierarchical decomposition of a software system's architecture, and hierarchical composition of a system's components, are important tools for managing a given system's complexity. The components of a given conceptual unit are grouped together into a larger, more complex component; that component may also be grouped with other like components into even larger components. Through the use of appropriate interfaces the underlying complexity is masked, allowing the system's architecture at its highest level to be more readily understandable.

For example, the Linux architecture is decomposed into seven key components (that is, Linux subsystems) and their dependencies. Each of these components exports an interface to the rest of the system, and thereby abstracts away the component's internal architecture. This is also frequently the case with off-the-shelf components discussed above, which may be systems in their own right. In principle, a hierarchically (de)composed system allows the architect to isolate the parts of a system that are relevant for a required adaptation.

There is a real danger in reducing guidelines and observations such as found in this chapter to a metric that is then applied blindly. Architects (and their managers) are expected to use their common sense.

For example, to artificially reduce a system's complexity, a simple "solution" may be to make a monolithic system, where all components and connectors are lumped together into one large module. That would clearly not be a good idea, and would not be the intended implication of these guidelines.

Beware of the Numbers Game

12.3 SCALABILITY AND HETEROGENEITY

Definition. Scalability is the capability of a software system to be adapted to meet new requirements of size and scope.

Even though a system's scalability refers to its ability to be grown or shrunk to meet changes in the size of the problem, traditionally the difficulty faced by software engineers has been in supporting *larger* and thus *more complex* systems. Therefore, we will restrict our discussion to scaling software systems *up*.

Software architecture plays a critical role in supporting scalability. There are several dimensions to scalability, which we will discuss along with the role software architecture plays in supporting each. It should be noted that scalability can be achieved in an arbitrary case, but at a potentially exorbitant cost. The objective of this section is to provide guidelines that will allow software architects and engineers to improve a system's scalability without also prohibitively increasing its complexity and deteriorating its performance. In other words, a software system can be said to scale well if its rate of growth is not greater than the corresponding rate of complexity increase.

Two other NFPs deal with system aspects related to scalability: heterogeneity and portability.

> **Definition.** *Heterogeneity* **is the quality of a software system consisting of multiple disparate constituents or functioning in multiple disparate computing environments.**

We will often want to speak of a system easily accommodating heterogeneous elements, that is, accommodating incorporation of disparate components and connectors into its structure, thus we will also use heterogeneity to refer to an ability:

> **Definition.** *Heterogeneity* **is a software system's ability to consist of multiple disparate constituents or function in multiple disparate computing environments.**

> **Definition.** *Portability* **is a software system's ability to execute on multiple platforms (hardware or software) with minimal modifications and without significant degradation in functional or non-functional characteristics.**

Portability can thus be viewed as a specialization of heterogeneity.

Like scalability, heterogeneity and portability are system properties reflective of the system's ability to accommodate change and difference. They refer to increasing numbers of types of execution environments, in the case of both portability and heterogeneity, as well as types of software elements and users, in the case of heterogeneity.

Heterogeneity can be looked at from two perspectives:

- *Internal heterogeneity:* A system's ability to accommodate multiple types of components and connectors, possibly written in different programming languages, by different developer teams, and even different organizations.

- *External heterogeneity:* A system's ability to adjust to and leverage different hardware platforms, networking protocols, operating systems, middleware infrastructures, and so on. This view of heterogeneity thus encompasses portability.

In the below discussion, for ease of exposition we will focus on scalability as the over arching property.

12.3.1   Software Components and Scalability

A software system's architecture may need to support the addition of new components. The components may be added as new requirements emerge during the system's life span. Alternatively, existing components may be replicated to improve system efficiency. In either case, architects should follow some general guidelines to ensure scalability. Again, the reader should remember that these are only guidelines. In general, one should adhere to them whenever possible, yet the reader will probably be familiar with, or will be able to conjure, software development scenarios that would argue against following these guidelines.

In addition to considering the impact of functional component design on scalability, this section also explicitly considers the impact of the system's data design. Many systems are highly data-intensive. Presently, that means storing, accessing, distributing, and processing terabytes and even petabytes of data. The World Wide Web can be thought of as such a system. Other examples include scientific applications deployed on a data grid [for example, Globus (Foster, Kesselman, and Tuecke 2001) and OODT (Mattmann et al. 2006)]; such systems are discussed in Chapter 11. In addition to the sheer overall size of the data used by a system, many systems must process that data within specific time constraints. We refer to the amount of data processed in a given amount of time as data *volume* (expressed in bytes per second). Architectural decisions will directly impact a system's ability to scale up to large data volumes. This section also identifies several heuristics architects should keep in mind when striving for data scalability.

Give Each Component a Single, Clearly Defined Purpose

This guideline has analogs in the cases of efficiency and complexity. An architect should avoid placing too much responsibility on any one component. Failing to adhere to this guideline will typically result in large, internally complex components with many dependencies on other components in the system. Such important components may also lack architectural integrity because they encapsulate multiple concerns. They may thus become single points of failure or performance bottlenecks. Scaling up a system that comprises such components will be a challenge because there is an increased chance that any newly added components will also need to rely on the important components, further adding to their workload. An example such component is Linux's `Process Scheduler` from Figure 12-5.

Give Each Component a Simple, Understandable Interface

A component should be easy to identify and understand, use and reuse, deploy and redeploy. A component with a simple interface will have few and clear dependencies on other components in the system. Adding new components will have a minimal impact on such a component. Connectors can be more easily adapted, or new ones introduced, to support interactions with such a component. Finally, such a component will be easier to replicate and distribute across multiple hardware hosts if needed.

Do Not Burden Components with Interaction Responsibilities

This is a common pitfall. Simply put, adding interaction facilities to a component violates the component's conceptual integrity. Furthermore, it decreases the component's reusability potential since reuse becomes an all-or-nothing proposition. As discussed previously, it also increases a component's size and complexity. This has a deleterious impact on scalability. For example, scaling up a system by replicating such a component may become an issue: It may be less clear how that component should interact with the rest of the system since it encapsulates interaction design decisions, which should be public and external to the component.

Avoid Unnecessary Heterogeneity

Component incompatibilities can be overcome, but typically at a price. While it may in some cases significantly reduce development costs and effort, reusing heterogeneous (typically off-the-shelf) components should be approached judiciously. Components that are not carefully tailored to work together can cause architectural mismatches. Many examples exist where the needed functionality that was embodied in different components could not be integrated because of discrepancies in the components' interfaces, assumptions, and constraints.

This, in turn has a direct impact on scalability: A system cannot scale up effectively if adding a single component can fundamentally alter the system's properties or, worse, break the system. Relying too much on sophisticated connectors is not the answer in such situations either; engineers may manage to integrate the needed functionality, but possibly at the expense of other properties, such as efficiency, adaptability, or dependability. This is why architectural analysis is an indispensable aid to system integration.

Distribute the Data Sources

It is possible to imagine a situation in which a system employs a single powerful database that is capable of storing all of its data. Such a decision may be justified for reasons of architectural simplicity or in order to decrease the project's costs. However, if the data needs to be accessed concurrently by many other components in the system, modified, and then stored again, the centralized database may not be able to support the needed data volume, especially if the system needs to grow. In other words, the data source component becomes the system's bottleneck. Furthermore, it becomes a single point of failure.

It is preferable in such situations to distribute the data sources, and possibly task each host with a specific, well-defined subset of the data and data consumer components. This enables multiple system components to access the needed data more efficiently and reliably. The added load on the data storage components that results from adding more data processing (that is, client) components will be distributed more evenly across the system. A significant growth in the size of stored data will be amortized across multiple components. Finally, even if one data source were to fail in such a situation, the remainder of the system could still function in a degraded mode. An example of this approach is BitTorrent (Cohen 2003), which is discussed in Chapter 11.

Replicate Data When Necessary

A common technique used to ensure scalable access to system data in distributed systems is data replication. Replication can help support growing numbers of data consumers; they do not all have to go to the same source. In many distributed systems data replication for local consumption—by a single software component or on a single host—is achieved by caching. Replication can also help the system's fault tolerance: If one of the components containing a copy of the needed data fails, requests for that data can be rerouted to another one of its copies.

Data replication must be approached with appropriate caution, however. Engineers must distinguish between mutable and immutable data. Immutable ("read only") data can typically be replicated with few concerns, except when the data is sensitive and access to it needs to be restricted. On the other hand, replicating mutable data requires that all replicas be synchronized. Constant synchronization of distributed copies of the same information can be very expensive in terms of performance, while stale (that is, unsynchronized) data can cause incorrect system behavior and may be unacceptable to the system's users.

12.3.2 Software Connectors and Scalability

As new functionality is added to a software system, the system will likely also need to grow in the number of interaction mechanisms, that is, connector types. New connector instances may also be added to improve the system's performance, for example, by reducing the load on existing connectors. As in the above case, we can identify some general guidelines that can help to improve a system's scalability in terms of interaction. Again, keep in mind that these are general guidelines and that it is possible to encounter software development scenarios that may not allow one to adhere to these guidelines.

Use Explicit Connectors

This guideline may appear obvious by now, but it needs to be stressed because the choice to adhere (or not adhere) to it will have significant implications on the given system's scalability. Connectors remove the burden of interaction from components. They are the natural points of scaling in a system. Even when a given connector, such as a remote procedure call, is unable to support the system's scaling up, architects have the opportunity to replace that connector with a more appropriate one, such as an event-passing or data-caching connector.

System adaptations such as adding new components, extending the system's distribution to new hosts, or increasing the amount of data and the number of data types, can be directly aided by the chosen connectors and, at the same time, should have minimal or no impact on the system's individual components. For example, a component should not need to be aware of the number of other components in the system with which it is interacting.

As discussed in Chapters 4 and 11, software architectures and architectural styles that result in highly scalable systems, such as publish-subscribe or REST, employ explicit, first-class connectors to achieve that scalability.

Give Each Connector a Clearly Defined Responsibility

If a connector is overburdened with supporting multiple interaction facets in a given system, large numbers of components, or large amounts of data, that connector may not be able to support adequately the system's further growth in size. There are scenarios in which a heavy burden on a connector clearly cannot be avoided. In other situations, a connector may be treated by architects as a software bus that should handle all of the interactions in a system or subsystem. An example is a message-oriented middleware product.

In such situations, using a larger number of connector instances of the same type is a simple remedy. Each individual connector thus ends up being simpler and responsible for a smaller portion of the overall system's interactions. As such, it will have the potential to support new interactions as needed in the future and hence to aid the system's scalability. Furthermore, adding new connectors becomes easier because their responsibilities are clearly delineated and component interaction points are clearly defined.

Decisions such as the above—to delegate interaction responsibilities to multiple connectors—may be only conceptual, design aids, but they will also likely manifest themselves in system implementations.

Choose the Simplest Connector Suited for the Task

An architect will often have multiple interaction choices at his disposal. For example, the architect may be able to choose between RPC or a publish-subscribe connector. A decision to go with the latter may be a result of envisioned future system growth, and the impulse may be to go with a far-reaching, more comprehensive solution.

This is not necessarily a wise strategy. Unnecessary complexity usually affects system performance. It is very likely that the system will, in fact, evolve. However, that evolution could be in a direction different from the one anticipated by the architect. Even if the architect turns out to be correct, future adaptations (in this case, future additions of new items such as components, users, points of distribution, and data) should be addressed by introducing the more complex connectors when they are needed. In the meantime, selecting the most appropriate connectors for the system as it currently stands helps to preserve the system's conceptual integrity and likely will speed implementation.

Be Aware of Differences Between Direct and Indirect Dependencies

Direct, explicit dependencies between components in a system, such as those captured by synchronous procedure call connectors, can aid architects with controlling the system's complexity and ensuring that its performance requirements are met. However, scaling up such a system may be nontrivial, precisely because the connectors ensure a tight fit among the system's *current* components.

The alternative is to use indirect, implicit dependencies, possibly simultaneously among multiple components, and possibly characterized by asynchronous interaction. In addition to better supporting scalability, such connectors can also aid system adaptability. Examples discussed previously are event broadcasting connectors and shared data access connectors. The advantages of connectors that support loose component coupling come at a cost, however. Such connectors can negatively impact both the system's complexity and performance. For example, how does one discover the sources of system defects when the component interactions are hidden? How does one ensure system efficiency when, in principle, multiple components can respond to a given request at arbitrary times and in arbitrary order?

A software architect must be aware of this fundamental trade-off and select connectors judiciously.

Do Not Place Application Functionality Inside Connectors

Placing application-specific functionality inside the ostensibly application-independent interaction facilities may be tempting for several reasons. For example, co-locating a connector's caching capability with some in situ data processing may accrue certain performance gains. However, doing so will violate the separation of concerns principle, and will result in an increase in the connector's complexity.

Such a decision will also impact the system's scalability. It likely will be more difficult for a connector to service an increasing number of components or route increasing data volumes if the connector is also encumbered with processing responsibilities. Furthermore, the processing done inside the connector may result in additional dependencies with the components, and possible architectural mismatches. Ironically, the ultimate epilogue may well be that the very property used to justify placing application processing inside the connector—improved system efficiency—may end up undermined.

Leverage Explicit Connectors to Support Data Scalability

There are certain types of application-independent data processing that are naturally housed inside a connector. These are techniques for bringing data closer to its consumers and serving it more efficiently or fluidly, and include buffering, caching, hoarding, and prefetching. Such services may need to be tailored to an application. For example, Should data be cached after the initial request or prefetched in anticipation of future requests? What is the volume of data that needs to be buffered before it is served to a component? Under what circumstances should a copy of the data be stored locally?

These services do not alter a system's functionality, hence the system's components should be completely insulated from them. On the other hand, these services can have a significant impact on the system's non-functional characteristics, in particular, its efficiency and scalability. Therefore, making connectors explicit, first-class entities in the system's architecture is a precondition to providing these data scalability services. Recall that this is a major lesson from the REST style (Chapters 1 and 11), which had to enable an unprecedented degree of data scalability in the REST-compliant systems, most notably the World Wide Web.

12.3.3   Architectural Configurations and Scalability

Avoid System Bottlenecks

If a large and growing number of components depend on services provided by a single other component in a system, that component may eventually become unable to provide its services efficiently or reliably to all of its clients. Similarly, if a large and growing number of components interact through a single connector, at some point that connector may become unable to satisfy the components' interaction needs. In such situations, the overburdened individual components and connectors may have a significant impact on the overall system's performance and may preclude further system growth. In other words, they may become system bottlenecks.

An explicit architectural model can aid with identifying and avoiding bottlenecks. Even a casual glance at the architectural configuration of certain systems can indicate possible bottlenecks. For example, Figure 12-4 suggests that the Library component is a potential bottleneck because all other major Linux components invoke it. In order to establish whether Library is indeed a bottleneck, additional information is needed: How frequently is it called? What is the latency of servicing requests? Are any requests dropped because of the component's inability to service them quickly enough? Is the performance of other system components significantly impacted by this component's performance?

If the component or connector is established as being a bottleneck in the system, the system may need to be redesigned to eliminate this problem. For example, a replica of the overburdened component may be introduced to service a portion of the requests; likewise, a new connector may be inserted to off-load the original connector by servicing a subset of the interacting components. In distributed systems literature, such techniques are commonly referred to as *load balancing*.

Make Use of Parallel Processing Capabilities

Certain types of problems lend themselves naturally to processing in multiple parallel threads. Examples are many scientific computing applications. In such cases, the system's scale in the amount of computation performed or the volume of data processed will depend upon the number of concurrently executing modules, each of which is likely executing on a separate physical processor. In other words, scalability is achieved through sheer distribution.

One limitation, of course, is that not all problems can be easily parallelized in this manner. Unless the *problem* is naturally, easily parallelized, increasing the scale can happen at the significant expense of efficiency.

Place the Data Sources Close to the Data Consumers

If components that need to access some data are distributed across a network, the decision to have a single, remotely located data storage component will result in a lot of network traffic. This, in turn, will affect the system's performance and its ability to accommodate additional client components that may yet further increase the data traffic. One solution is to always keep the data sources close to data consumers, minimizing the resulting network traffic, and even co-locating them on the same host whenever possible.

Clearly, this guideline will be difficult to apply in many distributed systems. Moving the data closer to the processing components can be done virtually through techniques such as caching and prefetching, as discussed earlier. However, in such cases the system needs to ensure that multiple copies of the same data are synchronized, which may add to the system's processing and communications load beyond the savings incurred by making data access local.

Another possibility is to co-locate the processing components. However, the application's location constraints may limit the architect's options. Furthermore, even if a given component could be redeployed to another host (that is, closer to the data), its interactions with other parts of the system may suffer as a result.

Try to Make Distribution Transparent

Relocating either processing or data to improve a system's performance or scalability in the manner discussed above requires some degree of location transparency. We have discussed the potential negative impact of a component's location transparency on efficiency. At the same time, location transparency can aid a system's scalability.

In a distributed setting, scaling up a system will often result in changing the deployment view of the system's architecture. For example, new users may need to be allowed to access the system via new hardware hosts. Processing or data components may need to be added in specific places in the architecture, or they may need to be relocated across hosts, to enable the new users. The outcome will be increased processing and data traffic in the system.

Redeployment may cause significant disturbances to a system. However, if connectors are capable of handling both local and remote interactions in a manner that is transparent to the involved components, then the system can be reconfigured in several ways, such as by redeploying consumer components closer to the needed data sources, replicating remote functionality locally for performance, or off-loading components to capacious remote hosts.

The impact of such adaptations always needs to be assessed carefully before they are effected.

Use Appropriate Architectural Styles

The architectural styles selected for a given system will have a significant influence on that system's scalability. As has been the case with other system properties, even if we do not take into account specific details of the system under development, certain architectural styles will be more appropriate for achieving scalability than others. Thus, for example, publish-subscribe and event-based architectures have been demonstrated to scale to very large numbers of components, users, devices, and data volumes. Other styles typically result in systems that scale well in one or more dimensions. For example, interpreter-based systems cannot easily accommodate growing numbers of users, but can usually handle addition of new functional operators. Likewise, pipe-and-filter may be unable to support increasingly large volumes of data, but can support increasing numbers of components, since arbitrarily long pipelines can be constructed.

12.4 ADAPTABILITY

> *Definition. Adaptability* is a software system's ability to satisfy new requirements and adjust to new operating conditions during its lifetime.

Adaptability can be manual or automated. A software system's architecture has an impact on either type of adaptability. Chapter 14 is dedicated in its entirety to architectural adaptation, so we will make only brief general observations here.

12.4.1 Software Components and Adaptability

Architecturally relevant adaptability occurs at the level of system components, their interfaces, and their composition. In other words, if adaptation is required entirely *within* an individual component or connector, that adaptation is not considered to be architectural. Such adaptations can still be effected with the aid of the system's architecture, for example, by replacing an entire component with its newer version. This observation informs several guidelines for designing for adaptability.

Give Each Component a Single, Clearly Defined Purpose
This guideline has been discussed above—twice—in the context of efficiency and complexity. Since architecture-level adaptation occurs at the level of entire components, it is imperative to separate different system concerns into multiple components. This allows the architects and engineers to minimize the amount of degradation the system experiences during adaptation.

Minimize Component Interdependencies
Adapting a complex system is difficult. Each modification may impact multiple parts of the system. For example, Figure 12-5 indicates that modifying any major subsystem of Linux will, in principle, have an effect on every other subsystem. Defining the system's components to have simple interfaces, in a manner that precludes unnecessary interdependencies, can help to control the effects of adaptation.

Avoid Burdening Components with Interaction Responsibilities
Again, this guideline was discussed previously in the context of other NFPs. In the context of adaptability, the objective is to separate the system's functionality and data from interaction.

Separate Processing from Data

Adaptations to the system's processing components should be handled independently of adaptations to its data.

Separate Data from Meta-Data

Changes to the data in a large, long-lived software system will occur regularly. If the data is separated from the meta-data (that is, the data about the data), then in principle each can be adapted independently of the other. Furthermore, the processing components will be able to adapt more easily to the changes in both the data and the meta-data.

12.4.2 Software Connectors and Adaptability

Connectors are the key enablers of architectural adaptability. Components should be insulated from their particular context to the greatest extent possible in order to appropriately separate system concerns and maximize their reuse potential. It is the task of connectors to provide the necessary facilities that enable a given component to operate appropriately in its environment. Several guidelines for adaptability stem from this observation.

Give Each Connector a Clearly Defined Responsibility

If a connector is in charge of enabling the interactions of a given type among a specific set of components, it will be easier for architects and engineers to manage the required adaptations to those components or their interactions. However, this requires one additional property of connectors, discussed next.

Make the Connectors Flexible

At the least, connectors must be able to support different numbers of components, and possibly component types. If a connector is unable to do so by itself, composing it with other connectors may produce the desired effect, as elaborated next.

Support Connector Composability

To enable interactions among heterogeneous components, which may be added to a system during run time, connectors must be composable with other connectors. For example, Figure 12-6 shows a connector composed from three separate object request brokers (ORBs)—recall the discussion on CORBA from Chapter 4. In the architecture depicted in Figure 12-6, each component exchanges information only with the connector to which it is directly attached; in turn, the connector will (re)package that information and deliver it to its recipients using one or more middleware technologies—whatever is necessary to achieve the desired communication. Each such middleware-enabled connector exposes the interface expected by its attached components. The connector may change the underlying mechanism for marshaling and delivering messages, but externally appears unchanged.

Such a composite connector has the added advantage that it can also preserve the topological and stylistic constraints of the application. For example, the application in Figure 12-6 was designed according to the C2 style (recall Chapter 4). This means that, for example, Component A and Component B can interact with one another, while Component A and

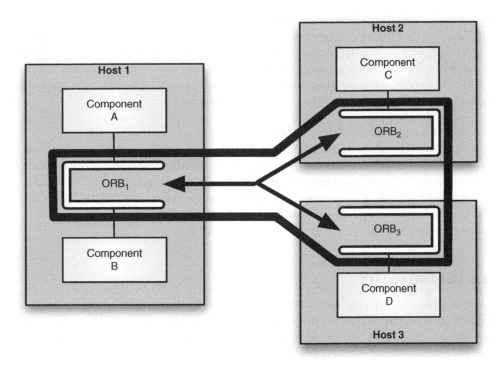

Figure 12-6.
*Distributed
components
interact through a
single conceptual
connector, which
is actually
composed from
multiple
interacting
ORBs. Each
ORB exports the
interfaces
expected by its
attached
components. To
do so, the ORB
may need to
include an
adaptor, depicted
as a highlighted
ORB edge.*

Component C cannot. Using a single ORB to connect the components—even if it were possible—would potentially violate these stylistic constraints.

Another advantage of such composite connectors is that they are independent of other connectors in the system, and can optimize aspects of communication in a homogeneous setting (for instance, if the interaction between Component A and Component B is local). Maintaining a connector's interface and semantics, coupled with its composability, allows much more flexibility in application development and deployment. For instance, if it were later decided that Component C and Component D should indeed run in the same process, it would be possible to make this change by simply reconfiguring the composite connector. The component code would not have to be changed at all.

Be Aware of Differences Between Direct and Indirect Dependencies

This guideline has been discussed above in the context of scalability. Much of the argument is applicable for adaptability. In principle, direct and explicit dependencies result in more efficient systems, while indirect and implicit dependencies allow the given system to adapt more easily.

12.4.3 Architectural Configurations and Adaptability

Leverage Explicit Connectors

A software system in which the connectors are implicit (that is, in which components are endowed with interaction capabilities) will be difficult to adapt since individual concerns may be distributed across multiple system elements.

Try to Make Distribution Transparent

As in the case of scalability, distribution transparency has its advantages when adaptability is concerned: Making modifications to a system is much easier if components are oblivious to the system's deployment profile. For example, the system or one of its parts may be redeployed without requiring changes to the system's components. Of course, the efficiency impact of such adaptations must be carefully taken into account.

Use Appropriate Architectural Styles

As with other NFPs, architectural patterns and styles can directly impact adaptability. Simply put, certain styles are better suited to support adaptability than others. For example, styles that support event-based interaction, such as publish-subscribe and implicit invocation, naturally and effectively support adaptability. On the other hand, styles that require direct dependencies among the components, such as virtual machines or distributed objects, can hamper adaptability.

12.5 DEPENDABILITY

Software dependability researchers Bev Littlewood and Lorenzo Strigini define dependability informally as a collection of system properties that allows one to rely on a system functioning as required (Littlewood and Strigini 2000). Dependability is a composite NFP that encompasses several other, related NFPs: reliability, availability, robustness, fault-tolerance, survivability, safety, and security. Security is discussed in detail in Chapter 13; here, we focus on the design guidelines required to ensure the remaining facets of dependability in a system's software architecture. The following definitions illustrate the interrelated nature of these different facets of dependability. The role of software architecture in ensuring a software system's dependability is then discussed.

> *Definition.* A software system's *reliability* is the probability that the system will perform its intended functionality under specified design limits, without failure, over a given time period.

> *Definition.* A software system's *availability* is the probability that the system is operational at a particular time.

Unlike reliability, which is a statistical measure of the system's overall health over a continuous period of time, availability represents the system's health at discrete snapshots in time.

> *Definition.* A software system is *robust* if it is able to respond adequately to unanticipated run time conditions.

Robustness deals with those run time circumstances that have not been captured in a system's requirements specification. It can be said that responding to conditions specified in the requirements is a matter of system correctness, while responding to all other conditions is a matter of robustness. The adequacy of the response will vary depending on different factors, such as application domain, user, and execution context.

> *Definition.* A software system is *fault-tolerant* if it is able to respond gracefully to failures at run time.

The failures affecting a system can be outside the system itself, whether caused by hardware malfunctions or system software defects, such as network or device driver failures. Alternatively, the system's own components may fail due to internal defects. What constitutes a graceful reaction to failure will depend on the system context. For example, one system may continue operating in a degraded mode; another one may introduce, possibly only temporarily, new copies of the failed components; yet another may offer the "blue screen of death" to the consternation of its users, requiring a reboot of the entire computer, after which the user might be able to continue with normal operation.

From a software architectural perspective, faults can be classified into the following.

1. Faults in the system's environment (that is, outside the software architecture).
2. Faults in components.
3. Faults in connectors.
4. Component-connector mismatches.

An NFP closely related to fault-tolerance is survivability.

> *Definition.* **Survivability is a software system's ability to resist, recognize, recover from, and adapt to mission-compromising threats.**

Survivability must address three basic kinds of threats, cited below.

1. *Attacks*, examples of which are intrusions, probes, and denials of service.
2. *Failures*, which can be due to system deficiencies or defects in external elements on which the system depends.
3. *Accidents*, which are randomly occurring but potentially damaging events such as natural disasters.

Therefore, fault tolerance and survivability are related because the goal of both is to effectively combat threats, and system faults can be viewed as one kind of threat.

It should be noted that the distinctions among the three categories of threats may not matter in the context of recovery from the threats. The key to survivability is to try to recover from these threats as gracefully as possible. In order to make a system survivable, the basic activities that can be performed are the following.

1. Resistance to threats.
2. Recognition of threat and extent of damage.
3. Recovery of full and essential services after a threat.
4. Adaptation and evolution to reduce the impact of future attacks.

The final facet of dependability that will be discussed here is software system safety. Several definitions of software safety are currently in use, and they usually are variations on the definition provided by software safety expert Nancy Leveson (Leveson 1995). We provide a similar definition.

> *Definition.* **Safety denotes the ability of a software system to avoid failures that will result in loss of life, injury, significant damage to property, or destruction of property.**

It should be noted that different degrees of property damage and destruction, and even human injury, may be considered acceptable in the context of different systems and/or system usage scenarios. The elaboration of such circumstances is outside the scope of this book, however.

12.5.1   Software Components and Dependability

More dependable software components will, on the average, result in more dependable software systems—though it should be noted that dependable components need not always result in dependable systems, and that highly dependable systems may comprise undependable individual components (recall the "Honey-Baked Ham" sidebar in Chapter 8). Practice has shown that it is seldom possible to develop components that are completely reliable, robust, and fault-tolerant. However, engineers can follow certain practices to help with achieving these properties. In particular, the guidelines below are targeted at the outwardly visible facets of a component.

Carefully Control External Component Interdependencies

Changes in the behavior of a given component, including anomalous behavior and failures, should have a minimal impact on the remaining components in the system. This can be achieved by properly insulating components from one another. One specific guideline is to restrict all intercomponent dependencies to be explicit and only at the level of the components' public interfaces. Recall from the discussion earlier in this chapter that following this guideline may compromise a system's scalability and adaptability. Another guideline is to minimize, or completely disallow, side effects from component operations.

Provide Reflection Capabilities in Components

While a given component in a system may be unable to provide certain desired dependability guarantees, it should be possible to partially mitigate that by enabling querying of the internal state of the component. This will allow other parts of the system to assess the health of the component at times that are deemed important.

Provide Suitable Exception Handling Mechanisms

When an individual component fails, the rest of the system may be able to adjust to that failure. In order for that adjustment to happen quickly and gracefully, the failing component should be able to expose the necessary information to the rest of the system. One way of doing this is by providing exception reporting mechanisms via the component's public interface. This will allow the other components and connectors in the system to adjust their operation accordingly.

Specify the Components' Key State Invariants

Architects can explicitly state conditions that must hold at different times during the component's execution. Such invariants will allow the component's users to establish best-case, normative, and worst-case guarantees when interacting with that component. Different actions taken in response to that information will then have the potential to improve the overall system's dependability.

12.5.2   Software Connectors and Dependability

Employ Connectors that Strictly Control Component Dependencies

Unintended or implicit dependencies among a system's components will likely harm a system's dependability. Explicit, first-class connectors can be used to manage all dependencies among system components. If necessary, connectors can completely insulate components from one another. It should be noted that widely used connectors such as shared memory and procedure calls give developers too much leeway in creating component interdependencies. Many distributed systems employ connectors that, by necessity, strictly enforce component boundaries and control remote interactions. However, recall from Chapter 5 that even within a single address space it is possible to leverage connectors, such as event buses, that will enforce any component interaction requirements.

Provide Appropriate Component Interaction Guarantees

In certain scenarios, it is imperative that a component receive the data sent to it, even if that means sending the information multiple times. In other scenarios, the system's hardware resources may be overtaxed to the point that, regardless of other needs, the system cannot afford to have the same data transmitted or processed more than once. In yet other circumstances, the recipient components may process each event, even though these are replicas of the same event. In that case, the system's state may erroneously change and the results produced may be wrong. This could have disastrous consequences in a safety-critical system: Consider receiving, multiple times, a command to change the pitch, roll, or yaw of an aircraft by a specified value.

In large, distributed systems—especially those composed with heterogeneous, possibly off-the-shelf components—the individual components may, for instance, make different assumptions about each other, the desired interaction profiles, or the state of the hardware resources. In such situations, it is the responsibility of connectors to ensure that all interaction guarantees (for example, at least once, at most once, or exactly once) are provided, and possibly adapted in response to changing circumstances during the system's execution.

Support Dependability Techniques via Advanced Connectors

A number of dependability concerns and needs in a system cannot be met simply by constructing solid components, properly composing them, and ensuring that they interact only in the prescribed ways. Large, complex, distributed, embedded, and mobile systems need to respond to many external stimuli, and can suffer failures induced by human users, hardware malfunctions, or interference—whether accidental or malicious—from other software systems.

To deal with such situations, connectors may need to support advanced interaction facilities. Examples include providing replicas of failing or failed components on the fly, run time replacement of components (also referred to as "hot swaps"), and support for multiple versions of the same functionality, for example, to ensure the correctness of calculations. These facilities will often need to be provided such that the system's existing, still correctly functioning components are unaware of them. In other words, connectors should support *seamless* dependability.

12.5.3 Architectural Configurations and Dependability

Avoid Single Points of Failure

In many large systems, a large portion of a system may depend on the services provided by one component or a small number of components. If those services are critical to the system's mission, the failure of the component, or components, providing them will significantly or completely incapacitate the system.

There are numerous examples of such systems. For instance, any data-intensive system with a centralized repository cannot afford to lose the repository. Likewise, a spacecraft with a centralized controller will be lost if the controller fails. Yet another example is a swarm of robots relying on a centralized planning engine; the robots may end up roaming aimlessly if the planner malfunctions.

There are several techniques that can be employed to deal with such concerns, including replicating the component in question, clearly separating into multiple components the different concerns it may embody, and employing connectors with advanced capabilities such as those discussed immediately above. At the same time, it should be acknowledged that in some situations it may be impossible to avoid creating a design that contains one or more single points of failure. Regardless of the circumstances (that is, whether the single point of failure can be avoided or not), software architects need to be aware of this issue throughout the design process.

Provide Back-Ups of Critical Functionality and Data

This guideline should be obvious. It also is not universally applicable. For example, it is possible that a lack of system resources or hard real-time constraints effectively prevent back-ups. However, as with one's personal computer or PDA, back-ups are ultimately the best way of ensuring that critical functionality and data are not lost. Different techniques may be used to implement this guideline, including employing advanced connectors such as those discussed above.

Support Nonintrusive System Health Monitoring

It may be too late to try to deal with system malfunctions once they have already occurred. Frequently, however, a system will exhibit anomalous behavior and give hints that something is wrong for some time before it, or a part of it, actually fails. Periodically monitoring the system for certain events that indicate its health status can help engineers to anticipate, and possibly eliminate, any unexpected behavior.

Nonintrusive monitoring can be achieved in a number of different ways. One possibility is to employ a component model that supports the inclusion of explicit monitors at the level of application components. Another, even less intrusive possibility is to include monitoring facilities within the system's connectors. Component containers used in many middleware platforms present another possible target for placing system health monitors.

Support Dynamic Adaptation

A dynamically adaptable system is able to respond to events at run time; a static system may not. Dynamically adaptable systems are able to support the addition, removal, replacement, and reconnection of both components and connectors while the system is running. In decentralized settings they frequently also support dynamic discovery of available services. A thorough treatment of the role of software architecture in dynamic adaptation is provided in Chapter 14.

It should be noted that dynamic adaptation can harm a system's dependability, at least temporarily. Recall the discussion of mobility in Chapter 10 and, in particular, the diagram in Figure 10-12. In addition to rendering the system at least temporarily undependable *during* the dynamic adaptation, it is possible that the result of adaptation will be a system whose critical properties, including its dependability, are compromised. This is a reason why the stakeholders of many highly safety-critical systems are leery of dynamically modifying their systems. In other words, while dynamic adaptation can be a very useful tool at an architect's disposal, it should be applied with caution.

12.6 END MATTER

Engineering a software system to provide the required functionality is often quite challenging. This is why historically a majority of the software design and implementation techniques have focused on supporting and improving a system's functional capabilities. Ultimately, however, good engineers will usually manage to produce almost any functionality, no matter how complex. What they will still struggle with are the non-functional aspects of their systems.

Recall the discussion of the "better-cheaper-faster — pick any two" software engineering maxim from Chapter 10. It suggests that, so long as the system stakeholders are willing to sacrifice one or more of the system's non-functional characteristics, such as schedule, cost, or performance, developers will be able to produce the desired functional capabilities.

Producing those capabilities *along with* the desired non-functional system characteristics is significantly more challenging. There is much less guidance available, in particular to software system architects, for how such characteristics are to be "designed into" the system in question. One reason is that many of these characteristics are loosely defined and qualitative in nature. The challenge becomes even more daunting when system stakeholders have to consider multiple, possibly clashing non-functional characteristics simultaneously.

This chapter has distilled a large body of experience and good software engineering practices into a set of guidelines [or "tactics," as they have been referred to elsewhere in literature, for instance, (Rozanski and Woods 2005)] that software architects can follow in achieving specific non-functional properties. The guidelines should work most of the time, but they should be applied with caution. Whenever appropriate, each of the guidelines in this chapter has been coupled with specific admonitions that reflect the difficulties a software architect may encounter in certain development scenarios.

Both the guidelines and the accompanying admonitions should be kept in mind when designing software systems. The reader should also realize that this chapter did not, and could not, provide a complete enumeration of all possible architectural design scenarios, or all possible trade-offs among the choices made in achieving the desired non-functional characteristics. Chapter 13, which follows, is a companion to this chapter, in that it provides in-depth treatment of security, an NFP of tremendous importance in modern software systems. Together, these two chapters are intended to serve as a rich foundation for software designers targeting NFPs.

The Business Case

Achieving desired non-functional properties often makes the difference between a successful product and a failure. There are many examples from the software development industry. Just recall the example of Microsoft Word 6.0, released in the mid-1990s. The Windows version of the product performed well and was successful. The Macintosh version, with roughly the same functionality, was large and slow, and resulted in a fair amount of bad publicity for Microsoft. This example is telling also in that attempts at patching the product proved unsuccessful, so that Microsoft eventually had to revert to Word 5.0 for its Macintosh user base.

While Microsoft was able to weather this particular storm, a smaller company in its place may not have been able to recover as easily. Inserting a non-functional property into a system after the system has been designed, and possibly implemented, is rarely a successful strategy, and it is fraught with dangers. A more appropriate approach is to plan for the desired properties from the project's inception and to ensure that the necessary architectural design decisions are made. In many situations, even knowing what *not* to do, or at least which pitfalls to avoid, in designing the system can be quite valuable. The guidelines provided in this chapter can serve as a useful tool in that regard.

12.7 REVIEW QUESTIONS

1. Define the following NFPs:
   a. Efficiency
   b. Complexity
   c. Adaptability
   d. Scalability

2. What are the different dimensions of dependability?

3. How is each of the above NFPs manifested in software architectures?

4. How can each of the above NFPs be addressed at the architectural level?

5. Identify at least three guidelines for achieving each of the above NFPs. Elaborate on the manner in which each of those guidelines supports the NFP in question.

6. Can multiple NFPs be achieved simultaneously? If so, under what conditions? If not, why not?

12.8 EXERCISES

1. It is often difficult to simultaneously satisfy multiple non-functional properties (NFPs). Discuss the trade-offs between the following NFPs with respect to their impact on a system's architecture. For each trade-off, provide the answer in three parts: Discuss how your architectural choices can help to maximize each of the two individual properties (possibly at the expense of the other property); then discuss architectural choices that can help you maximize both properties in tandem. Make sure to provide your answer at least in terms of the role and specific characteristics of components and connectors that impact the NFPs.
   a. Performance versus complexity
   b. Safety versus efficiency
   c. Reliability versus adaptability

2. Recall the example Lunar Lander architectures discussed in Chapter 4. Select any two of the architectures from Chapter 4. For each NFP discussed in this chapter, analyze what can and cannot be determined about the selected architectures. Can you recognize any of the NFP design guidelines in either of the two architectures? What is your assessment of the architectures' respective support for the NFP under consideration?

3. Now consider an ADL model of Lunar Lander from Chapter 6. Does the model aid or hamper your ability to answer the questions from the preceding exercise? Be sure to justify your answer.

4. Discuss how one of the architectures selected in the two preceding exercises can be adapted to improve:
   a. Efficiency
   b. Scalability
   c. Adaptability

5. The list of guidelines for achieving the different NFPs provided in this chapter is incomplete. Add at least one additional guideline for each existing NFP.

6. Devise a set of design guidelines for achieving additional properties, such as:
   a. Heterogeneity
   b. Compositionality
   c. Security

   If necessary, you should locate the definitions and any other necessary explanation of these properties. Note that security is discussed in Chapter 13.

7. Analyze the pair–wise trade-offs among one of the properties you devised in the previous exercise and those introduced in this chapter.

12.9 FURTHER READING

Several software engineering textbooks provide useful overviews of non-functional properties (NFPs). Carlo Ghezzi, Mendi Jazayeri, and Dino Mandrioli (Ghezzi, Jazayeri, and Mandrioli 2003) are particularly thorough in their treatment of NFPs. They divide the NFPs into internal (relevant to architects and developers) and external (relevant to customers and users). Furthermore, they divide NFPs into those relevant to the developed product and those relevant to the development process. The NFPs studied in this chapter are the internal product NFPs.

Ghezzi et al. do not focus on the design guidelines for accomplishing the various NFPs. A recent book by Nick Rozanski and Eoin Woods (Rozanski and Woods 2005) attempts to do just that. The authors identify a set of NFPs relevant to software architects. These include performance, scalability, security, and availability. They also propose a number of guidelines, called tactics, targeted at achieving the NFPs. Several of their tactics are relatively general (such as "capture the availability requirements"), and are not targeted separately at different architectural facets such as components, connectors, and configurations.

A volume on the *Future of Software Engineering (FoSE)* (Finkelstein 2000), accompanying the proceedings of the 22nd International Conference on Software Engineering (ICSE 2000), provided a set of useful overviews and research roadmaps for several NFPs, including reliability and dependability (Littlewood and Strigini 2000), performance (Pooley 2000), and safety (Lutz 2000). These topics have been revisited in the *FoSE* volume (Briand and Wolf 2007) accompanying the 29th International Conference on Software Engineering (ICSE 2007) by Michael Lyu on reliability (Lyu 2007), Murray Woodside et al. on performance (Woodside, Franks, and Petriu 2007), and Mats Heimdahl on safety (Heimdahl 2007).

Many of the architectural guidelines advocated in this chapter targeted at accomplishing NFPs emerged over time from general software engineering principles. For example, modularity and separation of concerns was articulated by David Parnas more than thirty years ago (Parnas 1972). More recently, Robert DeLine has argued for a decoupling of a component's "essence" from its "packaging" (DeLine 2001). Robert Allen, David Garlan, and John Ockerbloom have shared a very useful experience on the effects of off-the-shelf component integration on a system's NFPs, and the inherent architectural causes (Garlan, Allen, and Ockerbloom 1995; Garlan, Allen, and Ockerbloom 1995).

13

Security and Trust

The preceding chapter introduced several non-functional properties, such as efficiency, scalability, and dependability, and described architectural design strategies to help achieve those properties. Security is another non-functional property; its increasing, critical importance warrants the separate, in-depth look provided in this chapter. As with many other non-functional properties, it is most effectively addressed while designing a system's architecture.

Consider the example of building architectures introduced in Chapter 1. A building is designed with various structural properties and the owner's requirements in mind. If such requirements and design do not encompass security needs, problems can arise. For instance, if a building has windows or doors that are easy to access from the outside, or its structure prevents the installation of security alarms, the building may be vulnerable to unwanted visitors. If these considerations are addressed during the building's design, however, a secure structure at a reasonable price is achievable.

If the building is not designed from the outset with security in mind, it may still be possible to add external reinforcements to improve security when such demands later occur. For example, thin walls can be reinforced by adding extra layers; doors and windows that represent potential points of entry can be safeguarded using suitable lock mechanisms. In some cases, a building may not be securable by itself but it might be housed within a gated enclosure that can safeguard an entire community against external intruders.

The caveat of adding security afterward, though, is that it is generally more expensive than taking the proper measures from the beginning. Imagine opening up the walls, installing extra wires and cameras, then closing the walls. This is more expensive than envisioning the requirements from the start and designing the building around those requirements. The same is true for software. It is therefore imperative that security be considered and treated when developing a system's architecture. Using a software architecture-based approach for security allows developers to leverage experience and achieve desired security properties. Software architecture also provides a sound basis for reasoning about security properties.

Note that while external reinforcements can be used to provide a certain degree of security post-development, it still entails that the software be designed to allow addition of such reinforcements without compromising required functionalities. This makes reasoning about security at the architectural level even more important. Further, since software systems often go through an extended round of releases as new functionalities are added, a security-based architectural approach can provide guidance through the various software evolution cycles and help ensure that essential security properties continue to be achieved through each release.

Security, as important as it is, is only a part of the overall system. It has to be balanced with other non-functional properties. For example, encryption is generally used in software systems to keep data secret, but using encryption can be computationally expensive, and the performance of the system might be adversely impacted by such operations. Even more importantly, security, along with other non-functional properties, must be balanced against a system's general functional requirements. For example, a browser that displays and executes all types of content would provide the richest experience for users, but such indiscreet execution is almost doomed to bring malicious software into a user's computer. When facing such choices, uninformed stakeholders, such as end-users and product-planning teams, might choose functionality over other critical properties. A software architecture approach can ameliorate this condition by providing the necessary abstraction and tools that will help stakeholders to make sound decisions.

The chapter begins with introduction of the different aspects of security, including confidentiality, integrity, and availability. Section 13.2 discusses several general design principles for security. These principles have been developed by theoreticians and practitioners over the years and have been applied in many systems. We illustrate how these principles can be applied to software architectures. In some contrast to the preceding chapter, however, the design guidance provided is not as straightforward. Properties such as efficiency and dependability have been important to software designers since the beginning of software engineering, hence it is not surprising that the preceding chapter was replete with crisp techniques for achieving them. Security is of more recent prominence, and is arguably more subtle, so a broad understanding and application of general design principles is needed. In Section 13.3, a technique for architectural access control is presented that complements other design techniques with capabilities to specify and regulate intercomponent communication. The chapter concludes with presentation in section 13.4 of an architectural approach for constructing trust-enabled decentralized applications. These types of applications play an important role in the emerging collaborative Web world, where autonomous users communicate and collaborate in a community environment and require trust management to protect themselves from malicious users.

13.1 SECURITY

The National Institute of Standards and Technology defines computer security as, "The protection afforded to an automated information system in order to attain the applicable objectives of preserving the integrity, availability and confidentiality of information system resources (includes hardware, software, firmware, information/data, and telecommunications)" (Guttman and Roback 1995). According to this definition, there are three main aspects of security: confidentiality, integrity, and availability. We briefly introduce them here; for a comprehensive treatment, see the references in the "Further Reading" section at the end of the chapter.

Confidentiality

Preserving the confidentiality of information means preventing unauthorized parties from accessing the information or perhaps even being aware of the existence of the information. Confidentiality is also referred to as secrecy.

This concept is as applicable in the domain of building architectures as it is to computer systems. For example, in a large office complex having two buildings, if the office management does not want others to know when certain items are moved between the two buildings, the management could build a covered passage between them so that others outside the building are unable to see what is moved within the passage. Even better, the passage could be built underground so people would not even be aware of the existence of the passage.

Applying this concept to software architectures, software systems should take proper measures while exchanging information to protect confidential information from being intercepted by rogue parties. Likewise, systems should store sensitive data in a secure way so unauthorized users cannot discover the content or even the existence of such data.

Cryptography

A well-known measure to support secrecy in software systems is use of encryption techniques. Cryptography itself has been used since the beginning of civilization, and the wide use of computer systems facilitates the wide adoption of computer cryptography. A basic encryption mechanism can be described with the following equations:

$$Cipher = Encryption\,Function(Encryption\_Key, ClearText)$$

$$ClearText = Decryption\,Function(Decryption\,Key, Cipher)$$

When information needs to be encrypted to preserve confidentiality during communication or storage, the information, called clear text, is fed into an encryption algorithm, along with an encryption key, to produce a cipher. To retrieve the original information stored in the cipher, the cipher can be fed into a decryption algorithm, along with the decryption key, to produce the original clear text.

An encryption function has a corresponding decryption function. After using a specific encryption function, only the corresponding decryption function can be used to decrypt the cipher.

There are two forms of cryptography functions. With *shared-key cryptography* the same key is used by both the encryption and decryption functions. This type of scheme has been used since the earliest days of cryptography. Management of the shared key presents problems, however. Since the key is shared between the sender and the receiver, the key must be delivered to both the sender and the receiver, which can be awkward if a sender wants to communicate with many receivers. Moreover since best security practices demand that keys not be reused (in order to defeat cryptanalysis efforts by opponents), these key deliveries must be performed every time a key is changed.

To solve the key management problem with the shared-key scheme, *public key cryptography* was invented in 1970s. These systems use a key pair, which consists of two related keys that are generated at the same time. One key, the private key, is retained and kept secret by an individual party. The corresponding key, the public key, is published by the individual and shared with everyone. To send information secretly, the initiator encrypts the clear text with the public key of the *recipient*, and sends the cipher text. The recipient's private key is used by the individual to decrypt the message. If the keys are appropriately generated it is computationally infeasible for a third party to determine the individual's private key from the known public key, hence confidential communication is ensured.

Besides secrecy, public key cryptography can also be used to provide nonrepudiation. The private key can be used to generate a digital signature. Such a signature is similar to a regular handwritten signature in that only the person who possesses the private key can generate the signature. Thus, receiving information having such a digital signature is a sure sign that the sender has sent the information, since no one can generate the signature without the private key. Recipients can use the sender's public key to verify signatures, thus establishing that the information was indeed sent by the sender (nonrepudiation) and that it is authentic and was not modified along the way.

While a public key mechanism is flexible and mathematically sound, it suffers from a performance problem. It is generally orders of magnitude slower than a shared-key algorithm. Thus, a choice exists between private key and public key: the former is fast, but is inflexible, and requires complex key management mechanism; the latter provides scalability and ease of management, but is much slower. An architectural solution that combines both of them is to use a public key mechanism to negotiate a shared key in the beginning of the communication session, and then apply the negotiated key with a shared-key encryption algorithm in the ensuing communications.

An important principle while designing a cryptography based system is to avoid designing yet another encryption algorithm. Such algorithm design requires extensive mathematical skills, which is outside the scope of most projects. If you think you can design a secret encryption algorithm, then the admonition, "Do not depend on secrecy for security," is applicable here. It is almost inevitable that a determined hacker will expose the operational details of the newly proposed algorithm, and the "security" based on secrecy is lost. Instead, to design secure software based on cryptography to achieve secrecy and nonrepudiation, a designer should evaluate performance, architecture, and security requirements, choose a suitable public algorithm, and use frequently changing keys as the primary secrecy mechanism.

Integrity

Maintaining the integrity of information means that only authorized parties can manipulate the information and do so only in authorized ways. For example, in a building protected by a door that can be opened by entering an access code on a numeric panel, only the owner should be able to change the code. Moreover, when the code is changed, it should only be changeable to another numeric code—not to an alphanumeric one.

Analogous constructs exist at the programming language level, such as access modifiers of member fields and functions. For example, in Java, member fields and functions are given access levels as `private`, `package`, `protected`, and `public`, such that only certain parts of the class hierarchy can access those members. A `private` field of a class can only be accessed by the methods of the same class, whereas a `package` method can be called by all classes of the same package. Likewise, in C++, `const` pointers can be defined that enforce the condition that data accessed through those pointers cannot be changed.

At the software component and architectural level, similar protective mechanisms can be applied to the interfaces of components. For example, if a particular interface of a component changes the most critical information belonging to that component, invocation of that interface should be ensured to be limited to only authorized components. Therefore, such an interface should be designated and separated from the others and receive more scrutiny during design.

To establish the identity of a user—and hence to determine whether a user is authorized or not—an authentication process is used to verify that the user is really who the user claims to be. The most common form of authentication is the user name/password pair: If a user can correctly supply the password associated with a user name, then the user is authenticated as that specific user. This is a form of authentication that relies on what a user knows; other forms of authentication include checking who the user is (for example, by scanning the iris of the user and comparing it to a set of authorized irises) and what the user has. (For example, a user must posses a security token that can generate the correct number at the correct time.)

Depending on security requirements, different levels of authentication may be used for software components and connectors. For example, in the Microsoft DCOM middleware technology, authentication may be bypassed completely. However, if needed, authentication can be performed at the beginning of a communication session, for each method, or even for each communication packet. The most secure authentication level is, of course, the packet authentication level, but it is also the most computationally expensive. The authentication requirements of a communicating client and server determine what the DCOM middleware connector must do. In particular, the middleware connector ensures that both parties operate on the chosen authentication level.

To deter potential intruders, a software system can maintain an audit trail that records important historical information. By analogy, the security guard of a gated housing community can record every visitor's name, license plate, and visiting time, so any security incident could be correlated to possible suspects. Likewise, security cameras can be deployed to record the activities of residents. (Of course, such measures have to be balanced against privacy requirements!) Correspondingly, in the case of software components, audit trails can be maintained internally; that is, a component may log requests and responses from an authenticated user and then produce an audit trail of those requests and responses at a later time. Connectors may also be used to log component invocations that pass through the connector. Further, since the architecture provides a systemwide view of the configuration of components and connectors, an audit trail can be captured recording patterns of access through the system.

Availability

Resources are *available* if they are accessible by authorized parties on all appropriate occasions. In contrast, if a system cannot deliver its services to its authorized users because of the activities of malicious users, then its services are unavailable; it is said to be the victim of a denial of service (DoS) attack.

Applications that are distributed across a network, such as the Internet, may be susceptible to a distributed denial of service (DDoS) attack. Such attacks try to bring down the many distributed elements of an application. For example, the Domain Name System (DNS), which is in charge of resolving URLs to IP addresses and is distributed across different levels of operation, has occasionally been the target of such attacks. When such attacks succeed, access to Web resources, for example, may be denied.

13.2 DESIGN PRINCIPLES

Security aspects of software systems should be considered from a project's start. During system conception the security requirements should be identified and corresponding security measures designed. Patching security problems after a system is built can be prohibitively expensive, if not technically infeasible. Security requirements also evolve with other requirements. Thus, an architect should anticipate possible changes and design flexibility into the security architecture. The architecture of the system is the place for software developers to identify the security requirements, design the security solutions, and design to accommodate future changes.

This section highlights several design principles that help guide the design of secure software. These principles emerged from the research community and have since been applied in many commercial software systems. Such principles are by no means sufficient by themselves for the design of secure software, but do play an important role in guiding designers and architects through possible alternatives and choosing an appropriate solution.

- *Least privilege:* Give each component *only* the privileges it requires.
- *Fail-safe defaults:* Deny access if explicit permission is absent.
- *Economy of mechanism:* Adopt simple security mechanisms.
- *Complete mediation:* Ensure every access is permitted.
- *Open design:* Do not rely on secrecy for security.
- *Separation of privilege:* Introduce multiple parties to avoid exploitation of privileges.
- *Least common mechanism:* Limit critical resource sharing to only a few mechanisms.
- *Psychological acceptability:* Make security mechanisms usable.
- *Defense in depth:* Have multiple layers of countermeasures.

These principles adapted from (Bishop 2003), (Saltzer and Schroeder 1975), and (Gasser 1988).

Design Principles for Computer Security

Principle of Least Privilege

The principle of least privilege states that a subject should be given only those privileges it needs to complete its task. The rationale is that even if a subject is compromised, the attacker has access only to a limited set of privileges, which limits the damage to certain specific parts of the system.

Currently, many less-informed Windows users browse the Internet using an account with many administrative privileges. This is not only unnecessary for the simple task of browsing the Web but is potentially dangerous since it opens paths for malicious software to take control of the user's computer. This practice owes its origin to early versions of Windows that were generally shipped with only one account, the administrator account. Based on the principle of least privilege, a minimally privileged account should be used for daily simple activities such as browsing and e-mail. Embodying this principle, Internet Explorer 7, shipped in late 2006, can lower its privileges during execution to below those of the launching user's privileges.

Software architecture makes it easier to determine the least privileges components should have since explicit models of the architecture enable analysis of communication and control paths to determine the necessary attributes. A component should not be given more privileges than are necessary for it to interact with other appropriate components.

Principle of Fail-Safe Defaults

The principle of fail-safe defaults states that unless a subject is granted explicit access to an object, it should be denied access to that object. This scheme might deny some safe requests that otherwise would have been granted, but it assures that each granted access is a safe access.

A simple illustration of this principle is the case of Internet browsers requesting a resource ("GETing a URL") on behalf of a user's request. Fetching and displaying a resource is a form of granting permissions based on the user-selected URL. Since a URL can be expressed and encoded in different forms (such as using absolute paths versus relative paths), it is not always straightforward to list and reject *all* invalid URLs. Thus, this rule suggests that accesses to all URLs should be denied unless their form can be verified as belonging to a known, valid kind. Based on this principle, a connector connecting two components should only allow the specific communications that satisfy some approval criterion, rejecting all others.

Principle of Economy of Mechanism

The principle of economy of mechanism states that security mechanisms should be as simple as possible—also referred as the KISS principle (Keep it Simple and Small). While this rule generally is useful with any type of design, it is especially important for security systems. Complexity is the enemy of security because complex interactions make verifying the security of software systems more difficult and hence could possibly lead to a security breach.

One way to apply this principle is to isolate, consolidate, and minimize security controls. Redundant security mechanisms should be simplified. For example, in Internet Explorer prior to Version 7, there were multiple places where URLs were analyzed and results of these analyses were used to make decisions. Such redundancy and inconsistency led to security vulnerabilities. This issue was corrected in Internet Explorer Version 7 by centralizing the handling of URLs. An architecture description provides a suitable abstraction to apply this principle more generally. It allows architects to analyze the locations of security controls, identify potential redundancy, and evaluate alternatives to choose a suitable place for the control.

Principle of Complete Mediation

The principle of complete mediation requires that all accesses to entities be checked to ensure that they are allowed, irrespective of who is accessing what. The check should also ensure that the attempted access does not violate any security properties.

Applying this principle to a software system requires all communication to be checked thoroughly. Such an inspection is greatly facilitated through the systematic view of the system provided by an accurate architectural model. A security architect can evaluate each possible interaction among the components in all types of configurations to make sure that none of the interactions and configurations violate the intended security rules.

The principle of economy of mechanism helps achieve complete mediation. Where there are only a limited number of security control mechanisms it is easier to apply security control, verifying that each access actually goes through these mechanisms.

Principle of Open Design

The principle of open design states that the security of a mechanism should not depend upon the secrecy of its design or implementation. While secrecy is a desired security property, secrecy itself should not be used as a mechanism. A secure design should not rely on the fact that an intruder does not know the internal operations of the software system. While keeping the internals secret might initially make it more difficult for an attacker to break into a system, simply relying on such secrecy is unreliable. It is inevitable that such information will be discovered by malicious users in a world where many different types of information and computational resources are available to attackers. Trivially, employees could leak the secret, either intentionally or unintentionally. Among other options, the attacker can also try clever reverse engineering or simple brute force attacks.

Revealing the internals of a system can actually increase its security. In early stages of design other security reviewers can inspect and evaluate the design and provide insights.

Further, during its operation and evolution phases, the system can be studied and refined accordingly to make it more secure. For instance, a system's security should not rely upon a software connector implementing a proprietary (secret) communication protocol. The likelihood of that idiosyncratic communication protocol having flaws is very high. Rather, using a protocol that has passed extensive external scrutiny is far more likely to provide the security desired.

Principle of Separation of Privilege

The principle of separation of privilege states that a system should not grant permission based on a single condition. It suggests that sensitive operations should require the cooperation of more than one key party. For example, a purchase order request generally should not be approvable solely by the requestor; otherwise, an unethical employee could keep requesting and approving inappropriate purchase orders without immediate detection by others.

Software architecture descriptions facilitate the checking of this principle. If an architect discovers that some component possesses multiple privileges that should be separated, the architect should redesign the system and the component so that the privileges are partitioned amongst multiple components.

Principle of Least Common Mechanism

The principle of least common mechanism states that mechanisms used to access separate resources should not be shared. The objective of the principle is to avoid the situation where errors or compromises of the mechanism while accessing one resource allow compromise of all resources accessible by the mechanism. For instance, use of separate machines, separate networks, or virtual machines can help fulfill this principle and avoid cross-contamination.

In the context of software architectures, this implies the need for careful scrutiny when certain software architectural styles are used. For example, in the case of the blackboard style, where all data is maintained on the shared blackboard and access to it is mediated by the blackboard component, the architect must ensure that the existence of the shared store and common mechanism does not introduce unintended security problems.

Principle of Psychological Acceptability

The principle of psychological acceptability states that security mechanisms should not make the resource more difficult to access for legitimate users than if the security mechanisms were not present. Likewise, the human interface of security mechanisms should be designed to match the mental model of the users and should be easily usable. Otherwise, the users will either attempt to bypass the security measure because it is too difficult to use, or use it incorrectly because the user interface is error-prone.

This principle did not receive much attention in the past, but now that software has become a mainstream phenomenon and most computer users are not technically savvy, it is increasingly important to design security mechanisms keeping users' psychological acceptability in mind.

By analogy, a building may have several security capabilities to safeguard it, such as specially designed door and security alarms. Yet if the building owner does not use them because they are too cumbersome or error-prone, then essentially the building becomes as vulnerable to potential threats as if the safeguards did not exist. With regard to software systems, an application may support security techniques such as digital authentication and cryptography, but if the end users do not use those techniques because they do not understand the mechanisms or cannot use the mechanisms correctly, the resulting system may become vulnerable to security attacks such as impersonation and repudiation.

Bruce Schneier, on Security Systems, rather than Security Technologies	The principle of psychological acceptability has been emphasized by Bruce Schneier, a security expert and the author of *Applied Cryptography* (Schneier 1995). In the preface to his subsequent book, *Secrets and Lies* (Schneier 2000) he writes,

> Cryptography is a branch of mathematics. And like all mathematics, it involves numbers, equations, and logic. Security, palpable security that you or I might find useful in our lives, involves people: things people know, relationships between people, people and how they relate to machines. Digital security involves computers: complex, unstable, buggy computers.
>
> Mathematics is perfect; reality is subjective. Mathematics is defined; computers are ornery. Mathematics is logical; people are erratic, capricious, and barely comprehensible.
>
> The error of *Applied Cryptography* is that I didn't talk at all about the context. I talked about cryptography as if it were The Answer™. I was pretty naïve.
>
> The result wasn't pretty. Readers believed that cryptography was a kind of magic security dust that they could sprinkle over their software and make it secure. That they could invoke magic spells like "128-bit key" and "public-key infrastructure." A colleague once told me that the world was full of bad security systems designed by people who read *Applied Cryptography*.
>
> Since writing the book, I have made a living as a cryptography consultant: designing and analyzing security systems. To my initial surprise, I found that the weak points had nothing to do with the mathematics. They were in the hardware, the software, the networks, and the people. Beautiful pieces of mathematics were made irrelevant through bad programming, a lousy operating system, or someone's bad password choice. I learned to look beyond the cryptography, at the entire system, to find weaknesses. I started repeating a couple of sentiments you'll find throughout this book: "Security is a chain; it's only as secure as the weakest link." "Security is a process, not a product."
>
> Any real-world system is a complicated series of interconnections. Security must permeate the system: its components and connections.

Principle of Defense in Depth

The principle of defense in depth states that a system should have multiple defensive countermeasures to discourage potential attackers. Since an attacker will have to break through each of these countermeasures, it increases the likelihood of being able to identify and prevent an attack from occurring.

This principle requires each component in a path that leads to a critical component to implement proper security measures in its own context. This ensures that the security of the whole system will not be violated just because of one component's failure to implement proper security control.

A good example is the way Microsoft Internet Information Service (IIS) Version 6 (a Web server) handles WebDAV requests. By re-architecting IIS, utilizing the underlying support provided by the operating system, and applying appropriate security measures at

POTENTIAL PROBLEM	PROTECTION MECHANISM	DESIGN PRINCIPLES
The underlying dll (ntdll.dll) was not vulnerable because...	Code was made more conservative during the Security Push.	Check precondition
Even if it were vulnerable...	Internet Information Services (IIS) 6.0 is not running by default on Windows Server 2003.	Secure by default
Even if it were running...	IIS 6.0 does not have WebDAV enabled by default.	Secure by default
Even if Web-based Distributed Authoring and Versioning (WebDAV) had been enabled...	The maximum URL length in IIS 6.0 is 16 Kbytes by default (>64 Kbytes needed for the exploit).	Tighten precondition, secure by default
Even if the buffer were large enough...	The process halts rather than executes malicious code due to buffer-overrun detection code inserted by the compiler.	Tighten postcondition, check precondition
Even if there were an exploitable buffer overrun...	It would have occurred in w2wp.exe, which is running as a network service (rather than as administrator).	Least privilege (Data courtesy of David Aucsmith)

Figure 13-1. *Security for Microsoft IIS. Table data from Table 1 in (Wing 2003). (c) IEEE 2003.*

multiple points along the access path, IIS has become a far more secure system than its previous versions. The different mechanisms applied by different components along the WebDAV access path are shown in Figure 13-1.

This principle does not contradict the principle of economy of mechanism because it does not duplicate identical security checks, or worse, implement similar but inconsistent checks. Instead, each component provides unique security safeguards that are most appropriate in its local context and thus helps to collectively form a more secure system.

13.3 ARCHITECTURAL ACCESS CONTROL

Having introduced the design principles for building secure software, we now present one technique, architectural access control, to demonstrate how software architects can follow the above-described principles in designing secure software systems. We define the basic access control models in security, illustrate how these models can be applied during architectural design, introduce software tools that facilitate the utilization of these models, and, through examples, show how these concepts and techniques can be practiced.

13.3.1   Access Control Models

The most basic security mechanism used to enforce secure access is a *reference monitor*. A reference monitor controls access to protected resources and decides whether access should be granted or denied. The reference monitor must intercept every possible access from external subjects to the secured resources and ensure that the access does not violate any policy. Widely accepted practices require a reference monitor to be tamper-proof, non-bypassable, and small. A reference monitor should be tamper-proof so that it cannot be altered. It should be non-bypassable so that each access is mediated by the reference monitor. It should be small so that it can be thoroughly verified.

Two dominant types of access control models are discretionary access control (DAC) models and mandatory access control (MAC) models. In a discretionary model, access is based on the identity of the requestor, the accessed resource, and whether the requestor has permission to access the resource. This permission can be granted or revoked at the resource owner's discretion. In contrast, in a mandatory model, the access decision is made according to a policy specified by a central authority.

Classic Discretionary Access Control

The Access Matrix Model is the most commonly used discretionary access control model. It was first proposed by Butler Lampson (Lampson 1974) and later formalized by Michael Harrison, Walter Ruzzo, and Jeffrey Ullman (Harrison, Ruzzo, and Ullman 1976). In this model, a system contains a set of subjects (also called principals) that have privileges (also called permissions) and a set of objects on which these privileges can be exercised. An access matrix specifies the privilege a subject has on a particular object. The rows of the matrix correspond to the subjects, the columns correspond to the objects, and each cell lists the allowed privileges that the subject has on the object. The access matrix can be implemented directly resulting in an authorization table. More commonly, it is implemented as an access control list (ACL), where the matrix is stored by column, and each object has one column that specifies the privileges each subject has over the object. A less common implementation is a capability system, where the access matrix is stored by rows, and each subject has a row that specifies the privileges (capabilities) that the subject has over all objects.

Role-Based Access Control

A role-based access control (RBAC) model is a more recent extension of the classic access control model. In this model, an extra level of indirection, called a role, is introduced. Roles become the entities that are authorized with permissions. Instead of authorizing a user's access to an object directly, the authorization is expressed as a role's permissions to an object and the user can be assigned to the corresponding role. RBAC allows roles to form a hierarchy. In such a hierarchical RBAC model, a senior role can inherit from a junior role. Every user that takes the senior role can also take the junior role, thus obtaining all the permissions associated with the junior role. The RBAC model, thus, eases management of access control in large-scale organizations. Instead of granting and revoking permissions individually to many users, all relevant users can be assigned a single role, and the permissions can be granted and revoked to this role. Role-based access control allows a clear specification of the roles that cannot be performed simultaneously by a user.

Mandatory Access Control

Mandatory access control models are less common and more stringent than discretionary models. They can prevent both direct and indirect inappropriate access to a resource. The most common types of mandatory models work in a multilevel security (MLS) environment, which is typical in a military setting. In that environment, each subject (denoting a user) and each object are assigned a security label. These labels have a dominance relationship between them. For example, the top-secret label dominates the classified information label. A subject can only access information whose label is dominated by the label of the subject. Thus, a subject with only classified information clearance cannot access top secret information, but a subject with top secret clearance is able to access content that is labeled classified information.

13.3.2 Connector–Centric Architectural Access Control

This section presents a connector-centric approach that describes one way in which the above-described access control models can be applied and enforced at the architectural level. Specifically, we describe how an architectural description can be extended to model security and how the resultant description can be checked to examine whether the architecture successfully addresses the security needs of the system.

Basic Concepts

The core concepts that are necessary to model access control at the architecture level are *subject, principal, resource, privilege, safeguard*, and *policy*.

Subject. A *subject* is the user on whose behalf a piece of software executes. The concept of subject is key in security, but is typically missing from software architectural models. Many software architectures assume that (a) all of its components and connectors execute under the same subject, (b) this subject can be determined at design-time, (c) the subject generally will not change during run time, either inadvertently or intentionally, and (d) even if there is a change, it will have no impact on the software architecture. As a result, there is typically no modeling facility to capture the allowed subjects of architectural components and connectors. Consequently, the allowed subjects cannot be checked against actual subjects at execution time to ensure security conformance. In order to address these needs for architectural access control, basic component and connector constructs must be extended with the subject for which they perform, thus enabling architectural design and analysis based on different security subjects.

Principal. A subject can take upon it multiple *principals*. Essentially, principals encapsulate the credentials that a subject possesses to acquire permissions. There are different types of credentials. In the classic access control model, the principal is synonymous with the subject and directly denotes the identity of the subject. But there exist other types of principals that provide indirection and abstraction necessary for more advanced access control models. In a role-based access control model, each principal can denote one role that the user adopts. The results for accessing resources will vary depending on the different principals a subject possesses.

Resource. A *resource* is an entity for which access should be protected. Example resources and access controls on them are files that should be read-only, password databases that should only be modified by administrators, and ports that should only be opened by the root user. Traditionally, resources are *passive* and accessed by active software components operating for different subjects. However, in the case of software architecture, resources can also be *active*. Specifically, software components and connectors may also be considered resources, access to which should be protected. Such an active view is lacking in traditional architectural modeling. Explicitly enabling this view can give architects more analysis and design power to improve security assurance.

Permission, Privilege, and Safeguard. *Permissions* describe operations on a resource that a component may perform. A *privilege* describes what permissions a component possesses depending upon the executing subject. Privilege is an important security concept that is missing from traditional architecture description languages. Most current modeling approaches take a maximum privilege route wherein a component's interfaces list all the privileges that that component could possibly need. This could become a source for privilege escalation vulnerabilities that are caused when a less privileged component is given more privileges than it properly should be granted in a particular usage context. A more disciplined modeling of privileges is therefore needed to reduce such vulnerabilities.

There are two types of privileges corresponding to the two types of resources. The first type handles passive resources and enumerates, for instance, which subject has read/write access to which files. The second type deals with active resources. These privileges include architecturally important privileges such as instantiation and destruction of architectural elements, connection of components with connectors, execution through message routing or procedure invocation, and reading and writing architecturally critical information. These privileges are pivotal in ensuring secure execution of software systems.

A notion corresponding to privilege is *safeguard*, which describes conditions that are required to access the interfaces of protected components and connectors. A safeguard attached to a component or a connector specifies the privileges that other components and connectors must possess before they can access the protected component or connector.

Policy. A *policy* ties together the concepts above. It specifies what privileges a subject, with a given set of principals, should have in order to access resources that are protected by safeguards. It is the foundation needed by the architectural elements to make access control decisions. Components and connectors consult the policy to decide whether an architectural access should be granted or denied.

The Central Role of Architectural Connectors

Architectural access control is centered on connectors because connectors propagate privileges that are necessary for access control decisions. They regulate communication between components and can also support secure message routing.

Components: Supply Security Contract. A security *contract* specifies the privileges and safeguards of an architectural element.

In the ensuing discussion, for purposes of specific illustration, we will utilize and refer to modeling architectures using the xADL language (Dashofy, van der Hoek, and Taylor 2005), as presented in Chapter 6. For component types, the above modeling constructs are modeled as extensions to the base xADL types. The extended security modeling constructs describe the subject the component type acts for, the principals this component type can take, and the privileges the component type possesses.

The base xADL component type supplies interface signatures that describe the basic functionality of components of this type. These signatures become the active resources that should be protected. Thus, each interface signature is augmented with safeguards that specify the necessary privileges an accessing component must possess before the interfaces can be accessed.

Connectors: Regulate and Enforce Contract. Connectors play a key role in regulating and enforcing the security contract specified by components. They can determine the subjects for which the connected components are executing. For example, in a normal SSL (secure socket layer) connector, the server authenticates itself to the client, thus the client knows the executing subject of the server. A stronger SSL connector can also require client authentication, thus both the server component and the client component know the executing subjects of each other.

Connectors also determine whether components have sufficient privileges to communicate through the connectors. For example, a connector can use the information about the privileges of connected components to decide whether a component executing under a certain subject can deliver a request to the serving component. This regulation is subject to the policy specification of the connector. The recent version of DCOM, for example, introduces such regulation on local and remote connections.

Connectors can also potentially serve to provide secure interaction between insecure components. Since many components in component-based software engineering can only be used "as is" and many of them do not have corresponding security descriptions, a connector is a suitable place to assure appropriate security. A connector decides which communications are secure and should be allowed, which communications are dangerous and should be rejected, or which communications are potentially insecure and require close monitoring.

A Secure Architecture Description Language: Secure xADL. Secure xADL is a software architecture description language that describes security properties of a software architecture. Secure xADL combines the xADL language with the architectural access control concepts defined in the preceding paragraphs. Figure 13-2 depicts the core syntax of Secure xADL. The central construct is `SecurityPropertyType`, which is a collection of the subject, the principals, the privileges, and the policies of an architectural element. The `SecurityPropertyType` can be attached to component and connector types in xADL. Figure 13-2 illustrates that it is attached to a connector type to make a secure connector type. The `SecurityPropertyType` can also be attached to components and connectors, making them secure components and connectors. Finally, the `SecurityPropertyType` can also be attached to the specifications of subarchitectures and the description of the global software architecture.

An access control policy describes what access control requests should be permitted or denied. The policies for Secure xADL are embedded in the xADL syntax and written with the eXtensible Access Control Markup Language (XACML) (OASIS 2005). XACML is an open standard from OASIS (Organization for the Advancement of Structured Information Standards) to describe access control policies for different types of applications. It is utilized in an environment where a policy enforcement point (PEP) asks a policy decision point (PDP) whether a request, expressed in XACML, should be permitted. The PDP consults

Figure 13-2.
Secure xADL
schema.

```
<complexType name="SecurityPropertyType">
  <sequence>
    <element name="subject"
             type="Subject"/>
    <element name="principals"
             type="Principals"/>
    <element name="privileges"
             type="Privileges"/>
    <element name="policies"
             type="Policies"/>
  </sequence>
</complexType>

<complexType name="SecureConnectorType">
  <complexContent>
    <extension base="ConnectorType">
      <sequence>
        <element mame="security"
             type="SecurityPropertyType"/>
      </sequence>
    </extension>
  </complexContent>
</complexType>

<complexType name="SecureSignature">
  <complexContent>
    <extension base="Signature">
      <sequence>
        <element name="safeguards"
             type="Safeguards"/>
      </sequence>
    </extension>
  </complexContent>
</complexType>

<!-- similar constructs for component, structure, and instance -->
```

its policy, also expressed in XACML and makes a decision. The decision can be one of the following: `permit`, `deny`, `not applicable` (when the PDP cannot find a policy that clearly gives a permit or a deny answer), and `indeterminate` (when the PDP encounters other errors).

The core XACML is based on the classic discretionary access control model where a request for performing an action on an object by a subject is permitted or denied. In XACML, an object is termed a resource. Syntactically, a PDP has a `PolicySet`, which consists of a set of `Policy`. Each `Policy` in turn consists of a set of `Rule`. Each `Rule` decides whether a request from a subject for performing an action on a resource should be permitted or denied. When a PDP receives a request that contains attributes of the requesting subject, action, and resource, it tries to find a *matching* `Rule`, whose attributes match those of the request, from the `Policy` and `PolicySet`, and uses the matching rule to make a decision about permitting or denying access to the resource.

An Algorithm to Check Architectural Access Control

In xADL, each component and connector has a set of interfaces that represent externally accessible functionalities. An interface can be either an incoming interface, denoting functionality the element provides, or an outgoing interface, denoting functionality that the element requires. Each incoming interface can be protected by a set of safeguards that specify the permissions that components or connectors must possess before they can access that interface. Each outgoing interface can also possess a set of privileges that is generally the same as those of the owning element, that is, the privileges of the element having that outgoing interface.

The interfaces are connected to form a complete architecture topology. A pair of connected interfaces has one outgoing interface and one incoming interface. Such a connection specifies that the element with the outgoing interface accesses the element at the incoming interface. Each such connection defines an *architectural access*. For example, in the C2 architecture style, a component sends a notification from its bottom interface to a top interface of a connector if the component has sufficient privileges. Architectural access is not limited to direct connections between interfaces. Two components could be connected through a connector. Thus, a meaningful architectural access might involve two components that only indirectly communicate through a connector.

At the architecture level, the concerning decision is whether an architectural access in a software architecture description should be granted or denied. More precisely, *given a software architecture description written in Secure xADL, for a pair of components (A, B), should A be allowed to access B?* Finding the answer to this question can help an architect design secure software from two different perspectives. First, the answer helps the architect decide whether the given architecture allows intended access control. If there is some access that is intended by the architect but is not allowed by the description, the description should be changed to accommodate the access. Second, the answer can help the architect decide whether there are architectural vulnerabilities that introduce undesired access. If some undesired access is allowed, then the architect must modify the architecture and architectural description to eliminate such vulnerabilities.

From an architectural modeling viewpoint, the security-related decisions made by components and connectors might be based on factors, or contexts, other than the decision maker and the protected resource. The four most common types of contexts that can affect access control decisions are the neighboring components and connectors, the type of components and connectors, the subarchitecture containing components and connectors, and the global architecture.

Given knowledge of the executing subjects, an algorithm can be used to decide whether the outgoing interface of an accessing component carries sufficient privileges to satisfy the safeguards of the incoming interface of an accessed component. The accessing component can acquire privileges from multiple sources. The component may itself possess some privileges. It can also get privileges from its type, the containing subarchitecture, and the complete architectural model. Further, privileges can also propagate to the accessing component through connected components and connectors, subject to the privilege propagation capability of the connectors. The accessed components can acquire safeguards from similar sources. One notable difference in acquiring safeguards is that this process does not involve the connected element context, and thus does not go through a propagation process.

The simplest approach to make a decision whether to allow such access is to check whether the accumulated privileges of the accessing element covers the accumulated permissions of the accessed element. However, the accessed element can choose to use a different policy, and the sources of the policy can be from the accessed element, the type of the element, the subarchitecture containing the element, and the complete architecture.

Figure 13-3.
Access control
check algorithm.

```
Input: an outgoing interface, Accessing,
       and an incoming interface, Accessed

Output: grant if the Accessing can access
        the Accessed, deny if the Accessing
        cannot access the Accessed

Begin
  if (there is no path between Accessing and Accessed)
    return deny;
  if (Accessing and Accessed are connected directly)
    DirectAccessing = Accessing;
  else
    DirectAccessing = the element nearest to Accessed in the path;
  Get AccumulatedPrivileges for
    DirectAccessing from the owning element, the type, the containing
    sub-architecture, the complete architecture, and the
    connected elements;
  Get AccumulatedSafeguards for Accessed from the owning element, the
    type, the containing sub-architecture, and the complete architecture;
  Get AccumulatedPolicy for Accessed from similar sources;
  if (AccumulatedPolicy exists)
    if (AccumulatedPolicy grants access)
      return grant;
    else
      return deny;
  else
    if (AccumulatedPrivileges contains AccumulatedSafeguards)
      return grant;
    else
      return deny;
End;
```

A simple architectural access control check algorithm is sketched in Figure 13-3. The algorithm first checks whether the accessing interface and the accessed interface are connected in the architecture topology. If not, the algorithm denies the architectural access. However, if they are connected, the algorithm proceeds to find the interface in the path that is nearest to the accessed interface, namely the direct accessing interface. If the accessing interface and the accessed interface are directly connected, this direct accessing interface is the same as the accessing interface. Then, the privileges of the direct accessing interface are accumulated using various contexts. Similarly, the safeguards and policies of the accessed interface are also collected. If a policy is explicitly specified by the architect, then the policy is consulted to decide whether the accumulated privileges are sufficient for the access. If there is no explicit policy, then the access is granted if the accumulated privileges contain the accumulated safeguards as a subset. This simple algorithm assumes a known, fixed assignment of subjects on whose behalf the architecture operates. Changing subjects requires re–analysis. Dynamic contexts require a more sophisticated approach.

The algorithm in Figure 13-3 checks architectural access control for a pair of interfaces. Extending it to the global system architecture can be achieved by enumerating each pair of interfaces and then applying the algorithm to each pair. If the global architecture contains subarchitectures, then a completely flattened architecture graph, where containers' privileges are propagated to the contained elements, is first constructed. Afterward, the algorithm is used to check architectural access control between relevant pairs of interfaces belonging to this architecture graph.

We now examine how the models and techniques for architectural access control can be applied to two applications, one based on secure cooperation and Firefox as the other.

Example: Secure Cooperation

The first example of architectural access control is a simplistic, notional application that requires secure cooperation between its participants. The software architecture of the application is expressed in the C2 architectural style. The application allows two parties to share data with each other, but these two parties do not necessarily fully trust each other; thus, the data shared must be subject to the control of each party.

The two parties participating in this hypothetical application are an insurance company and a hospital. Each can operate independently and display the messages they receive from their own information sources. For example, the insurance company may internally exchange messages about an insured person's policy status and the hospital sends a patient's medical history among its departments. The two parties also need to share some messages so the insurance company can pay for the service the hospital provides to patients. To accomplish this, the hospital sends a message to the insurance company, including the patient's name and the service performed. After verifying the policy, the insurance company sends a message back to the hospital, authorizing paying a certain amount from a certain account. While the two parties need to exchange information, such sharing is limited to certain types of messages. Governing laws, such as the United States' Health Insurance Portability and Accountability Act (HIPAA), might prohibit one party from sending certain information to the other, such that the hospital cannot send a person's full medical report to the insurance company. Moreover, maintaining business competitiveness also requires each party to not disclose unnecessary information.

Figure 13-4 depicts the application architecture that uses a secure connector on each side that securely routes messages between the insurance company and the hospital. When the insurance-to-hospital connector receives a notification message, it inspects the message, and if the message can be delivered to both the company and the hospital, such as a payment authorization message, then the message is forwarded to both sides. Otherwise, the message is only transferred within the insurance company. The hospital-to-insurance connector operates in a similar fashion.

The data sharing can be controlled in a number of ways by setting different policies on the connectors. For instance, each of the connectors can be denied instantiation that will prevent any sharing to occur. Even if both connectors are instantiated, the connections with other components and connectors can still be rejected to prevent message delivery and data sharing. When the connectors are instantiated and properly connected with other elements, each of them can use its own policy on internal message routing to control the messages that can be delivered to its own and the other side.

This architecture also promotes understanding and reuse: Only two secure connectors are used; these connectors perform a single task of secure message routing, and they can be used in other cases by adopting a different policy.

Example: Firefox

Firefox is an open-source Web browser first released in November 2004. It uses three key platform technologies: XPCOM, a cross-platform component model; JavaScript, the Web development programming language that is also used to develop front-end

Figure 13-4.
*Insurance-
hospital
interorganization
information
routing.*

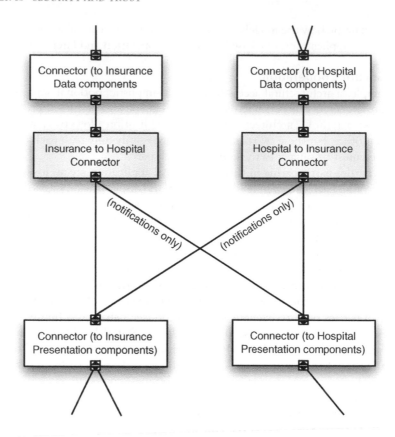

components of Firefox; and XPConnect, the bidirectional connection between native XPCOM components and JavaScript objects.

Trust Boundary Between Chrome and Content. When a user uses the Firefox browser to browse the Web, the visible window contains two areas. The chrome, which consists of decorations of the browser window, such as the menu bar, the status bar, and the dialogs, are controlled by the browser. The browser is trusted to perform arbitrary actions to accomplish the intended task. Borrowing the chrome term that originally refers to the user interface elements, the browser's code is called the *chrome code*. Such code can perform arbitrary actions. Any installed third-party extensions also become a part of the chrome code.

The other area, the content area, is contained within the browser chrome. The content area contains content coming from different sources that are not necessarily trustworthy. Some of this content may contain active JavaScript code. Such *content code* should not be allowed to perform arbitrary actions unconditionally and must be restricted accordingly. Otherwise, such code could abuse privileges to cause damage or harm to the users. This boundary between the chrome code and the content code is the most important trust boundary in Firefox.

Because of the architectural choice of using XPCOM, JavaScript, and XPConnect to develop the Firefox browser and extensions, both chrome code and content code written in JavaScript can use XPConnect to access interfaces of XPCOM components that interact with the underlying operating system services. The XPCOM components are represented as the global Components collection in JavaScript.

XPConnect, as the connector between the possibly untrustworthy accessing code and the accessed XPCOM components, should protect the XPCOM interfaces and decide whether the access to those interfaces should be permitted.

Trust Boundary Between Contents from Different Origins. Another trust boundary is between contents having different origins. The origin of content is determined by the protocol, the host name, and the port used to retrieve the content. Contents differing in either the protocol, the host name, or the port would be considered to have different origins. Users may browse many different sites, and any page can load content from different origins. The content coming from one source should only be able to read or write content originating from the same source. This is called the *same-origin* policy. Otherwise, a malicious page from one source could use this cross-domain access to retrieve or modify sensitive information from another origin, such as the password that the user uses for authentication with the other origin. This is an architectural access control process where interfaces of a content component from one origin should not be inappropriately accessed by another content component from another origin.

Principals. Since the JavaScript language does not specify how security should be handled, the Firefox JavaScript implementation defines a principal-based security infrastructure to support enforcing the trust boundaries. There are two types of principals. When a script is accessing an object, the executing script has a *subject principal* and the object being accessed has an *object principal.*

Firefox uses principals to identify code and content coming from different origins. Each unique origin is represented by a unique principal. The principal in Firefox corresponds to the Subject construct in Secure xADL. Such Subjects are used to regulate architectural access control.

XPConnect: Secure Connector. The security manager within the XPConnect architectural connector coordinates critical architectural operations. It regulates the access by scripts running as one principal to objects owned by another principal (if the subject principal is not the system principal, then both principals should be the same for the access to be allowed), it decides whether a native service can be created, obtained, and wrapped (one type of architectural instantiation operation), and it also arbitrates whether a URL can be loaded into a window (another type of architectural instantiation operation).

Figure 13-5 depicts the Firefox component security architecture. Interfaces of the native XPCOM components executing with the chrome role are accessible from other chrome components but should be protected from other content components. The XPConnect connector maintains this boundary between content code and chrome code. The content components from one origin, including the containing window or frame and the DOM nodes contained within them, form a subarchitecture. Their interfaces can be manipulated by chrome components, but should be protected from content components from other origins. The XPConnect connector maintains this boundary of same origin and helps achieve the needed protection.

Figure 13-5.
*Firefox
component
security
architecture.*

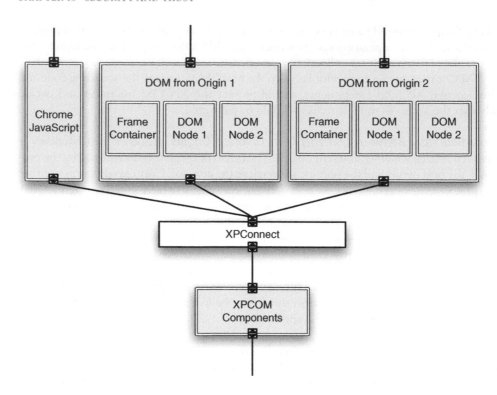

To briefly summarize this section, we first defined the access control models needed to enforce security and illustrated how they can be applied at the architecture level through the use of concepts such as *subject, principal, resource, privilege, safeguard,* and *policy*. We next demonstrated how these concepts can be incorporated into an architecture description using the Secure xADL architecture description language as an example. The resulting architecture description can be checked to verify that the architectural accesses occur only as intended. The concepts, languages and algorithms allow an architect to evaluate the security properties of alternative architectures and choose designs that suit secure requirements. We also discussed two example applications to illustrate these benefits.

In the next section, we discuss another security notion—trust—and show how an architecture approach can be successfully used to integrate trust management within environments where participants are decentralized and make independent trust decisions in the absence of a centralized authority.

13.4 TRUST MANAGEMENT

Trust management concerns how entities establish and maintain trust relationships with each other. Trust management plays a significant role in decentralized applications (such as the peer-to-peer architectures discussed in Chapter 11) where entities do not have complete information about each other and thus must make local decisions autonomously. Entities must account for the possibility that other entities may be malicious and may indulge in attacks with an intention to subvert the system. In the absence of a centralized authority that can screen the entry of entities in the system, manage and coordinate the peers, and implement suitable trust mechanisms, it becomes the responsibility of each decentralized entity to adopt suitable measures to safeguard itself. Trust relationships, in such applications, help entities gauge the trustworthiness of other entities and thus make informed decisions to protect themselves from potential attacks.

It is therefore critical to choose an appropriate trust management scheme for a decentralized application. This by itself is not enough, however. Consider the analogy of a house, access to which is restricted by a lock on the front door. The owner may be worried that the lock may be easily picked by thieves and so may explore new kinds of locks that are harder to break; however, the owner may not realize that the windows are unsecured and can be easily penetrated. Thus, it is important to focus on the lock as well as the windows to ensure the integrity of the house. Similarly, it is important to focus not only on a reliable trust management scheme but also on fortifying each entity in a decentralized application. This is possible through a software architecture approach that guides the integration of a suitable trust model within the structure of each entity and includes additional security technologies to address the pervasive concerns of security and trust.

Our focus in this section is primarily on incorporating reputation-based trust management systems within the architecture of decentralized entities. Reputation-based trust management systems are those that use an entity's past reputation to determine its trustworthiness. However, before delving deeper into reputation-based systems, we present a brief introduction to the concepts of trust and reputation.

13.4.1 Trust

The concept of trust is not new to humans and it is not limited only to electronic entities. Trust is an integral part of our social existence: Our interactions in society are influenced by the perceived trustworthiness of other entities. Thus, in addition to computer scientists, researchers from other fields such as sociology, history, economics, and philosophy have devoted significant attention to the issue of trust (Marsh 1994). Given the fact that trust is a multidisciplinary concept, several definitions of trust exist in the literature. However, since the discussion here is in the context of software development, we adopt a definition of trust coined by Diego Gambetta that has been widely used by computer scientists. He defines trust as

> ... a particular level of the subjective probability with which an agent assesses that another agent or group of agents will perform a particular action, both *before* he can monitor such action (or independently of his capacity ever to be able to monitor it) *and* in a context in which it affects his own action. (Gambetta 2000)

This definition notes that trust is subjective and depends upon the view of the individual; the perception of trustworthiness may vary from person to person. Further, trust can be multidimensional and depends upon the context in which trust is being evaluated. For example, A may trust B completely to repair electronic devices but may not trust B to repair cars. The concept of context is thus critical since it can influence the nature of trust relationships significantly.

Gambetta also introduced the concept of using values for trust. These values may express trust in several different ways. For example, trust may be expressed as a set of continuous real values, binary values, or a set of discrete values. The representation and expression of trust relationships depends upon the application requirements. For example, binary values for trust may be used in an application that needs only to establish whether an entity can be trusted. If instead the application requires entities to compare trustworthiness of several entities, a richer expression of trust values is required, motivating the need for continuous trust values.

Trust is conditionally transitive. This means that if an entity A trusts entity B and entity B trusts entity C, it may not necessarily follow that entity A can trust entity C. There are a number of parameters that influence whether entity A can trust entity C. For example, entity A may trust entity C only if certain possibly application-specific conditions are met, or if the context of trust is the same.

13.4.2   Trust Model

A trust model describes the trust relationships between entities. Realizing the immense value of managing trust relationships between entities, a number of trust models have been designed. These models are geared at different objectives and targeted at specific applications and hence embody different definitions of "trust model." For some, the model may mean just a trust algorithm and a way of combining different trust information to compute a single trust value; for others, a trust model may also encompass a trust-specific protocol to gather trust information from other entities. Yet others may want a trust model to also specify how and where trust data is stored.

> *Definition.* **A *trust model* describes the trust information that is used to establish trust relationships, how that trust information is obtained, how that trust information is combined to determine trustworthiness, and how that trust information is modified in response to personal and reported experiences.**

This definition of a trust model identifies three important components of a trust model. The first component specifies the nature of trust information used and the protocol used to gather that information. The second component dictates how the gathered information is analyzed to compute a trust value. The third component determines not only how an entity's experiences can be communicated to other entities but also how it can be incorporated back into the trust model.

13.4.3   Reputation-Based Systems

Related to trust is the concept of *reputation*. Alfarez Abdul-Rahman and Stephen Hailes (Abdul-Rahman and Hailes 2000) define reputation *as an expectation about an individual's behavior based on information about or observations of its past behavior*. In online communities, where an individual may have little information to determine the trustworthiness of others, reputation information is typically used to determine the extent to which they can be trusted. An individual who is more reputed generally is considered to be more trustworthy.

Reputation may be determined in several ways. For example, a person may rely on his direct experiences, the experiences of other people, or a combination of both to determine the reputation of another person. Trust management systems that use reputation to determine the trustworthiness of an entity are termed reputation-based systems. There are several applications, such as Amazon.com and eBay, that employ such reputation-based systems.

Reputation-based systems can be either centralized or decentralized. A decentralized reputation-based system is one where every entity directly evaluates other entities, maintains those evaluations locally, and interacts directly with other entities to exchange trust information. A centralized reputation-based system, on the other hand, relies on a single centralized authority to either facilitate evaluations and interactions between entities or to store relevant trust information. Amazon.com and eBay provide a central repository to store reputation information provided by their users while XREP, a trust model for P2P file-sharing applications, is an example of a decentralized reputation-based system. Next, we next take a deeper look at eBay and XREP.

eBay

eBay is an electronic marketplace where diverse users sell and buy goods. Sellers advertise items and buyers place bids for those items. After an auction ends, the winning bidder pays the seller for the item. Both buyers and sellers rate each other after the completion of a transaction. A positive outcome results in a $+1$ rating and a negative outcome results in a -1 rating. These ratings form the reputation of buyers and sellers. This reputation information is stored and maintained by eBay instead of by its users. eBay is, thus, not a purely decentralized reputation system. If eBay's centralized data stores were to become unavailable, eBay users would have no access to the trust information of other users.

eBay allows this trust information to be viewed through feedback profiles. A user can click on the feedback profile of buyers or sellers to view their past interaction histories and trust information. The profile includes the number of total interactions a user has been involved in along with his total trust score. This score, called the feedback score, is computed as follows: A positive rating increases the feedback score by 1, a negative rating decreases the feedback score by 1, and a neutral rating leaves the feedback score unaffected. A user can only affect another user's feedback score by one point per week. For example, if one user were to leave three positive ratings for another user, the feedback score would only increase by 1. Similarly, even if a user were to leave five negative ratings and two positive ratings, the feedback score would only decrease by 1. The profile also lists the user's total number of positive, negative, and neutral ratings. The profile also displays the aggregate of the most recent ratings received in the last one month, six months, and twelve months. A user viewing a profile can also choose to read all the comments written about a particular buyer or seller.

Such a system can be manipulated to defeat its purpose, of course. The case of eBay in 2000 is a classic example of a set of peers engaging in fraudulent actions (Dingledine, 2003 #2984). A number of peers first engaged in multiple successful eBay auctions (to establish strong trust ratings). Once their trust ratings were sufficiently high to engage in high-value deals, they used their reputations to start auctions for high-priced items, received payment for those items, and then disappeared, leaving the buyers defrauded.

XREP

XREP, proposed by Ernesto Damiani and colleagues (Damiani et al. 2002), is a trust model for decentralized peer-to-peer (P2P) file-sharing applications. Development of trust models is an active area of research and XREP is chosen here to serve as an example. P2P file-sharing applications consist of a distributed collection of entities, also called peers, that interact and exchange resources, such as documents and media, directly with other peers in the system. A decentralized P2P file-sharing application, such as one based on Gnutella, is characterized by the absence of a centralized authority that coordinates interactions and resource exchanges among peers. Instead, each peer directly queries its neighboring peers for files and this query subsequently is forwarded to other peers in the system. Each queried peer responds positively if it has the requested resource. Upon receiving these responses, the query originator can choose to download the resource from one of the responding peers.

While such decentralized file-sharing applications offer significant benefits, such as no single point of failure and increased robustness in addition to allowing users at the edge of the network to directly share files with each other, they are also prone to several attacks by malicious peers. This is because such decentralized P2P file-sharing applications are also open, implying that anyone can join and leave the system at any time without any restrictions. Peers with malicious intent may offer tampered files or may even disguise Trojan horses and viruses as legitimate files and make them available for download. In the January 2004 issue of *Wired* magazine, an article by Kim Zetter, "Kazaa Delivers More Than Tunes" (Zetter 2004) mentions a study in January 2004 that reported that 45 percent of 4,778 executable files downloaded through the Kazaa file-sharing application contained malicious code such as viruses and Trojan horses. When unsuspecting users download such files, they may not only harm their own computers but also unknowingly spread the malicious files to other users.

Clearly, there is a need for mechanisms that will help determine the trustworthiness of both peers and the resources offered by them. Decentralized reputation-based trust schemes offer a potential solution to this problem by using reputation to determine the trustworthiness of peers and resources. XREP is an example of such a reputation-based scheme for decentralized file-sharing applications. XREP includes a distributed polling algorithm to allow reputation values to be shared among peers, so that a peer requesting a resource can assess the reliability of both the peer and the resource offered by a peer.

The XREP distributed protocol consists of the following phases: resource searching, resource selection and vote polling, vote evaluation, best servent check, and resource downloading, as illustrated in Figure 13-6. Resource searching is similar to that in Gnutella and involves a servent (that is, a Gnutella peer; *servent* is a neologism formed from *server* and *client*) broadcasting to all its neighbors a *Query* message containing search keywords. When a servent receives a *Query* message, it responds with a *QueryHit* message. In the next phase, upon receiving *QueryHit* messages, the originator selects the best matching resource among all possible resources offered. At this point, the originator polls other peers using a *Poll* message to ask their opinions about the resource or the servent offering the resource. Upon receiving a *Poll* message, each peer may respond by communicating its votes on the resource and servents using a *PollReply* message. These messages help distinguish reliable from unreliable resources and trustworthy from fraudulent servents.

In the third phase, the originator collects a set of votes on the queried resources and their corresponding servents. Then it begins a detailed checking process that includes verification of the authenticity of the *PollReply* messages, guarding against the effect of a group of malicious peers acting in tandem by using cluster computation, and sending

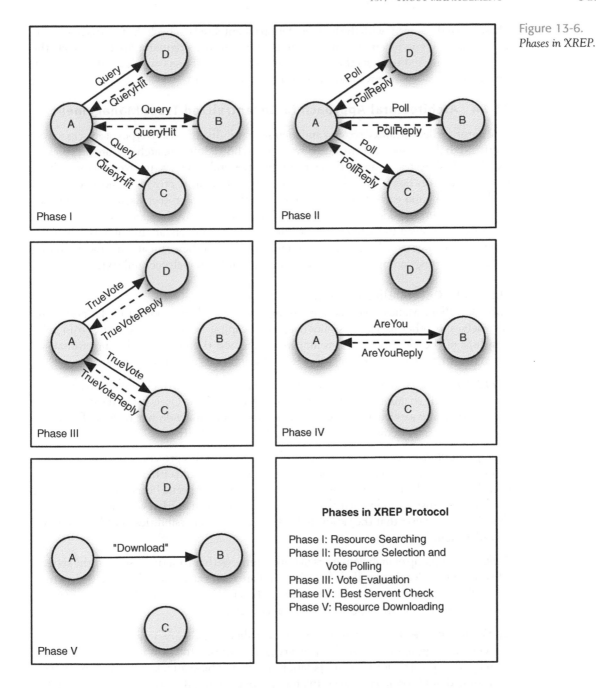

Figure 13-6.
Phases in XREP.

TrueVote messages to peers that request confirmation on the votes received from them. At the end of this checking process, based on the trust votes received, the peer may decide to download a particular resource. However, since multiple servents may be offering the same resource, the peer still needs to select a reliable servent. This is done in the fourth phase when the servent with the best reputation is contacted to check the fact that it exports the resource. Upon receiving a reply from the servent, the originator finally contacts the chosen servent and requests the resource. It also updates its repositories with its opinion on the downloaded resource and the servent who offered it.

13.4.4 Architectural Approach to Decentralized Trust Management

The nature of decentralized systems and their susceptibility to various types of attacks makes it critical to design such decentralized systems carefully. Software architecture provides an excellent basis to reason about these trust properties and can serve to provide comprehensive guidance on how to build such systems. In particular, it provides guidance on how to design and build each decentralized entity so that it can protect itself against attacks, as well as retain its independence to make local autonomous decisions. There are three main steps involved in such an architectural approach: understanding and assessing the real threats to a system, designing countermeasures against these threats, and incorporating guidelines corresponding to these countermeasures into an architectural style.

Threats to Decentralized Systems

Impersonation. Malicious peers may attempt to conceal their identities by portraying themselves as other users. This may happen to capitalize on the preexisting trust relationships of the identities they are impersonating and the targets of the impersonation. Therefore, the targets of the deception need the ability to detect these incidents.

Fraudulent Actions. It is also possible for malicious peers to act in bad faith without actively misrepresenting themselves or their relationships with others. Users can indicate that they have a particular service available even when they knowingly do not have it. Therefore, the system should attempt to minimize the effects of bad faith.

Misrepresentation. Malicious users may also decide to misrepresent their trust relationships with other peers in order to confuse. This deception could either intentionally inflate or deflate the malicious user's trust relationships with other peers. Peers could publish that they do not trust an individual that they know to be trustworthy. Or, they could claim that they trust a user that they know to be dishonest. Both possibilities must be taken into consideration.

Collusion. A group of malicious users may also join together to actively subvert the system. This group may decide to collude in order to inflate their own trust values and deflate trust values for peers that are not in the collective. Therefore, a certain level of resistance needs to be in place to limit the effect of malicious collectives.

Denial of Service. In an open architecture, malicious peers may launch an attack on individuals or groups of peers. The primary goal of these attacks is to disable the system or make it impossible for normal operation to occur. These attacks may flood peers with well-formed or ill-formed messages. In order to compensate, the system requires the ability to contain the effects of denial of service attacks.

Addition of Unknowns. In an open architecture, the cold start situation arises: Upon initialization, a peer does not know anything about anyone else on the system. Without any trust information present, there may not be enough knowledge to form relationships until a sufficient body of experience is established. Therefore, the ability to bootstrap relationships when no prior relationships exist is essential.

Deciding Whom to Trust. In a large-scale system, certain domain-specific behaviors may indicate the trustworthiness of a user. Trust relationships generally should improve when good behavior is perceived of a particular peer. Similarly, when dishonest behavior is perceived, trust relationships should be downgraded accordingly.

Out-of-Band Knowledge. Out-of-band knowledge occurs when there is data not communicated through normal channels. While trust is assigned based on visible in-band interactions, there may also exist important invisible interactions that have an impact on trust. For example, Alice could indicate in person to Bob the degree to which she trusts Carol. Bob may then want to update his system to adjust for Alice's out-of-band perception of Carol. Therefore, ensuring the consideration of out-of-band trust information is essential.

Measures to Address Threats
Use of Authentication. To prevent impersonation attacks, it is essential to use some form of authentication so that message senders can be uniquely identified. For instance, entities sign outgoing messages and receiving entities verify those signatures to validate the authenticity of those messages. Signature-based authentication, such as that discussed at the beginning of this chapter, also helps protect against potential repudiation attacks—attacks where an entity may falsely claim that it never sent the message.

Separation of Internal Beliefs and Externally Reported Information
In a decentralized system, each entity has its own individual goals, which may conflict with those of other entities. It is therefore important to model externally reported information separately from internal beliefs. This separation helps resolve conflicts between externally reported information and internal perceptions. For example, a peer may favor information it has perceived directly and believes to be accurate over information reported by others. A peer may also not want to disclose sensitive data, so it must have the ability to report information that differs from what it actually believes. ("What I've heard is . . . ")

Making Trust Relationships Explicit. Without a controlling authority that governs the trust process, peers require information to make decisions whether or not to trust what they perceive. Active collaboration between peers may provide enough knowledge for peers to reach their local decisions. Thus it is important that information about trust relationships be explicit and exchangeable between peers. There is a possibility that exposing trust information may be misused by malicious peers to take advantage of certain peers; however, it should be remembered that exchanged information may not truly reflect the trust perceptions of the entities.

Comparable Trust. Ideally, published trust values should be syntactically and semantically comparable; that is, equivalent representations in one implementation should have the same structure and meaning in another. If the same value has different meanings across implementations, then accurate comparisons across peers cannot be made.

Corresponding Guidelines to Incorporate into an Architectural Style

Digital Identities. Without the ability to associate identity with published information, it is a challenge to develop meaningful trust relationships. Thus, the concept of identities, both physical and digital, is necessary to facilitate meaningful relationships. However, it is important to understand the limitations of digital identities with respect to physical identities.

There may not be a one-to-one mapping between digital and physical identities as one person may utilize multiple digital identities or multiple people may share the same digital identity. Additionally, anonymous users may be present who resist digital identification. Therefore, it is not always possible to tie a digital identity to one physical individual and make accurate evaluations of a person. Instead, a critical criterion of trust relationships in decentralized applications should be the actions performed by digital identities, not by physical identities. The architectural style should therefore consider trust relationships only between digital identities.

Separation of Internal and External Data. Explicit separation of internal and external data supports the separation of internal beliefs from externally reported information within a peer. Therefore, the architectural style should adopt the explicit separation of internal and external data.

Making Trust Visible. Trust information received externally from entities is used within the peer architecture to make local decisions. In order to process this trust information internally across the architecture, trust cannot be localized to only one component. Each component responsible for making local decisions needs the ability to take advantage of this perceived trust. If the perceived trust is not visible, then accurate assessments may not be made. Therefore, the architectural style should require trust relationships to be visible to the components in the peer's architecture as well as be published externally to other peers.

Expression of Trust. There has been no clear consensus in the trust literature as to which trust semantics provide the best fit for applications, therefore it is believed that indiscriminately enforcing a constraint at the architectural level to use a particular trust semantic is inappropriate. While trust values should be semantically comparable, a generic architectural style might impose only the constraint that trust values must at least be syntactically comparable. For example, this can be done by enforcing that trust values be represented numerically.

Resultant Architectural Style

The principles and constraints identified above can be combined to create an architectural style for decentralized trust management. In addition to these constraints, based on the common elements of trust models, four functional units of a decentralized entity are first identified. These are Communication, Information, Trust, and Application. The Communication unit handles interaction with other entities, the Information unit is responsible for persistently storing trust and application-specific information, the Trust unit is responsible for computing trustworthiness and guides trust-related decisions, and the Application unit includes application-specific functionality and is responsible for enabling local decision making. The Communication unit does not depend upon any other units while the Information unit depends upon information received from other entities and thus depends upon interaction with them. The Trust unit depends upon the Communication and Information units and the Application unit builds upon all the other three units.

Given this interplay between the four units, adopting a layered architectural style enables a natural structuring of these units according to their interdependencies and also offers several benefits such as reusability of components. Since decentralized entities are autonomous, they have the privilege of refusing to respond to requests of other entities. As a result, decentralized applications typically employ asynchronous event-based communication protocols. In order to reflect this communication paradigm within the internal architecture of an entity, an event-based architectural style for the architecture of an entity is natural. Moreover, event-based architectural styles have been known to successfully facilitate loose coupling among components. This can, for instance, allow for the replacement of trust models and protocol handlers in the architecture.

C2 is one such event-based layered architectural style. As discussed in Chapter 4, C2 includes specific visibility rules—components belonging to a layer are only aware of components in layers above them and are unaware of components below them. C2 thus naturally fits in with the constraints of a trust–centric architectural style. Further, C2 also has existing tool support that can be leveraged by an architectural style based on C2. Therefore, the PACE architectural style, (Practical Architectural Style for Composing Egocentric applications) described next, extends the C2 style.

PACE Architectural Style

The PACE architectural style includes all the above-described guidelines and constraints and provides guidance on the components that must be included within the architecture of an entity and how they should interact with each other. The style is described here to illustrate one way of combining insights from the preceding discussion into a coherent architecture. Corresponding to the four functional units, PACE divides the architecture of a decentralized entity into four layers: Communication, Information, Trust, and Application. Each of these layers, along with their components, is illustrated in Figure 13-7.

The Communication layer is responsible for handling communication with other peers in the system. It consists of several components designed to support various standard communication protocols, the Communications Manager, and the Signature Manager. The communication protocol components are responsible for translating internal events to external communications. The Communications Manager instantiates the protocol components while the Signature Manager signs requests and verifies notifications.

To separate the internal trust beliefs of a peer from those received from other peers, the Information layer consists of two components: the Internal Information component that stores self-originating messages and the External Information component, which stores messages received from others.

The Trust layer incorporates the components that enable trust management. This layer consists of the Key Manager, which generates the local PKI keypair; the Credential Manager, which manages the credentials of other peers; and the Trust Manager, which computes trust values for messages received from other peers.

The Application layer encapsulates all application-specific components. The Application Trust Rules component encapsulates the chosen rules for assigning trust values based on application-specific semantic meanings of messages, and supports different dimensions of trust relationships. The Application subarchitecture represents the local behavior of a peer. While components in the other layers can be reused across different applications, components in the Application layer are application-dependent and hence not reusable

Figure 13-7.
PACE
components.

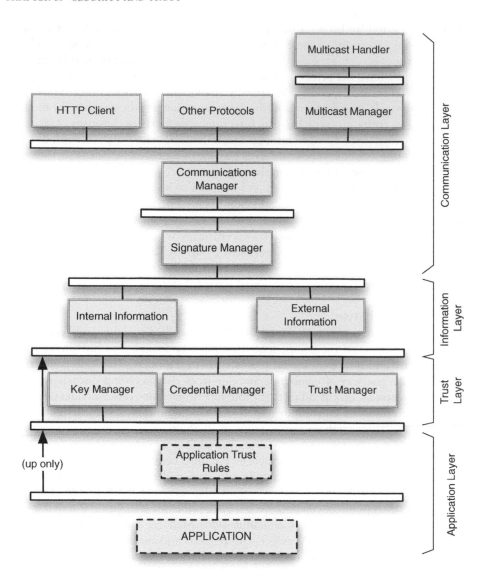

Figure 13-7. *PACE components.*

across domains. The application developer is thus expected to implement components for this layer depending upon the application's needs; its internal architecture may be in an entirely different style. All external communication must go through the PACE stack, however.

PACE-Induced Benefits

PACE's guiding principles induce properties that act as countermeasures against threats to a decentralized system. Some of these properties are effected by the PACE architectural style and canonical implementations of its standard components; others are application specific and so involve the Application layer. We now take a look at some of the common threats and the way PACE helps address them. It should be noted that it is not mandatory for all peers participating in a decentralized system to be built in the PACE architectural style in order to function and interact with PACE-based peers. However, those peers cannot avail themselves of the benefits of the PACE style.

Impersonation. Impersonation refers to the threat caused by a malicious peer posing as another in order to misuse the peer's privileges or reputation. PACE addresses this threat through the use of digital signatures and message authentication. All external communication in the PACE architecture is constrained to the Communication layer, thus it offers a single point where impersonation can be detected. A malicious peer that tries to impersonate a user without the correct private key or does not digitally sign the message can be detected by verifying signatures. Additionally, if a private key has been compromised, a revocation for that key can be transmitted. PACE components can then refuse to assign trust values to revoked public keys.

Fraudulent Actions. Malicious peers may engage in fraudulent behavior including advertising false resources or services and not fulfilling commitments. Since PACE is designed for open, decentralized architectures, there is little that may be done to prevent the entry of malicious peers. However, malicious actions may be detected by the user or through the Application layer. Explicit warnings can then be issued concerning those malicious peers, which may help others in their evaluations of these peers.

Misrepresenting Trust. A malicious peer may misrepresent its trust with another in order to positively or negatively influence opinion of a specific peer. Since PACE facilitates explicit communication of comparable trust values, a peer can incorporate trust relationships of others. By using a transitive trust model in the Trust Manager, if Alice publishes that she distrusts Bob, then Carol can use that information to determine if she should trust Bob's published trust relationships.

Collusion. Collusion refers to the threat caused by a group of malicious peers that work in concert to actively subvert the system. It is thus of greater concern than a single peer misrepresenting trust. It has been proven that explicitly signed communication between peers can overcome a malicious collective in a distributed setting. Adapting and combining these results with efficient schemes to identify noncooperative groups in a decentralized setting [such as in NICE (Lee, Sherwood, and Bhattacharjee 2003)] with PACE's ability to detect impersonation allows collusion to be addressed.

Denial of Service. Malicious peers may also launch attacks against peers by flooding them with well-formed or ill-formed messages. The separation of the Communication layer allows isolation and response to the effects of such denial of service attacks. Incorrectly formed messages can be disposed of by the protocol handlers. The Communications Manager can also compensate for well-formed message floods by introducing rate limiting or interacting with neighboring firewalls to prevent further flooding.

Addition of Unknowns. When the system is first initialized, there can be a cold-start problem because there are no existing trust relationships. Even though a peer may not have previously interacted with another peer or a message may be known to be forged, PACE's Application layer can still receive these events. Without enough information to make an evaluation, the message will not be assigned a trust value by the Trust Manager.

However, the user can still make the final decision to trust the contents of the message based on out-of-band knowledge that is not captured explicitly.

Deciding Whom To Trust. In a large-scale system, certain domain-specific behaviors may indicate the user's trustworthiness. Trust relationships should generally improve when good behavior is perceived of a particular peer and vice versa. In PACE, the application trust rules component allows for automated identification of application-dependent patterns. The detection of good or bad behavior by this component can cause the trust level of the corresponding peer to be increased or decreased respectively along a particular trust dimension.

Out-of-Band Knowledge. It is essential to ensure that out-of-band information is also considered in establishing trust relationships. While PACE confines all electronic communication to the Communication layer, out-of-band trust information can originate as requests from the user through the Application layer.

Building a PACE-Based Trust-Enabled Decentralized File-Sharing Application

In this section, we present a walk-through of how PACE can be used to design and construct applications. Specifically, we explore how the PACE architectural style can be used to guide the construction of a trust-enabled decentralized file-sharing application. Since the XREP trust model for file-sharing applications was presented earlier, it will be used as the candidate trust model for integration within the PACE style.

The first step in designing an appropriate architecture for each file-sharing entity is to identify the components in the four layers. Since the PACE architectural style already specifies components for the Communication, Information, and Trust layers, the main task here is to identify the components of the Application layer. For the file-sharing application, the Application layer can be decomposed, for example, into eight different components organized into three sublayers as shown in Figure 13-8.

The top sublayer contains only the Application Trust Rules component while the bottom sublayer comprises the User Interface. The middle sublayer consists of the components: Library, Search Manager, Poll Manager, File Exchanger, Evaluator, and Preferences. The Library component maintains the list of files that have been downloaded and that can be shared with other peers; the files themselves are persistently stored in the Internal Information. The Search Manager component is responsible for issuing *Query*, *Poll*, and *TrueVote* messages and displaying received responses to those messages through the user interface.

The Poll Manager component responds to *Poll* messages by sending *PollReply* messages. The File Exchanger component is responsible for uploading and downloading files, displaying uploaded and downloaded files to the user interface, saving downloaded files to the Internal Information storage, and deleting files from the Internal Information. The Evaluator component is responsible for checking the authenticity of *PollReply* messages and analyzing peer votes received about resources. The Preferences component manages login information for the user and enables the user to specify preferences including whether to automatically connect to the P2P network, the number of hops, the number of permissible uploads and downloads, and the destination for the library folder.

Once the components of the Application layer are identified, it is important to determine the interactions between the components in order to identify the relevant request and

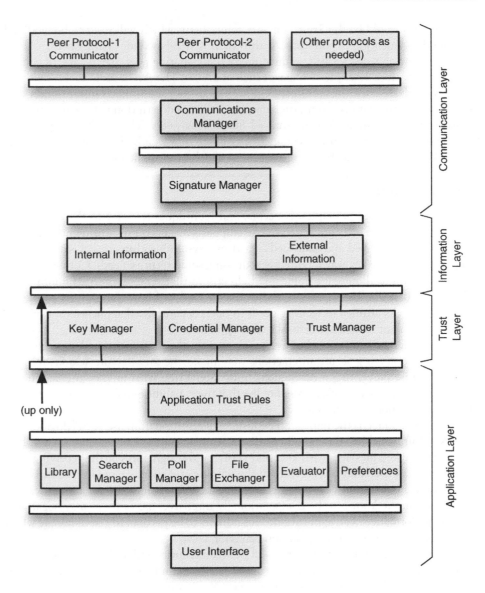

Figure 13-8.
*XREP-based
architecture of
file-sharing peer.*

notification messages that traverse the architecture. This includes modeling the different kinds of trust messages exchanged between peers as dictated by the XREP trust model so the relevant components can appropriately react to them.

In the next step, components belonging to each layer must be appropriately implemented. If existing implementations for any of these components exist, the application developer can choose to reuse them as long as the PACE style is not violated. Since PACE prototypes in other application domains already exist, it is possible to reuse all components from the Communication, Information, and Trust layers without any modifications. The only exception would be the Trust Manager component, which will need to be modified to enable the evaluation of poll results within each XREP-based file-sharing peer.

Finally, the above-described architecture of a file-sharing peer may be described in a suitable architecture description language such as xADL. The ArchStudio tool suite could be used to both describe the architecture as well as instantiate it. Each instantiation corresponds to a particular peer; thus, the same architectural description may be instantiated repeatedly to create multiple trust-enabled file-sharing peers. The resulting application then could be subjected to threat scenarios to evaluate how well XREP-enabled peers built in the PACE style counter the threats typical to file-sharing applications.

13.5 END MATTER

This chapter presented principles, concepts, and techniques relevant to the design and construction of secure software systems. The emphasis has been on showing how security concerns may be assessed and addressed as part of a system's architecture. Use of explicit connectors offers one key way for directly addressing some security needs. Connectors can be used to examine all message traffic and help ensure that no unauthorized information exchange occurs. The latter portion of the chapter explored how the use of a particular architectural style, attuned to security needs in open decentralized applications, can help mitigate risks. Trust models are central to this approach.

Making a system secure may, however, compromise other non-functional requirements. For example, enforcing secure interactions may make the architecture less flexible. In particular, while preventing a component from interacting with unknown components may discourage security attacks, it also implies that the capabilities offered by the untrusted components cannot be leveraged.

Another example is the impact on performance resulting from use of SPKI (Standard Public Key Infrastructure) for digitally authenticating messages. This mechanism involves signing transmitted messages with keys and verifying the signatures at the receiving end. Message content itself may be encrypted at the sending end and decrypted at the receiving end to ensure confidentiality of message content. Since algorithms used for authentication and encryption are known to be computationally intensive, use of them may negatively affect the performance of an application. This is likely to be particularly troublesome when message-exchange dominates application behavior.

A third example relates to the trade-off between security and usability. If the security mechanism in a software system requires a user to perform cumbersome or repetitive actions (for instance, by showing redundant or unnecessary dialog prompts repeatedly), the user may choose to completely turn off the security mechanism.

These examples illustrate the importance of properly considering such trade-offs. It is critical for software architects and application developers to apply careful analysis while designing and constructing secure software systems.

The Business Case	In a television advertisement for a motor oil additive, auto racing legend Andy Granatelli said, "You can pay me now, or you'll pay me later," referring to the benefits of regular engine maintenance. The implication was that failure to tend to the preventive needs of an engine in a timely manner could lead to expensive, if not catastrophic, failure later on. So it is with software security.

As with other software qualities, it is far more cost effective, and technically easier, to plan for and design in security from a project's outset, rather than waiting until a security breach either lands a company unfavorably in the public eye or causes a significant financial loss. Moreover, an architecture-based approach focuses on a comprehensive analysis and solution strategy, not a "plug this leak and wait for the next disaster" reactive response.

The serendipity that accompanies architectural design for security and trust is that the discipline of analyzing a design and introducing security-focused separations and mechanisms at the outset can yield a clean design able to accommodate other, nonsecurity focused, demands for change that arise over time.

Trust management for open, decentralized systems will continue to rise in importance as Web services and other forms of open commerce increase in adoption. As the main text of this chapter has shown, the techniques available have numerous limitations. These limitations are no different from those that have always existed in business, long before the advent of electronic commerce. Should you trust another vendor? Will your invoice be paid? How do you know? The legal remedies that society provides, the out-of-band communication people depend upon—these can apply in e-commerce as well. The increased difficulty, and hence the need for trust management techniques such as those described here, arises from the speed with which transactions—both legitimate and fraudulent—can take place.

Chapter 12 began exploration of architecturally-based techniques for achieving a variety of non-functional properties. This chapter continued that theme, focusing on the specific NFPs of security and trust. Chapter 13 completes the theme, by focusing in-depth on the NFP of adaptability.

13.6 REVIEW QUESTIONS

1. What is security? What are the properties that a software system must exhibit in order to be called secure?

2. List and briefly describe each design principle explained in this chapter.

3. What challenges to security are introduced by decentralized applications? What is trust management?

13.7 EXERCISES

1. Identify and describe any trade-offs between the design principles explained in the chapter.

2. What are the security benefits and the security risks associated with the following architectural styles from Chapter 4?
   a. Pipe-and-filter
   b. Blackboard
   c. Event-based
   d. C2

   In your answer, consider how malicious actions in one component can or cannot affect the actions of other components.

3. Choose any software application, such as Firefox, and use UML sequence diagrams to show how the security mechanisms within the application operate.

4. Describe at least two applications, other than online auctions and file sharing, where trust or reputation management may prove useful, and explain the rationale for your choices.

5. Evaluate whether the PACE architectural style could be used to build the participants in the above applications.

6. Study the architecture of Internet Explorer 7 and evaluate whether IE 7 has any architectural security deficiencies. If so, how can these vulnerabilities be addressed? Use xACML and Secure xADL to propose a more secure architecture for IE 7.

13.8 FURTHER READING

An excellent introduction to the field of computer security is given by Bruce Schneier in (Schneier 2000). This highly readable book explores the interplay of technical and nontechnical issues in achieving system security. Matt Bishop's text (Bishop 2003) provides details of the technologies involved. Pfleeger and Pfleeger's book (Pfleeger and Pfleeger 2003) is another comprehensive reference.

Research frontiers for software engineering for security are presented in Devanbu and Stubblebine's roadmap paper (Devanbu and Stubblebine 2000) from the 2000 International Conference on Software Engineering.

Further details on the PACE architectural style can be found in (Suryanarayana et al. 2006; Suryanarayana, Erenkrantz, and Taylor 2005). Further details on the connectorcentric approach to security are available in (Ren et al. 2005; Ren and Taylor 2005).

More recently, new results have been presented at the International Workshop on Software Engineering for Secure Systems, beginning with the 2005 workshop.

14

Architectural Adaptation

Few applications are designed, built, used, and ultimately discarded without undergoing change. Change is endemic to software: Both the perceived and actual malleability of the medium, coupled with the ease of altering code, induces everyone associated with an application to initiate changes. Users change their minds about what they want and hence what they require of an application. Designers seek to improve their designs with respect to performance, or appearance, or some other property. The application's usage environment can change. Whatever the reason, software developers are faced with the challenges of coping with the need to modify an application. We group all of these types of changes under the term *adaptation*: modification of a software system to satisfy new requirements and changing circumstances.

Adaptability was introduced in Chapter 12 as one of several non-functional properties for which architects must frequently design. Several basic architectural techniques supporting adaptation were presented. Just as Chapter 13 was devoted to in-depth exploration of the non-functional properties of security and trust, so this chapter delves further into adaptability. Nonetheless, this chapter does not aspire to present techniques for dealing with all possible types of adaptation at all levels of granularity and abstraction—to do so would require a book of its own. Consistent with the focus of the book, our discussion is centered on facilitating change in the context of software architectures: We focus on adaptation to a system's principal design decisions—its architecture—and on changes that proceed from a strong architectural foundation. We consider processes for effecting change that are conceptualized in terms of the system's architecture, and show the value and role of explicit architectural models in supporting and effecting adaptation. We also consider one of the more difficult types of change: modifying applications on-the-fly, showing how this can be achieved using an architecture- and connector-centric approach.

The goals of the chapter are to:

- Characterize adaptation, showing what changes, why, and who the players are.
- Characterize the central role software architecture plays in system adaptation.
- Present techniques for effectively supporting adaptation, based on an architecture-centric perspective.

This chapter reveals the particular power of connectors in supporting adaptation, especially in those situations where the connectors remain first-class entities in the implementation and where communication is event-based. Highly dynamic applications are possible in such situations and offer the opportunity for creating novel, flexible, highly adaptable applications.

14.1 CONCEPTS OF ARCHITECTURE-CENTRIC ADAPTATION

14.1.1 Sources and Motivations for Change

Several motivations for change are familiar to developers. Perhaps the most common is *corrective change*, where the application is adapted to conform to the existing requirements. Put in other words, corrective change means bringing the descriptive architecture into conformance with the prescriptive architecture. Put most simply, bug fixing. Whether bug fixing is easy or highly disruptive, however, may depend on the root cause of an error: Did the observed problem with the application stem from a small, localized error in the code, or result from a profound mistake made at the highest level of system structure? Understanding the root cause is essential for determining how to effect the fix; attempting to patch a deep problem with localized change usually is not effective.

A second common motivation for change is *modification to the functional requirements* for a system—new features are needed, existing ones modified, perhaps some must be removed. Rather than thinking that the existence of such needs for change reflect an inadequate system planning or analysis process, functional change requests often proceed from success with the existing application. Once applications are in use they inspire users to think of their task in new ways, leading to new ideas for what might be accomplished. Applications in use may change the usage context, or the usage context may change for extrinsic reasons. Whatever the source, feature change requests typically represent changes to the application's architecture.

A third motivation for change is the requirement to satisfy *new or changed non-functional system properties*. Such properties include security, performance, scale, and so on, as discussed in Chapters 12 and 13. New non-functional properties may induce profound changes to a system's architecture. One example is the World Wide Web. Prior to 1994 the Web's governing protocol was HTTP/1.0, a point-to-point protocol with no provision for proxies or caching. The change to HTTP/1.1 was accomplished by the adoption of a new architectural style for the Web (viz., REST), enabling the Web to scale from thousands of servers and tens of thousands of clients, to many millions of each. Similarly, as security attacks on Microsoft's IIS Web server increased, a significant redesign was required to meet the new threats. Another non-functional property that may cause significant architectural change is "better organization"—restructuring an application in *anticipation* of future change requests. For instance, a new middleware platform (that is, connector technology) may be put in place as a proactive step toward supporting potential future modifications.

A fourth common motivation for system adaptation is the need to conform to a *changed operating environment*. In this situation, neither the application's functions, nor its non-functional properties are altered, but the application's structure must be adapted to run, for example, on new hardware or to accommodate changes in interfaces to external systems.

More obviously germane to the software architect are motivations for change that *arise from product-line forces*. Strictly speaking, such changes can be classified under one of the preceding types of change, but such classification would obscure the insights.

The first of these product-line motivations is the desire to *create a new variant* within a product line. The notion here is that the architects have previously identified a branch point within a product-line architecture and at that branch point a new variant is identified. For example, in consumer electronics, a branch point within the design for integrated television systems is the interface to a high-capacity storage/replay subsystem—a hard disk, a DVD recorder/player, or a tape system perhaps. If it becomes desirable to interface with a different technology, perhaps Blu-ray, a new variant at that branch point is created. In our long-running example of the Lunar Lander video game, a new variant might be based upon the desire to utilize a new wireless joy-stick for controlling the lander or to incorporate a new three-dimensional graphics engine having improved performance.

Another of the product-line motivations is *creation of a new branch point*, thereby identifying a new opportunity for product marketplace segmentation. For instance, an electronics manufacturer may decide to adapt the design of its television products to enable them to work with home security systems, perhaps by using picture-in-picture technology to allow continuous display of surveillance camera data while watching broadcast TV. The existence of many types of external security systems implies many possible variants within this branch point; other variants are implied by the many ways of integrating surveillance information into the television display environment. New branch points in the Lunar Lander design might focus on multiplayer environments or on extensibility to allow missions to other solar system objects.

Yet another product-line motivation comes from the desire to *merge product (sub-)lines*, thereby rationalizing their architectures. A successful effort of this type will yield a common product-line architecture without requiring the complete creation of a new architecture. The goal, ostensibly, is to preserve as much as possible from the contributing architectures.

One type of adaptation that will be discussed later in this chapter is on-the-fly adaptation. The difficulty of supporting such change is typically greater than for non-real-time adaptation, so a few words are needed here to prompt its consideration. A simple but perhaps extreme example motivating this type of change comes from planetary exploration. The Cassini/Huygens spacecraft were launched from Cape Canaveral in October 1997; they did not reach their intended destination, Saturn, until July 2004. During transit to Saturn the onboard software systems were upgraded several times. As the Cassini Web site (NASA Jet Propulsion Laboratory) puts it, "This development phase will never really be complete, since new command sequences are continually being created throughout Cassini's operation. New flight software will also be developed and loaded aboard the spacecraft periodically, to run in the Command Data Subsystem, Attitude and Articulation Control Subsystem, as well as in the physical science instruments onboard." As a *system* it is clear that Cassini could not be stopped and reloaded with the new software; rather the updates had to take place while the system was in continuous operation.

Spacecraft Software Updates	The updating of spacecraft software while in space light is an extreme case of adaptation on the fly. The needs for updating reflect many sources, from new directions or priorities for a mission based upon recently discovered phenomena to bug fixes. Another source is time pressure and astrophysics: Because of the relative orientation of the planets it may be essential to launch an exploration mission in a fairly narrow time frame. If the mission software is not ready by the time of launch, a workable strategy is to launch with a skeletal system and then upgrade while the craft is en route to the mission's destination. All of these factors have arisen in the Cassini mission to Saturn. Needless to say, the stakes are high in on-flight software updates, hence a very conservative, patch-oriented update strategy is applied. A few documents are available online that describe the processes involved [such as (Paczkowski and Roy 2004)].

A more prosaic example is the extension of Web browser functionality. If when surfing the Web a resource is encountered that requires a novel type of display software (such as for a new type of audio encoding, perhaps), the browser must be extended. If the browser requires the user to download the new extension, perform some installation steps, and then restart the browser—or worse yet, the computer—before being able to continue, the user is inconvenienced. After restart the user will have to renavigate to the resource that demanded the extension in the first place. A more pleasant strategy, from the user's perspective, is to support the download and installation of the new software (that is, adaptation of the browser) *dynamically*, so that the user may continue usage in an uninterrupted manner.[1]

Motivations for supporting online (dynamic) change thus include:

- Nonstop applications: Ones in which the software cannot be stopped because the application cannot be stopped—the services of the software are continually required or safety-critical.
- Maintaining user or application state: Stopping the software would cause the user to lose mental context or because saving and/or re-creating the software's application state would be difficult or costly.
- Re-installation difficulty: Applications with complex installation properties, such as software embedded in an automobile.

Finally, all software adaptation is motivated by *observation and analysis*. While perhaps this is an obvious point, the role of observation and analysis is critical in the process of supporting software adaptation, and will be discussed later in the chapter. The behavior and properties of the extant system are observed and compared with, for instance, goals and objectives for the system, and to the extent that analysis reveals a discrepancy, adaptation activities are initiated.

14.1.2 Shearing Layers

Before going further in consideration of the adaptation of software systems it is worth a moment to consider change in physical, building architecture. Stewart Brand's insightful book, *How Buildings Learn—What Happens After They're Built* (Brand 1994), examines how, and why, buildings change over time. We have all seen this process, of course: We rearrange the furniture in our offices and homes, we install new cabling in our homes to accommodate new audio systems, we install new windows to remove drafts and make a building more energy-efficient. On infrequent occasions we remodel our homes, adding new space or reconfiguring existing space. On very rare occasions we might even see a house physically moved—for instance, if it is of historical significance but is in the way of a new civic development.

Brand categorizes the types of change that can be made to a building in terms of "shearing layers." Building upon earlier work by Frank Duffy, Brand cites six layers.

> Site. This is the geographical setting, the urban location, and the legally defined lot, whose boundaries and context outlast generations of ephemeral buildings.
>
> Structure. The foundation and load-bearing elements are perilous and expensive to change, so people don't. These *are* the building.
>
> Skin. Exterior surfaces now change every twenty years or so, to keep up with fashion or technology, or for wholesale repair.
>
> Services. These are the working guts of a building: communications wiring, electrical wiring, plumbing, sprinkler systems, . . .
>
> Space Plan. The interior layout—where walls, ceilings, floors, and doors go.

---

[1]Strictly speaking, any browser that supports JavaScript is dynamically adaptable. Whenever JavaScript is downloaded from a Web site and executed in the browser the user is taking advantage of dynamic extensibility. Most contemporary browsers are so good at this that the experience is completely transparent to the user.

Figure 14-1.
*Shearing
layers of change
[from Stewart
Brand's* How
Buildings Learn
(Brand 1994)].

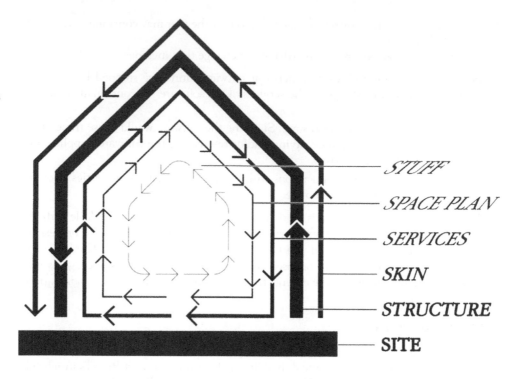

Stuff. Chairs, desks, phones, pictures, kitchen appliances, lamps, hairbrushes; all the things that twitch around daily to monthly.

(Brand 1994)

These six shearing layers are illustrated in Figure 14-1, with the arrangement of the layers in the diagram corresponding to where, approximately, the layers appear in a physical structure.[2]

Software is like this too. Though software is intrinsically more malleable, the constraints and dependencies that we impose during the process of design and implementation make it behave much like a building. As we have seen, any software system has an architecture, which determines its load-bearing elements. It has a site in its installation, that is, the usage context, whether it is a home business, a research laboratory, or a bank. Similarly, software has a "skin" with its user interfaces; further analogies can be found for the other layers. The difficult thing about software, however, is that we cannot examine a software system by looking at the source code and readily distinguish one of the system's load-bearing elements from a mere incidental—an item as incidental as the placement of a hairbrush in a house.

---

[2]Layers, as used by Brand and shown in Figure 14-1 do not correspond exactly to layers as used in software. In particular, the relative juxtaposition of layers in a software system, such as found in the layered style of Chapter 4, differs from the ordering of the shearing layers. As shown in this diagram, for instance, the relatively immutable structure layer is adjacent to the relatively mutable skin.

One value of Brand's observations is the categorization of types of change according to the nature and cost of making a change within those dimensions. Put another way, our understanding of building layers, either as sophisticated housing developers or simply as occupants, informs us regarding what can be changed, how quickly, and roughly for what cost. For instance, as Brand noted, changes to a load-bearing element of a building—such as a steel girder—are just not done; to do so would likely endanger the structural integrity of the building. If we could make a similar categorization for software, one that would allow us to dependably identify the load-bearing elements of an application, it would help us understand the necessary techniques to effect a given change, and allow us to effectively estimate the time and cost to achieve the goals. Our intuition as to understanding the costs, difficulty, and time to make changes in any of these aspects to a building is pretty good, due at least in part to our long experience with buildings and their visible, material nature. Unfortunately, we do not usually have that kind of intuition with software, for we often cannot associate a change request with a particular type of layer in the software.

One of Brand's objectives in identifying shearing layers with their different properties is that it provides design guidance. Recognizing that the layers change at different rates, change is facilitated by limiting the coupling between the parts of a building that correspond to different shearing layers. (A simple example admonition that comes from this is, "Don't inextricably associate the appearance of a building with its services"—an admonition famously contravened by Paris's Pompidou Center, as illustrated in Figure 14-2. By making the services—such as escalators—part of the skin, changing one requires changing the other. Maintenance costs for the services now must also include costs for maintaining their very public appearance.)

These layer notions can be applied to software. In particular, the observation of layers and the admonition to decouple them is consistent with David Parnas's dictum that software engineers should "design for change." The layer concept goes beyond that simple platitude,

Figure 14-2.
The Pompidou Center: A good lesson in why appearance should not be inextricably linked with services.

however, to suggest specific ways of assessing whether a proposed connection between two elements of a system is appropriate or not. Are the elements proposed for connection in separate layers? In layers that are widely separated? Is the proposed connection one that maintains the essential aspects of independence for those layers?

In Brand's analysis, structure plays a somewhat distinguished role. Its relative immutability in building architecture means that it must be understood well, for it provides the bounds to the types of changes that can be applied. In the case of software, with its relative mutability, we have the opportunity for accommodating a great range of change—but only under certain conditions. We can achieve effective adaptation if we make the structure of software explicit (that is, the system's architectural configuration of components and connectors), and provide ways for manipulating that structure. At a minimum, understanding a software system's architecture enables us to assess the potential for future changes.

Finally, Brand makes a trenchant observation about building architectures that provides key insight into software adaptation: "Because of the different rates of change of its components, a building is always tearing itself apart." As introduced in Chapter 3, a concern with software change is architectural erosion, the regressive deviance of an application from its original intended architecture resulting from successive changes. If a programmer modifies an application based only upon local knowledge of the source code, it can be quite difficult to determine if the changes made cut across the software's shearing layers. Put another way, the changes to code may not respect the principal design decisions that govern the application. To the extent that the boundaries are ignored while making changes, the structure is degraded. The preventative strategy for avoiding architectural erosion of this type is to base change decisions not on local analysis of the code, but on the basis of understanding and modifying the architecture, and then flowing those changes down into the relevant code, a theme we explore below.

14.1.3 Structural Elements Subject to Change

Any of a system's structural elements, its components, connectors, and their configuration, may be the focus of adaptation. The particular characteristics of these elements as found in a specific system will significantly determine the difficulty of accommodating change and the techniques useful for achieving it.

Components

Some changes may be confined to a component's interior: Its interface to the outside world remains fixed, but, perhaps to achieve a particular non-functional property, the component's interior must be altered. A component's performance may be improved, for example, by a change to the algorithm that it uses internally. In many cases, however, adaptation to meet modified functional properties entails changing a component's interface.

Beyond this simple dichotomy a component may possess capabilities that facilitate its adaptation, or its role in the adaptation of the larger architecture within which it resides.

First among these capabilities is knowledge of self and exposure of this knowledge to external entities. A component may be built such that its own specifications are explicit and included within the component. A straightforward form and use of such specifications are as run time assertions that validate that incoming parameters satisfy the assumptions upon which the component's design depends. In a verified, static (that is, non-adaptive) world, such run time assertion checking may well be considered wasteful, but in an uncertain, adaptive world, such checking may be a useful adjunct in maintaining a robust application. A less obvious use of such assertions is in gathering information that may motivate adaptations. Assertions may repeatedly detect violation of input assumptions. If a component retains a history of such violations and exposes that history to a monitoring agent, that information may guide the architect in identifying ways in which the architecture needs to be changed. More generally, a component may make its full specifications available for inspection by external entities. Such a capability enables dynamic selection of components to achieve system goals and hence is strongly supportive of adaptation. While not supported in all programming languages, component reflection is supported in Java.

Second is (self-)knowledge of the component's role in the larger architecture. For instance, a component could be built to monitor the behavior of other components in an architecture and to change its behavior depending upon the failure of an external component. A component may be able to query whether other components exist in an architecture that could be used to obtain an equivalent service. Similarly, if a component monitors its own behavior and realizes, for example, that it is not performing fast enough to satisfy its client components, it could request an external agent to perform some load leveling or other remedial activity.

Third is the ability to proactively engage other elements of a system in order to adapt. Continuing the previous example, rather than asking an external agent to reduce the load, a component might query whether external (sub-) components are available that could be used within the component to enable it to improve its own performance. While such a scenario is currently pretty far-fetched, such a capability is only a natural progression from components that are not self-aware and not reflective, to components that are reflective but passive, to components that not only are reflective but (pro)active in supporting system adaptation.

The capabilities listed above prefigure the general adaptation techniques discussed later in this chapter. The common theme is explicit knowledge and representation of a component's specifications and knowledge of its role within the wider architecture.

Component Interfaces. Changes to component interfaces are often inevitable when modifying functionality. Changing a component's interface, however, requires changes to the interface's clients as well: The input and output parameters must match at both ends of the interaction. Many client components may not be "interested" in the new functionality represented by the new interface, yet must be modified nonetheless.

This undesirable ripple effect of change has motivated creation of techniques for mitigating such impacts. A popular technique is the creation of adaptors, whereby components wanting to use the original interface invoke an adaptor component, which then passes along the call to the new interface, as illustrated in Figure 14-3. A client needing the new interface calls the modified component directly.

Use of a technique such as this clearly has architectural implications: New components are introduced and tracing interactions to understand system functioning becomes more involved. Subsequent changes to one of the previously unmodified methods become even more complex: Should yet another adaptor be introduced? Should the method be changed in the root component and in all the previously created adaptors? Suffice it to say for now that "local fixes" that attempt to mitigate changes to component interfaces can have

Figure 14-3.
*Use of adaptor
components to
preserve
interfaces.*

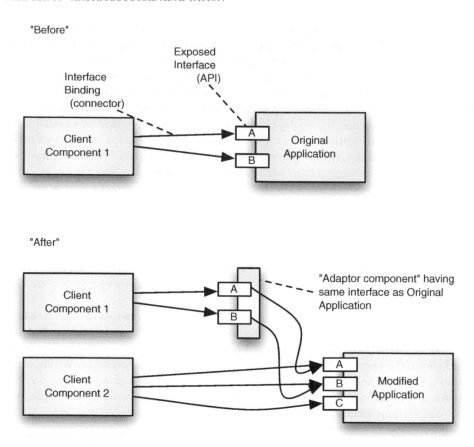

serious repercussions; the architect is wise to consider, in advance, a range of techniques for accommodating change, as discussed later in this chapter.

Connectors

Just as components may be required to change, so may connectors, and depending on the type of change, the architectural implications may be profound or may be negligible, similarly for the resulting changes in the implementation. Typically, the motivation for changes to connectors is the desire to achieve altered non-functional properties, such as distribution of components, heightened independence of subarchitectures in the face of potential failures, increased performance, and so on.

Changes to connectors may be along any of the dimensions of connector design discussed in detail in Chapter 5. As the latter part of this chapter will show, choice of connector type is a major determinant of the effort involved in supporting architectural evolution. Roughly speaking, the more powerful the connector, the easier the architectural change. Connectors that remain explicit in the implementation code and that support very strong decoupling between components (such as those connectors supporting event-based communication) are superior for supporting adaptation.

Configurations

Changes to the configuration of components and connectors—that is, how they are arranged and linked to one another—represent fundamental changes to a system's architecture. Such changes may occur at any level of design abstraction, and may be motivated by the need to meet new functional requirements or to achieve new non-functional properties. For instance, a common, large-scale configuration change is to move from an integrated business-to-business application model to an open, service-oriented architecture. The custom application may enable two businesses to communicate and transact business very efficiently, but a move to an open, service-oriented architecture may allow each party to more easily add new functionality, or support interactions with other business partners. Many of the core components may remain unchanged, but the way the components interact with each other and the connectors through which they communicate may be profoundly altered.

Effectively supporting such a modification requires working from an explicit model of the architecture. Many dependencies between components will exist, and the architectural model is the basis for managing and preserving such relationships. Most importantly, the constraints that governed creation of the initial architecture must be maintained if the architecture is to retain the same style. If maintaining the governing style constraints is not possible, then deliberative analysis should take place to determine an appropriate style for the new application. The move from custom, tightly integrated business-to-business applications to service-oriented architectures is precisely such a change: The fundamental architectural style of the application is altered.

The architectural model will need to manage deployment characteristics too, as basic component-connector relationships, in keeping with the discussion of Chapter 10.

14.1.4 Change Agents and Context

Techniques for effecting change are determined not only by what is ultimately changed, but also by the *context* for the change and the character of the *agent(s)* performing the change. Important aspects of the context for change include:

- The factors behind the change motivation: how a system is observed and what analysis can be performed on those observations.
- The timing of the change: when in the development/deployment/use time line the change occurs.

The agents for achieving change include both people and software. Important attributes of the change agents include:

- The location of the agent with respect to the system being changed.
- The knowledge possessed by the change agent about the system, whether complete or partial.
- The degree of freedom possessed by the change agent.

Each of the above items is considered in the following paragraphs.

Motivations, Observations, and Analysis

Several types of motivation for change were discussed earlier. Depending on the particular motivation that is at work, different problems and opportunities for dealing with the change arise. All motivations spring from a combination of observations about a system and analysis of those observations. For example, a system may not perform some newly desired function (as determined by comparing its current behavior to the newly sought behavior), or it may need to be fixed (as determined by comparing its current behavior to the original specification). The key issue is where the observations about a system originate.

Some observations may be drawn from the engineer's review of the system's architecture. More likely is the situation where a user, or some external agent, observes the run-time behavior of the application. To the extent that these observations are tied or related to information about the architecture of the application, the adaptation task is eased. If the only observations are those that come from seeing an application's external functional behavior, then determining the related structure is a task akin to debugging: The offending behavior has to be (possibly laboriously) examined to see what parts of the application are responsible. If the application has, or can have, probes included within it that are designed to assist the analyst determine which internal elements are relevant, the adaptation can proceed more quickly. Every beginning programmer is familiar with this technique in its simplest form: the inclusion of dozens of `println` functions, to repeatedly indicate where the program is executing and the values that particular variables have.

As architectures become more complex the beginning programmer's print line technique becomes inadequate. The concept, though, is still valuable. Monitors of the architecture can be included in a system (typically in the connectors) to enable high-quality monitoring of the behavior. The more precise the information and the analysis based on that information, the better the change can be planned and managed. In extreme cases, the absence of a good technique for identifying the components responsible for a particular behavior may cause an engineer to replace an entire subsystem. With good information, however, a much more localized change may suffice. We return to the topic of embedded probes in Section 14.3.1 below.

Timing

The positioning of change within a project's time line greatly affects the techniques available for accommodating the change. In short, the earlier the better. Rather than just repeating the old maxim that fixing problems in requirements is substantially cheaper than fixing them in code, we expand the time line to include system deployment and system use, for indeed some applications may need to be changed in situ, on the fly. A notional graph showing the relationship between cost and timing is found in Figure 14-4.

In Figure 14-4, the steep rise in cost is associated with accommodating change once a system is deployed; the costs top out when a deployed system must be changed on the fly. Deployment adds the costs of dealing with each individual installation of a system—possibly behind firewalls and customized at time of installation. On-the-fly adaptation requires special mechanisms and circumstances, a topic we treat on its own in Section 14.3.3.

Accommodating change early in a project's life is not the same, however, as fixing problems in the requirements. Identification, early in a system's design, of types of potential changes enables insertion of mechanisms specifically intended to facilitate those changes when they happen later. Far beyond a banal "design interfaces to be resilient in the face

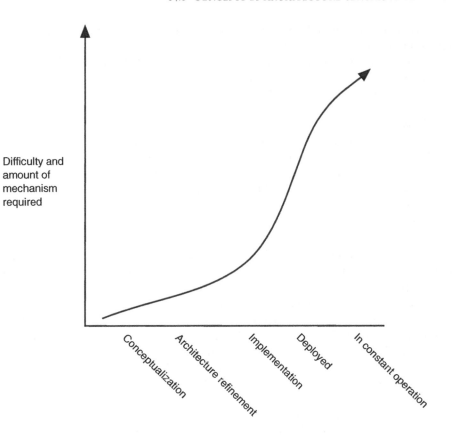

Figure 14-4.
Notional relationship between the timing of the identification of a change and the difficulty of and mechanism required for supporting that change.

of potential, identifiable changes to the internals of a module," numerous sophisticated techniques designed to enable broad adaptation have been created. These include plug-in architectures, scripting languages, and event interfaces. These and others will be described in Section 14.3.2.

Change Agents: Their Identity and Location

The processes that carry out adaptation may be performed by human or automated agents, or a combination thereof. Some trade-offs between these two types of agents are obvious, such as noting that humans can deal with a much wider range of problems and types of change or that automated agents can act with greater speed. Other issues may not be so obvious. One particular value of automated change agents is in the domain of deployed and continuously operating systems. If an adaptation change agent is part of a deployed application from the outset, the potential is present for an effective adaptation process: Getting to the deployed application is not a question. Moreover, the agent may have access to contextual information, whereby details of any local modifications and customizations are available. This potentially enables the change agent to act differently in every individual deployment. Users of modern desktop operating systems are familiar with such agents: Periodically a user is notified when an OS or application upgrade is available. If the agent is at all sophisticated, the advice given regarding the updates to be performed will be based upon knowledge of any local optimizations. (Often the downloaded update will perform a repeat or supplementary analysis, presenting messages such as "Locating installed components.")

In the case of dynamic adaptation the local presence of an automated change agent is essential. Managing the state of the application during the update can be a complicated matter, and is specifically discussed later in this chapter.

Knowledge

The knowledge possessed—or not—by the change agent can be a major determinant of the adaptation strategy followed. For example, there may be uncertainty surrounding the new behavior or concerning the new properties that are believed to be required. In such a case, an adaptation approach that deliberately works to mitigate risk is needed. This might involve processes that allow the engineer to easily retreat from a change if the change is not satisfactory. Prototypes or storyboards of potential changes are other strategies that could be employed when there is uncertainty.

Another key aspect of knowledge that governs adaptation strategy is knowing the constraints that must be retained in the modified system. More specifically, an adaptation should be performed with full knowledge of the architectural style of the application. Since the style is (typically) an intangible attribute of a system's structural architecture, knowing it and ensuring that any changes made are consistent with it requires extra work on the part of the adaptation team. The penalty for failing to know and respect the style is architectural degradation. That penalty may not have immediate repercussions, but through the course of successive changes the system's qualities will degrade and the difficulty of performing new changes will increase, sometimes reaching the point where further changes cannot be made at all.

Other important aspects of system knowledge include some obvious things. If the system's architecture has not been retained, then architectural recovery will be required. If a system component is a purchased binary, for which no information is available concerning its adaptation properties (if any), then large granularity changes will be needed ("component transplants"). If no analysis tools are available to help assess properties of a proposed change, then perhaps a more iterative approach to the adaptation should be followed. When it comes to adaptation, the more knowledge of the system and the change, the better.

Degree of Freedom

The final aspect of the context of change is the degree of freedom that the engineer has in designing the changes. One might think that greater freedom is always better. Unfortunately, greater freedom comes at a significant cost: The search space for solutions is larger, there is less immediate guidance for the engineer on how to proceed, and assessing all of the consequences and properties of a possible change will take more effort. The assumption of this statement, of course, is that the engineer is attempting to do a high-quality job; the cost can always be kept down in the short term by simply adopting whatever adaptation scheme first comes to mind, and doing the work in the same manner or style as the engineer always does. The price is paid in the future, when, for example, it is discovered that the change inhibits further growth or otherwise degrades the system's architectural quality. The alternate approach is to know or learn the constraints of the application and work within those constraints to satisfy the needs. With this approach, coherency is retained and the engineer's energies are directed toward solutions within the current architectural style.

14.1.5 Architecture: The Central Abstraction

The final concept of architecture-centric adaptation is the central one: the architectural model. An explicit architecture is assumed in much of the preceding discussion. In the absence of an explicit architecture, the engineer is left to reason about adaptation from memory and from source code—neither of which has proven very effective in managing change. The presence of an explicit architecture provides a sufficient basis for the planning and execution of system adaptation. Since the architecture *is* the set of principal design decisions governing the system, adaptation based on the architecture proceeds from knowledge of those things that are most intrinsic to the system's design.

The critical need, of course, is to maintain the integrity of the architecture and its explicit representation throughout the whole course of adaptation. As discussed earlier, in Chapters 2 and 9, the most important and most difficult aspect of this task is maintaining consistency between the architecture and the implementation. As long as the implementation is faithful to the architecture, the architecture can serve as the primary focus of reasoning about potential adaptations. As soon as the architectural model fails to be a reliable guide to the code it loses its value for guiding changes; the engineer is left with just the code—the "software engineering" of the 1970s.

Note that apropos of the discussion above regarding the location of change agents, if the agent is an automated part of a deployed system, then for architecture to be the central abstraction governing adaptation, the architectural model must either be deployed with the application or communication with an outside reference must be possible. If the model is not available, the agent does not have any basis for architecture-based adaptation.

The next section places all the concepts discussed above into a comprehensive framework for architecture-based adaptation.

14.2 A CONCEPTUAL FRAMEWORK FOR ARCHITECTURAL ADAPTATION

The first comprehensive conceptual framework for architecture-based adaptation was presented in 1999 (Oreizy et al. 1999). The framework, shown in Figure 14-5, shows the principal activities and entities and the key relationships among them. The diagram is simple enough to explain how a very static, requirements-based adaptation process proceeds, but sophisticated enough to indicate how a highly dynamic, automated adaptation process can work. Quoting from Peyman Oreizy and his colleagues' article,

> The upper half of the diagram, labeled "adaptation management," describes the lifecycle of adaptive software systems. The lifecycle can have humans in the loop or be fully autonomous. "Evaluate and monitor observations" refers to all forms of evaluating and observing an application's execution, including, at a minimum, performance monitoring, safety inspections, and constraint verification. "Plan changes" refers to the task of accepting the evaluations, defining an appropriate adaptation, and constructing a blueprint for executing that adaptation. "Deploy change descriptions" is the coordinated conveyance of change descriptions,

Figure 14-5.
*Conceptual
architecture for
adaptation. From
(Oreizy et al.
1999). (c) IEEE
1999.*

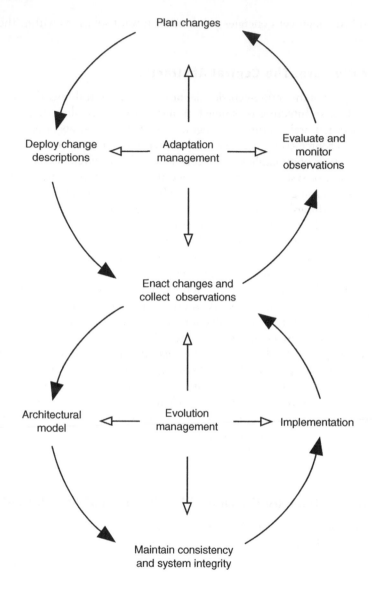

components, and possibly new observers or evaluators to the implementation platform in the field. Conversely, deployment might also extract data, and possibly components, from the running application and convey them to some other point for analysis and optimization.

Adaptation management and consistency maintenance play key roles in our approach. Although mechanisms for runtime software change are available in operating systems (for example, dynamic-link libraries in Unix and Microsoft Windows), component object models, and programming languages, these facilities all share a major shortcoming: they do not ensure the consistency, correctness, or other desired properties of runtime change. Change management is a critical aspect of runtime-system evolution that identifies what must be changed; provides the context for reasoning about, specifying, and implementing change; and controls change to preserve system integrity. Without change management, the risks engendered by runtime modifications might outweigh those associated with shutting down and restarting a system. . . .

The lower half of [the diagram], labeled "evolution management," focuses on the mechanisms employed to change the application software. Our approach is architecture-based: changes are formulated in, and reasoned over, an explicit architectural model residing on the implementation platform. Changes to the architectural model are reflected in modifications to the application's implementation, while ensuring that the model and the implementation are consistent with one another. Monitoring and evaluation services observe the application and its operating environment and feed information back to the diagram's upper half.

Figure 14-6 presents a further refined framework. Rather than the somewhat arbitrarily labeled "adaptation management" and "evolution management" of Figure 14-5, this figure

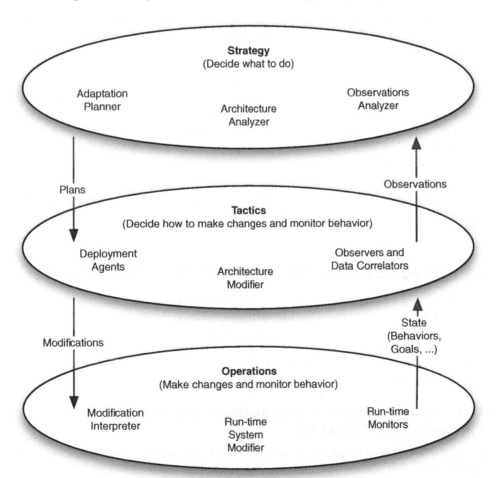

Figure 14-6.
Activities, agents, and entities in architecture-based adaptation.

separates the activities into three types and shows the entities and agents involved in carrying out the activities. The essential insights of the earlier framework are present, but now with additional detail and precision.

The three activities are characterized as strategic, tactical, and operational. Strategy refers to determining what to do, tactics to developing detailed plans for achieving the strategic goals, and operations to the nuts-and-bolts of carrying out the detailed plans.

Within the Strategy activity layer are agents for analyzing information about the system and the architecture, then planning adaptations based on that analysis. These agents may simply be tasks that a human user performs, or may be automated programs that carry out such tasks.

Within the Tactics activity layer are agents for making specific architectural modifications based upon the plans received from the strategy layer and deployment agents for seeing that those modifications are conveyed to all deployed instances of the architecture to be modified. Also found here are agents for determining how to correlate raw monitoring information received from deployed instances of the system such that the collected data is suitable for analysis at the strategy level.

Within the Operations activity layer are the specific mechanisms for modifying the architecture models (such as may reside on deployed instances) and modifying the implementation, maintaining consistency between them, and mechanisms for gathering data from an executing instance.

Keep in mind that one purpose of a framework such as this is to provide the engineer with a checklist of issues. Not all parts of the framework will be equally useful in all adaptation contexts. Similarly, the location of the various entities involved (both the agents performing the changes and the entities being analyzed or being changed) may vary. The architectural model is a good example: Any agent that needs to analyze or modify the architecture must have access to it. If the application is embedded in an isolated, autonomous system, then all the agents required, and the model, must be present on that system. If, on the other hand, the system can be stopped, reloaded, and restarted, all the adaptation agents and models may be found (only) on the development engineer's workstation. The deployment activity might only involve the object code.

14.3 TECHNIQUES FOR SUPPORTING ARCHITECTURE-CENTRIC CHANGE

In this section, we first present a selection of techniques that can be used to support the activities of the conceptual framework presented above, such as observing the application state and modifying the architecture. Since not all architectures or architectural styles are equally adept at supporting adaptation, we then present an overview of styles—some more architectural than others—that facilitate change. The section concludes with discussion of the special problems of autonomous change.

14.3.1 Basic Techniques Corresponding to Activities of the Conceptual Framework

Adaptation is triggered when someone—user, developer, auditor—determines that the current behavior of a system is not what is desired. That determination is based upon observation, the cornerstone activity.

Techniques for Observing and Collecting State

Determining the techniques that are most useful for observing and collecting state information presupposes knowing what "state" is. In its most obvious form, state consists of the run time values of a program's objects. Since values are continually changing, state is relative to time, and since only a small subset of a program's state is likely to be of use in adaptation, the observed state is usefully a time-stamped sequence of a subset of the run time values of the program's objects.

Other information beyond the values of a program's variables may also be important parts of state used for adaptation purposes. For instance, properties of the program's environment that are not represented in the program may be essential in determining how an application should be adapted. It may be, for example, that the behavior of a system should be a function of some currently unrepresented attribute of the external environment. An automated teller machine, for instance, should perhaps enter a safe mode and wirelessly signal an alarm whenever the ATM is subjected to G-forces in any direction (such as might be caused by an earthquake—or by someone attempting to abscond with the machine). Gathering this enhanced notion of a program's state would entail monitoring more than just the program.

A more prosaic example of external information that may be critical in determining an adaptation strategy is deployment information. The behavior of a system may be impacted by the presence of certain platform-specific options—the presence of certain device drivers, the amount of memory available, or the version of the operating system, for instance. Such information is usually easy to gather (for instance, from "registries" such as MS Windows registry database or Mac OS X's library files) and may be essential in the analysis phase.

System specifications and the system's architectural model may also be aspects of state that need to be observed on the target system and brought to the analysis context. One might expect this information to be static and already known to the adaptation analyst/planner, but in some contexts that may not be true. For example, if an application is highly configurable, each running instance of the application may be unique—perhaps because of customization to reflect installed hardware options. This information is thus akin to the deployment information mentioned above: In that case, the site-specific information concerns properties external to the application to be adapted; in this case, the information is about the application itself. The observed architecture, therefore, is the architecture of the application as it exists in its fielded state. Its set of components, connectors, and their current configuration may be unique. In some more esoteric situations, such as autonomous adaptation, the fielded system may also contain explicit and dynamically changing goal specifications for the application. These would also constitute part of the state subject to observation and reporting to the adaptation analyst.

Gathering the State. Numerous techniques exist for gathering the state of a program's objects; the numerous techniques developed to support program debugging all apply. Most primitively, the analyst may manually observe the program's user interface. More usefully, observation code may be part of a special run time system that enables monitoring of a program without requiring any modification to it. In some contexts, such as specialized embedded systems, "bolt-on" hardware analyzers may allow inspection of program state without any disturbance to the run time software environment.

If modification of the subject software system is feasible, a variety of more specialized and targeted approaches are possible. Again, at the most primitive level, the beginning programmer's technique of seeding a program with print statements may be sufficient. As program and problem complexity increase, more powerful and thoughtful approaches are required. Customized monitors may be inserted in the application code and function similarly to assertions. Such assertions can check for specified conditions and, if satisfied, record some value or otherwise emit an observation of the program's state. Whether a given programming language's assert statement is appropriate for this use depends on the language semantics: If satisfaction of the assert's condition necessarily interrupts the program's flow of control following the assertion, then use of that language feature would not be appropriate. Monitoring should allow execution to proceed unimpeded.

To the extent that creation of custom monitors is a manual process, it is an expensive process. Moreover, the use of custom monitors such as described above is only feasible when the source code is available and the application can be recompiled. One alternative is to focus on capturing information only at component boundaries, and to do so by capturing information that passes through an application's connectors. This technique can be based upon commercial middleware when used for connectors, or may take other forms. If the information gathering is automatic and does not filter "uninteresting" data, then it must be coupled with other tools to support filtering after the raw data has been gathered.

The concept is illustrated by the MTAT system (Hendrickson, Dashofy, and Taylor 2005), which creates a log of all messages sent between components in an architecture during its execution. This log is created by automatically implanting trace connectors in an architecture (see Figure 14-7). Trace connectors intercept all messages passing through them, make a copy of each message, and send each copy to a distinguished component that logs the messages in a relational database. The original messages are passed on unmodified. The trace connectors are first-class connectors. Figure 14-8 shows an architecture before modification as well as the architecture after inserting trace connectors.

The MTAT analysis system includes a tool that examines an xADL description of a system's structure and inserts trace connectors into that description automatically. The system's structure is modified so that each link in the original architecture is split into two links, with a trace connector between. Because the infrastructure provided by xADL and its supporting ArchStudio tool set instantiates architectures directly from their descriptions,

Figure 14-7.
A trace connector.

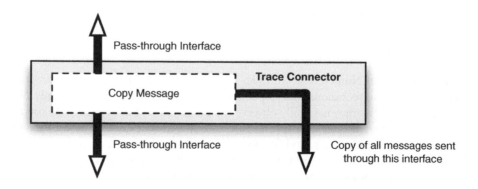

Original Architecture

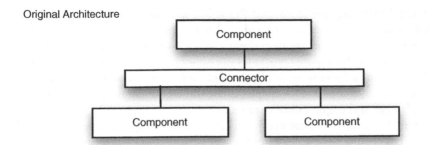

Figure 14-8.
*Instrumented
architecture and
original
architecture.*

Instrumented Architecture

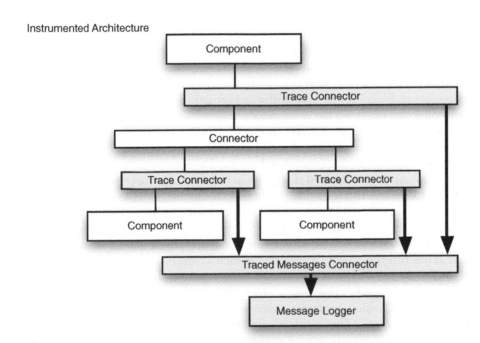

no recoding of components is needed for instrumentation. Consequently, components in the application remain unaware of any architectural changes or the presence of the trace connectors once the architecture is modified. The approach works in both single-process and distributed systems. In distributed systems, connectors that bridge process boundaries are broken into two halves—one in each process they connect. In terms of instrumentation, distributed connectors are treated the same way single-process connectors are; a trace connector is placed on every link in every process.

Finally, depending on the adaptation context, the technique used for gathering the observations may also need to be responsible for transmitting them from the platform where the target application is running to the host where the adaptation analysis will take place. To the extent that the target is an embedded system this off-board transmission is likely to be a necessity.

Techniques for Analyzing the Data and Planning a Change

Analyzing the Data. Analyzing the data gathered from observing a system and consequently determining the adaptations to perform is a wide-open problem. The range of types of changes that may be required precludes the prescription of a small set of standard techniques. Indeed, the problem is essentially the same as program understanding and program debugging. For some situations, a simple, canonical technique may suffice; for most situations, ample human thought will be required.

To the extent that kinds of change may be anticipated while a system is being designed, techniques may be put into place to monitor for specific situations, triggering preplanned strategies for coping with the change when the monitors detect the key values. The data analysis is simply comparing a value to a reference. Consider the example of an electronic commerce application. As the number of customer transactions increases the back-end servers must perform more work. As a maximum threshold is approached, additional servers must be brought online to avoid degradation of the user experience. Since much of the transaction processing in such e-commerce applications can be performed by independent servers, a simple load-sharing design can be used wherein additional servers are brought online automatically, becoming part of the "server farm" as the result of monitoring a threshold value and triggering the preplanned response.

An easy step up from this situation is using a set of rules to monitor a set of observed values. The guarding conditions in the rules may be complex; so, too, may be the corresponding actions. In essence, though, the approach is the same: The system's design has explicit provision for accommodating anticipated change, including the specific approach for monitoring and analysis. One use of this technique might be in comparing observed behavior of a system with behavior predicted by an analysis of the architecture before its implementation. For example, a simulation may show that a system correctly aborts a transaction if any one of its subtransactions fails; but monitoring of the implementation may show that the transaction was (inappropriately) completed in such a case, requiring correction.

Beyond these simple approaches there are few general techniques focused on analyzing observational data to guide adaptation. One example is illustrative, however. The MTAT system is targeted at helping engineers understand the behavior of applications having an event-based architecture. (The Rapide system of Chapter 6 is similar.) The trace connectors shown in Figure 14-7 feed copies of all messages sent in the architecture to a relational database. This database can then be examined in various ways to determine, for instance, communication patterns in the application or causality chains. Causality chains are particularly useful: When an engineer understands that message a from component A causes message b to be sent from component B and so on, changes can be made that reflect a deep understanding of the interrelationships between elements of a system's architecture. Note that, in essence, this approach is similar to techniques employed in debugging source code; the difference is in bringing the analytic approach to bear at the level of architectural concepts, and focusing on the particular kind of communication used at the architectural level.

Analyzing the Architecture and Proposing a Change. Assuming that observations of a system have been obtained and analyzed, it remains to develop a modification to the architecture to meet the needs with which the architect is concerned. Again, the challenge may be very simple or very complex.

If the architecture was originally designed to accommodate certain types of change, and analysis of the data shows that the needed change is within the expected scope, then proposing a responsive change is straightforward. For instance, if a component is shown to be a performance bottleneck, and a faster replacement component having the same interfaces can be produced (that is, the change is confined to the component's internal "secrets"), then simply swapping the original component for the improved one is all that is required. If a system's architecture is in the client-server style and a new client is needed, modification is simple. If a system's architecture is in the publish-subscribe style and a new publisher is available, then again the path to change is straightforward. The pattern here is clear: If the needed change fits within the type of change anticipated and accommodated by the application's architectural style, then the approach to take is clear.

If analysis shows that the needed change does not fall within an anticipated pattern, then the architect has to revert to the general analysis and design techniques discussed earlier in Chapters 4 and 8.

Commercial systems use a variety of techniques and terminology in supporting "upgrades" of deployed software products. The terms *upgrades*, *releases*, *service packs*, *patches*, and others are all used. There is little consistent technical meaning for these terms. Patches were initially used to refer to small changes to a file, but some have used the term for what amounts to wholesale replacement of the original file. Patches can be applied to binary as well as textual files. The term *service pack* is usually used to denote a collection of changes to an application, but there is no consistency on this either.

The means of deployment and installation of patches (whichever term is used) can vary significantly. Some deployments are initiated by the deployed software itself—that is, an instance of a system checks with the home site for available upgrades and, if found, proceeds to initiate a download. In other occasions, the vendor will initiate the deployment, attempting to notify all user sites of the need for the upgrade. Once deployed the patch may be installed automatically or may require active user involvement.

The installation activity may be unsophisticated or may involve checking the context—determining the other components or applications that are installed that might determine the particular change to make.

All of these activities echo or embody some of the techniques involved in a robust architecture-based adaptation process, such as described in this chapter.

Patches, Service Packs, Upgrades, and Releases

Analyzing the Proposed Change. After a proposed change to an architecture has been developed it should be checked to determine if it is complete and appropriate for deployment to its target platforms. Checking a proposed change seems so obvious that it should go without saying, but consider some of the possible items that may need to be checked:

- Are there any unattached ("broken") links in the new architecture?
- Have all interface links been type-checked for consistency?
- Are all components properly licensed for use in the target environments? (For example, if the target environment is a commercial product, do any of the new components have GPL licenses attached?)
- Are communications between the components performed consistently with the application's security requirements? (For example, if two components communicate over an open network, are the messages encrypted?)

- Is every component and connector in the revised architecture mapped to an implementation?
- Is everything in the deployment package that the change agent on the target platform requires? (For example, license keys and configuration parameters.)

The number of issues that may need to be checked is large, and hence an explicit process step to verify them is usually warranted.

One situation that calls for special attention is when each target system to which the revised architecture is to be deployed may be unique. That is, due to the possibility of local modifications, each target needs, in essence, to be individually checked. If the number of targets is at all significant, the analysis will have to be automated.

Techniques for Deploying Change Descriptions and Modifying the Architecture

Describing Changes to an Architecture. To effect a repair on a running software system, the changes to the system that will occur because of the repair must be specified and machine-readable. There are three primary ways that concrete architectural changes can be expressed, as follows.

- *Change scripts:* Change scripts are executable programs that operate on a system to make changes. In general, these scripts leverage underlying adaptation APIs provided by the implemented system (or its architecture implementation framework or its middleware). Adaptation APIs provide high-level functions, for instance, for instantiating and removing components and connectors, creating and destroying links, exposing or withdrawing provided services, and so on. Sometimes, change scripts will be accompanied by implementation artifacts (for example, new source or binary files) that are merged with the implemented system.
- *Architectural differences:* Rather than executable programs or scripts, architectural changes can be expressed as a set of differences between one architecture and another. In general, these differences, also known as "diffs," contain a list of additions, removals, and (optionally) modifications to architectural elements. For example, a diff might indicate the addition of two components, new interfaces on those components and new architectural links to hook those components into the architecture, as well as the removal of links that are no longer needed. Given two concrete architectural models of the system—as it is and the system as it should be—tools can create a diff automatically.
- *New architectural models:* In some cases, especially cases where the current state of the system to be adapted is unknown, a complete architectural model is used to describe the target adaptation architecture. In this case, an architectural difference is generally created by examining the elements in the current system as well as those in the new model and determining what to add and what to remove to bring the current system in line with the new architecture. Whether or not this architectural difference is expressed as a new artifact or is simply a side effect of determining the changes depends on the approach.

Applying Changes to an Architecture. In any of these three cases, two worlds are involved—the world of architecture and the world of implementation. In general, for any of these change artifacts to be effective in adapting a real, implemented system there must be a tight correspondence between elements in the architectural model and elements in the implementation. The use of architecture implementation frameworks or flexible middleware (see Chapter 9) can be used to facilitate this.

In the absence of tight bindings between architecture and implementation, it is conceivable to employ a human as the change agent on the target system. That is, the change artifact is reviewed by a person, and that person is responsible for making the corresponding changes to the system. Certain software systems [for example, enterprise resource planning (ERP) systems] are so complex to deploy, install, and configure that customers simply cannot do it themselves. In general, an organization that purchases such software also hires a team of consultants or product experts to deploy, install, and configure the software for their own organization. In this case, architectural changes might be deployed from the vendor to the consulting team, which could then make the configuration changes to the system manually.

Once changes to a system's architecture are described concretely in one of the above forms, they must be actually applied to that system. In the case of change scripts, the change script is executed in some run time environment co-located with the target application. Software underlying the target application, usually the architecture implementation framework or middleware, is called upon to actually make the changes to the system. In the case of architectural diffs, a change agent running alongside the target application must interpret the diff and make the changes specified therein, a process known as merging. In the case of new architecture specifications, a change agent must determine the difference between the current and intended application configuration and make changes as needed.

Issues with Deployment. No matter what form of change artifact is used—change scripts, architectural diffs, or new architectural specifications—that artifact needs to be deployed to the target system (or its associated change agent). The issues involved with deploying these change artifacts are similar to those found in software deployment in general, and so most of the advice in Chapter 10 on deployment applies here as well. If the target system is running on a single remote host, deployment is generally straightforward: The change artifact can be sent over any number of network protocols such as HTTP or FTP to the change agent, which then executes the changes. Distributed and decentralized systems can use push-based or pull-based approaches to distribute change artifacts.

In any of these approaches, a change agent must be located on the target machine to actually effect the changes on the architecture—to execute the change script, to parse the architectural diff, and so on. This agent can be deployed with the original system, or it can be sent along with the change artifact. For example, a change script could be compiled into executable form (as an "installer" or "patcher") and then sent over the network to the target system, where it is executed by the operating system directly. This is convenient as it avoids the problem of having to update change agents themselves. This strategy carries some security risk—running arbitrary executables on target platforms is an easy way to spread malicious software if the code is not trusted. Code signing and other strategies can be used to mitigate this risk.

Issues with Applying Changes. Making on-the-fly architectural changes (see Section 14.3.3 below) is more difficult. All issues identified below with respect to ensuring that the application is in an appropriate quiescent state to be adapted apply with these strategies.

Making on-the-fly changes to a distributed system is even more difficult, since the change must first be deployed to all appropriate parts of a distributed system, and then the system as a whole must be put into a quiescent state for update. This involves additional risk, since network and host failures during the update process can make it difficult to get the system into a consistent state.

An Example: ArchStudio

The ArchStudio environment supports architecture-based adaptation with a combination of techniques listed above. Specifically, it uses an architecture-implementation framework to ensure a mapping between architecture and implementation. Then, architectural diffs are used as change descriptions to evolve a system at run time. The process for evolving a system occurs in four steps.

Step 1 of the process is shown in Figure 14-9. An architecture description in xADL is provided to a tool in ArchStudio, the Architecture Evolution Manager (AEM). The AEM reads through the model and uses the Flexible C2 Framework, described in Chapter 9, to instantiate the system. Implementation bindings in the xADL model facilitate the mapping from architectural components and connectors to Java components.

Step 2 of the process is shown in Figure 14-10. A new architectural model is created in the environment, possibly by making a copy of and modifying the old model. Then, the old model and the new model are both provided as input to another ArchStudio tool, the Differencing Engine, "ArchDiff." ArchDiff creates a third document, an architectural diff, that describes the differences between the two.

Step 3 in the process is shown in Figure 14-11. Here, the new model is no longer needed. The original model, still describing the running system, and the diff are both provided as input to another ArchStudio tool, the Merging Engine, "ArchMerge." The merging engine, acting as a change agent, modifies the original model with the changes in the diff.

Step 4 in the process is shown in Figure 14-12. Here, the AEM notices that changes were made to the original model (by way of events emitted from the model repository

Figure 14-9.
*ArchStudio
adaptation step1:
instantiation.*

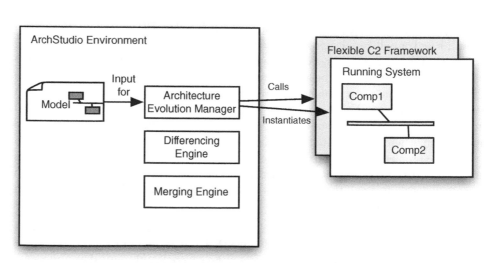

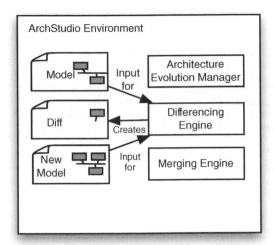

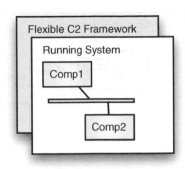

Figure 14-10.
ArchStudio
adaptation step 2:
differencing.

within ArchStudio). AEM then makes the corresponding changes to the running architecture by making more calls to the underlying Flexible C2 Framework, instantiating new elements and changing the application as necessary. Although only additions are shown in these simple diagrams, ArchStudio supports additions, modifications, and removals of elements.

14.3.2 Architectures/Styles that Support Adaptation

The preceding sections focused on generic techniques that support parts of the conceptual framework for architecture-based adaptation presented in Figure 14-6. The difficulty of making changes—even using these techniques—will vary enormously from one application

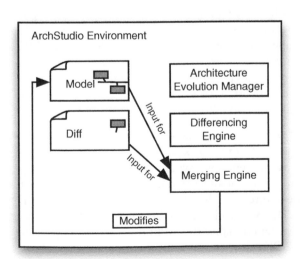

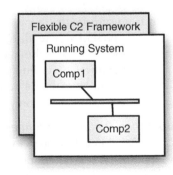

Figure 14-11.
ArchStudio
adaptation step 3:
merging.

*Figure 14-12.
ArchStudio
adaptation step 4:
applying changes.*

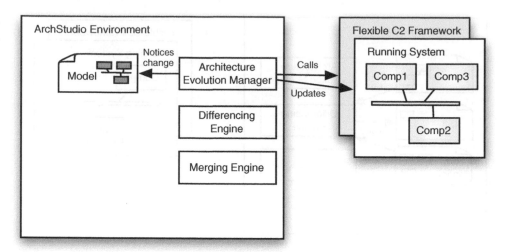

*Figure 14-12.
ArchStudio
adaptation step 4:
applying changes.*

to another, depending on the type of change required and the nature of the architecture to be changed. The discussion of shearing layers early in this chapter indicated, in generic terms, why some changes are more difficult to effect than others. The discussion of the many architectural styles in Chapter 4 showed in particular how some styles are more adept at handling particular types of change than others. Client-server architectures, for example, are designed to easily accommodate the addition or deletion of clients.

In the subsections below we revisit the topic of styles, introducing some specific interface-focused architectural approaches to facilitating change, and then briefly reconsider some concepts from Chapter 4 that are particularly effective in supporting change.

Interface-Focused Architectural Solutions

Since developers have been charged with changing software since the advent of computing, it is no surprise that a variety of techniques have emerged to help this process. The techniques presented here all reflect application of the dictum "design for change." We have categorized these techniques as interface-focused since they rest upon application-programming interfaces or interpreter interfaces presented by the original application.

These techniques do not purport to support all types of change. Indeed, the primary focus of these techniques is only in *adding* functionality in the form of a new module.

Application Programming Interfaces (APIs). APIs are perhaps the most common technique for enabling developers to adapt an application by extending it. With this technique, the application exposes an interface—a set of functions, types, and variables—to developers. The developers may create and bind in new modules that use these interface elements in any way the developers choose. (The interrelationships between the new modules themselves are unconstrained by the API.) The type of change to the original application that can be supported is limited to whatever functionality the API presents. Many operating systems and commercial packages use APIs.

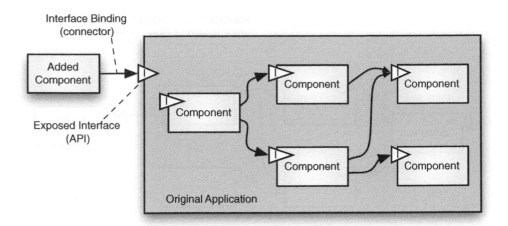

Figure 14-13.
*Using an API to
extend an
application with a
new module.*

This approach is illustrated in Figure 14-13, which presents a notional picture of an application to which one new component has been added. The added component can make use of any of the features of the original application that are exposed by the API, but it cannot access the interfaces of any of the components internal to the application, nor can it modify any of the connections internal to the application. The added component makes calls to the original application; nothing in the original application can make calls to the added component.

Plug-Ins. Plug-ins are sort of a mirror-image of APIs: Instead of the added component calling the original application, the application calls out to the added component. To achieve this, the original application predefines an interface that third-party add-ons or plug-ins must implement. The application uses and invokes the plug-in's interface, thereby altering its own behavior. To initiate the process, the original application must be made aware of the existence of the plug-ins; they must become registered with the application. Typically, the registration happens on application start-up, when the application inspects predefined file directories. Components found in those directories that meet the interface specification are registered and may then be called. The technique is illustrated in Figure 14-14.

Adobe Acrobat and Adobe Photoshop are applications that historically have made significant use of the plug-in mechanism. Direct interactions between multiple plug-ins are possible, but such interaction is not part of the plug-in architecture as such.

"Component/object Architectures". With this technique, the host application exposes its internal entities and their interfaces to third-party developers so that they can be used during the adaptation process. This is in contrast, for example, with the API and plug-in approaches that view the original application as a monolithic entity whose internal structure is opaque and immutable. Here, add-ons alter the behavior of the host application by adding new components that interact with existing components. Exposing the internal entities also allows a component to be replaced by one that exposes a compatible interface. This approach is illustrated in Figure 14-15.

Figure 14-14.
*Using a plug-in
interface to
extend an
application.*

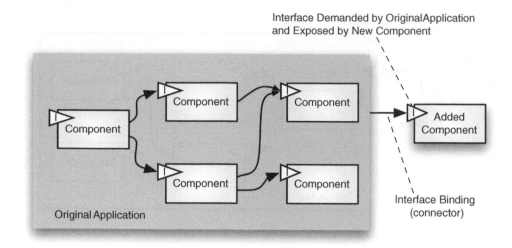

This approach to adaptation is more powerful than either APIs or plug-ins, since more interfaces are exposed, and the approach seems architecture-centric because the key items in the vocabulary are a system's components. Typically missing in common application of this technique, however, is an explicit architectural model. The developer is (just) confronted with the system's source code; nothing at a higher level of granularity can be manipulated to achieve the desired changes.

CORBA-based systems, discussed in Chapter 4, are members of this category, as are systems built with Microsoft's Component Object Model (COM). Such systems can be very fluid, but management of them can be difficult because there is no explicit model capable of serving as the fundamental abstraction.

Figure 14-15.
*Application
modification
via the
component/object
architecture
approach.*

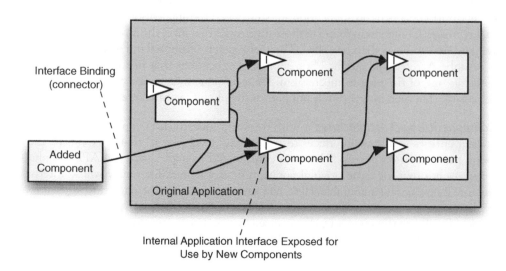

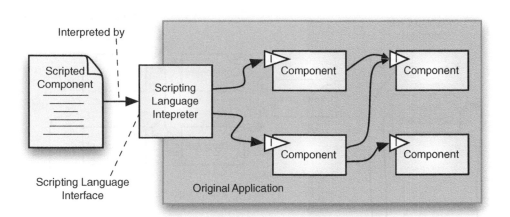

Figure 14-16.
*Application
adaptation by
means of a
scripting
language.*

Scripting Languages. With this approach, the application provides its own programming language (the "scripting language") and run time environment that the architect uses to implement add-ons. In essence, this is a use of the interpreter style from Chapter 4. Add-ons, when executed by the interpreter, alter the behavior of the application. Scripting languages commonly provide domain-specific language constructs and built-in functions that facilitate the implementation of add-ons, especially for users who lack programming expertise. Spreadsheet formula languages, macro systems, and programming-by-demonstration systems are essentially scripting languages optimized for specialized needs. Microsoft Excel is a prime example of an application that provides this means of extension. The technique is illustrated in Figure 14-16.

Event Interfaces. With this technique—a simple application of the event-based architectural style of Chapter 4—the original application exposes two distinct interfaces to third-party developers. The first is an incoming event interface, specifies the messages it can receive and act on; the second, an outgoing event interface, specifies the messages it generates. Messages are exchanged via an event mechanism. Add-ons alter the behavior of the application by sending messages to it or by acting on the messages they receive from it. As discussed in Chapter 5, event mechanisms commonly provide a message broadcast facility, which sends a message to every add-on attached to the event mechanism. The event mechanism acts as an intermediary, encapsulating and localizing program binding and communication decisions. As a result, these decisions can be altered independently of the original application or add-on components. This is in sharp contrast to the other techniques, in which programs directly reference, bind to, and use each other's interfaces. The technique is illustrated in Figure 14-17.

(Strong) Architecture-Based Approaches

Should changes to a system be required that involve more than just adding a new module, a richer approach to adaptation is needed than what the interface-focused solutions above offer. The core of any architecture-based solution, as we have discussed, is an explicit architectural model, faithful to the implementation, which can serve as the basis for reasoning about changes.

Figure 14-17.
*An event
architecture used
to support
extension.*

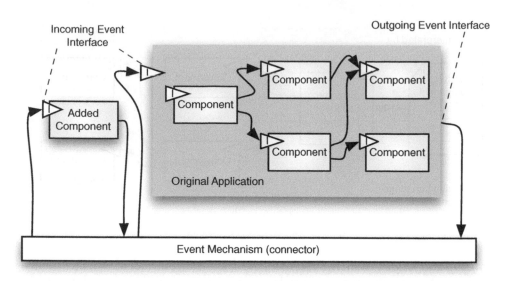

Figure 14-17. *An event architecture used to support extension.*

Simply having an explicit architecture is no panacea, of course. Complex dependencies between architectural elements and inflexible connectors may render difficult any adaptation problem. Consistent use of any of the architectural styles of Chapter 4 can remove some of the inherent difficulties. Ill-conceived custom styles that combine simpler styles in complex ways can vitiate those benefits, however.

The fundamental issue is *bindings*. To the extent that an architectural style enables easy attachment and detachment of components from one another, that style facilitates adaptation. The consistent emphasis of this text on the use of connectors stems from the benefits that explicit connectors can provide in supporting such attachments and detachments. The wide range of connector techniques discussed in Chapter 5 reveals that not all connectors are equally supportive of adaptation, however. Since a direct procedure call is one kind of connector it is obviously possible for the internals of one component to be strongly tied (via a procedure-call connector) to the details of an interface provided by another component. In the extreme (and hence rather useless) case of treating shared memory as a connector, arbitrary interdependencies between components may be achieved. These negative examples do serve to indicate what makes a good connector and what makes a style supportive of adaptation: independence between components. At a minimum, this means lack of dependency on interfaces. (As we shall see later, however, this is not a sufficient condition.) Use of particular types of connectors can achieve this independence, wherein one of the roles of the connector is to facilitate communication between two components while insulating them from dependence.

Perhaps the best example of this kind of connector and the independence provided is the event-based connector discussed in Chapter 4 in conjunction with the implicit invocation architectural styles. Components send events to connectors that route them to other components. The events are capsules of information; the sending component may not know which components receive the sent event; a receiving component may not fully understand all the information in the event, but still can process it such that its own objectives are satisfied. A network protocol (such as HTTP/1.1) can be used, for example, to support this type of communication. The protocol supports moving MIME-encapsulated data throughout a distributed application; how a receiving component interprets and processes the encapsulated payload is a decision local to that component. Ensuring that the collection of components and connectors cooperate to achieve the objectives for the application is the responsibility of the system architect. For detailed examples of this type of architecture, see Chapter 4, including the discussion of the C2 style.

14.3.3 The Special Problems of On-the-Fly and Autonomous Adaptation

Adapting a system while it remains in operation presents special challenges, complicating the adaptation process. Some example situations where that complication cannot be avoided were given at the beginning of the chapter, and include applications whose continuous operation is essential to the success of some larger system, such as control software in a continuously operating chemical refinery.

Autonomous adaptation means that human involvement in the adaptation process is absent, or at least greatly minimized. Autonomous adaptation can be a complicating addition to on-the-fly adaptation, such as when the continuously operating system is isolated from external control, as in robotic planetary exploration. Such extreme circumstances are not the only ones where autonomous adaptation may be required, however. It may be, for instance, that rapid response requirements to partial system failure dictates the use of autonomous adaptation techniques.

Some of the challenges of on-the-fly adaptation can be seen through analogies. Living in a house that is undergoing a major renovation is sometimes necessary, and is seldom pleasant. The unpleasantness comes from attempting to carry on daily life while portions of the service architecture that we depend upon—plumbing, electricity, heat, security, and so on—are only partially or intermittently available. Life goes on, but not in the regular rhythms or with the usual comforts.

A more vivid, and instructive, example is surgery. The patient corresponds to the system being "adapted." Clearly it is essential that while the adaptation is taking place—repair to a heart valve, for example—the patient must be kept alive. The various subsystems of the human (must) continue to function even though major disruptions take place. The various techniques and technologies of heart surgery, from anesthesia to cardiopulmonary bypass, are designed to maintain basic system performance while enabling major restructuring of a key component.

The key additional issues in on-the-fly adaptation are as follows:

- *Service strategy:* While the adaptation is taking place, will the system continue with a temporary service to fully replace the one being changed? Will it continue with a reduced level of service? A missing service? Can some service errors be tolerated? System functioning during adaptation may be maintained through the use of auxiliary components (such as the heart-lung machine in the surgery analogy), or may be degraded to a lower level of functionality (such as using a bathroom sink to wash dishes while the kitchen is remodeled in the home remodeling analogy).

- *Timing:* Identifying the occasions when the subject parts of the system can be altered. Depending on the service strategy adopted, the conditions under which the adaptation may proceed can be identified. Replacement of a component may only be allowed, for example, when it has finished servicing all outstanding requests to it, and has not initiated any requests on other components in the application.
- *Restoration or transfer of state:* If a component is replaced, does the replacement component need to know some or all of the state information that was held by its predecessor? The first calculations made by the new component may necessarily be functions of previous values computed and stored, in which case that state would have to be restored at the time the new component is started up.

An example may help make these concepts more clear. (Throughout this section we assume, consistent with the preceding parts of this chapter, that the smallest unit of change is a component and that component identity and boundaries are maintained in the implementation.)

Consider the case of a processor that controls the opening and closing of a valve in a chemical refinery based upon command inputs, temperature sensors, and flow meters. Such a processor may be designed in the sense-compute-control pattern discussed in Chapter 4. It may become necessary to replace one of the control components onboard, due to identification of an error in one of its algorithms. One plausible adaptation strategy is, at an arbitrary time, to cease processing of any incoming signals on its sensors, leave the valve's opening at whatever position it is in, swap out the offending component, swap in the new component, and then start the replaced component by first sampling all the input sensors, and then issuing new commands to the valve. Whether this strategy will work depends on, for example, whether any inputs missed during the swap were critical to the refinery's safety, or whether leaving the valve open in its last position could endanger the refinery before the new component was in place. For instance, if the valve was left in the "full on position" while the upgrade was taking place, and if the upgrade took very long to transpire, some downstream reaction in the refinery may be put at risk. A better strategy would likely entail buffering all inputs to the valve controller so that when the new component comes online it would ensure that every incoming value was processed, and instead of leaving the valve at its last setting, putting it into some safe position.

The appropriate service strategy for this example would likely be determined in consultation with the plant's chemical engineers. The amount of time the control processor could safely be preoccupied with the adaptation might well be determined by properties of the chemical processes in the refinery. If the valve is highly critical, a temporary controller may need to be put into place. Timing of the adaptation could be determined by properties of the plant, or perhaps by the state of the value itself (perhaps the adaptation would occur only when the valve is closed).

Determining the Conditions for When to Effect a Change

The determination of the precise conditions under which it is appropriate to replace a component can be a function of the system as well as of the architecture. The system, as illustrated in the refinery example, may dictate that change happen only under certain external conditions. Alternatively, system domain analysis may reveal that change can happen at any time—even if it means that some outputs produced are erroneous—simply because the system is so robust that it can tolerate some significant degree of error on the part of the software. For example, a satellite that gathers weather data, processes it, and sends the resulting information to the ground may be in this category. Weather data is continuous and is a phenomenon that changes slowly (relative to computer processing, at least), so simply losing some amount of the telemetry data is unlikely to matter.

Some applications will demand a much more conservative analysis, however. The principle is that it is safe to remove/replace a component only when such change will not adversely affect the functioning of the rest of the application. While precisely identifying all such conditions may be quite difficult, it is easier to specify sufficient conditions. Some sufficiency conditions are captured in the notion of *quiescence*. The intuition is that it is safe to replace a component when that component is inactive. A simple understanding of quiescence is that the component is not engaged in sending or receiving information, and internally is idle (all of its threads are idle). Inactivity, however, needs to be understood more comprehensively, in terms of any transactions to which the component may be a party. That is, a component C may initiate a set of actions that are performed by other components, itself staying inactive until the other components complete their task and return control to C. In this case, C is not quiescent until all actions that are part of a (conceptual) transaction are complete. Various shades of quiescence are defined in the sidebar, drawing from the work of Professors Jeff Kramer and Jeff Magee, who pioneered this area.

If an application is implemented with powerful, explicit connectors, such as message buses, then determining whether a component is engaged in communication is easy—the connectors may be used to make this determination. Knowing whether a component is engaged in a multiparty transaction, however, requires deeper analysis and will have to consider the behavioral characteristics of the architecture as a whole. The stronger the notion of quiescence required, the more complex will be the determination of when it is achieved.

A node in the active state can initiate and respond to transactions. The state identified as necessary for reconfiguration is the passive state, in which a node must respond to transactions, but it is not currently engaged in a transaction that it initiated, and it will not initiate new transactions. This passive state is so defined as to permit connected nodes to progress towards a passive state by completing outstanding transactions. In addition it contributes to system consistency by completing transactions.

For consistency during change we require a stronger property, that the node is not within a transaction and will neither receive nor initiate any new transactions i.e. all outstanding transactions are complete and no new ones will be initiated. Change quiescence of a node is defined as that state when the node is both passive and there are no outstanding transactions to which it need respond. Such a state depends not only on the node itself, but on the connected nodes. From "Change Management of Distributed Systems" (Kramer and Magee 1988). © 1988 ACM, Inc. Reprinted by permission.

Quiescence, According to Kramer and Magee

Management of State

A component's *state* is the set of values that it maintains internally. When a component A is replaced with a component B, the question arises as to what B's state should be initialized to upon its startup. The easiest situation is one where no transfer or re-creation of corresponding state is needed. For example, many Unix filters do not maintain state; the output they produce is solely a function of the most recently read input, unaffected by any preceding computation. Other applications may not be so designed. For instance, the user may have set a number of preferences; should the application be modified while the user is working with it, the preferences should be transferred. One effective strategy for dealing with transference of state is simply to externalize it: copy whatever state needs to be moved to a third party; when the replacement component comes online its first action is to initialize itself by drawing from the third party. This strategy, of course, presumes that the components were designed for replacement—a condition not often true.

Practical Tips

While the principles and issues discussed above apply to architectures generally, there are some practices and approaches that definitely ease the practical problems of supporting on-the-fly adaptation. Foremost are use of explicit, discrete, first-class connectors in the implementation and use of stateless components. To see the success of this simple advice, consider the architecture of the Web. As described elsewhere in this text, the Web is based upon these principles—and manifestly the Web is an application that continuously is undergoing change. Proxies and caches can be added and deleted; new Web server technologies put into place, new browsers installed. It all works because the interactions between the various components are discrete messages and the core protocol (HTTP/1.1) requires interactions to be context-free ("stateless" in the Web jargon)—a server does not need to maintain a history of interactions with a client in order to know how to respond to a new request.

Autonomous Change

Autonomous change is adaptation undertaken without outside control. The distinctive character of autonomous change is not the challenge of working without connection to, say, the Internet, but rather effecting the change process without involving humans. The desire to avoid involving humans is readily motivated: A self-adaptive system can change much more quickly than one involving people; consequently, self-adaptive change is likely to be much cheaper. Other situations may similarly motivate autonomous change. For instance, if a large number of very similar systems must be changed, but each with minor variances, an autonomous approach may work not only faster, but more accurately, as such repetitive tasks are often poorly performed by people—the tasks are simply too boring to keep one's attention.

The difficulties entailed in achieving autonomous change are equally clear: All the activities discussed above must be completely realized as executable processes, from data observation, to analysis, to planning, to deployment, to run time system modification. More-over, all these executable processes, and all the information involved in their execution, must reside on the autonomous system. Preeminent in this information is the architectural model of the system. Note that with this onboard, and kept faithful to the implementation, the system is continuously self-describing.

In practical terms, self-adaptive systems today are limited to rather simplistic situations for which a set of rule-based adaptation policies can be formulated. As previously discussed, this is appropriate for systems where the types of adaptation needs can be anticipated and encoded in simple terms. Expanding the range of systems and types of change for which autonomous solutions can be developed is an area of active research.

According to IBM, "Autonomic computing is an approach to self-managed computing systems with a minimum of human interference. The term derives from the body's autonomic nervous system, which controls key functions without conscious awareness or involvement. Autonomic computing is an emerging area of study and a Grand Challenge for the entire I/T community to address in earnest."

The initial autonomic computing manifesto (IBM 2001), as issued by IBM, focused attention on installation and management of IT infrastructure, such as corporate servers and networks, and their use in business processes. According to this manifesto there are at least eight key characteristics of autonomic systems:

"Autonomic Computing," IBM's Grand Challenge for the IT Industry

1. "To be autonomic, a computing system needs to 'know itself'—and comprise components that also possess a system identity."

2. "An autonomic computing system must configure and reconfigure itself under varying and unpredictable conditions."

3. "An autonomic computing system never settles for the status quo—it always looks for ways to optimize its workings."

4. "An autonomic computing system must perform something akin to healing—it must be able to recover from routine and extraordinary events that might cause some of its parts to malfunction."

5. "A virtual world is no less dangerous than the physical one, so an autonomic computing system must be an expert in self-protection."

6. "An autonomic computing system knows its environment and the context surrounding its activity, and acts accordingly."

7. "An autonomic computing system cannot exist in a hermetic environment."

8. "Perhaps most critical for the user, an autonomic computing system will anticipate the optimized resources needed while keeping its complexity hidden."

–IBM 2001

Clearly IBM's vision for autonomic computing is consistent with the architecture-based approach to adaptation articulated in this chapter. Indeed, the first characteristic listed above is essentially a restatement of the requirement of maintaining an onboard model of a system's architecture, as discussed in the main body of the text.

References: (IBM 2002; Kephart and Chess 2003); Autonomic Computing Conference www.autonomic-conference.org/.

14.4 END MATTER

There is little question that applications will be adapted and changed over their lifetime. The real question is how expensive and how difficult will it be to effect those changes. While "designing for change" and the use of encapsulation is an important principle for assisting with change, much more powerful and capable mechanisms are required for meeting contemporary adaptation needs. This chapter has presented such mechanisms:

- A conceptual framework for governing the entire adaptation process.
- Architectural styles that assist with accommodating large-scale system change.

- Specific techniques for assisting with the major tasks of adaptation: monitoring, analyzing, planning, and effecting.

If a system's descriptive architecture and its prescriptive architecture are consistent, then adaptation can be orchestrated around changes to the architectural model. This approach, besides providing the intellectual tools for managing ordinary adaptation, opens the door to novel types of application evolution, such as wherein the architectural model is deployed with the application and adaptation processes on the target machine utilize the model in determining and carrying out changes.

This chapter concludes a three-chapter sequence on designing systems for nonfunctional properties. Chapter 12 introduced the main concepts and covered a variety of NFPs. Chapter 13 delved into the NFPs of security and trust; this chapter has examined the NFP of adaptability. The next chapter returns to a subject introduced in the very first chapter of the text: program families. With all the various elements of architecture-based development laid out in the intervening chapters, we next explore in depth how cost-effective development of a related set of applications can be achieved.

The Business Case	Adaptation is the means for preserving and leveraging sunk investment in software. To not adapt is to abandon the investment; the challenge is cost-effective adaptation. An architecture-based approach to adaptation offers: • New opportunities for products/applications. • Better opportunities for maintaining deployed products. • Better opportunities for responding to customer enhancement requests. • Less downtime. • New opportunities for third-party enhancement, while maintaining control of intellectual property. The concept behind the last bulleted entry above is to expose parts of the architecture that enable third parties to add value through their proprietary extensions, but to do so without exposing the internals of components, or even allowing the third parties to become aware of the existence of large portions of the primary architecture. This strategy appears to be successful in, for example, commercial image-processing applications. One risk of supporting adaptation is abuse based upon perceived ease. That is, if marketing, for example, is led to believe that the organization can effectively support product evolution with ease, then they may be less likely to carefully analyze new customer requests or to bundle requests for changes into meaningful packages.

14.5 REVIEW QUESTIONS

1. What are the fundamental causes or motivations for software adaptation?

2. What are the major activities of software adaptation?

3. For each of the major activities of adaptation, describe a technique that assists in performing that activity.

4. How can architectures be designed to make the task of third-party extension easier?

5. How do plug-in architectures work?

6. Why may quiescence be needed for run time replacement of a component?

14.6 EXERCISES

1. Consider the problem of modifying several of the Lunar Lander designs of Chapter 4 to serve as a Martian lander. Would the changes required be confined to components, or would connectors be involved?

2. Consider the problem of adapting the Lunar Lander designs of Chapter 4 to work by remote control. That is, instead of the Lander having a pilot on board, the craft is unmanned and a pilot on Earth must control the descent. What type of changes would be required to the components? To the connectors?

3. Consider the challenges faced in adapting a planetary exploration vehicle, such as the Cassini mission to Saturn. What would be a suitable architectural style for supporting in-flight system adaptation? Would you have a kernel that is nonupdatable? Why or why not?

4. What degree of quiescence would be required in your answer to question 3 when performing an update? To what extent does your answer depend on the type of update (that is, the degree of change involved)?

5. What are the differences (if any) between software architectures that support dynamic adaptation and fault-tolerant architectures? What circumstances are the approaches suited for?

6. Suppose you had optimized a connector in the implementation of a system for performance reasons and then need at some later date to modify the architecture. How would you approach adaptation of this system if the adaptation is performed offline? What if the adaptation must be performed dynamically?

7. Analyze the robotic architectures of Chapter 11 with respect to their ability to effectively accommodate changes such as requiring the robot to (a) perform a minor variation to an existing task, and (b) utilize a new tool, such as a new robotic arm, to perform an entirely new task.

8. Is preplanned change really an instance of dynamic architecture? Why or why not? What should the litmus test be?

9. (Research question) What is the role of dynamic adaptation (or just "adaptation") in the context of software product families? When should adaptation of a member of a family be considered creation of a new product?

10. (Research question) Does design of an application to support ease of adaptation conflict with the ability to ensure that any given instance of the application performs its intended task? In general, does ease of adaptation conflict with analyzability?

14.7 FURTHER READING

Since change has accompanied software development from the outset of the field there is no shortage of literature discussing how to adapt software. Indeed, the entire "Millennium Bug"/Y2K problem was one massive effort in software adaptation. In that case, of course, the change being effected was extremely narrowly focused. Sadly, for some Y2K systems, architecture changes were required since the two-digit fault was so implicitly part of those systems' design.

Stewart Brand's book on change in physical architectures (Brand 1994) is well worth an extensive read, for it has numerous insights on adaptation that have correspondences in software adaptation. If nothing else, you will discover why you love some buildings and hate others.

Some of the earliest work in architectural approaches to adaptation was performed at Imperial College by Jeff Kramer and Jeff Magee as part of the Regis (Magee,

Dulay, and Kramer 1994; Ng, Kramer, and Magee 1996) and Conic projects (Kramer and Magee 1990). Successive work with Darwin continues this theme (Magee and Kramer 1996).

Peyman Oreizy and colleagues are responsible for many of the key insights presented in this chapter, including the original conceptual model for the management of self-adaptive systems (Oreizy, Medvidović, and Taylor 1998; Oreizy et al. 1999) and the characterization of the architectural styles promoting adaptability presented in Section 14.3.2. The first of these two papers received an award in 2008, when it was recognized as the most influential paper from the 1998 International Conference on Software Engineering. As part of the award, the authors were invited to present a new paper on the topic, retrospectively analyzing the past decade's work in software adaptation and prospectively offering challenges for work still to be done (Oriezy, Medvidović, and Taylor 2008). Additional recent work includes approaches based on knowledge-based systems (Georgas and Taylor 2004; Georgas, van der Hoek, and Taylor 2005). Gomaa has explored the use of patterns to facilitate reconfiguration in (Gomaa and Hussein 2004), and addresses the issue of quiescence.

Many more references are available from the proceedings of the leading workshops in the field, which include the Workshop on Software Engineering for Adaptive and Self-Managing Systems and the Workshop on Architecting Dependable Systems.

15

Domain-Specific Software Engineering

Software systems differ in terms of their purpose, size, complexity, provided functionality, quality needs, intended usage, expected or required execution context, involved stakeholders and their concerns, level of criticality to system users, and so on. An argument can be made that this is precisely why software is difficult to develop. However, such differences across individual systems are not unique to software engineering. They can be found in any complex system and any engineering discipline.

As an example, consider two different products of modern engineering: airplanes and television sets. Both airplanes and televisions are complex systems, but their functionalities differ a great deal. They also have very different quality requirements. While it is certainly important for a television to function reliably, in the case of airplanes reliability can be a matter of life and death. Travelers expect airplanes to be robust in the face of atypical situations such as storms, turbulence, loss of cabin air pressure or engine or electrical power, and physical damage to the aircraft. On the other hand, consumers understand when, say, an electrical power surge damages their TV set and are content to wait for the TV to be repaired or simply will buy a new one. People expect that an airplane may be in use for decades and that it will need to be refurbished and upgraded during that time. They do not have the same expectations of a television.

Airplanes and televisions are products of (very) different engineering problem *domains*. As a result of these differences, the respective skill sets of the engineers working in the two domains also are likely to be specialized and very different: It would be unrealistic to expect an electrical engineer working on airplanes to be able to switch to building televisions without (perhaps significant) retraining, and most people would feel uneasy if they were flying on an airplane built by engineers who usually design televisions. There are many obvious reasons for this—the main one is that the problems solved in the two domains require different principles, techniques, processes, and tools that are honed separately over years or decades. Simply put, the two problem domains demand different solutions, and those developed for one domain are highly unlikely to fit the other.

Each application domain may further have several *subdomains*. For example, in the context of avionics, different subdomains may encompass rotary-wing aircraft (helicopters) versus fixed-wing aircraft (airplanes), military versus commercial aircraft, jet engine versus propeller engine aircraft, and so on. Within a single domain or one of its subdomains, organizations often focus on constructing *populations* of related systems. For example, Boeing engineers work on a wide variety of commercial and military aircraft that are likely to share some engineering characteristics. More easily recognized are the more closely related *families* of systems, or *product lines*, that exist within those populations. In the case of Boeing, an example would be the 7X7 family of passenger airliners. A family may be defined even more narrowly, for example, to encompass different models of the Boeing 747 jumbo jet.

It is reasonable to expect that even within the domain of avionics, the skills of an engineer working on rotary-wing aircraft may differ from those of colleagues working on fixed-wing aircraft. Likewise, an engineer building a military jet may have different experience and expertise than an engineer building a commercial airliner. Even more specifically, engineers working within Boeing's commercial airliner division likely approach certain aspects of their craft differently from their counterparts at Airbus. Additionally, there is a great deal of overlap regarding *how* different members of the Boeing 7X7 family of passenger jets are constructed; while many of the underlying principles are the same, the comparable Airbus airliners are likely to have been designed and built differently.

An analogous narrowing of the problem scope and specialization of the engineers' skills can be observed in other domains. For example, in the consumer electronics domain, a Philips engineer is likely to have somewhat different skill sets from, say, a Sony engineer. As another example, within the automotive domain, some General Motors engineers may focus on the broad population of GM vehicles while others may focus more narrowly on, say, the family of Cadillacs. Figure 15-1 illustrates this progressive narrowing of the problem scope and the resulting growth in commonality among systems.

As with any profession, software engineers have basic skills, techniques, guidelines, and tools that are applicable independent of the target domain. Separation of concerns, modularity, object-orientation, design patterns, UML, Java, CORBA, and so on, comprise a common "toolbox" at the disposal of software engineers. It would not be unfair

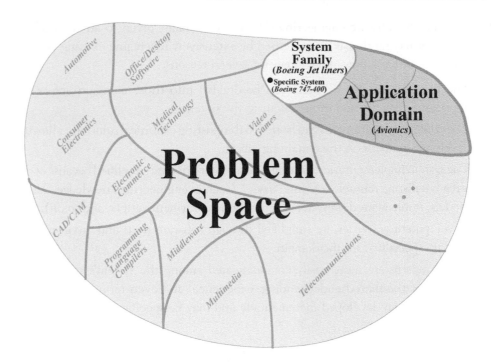

Figure 15-1.
*Engineers
construct systems
within many
problem
domains, which
are broken down
into subdomains,
which in turn are
broken down into
families.*

to think of these as equivalent to, say, Maxwell's laws, soldering irons, capacitors, resistors, and so on, that are at the disposal of an electrical engineer.

However, these basic tools and principles are only a rudimentary foundation for the construction of complex systems. They neither attempt to leverage the useful properties of a given problem domain nor help to identify and exploit the similarities that are likely to exist across systems in a given family. It would be too difficult, risky, and costly to attempt to build every software system using only these primitive tools. In the early days of computing, software engineers were forced to do exactly that. They had little or no knowledge about building software, especially within particular domains, so they had to develop software systems from "first principles."

The situation today is very different. A large amount of software engineering knowledge has been acquired through extensive experience (and costly failures) in many domains. Within these domains, many product populations and product lines have been developed and evolved. By leveraging knowledge from these experiences, engineers can build subsequent systems within the same domain or family more quickly, cheaply, and reliably. To use our earlier analogy, while the ability to build a television may not translate to the ability to build an airplane, the ability to build one airplane imparts a large amount of information about how to build another.

Domain-specific software engineering (DSSE) is the name given to an approach to software engineering that is characterized by extensively leveraging existing domain knowledge. DSSE is a powerful strategy for several reasons:

- The requirements for a system can be divided into those common across the application domain and those unique to the system.
- The common requirements can be tied to the existing canonical solutions, allowing developers to focus on the remaining subset.
- The system implementation, testing, and maintenance are simplified because of the already-existing reusable software "assets" (such as engineering knowledge, design models, implemented subsystems, test suites, deployment scripts, and so on).
- Development activities are simplified through software tools and environments that are specialized for the domain.
- Any concerns are more easily communicated among the system's stakeholders because of the shared understanding, experience, and even terminology, which may have been developed incrementally and may be specific to the application domain.

As we will elaborate in this chapter, DSSE combines insights from three principal areas:

1. The *domain*, which scopes the discourse, the problem space, and the solution space.
2. *Business goals*, which motivate the work and help engineers decide why they are doing what they are doing.
3. *Technology*, which is used to facilitate development and reuse of domain- and business-specific assets.

The respective roles of and relationships among these areas are depicted in Figure 15-2, which provides a conceptual basis for the remainder of this chapter. It allows us to define, relate, and explain appropriately two key facets of DSSE: domain-specific software architectures (DSSA) and product families, also referred to as product lines (PL). Even though they are closely related, these two areas of software engineering have received mostly separate treatments in the literature.

This chapter introduces and discusses the DSSE concepts foreshadowed above, with a particular focus on the role of software architecture in DSSE. By the end of the chapter, the reader will better understand how DSSE is different from ordinary architecture-based software engineering, its benefits, the relationship between DSSAs and product lines, and how to apply the resulting concepts to capture explicitly and effectively architectural solutions that span multiple systems across a domain or, more narrowly, across a system family.

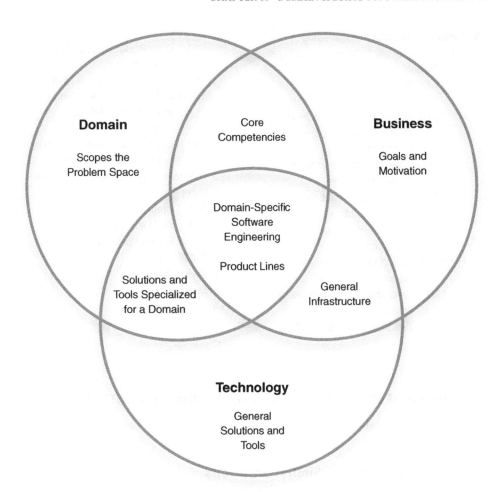

Figure 15-2.
Domain-specific software engineering requires organizations and engineers to leverage different aspects of three inter-related areas: domain, business, and technology.

15.1 DOMAIN-SPECIFIC SOFTWARE ENGINEERING IN A NUTSHELL

Before we go on to the specifics of DSSAs and product lines, let us provide a brief context for them.

15.1.1 Similar Problems, Similar Solutions

For the purpose of illustrating our discussion, we show a highly simplified view of traditional software development in Figure 15-3: A team of software engineers is typically given a description of a problem that they are to solve. That description may be detailed or may be cursory; it may be written down precisely or stated verbally (and ambiguously) by a human customer or prospective user; the description may be relatively complete or it may emerge incrementally during the development process. In any case, the principal task of the software engineers is to find a way of taking the problem description, which exists in the *problem space*, and mapping it to a software system, which exists in the *solution space*. Doing so in general is difficult because the two spaces usually are characterized by different concepts, with different terminologies and different properties. Doing so is also difficult because, in general, there are often many possibilities for addressing a given software requirement, ranging from the programming language in which the requirement will be implemented, to the code-level constructs used to realize the requirement, to the hardware platform on which it will execute, to the different ways of modularizing the system (including choosing not to modularize it at all), and so on. This is, in part, why historically it has been such a challenge for developers to ensure desired properties in software systems: too many choices without a clear indication of which choice works best, and why.

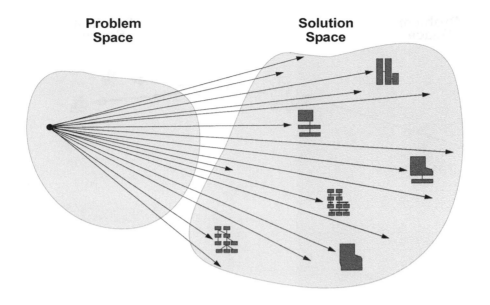

Figure 15-3.
A deliberately simplified view of traditional software development: Any given software development problem can be solved in a large number of different ways.

Software architecture-based development addresses this problem in part by elevating the discourse to a higher plane with fewer choices: What are the principal components needed for the given system? What are their interactions? What are their compositions into system configurations that effectively solve the problem at hand? Figure 15-4 depicts this approach to system development. Again, the picture is deliberately oversimplified to illustrate the point: A problem will often have a more constrained number of software

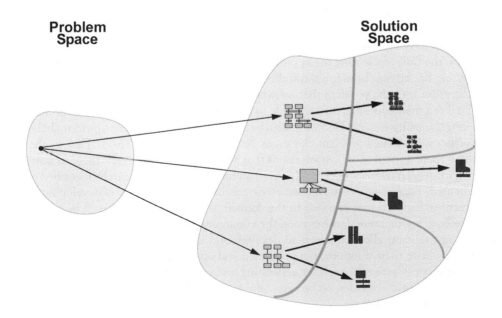

Figure 15-4.
A deliberately simplified view of architecture-based software development: Any given software development problem can be solved by a finite number of software architectures.

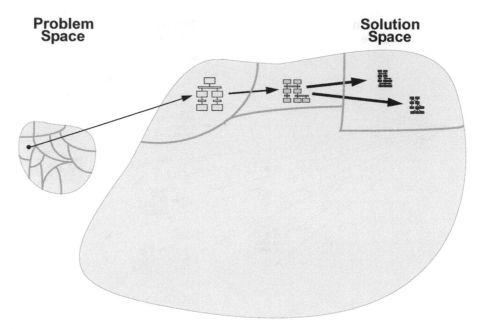

Figure 15-5. *A deliberately simplified view of DSSE: Some software development problems belong to specific classes of problems for which known (partial) architectural and implementation solutions exist. Those partial architectures are then tailored to the specific problem at hand and implemented using well-understood techniques.*

architectural solutions that are known to be effective for solving it. In turn, each of those architectures will have a comparatively smaller number of possible implementations (for reasons that have already been discussed in the preceding chapters).

Still, the task of selecting the appropriate software architecture and implementing it is anything but trivial. In many ways, this problem only interposes one additional level of indirection into the problem that software engineers faced in the past. This is where DSSE takes a markedly different approach, as depicted in Figure 15-5: Instead of primarily attacking the solution space, DSSE is guided by the observation that certain *problems* belong to specific, well-defined problem classes, or *domains* (recall Figure 15-1). That is, these problems share a number of characteristics that allow engineers to attack them in similar ways. Within each domain, effective (partial) architectural solutions can be identified and documented. These solutions are known as *reference architectures*. Instead of developing new architectures for each new problem in the domain, solutions can be derived by tailoring the reference architecture. Furthermore, the commonalities across the different problems in the same domain allow engineers to develop solid intuitions about a system before it is built, evaluate their solutions in a principled and often rigorous manner, and leverage a large number of powerful tools for generating and evaluating system implementations. All of the resulting activities, techniques, and tools are aided by their relatively narrow, well-defined focus and scope.

15.1.2 Viewing DSSE Through the Prism of Domain, Business, and Technology

As argued in the chapter's introduction and depicted in Figure 15-2, three principal concerns of DSSE are domain, business, and technology (Medvidović, Dashofy, and Taylor 2007). The prominence of each of the three concerns, and their exact mix, will differ across organizations and projects. Those differences have clear implications on the organizations and projects concerned, as well as on the stakeholders, the processes, and ultimately the products. We discuss each area in the diagram from Figure 15-2 in more detail below.

Domain: The domain, independent of business and technology concerns, establishes a problem space. It has defined characteristics, a vocabulary, a motivation (why this domain exists), and so on. This area will be further expanded below.

Business: Business, independent of any domain or technology concerns, is largely concerned with human goals: improving people's quality of life through the creation of new products, attaining money, power, notoriety, and so on. These goals motivate people to solve problems. Note that this is not meant to imply that domain-specific software must be sold or otherwise developed for the purpose of attaining monetary profits. However, the goal of using DSSE is to optimize certain aspects of software engineering: reducing cost or time to develop, improving the quality of products in the market (even open-source products), and so on.

Technology: Technology, independent of a domain or business goals, comprises tools, applications, reusable components, infrastructure, and methods that can be applied generally. In this sense, technology could be characterized as "solutions without problems."

Domain + Business: When business goals are applied to a particular domain, expertise and core competencies emerge. Business organizations specialize their skills to optimize them for particular domains: building televisions or airplanes, for example.

Business + Technology: Regardless of the domain(s) in which it operates, a business organization will acquire and develop technologies that are relevant to its overall goals but that can be applied to many domains. For example, any software development organization undoubtedly will have an infrastructure containing compilers, operating systems, networks, office applications, and so on that does not apply specifically to any domain.

Domain + Technology: This intersection contains tools, methods, and even architectures that are specifically applicable to a particular domain, but are independent of any particular business goal. For example, a programming language and compiler that are specifically developed for building aircraft software would fall into this category.

Domain + Business + Technology: This is the core of domain-specific software engineering: business goals motivating the identification and creation of a solution in the problem space of a domain, facilitated by the use of technology.

We have outlined the various concepts and interactions that comprise domain-specific software engineering. Now, we will examine how software architecture can be leveraged and specialized for application in the context of DSSE. We will study two key architecturally relevant areas of DSSE: domain-specific software architectures and product lines.

15.2 DOMAIN-SPECIFIC SOFTWARE ARCHITECTURE

A domain-specific software architecture (Tracz 1995; Coglianese, Smith, and Tracz 1992; Tracz 1994; Tracz, Coglianese, and Young 1993) comprises a codified body of knowledge about software development in a specific application domain. Barbara Hayes-Roth (Hayes-Roth et al. 1995) provides a useful operational definition of a domain-specific software architecture:

> *Definition.* A domain-specific software architecture (DSSA) comprises:
> - A reference architecture, which describes a general computational framework for a significant domain of applications.
> - A component library, which contains reusable chunks of domain expertise.
> - An application configuration method for selecting and configuring components within the architecture to meet particular application requirements.

Figure 15-6 provides an generalized overview of a DSSA-centric software development process. In addition to the usual *application engineering* activities in which developers engage, DSSAs involve a number of *domain engineering* activities. These activities result in models of the application domain's relevant entities, their characteristics, and their relationships; definitions of the key terminology; canonical requirements; design- and implementation-level solutions that are reusable across systems in the domain; and tool support specialized to aid development within the domain.

This body of assets does not come for free. Instead, it is built over time, as engineers amass experience (both good and bad) of building individual systems within a domain and try to generalize that experience for use in future systems. In the remainder of this section we will discuss the characteristics of application domains and domain models, the requirements that remain stable and those that change within a domain, and the corresponding solution strategies. We will illustrate the discussion with an example DSSA derived from the different Lunar Lander architectures discussed in the preceding chapters.

15.2.1 Domain Knowledge

As we have discussed, one of the main concerns of domain-specific software engineering is the problem domain itself. In order to exploit the properties of the domain, its key characteristics must be captured in a domain model. Simply put, a *domain model* (Batory, McAllester et al. 1995) is a representation of what happens in an application domain. This includes the *functions* being performed, the *objects* (also referred to as *entities*) performing the functions and those on which the functions are performed, and the *data* and *information* flowing among the entities and/or functions. In the parlance of the preceding section, a domain model deals with the problem space. Therefore, the above terms are used in their ordinary sense (for example, function as an operation performed on or by an entity "living" in the domain), rather than in the sense that software engineers typically assign to them (for example, function as a method that returns a value in a C++ program).

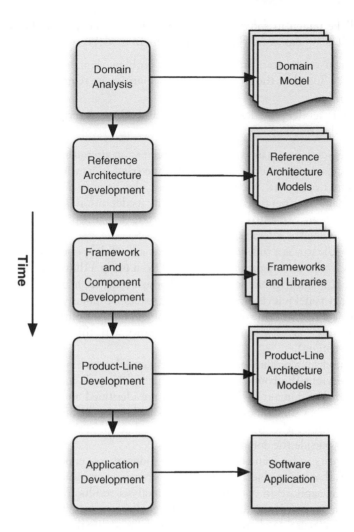

Figure 15-6.
*Overview of the
DSSA process
and managed
artifacts.*

If we take avionics as an example domain, the functions of interest would be aircraft takeoff, landing, taxiing, flying, pitch, roll, yaw, fueling, refueling (possibly in-flight), maintenance, and so on. Data and information flowing among these functions would be various pilot commands, instrument signals, warnings, status check messages, fuel consumption rates, data collected for the black boxes, and so on. The entities in the domain would include the flight instruments, the aircraft's rudder and wing flaps, the fuel tanks, the fuel transferred into the tanks during fueling and from the tanks to the engine during flight, the hydraulic fluids used to control the aircraft, and so on. It is this type of terminology, entities, their relationships, and operations on them that go into constructing a domain model.

Note that nothing in the above (very brief and informal) domain description belies the fact that a significant portion of a given avionics system's functions, data, and entities eventually will be reified in software. Remember, the domain model characterizes the problem space. The fundamental objective of a domain model is two-fold:

1. A domain model standardizes the given problem domain's *terminology* and its *semantics*. Together, the terminology and semantics are referred to as the domain's *ontology*.

2. A domain model provides the basis for standardized descriptions of problems to be solved in the domain.

For example, *yaw* is a term used in avionics to refer to an aircraft's rotation about an axis that is perpendicular to the aircraft's horizontal plane (that is, its wings) and goes through the aircraft's center of gravity. We would, of course, also have to define what a center of gravity is, and then any other terms needed to clarify its definition, and so on, until all the terms related to yaw are explained using the appropriate domain-specific terminology. Yaw is produced by moving the aircraft's rudder.

Note that while yaw is a widely known term because of the popularity and ubiquity of flight in today's world, nothing really prevents us from using a different term to describe this same concept in another problem domain. For example, we might call the analogous movement of a flat-panel television screen *left-right rotation*. Similarly, we can use this same term to describe a different concept in another problem domain (although in this case we would risk confusing matters given the broad familiarity with this particular term and its above-defined meaning).

A domain model is a product of context analysis and domain analysis. *Context analysis* is the activity whereby the boundaries of a domain are defined, and the relationships of the entities inside the domain to those outside it are identified and captured. This is an important activity that sometimes remains overlooked, since DSSE focuses primarily on things *within* a domain, rather than the bounds of the domain or the relationship between things inside and outside the domain.

Domain analysis can be defined as the activity of identifying, capturing, and organizing the *domain assets*, that is, the objects, operations, and data recurring across a class of similar systems within an application domain. Domain analysis results in a description of the domain assets using a standardized vocabulary. Its goal is to set the foundation of making the assets usable and reusable when solving new problems within the domain. For example, yaw is a usable asset if it is described in a manner that allows an avionics (software) engineer to find it easily and understand its meaning unambiguously whenever needed. Yaw is *reusable* if it describes an operation of all, or at least most, aircraft within the domain (for example, large passenger airplanes). Note that this level of reuse, while clearly important to multiple projects conducted by an engineering organization, including its software engineering divisions, has little if anything to do with code.

A domain model will usually comprise several pieces of information that together present a useful picture of the domain assets and their interrelationships. These models can be grouped into four categories:

- Domain dictionary
- Information model
- Feature model
- Operational model

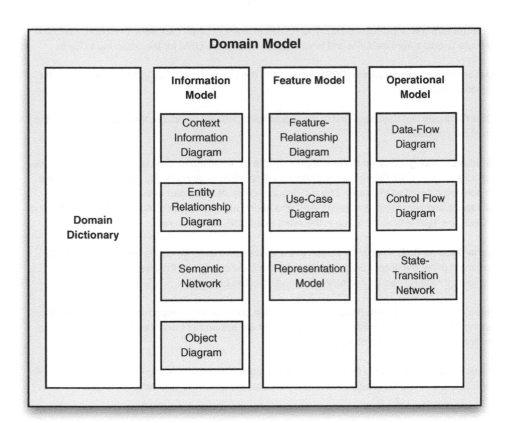

Figure 15-7.
*Elements of a
domain model.*

The different models and a broad cross-section of their associated diagram types are shown in Figure 15-7. We now discuss each of them in more detail.

Domain Dictionary

A domain dictionary represents the identification and definitions of terms used in the domain model. These terms may be widely used and understood outside the domain, in which case the goal of including them in the domain dictionary may be to define them carefully and avoid any inconsistencies and ambiguities in their usage. On the other hand, the terms may be specialized, or even invented for the sole purpose of fostering human stakeholders' communication and understanding within the domain. The domain dictionary should be updated over time with new terminology and with new or clearer understandings of existing concepts. A domain dictionary also becomes an indispensable tool for training new engineers working within the application domain. Figure 15-8 shows a partial domain dictionary from a hypothetical Lunar Lander DSSA.

Information Model

An information model is actually a collection of multiple models that may be used in different organizations and different DSSAs. The information model is a result of context analysis and information analysis. Context analysis results in defining the boundaries of

Figure 15-8.
*Partial domain
dictionary for a
Lunar Lander
DSSA.*

Command/Service Module (CSM): The section of the spacecraft that orbits the moon; the Lunar Module undocks from the CSM and lands, redocking with the CSM for the return trip to Earth.

Descent Propulsion System (DPS): A system of the Lunar Module that includes fuel tanks and descent engine.

DSKY: Display and Keyboard Unit of the spacecraft's onboard computer; the user interface of the onboard computer.

Guidance, Navigation and Control System (GN&C): A system on the Lunar Module responsible for collecting and calculating data (including position, altitude, and velocity) to aid navigation and to achieve a specified trajectory. The two onboard computers are part of this system: Primary Guidance and Navigation System (PGNS) and Abort Guidance Section (AGS). Independent of the PGNS, the AGS acts as a backup in the event that PGNS malfunctions.

Lunar Module (LM): This is the portion of the spacecraft that lands on the moon. It consists of two main parts: the Ascent Stage (which holds the crew cabin) and the Descent Stage, which contains thrusters used for controlling the landing of the LM.

Reaction Control System (RCS): A system on the Lunar Module responsible for the stabilization during lunar surface ascent/descent and control of the spacecraft's orientation (attitude) and motion (translation) during maneuvers.

Vertical Velocity (see also One-Dimensional Motion): For a free-falling object with no air resistance, ignoring the rotation of the lunar surface, the altitude is calculated as follows:

$$y = \tfrac{1}{2} * a * t^2 + v_i * t + y_i$$

where:

   y = altitude
   a = constant acceleration due to gravity on a lunar body
   (see **Acceleration** for sample values)
   t = time in seconds
   v_i = initial velocity
   y_i = initial altitude

When thrust is applied, the following equation is used:

$$y = \tfrac{1}{2} * (a_{burner} - a_{gravity}) * t^2 + v_i * t + y_i$$

where:

   y = altitude
   a_{burner} = constant acceleration upward due to thrust
   $a_{gravity}$ = constant acceleration due to gravity on a lunar body
   (see **Acceleration** for sample values)
   t = time in seconds
   v_i = initial velocity
   y_i = initial altitude

the domain and preserves information that may be otherwise implicit and scattered across many different systems and their artifacts. Information analysis then takes the result of context analysis (that is, the contours of the domain) and represents the intradomain knowledge explicitly in terms of domain entities and their relationships.

The information model ensures that the DSSA employs appropriate data abstractions and decompositions. Different elements of the information model are used by at least three types of stakeholders.

1. Requirements engineers use the information model as an aid in precisely specifying the reference requirements, that is, the requirements common across the applications in the DSSA (see the "Canonical Requirements" section below for a detailed discussion of reference requirements). They also use the information model to relate appropriately the application-specific requirements to the reference requirements.

2. Software architects use the information model to identify and appropriately relate the modules in the software system in the manner that reflects the characteristics of the domain, the interfaces exported by those modules, the data exchanged among them, and the mechanisms by which and constraints under which data is exchanged. This activity results in a reference architecture (see the "Canonical Solutions" section below for a detailed discussion of reference architectures). Software architects also use this information to relate application-specific architectures and designs to the reference architecture.

3. Software system maintainers use the information model to understand the manner in which any given application in the DSSA addresses problems. This enables them to relate properly the system maintenance and evolution requirements to the reference requirements and application-specific requirements, and to relate their proposed realization in the system to the reference architecture and application-specific architecture.

An information model usually consists of one or more of the below types of diagrams.

Context Information Diagram. This diagram captures the high-level data flow between the major entities in the system, their relationship to the entities outside the system (as well as outside the domain), as well as any data that is assumed to come from external sources. For example, in the Lunar Lander DSSA, the information exchanged among the spacecraft's sensors, actuators, and computers is part of the context information diagram. At the same time, the topology of the moon's (or planet's) surface on which the spacecraft is landing is considered to be outside the domain. An example context information diagram from the Lunar Lander DSSA is shown in Figure 15-9.

Entity/Relationship (ER) Diagram. This diagram captures aggregation ("a-part-of") and generalization ("is-a") relationships among the entities within the domain. For example, in the Lunar Lander DSSA, fuel level is "a-part-of" the spacecraft entity, while a given thruster "is-a" Lunar Lander actuator. An example ER diagram from the Lunar Lander DSSA is shown in Figure 15-10.

Object Diagram. This diagram identifies the objects in the application domain rather than in the software. In other words, the object diagram describes entities in the problem space;

Figure 15-9.
*Example context
information
diagram from the
Lunar Lander
DSSA.*

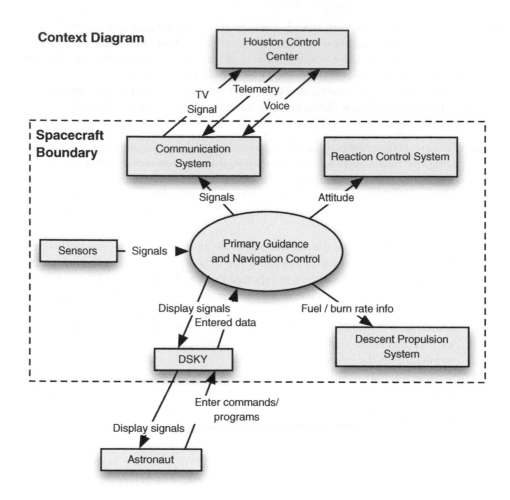

the solution-space components used to realize the problem-space entities will be captured
in the reference architecture, discussed below. The object diagram captures the attributes
and properties of each object, as well as their interdependencies and interactions with
other objects in the domain. An example object diagram from the Lunar Lander DSSA is
shown in Figure 15-11.

Feature Model

The feature model is, in fact, a collection of several models. A feature model results from
feature analysis. The goal of feature analysis is to capture and organize a customer's or end-
user's understandings and expectations of the overall (shared) capabilities of applications in
a given domain. The feature model is considered to be the chief means of communication
between the customers and the developers of new applications. The feature model explicitly
delineates the commonalities and differences among systems in the domain. Examples
of features include function descriptions, descriptions of the mission and usage patterns,
performance requirements, accuracy, time synchronization, and so on (Kang et al. 1990).

ER Diagram

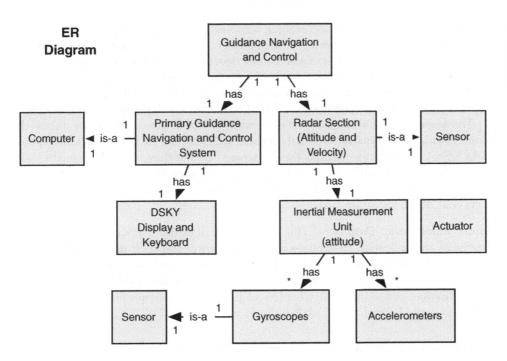

Figure 15-10.
Example ER diagram from the Lunar Lander DSSA.

Such features are meaningful to the users and can assist the engineers in the derivation of DSSA that will provide the desired capabilities.

Features may be defined as mandatory, optional, or variant. Mandatory features are expected to recur across all systems in the domain. In the case of the Lunar Lander system, *Compute Altitude* is a mandatory feature: Any implementation of the Lunar Lander must be able to continuously compute the spacecraft's altitude. Optional features are those that are identified as useful for a subset of the systems within the given DSSA. For example,

Object Diagram

Object	Attributes	Operations
Landing Radar	Attitude Velocity	Sense Altitude Sense Velocity
Descent Engine	Throttle Level Nozzle Direction	Set Throttle Level Change Nozzle Direction (Gimbal) Turn On / Off
Thrust Engines	Firing Mode Attitude Translation	Set Pulse or Continuous Change Altitude Change Translation

Figure 15-11.
Example object diagram from the Lunar Lander DSSA.

Get Burn Rate is an optional feature: Some versions of the Lunar Lander are able to ask the system user for the preferred fuel consumption rate. Finally, variant features exist in most (or all) systems within a DSSA, but differ depending on the values of one or more parameters. For example, *Compute Velocity* is a variant feature within the Lunar Lander DSSA, whose exact realization may depend upon the size and mass of the spacecraft as well as the size, mass, and atmosphere of the celestial body onto which the spacecraft is landing.

The feature model also encompasses several types of diagrams, which are discussed below. As with the information model, the architects developing the feature model for a particular DSSA would decide which of these diagrams best suit their needs. They might also choose other types of similar diagrams. For example, Software Engineering Institute's Feature Oriented Domain Analysis (FODA) approach advocates the use of semantic networks (Kang et al. 1990) in feature modeling.

Feature Relationship Diagram. [1] This diagram describes the overall mission or usage patterns of an application. It captures the major features and their decomposition into subfeatures. This model can also include any quality requirements associated with individual features such as dependability, security, performance, accuracy, real-time requirements, synchronization, and so on (recall Chapters 12 and 13). An example feature relationship diagram from the Lunar Lander DSSA is shown in Figure 15-12.

Figure 15-12.
Example feature relationship diagram from the Lunar Lander DSSA.

Feature Relationship Diagram—Landing Phase

Mandatory: The Lunar Lander must continually read altitude from the Landing Radar and relay that data to Houston with less than 500 msec of latency. Astronauts must be able to control the descent of the Lunar Lander using manual control on the descent engine. The descent engine must respond to control commands in 250msec, with or without a functioning DSKY…

Optional/Variant: Lunar Lander provides the option to land automatically or allow the crew to manually steer the spacecraft.

Quality Requirements:

Real-time requirements: The thrusters and the descent engine must be able to respond to commands from the computer system in real-time.

Fault tolerance: Lunar Lander must be able to continue in its flight path even when the main computer system (Primary Navigation Guidance & Control) goes down. Lunar Lander must be able to maintain system altitude even when one of the thrusters and propellant supplies goes down in the Reaction Control System.

Lunar Lander's computer system must function properly after a restart (restart protection).

---

[1] The feature model is sometimes also referred to as "context model," and the feature relationship diagram as "context diagram." We deliberately refrain from using "context" in this setting to avoid confusing matters with the context diagram in the information model.

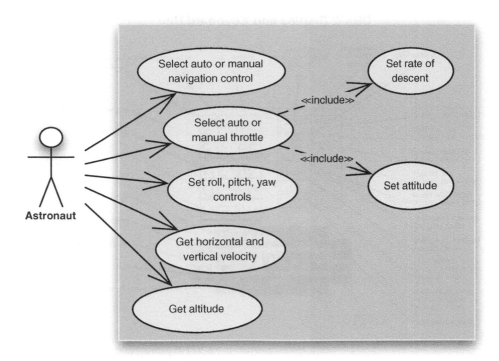

Figure 15-13.
*Example use-case
diagram from the
Lunar Lander
DSSA.*

Use-Case Diagram. This diagram captures the usage scenarios in the system. Use cases have become prevalent with the introduction of the Unified Modeling Language (see Chapters 6 and 16). Use-case diagrams are elicited from domain experts, system customers, and system users, and encompass the manner in which a feature is expected to be used, as well as control- and data-flow among multiple features. An example use-case diagram from the Lunar Lander DSSA is shown in Figure 15-13.

Representation Model. This diagram describes how information is made available to a human user. In other words, the representation model details what the appropriate user interfaces are for the systems within the DSSA. This model also captures the information produced for another application: What kinds of input and output capabilities are available, and what is the expected, common format for the exchanged information? An example partial representation model from the Lunar Lander DSSA is shown in Figure 15-14.

Operational Model

The operational model is the foundation upon which the software designer begins the process of understanding (1) how to provide the features for a particular system in a domain, and (2) how to make use of the entities identified in the resulting domain model. The operational model identifies the key operations (that is, functions) that occur within a domain, the data exchanged among those operations, as well as the commonly occurring sequences of those operations. In other words, the operational model represents *how* applications within a domain work.

Figure 15-14.
*Example
representation
model from the
Lunar Lander
DSSA. Original
DSKY diagram
from Apollo
Operations
Handbook,
Lunar Module
LM5 and
Subsequent,
Volume 1:
Subsystems Data
(LMA790-3-
LM5).*

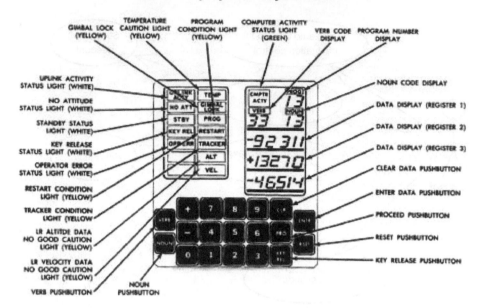

DSKY: Display and Keyboard Unit

Three 5-digit registers
  (General Purpose)
Three 2-digit registers
  (Indicate landing phase)
19 Keys
Warning Lights

Issue commands via VERB (action) and NOUN (object)
- E.g.: VERB 6 NOUN 20
- VERB 6: Display in Decimal
- NOUN 20: Angles
70 pre-defined PROGRAMS
- E.g., PROGRAM for each descent phase:
- P63 (Braking)
- P64 (Approach)
- P65 (Landing)

The operational model is a result of operational analysis, which identifies the commonalities as well as differences in control-flow and data-flow among the entities in a domain. The domain-wide entities identified in the information and feature models, discussed above, form the basis for the operational model: The information model captures the data exchanged by the operations, while the feature model captures the operations themselves. The control- and data-flow of each individual application within the DSSA can be derived from the operational model.

Three representative types of diagrams used within the operational model are discussed below.

Data-Flow Diagram. This diagram focuses explicitly on the data exchanged within the system, with no notion of control. An example data-flow diagram from the Lunar Lander DSSA is shown in Figure 15-15.

Data-flow Diagram

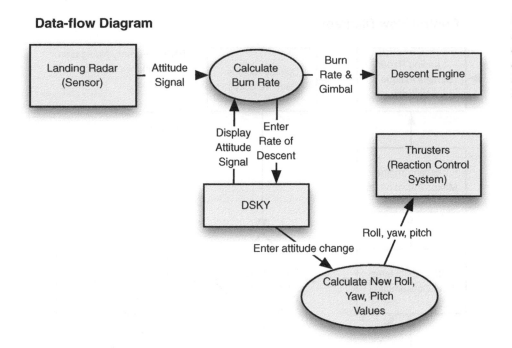

Figure 15-15.
*Example
data-flow
diagram from the
Lunar Lander
DSSA.*

Control-Flow Diagrams. This diagram focuses on the exchange of control within the system, without regard for data. An example control-flow diagram from the Lunar Lander DSSA is shown in Figure 15-16.

State-Transition Diagram. This diagram models and relates the different states that the entities in the domain will enter, events that will result in transitions between states, as well as actions that may result from those events. An example state-transition diagram from the Lunar Lander DSSA is shown in Figure 15-17.

15.2.2 Canonical Requirements

A critical element of a DSSA is the canonical or *reference* requirements. These are requirements that apply across the entire domain captured by a DSSA. Such reference requirements will be incomplete because they must be general enough to capture the variations that occur across individual systems and because individual systems also will introduce their own requirements. However, reference requirements directly facilitate the mapping of the requirements for each system within a given domain to the canonical domain-specific solution (discussed in the next section).

Similar to the requirements for any software system, the starting point for reference requirements is the customer's statement of needs. In a DSSA, this statement is general enough to apply to any system in the domain. A DSSA is an exercise in generalization from specific experience, so the statement may emerge over time from similar statements that were specific to individual systems constructed previously within the domain. The

Figure 15-16.
*Example
control-flow
diagram from the
Lunar Lander
DSSA.*

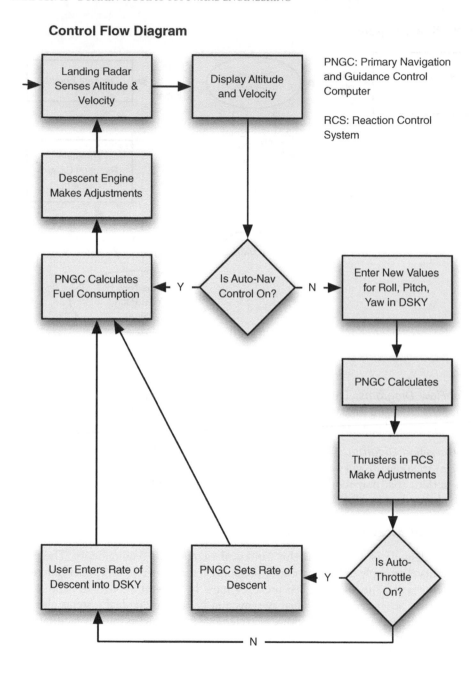

Control Flow Diagram

PNGC: Primary Navigation and Guidance Control Computer

RCS: Reaction Control System

customer needs statement identifies the functional requirements for the DSSA at a high level of abstraction. It is usually informal, ambiguous, and incomplete. It is a starting point for deriving (reference) requirements, but it is not the same as reference requirements. As an example, Figure 15-18 shows a partial customer needs statement for the Lunar Lander DSSA.

State Transition Diagram

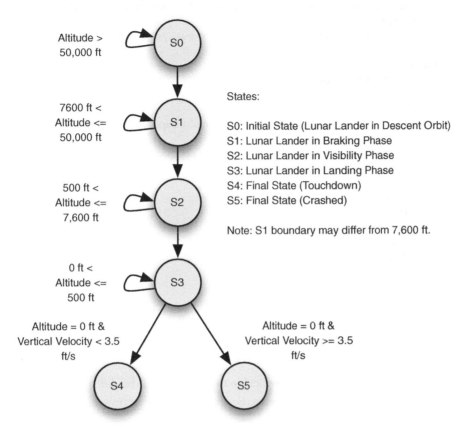

Figure 15-17.
*Example
state-transition
diagram from the
Lunar Lander
DSSA.*

States:

S0: Initial State (Lunar Lander in Descent Orbit)
S1: Lunar Lander in Braking Phase
S2: Lunar Lander in Visibility Phase
S3: Lunar Lander in Landing Phase
S4: Final State (Touchdown)
S5: Final State (Crashed)

Note: S1 boundary may differ from 7,600 ft.

Reference requirements are then derived from the customer needs statement as well as the requirements of the individual legacy systems within the domain. The reference requirements contain the defining characteristics of the problem space. These are the *functional requirements*. Reference requirements also contain limiting characteristics (that is, constraints) in the solution space. These are the *non-functional requirements* (such as security, performance, reliability), *design requirements* (such as architectural style, user

A family of related systems is needed that
1. *Supports the Lunar Lander video game for different platforms (e.g., PC, Mac, Pocket PC, cell phone, etc.).*
2. *Supports different user interfaces, from simple textual to a sophisticated 3-D GUI.*
3. *Runs on a single machine or is decentralized across a network.*
4. *Works in a single-user or multi-user competition mode, and supports different variations (e.g., only landing from a given height, first entering orbit and then landing, landing on different types of terrain, landing on different types of celestial bodies, etc.).*

Figure 15-18.
*Example
customer needs
statement from
the Lunar Lander
DSSA.*

Figure 15-19.
*Example
reference
requirements
from the Lunar
Lander DSSA.*

Mandatory
- Must display the current status of the Lunar Lander (horizontal and vertical velocities, altitude, remaining fuel)
- Must indicate points earned by player based on quality of landing

Optional
- May display time elapsed

Variant
- May have different levels of difficulty based on pilot experience (novice, expert, etc.)
- May have different types of input depending on whether:
    Auto Navigation is enabled
    Auto Throttle is enabled
- May have to land on different celestial bodies:
    Moon
    Mars
    Jupiter's moons
    Asteroid

interface style), and *implementation requirements* (such as hardware platform, programming language).

Similar to the feature model discussed above, reference requirements must distinguish among three types of requirements:

1. *Mandatory requirements* are applicable to all systems in the domain.
2. *Optional requirements* are known to be applicable to a certain set of systems within the domain.
3. *Variable requirements* are application-specific, and may be unknown at the time the DSSA, and more specifically reference requirements, are formulated.

In general, each requirement—whether functional, non-functional, design, or implementation—can be of any one of the three types (mandatory, optional, or variable). We provide examples of mandatory, optional, and variable requirements for the Lunar Lander in Figure 15-19.

15.2.3   Canonical Solution Strategies—Reference Architectures

When business goals and technology are applied to a problem within a domain, solutions emerge. A single product architecture represents a single solution. However, as we have covered extensively, when attacking problems in the same domain with similar business goals in mind and leveraging similar technology, similarities will emerge in solution architectures. These similarities can be captured in a *reference architecture*. Here, we repeat the definition found in Chapter 3.

> **Definition. Reference architecture** is the set of principal design decisions that are simultaneously applicable to multiple related systems, typically within an application domain, with explicitly defined points of variation.

As sets of principal design decisions, reference architectures are themselves architectures. However, they are generic or variegated such that they are applicable to multiple systems simultaneously—in the context of the terms we have used in this chapter, to a population or a product line of systems. Points where the architecture can vary from family member to family member are explicitly defined as part of the reference architecture.

There are many different kinds of reference architectures; this definition is intentionally broad. They differ in how they express the commonalities and the points of variation in a population or product line. Three classes of reference architectures are:

Complete single-product architecture: An ordinary product architecture of a simple toy example or a complete system for a particular domain can be considered a reference architecture, since it might serve as an exemplar for future products in the same domain. Such reference architectures are relatively weak because they do not provide much engineering guidance as to how to use the reference architecture to create new systems, and they do not explicitly call out variation points.

Incomplete invariant architecture: A partial architecture can be specified that is constant and unchanging among all products. Parts of the architecture that vary from product to product are left unspecified, although some design guidance might be provided as to how to "fill in the blanks" in the architecture.

Invariant architecture with explicit variation: This kind of reference architecture can be used to simultaneously capture both the invariants *and* the variants in products in a domain. For each variation point, permitted alternatives are specified in detail.

Developing a Reference Architecture

Developing a reference architecture is a serious decision because it will be the guiding foundation for a number of future products. Determining when, how, and why to develop a reference architecture is critical to success.

When to Develop a Reference Architecture. An obvious question that arises in DSSE is, "When is the right time to develop a reference architecture?" Choosing an appropriate time is critical because a reference architecture will constrain and bind all solutions in the domain. Premature development of a reference architecture can be disastrous if the architecture is not validated or the stakeholders' understanding of the domain is too incomplete: Instead of affecting just one product, a mistake made in a too-early reference architecture will propagate to many products and vastly increase the costs of that mistake. On the other hand, developing a reference architecture too late can be equally costly: If many diverse solution architectures have already been developed in a domain, then there will be little opportunity to adapt these existing architectures to fit the reference architecture (they will become "legacy systems"), and therefore substantially limit reuse benefits.

A good tactic that mitigates some risk is to adopt an incremental approach with respect to reference architecture. The reference architecture should still be developed with the entire family of products in mind—if this is not done, it may take on the characteristics of a single product and later have to be significantly adapted to incorporate the full family. If, as is often the case, a number of products have already been developed and they are being adapted to use a reference architecture, it is usually easier to adapt one or two products at a time to use the reference architecture rather than try to unify the family all at once. Starting with the products whose existing architecture is closest to the target reference architecture is generally a good idea. This allows the reference architecture to be evaluated and refined without affecting too many products simultaneously.

Choosing the Form of a Reference Architecture. Deciding how to capture a reference architecture depends on the domain, the stakeholders, and the underlying business needs of the organization(s) involved. More precise modeling techniques (such as the use of explicit variation points) make it easier to detect and prevent phenomena such as architectural drift and erosion, but might also limit creative freedom and opportunities for innovation.

A complete single product architecture offers the least guidance to architects as to how to elaborate it into a family of products (unless the products in that family have architectures that are very close to the reference architecture). If this form is chosen for the reference architecture, explicit documentation of the underlying style and what is and is not allowed to change should be provided as well. It may also be useful to include several examples of complete product architectures in a family to illustrate this.

Incomplete invariant architectures have the advantage that they tell architects directly what must be present in a family member's architecture. However, they may lack details about how to actually complete the elaboration process. Again, important documentation about the style and how elaboration should proceed is important. Another (somewhat costlier) alternative is to combine this with complete product architectures: that is, as part of the reference architecture, provide both the incomplete invariant architecture *and* one or more elaborated product architectures (even if these are only samples or demonstration architectures) as these can serve as examples for future elaborations.

Invariant architectures with explicit variation points provide the most direction to architects; not only do they say exactly what must be present in every family member's architecture, but they also effectively define all the members of the family. A reference architecture in this form may have a large number of variation points, and the sum of all possible alternatives will far exceed the business needs of the developing organization. For example, imagine such a reference architecture that defines eight optional features that may be included or not included. This reference architecture defines a family of $2^8 = 256$ possible architectures. Not all of these architectures will be feasible (due, perhaps, to feature conflicts) or desirable to produce (due to market conditions). These reference architectures make it easy to select family members, but limit the scope of the products that can be in the family at all.

For a complex domain, a reference architecture will be extremely detailed, with multiple coordinated views, extensive documentation capturing the invariants and variation points, and guidance on how to refine the reference architecture into a concrete application. Rationale for the various decisions embodied in the architecture would also be included. A structural view such as the one shown in Figure 15-20 might be part of such a reference architecture. This depiction alone is not enough to interpret its intent; supporting documentation also is needed. For example, it may be that the components shown are intended to be the only components in the system, or implementers may be advised to add additional components as necessary. Certain points of variation are obvious: whether or not a relay satellite is used, the type of middleware, the implementation of the space link, the other sensors on the lander, and so on. The intended interpretation of all these

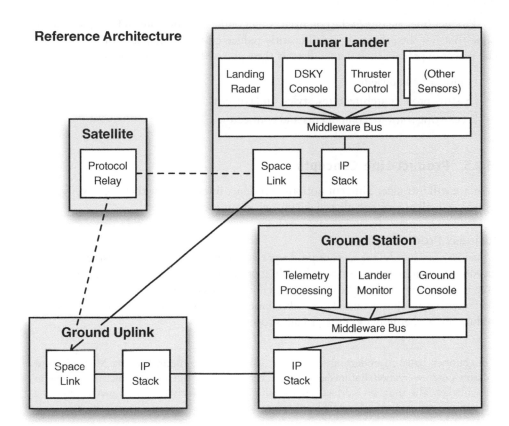

Figure 15-20.
*Example
reference
architecture
structural view
for a Lunar
Lander system.*

elements should be contained in ancillary documentation; this is typical of a reference architecture.

15.2.4 Product Lines and Architecture

There are many significant differences between designing a single-product architecture and a reference architecture; chief among them is that a reference architecture must serve as the basis for many different products simultaneously. This introduces a whole host of new issues: Not only must the architecture suffice for a single solution, but must be developed, visualized, and evaluated in terms of a large number of potential solutions (many of which may never be realized).

Here is where the technologies and techniques developed in the *product-line architecture* community are applicable. Product-line architectures give stakeholders tools with which to diversify an ordinary product architecture into an artifact suitable for describing many similar/related products: a *product line*. The techniques presented here allow stakeholders to develop multi-product architectures without losing the benefits that we have identified in the single-product case: explicit models, visualization, analyzability, and so on.

Product lines are one of the potential "silver bullets" of software architecture—a technique that has the potential to significantly reduce costs and increase software qualities. The power of product lines comes directly through *reuse*, specifically the reuse of:

- Engineering knowledge.
- Existing product architectures, styles, and patterns.
- Preexisting software components and connectors.

15.2.5 Product-Line Concepts

Here, we will introduce different notions of product lines and how they are developed and defined, as well as elements that make up a product line.

Business Product Lines

A business product line is a set of products tied together to achieve a business/monetary purpose, such as increasing sales by bundling products. These products do not necessarily have to have any similarity from an engineering perspective—it is not uncommon for a company that has just acquired new subsidiaries to put all the new products into a single product line to better market the products together.

Business Goes Where Money Flows

In a business based on product sales, there is a gap between expense and income. Money is spent during product creation, but income does not begin to arrive until the product is available in the market. This situation is depicted in the following graph, with the shaded area representing the initial outlay of capital required for product development.

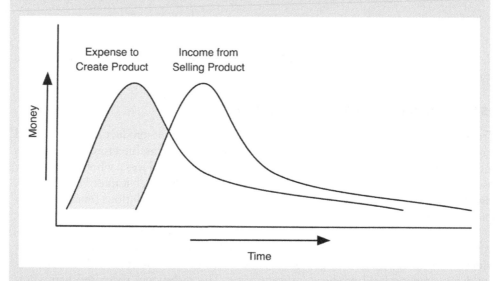

If traditional development practices are used, additional products will have similar expense/income curves, like so:

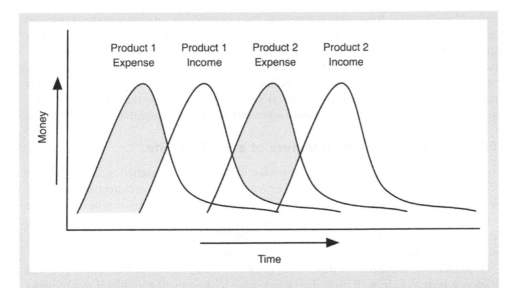

The use of product lines, however, lowers the development cost and time for making a new product in the product line. In doing so, additional revenue can come in earlier, reducing the effect of expenses that are incurred, like so:

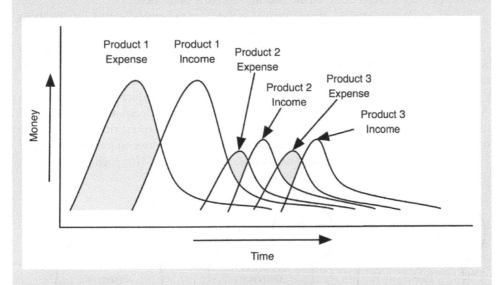

Note that the shaded areas (times when expenses exceed revenues) are much more limited when product lines are used.

Engineering Product Lines

Products in an engineering product line are tied together by similarities in how they are designed or constructed. Often, a product line will be both a business and engineering product line, but this is not always the case. For example, an auto manufacturer, such as Ford, will build a number of cars on the same engineering platform but market them under different brand names, such as Lincoln, Mercury, and Mazda. Engineering product lines often share significant portions of their architecture, and the products within them may all conform to a broader DSSA. The product lines discussed in the remainder of this chapter are engineering product lines; however, Section 15.2.10 discusses strategies for unifying disparate products (perhaps those in a business product line) into an engineering product line.

15.2.6   Specifying the Architecture of a Product Line

The architectures of product lines are somewhat different from reference architectures in a DSSA. In general, product-line architectures capture the complete architectures of multiple related products simultaneously. Conversely, reference architectures can be incomplete or partial. They may, for example, specify the architecture of a single product with loose guidance about how to adapt it to other contexts. They may also specify only invariant parts of an architecture and leave the rest up to solution developers.

Product-line architectures differ from reference architectures in two ways. The first difference is one of scope: Rather than attempting to describe the architectures of many (potentially diverse) solutions within a domain, product-line architectures focus on a specific, explicit set of related products, often developed by a single organization. The second difference is one of completeness: Product-line architectures generally capture multiple complete product architectures rather than leaving parts undefined.

Recall our characterization of architecture as the set of principal design decisions about a system. A product-line architecture can be similarly defined: A product line architecture captures simultaneously the principal design decisions of many related products. Some of these design decisions will be common among all the products, some will be common among a subset of the products, and some will be unique to individual products.

Figure 15-21 shows a product-line architecture with two products conceptualized as a Venn diagram. The large center circle represents the design decisions common to all products in the product line. The "A" shape represents the decisions that are unique to Product A. The "B" shape represents the decisions that are unique to product B. Figure 15-21(a) shows the three groups of design decisions. Figure 15-21(b) highlights Product

Figure 15-21.
A *product-line architecture conceptualized as a Venn diagram.*

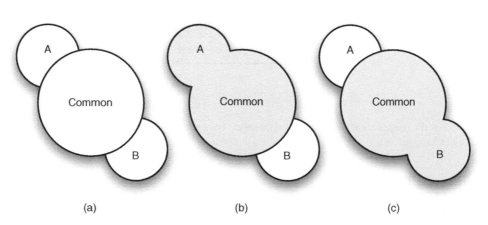

(a)   (b)   (c)

A: the union of the common design decisions and the "A" design decisions. Figure 15-21(c) shows Product B: the union of the common design decisions and the "B" design decisions.

To further discuss product-line architectures, we turn again to the Lunar Lander example. We have discussed different variants of the Lunar Lander game in earlier chapters, but each has been discussed in isolation. Product-line architectures give us the power to specify and discuss a family of Lunar Lander games in terms of explicit differences among the family members. The constructs that make this possible are *variants* and *versions*.

Variants

Extending an ordinary software architecture into a product line architecture can be accomplished through the addition of *variation points* to create *variant* architectures. Each variant architecture represents a different product—a member of the product line. A *variation point* is a set of design decisions that may or may not be included in the architecture of a given product. Variation points identify where the design decisions for a specific product architecture diverge from the design decisions for other products. Each variation point is accompanied by a condition that determines when the design decisions for that variation point are included in a product's architecture. In the above example, the inclusion of the "A" design decisions can be seen as a variation point. The condition for this variation point is simple: The decisions are only included if the product being built is Product A.

By isolating and codifying variation points, a large number of product architectures can be described compactly by exploiting the different combinations of variations. Consider a hypothetical product line of Lunar Lander games that consists of three slightly different Lunar Lander products: Lunar Lander Lite, Lunar Lander Demo, and Lunar Lander Pro.

Lunar Lander Lite is intended as a freely distributed Lunar Lander game with a text-based user interface. It resembles the Lunar Lander games discussed in earlier chapters, such as those implemented in Chapter 9. Lunar Lander Pro is intended as a commercially sold Lunar Lander game with a fancier graphical user interface. Internally, the data store and game logic are identical to Lunar Lander Lite's; the only difference is in the user interface component. Lunar Lander Demo is a freely distributed but time-limited version of Lunar Lander Pro. It has the same graphical user interface as Lunar Lander Pro, but it expires and is not playable thirty days after installation. Periodically, it reminds users that if they want to continue playing beyond the thirty-day limit, they are required to purchase or upgrade to Lunar Lander Pro.

The architectural structures of all three Lunar Lander products are shown in Figure 15-22.[2] Figure 15-22(a) shows Lunar Lander Lite, consisting of a data store and game logic component, along with a text-based UI. Figure 15-22(b) shows Lunar Lander Demo, with a graphical UI component in place of the text-based UI, and an additional demo reminder and system clock that plug into the user interface to remind the user to register. Figure 15-22(c) shows Lunar Lander Pro, identical to Lunar Lander Demo but missing the Demo Reminder and System Clock components.

Table 15-1 shows the elements—in this case components and connectors—included in each of the three product-line members. This kind of table is good for deciding whether

---

[2]The Lunar Lander example in this chapter will focus on structural design decisions; however, the techniques described apply, in general, to broader kinds of design decisions that go beyond just components and connectors.

Figure 15-22.
*Architectures of
Lunar Lander:
(a) Lite, (b)
Demo, and (c)
Pro.*

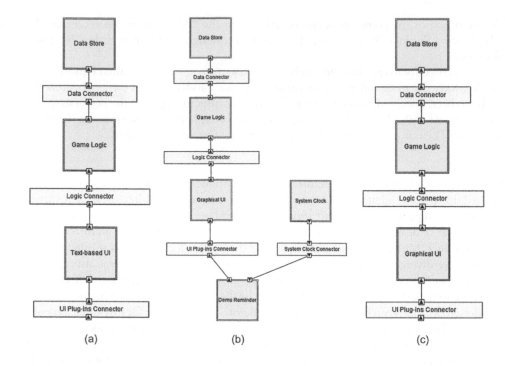

Figure 15-22. *Architectures of Lunar Lander: (a) Lite, (b) Demo, and (c) Pro.*

and how to create a product line. Here, it is obvious that there is significant commonality and overlap among the three products—good motivation for creating a product line.

Once the creation of a product line begins, it is a good idea to group low-level elements into variation points. Recall that each variation point represents a set of design decisions that may or may not be included in the architecture. This allows product-line architects to think about products in terms of features rather than low-level elements. For example, while it is conceivable to think of a product that contains a System Clock Connector but no System Clock, in practice this does not make much sense.

Table 15-1
*Elements present
in each Lunar
Lander
product-line
member.*

| | Product | | |
Components and Connectors	Lite	Demo	Pro
Data Store	X	X	X
Data Store Connector	X	X	X
Game Logic	X	X	X
Game Logic Connector	X	X	X
Text-Based UI	X	X	
UI Plug-Ins Connector	X	X	X
Graphical UI		X	X
System Clock		X	
System Clock Connector		X	
Demo Reminder		X	

Components and Connectors	Core Elements	Text UI	Graphical UI	Time Limited
Data Store	X			
Data Store Connector	X			
Game Logic	X			
Game Logic Connector	X			
Text-Based UI		X		
UI Plug-Ins Connector	X			
Graphical UI			X	
System Clock				X
System Clock Connector				X
Demo Reminder				X

Table 15-2
Grouping architectural elements into variation points.

A mapping of elements to variation points is shown in Table 15-2. Here, elements common to all products are grouped into Core Elements. Three other variation points are defined as well: the inclusion of a textual UI, a graphical UI, and whether or not the product is time-limited. The grouping of architectural elements or design decisions into features is often motivated by domain constraints, business goals, and the individual dependencies and exclusion relationships among the elements. Ultimately, these groupings must be chosen and defined by system architects—their creation is not an algorithmic process. Variation points will have dependencies and exclusion relationships as well: For example, all variation points depend on the inclusion of the Core Elements, and at least one of the two user interface variation points must be included in a product. These relationships and constraints must be carefully documented.

Once the variation points have been defined, individual products can be specified as combinations of the variation points. For business reasons, or reasons of variation point compatibility, not all combinations of variation points will be made into products.

Table 15-3 shows the creation of the three Lunar Lander products from the variation points defined in Table 15-2. Assuming that the core elements are always included, the three variation points altogether create 2^3 or eight potential products, of which three have been selected for construction. In addition to helping people understand the differences between the different product-line members, this kind of table is often useful in generating ideas for new products using the variation-point combinations *not* selected. For example, one could conceive of a Lunar Lander game that includes both a textual *and* a graphical user interface, perhaps giving the user multiple ways of interacting with the game and viewing its state. One could also imagine a time-limited version of the game with a textual UI, or a time-limited version with both user interfaces.

	Lunar Lander Lite	Lunar Lander Demo	Lunar Lander Pro
Core Elements	X	X	X
Text UI	X		
Graphical UI		X	X
Time Limited		X	

Table 15-3
Products as combinations of variation points.

By unifying common features and documenting these explicit variation points, we can combine these three individual architecture descriptions into a single product-line architecture. A few architecture description languages such as Koala (van Ommering et al. 2000) and xADL (Dashofy, van der Hoek, and Taylor 2005) allow you to do this directly.

The combined product line is shown in Figure 15-23, here in xADL's graphical visualization using xADL's product-line features (Dashofy and van der Hoek 2001) to express the points of variation. All elements from all products are shown together. Elements such as the *Data Store* and *Game Logic* components that are part of the core are represented normally. Elements that are included in one or more variation points are represented as

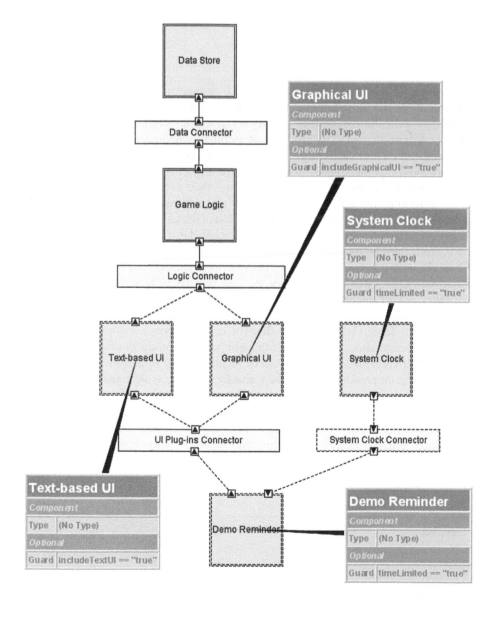

Figure 15-23.
Lunar Lander product line architecture.

optional. Each optional element is accompanied by a guard condition that indicates when it should be included in a product. In this product line, three variables—`includeTextUI`, `includeGraphicalUI`, and `timeLimited`—correspond to the variation points defined in Table 15-2. By setting the value of any of these variables to "true," the elements corresponding to that variation point will be included in the architecture.

xADL's use of a Boolean expression language to document these guard conditions gives it additional expressive power, including some ability to constrain relationships between features. For example, the *Text-based UI* and *Graphical UI* features could be made mutually exclusive by unifying the `includeTextUI` and `includeGraphicalUI` variables into a single variable, say '`uiType`,' whose value would be either "graphical" or "textual," but not both.

Selection

The process of reducing a product line into a smaller product line or a single product is known as *selection*. Selection involves evaluating the conditions associated with each variation point and either including or excluding the associated design decisions.

Consider the Lunar Lander product line. By fixing the `includeTextUI` variable to "false," we have selected only products that do not include a textual UI. This reduces the total number of potential products from 8 to 4. By also fixing "`includeGraphicalUI`" to "true," we can select only those products that include a graphical UI. Now, the total number of potential products is two. By fixing the final variable, `timeLimited`, to "true," we can reduce the product line to a single product—one without a textual UI, with a graphical UI, and that is time-limited. This product, incidentally, is the Lunar Lander Demo product—something easily seen by referring to Table 15-3.

Without tool support, product-line selection must be performed manually—either on the fly in the minds of the stakeholders interpreting architectural models or by creating and maintaining explicit models of each product in the product line. Using an approach that supports the explicit specification of variation points and product lines such as Koala or xADL can make the selection process substantially easier. Specifically, in these approaches product-line selection can be performed automatically through the use of tools. xADL's product-line selector tool allows users to bind values to guard variables, and then reduce a product-line architecture such as the one shown in Figure 15-23 into a single-product architecture such as the one shown in Figure 15-22 with a few clicks of the mouse.

15.2.7 Capturing Variations Over Time

The products in a product line are often alternatives to one another, intended for simultaneous development and release, as is the case with the Lunar Lander product line described above. However, product-line architectures also can be used to capture different versions of the same product over time. In general, different versions of the same product will have relatively similar architectures (unless something drastic such as a complete redesign or rewrite occurs). When this is the case, it is possible to enumerate the design decisions in both architectures and determine what changed from one version of a product to the next. These can be turned into variation points and encoded into a product line, where the different products are not alternatives, but rather the same product at different times.

Figure 15-24.
Two versions of a Lunar Lander game: (a) version 1, and (b) version 2.

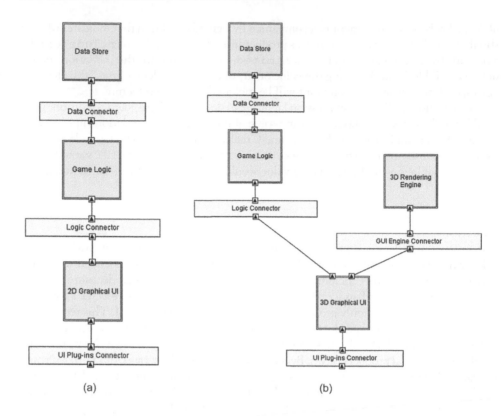

(a)   (b)

Consider an evolving Lunar Lander game. The first version of the game might include a graphical user interface with two-dimensional graphics. A second version of the same game might differ by including a graphical user interface with three-dimensional graphics, supported by an off-the-shelf three-dimensional rendering engine. These two product architectures are shown in Figure 15-24(a) and (b), respectively.

Clearly, this situation mirrors the situation seen earlier when the products were different games to be marketed, rather than versions of the same game. Using the same mechanisms described above, the two versions of the game might be encoded into a single product line, with each product representing one version of the game. This product line is shown in Figure 15-25. Here, the version is selected using a single variable, version, rather than by choosing a combination of variation points.

15.2.8   Using Product Lines as Tools for What-If Analysis

Product lines can be used to capture variations across related products and across different versions of the same product. Another application of product lines is to capture design alternatives. Design is often an exploratory process—it involves making decisions and trade-offs that will affect the properties and construction of the target products. Questions arise: Should we include this component or that component? Should this part of the application run on the client or on the server? Often, it will be unclear which path is best, so multiple alternatives are considered and pursued until more information becomes available.

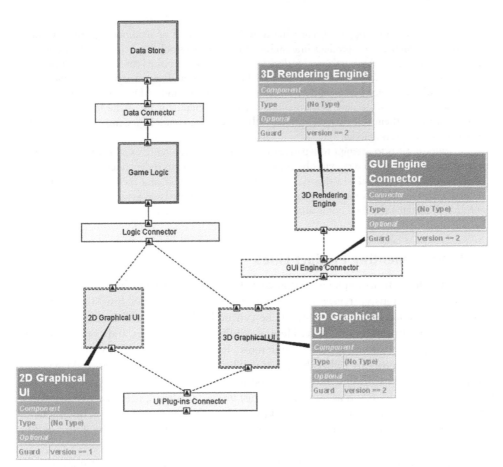

Figure 15-25.
*Product line of
Lunar Lander
games where each
product is a
version of Lunar
Lander.*

When this happens, product-line techniques can be used to simultaneously capture alternative architectures. Here, each product is not a system that is intended to be built, but one of many potential product designs. Points of variation in these product lines are decision points. The selection process can be used as a form of "what-if" analysis.

Software engineers have had to deal with variations, evolving artifacts, forking, branching, merging, and related concepts for years, particularly in the area of source code. In general, they are assisted in these regards by software configuration management systems. Configuration management systems can also be used to help address these concerns when dealing with artifacts such as architectural models, especially when the artifacts themselves offer no explicit support for these concepts.

One simple approach is simply to put architecture models into a version control system such as RCS (Tichy 1985), CVS (Fogel 1999), Subversion (Collins-Sussman, Fitzpatrick, and Pilato 2004), or ClearCase (Atria Software 1992). This is a viable option for versioning architectures as a whole, and it helps track the evolution of architectures over time. To some extent, alternatives can be created through branching revisions.

Configuration Manage-ment of Architec-tures

This approach does not work particularly well for creating or maintaining product-line architectures. Managing a product-line architecture means establishing a core set of design decisions and then combining those core decisions with variation points consisting of additional decisions. In general, design decisions are spread throughout and across architectural models, and this is why architecture description languages such as Koala and xADL embed the variation points within models. Because version control systems generally work at the level of files, it is difficult to use them to manage elements within files—for example, a component specified inside an architectural model.

A compromise is to attempt to separate out core parts of architectures and variation points into separate files, and then manage the evolution of these elements independently in a version-control system. This works in theory, but in reality it is difficult and inconvenient to have related design decisions for a single product-line member scattered across files, especially when automated merging tools are not available to merge them together again.

15.2.9 Implementing Product Lines

The major reductions in implementation costs from using a product line come about primarily through extensive reuse: Where two products in a product line share a similar architecture, the implementations should be (virtually) identical. Achieving this level of reuse must start in the architecture. Here, flexibility in connectors and communication methods is a primary driver of product-line reuse. If an architecture is chosen where components and connectors are tightly bound, it will be extremely difficult to introduce points of variation without recoding existing components. However, if flexible connectors and communication styles (such as message passing) are used instead, it is easier to introduce variations in the architecture without making extensive changes. However, having flexibility at the architectural level does not necessarily mean that the same flexibility will be present at the implementation level.

Chapter 9 discussed how implementing a system built using software architecture techniques is largely a mapping problem: understanding and controlling how design decisions made in the architecture map to implementation artifacts. In general, all the advice in Chapter 9 applies here as well. Implementing a product-line architecture is still a mapping problem, except that multiple products composed of core elements and variation points are involved. In this case, separating concerns in the implementation artifacts along the boundaries of variation points in the product line is critical.

Consider the situation presented in Figure 15-26. In Figure 15-26(a), good separation of concerns has not been maintained in the implementation. Various source files (File1.java, File2.java, and File3.java) are responsible for implementing both core and product-specific concerns. In this case, neither Product A nor Product B can be constructed without importing at least part of the implementation of the other. This makes it hard to evolve the products independently, and to integrate new products into the product line. Figure 15-26(b) shows a good separation of concerns: Here, implementation artifacts corresponding to products are kept separate from the common core and from each other. Both products can be built without using artifacts that (partially) implement other products.

One way of maintaining this separation of concerns is to use flexible architecture implementation frameworks, as discussed in Chapter 9. Many implementation frameworks help to enforce loose coupling between component and connector implementations, such

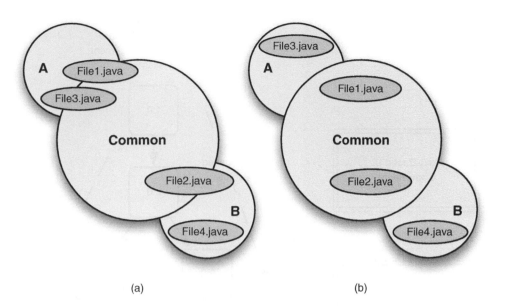

that components and connectors can have their dependencies changed easily and automatically. Implementation frameworks often allow components and connectors to be bound to each other "late"—either at product build time or even dynamically at run time. Implementations that employ late bindings of components generally enforce better separation and independence of components and help to drive reuse. Interface-implementation separation is also important: Well-defined implementation-level interfaces help to establish the services that are provided and required by a component (or set of components) without requiring a particular implementation. This separation of concerns further increases flexibility: Changes to the implementation of one component will not require changes to other components if the contract of the interface is maintained.

This is not always easy to achieve. Often, legacy products are incorporated into a product line. These products may not use flexible components, connectors, and communication methods. In this case, a careful refactoring should be considered, driven by the product-line architecture. Tight bindings in a product line are workable as long as they do not interfere with or cross the points of variation. For example, if three core components that are part of every product in the product line are tightly coupled, this is not a major problem: These components never will be separated, so making their bindings to each other flexible will be of limited near-term value. Instead, developers and architects should focus on making the bindings to components that exist only in a few products more flexible.

Product Lines and Source-Code Management Systems

Any mature development project will leverage some form of configuration management tool set to keep track of different versions of lower-level implementation artifacts: code files, resource files, and so on. Successfully managing product-line implementations requires an understanding of the relationship between versions of architecture-level elements (components, connectors) and versions of implementation-level elements (code, resource files)

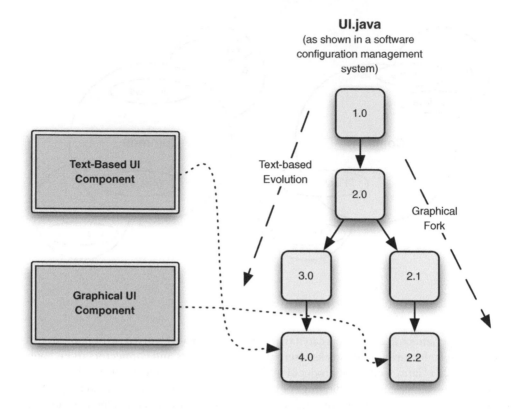

Figure 15-27.
Dealing with versions and development branches in a configuration management repository.

as stored in a configuration management repository. Implementations that are cleanly separated along the lines of architectural elements greatly simplify the mapping problem.

One phenomenon that occurs more often in product-line development than in single-product development is the use of multiple versions of the same implementation artifact (for example, source file) in different places in the product line architecture. For example, recall the Lunar Lander product line shown in Figure 15-23. Perhaps, for whatever reason, the implementation of the text-based user interface and the graphical user interface were based on the same code, a single file called UI.java, that has evolved over time. At some point in the past, a fork of UI.java was created in the configuration management repository, without renaming the file. Thus, there are two development branches of UI.java: one for a textual UI and one for a graphical UI.

This situation is depicted in Figure 15-27. Here, the *Text-Based UI* component uses version 4.0 of UI.java, while the *Graphical UI* component uses version 2.2. In a situation like this, implementation mappings must not only refer to individual files, but also individual *versions* of individual files.

15.2.10   Unifying Product Architectures with Different Intellectual Heritage

Unfortunately, product lines are not always considered at the inception of a group of related products. The idea of using product lines often appears on an organization's radar only after it has developed many products that have similar functionality and has duplicated an enormous amount of effort in doing so. Alternatively, company mergers and acquisitions can leave a single organization with the responsibility for developing, maintaining, and evolving very similar (and at one time, competing) products. At this time, the use of product lines becomes extremely attractive as a way of cutting costs by reusing engineering knowledge and architectural decisions from one product to the next. The difficulty is that the existing products in the product line often share little intellectual heritage, and the product architectures differ widely.

This is one of the most difficult problems in product-line development. The primary tension is that the goal of using a product line is to enable reuse, but the existing products exhibit little to no reuse. When this is the case, attempting to develop a product-line architecture that includes all the existing products may be of limited value, except as a historical artifact. Instead, processes should be forward-looking, attempting to extract the architectural lessons of previous projects and unify them into a product line for future products (or future product versions).

Before a product-line architecture can be developed, individual product architectures must be obtained. Architecturally savvy organizations already will have documented architectures for their products, but, as we have discussed, many product architectures evolve organically or diverge from their original intentions. In this case, architectural recovery (discussed in Chapters 3 and 4) is the first step toward product-line development.

The next step of the process is to normalize the existing product architectures (if necessary). Often, even when architectures for each product are available, they may not capture the same aspects of the systems under development, or capture those aspects at the same level of detail. They may not use the same terminology to refer to similar concepts. When this is the case (and it nearly always is) some amount of normalization must occur—some of the architectures must be adapted so that the commonalities and differences among the product architectures can be more readily identified. Luckily, architecture elaboration in this situation is made easier by the fact that there are actual, implemented products from which to extract the additional necessary information.

When normalized product architectures are available, they can be compared to identify common aspects and points of variation. Unless all of the architectures are expressed in the same notation at the same level of detail, it is probably not possible to automate much of this process. Instead, it is more useful to gather the architects and other stakeholders from each product into a series of meetings. Developing tables similar to Table 15-1 and Table 15-2 in order to understand the overlap between features and elements in the various products may be a useful exercise.

Developing a product-line architecture from this point forward is then a stakeholder-centric activity. There is no one right way to go about this, and depending on the domain and the organizational goals, the effort may go in one of many different directions:

No Product Line: It may be determined that, after examining the architectures, less reuse is possible than previously imagined. Perhaps the products were thought to perform many similar functions, but in reality they do not. Alternatively, the products may be so architecturally different that attempting to unify future versions of the products into a product line would cost more than the potential reuse would save. Here, the best alternative might be to abandon the idea of developing a product line entirely, and focus on further distinguishing the products from one another in separate development efforts.

One Master Product: Often, the easiest course of action in developing a new product line is to identify the best existing product and use its architecture as a basis for a product line. In this way at least one product will fit naturally into the emergent product line, and innovative features from other products can be integrated as appropriate.

Hybrid: When no one product can be identified as the master for the purpose of developing a product line, the "best of breed" features of each product in the domain can be extracted and unified into a hybrid product line. Here, no one existing product will fit totally naturally into the product-line architecture. This is most useful when new products are not intended to be direct descendants of old products or when existing products are being unified.

15.2.11   Organizational Issues in Creating and Managing Product Lines

This chapter has largely covered the creation and management of product lines and product-line architectures from a technical perspective. However, using product lines is not a solely technical activity. A product-line–based approach needs to be as much organizational and cultural as it is technical. Creating a product line often means integrating the needs and opinions of stakeholders from fundamentally different perspectives into the same effort. This can foster all kinds of organizational and technical issues: friction between the teams, feature creep, difficulty prioritizing customers, least-common-denominator architectures, and so on.

Furthermore, an organization's investment strategy in its products needs to change to match a product-line approach. Creating a product line incurs substantial costs that do eventually pay off, but not in the context of a single product. Rather, they are recovered through lower maintenance expenses across multiple products, the increased profits from selling more product variants, and the lower costs of developing future versions of the products. This requires organizations to think *horizontally*, across product and team boundaries, which often requires both an organizational and cultural shift.

Paul Clements and Linda Northrop have written extensively about these issues in their book *Software Product Lines: Practices and Patterns* (Clements and Northrop 2001); we encourage those interested to look to this and other sources for more detailed guidance in this regard.

15.3 DSSAS, PRODUCT LINES, AND ARCHITECTURAL STYLES

We have discussed domain-specific software architectures (DSSAs) and product lines, as well as their relationship to each other. A natural question arises at this point: What are the relationships among DSSAs, product lines, and architectural styles?

Recall that architectural styles represent a reusable package of design decisions that can be applied to different products to elicit desired qualities. In some sense, both DSSAs and product-line architectures can be seen in the same light. Usually, however, architectural styles are far more general than DSSAs or product lines. Most architectural styles can be applied across many domains. For example, the pipe-and-filter style has been used to develop text-processing applications, typesetting systems, and program compilers. Typically, such diverse applications would not all be members of the same DSSA or product line.

Styles do, however, play an important role in the development of both DSSAs and product lines. It would be unusual for different products in the same DSSA or product line to have significantly different architectural styles. As noted above, one of the most common canonical requirements in the development of a DSSA is the architectural style that will be used to create applications within the DSSA. Typically, a reference architecture for a DSSA will follow this prescribed style. Similarly, individual products in the same product-line architecture will generally follow the same style. The use of a common style across a DSSA or product line is ultimately an effort to ensure consistent qualities in the products that emerge and to keep them from drifting away from the original intent of the product line.

Just as there can be points of variation in architectures, there can also be points of variation in architectural styles themselves: different sets of constraints to solve related problems. By applying product-line architecture techniques to the decisions that compose architectural styles rather than architectures, it is possible to create a family of architectural styles.

Recall two of the most basic architectural styles from Chapter 4: batch-sequential and pipe-and-filter, as shown in Figure 15-28. These styles actually have many constraints in common. For example, both enforce a linear ordering of components, each of which has one input and one output, and data moves unidirectionally through the line, being processed individually by each component. They differ in a few details: batch-sequential systems pass the data wholesale in a chunk, and only one component operates on the data at a time; pipe-and-filter systems pass data as it is available and components execute in

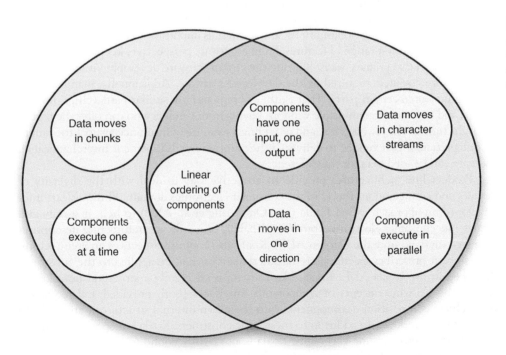

Figure 15-28.
An example of related architectural styles.

parallel when possible. Here, explicit variation points can be used to express and reason about the relationship between architectural styles just as they are used to reason about the relationship among software products.

15.4 DSSE EXAMPLES

We now present two examples of how domain-specific software engineering techniques, including product-line architectures, have been applied in software development practice. The first example is Philips Electronics's use of the Koala architecture description language in the development of software for devices in the consumer electronics domain. The second example is the domain of software-defined radios, configurable devices that communicate using radio waves, with their internal functionality implemented by software.

15.4.1 Koala and Consumer Electronics

Consumer electronics is a dynamic and highly competitive domain of product development. For decades, devices such as televisions and cable descramblers were relatively simple with a few, well-defined capabilities. Over the years, they have become more and more complex, largely due to enhancements in their embedded software. The latest incarnations of these devices include graphical, menu-driven configuration, on-screen programming guides, video on demand, and digital video recording and playback. In a global marketplace, each of these devices must be deployed in multiple regions around the world, specifically configured for the languages and broadcast standards used in those regions.

The increasing feature counts of consumer electronic devices are accompanied by fierce competition among organizations, and it is just as important to keep costs down as it is to deploy the widest range of features. From a software perspective, keeping costs down can be done in two primary ways: limiting the cost of software development and limiting the hardware resources required by the developed software. Additionally, manufacturers often multisource certain parts. That is, they obtain and use similar parts (chips, boards, tuners, and so forth) from multiple vendors, buying from vendors who can offer the part at the right time or the lowest price, and providing a measure of insurance against the failure by one particular part vendor to deliver. If the parts are not 100 percent interchangeable, software can be used to mask the differences.

Product-line architectures provide an attractive way to deal with the diversity of devices and configurations found in the consumer electronics domain. Philips Electronics developed an approach called Koala (van Ommering et al. 2000) to help it specify and manage its consumer electronics products. Koala is primarily an architecture description language (derived from the Darwin ADL). Koala also contains aspects of an architectural style since it prescribes specific patterns and semantics that are applied to the constructs described in the Koala ADL. Koala, like Darwin, is effectively a structural notation: It retains the Darwin concepts of components, interfaces (both provided and required), hierarchical compositions (components with their own internal structures), and links to connect the interfaces. In addition to these basic constructs, Koala has special constructs for supporting product-line variability. Koala is also tightly bound to implementations of embedded components: Certain aspects of Koala (such as the method by which it connects

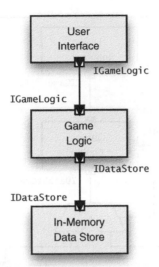

Figure 15-29.
*Basic Koala
diagram of Lunar
Lander.*

required and provided interfaces in code) are specifically designed with implementation strategies (such as static binding through C macros) in mind.

A basic Koala diagram with no product line variability for a Lunar Lander application is shown in Figure 15-29. As you can see, basic Koala diagrams are effectively equivalent to Darwin diagrams. Koala extends Darwin in the following ways:

IDL-based interface types: An interface type in Koala is a named set of function signatures, similar to those you would find in C. For example, the interface to the Lunar Lander data store in Koala might be declared like this:

```
interface IDataStore{
    void setAltitude(int altitudeInMeters);
    int getAltitude();
    void setBurnRate(int newBurnRate);
    int getBurnRate();
    ...
}
```

The IDataStore interface type may be provided (or required) by any number of Koala components. When a provided and required interface are connected, the provided interface type must provide at least the functions required by the required interface type.

Diversity interfaces: One of the philosophies of Koala is that configuration parameters for a component should not be stored in the component; instead, configuration parameters should be accessed by the component from an external source when needed. This allows the application to be configured centrally, from a single component (or set of components) whose purpose is to provide configuration data for the application. Diversity interfaces are special required interfaces that are attached to components and are used by the component to get configuration parameters.

Figure 15-30.
*Koala diagram of
Lunar Lander
with a variation
point.*

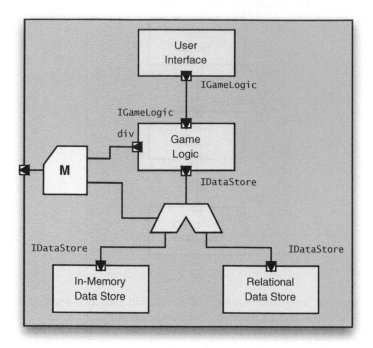

Switches: A switch is a new architectural construct that represents a variation point. It allows a required interface to be connected to multiple different provided interfaces. When the variation point is resolved, only one of the connections will actually be present. A configuration condition determines which provided-required interface pair is connected. These configuration conditions are analogous to the guards discussed earlier in this chapter. A switch is connected to a diversity interface to get its configuration parameters, just as a component would. Depending on the values returned through the diversity interface, the switch will route calls to one of the required interfaces connected to it. This may result in disconnected components (that is, components that will never be involved). Disconnected components are not instantiated to save resources.

Figure 15-30 shows a Lunar Lander architecture in Koala with a variation point. Here, the application can use an in-memory data store or a relational data store to maintain application state. The required interface of the *Game Logic* component is now routed through a switch, which is configured by configuration parameters provided externally. The *Game Logic* component includes a new diversity interface `div` that allows it to access those external configuration parameters.

Optional Required Interfaces

Several components may provide similar, but not identical, services. For example, a basic TV tuner component may have only the ability to change frequencies, but an advanced TV tuner may be able to search for valid frequencies as well. It is possible for callers to a TV tuner to include an optional required interface and query whether the interface is actually connected or not. If it is connected, the caller can make calls on the optional interface; if not, the caller should behave/degrade gracefully.

Through these mechanisms, Koala gives architects the power to specify and implement product lines of embedded systems. Koala's main strengths are its straightforward notation, intuitive graphical visualization, and tool support for implementing product lines efficiently. Although developed for the consumer electronics domain, Koala is generic enough for use in many domains.

A drawback of Koala is its lack of support for explicit software connectors (a trait it inherits from Darwin). Koala implies that communication among components happens exclusively through synchronous request-response procedure calls. There is no explicit support for asynchronous or message-passing interaction (message passing, in particular, is a well-known mechanism for supporting flexibility and diversity). However, in the target domain (embedded systems in consumer electronics devices), synchronous procedure calls are a very typical mode of interaction.

Using an architecture-centric approach gave Philips the ability to break up its software systems into reusable components that communicate through explicit interfaces, while still retaining the small size and efficiency necessary for embedded systems development. Taking inspiration from an existing architecture description language (Darwin), Philips defined a domain-specific ADL (Koala) with semantics that mapped well to its application domain. Additionally, Philips incorporated explicit support for variability into Koala. This gave it the ability to deal with the many market-induced variations in its product lines (to deal with multiple grades of products with different feature combinations, different requirements due to internationalization, and so on). Rather than maintaining separate architectural descriptions for each product, entire product lines can be captured in a single model. More than 100 engineers at Philips have used Koala, making it one of the most successful industrial applications of ADLs and domain-specific architecture-centric development.

15.4.2 Software-Defined Radios

Communication over the air has been used to facilitate all kinds of social advances, from early audio and Morse-code transmissions to video transmissions for television, to the latest advances in cellular phones and broadband WiFi connections. Traditionally, radio hardware has been specialized for a particular kind of application: For example, an ordinary car stereo is limited to receiving analog AM/FM audio transmissions. It cannot, for example, decode TV signals (even the audio portion) or act as an Internet WiFi repeater. To do so would require hardware components to be changed out or adapted.

The increased capabilities of digital signal processing components as well as advances in reconfigurable hardware (FPGAs[3] in particular) have made it possible to rethink how communication-over-radio devices are built from both a hardware and software perspective. The result has been an effort to develop so-called software-defined radios (SDRs) (Dillinger, Madani, and Alonistioti 2003). A software-defined radio is a device that can transmit,

---

[3]FPGA stands for Field Programmable Gate Array. An FPGA is effectively an integrated circuit consisting of an array of logic gates that can be reconfigured through software. Once reconfigured, the circuit can perform any function it is programmed for—processing data, cracking encryption, emulating a microprocessor, and so on. In general, FPGAs are slower and larger than special-purpose hardware, but the performance is reasonably close.

Figure 15-31.
*Basic data
pipeline of a
software-defined
radio.*

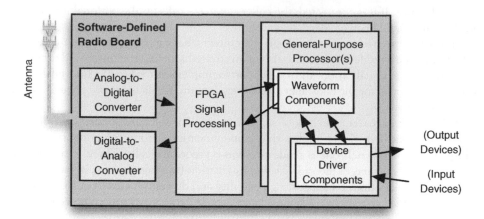

receive, and process signals over the air for a variety of applications, where the application is defined by the software that is loaded on the radio. Standard components of a software-defined radio include an antenna, analog-to-digital conversion, FPGAs for high-frequency digital signal processing, and general-purpose processors (such as PowerPCs) for further signal processing duties, as well as various I/O ports for interfacing with audio and video devices (displays, microphones, speakers, and so on).

The basic data flow through a hypothetical software-defined radio board is shown in Figure 15-31. Depending on the configuration of the FPGA(s) and the components and connectors loaded on the general-purpose processors, the radio can be used for all sorts of applications. In theory, a software-defined radio could act as everything from an ordinary FM radio to a television set to a wireless access point simply by loading different software onto the radio.

The domain of software-defined radios is ideal for the application of DSSE principles. A domain-specific software architecture has been developed for software-defined radios called the Software Communications Architecture (Modular Software-programmable Radio Consortium 2001); see the accompanying feature titled, "The Software Communications Architecture (SCA)." This particular DSSA is not a panacea, however, and the sidebar touches on many issues that may make it less than ideal.

**The
Software
Communica-
tions
Architecture
(SCA)**

The organizations interested in developing software-defined radios are keenly interested in the design, particularly the software design, of such radios. This resulted in the development of a standard known as the Software Communications Architecture (SCA), which governs the design of SDRs (although, as the name implies, it is intended for future application to other kinds of communications systems).

The SCA is an interesting document to study, since it is the standard architecture that many organizations implementing SDRs are intended to follow.

The SCA looks at the software architecture of a software-defined radio as a set of interacting software components. These components are defined and interact via CORBA (see Chapter 4). As one might expect, the choice of CORBA as the sole software interconnection technique induces several architectural consequences on SCA systems, among them:

- The style of an SCA-based software-defined radio is a distributed objects style.

- Interfaces are a primary driver of interaction.

- Provided interfaces for various kinds of components are defined using CORBA IDL.
- Components communicate primarily through synchronous procedure calls to provided interfaces.

The bulk of the SCA specification is a collection of CORBA IDL interface definitions for various kinds of components. For example, filesystem components implement an interface very similar to the POSIX filesystem interface. Other interface definitions exist for different kinds of drivers and other service components.

Actual signal data in the architecture is broken up into digital data packets. Packets of data are passed from one component to another through a de facto call named `PushPacket`. A component that is to send a packet of data to another component will call `PushPacket` and pass the data packet to the target component. Chains of these components create processing pipelines and data flows.

The SCA raises a number of important questions based on what is and is not specified. For example, the architectural style embodied by the SCA is a distributed objects style, with a library of different kinds of components (objects) that can be used to construct SDRs.

It is unclear which came first: the style or the choice of middleware. The SCA developers may have decided that a distributed objects style was the right style for constructing software-defined radios and then chose CORBA as a middleware platform or framework for implementation. However, it is also possible that the SCA developers, encountering heterogeneous hardware platforms and component implementations (especially legacy component implementations embedded in non-software-defined radios), chose CORBA for its services in masking these differences, and the distributed objects style was just fallout from this decision. For the low-bandwidth control pathways in the architecture, distributed objects makes sense, but distributed objects is not a style that comes to mind for dealing with high-throughput data flows of packets passing through a radio. In this case, a hybrid style that had explicit support for streams, or at least asynchronous message-based data flows, might have been more appropriate.

Another question to ask is why CORBA itself was specified in the SCA, as opposed to other middleware that supports a distributed objects style such as COM, or an architecture framework that can be implemented with different kinds of middleware. The intent was likely to support interoperability among independently developed components: Because CORBA is not tied to one particular vendor, many CORBA implementations exist. However, interoperability between CORBA implementations is rarely perfect, and components developed against one implementation may have difficulty working in the context of another. It could be argued that the calling out of CORBA as a core aspect of SCA-based systems is a case of overspecification in the architecture.

The above descriptions talk about which aspects of a software-defined radio are specified by the SCA. It is perhaps more important to understand which aspects *are not* specified. The SCA surprisingly provides almost no guidance as to how to develop a radio based on the components and interfaces it defines. It contains little information about how to configure the components, to structure the radio application as a whole, or how to implement them. This leaves perhaps the most important and difficult decisions about constructing a radio entirely up to the radio developers themselves.

A final question to ask concerns the kinds of software qualities that are enabled by the use of the SCA. Portability, composability, and ease of integration may be enabled by this architecture because of the detailed interface specifications and the identification of specific middleware to connect elements. However, are these qualities the most important qualities in the development of a software-defined radio? Arguably, more important qualities such as performance and reliability are largely ignored by the SCA, and this is perhaps its biggest problem. At this time, the jury is still out on the success of the SCA; several commercial and

> military efforts are underway to implement SCA-based radios. However, open-source and hobbyist groups also are implementing software-defined radios using their own architectures and frameworks and meeting with a measure of success. Time will tell whether the SCA will bear fruit or not.

The software-defined radio domain is also an example of where product lines can make a significant impact because the domain encompasses so much variability. Variability exists at many different levels of abstraction:

Network Topology: In this domain, radio devices do not stand alone: They communicate (via radio links) with other radios running other applications. Although software-defined radios can remain in one location, it is often the case that the radios themselves are mobile—mounted to vehicles or carried by individuals who move around. As such, the topology of devices can change as they move around or devices go on or offline.

Radio Configuration: A single software-defined radio board comprises a channel: a device that can be configured for one particular application at a time. In general, these devices are configured on a single board. More complicated radios support multiple channels by having multiple hardware boards mounted in the same radio backplane. Two-to-eight–channel radios are not uncommon for commercial or military applications.

Board Configuration: Each board in a software-defined radio can be implemented in a number of different ways. Although the basic elements (antenna, analog-to-digital conversion, and signal processing) are basically the same, they can be configured in different ways. Boards may include different FPGAs, different general-purpose processor configurations, different I/O ports and controllers, or different amounts of memory or storage.

Software Configuration: Each board generally has a number of processing elements on it that can be loaded with software: FPGAs and general-purpose processors, for example. Depending on the application, different components will be loaded onto the different processing elements.

Variability at each of these levels must be understood, controlled, and managed. The first thing to note is that these levels of abstraction are more or less hierarchical: Vehicles contain radios, radios contain boards, boards contain processing elements, and processing elements contain software elements. Modeling notations that directly support hierarchical architectures, such as Darwin, Koala, or xADL 2.0, are all good candidates for modeling such an architecture. Variability at each level is also somewhat limited: Specific software-defined radios will be developed for specific purposes (military, commercial, and so on). Thus, network topologies will have certain common characteristics. For a given organization, only a few different radio and board configurations will be produced: An organization may produce only a two-channel and a four-channel radio, for example. Board configurations may be limited to a "test board" and a "production board." Software configurations will be partially driven by board configuration: Each device or controller on the board will likely have an associated device driver component; other components will be driven by the various applications loaded on the radio.

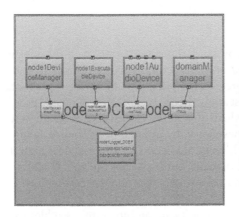
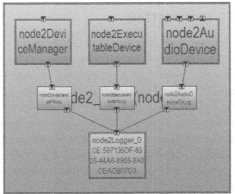

(a)

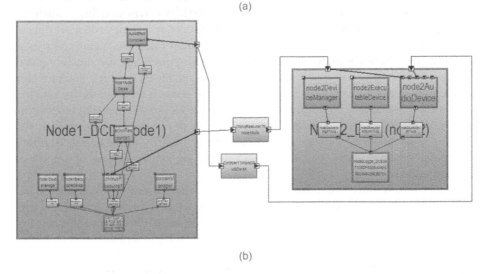

(b)

Figure 15-32.
*Software-defined
radio structure
with (a) just
drivers and
operating
environment
loaded, and (b)
with a waveform
application
deployed.*

Figure 15-32 shows two variants of the architecture of a software-defined radio called the SCA Reference Implementation (SCARI), modeled in xADL and depicted in xADL's graphical visualization. SCARI is a simple example of an SCA-based software-defined radio, intended to demonstrate how the SCA can be used to implement an SDR. Figure 15-32(a) shows the radio with only the device drivers and operating environment deployed. Figure 15-32(b) shows the same radio with an additional waveform application deployed. Each represents a different product-line variant, and by assigning guards to each the waveform components using techniques shown earlier in this chapter, waveform deployments can be selectively applied to the radio using product-line selection.

The extreme flexibility in the domain is induced by increasingly adaptable hardware, but is primarily enabled by software. Since software is so malleable, this should come as no surprise. Because of this, as well as other constraints that must be considered when dealing with SDRs—size, power consumption, performance, time to load and unload waveforms, and so on—SDRs are yet another domain where the capture and reuse of specialized engineering knowledge and experience can substantially reduce costs and risks in the development of new systems.

15.5 END MATTER

Domain-specific software engineering is, in many ways, the culmination of all the advice given in this book. It broadens the challenge of architecture-based development substantially: Instead of just applying architecture-centric principles to a single product, organizations and even entire communities must apply them across a range of related products. This is complicated by the fact that the products already developed in the domain were developed for different, often competing business goals, by isolated development groups that did not share engineering knowledge or architectural assets. This is perhaps the biggest challenge in architecture-centric software development, but it also has the greatest potential reward: a substantial reduction in costs and risks to develop new systems within an entire domain.

In some ways, the creation of a domain-specific software architecture resembles the development of an architecture for a single product—it still involves modeling, visualizing, analyzing, and applying principal design decisions. However, it is made even more difficult by the fact that the architecture must work for a wide range of systems. A constant tension exists between overspecification and underspecification—specifying too much and constraining the kinds of systems you can construct versus specifying too little and providing insufficient guidance and value. Key contributors may come from different backgrounds and organizations and may have fundamentally different ideas about how the architecture should be constructed. This chapter has provided a survey of the kinds of artifacts that make up a domain-specific software architecture, and provided some advice about how to create them. However, in the end, it still is a very human-centric process of negotiation and cooperation.

Product-line architecture techniques provide a more concrete way to apply domain-specific software engineering "in the small." Product lines are typically developed within a single organization and target a much narrower set of products. Because of this narrower focus, product-line architectures are often far easier to develop and maintain than DSSEs, since there is far less variation in business goals and there are fewer organizational boundaries to cross. Substantial cost reduction and risk mitigation can still be achieved within the product line, especially if automated tools can help with activities such as product-line selection.

Domain-specific software engineering highlights how software architecture in practice is both an organizational and a technical issue. We have highlighted how business concerns motivate certain development practices and techniques. The next chapter will continue this theme by focusing on architecture-related standards. The creation, adoption, and use of standards are also driven by business goals, and standards are a big part of how software architecture is viewed and used in practice.

| The Business Case | The primary attraction and benefit of domain-specific software engineering is found through *reuse*. Reuse, continual learning, and refinement of knowledge about how to build systems is the hallmark of any engineering discipline. Software reuse has therefore been widely recognized and often touted as a way of controlling the complexity of software systems, improving their reliability, speeding up their development, reducing their associated costs, and so on. However, a cursory look at the practice of software reuse indicates that most frequently it entails *scavenging* |

source files for needed code fragments, *cloning* modules needed in multiple places in a system (which is, incidentally, something that good software engineering practice discourages), or *purchasing* entire commercial-off-the-shelf (COTS) solutions.

Therefore, reuse in software development is predominantly focused on source code. However, this is misaligned with the near-universal awareness that the key software engineering costs lie elsewhere—in requirements elicitation and system design—and that software architecture is a system's (and, often, a development organization's) principal asset. In other words, source code-level reuse is not the most effective reuse.

DSSE recognizes and addresses this discrepancy. It provides mechanisms for expanding the notion of reuse to include all concerns in the development of a software system (so long as that system falls within a particular application domain). This includes:

- The canonical, *reference* system requirements that are in some significant way shared across all systems in the domain.
- The terminology specific to a domain, and sometimes *invented* for the sole purpose of enabling effective software development in that domain.
- The canonical, *reference* architecture, with clearly identified variation points.
- The canonical, low-level system designs that realize the architecture.
- The analysis, simulation, and testing models and tools.
- The domain-specific implementation techniques, off-the-shelf components, and code generators.
- The system construction and deployment scripts.
- The predicted evolution patterns and associated mechanisms.
- The required knowledge and training of software engineers.
- The processes for managing different projects with shared characteristics, existing domain-specific assets, already developed systems, and systems currently under development, as well as planning future systems.

The argument here is that, in theory, this could be done for any software system. In practice, it is not possible. But if your domain is reasonably well defined and stable, and if you have a base of experience to draw from, leverage it!

If it seems as if this is a lot to manage, it is. But it is still easier, and less expensive, to manage known assets than it is to discover them. Organizations and communities constructing complex systems within a domain will undoubtedly still have to consider, capture, and codify all the aspects that are part of a DSSA. This cost, while high, provides adequate return on investment—the goal here is to capture once, reuse forever.

The explicit capture and use of product lines is an even more business-centric practice. Product lines facilitate reuse at the architectural level, and allow organizations to construct and manage new product variants with only incremental costs. As markets diversify and organizations do business with an increasing array of cultures, countries, standards, and customer needs, being able to tailor and market a wide variety of similar products becomes increasingly important. As a side benefit, the same product-line techniques can be used to help understand the evolution of individual products over time and to capture what-if decisions and rationale in more explicit ways, further bolstering an organization's core business knowledge.

A caveat: Domain-specific software engineering is largely a horizontal endeavor; it means surveying and unifying engineering activities across products, and perhaps even across business areas. Organizations that can adapt to this style of engineering can exploit DSSE. However, many organizations still treat product development as a series of independent "stovepipes,"

> where personnel, engineering knowledge, and budgets are strictly partitioned across product boundaries. If this remains the case, an organization will never be able to exploit DSSE, because it cannot make the horizontal investments necessary to exploit commonalities and reuse.

15.6 REVIEW QUESTIONS

1. What is domain-specific software engineering (DSSE)? What problems in software development does it address?

2. What are the three main concerns addressed by DSSE? How do they relate to one another?

3. How does DSSE help to partition problem spaces and solution spaces? How does this make software development easier?

4. Enumerate the various artifacts that are part of a DSSA. What information does each artifact contain? What is its purpose?

5. What is a reference architecture? How does it differ from an ordinary software architecture? What different kinds of reference architectures can be created?

6. When should a reference architecture be developed?

7. What is a product line? How does it differ from a domain?

8. What is a product-line architecture? What is the relationship between a reference architecture and a product-line architecture? What are variation points?

9. Identify strategies for unifying multiple related products into a product line.

10. What is the relationship between architectural design decisions, features, and products in a product line?

11. How can product lines be used to capture variations in a single product over time?

12. How can product lines be used to capture what-if scenarios in product development?

13. What is product-line selection and how is it performed?

14. What are some strategies for unifying products with different intellectual heritages into a product line?

15. What is the relationship among DSSAs, product lines, and architectural styles?

16. How does Koala assist developers in domain-specific software engineering? What Koala features enable it to capture product-line architectures?

17. How can domain-specific software engineering techniques help in the construction of software-defined radios? How can software-defined radios form a product line?

15.7 EXERCISES

1. Select a problem domain with which you are familiar and try to produce a domain model as described above. Which of the domain modeling activities pose the greatest challenges? Why?

2. Survey some of the architecture-based development approaches presented in this book, and identify how (or if) they address the three primary concerns of domain, business, and technology. Is any one concern favored over others? Why?

3. Find two to four examples of systems that are in the same domain but are not built by the same organization. Create tables, like those in this chapter, showing the elements in each product, grouping them into

features, and showing how features are composed into the products. Speculate on how you might use DSSE and product-line techniques to unify these products into a product line, or to extract a DSSA from them.

4. Use an architecture description language that supports product-line modeling such as Koala or xADL to capture at least three different Lunar Lander games with different features.

5. Download and review the SCA specification. Which aspects of a DSSA are covered by this specification and which are not? Is it an adequate reference architecture for the domain of software-defined radios?

6. Find an open-source project that has multiple product variations—perhaps for reasons of running on different platforms, providing different services, or working in an international context. Determine how these product variants are managed. Is an architectural approach at work?

15.8 FURTHER READING

A tremendous amount of the general DSSE/DSSA information in this chapter comes from early work on domain-specific software engineering in the avionics domain by Will Tracz and Don Batory et al. (Tracz 1995; Tracz 1993; Tracz, Coglianese, and Young 1993; Tracz 1996; Batory, McAllester et al. 1995; Batory, Coglianese et al. 1995; Tracz, Coglianese, and Young 1993). These references not only provide deeper background on DSSE and DSSAs in general, but also discuss yet another application domain in which these techniques have been applied. Tracz has also written extensively on reuse in general, with most of his articles compiled into his book *Confessions of a Used Program Salesman* (Tracz, 1995).

The Koala (van Ommering et al. 2000) work is another excellent example of the successful use of architecture-centric development in practice. Although the early Koala work was focused on individual product lines, Rob van Ommering has expanded his work to cut across product lines and address product populations (van Ommering 2002) as well.

There is extensive literature on product lines. Paul Clements and Linda Northrop (Clements and Northrop 2002) write about product lines from a high-level perspective, focusing on management issues, processes, patterns of practice, and case studies. Hassan Gomaa (Gomaa 2004) takes a UML-centric approach to modeling both product lines and patterns found therein. Klaus Pohl et al. (Pohl, Böckle, and van der Linden 2005) also take a primarily process-centric approach.

Another substantial body of work on product-line architectures and modeling comes from Andrévan der Hoek et al. in the Ménage project (van der Hoek 2000; Roshandel et al. 2004; van der Hoek 2004), which captured options, variants, and versions explicitly in architectural models and which inspired the product-line features in xADL.

16

Standards

Over the years, various organizations have attempted to create standard architectural approaches, techniques, and tools for software systems. Other standards simply emerged as a result of common use among many organizations, such as the Unified Modeling Language (UML).

Some of these standards have achieved widespread adoption and significant backing in industry and government, and often are mandated for use on different projects. In general, these standards encapsulate a significant amount of engineering knowledge and guidance. However, it is important for software architects and other stakeholders to establish and maintain a rational perspective concerning these standards: what they are good for, what they can provide, and what they fail to provide. Often, the momentum behind a standard creates a (vastly) overinflated perception of its real value and impact. This chapter puts some of the most influential standards in context and identifies their strengths and weaknesses.

16.1 WHAT ARE STANDARDS?

Definition. A *standard* is a form of agreement between parties.

From a software architecture perspective, there are many different kinds of relevant standards: standards for notations, tools, processes, interfaces, organizations, and so on. Standards can come from different sources: individuals, teams, single-practitioner organizations, coalitions of such organizations, governments, or organizations whose specific goal is to create and codify standards such as the American National Standards Institute (ANSI), Ecma International, the International Organization for Standardization (ISO), and the World Wide Web Consortium (W3C). When a standard is controlled by a body that is considered to be authoritative, the standard is often called a de jure standard (meaning "from law"). De jure standards often:

- Are formally defined and documented.
- Evolve through a rigorous, well-known process.
- Are managed by an independent body, governmental agency, or multi-organizational coalition rather than a single individual or company.

Because of these characteristics, de jure standards tend to be the ones that are externally mandated for use in specific projects. The other kind of standard is a de facto standard (meaning "in fact" or "in practice"). De facto standards often:

- Are created by a single individual organization to address a particular need.
- Are adopted due to technical superiority or market dominance of the creating organization.
- Evolve through an emergent, market-driven process.
- Are managed by the creating organization or the users themselves, rather than through a formal custodial body.

The line between a de jure and a de facto standard is not always clear. For example, HTML is a standard notation for encoding Web pages and has all the above characteristics of a de jure standard, but the W3C has no authority to force individual Web publishers to follow the HTML standard—instead, market issues of browser compatibility tend to be the factor driving adoption. Similarly, de facto extensions to HTML have been created by companies such as Microsoft and Netscape that are widely used simply because of their creators' dominance in the browser market. In the computing world, popular de facto standards often evolve into de jure standards: Netscape developed the JavaScript Web scripting language on its own and included support in its browser. Microsoft created a workalike language for its Internet Explorer browser called JScript. As more and more people became dependent on this technology, Netscape submitted it to a standards body (Ecma International), where it has been standardized as ECMAScript.

Both de jure and de facto standards can be *open*, *proprietary/closed*, or somewhere in between. Totally open standards allow public participation in their development; anyone is free to come in and suggest improvements or changes. Totally proprietary or closed standards mean that only the custodians for the standard can participate in its evolution. Standards bodies such an ANSI, ISO, and Ecma International tend to fall somewhere in the middle; some of these allow virtually open membership, while others have a higher barrier to entry (voting of the existing members or a steep membership fee, for example).

Stakeholders and architects should be keenly familiar with the state of a particular standard before adopting it by asking key questions: Who supports the standard? How does it evolve? Is it dependent upon one specific company—that may be a competitor? What are its success and failure stories? How can feedback be incorporated into the standard's future development?

16.1.1 Why Use Standards?

Standards can provide many different tangible benefits to their users. Many of these benefits derive from standards' ability to create *network effects*. A network effect occurs when the value of a particular service or product goes up as more users employ it. The Web exhibits a classic example of a network effect: As more and more users publish content on the Web through the HTTP (Fielding et al. 1999) and HTML (Raggett, Le Hors, and Jacobs 1999) standards, the value of the Web as a whole increases for each of its users, since each of these users can access the new content without any additional investment.

Standards can ensure consistency across projects or organizations. Consistency is often the key driver of a network effect. Consider the value of the use of consistent symbology in a notation such as UML: As more stakeholders describe systems using UML, more people can develop an understanding of those systems without investing in learning a new notation.

Certain kinds of standards, such as interface or behavior standards applied to products, can be used to ensure interoperability or interchangeability. For example, the HTTP protocol can be seen as an interface standard; it dictates how to interact with a component, but not how that component must be implemented internally. Therefore, components developed by diverse organizations can all interoperate (on some level) as long as they conform to the HTTP standard. Interchangeability is a higher level of standardization; interchangeable software components can be swapped out for one another with little or no effort. In the world of software, interchangeable parts often exhibit different quality characteristics: One may be optimized for use in a single-processor system while another may be optimized for use in a distributed system.

Standards are bearers of engineering knowledge and can carry it from project to project. Often, standards are developed because organizations continue to reinvent the same basic techniques or tools over and over, at great expense. Standards reduce costs for the entire market by collecting and making the engineering knowledge available to everyone.

Standards also serve as targets for tool vendors. Organizations that adopt widely accepted standards generally will have the ability to buy off-the-shelf tools that implement the standard along with training supplements such as books, videos, and so on, instead of investing time and money to develop their own. For the most popular standards, adopting organizations often will have a choice of several competing tools, and market competition can drive further improvements in these tools.

Standards can also reduce the cost of powerful software tools. While software initially is expensive to produce, once it is created it can be replicated infinitely at little to no additional unit cost. In economic terms, software makes excellent use of *economies of scale*. By conforming to a standard, a tool can gain wider appeal and thus sell more units. As more units are sold, the developing organization can amortize the initial development cost across all the units, greatly reducing the price it needs to charge to be profitable. For example, consider two software tools that both cost $1 million to develop. If one tool sells 100 copies, then the price for each unit must be above $10,000 just to recover the development cost. However, if the tool sells 100,000 copies, then the price could drop to only $10 per unit. A tool that conforms to a widely accepted standard is much more likely to sell many copies than a tool that does not.

Over time, standards evolve. The procedure for evolving a standard is generally governed and managed by the standard's custodial organization. As standards are adopted and used, various weaknesses or drawbacks will be identified, and future versions of the standard can be developed to rectify some of them. Organizations that adopt the standard can take advantage of these lessons and the resulting improvements in the standard without bearing the entire brunt of the costs of developing them.

Having substantial control over a widely accepted standard can grant an enormous amount of market power to a custodial organization. If a single organization, such as a commercial company, develops a standard that becomes widely adopted, then that company has a great deal of control over how the standard is used and how the standard evolves. It can guide the standard's evolution in directions that match its own business interests—or drive it away from a competitor's interests.

Overall, the use of standards can carry many benefits. However, standards are not a panacea, and must always be evaluated with a critical eye.

16.1.2   Drawbacks of Standards

A host of benefits can be conferred upon organizations that adopt and develop standards. In doing so, organizations must work to mitigate or avoid some of their drawbacks.

The very nature of standards is somewhat at odds with the realities of software architecture. One message that this book has conveyed is that stakeholder needs and desired qualities of software vary widely from project to project and domain to domain. In contrast, standards often attempt to apply the same concepts and processes to widely different development efforts. This is probably the key weakness of most architecture-related standards in use today.

A related drawback is that the most widely adopted (and thus best-supported) standards are those that are the most general. This should not be surprising—the adoption potential of a particular standard is proportional to its applicability. However, this means that domain-specific standards that can impart a lot of specific guidance and value to projects within a domain are often the ones that have the least support—from tools, researchers, and so on.

The primary tension in standards development exists between overspecification—prescribing too much and limiting the utility of the standard—and underspecification—prescribing too little and limiting the benefits of the standard. As you might expect, the most broadly accepted standards tend to be the ones that are underspecified, leaving out significant semantic details. Without well-defined semantics, it is difficult to make quality judgments about a product simply because it conforms to a standard.

A related problem is the *least-common-denominator* problem. Because standards are often developed by a committee of diverse, often competing organizations, the individual goals of the organizations will tend to diverge along many dimensions. When many organizations are involved, divergent viewpoints are often simply left out of the standard, with only agreeable elements included. When this occurs, the standards that emerge tend to be small and underspecified.

The opposite problem can also occur: When divergent opinions occur among the developers of a standard, everyone's solutions are included, usually leaving the choice of approach up to the user of the standard. These standards are underspecified in a different way: While there is no shortage of options for users, there also is little guidance as to which approach to choose; the fundamental benefits of using a standard such as interoperability and consistency are reduced.

De Jure Standards: The Ivory Towers of Industry?

One critical element that distinguishes de jure standards from de facto standards is market adoption. A de facto standard has become a standard because it fulfills some need for a significant number of users. For these standards, market forces and network effects are primary drivers of adoption.

De jure standards (at least, those that have not emerged from de facto standards) are not similarly motivated. They are often developed and codified without preexisting market adoption. The quality of these standards is thus brought into question—they have not competed in an open marketplace of ideas and thus may be inadequate solutions even for the problems they are intended to address. This mirrors a common criticism levied at academic solutions to problems: that they come from the "ivory tower" in that they may be well-grounded in theory but are untested in practice. This is especially troubling when these standards are mandated for use in projects. Here, there is a significant danger that being *standards-compliant* will be more important than being *good*.

De jure standards usually arise from good intentions. Often, recognized experts in a particular domain are tapped to help produce the new standard. Sometimes, these standards result from composing existing de facto standards as well.

De facto standards are not a panacea either—there are many examples of de facto standards that have different problems—for example, poor support for evolution of the standard, or widespread adoption inhibiting innovation.

The key questions to ask about *any* standard are:

- What problem does this standard address?
- What are the limitations of this standard? (That is, what problems does this standard *not* address?)
- Has the standard been successfully applied?
- Whether or not it has been applied, is the standard theoretically sound?
- Are the practical reasons for adopting this standard compelling?
- What benefits can be expected from using this standard? Alternatively, what work can be avoided by adopting the standard?
- Are there alternatives to adopting the standard? What are the costs and benefits of the alternatives?
- What strategy is in place for dealing with the evolution of the standard?
- What contingency plans are in place if the standard fails to evolve?

16.1.3 When to Adopt

One of the critical questions that every development organization must answer when faced with a new standard is when to consider adoption. How an organization affects and is affected by a standard is largely governed by how and when it chooses to adopt that standard. Both early and late adoption have advantages and disadvantages.

Some of the benefits of early adoption include:

Ability to influence the standard: Early adopters can often become significant participants in the body that is responsible for creating the standard. They may then be able to move or evolve the standard in a way that is advantageous for them, or work to exclude competitors from similar participation.

Early to market: If the standard becomes successful, early-adopter organizations are the first to benefit. If the standard can be leveraged in the product market, then the organization's products will be among the first to support the standard.

Early experience: If the standard is successful or useful, early adopters will have more experience than others with using the standard, and can leverage this experience to their benefit.

Some of the drawbacks include:

Risk of failure: If the standard ends up not being successful, early adopters can be left holding the bag. Investment in the standard will not pay off because the standard will not be supported.

Moving target: As standards are initially developed, they go through numerous changes. Early adopters will have to adapt to these changes as they occur; if they develop products based on an early version of a standard, they may not be fully standards-compliant when the standard is eventually released.

Lack of support: Early in their development, standards will not have extensive support. Certain problems may not have been ironed out. Without support, organizations may end up developing support of their own, thus negating some of the cost benefits of adopting a standard at all.

Some of the benefits of late adoption include:

Maturity of the standard: Older standards tend to be more mature. They are more stable and undergo fewer changes; the changes that are made are done through a more principled process. Bugs in the standard likely have been worked out, or at least documented and worked around.

Better support: Older standards tend to be better supported in terms of tools, documentation, training materials, and so on. This support may be developed by other organizations, and can be bought rather than developed.

Some of the drawbacks of late adoption include:

Inability to influence the standard: It is, in general, more difficult to influence a standard after it has been developed and supported for a long time. Existing organizations in the standards body will have formed a community with its own culture, and the barrier to entry into this community will gradually grow over time.

Restriction of innovation: Older standards may not track cutting-edge developments in technology or methods. Becoming attached to an older standard may limit an organization's view to innovation.

So, when should an organization adopt a standard? The answer depends on the organization's goals. If the standard will substantially influence an organization's core business, it is probably more useful for the organization to take the risk and absorb the costs of getting involved early. If the standard fails and the organization has become involved, then only the original investment is lost; if the standard succeeds and the organization has not become involved, the organization may find itself being unduly influenced by a standard it cannot control. Alternatively, if the standard is simply a tool that the organization will use to improve its own products but will not be part of its core business, then waiting for others to foot the bill for maturing the standard is a smarter decision.

16.2 SPECIFIC STANDARDS

There are many standards related to software architecture that are widely accepted and in use today. We will attempt to categorize each standard based on its primary purpose, but recognize that many of these standards are difficult to peg in any one category.

16.2.1 Conceptual Standards

Conceptual standards tend to address the range of activities that go into creating and using architecture. Because of their wide scope, they tend to provide high-level guidance. For example, many focus on what should be documented, but not how (that is, in what notation) it should be documented. Conceptual standards often dovetail with other, more specific standards for methods or notations to form more complete and detailed approaches to software and systems development.

IEEE 1471

IEEE 1471 (IEEE-SA Standards Board 2000) is an IEEE recommended practice for architectural description that is often mandated for use by government contractors and other organizations. It recognizes the importance of architecture in helping to ensure the successful development of software-intensive systems. IEEE 1471's scope is limited to architectural descriptions; that is, architectural descriptions can be conformant to the standard, while other artifacts (products, processes, organizations) cannot. Architectural descriptions are a collection of products used to document an architecture: In this book, we refer to these artifacts as architectural *models*. The standard itself does not describe a specific notation for these models, however. Instead, it only specifies a minimal amount of required content in the models.

IEEE 1471 takes a stakeholder-driven view of architectures, much as we have done in this book. Architecture descriptions in IEEE 1471 specifically identify system stakeholders and their concerns. A complete architectural description will address all the concerns of all the stakeholders, although in practice this is more often an ideal than a reality.

IEEE 1471 architecture descriptions are also composed of views that are instances of viewpoints. The IEEE 1471 notion of views and viewpoints is consistent with the one used in this book. As we have discussed, views and viewpoints organize the architecture according to stakeholder concerns. Just as the standard does not advocate the use of any particular notation, it also does not advocate the use of any particular set of viewpoints—adopters of the standard are expected to choose viewpoints that correspond to its stakeholders' concerns. The standard encourages implementers to maintain consistency among views and to document any known inconsistencies in the architecture description. It does not explain how consistency is supposed to be achieved or measured or the methods that should be employed to do so.

As a standard, IEEE 1471 is purposefully light on specification (it is difficult to call it underspecified because the limits of its scope are obvious and deliberate). The standard provides a good starting point for thinking about capturing architectures, and does not try to advocate a single approach for every domain. The definitions and concepts that it uses are more or less consistent with those found in this book.

Users must be careful not to attribute too much capability to the standard, however. Our experience is that there is a belief among many organizations that being IEEE 1471–compliant is the equivalent of "doing good architecture." In fact, being IEEE 1471–compliant indicates that a set of "architecture description" products have been developed and designated by the system's engineers, but does not ensure that these products are of high quality, that they capture the critical aspects of the system, that they are expressed in appropriate notations, or that any reasonable methodology has been used to develop and check these products for consistency. As such, IEEE 1471's contributions are largely in defining a vocabulary of concepts and their relationships to one another.

DoDAF: The Department of Defense Architecture Framework

DoDAF (DoD Architecture Framework Working Group 2004) is a U.S. Department of Defense standard for documenting system architectures. It is the successor to the previous C4ISR architecture framework and supercedes it. DoDAF (and standards like it) are often referred to as architecture frameworks. Here, "framework" generally designates a process or set of viewpoints that should be used in capturing an architecture. This sense of framework is different from the architecture implementation frameworks we discussed in Chapter 9.

Like IEEE 1471, DoDAF's contributions are mostly at the conceptual level. DoDAF more deeply prescribes the kinds of things that should be captured in an architecture description. Unlike IEEE 1471, it advocates a specific approach that is more divorced from stakeholder concerns, as it identifies specific viewpoints and the sorts of information that should be captured in each of them. Like IEEE 1471, DoDAF leaves many choices up to the user: for example, the kind of notation(s) to use to document the architecture views and how to ensure consistency among them.

DoDAF terminology conflicts somewhat with the terminology used in this book with respect to views and viewpoints. The correspondence is roughly as shown in Table 16-1. Throughout the remainder of this discussion, we will use our terminology (viewpoint set,

Concept	Our Term	DoDAF Term
A set of perspectives from which descriptions are developed	Viewpoint set	View
A perspective from which descriptions are developed	Viewpoint	(Kind of) product
An artifact describing a system from a particular perspective	View	Product

Table 16-1
*Terminology
Differences*

viewpoint, and view). However, the DoDAF standard itself uses the alternative terms (view and product).

DoDAF is a multi-viewpoint approach. The various viewpoints address architectural design decisions at many levels, from the most abstract (concepts, missions) to the reasonably detailed (individual topologies of components and connectors). DoDAF viewpoints are grouped into four sets.

The operational view (OV): Views in the OV viewpoint set identify "what needs to be accomplished, and who does it." They define processes and activities, the operational elements that are part of those activities, and the information exchanges that occur between the elements.

The systems view (SV): Views in the SV viewpoint set describe the systems that provide or support operational functions and the interconnections between them. The systems in the SV are associated with elements in the OV.

The technical standards view (TV): The views in the TV viewpoint set identify standards, (engineering) guidelines, rules, conventions, and other documents intended to ensure that implemented systems meet their requirements and are consistent with respect to the fact that they are implemented according to a common set of rules.

All views (AV): DoDAF also recognizes some cross-cutting concerns that affect all views (AV). AV views include high-level overviews of the system and the environment in which the system will be deployed and a unified dictionary that defines terms used throughout all other views.

The DoDAF viewpoints are optimized for documenting complex architectures consisting of many interconnected and communicating nodes. These architectures are often called system-of-systems because the system as a whole is made up of constituent parts that are themselves complex systems with their own architectures.

To illustrate how the DoDAF is used to model a system-of-systems, we present a Lunar Lander application modeled in a subset of the DoDAF viewpoints. An OV-1 view is a stylized graphical representation of the system's operation. It is a free-form overview of the application and important elements in it. The DoDAF views are not optimized for simple one-node systems like the basic Lunar Lander application we have covered in this book so far. However, in a more complex Lunar Lander system, communicating nodes such as ground stations, satellites, sensors, and so on might be depicted in such a view. Figure 16-1 shows an OV-1 view of a system-of-systems Lunar Lander example. Here, the Lunar Lander itself communicates with the ground utilizing a satellite to relay data to a satellite communication station, which in turn is connected to a ground station. This is the most conceptual and least rigorous DoDAF viewpoint; other OV products are less conceptual and more concrete.

Figure 16-2 shows another DoDAF OV view, an OV-4 "Organizational Relationships" view. This diagram shows the relationships among various organizations and suborganizations that are involved in a project. Here, the main space agency oversees various subagencies, with assistance from an oversight organization. One subagency, the *Lander Crew*, is expanded to show the individuals roles that are assigned to personnel within that subagency. Note that the OV-4 diagram primarily depicts the relationships between people and not technological artifacts. The blending of organizations, personnel, and technology typifies OV diagrams in DoDAF.

Figure 16-1.
*DoDAF OV-1
view of Lunar
Lander.*

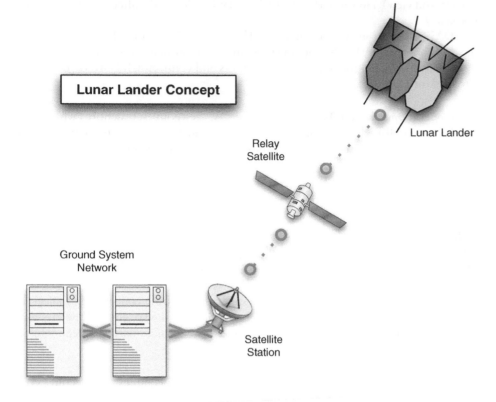

Figure 16-2.
*DoDAF OV-4
diagram of Lunar
Lander.*

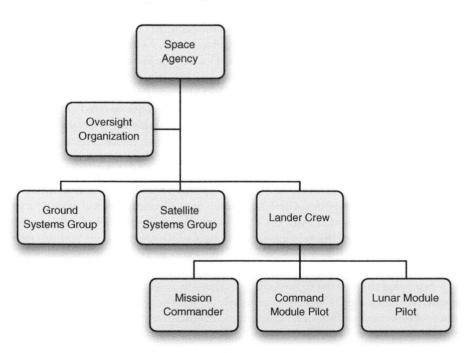

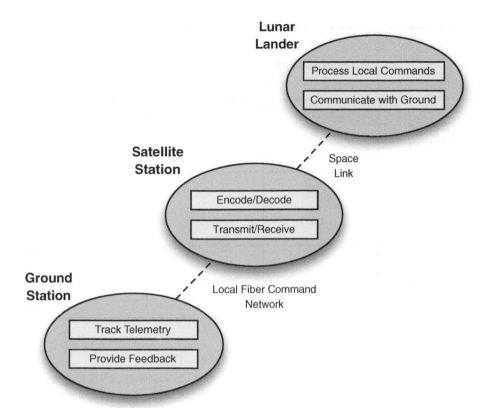

Figure 16-3.
*DoDAF SV-1
diagram of Lunar
Lander.*

DoDAF SV views tend to be more technical in nature. Figure 16-3 shows an SV-1 "Systems Interface Description" view. The nodes are intended to correspond to nodes shown in OV diagrams. This shows an initial breakdown of functional responsibilities among the nodes, as well as the interconnections between them. Many such SV-1 views can be created for the same system, depicting the system at different levels of abstraction or showing interconnections between individual functions on nodes, rather than just the nodes themselves.

DoDAF makes extensive use of what it calls matrix views, also known as "N^2 diagrams." These views are generally depicted as tables. Both axes of the table are populated with an identical set of nodes. These nodes generally represent concrete elements such as systems, subsystems, hosts, or devices. Each cell in the body of the table represents a possible interconnection between two of the nodes. If the two nodes are connected, details about the connection are listed at the intersection cell; otherwise, the cell is left blank. A matrix view contains all possible connections between elements.

Matrix views are often directly correlated with graph (that is, box-and-arrow) views of a system. Each node in the graph is listed on the axes of the table, and each line on the graph corresponds to a filled cell in the body of the table.

Figure 16-4 shows one such diagram, an SV-3 "Systems-Systems Matrix" diagram. In this diagram, the nodes on the axes are drawn from the earlier SV-1 diagram shown in Figure 16-3. Nodes on the diagonal are grayed out; communication between a node and

Figure 16-4.
DoDAF SV-3 diagram of Lunar Lander.

from \ to	Ground Station	Satellite Comm	Lunar Lander
Ground Station		Ground Feedback (TCP/IP)	
Satellite Comm	Lander Transmissions (TCP/IP)		Ground Feedback (Space Protocol)
Lunar Lander		Lander Transmissions (Space Protocol)	

itself is not considered. Each remaining node describes information exchange from the node named on the vertical axis to the node named on the horizontal axis. Nodes where no information is communicated, or no link exists (for example, from the *Ground Station* directly to the *Lunar Lander*) are left blank. Here, as with other DoDAF diagrams, the amount of detail present is determined by the user. The diagram in Figure 16-4 is relatively simple, showing only the kind of data transmitted and the protocol used. However, the DoDAF standard lists many types of information that can go in each node: status, purpose, classification level (such as unclassified or secret), means (such as the kind of network or protocol used), interface standard, and so on.

DoDAF TV products focus on identifying and tracking the technical standards that will be used to implement the described system-of-systems. DoDAF assumes that many aspects of these systems will be implemented using reusable off-the-shelf components that conform to various published standards. TV products provide ways of identifying what those standards are.

A portion of a TV-1 diagram for the Lunar Lander is shown in Figure 16-5. The leftmost column of the table shows a number of areas in which standards apply. The second column shows subareas. The DoDAF and a partner specification called the Joint Technical Architecture (JTA) enumerate these areas. Each system or subsystem, drawn from the earlier SV-1 view in this case, is associated with standards drawn from these areas. Each system or subsystem can also be given an absolute or relative time frame in which it will comply with or leverage the standard. For example, in this diagram, the *Ground Station*, *Satellite Station*, and *Lunar Lander* are all running operating systems that conform to the POSIX standard (IEEE 2004). Not all subsystems must use all selected standards, of course. Here, the *Ground Station* communicates with the *Satellite Station* using XML, sent over a Fiber Distributed Data

Standards for SV-1 Systems			Ground Station	Satellite Comm	Lunar Lander
Service	*Service Area*	*Standard*			
Information Technology Standards	Operating System Standard	ISO/IEC 9945-1:1996, Information Technology - Portable Operating System Interface (POSIX) - Part 1: System Application Program Interface (API)	Baseline: 1 Jan 2020	Baseline	Baseline + 3 mos
Information Transfer Standards	Data Flow Network	Extensible Markup Language (XML) 1.0 (Fourth Edition) W3C Recommendation 16 August 2006	Baseline + 6 mos	Baseline + 6 mos	
	Physical Layer	FDDI / ANSI X3.148-1988, Physical Layer Protocol (PHY) -- also ISO 9314-1	Baseline + 3 mos	Baseline + 3 mos	

Figure 16-5. *DoDAF TV-1 diagram for Lunar Lander.*

Interface (FDDI) physical network. Different standards (not shown here) would facilitate the communication between the *Satellite Station* and *Lunar Lander* subsystems.

DoDAF describes, in great detail, the breadth of information that can be captured in an architecture description. It also categorizes that information into viewpoints and, where appropriate, describes potential points of correspondence between viewpoints. While it introduces substantial complexity, this breadth is DoDAF's primary strength. In some sense, DoDAF can be seen as a huge checklist of items that may be useful to capture or think about in the development and modeling of a system's architecture. As with any modeling notation, users must decide for themselves the kinds of models to create, the level of detail, and so on. DoDAF offers some advice in this regard, discussing different uses for architecture models and the viewpoints that are (in whole or in part) applicable to that use. However, even with this advice, users must still decide how they want to use the DoDAF on a case-by-case basis.

DoDAF does not, in general, mandate any particular method or notation for documenting the various viewpoints. Therefore, its users can choose any subset of the viewpoints they want and document them using any notation or tool they want. To its credit, the DoDAF specification provides examples for each viewpoint, including UML examples.

However, these examples rarely exercise all possible details that can be captured in a view. Following the examples too closely would result in a set of views that left out major details. To strengthen the connection between DoDAF and UML, the OMG has submitted a request for proposals for DoDAF UML profiles (Object Management Group 2005). However, UML is not ideal for all DoDAF viewpoints (UML has no tabular diagram that would work for the matrix viewpoints, for example). Users must select notations and then weigh the advantages and disadvantages of their selection. Choosing several notations will increase the difficulty of coordinating them. Selecting a single notation might leave out important details, or make some viewpoints cumbersome.

Takeaway Message. Compared to the leanness of IEEE 1471, DoDAF takes the same high-level approach but goes into much more detail. It is optimized for capturing the relationships among people, organizations, system design decisions, and technical standards for complex and composite systems. It provides users with an extensive amount of information about *what* sorts of things to capture when developing an architecture, but far less information about *how* to capture that information or evaluate the results. Additional extensions to the standard, such as the aforementioned mapping of DoDAF views to UML, can fill in this gap. Because of the wide scope of the standard, it may be difficult for users to identify the views that are important to capture for a particular system. Because of its specificity, it may give users a false sense of security—that everything has been covered when, in fact, there are some stakeholder concerns that are being short-changed. A remedy for this is to focus first on stakeholders and concerns (as IEEE 1471 suggests) and then identify which DoDAF views map onto these concerns.

TOGAF: The Open Group Architecture Framework

The Open Group Architecture Framework (TOGAF)* (The Open Group 2003) is the product of an iterative collaborative effort by members of The Open Group, a collection of more than 200 companies and other organizations. TOGAF is an "enterprise architecture framework." It takes into account concerns beyond hardware and software, such as human factors and business considerations. Enterprise architectures tend to focus on organization-wide solutions to implement business goals. Elements in an enterprise architecture might include databases, applications such as spreadsheets and Web browsers, various client and server machines, as well as people in various roles. TOGAF borrows concepts and terminology from IEEE 1471; its notions of architecture, views, viewpoints, and so on are consistent with those discussed above in the context of IEEE 1471. Various versions of TOGAF have been developed over the years; each version has grown to encompass more aspects of architecture. TOGAF version 8 encompasses:

Business concerns, which address business strategies, organizations, and processes.

Application concerns, which address applications to be deployed, their interactions, and their relationships to business processes.

Data concerns, which address the structure of physical and logical data assets of an organization and the resources that manage these assets.

Technology concerns, which address issues of infrastructure and middleware.

---

*TOGAF is a trademark of The Open Group.

TOGAF consists of three major elements: an architecture development process called the ADM (architecture development method); a "virtual repository" of architecture assets (such as models, patterns, and architecture descriptions) extracted from architectures developed in practice, called the Enterprise Continuum; and a resource base consisting of guidelines, templates, background information, and so on to assist enterprises in following the ADM.

The centerpiece of TOGAF is the ADM, a process for developing enterprise architectures. Like many other modern software processes such as spiral model-based processes (Boehm 1988) and RUP (Kruchten 2003), ADM is iterative, meaning that activities are visited and revisited, with each subsequent iteration refining decisions made in earlier iterations. It recommends a sequence of steps and activities that should be taken, but leaves much up to the implementing organization—how to scope the project, how to make decisions within those phases, and so on. As shown in Figure 16-6, there are eight primary phases of the ADM, beginning with Architecture Vision (which is an effort to lay out

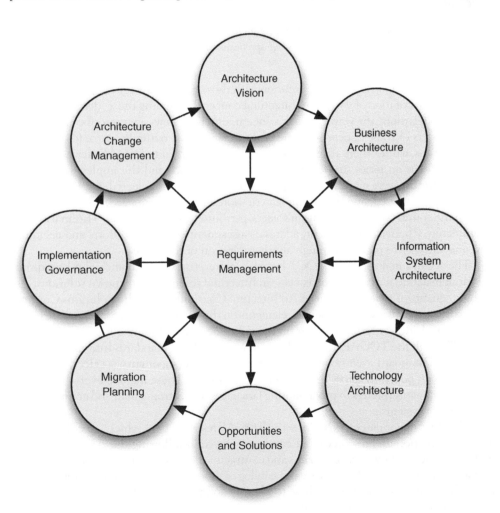

Figure 16-6.
TOGAF ADM
*process main
steps (redrawn
based on
TOGAF
specification).*

Architecture Continuum

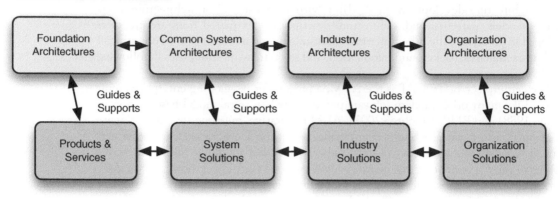

Solutions Continuum

Figure 16-7. *TOGAF Enterprise Continuum, consisting of the Architecture Continuum and the Solutions Continuum (redrawn based on TOGAF specification).*

what will be done and align the organization with those goals). Subsequent phases proceed through the elaboration of various architectural concerns including those identified above, creating models along the way. For each concern, different views are prescribed as ways to capture aspects of those concerns. Some of those views map naturally onto, for example, UML diagrams, while others are defined more generally, similar to DoDAF views. Remaining phases focus on issues surrounding reduction to practice and the implementation of the decisions that were made in earlier phases. Technologies are selected, implementation projects are prioritized, and actual implementation efforts are managed, all of which are done in the context of the organization's assets, personnel, and capabilities. The final phase, Architecture Change Management, addresses assessment of previous efforts and deciding how and whether to proceed through another iteration of the process.

The second major part of TOGAF is the "Enterprise Continuum." The Enterprise Continuum acts as a repository of assets—architectural resources and known solutions. As such, it consists of two portions: the Architecture Continuum and the Solutions Continuum, as shown in Figure 16-7. Roughly, elements on the left side of the continuum are more technological and concrete; elements on the right side address business and organizational issues. Through the TOGAF Technical Reference Model and Standards Information Base, the TOGAF standard itself taxonomizes various types of components, services, and standards that can be found across the enterprise continuum. These include everything from command-line interpreters to programming languages to electronic mail and configuration management systems.

The third major part of TOGAF is the TOGAF resource base, which is a collection of useful information and resources that can be employed in following the ADM process. It includes advice on how to set up boards and contracts for managing architecture, checklists for various phases of the ADM process, a catalog of different models that exist for evaluating architectures, information on how to identify and prioritize different skills needed to develop architectures, and much more.

TOGAF is distinguished from other approaches by its large size and broad scope; the summary in this section only covers the major elements of the standard. TOGAF focuses on *enterprise* architecture, which is different in character from the kind of software architecture discussed in this book. Enterprise architecture is as much about the architecture of an organization as the architectures of its products. Elements in TOGAF architectures tend to be organizations, people, and large-grained assets (applications, platforms, machines, enterprise-wide services, and so on). Otherwise, TOGAF collects a large and diverse set of best practices for architecture. It prescribes not only an architecture development process, but defines a wide variety of views and concerns, as well as solution elements that can be used to satisfy those concerns.

Takeaway Message. TOGAF complements other architectural approaches by taking into account more business and organizational concerns. Its high-level approach, focusing on enterprise architecture, means that it is best used for dealing with coarse-grained elements and assets, constructing entire information systems and not just software applications. Like DoDAF, TOGAF provides a substantial set of best practices to follow and checklists to use for assessment, but individual users are responsible for the details. Following TOGAF helps to ensure thoroughness, but not necessarily quality.

RM-ODP

RM-ODP (ISO/IEC 1998) is an ISO standard for describing open distributed processing (ODP) systems. Although the characteristics of ODP systems are described over several pages of the RM-ODP standard, they can generally be described as information systems developed to run in an environment of independent, heterogeneous processing nodes connected by a network. Primarily, the RM-ODP standard defines five viewpoints and describes associated viewpoint languages for documenting the architecture of an ODP system. These viewpoints are:

Enterprise: A viewpoint focusing on the system, its environment, and its surrounding context.

Information: A viewpoint focusing on information and information processing.

Computational: A viewpoint focusing on the architectural structure of the system and how different components or objects are distributed across hosts.

Engineering: A viewpoint focusing on the infrastructure required to support distribution.

Technology: A viewpoint focusing on technology choices for the system.

These viewpoints (and their associated languages) have various levels of concreteness. The computational and engineering viewpoints are more concrete and thus more constrained because they have the goal of helping to guarantee interoperability and portability of components. The enterprise and information viewpoints are more general, and therefore their languages are less constrained.

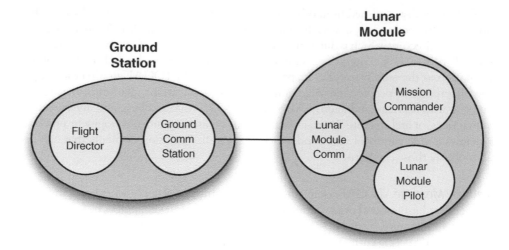

Figure 16-8 shows a sample RM-ODP enterprise view. Enterprise view elements include personnel and high-level application components, reminiscent of the kinds of elements addressed by TOGAF. The enterprise viewpoint looks at the system holistically, in terms of overall scope and its place inside the larger organization. Enterprise views can also describe agency boundaries—boundaries of responsibility or control.

In contrast, Figure 16-9 shows an example RM-ODP engineering view. This view shows how a ground system might communicate with a Lunar Lander via a complex communication channel implemented by two communicating network stacks. Here, the elements are more technologically oriented, and human elements do not appear. In general, both these views would be accompanied by text explaining the diagrams, the various elements, and their interconnections. The notation used above, with ovals and interconnections, is used in the RM-ODP specification but is not canonical: Many different notations (including, for example, UML) could be used to draw these diagrams.

Like DoDAF and TOGAF, RM-ODP focuses on *what* kinds of things should be modeled in an architecture, but not specifically *how* those things should be modeled. RM-ODP goes a step further than these two standards, however: Instead of prescribing a particular notation for each viewpoint, the RM-ODP specification prescribes a number of characteristics that a notation describing the viewpoint must have. Therefore, RM-ODP viewpoint languages are not languages in the traditional sense, but rather sets of requirements for languages. RM-ODP does include a separate specification describing, at a very high level, how various formal specification languages [for example, LOTOS (ISO 1989), Z (Spivey 1988), or SDL-92 (Telecommunication Standardization Sector of ITU 2002)] could be used to describe architectural semantics for RM-ODP architectures. Here, it lists an RM-ODP concept, and then identifies a formal specification language concept that could be used to implement that concept. This level of correspondence is not enough to give users serious guidance as to how to leverage these formal specification languages to implement RM-ODP.

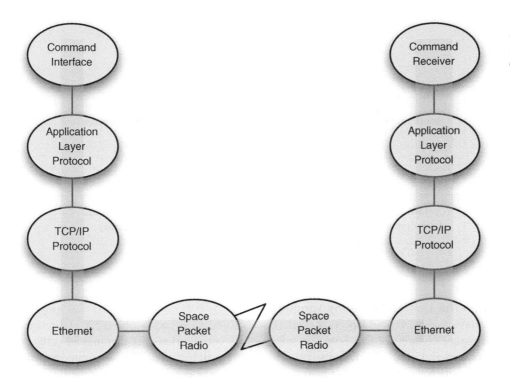

Figure 16-9.
*Sample
RM-ODP
engineering view.*

Takeaway Message. As a standard, RM-ODP is very similar to DoDAF, although the number of viewpoints is more limited and focused. Like DoDAF, an architecture specified according to the RM-ODP standard may or may not achieve certain qualities; the primary value added by RM-ODP is to ensure that architects think about and document certain aspects of architecture that impact various qualities—distributability, interoperability, and so on. It is eventually up to the architects to actually ensure those qualities. Although some mappings between RM-ODP concepts and formal methods are specified, there is a large gap between them that must be bridged by individual users. This gap is too large to assert that RM-ODP is particularly supportive of formal analysis activities.

16.2.2 Notational Standards

Notational standards define standard notations for writing down design decisions. Notational standards can be used to realize/implement certain elements of conceptual standards; for example, a notation such as UML can be used as a way of documenting the various DoDAF views. In a way, any codified architecture description language, such as those surveyed in Chapter 6, could be viewed as a de facto notational standard. In this section, we examine notations that have actually gone through a standardization process or committee and that have gained notoriety or use because they are standards.

Figure 16-10.
*UML diagram
without profile.*

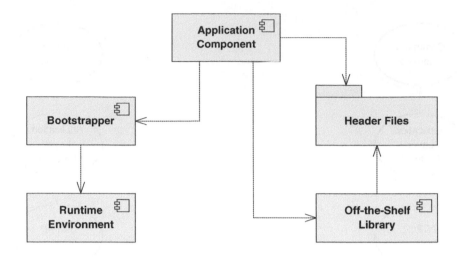

UML—The Unified Modeling Language

We have covered various aspects of UML (Booch, Rumbaugh, and Jacobson 2005) through-out earlier chapters of this book: its notation, its visualizations, its metamodel (Object Management Group 2002), and so on. This section will focus on UML as a standard and describe its advantages and disadvantages from that perspective.

UML provides a standard *syntax* for describing a wide variety of aspects of software systems. Basic UML (without extensions) prescribes very few semantics to go along with this syntax. It is possible for the same element or diagram to mean entirely different things. For example, the dashed arrow connector in UML indicates a dependency between two linked elements. That dependency could mean "needed to build" or "plugs-into" or "calls." There is no way, without additional context or information, for a stakeholder to look at a dependency arrow in UML and have any clear idea what it means. This situation is depicted in Figure 16-10—the dependencies are all specified but the reader knows little about them.

UML that follows only the basic standard establishes a common symbolic representa-tion of elements and their relationships. The fact that a system is described in UML implies little about the quality of that system—good designs can be documented in UML as easily as bad ones.

UML's value can be substantially increased through the use of UML extensions and profiles. Recall that a UML profile is a coordinated set of extensions to UML. In a way, UML profiles are themselves standards that specialize the base UML standard for different domains. OMG, the organization that manages the UML standard, also manages a num-ber of de jure standard UML profiles, including profiles for CORBA systems, enterprise application integration, and system engineering. The latter, called SysML, is discussed below.

Profiles may include stereotypes, tagged values, and constraints. UML stereotypes allow users to specialize existing UML symbols to add project- or domain-specific semantics. Stereotypes can specialize the dependency arrow to mean <<calls>> or

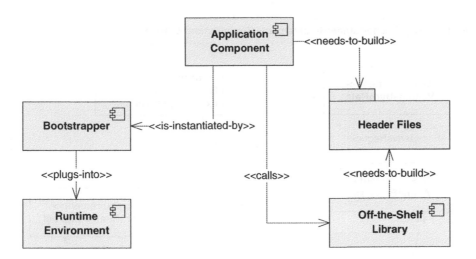

Figure 16-11.
*UML diagram
with profile.*

<<needed-to-build>> or <<plugs-into>>. For example, Figure 16-11 shows the same UML diagram as Figure 16-10, except the dependencies are stereotyped. This diagram is much more readable and provides substantially more information. To be fully useful, however, a UML profile for a project *must* be accompanied by detailed documentation explaining when and how to use the various stereotypes, tagged values, and constraints, as well as their meaning. With the proper use of profiles, a UML description becomes a valuable tool for stakeholder communication and system understanding, and also has positive impacts on traceability and analyzability.

Even with profiles, however, UML and its accompanying tools are (currently) not well-suited to the verification of specific quality properties. Will the described system satisfy its requirements? Be efficient? Be cost-effective? Be free of deadlock? To determine answers to questions like these, additional methods above and beyond UML, ranging from inspections to testing to formal verification, must be integrated separately into the development process.

Takeaway Message. UML is not a panacea for architecture-based software development. UML provides a set of common, symbolic notations for architects to write down and communicate certain kinds of design decisions. The diagram types that have been provided in UML allow architects to model a wide variety of concepts, although there are certainly architectural design decisions that cannot be easily captured in UML. UML profiles should be used to improve the rigor and understandability of UML diagrams, but profiles have their limits. Profiles can decorate existing diagrams, but they cannot create entirely new diagrams. Modeling a system in UML makes few guarantees about that system—UML can be used to document both good and bad architectures (although UML does make it easier to understand, communicate about, and evaluate architectures).

16.2.3 SysML

Despite the wide variety of modeling concepts supported in UML, different engineering efforts require even more modeling breadth. A good example of this is SysML (SysML Partners 2005). SysML is an effort by a coalition of more than twenty engineering organizations (primarily corporations, but also universities and other organizations) (SysML.org 2007)

Figure 16-12.
*SysML
requirement
diagram for
Lunar Lander.*

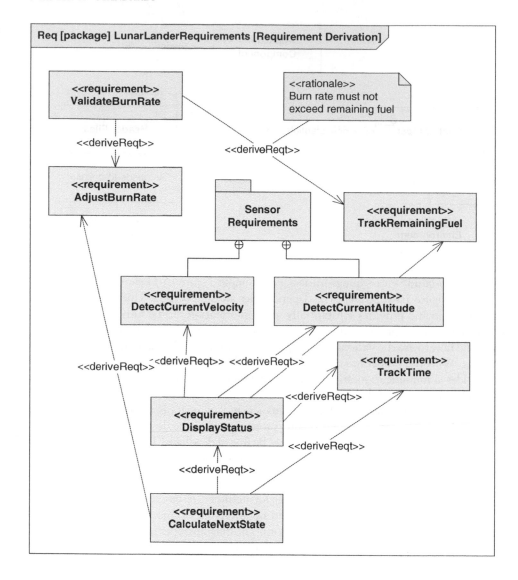

to customize UML for systems engineering. With respect to standardization, the SysML community has taken an interesting two-pronged approach. One group is developing and promulgating an open-source version of the SysML standard under a license that allows users to redistribute and modify SysML on their own. From this open-source version, an official OMG standard version of SysML has been created. "OMG SysML" is trademarked, and evolves, like UML, through the standards committees and processes of the OMG.

Many individuals and organizations perceive UML to be too software-biased for modeling systems engineering concerns that include elements such as hardware, networks, development organizations, and so on. Of course, many UML diagrams can be interpreted in ways that do capture these concerns (for example, a traditional systems engineering block diagram closely resembles a class diagram in many ways). SysML includes a subset of UML, but also extends it. Diagrams reused from UML are the activity, class, composite structure, package, sequence, state machine, and use case diagrams. Two of these diagrams are renamed for SysML: Class diagrams are called "block definition" diagrams and composite structure diagrams are called "internal block" diagrams. SysML also adds stereotypes to UML as well as two new diagram types: requirement and parametric diagrams. Requirement diagrams show system requirements and their relationships with other elements. Parametric diagrams show parametric constraints between structural elements, which are useful for performance and quantitative analysis.

Figure 16-12 shows a SysML requirement diagram for the Lunar Lander application. This diagram shows only requirements and their relationships; a more complex requirement diagram might actually include additional detail for each requirement such as the actual text describing the requirement, a unique ID, and so on. Requirement diagrams can also be used to associate requirements with elements from other diagrams such as use cases. Syntactically, requirement diagrams primarily reuse and specialize elements from class diagrams, using stereotypes on classes and relationships to make those elements specific to requirement diagrams.

Figure 16-13 shows a SysML parametric diagram. Parametric diagrams are specializations of SysML internal block diagrams—composite structure diagrams in UML. These diagrams allow architects to associate quantitative parameters with various model elements. These parameters can then be associated with mathematical models, equations, or analysis techniques that can be used to evaluate or assess parts of the system quantitatively. For example, several state-storage elements (the *Clock*, the *Lander State*) provide values to the next-state equation, which is used to calculate the next state of the Lunar Lander simulation.

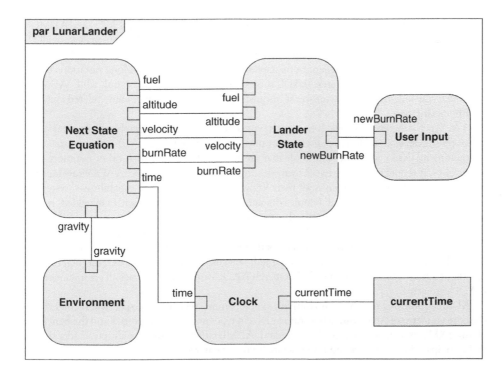

Figure 16-13.
SysML parametric diagram for Lunar Lander.

The development of SysML is consistent with our earlier assertion that UML is not necessarily a complete solution for architectural modeling. The SysML developers left out certain UML diagrams they believed were extraneous or unnecessary, and added new diagrams that were missing. SysML has not been as universally supported or adopted as UML, despite the fact that it is not a radical departure from traditional UML 2. Tool support in the form of modeling environments, for example, has lagged behind UML, and while some UML modeling environments such as Telelogic Rhapsody have some explicit SysML support, many others do not. This indicates that even a large group of influential organizations cannot necessarily force the adoption of any particular standard. Note also that even the new SysML diagrams reuse and overload existing UML symbols, likely a compromise to provide some degree of modeling support in tools that are not SysML-aware.

Takeaway Message. SysML is an example of how standards can evolve, change, and fork apart. By reusing substantial parts of the UML standard, the SysML partners were able to save a tremendous amount of effort as well as allow users to apply their existing UML knowledge in a systems-engineering context. However, the changes and extensions they made to UML—conservative as they are—have been a double-edged sword. On one hand, they provide increased expressiveness for systems engineers. On the other hand, they have reduced the amount of tool support that exists for users. Even standards that are supported by a substantial amount of influential organizations must still win many hearts and minds on technical and business merits to achieve widespread success.

A Tale of Two Standards

Chapter 6 described two modeling languages, AADL (Feiler, Lewis, and Vestal 2003) and ADML (Spencer 2000), from a technical perspective. However, these two modeling languages are also standards—AADL is standardized by the Society of Automotive Engineers (SAE) and ADML is standardized by The Open Group. Both standards describe new, stand-alone notations that can be used to model architectures. AADL is becoming increasingly successful, while ADML has effectively failed. Why? The answer is not necessarily clear or simple; many related factors are interacting here.

AADL is a complex language. It has a rich syntax and, to an extent, graphical visualizations still are being developed. However, the primary motivation for adopting AADL is that it provides compelling analysis capabilities and tools that are not easy to obtain with other notations or approaches. It is not just a minor tweak to an existing notation such as UML. AADL's developers began by focusing on a community of users known to need its unique capabilities—systems engineers in the automotive and avionics domains, and others working with embedded, real-time system development. Leveraging the existing support and user community of UML is also part of the AADL strategy; a UML profile for AADL is being developed and refined. In AADL's case, standardization is only a small part of why AADL seems to be winning hearts and minds. Providing novel capabilities, making judicious use of other standards, and targeting a specific community of users with needs that match AADL's unique capabilities all are influencing AADL's growth.

ADML, compared to AADL, is relatively simple. From a technical perspective, it combines the core concepts of Acme with a few innovations in types and meta-properties and the benefits of using XML as a meta-language. As a standard, ADML failed to achieve widespread adoption, and anticipated tool support and interoperability never emerged.

It is difficult to say why. Unlike AADL, ADML's improvements over previous technologies are incremental. ADML was not targeted at a specific domain or user community, although some ADML documentation notes its usefulness in enterprise architecture modeling and points out deficiencies in UML in this regard. ADML may have also suffered because of the availability of contemporary alternatives such as Acme, Darwin, and xADL 1.0, lack of initial tools to help motivate community growth, and so on.

On a positive note, however, many of the concepts of ADML did eventually appear in UML 2 (and thus also in XMI). UML already had a huge user base, and these contributions shored up support for structural modeling that was considered to be a deficiency of UML 1.x. The ideas of the ADML standard were much better received when they became part of UML. Of course, defining a new standard like ADML is much easier than convincing the already-mature UML community to incorporate these new ideas. However, ADML's contributions were a natural fit, addressing well-known drawbacks of UML. Incorporating a complex standard with many new and conflicting ideas like AADL into UML would likely cause much more friction in the UML community, and may be infeasible.

There are several lessons to be learned from the AADL and ADML experience. Standardization alone does not ensure the success of an approach. Success is largely dependent on the size and passion of the user community surrounding the approach, and standardization is just one way to catalyze the development of a community. Another important element is to "prime the pump" with support for the standard: Developing initial tools, documentation, and training for a standard, even if they are not perfect, can entice early adopters much more than a simple specification. For incremental improvements, or improving deficiencies in an existing standard, it is often best to focus efforts on improving or evolving the existing standard rather than trying to develop a new, parallel standard.

16.2.4 Standard Tools

Many organizational cultures will standardize on a particular tool as much as (or more than) more abstract approaches. Corporations often evaluate a spectrum of tools and then purchase one (or a small number) of them in bulk, and that tool becomes mandatory for use within the company. Standard tools tend to be de facto standards, because they generally are developed and controlled by a single organization.

Standard UML Tools

The wide adoption of the UML standard generally induces organizations to adopt one or more standard tools for working with UML. This is often motivated by a desire for consistency and interoperability across an organization, as well as market pressures: Organizations buying tools from a single vendor can often get volume discounts and negotiate enhanced support agreements. UML itself, however, is not bound to any particular tool. Tools that have become de facto standards for UML editing include IBM's Rational Rose (Rational Software Corporation 2003), Microsoft Visio (Microsoft Corporation 2007), Telelogic System Architect (Telelogic AB 2007), ArgoUML (Argo/UML), and others.

These tools vary in their exclusivity of support for UML. Tools such as ArgoUML and Rose focus their support almost exclusively on UML, while tools such as Visio and System Architect support diagrams in many notations. All the tools support the creation and manipulation of UML diagrams, generally through a point-and-click graphical interface. The form of this interface—what menu options are available and so on—depends on the individual tool. UML does not standardize how users are to interact with these diagrams. For example, Rose uses a tree-based view to organize diagrams within the model and property sheets to decorate various model elements.

The tools differ widely in their support for additional capabilities beyond plain UML modeling: design aids, artifact generation, constraint analysis, and so on. Sometimes, third parties will create plug-ins for the tools that add additional features.

A generic diagramming tool such as PowerPoint can be (and often is) used to create UML diagrams, even though it has no specific understanding of UML's (graphical) syntax and semantics. These tools, then, cannot provide any guidance to UML users to help create consistent or complete documents. UML-aware tools, on the other hand, provide design guidance as users create and edit UML. These features include:

Support for UML's built-in extension mechanisms: Recall that UML profiles allow users to specialize elements and introduce additional commonalities among them. UML tools may allow a user to define stereotypes and manage associated tagged values, applying the stereotype's tagged values to all elements of the stereotype, for example. The user interface may also provide new options when stereotypes are applied: The visual appearance of an element may change (adding an icon, for example) and new options may be presented to the user to manipulate the properties associated with that stereotype.

Support for consistency checks: The ability to specify and automatically check constraints can increase stakeholders' confidence in the quality of the architecture. Most UML tools guide the user in making syntactically correct UML documents. The syntactic constraints of UML are generally basic well-formedness checks—that links have valid endpoints, or that two elements do not have the same name, for example.

Many tools go further, and allow the user to check semantic and cross-diagram consistency constraints. For example, a tool may warn a user when a sequence diagram indicates an invocation on an object whose class does not implement a method with the same name as the message. Not all of these constraints are necessarily part of the UML standard, but they are commonly accepted conventions about particular relationships in UML and help to increase the internal consistency of UML models. One danger in this regard is that users of a particular tool may not be able to distinguish easily which constraints are part of UML itself, and which are just being enforced by the local tool.

Beyond these generic syntactic and semantic checks, UML includes a constraint language, OCL (Warmer and Kleppe 1998), that allows users to specify constraints on UML elements and element relationships. Tools are available that can assist users in specifying OCL constraints, and then check them automatically. UML does not mandate the use of OCL as its only constraint language, however, so it is possible for UML tools to incorporate additional constraint languages.

Generation of other artifacts: UML models can be used as the basis for generating artifacts useful in other life cycle activities, such as implementation or testing. Some UML tools include facilities for generating these artifacts, or parts of them. For example, Rose has an internal tool called SODA that focuses on the generation of other artifacts from Rose models. SODA effectively transforms UML models into other formats using user-definable templates. Different templates will transform UML models into different kinds of artifacts: One template may output documentation in a Microsoft Word file; a different template may take the same UML model and generate code skeletons for each of the defined classes. Automatic generation of artifacts that are important in non-design phases of the software engineering life cycle (such as code artifacts for the implementation phase) is especially useful in preventing architectural drift and architectural erosion.

Generation of UML: Some UML tools can take other artifacts (usually implemented systems) and automatically generate partial UML models for them. For example, some tools can iterate over a series of Java classes and automatically generate a corresponding class diagram. These inferences are not always 100 percent correct or useful. They may fail to make inferences about dependencies between classes because a mechanism such as dynamic class-loading or reflection is used. They may also generate every class dependency, when only some of them are architecturally important. For this reason, automatically generated UML needs to be reviewed and "tuned" by hand.

Traceability to other systems: Generation is not the only connection that UML tools may use to interoperate with other artifacts; traceability and links can be used as well. Linking mechanisms may be provided to connect UML elements with system requirements in a requirements management environment such as Telelogic DOORS (Telelogic DOORS), with configuration management repositories, with code-based integrated development environments, with simulation environments, and so on. When such links are available, additional consistency constraints can be checked as well. This can extend the scope of a UML modeling environment beyond UML itself and incorporate other architectural (and nonarchitectural) concerns into the modeling process.

Takeaway Message. UML tools have a profound effect on how users experience modeling in UML. While all tools provide basic support for drawing UML diagrams, the real value in the tools often comes from features provided above and beyond basic drawing: checking additional constraints above and beyond "plain" UML, customizability, generation of other artifacts, reverse engineering code, traceability to other artifacts managed in different environments, and so on. These features generally automate processes that would otherwise be tedious, manual, and error-prone. It is important to be cognizant of any differences between the standard UML language and peculiarities or limitations introduced by specific UML tools. Also, UML tools may lag behind the latest developments in the UML standard itself.

16.2.5 Telelogic System Architect

Telelogic System Architect (formerly Popkin System Architect) (Telelogic AB 2007) is a popular tool among system engineers. It is used to manage diagrams of many different views of a system in multiple diagrammatic styles. It has support for more then fifty different types of diagrams drawn from different modeling methodologies—all the UML diagrams, IDEF, OMT, generic flowcharting, and more. Beyond the basic System Architect tool, a number of variants are also marketed: for DoDAF, for Service Oriented Architectures, for designing enterprise-resource planning (ERP) systems, and so on.

System Architect can support this wide breadth of diagram types because of its internal construction. Internally, diagram data is stored in a relational database that is updated as the user creates and manipulates diagrams. Each diagram type is associated with a particular vocabulary of symbols and interconnections, as well as constraints that assist the user in creating syntactically correct diagrams.

System Architect is an example of a "standard" tool that trades semantic strength for breadth. It can be viewed as a very good domain-specific diagram editor. That is, it has specific support for drawing diagrams with the syntax of UML, IDEF, OMT, or any number of other types of diagrams. However, it has little understanding of the semantics of these diagrams. The specialized versions of the product (for example, System Architect for DoDAF) have some additional semantic knowledge built in such as the ability to generate or check the consistency of different diagram types.

Takeaway Message. Telelogic System Architect is a de facto standard, flexible drawing tool that gives users a plethora of diagram types in which to express architectural decisions. On one hand, the construction of the tool makes it very easy for Telelogic to incorporate new diagram types and adapt to new diagrammatic languages and standards that emerge. However, this comes at the cost of having more limited associated support for the semantics of those notations. In System Architect, it is certainly easier to draw diagrams with complex syntactic vocabularies than in a completely generic tool like PowerPoint, but it provides little guidance to users as to the quality, correctness, or consistency of their architectures.

16.3 PROCESS STANDARDS

The standards we have covered thus far are mostly related to how to capture an architecture, either conceptually, in a specific notation, or using a particular tool. Process standards dictate the process—that is, the steps—that are used to develop software. These standards focus less on artifacts and more on the methods used to create them.

16.3.1   Rational Unified Process

The Rational Unified Process (RUP) (Kruchten 2003) is a standard that was created by the Rational Software Corporation, now IBM. Fundamentally, the RUP is an iterative process, and is inspired by Barry Boehm's spiral model (Boehm 1988). Rather than prescribing a single, concrete sequence of steps to follow when developing software, the RUP is an adaptable process *framework*, intended to encompass many different iterative processes and to be tailored for each of them. RUP describes software construction as a whole and is not focused primarily on architectural development (like TOGAF's ADM).

A RUP project is done in *phases*. The RUP identifies four specific phases:

Inception phase: The inception phase includes initial activities that determine the goals and success criteria for an iteration; it includes making a business case, describing basic use cases, assessing risks, establishing budgets, and so on.

Elaboration phase: Here, use cases are further elaborated and architectural design decisions are made to satisfy them. Business plans and risk assessments made in the inception phase are refined and revisited. Prototypes may be developed.

Construction phase: This phase largely encompasses the implementation and construction of elements that are designed and specified in the elaboration phase.

Transition phase: In this phase, the developed product is transitioned to the end users. It is validated and tested, and its functionality and quality are assessed against the goals set in the inception phase. Deployment, installation, and training are performed in this phase.

The goal of each phase is to reach a *milestone*. For example, the inception phase ends with the "Life Cycle Objective Milestone," which requires stakeholder agreement on scope, cost, and schedule, elaboration of high-level use cases, agreement on credible risk assessments, and so on. Internally, each phase consists of smaller activities apportioned to various personnel. These activities are broken up by *disciplines* such as requirements, design, implementation, testing, and so on. Iterations of these activities may occur within each phase. While the inception phase is expected to be short and is usually done in a single iteration, the other phases often involve multiple iterations.

Figure 16-14 shows the relationship among phases, iterations, and disciplines in a hypothetical instance of RUP. Time proceeds from left to right. Note how the development

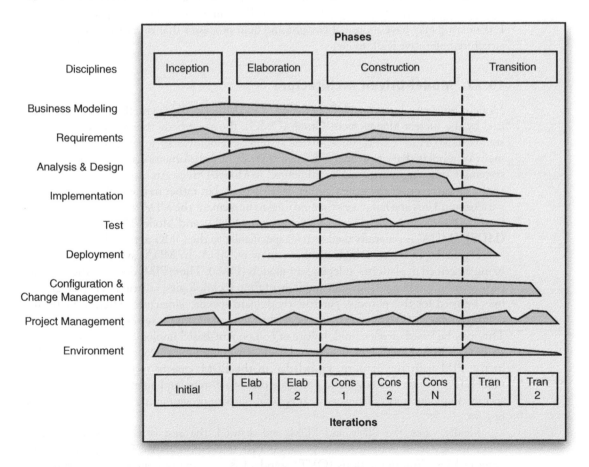

Figure 16-14. *Rational Unified Process phases, iterations, and disciplines (adapted from Kroll and Kruchten, The Rational Unified Process Made Easy: A Practitioner's Guide to the RUP).*

effort is partitioned by the phases and iterations occur within each phase. The dotted breakpoints between the phases indicate milestones that must be reached. Although all disciplines may be addressed during each phase/iteration, some disciplines are more prominent than others in different phases. For example, very little implementation occurs in the inception phase (perhaps proofs-of-concept or initial prototypes), while a large amount occurs during the construction phase. Likewise, requirements are a heavy focus during inception but are only revised and refined during the construction phase.

Takeaway Message. Ever since the development of the spiral model, software engineers have widely recognized that the use of iteration and risk analysis are important. RUP is a meta-process or process framework in which many iterative (and linear) processes are instances. For example, one could view the traditional waterfall model as a single-iteration instance of RUP. RUP has a tendency to view architecture as a design artifact, rather than as a pervasive discipline—as we have advocated in this book—but the two notions are not entirely incompatible. RUP is not necessarily a universal meta-process; certain development strategies such as Extreme Programming or Domain-Specific Software Engineering may have more lightweight and fluid processes that do not fit naturally in a structured, iterative RUP model.

16.3.2 Model-Driven Architecture

Model-Driven Architecture (MDA) (Mukerji and Miller 2003) is a methodology standardized by the Object Management Group (OMG), the same body that manages the UML standard. MDA aims to reconceptualize system development by leveraging the development of models that are refined, through a series of transformations, into implemented systems. Confusingly, the word "architecture" in Model-Driven Architecture does not refer to the architecture of the system under development, but rather to the architecture of the various standards and languages that are used to implement the MDA approach. Synonyms for MDA include Model-Driven Development (MDD) and Model-Driven Engineering (MDE); "MDA" is generally used to refer specifically to the OMG approach.

Figure 16-15 shows a high-level overview of MDA. In MDA, systems start out by being described in platform-independent models (PIMs). These PIMs describe the application without binding it to specific implementation technologies; any number of languages may be used for this purpose, particularly domain-specific languages. Then, a platform-definition model (PDM) is used to specify the target platform for system implementation. This may be based on some middleware or component-based implementation technology such as CORBA, .NET, JavaBeans, and so on. By combining the application knowledge in the PIM with the platform knowledge in the PDM, one or more platform-specific models (PSMs) are created. These PSMs are part of a system implementation in a domain-specific implementation language or a general-purpose programming language such as C or Java.

Ideally, once the PIMs and PDMs are defined, the rest of the translations can occur using (or at least leveraging) automated translation tools. The separate OMG Queries/Views/Transformations (QVT) standard is one way of defining model transformations. Assuming the translations are correct and preserve salient properties, the result of MDA should be a system that is faithful to the original models.

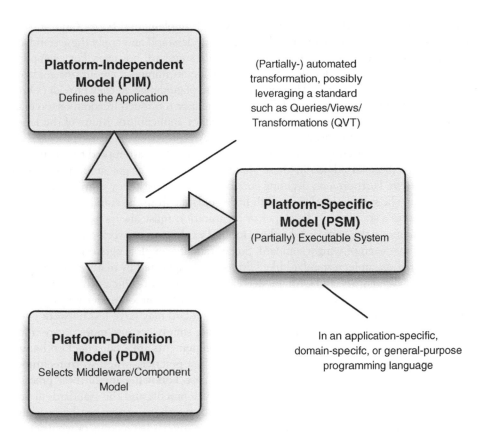

Figure 16-15.
*High-level
overview of
MDA.*

Takeaway Message. As a general approach, MDA is compatible with many of the mechanisms and ideas espoused in this book. For example, Chapter 9 on implementation discusses how generative technologies can be used to automatically generate (partial) implementations from architectural models, especially when an architecture implementation framework is used. The idea behind MDA is easy to grasp, but the practical details are somewhat more elusive. Making automated transformations from models into implementation artifacts is difficult. Developing completely platform-independent models of an application also is hard to do, since knowledge of available implementation technologies always informs and constrains architectures. MDA is much easier to employ in the context of DSSE, where a well-understood and constrained domain, reference architectures, and existing frameworks provide a much better-elaborated foundation.

16.4 END MATTER

This chapter has attempted to provide high-level overviews of some of the most popular and well-known standards used in practice. One thing that is not evident from this chapter is the level of detail at which many of these standards are specified. Specifications for some of the standards exceed the length of this book, and supplemental books (and, in some cases, book *series*) have been written to help people understand and apply these standards.

Size is rarely a good way to assess the value of a standard, however. For example, it stands to reason that large, detailed standards provide an immense amount of guidance, and indeed this is often the case. However, what kind of guidance do they provide? Often, large standards remain underspecified: They give the user too much freedom or too many options, often in an attempt to broaden their appeal or applicability. Many of the largest and broadest standards (for instance, DoDAF, TOGAF) prescribe extensive processes and checklists. These are often impossibly detailed—a project that attempted to satisfy every requirement or piece of advice in these standards would never get around to actually building a system. Furthermore, deciding correctness and consistency is an exercise most often left up to the system developers, with little guidance from the standards.

When using a standard, a developer or organization must always keep in mind the costs and benefits of the standard. Looking for and exploiting network effects should be a priority of anyone employing a standard. Some standards exploit network effects better than others. For example, a standard like UML is well supported by mature tools because of its large user community, and UML models can be used to more efficiently communicate ideas among different people and organizations because of common understanding of the meaning of different symbols. However, a process standard may have less network effect: The value of the process does not necessarily increase simply because more organizations use the it, unless improved tool support or process refinements are a side effect of that use.

The standards in this chapter document many best practices—well-worn techniques that have been successfully used on projects in the past. Following any of these practices is undoubtedly better than a completely ad hoc development, and the standards at least provide a yardstick against which completeness or comprehensiveness can be measured. Many important decisions, such as when enough modeling has been done, or what specific process to follow, or how to define individual project goals still must be made on a case-by-case basis. More specific and detailed guidance will not be found in the most generic (and unfortunately, well-known and well-supported) standards. Developers may have more luck combining the breadth of generic standards with more specific domain-specific standards—if such standards exist.

Standards are a big part of using software architecture in practice: Their creation, development, and use are motivated as much by business and organizational goals as technical ones. In the next chapter, we continue the theme of software architecture in practice by focusing on organizational concerns: people, roles, and teams.

The Business Case	From a business perspective, standards can be seen as a make-or-buy decision. Adopting a standard confers many benefits: Adopters are essentially buying the experience and time of previous engineering efforts, vendors, and so on. As those organizations evolve the standard, the quality of the standard is upgraded, effectively for free, and organizations can make decisions on when and whether to move to the latest version of a standard.
	Standards provide tremendous value by creating network effects: The more organizations that use the standard, the more valuable the standard becomes. If multiple organizations are involved in a single development effort, standards are often the best way to minimize communication breakdowns and integration difficulties that can kill an otherwise successful project.

When dealing with standards, businesses must keep in mind two primary threats. The first is becoming overly invested in or faithful to a particular approach when that is not warranted. The most reasonable approach is to adopt the standards that make sense, but prepare for a moderate investment in figuring out how to tailor those standards for your purposes.

Many businesses and organizations adopt standards with the mistaken assumption that all their business problems will be addressed if they simply follow the standard to the letter. As we have attempted to convey in this chapter, many of the most well-known, well-supported, and popular standards are often the most general and underspecified. Keeping a rational perspective on the scope of these standards is a must for any development organization. Organizations should define their business goals and the strategies for achieving them independently of any particular standard, and then choose and adapt standards that help them meet their goals based on those strategies.

The second threat is ignoring a standard that eventually becomes popular and finding the standard manipulated by competitors. For this reason, many large companies simply participate in every standardization process related to their business. For organizations that do not have the resources to do this, a more judicious and agile approach is appropriate. These organizations should minimally track the development of all relevant standards, but internally avoid getting too attached to any one standard.

16.5 REVIEW QUESTIONS

1. What is a standard?
2. What is the difference between a de facto and de jure standard?
3. What is a network effect? How do standards help to create a network effect?
4. What are some drawbacks of standards?
5. What are the advantages and disadvantages of adopting a standard early? What are the advantages and disadvantages of adopting a standard late?
6. What is the scope of IEEE 1471? How does it advise and guide users?
7. Describe DoDAF. How does DoDAF help its users? What does DoDAF not provide?
8. What is TOGAF and how does it differ from DoDAF? What is the difference between enterprise architec-

tures and software architectures, as they have been described in this book?
9. What are the five RM-ODP viewpoints? What kinds of systems is RM-ODP targeted for?
10. What are UML profiles and how do they help users in applying the UML standard?
11. What is SysML and how does it differ from UML?
12. What lessons can be learned from the standardization efforts behind ADML and AADL?
13. Enumerate some standard architecture tools. How do standard tools augment standard notations? How can they hinder the use of a standard notation?
14. Enumerate some process standards. How do process standards augment and interact with other standards?

16.6 EXERCISES

1. Obtain and read one of the standards listed in this chapter. Choose a system with which you are familiar (or one of the ones used as an example in this book, such as Lunar Lander or the World Wide Web) and outline how it would be described or implemented using that standard. Identify the standard's strengths and weaknesses in the context of your experience.

2. Draw out and discuss the relationships between the standards discussed in this chapter. Are they mutually exclusive? Do they dovetail with one another? Are they sequential? Identify some software development standards not discussed in this chapter and add them to your diagram.

3. Find an architectural model that claims to conform to one of the standards in this chapter. Check it for conformance against the standard itself.

4. Choose a standard and investigate how it is described and marketed by its creators and others. Assess whether the benefits (and drawbacks) claimed of the standard are accurate or not.

5. Contact one or more software development practitioners and find out about their use of standards. Ask what benefits they believe they are deriving from the use of the standard, and assess whether their development experiences have borne these out.

6. Find a tool set that purports to support a particular standard. Select various elements of the standard and determine how they are supported by the tool set. Identify how the tools help or hinder the use of the standard.

16.7 FURTHER READING

This chapter attempts to distill and extract the essence of some of the most well-known and influential standards in software engineering today. Still, the few pages dedicated to each standard cannot capture the scope of most of them. As noted above, the length of several of these standards exceeds the length of this book.

The best way to learn about a standard is often to go to the source. References are included in the bibliography for IEEE 1471 (IEEE-SA Standards Board 2000), DoDAF (DoD Architecture Framework Working Group 2004), TOGAF (The Open Group 2003), RM-ODP (ISO/IEC 1998), UML (Booch, Rumbaugh, and Jacobson 2005) and its meta-model the MOF (Object Management Group 2002), SysML (SysML Partners 2005), AADL (Feiler, Lewis, and Corporation 2003), ADML

(Spencer 2000), Rational Rose (Rational Software Corporation 2003), Telelogic System Architect (Telelogic AB 2007), RUP (Kruchten 2003), MDA (Mukerji and Miller 2003), and others. Beware of the "executive summaries" contained in some of these standards or related documentation; these descriptions are often heavy with hype and it is difficult to get a clear assessment of a standard from them. For comparative purposes, it might be useful to examine standards not related to architecture such as POSIX (IEEE 2004) and HTTP (Fielding et al. 1999) or domain-specific standards such as the Software Communications Architecture (SCA) (Modular Software-programmable Radio Consortium 2001), introduced in Chapter 15.

People, Roles, and Teams

It has become quite common for a software engineer to be granted a title such as "software architect," "senior software architect," or "chief systems architect" in a software development organization. Such a title appears to carry with it a certain amount of prestige. The usual assumption is that the engineer in question has exhibited exceptional skills in software system design, familiarity with the modern development technologies, an ability to communicate a vision for a project, effectively interact with system customers and managers, and lead his fellow engineers in completing the project successfully. At the same time, it is likely that someone looking a bit further will find many different descriptions of what software architects actually do from one company to another, and even from one project to another within a single company. In some companies, "chief architects" are brilliant engineers who worked in the trenches for many years and emerged as technically savvy sages; in other cases, they are former CEOs who decide to step down and shift their focus to ensuring their company's marketplace presence and setting the company's long-term technical strategy. What this means is that, in fact, simply having the title does not mean one has the qualifications.

Clearly, this is very different from, say, an electrical engineer or even a software engineer: Becoming one usually requires completing at a minimum an appropriate four-year college degree, and perhaps a further number of years of practical experience with specific additional training. By contrast, it is not unusual that a person with "software architect" in his title is not even a software engineer by training. This carries with it a significant danger: Identifying, nurturing, and promoting a software architect becomes similar to building an underspecified software system. In software development this is sometimes referred to as the IKIWISI syndrome, or "I'll know it when I see it." Discovering the right software system, just like discovering a good software architect, under such conditions can be too time consuming, too risky, too unpredictable, and too expensive. Moreover, it is also unclear how one can go about becoming an architect: The title tends to be bestowed upon, or sometimes assumed by, a person rather than being earned through a well-understood set of steps. And should that person move to a different organization, or even a different division within the same organization, the same set of job responsibilities might carry a completely different title. Finally, with very few exceptions, one will not find a training program within a (future) development organization that helps an individual get that job or an appropriate title.

If our goal is to study software architecture as a mature discipline with well-understood and codified objectives, principles, and practices, then we must define more clearly the roles and responsibilities of the discipline's practitioners, namely, software architects. This chapter will do just that. We are guided by the observation that software engineering is a multifaceted discipline that combines:

- *Core engineering skills*—for example, formal system modeling, code production, and product testing and measurement.
- *Organizational skills*—for example, project management, cost estimation, and adherence to industrial and government standards.
- *Interpersonal skills*—for example, communication with many stakeholders, honoring one's roles and obligations within a team, and putting the project's success before one's own personal goals.

Software architecture permeates the entire software engineering process, and in many ways forms its core; it is not unreasonable to require that software architects possess a large cross-section of these skills. The goal of this chapter is to answer four key questions:

1. Who are software architects?
2. What do software architects do?
3. How do they go about doing their job?
4. How do architects relate to, and interact with, other stakeholders in designing, implementing, and evolving a system's architecture?

The first question deals with the core set of skills a software architect must possess, including both technical and nontechnical skills. The second question sheds light on what a software architect's job actually entails. The third question addresses how software architects are organized into teams, and how and when they move from one project to another. Finally, the last question takes a broader perspective on software architecture in practice as an exercise in consensus building in order to satisfy all of a system's stakeholders. We will address each of these questions in more detail.

Outline of Chapter 17

17.1 WHO ARE SOFTWARE ARCHITECTS?

It has been said that software architecture is a result of applying "method, theft, and intuition" (Kruchten 1995).

- *Method* refers to a well understood, codified set of steps that can be repeatedly executed to solve a particular problem, or category of problem.
- *Theft* refers to the reuse of solutions that have been shown successful in the past.
- *Intuition* is the ability to conceive, understand, and apply ideas without necessarily being able to communicate or explain the entire rationale behind them.

In fact, the reader has seen different elements of method and "theft"—that is, reuse—discussed throughout this book. These include reliance on effective techniques, processes, and existing solutions, such as styles, patterns, and entire DSSAs.

In many ways, the essence of a software architect's job is to be able to apply and find the right balance among these three "sources" of architecture. In addition, by definition an architect is given a great deal of responsibility on a project; the project will succeed or fail depending on the architectural solutions employed. In many software development organizations that responsibility is not accompanied with specific authority. Instead, the architect is usually considered by the management as one of the engineers or, at best, as "first among equals." In order to do his job effectively, the architect must then find another way to exert influence and lead. He must possess and rely on a number of skills. An architect must be:

1. A software designer.
2. A domain expert.
3. A technologist.

4. A standards compliance expert.

5. A software engineering economist.

17.1.1 Architect as a Software Designer

First and foremost, a software architect must be an excellent designer of software systems. He must be able to recognize, reuse, or invent effective design solutions and apply them appropriately. He must be familiar with the key architectural styles and patterns that underlie the discipline of software architecture. An architect may even have some patterns and/or styles that are part of his private arsenal of design tools, amassed over time, possibly as a result of work within a specific domain or application family. Conversely, an architect must also be able to recognize ineffective or suboptimal designs, inappropriate styles and/or patterns, and design decisions "with strings attached."

In an ideal world, a good architect would always be able to provide rationale for all his decisions. However, we should also recognize that truly great architects—software or otherwise—often leave their mark when they depart from the conventional wisdom, for example, when they are faced with an unprecedented problem, or when they realize that an existing problem can be solved in a better way. Their inspiration in such cases may be difficult to rationalize.

To be a great designer of software systems, a software architect must be a skilled software or systems engineer, with years of experience that is both rich and varied, good communication skills, and a keen sense of aesthetics. A software architect must be an engineer because ultimately he is solving engineering problems. More specifically, he must have training as a *software* engineer because software systems exhibit many properties not shared by other types of engineered systems.

A good architect must have extensive experience because he must strive for the most effective balance of method, theft, and intuition for the problem at hand. For example, if he is dealing with an unprecedented system, he might need to rely on intuition honed by working on many different types of problem over the years and apply generic methods, such as object-orientation. On the other hand, if he is dealing with a variation on a known problem, he will be able to leverage directly his experience, and apply both specific methods and reuse solutions from prior systems.

The architect must also be a good communicator since he must convince many other people of his vision for the system. This includes, for example, other engineers who actually will build the system, but may also include the managers, external project collaborators, project customers and users, venture capitalists, and perhaps even the company's board of directors.

Finally, the architect must have a good appreciation for aesthetics. Those who cultivate such appreciation of design in the real world do a better job of designing in the software world. This point is only briefly stressed here, but has been discussed throughout the book (for example, see Chapters 1, 4, and 11). Elegant designs promote excitement about a project among its stakeholders, including the developers. They are remembered, studied, and emulated. In contrast, boring designs are not.

17.1.2 Architect as a Domain Expert

Many software development organizations produce multiple systems within the same application domain. For example, Microsoft works primarily within the domain of desktop applications; Google's primary domain of interest is information dissemination and use over the Internet; companies such Boeing and Lockheed Martin have an extensive focus on embedded systems; NASA produces ground-, Earth orbit-, and space-based systems.

In some cases, the domain of focus will be accompanied by one or more domain-specific software architectures (DSSAs) (recall Chapter 15) that codify the characteristics of the problem being tackled as well as the solution developed in response. The burden of intimate familiarity with the application domain and the greatest risks of inappropriate and ineffective solutions are removed from the architects in such systems; they need only familiarize themselves with and stick to the prescription contained in the DSSA.

However, the systems being developed in some companies will be related only loosely, such that they cannot be consolidated into a DSSA. In those cases, each system creates its own challenges. The software architects working on such systems will need to have an intimate understanding of each application domain, its major properties, and its idiosyncrasies. Otherwise, regardless of their skills as designers, architects are likely to produce designs that do not work well for the type of task at hand. They may have problems communicating with other stakeholders, including other engineers. And they may not be able to use the properties of the domain to their advantage when facing a problem with their architecture.

17.1.3 Architect as a Software Technologist

A software architect must know that his solutions actually will work once fully developed. Just like a building architect needs to ensure that his designs can be constructed, so a software architect needs to ensure that the software technology exists to support his ideas. A beautiful design is useless if it cannot be implemented.

An architect's primary role, and likely even his main strength, is not as a programmer. Indeed, experience has shown that outstanding programmers do not necessarily make outstanding architects. At the same time, the architect cannot divorce himself completely from programming. The reasons behind this are analogous to the arguments made throughout this book for why it is unrealistic to isolate completely a system's architecture from its implementation. Architects must progressively elaborate design concepts into concrete elements. To do so, they may need to prototype specific elements of their solutions to ensure that those elements will behave in practice as envisioned. They may need to test out ideas on the exact execution platform on which the system will run. The architects may also need to convince either managers or developers that a particularly controversial idea is worth pursuing, by showcasing its benefits in practice.

Architects also must have a grasp of the generic capabilities software developers will have at their disposal when implementing the architecture. In the previous chapters we have covered many such technologies and shown that they can have a direct bearing on a system's architecture. This may include the details of the operating systems and programming languages on which the eventual application will run. It may also require the architect to familiarize himself with the latest advances in software libraries, frameworks, middleware platforms, networking solutions, and so forth. The architect's job is not only to ensure that his ideas can be implemented; it is to ensure that they can be implemented effectively and that the process of creating that implementation is efficient.

Additionally, the architect may need to play the technologist card because of perceptions. Due to the nature of the job, the architect must project authority with different stakeholders. Since an architect often is not a manager on whom authority is explicitly bestowed, that authority must be earned. This is especially the case in the architect's interactions with engineers who have no competence in software development, yet who may be the architect's most important clients. Engineers are typically highly educated and skilled themselves, very protective of their work, and may believe that they are capable of solving a particular problem just as well as the architect—regardless of their lack of any genuine qualifications in software. Being able on occasion to demonstrate technical prowess will help the architect remind the engineers that he is one of them, of the reasons he holds the job, and that he does not live in the proverbial ivory tower.

17.1.4 Architect as a Standards Compliance Expert

Many government, legal, and technical bodies produce standards to which a development organization must adhere. Some of those standards are mandated externally and are the precondition for bidding on contracts. For example, many projects funded by the U.S. Department of Defense must adhere to the C4ISR architectural framework. Other standards may be required by the company's management. For example, a company may decide to use UML 2 as an architecture documentation tool.

In either case, a software architect must be intimately familiar with the relevant standards. They must be able to accurately assess and communicate the value of specific standards, or the lack of appropriate standards. They must understand a given standard's expected impact on the architecture and on the eventual product—both positive and negative—and be able to explain that impact to other stakeholders. Finally, they must be able to demonstrate that their architectural solutions adhere to any chosen standards, for example, in the case of a project audit.

The architect should also follow newly initiated standards efforts. A standards body may produce a technology that will significantly simplify development of future products, improve modeling and analysis capabilities for existing architectures, or ensure easy interoperability with important third-party software. For example, the emerging Architectural Analysis and Design Language (AADL), which was discussed in Chapter 6, may provide modeling capabilities that UML does not possess; a given extension to the CORBA standard may ease system implementation; and so on. Additionally, actual participation in standardization efforts may help prevent ill-conceived and resource-wasting standards from being imposed on future projects and software architects.

Standards Compliance Roadblocks

Despite his best efforts, a software architect may at times be unable to ensure full compliance of a given architecture with a given standard. There are at least two possible reasons for this.

First, the standard may be loosely defined. It may provide a set of general guidelines, rather than a rigorously specified notation, technique, or process that an organization can follow and use. An example of a loosely defined standard is DoDAF, which was discussed in the preceding chapter. Another example is UML itself: While its syntax is precisely defined, its semantics is not.

The second reason a standard may be hard to comply with is that the tools built to support the standard may, in fact, deviate from it. For example, a leading UML-based software modeling environment is IBM/Rational Rose. However, throughout UML's existence and evolution since the late 1990s, Rose has tended to deviate from the Object Management Group (OMG) standard, even if only in subtle ways. In such a situation, an organization that purchased Rose for modeling its software systems would be induced to deviate from standard UML.

Of course, the opposite of this argument also holds: These very reasons make it difficult to argue that an architecture does *not* comply with a standard.

17.1.5 Architect as a Software Engineering Economist

A great software designer is not necessarily a great software architect. His designs may indeed be superior when looked at in isolation, but in the context of a particular organization or project, those designs may be unrealistic, too expensive, technologically too ambitious, in violation of certain technological agreements or legal codes, or too risky for a multitude of other reasons. In other words, an architect must be more than just a (great) designer. An effective architect must produce an architecture that effectively addresses the problem at hand while simultaneously respecting the constraints placed on the project. If it fails on either count, that architecture will very likely result in a failed project.

One of the frequent constraints in real-world projects is money. Some companies competitively bid for contracts whose size constrains what can be done in the course of the project. Examples of such companies are large enterprises that work on government-funded projects in the United States and Europe: Lockheed Martin, Boeing, BAE Systems, and so on. Other companies get a finite, frequently quite small amount of venture capital to produce a successful system. Examples include many dot.com start-ups. Yet other companies go to their own coffers to fund a project that is expected eventually to turn a profit. Such companies include large commercial software outfits, such as Microsoft, Yahoo, and Google.

In each case, when producing an architecture for a system under development, the architect must not only be aware of the monetary constraint, but must also be able to determine whether his solution can be implemented effectively within the project's budget. This means that the architect must have some, at least basic, understanding of the economics of software development, and must accompany his design decisions with, possibly quick and crude "back of the envelope" calculations of how much their implementation is likely to cost. Budgetary considerations may also lead the architect to opt for adopting or adapting existing architectures and for going with off-the-shelf functionality. Being able to provide appropriate economic justification for all such decisions is an integral part of the architect's job. Ultimately, the architect must be constantly aware that the solution he produces may very well be technically suboptimal.

17.1.6 Some Bad Habits

There are also certain tendencies an architect must avoid. Some obvious bad habits are discussed here; the reader may be able to identify others as well.

Perfectionism. The constraints inherent in the architect's job often will make it impossible to produce the perfect architecture for the given problem. Among the many reasons discussed throughout this text, at any given time the architect is likely to possess only partial information. That information may change over time such that, as the architect discovers new details about the system he is working on, previously held beliefs become invalid.

Striving for perfection in such a fluid environment is impractical. In fact, one's ability to acknowledge, respond to, and even embrace change will be a mark of one's success as a software architect. This leads to the second bad habit.

Inflexibility. An architect should avoid insisting on a single correct or best way of constructing a system. A basic, positive, tendency of a designer should be to produce a clean and simple design. When constructing a building, bridge, or dam, this may mean clearing the building site so that the site fully reflects the architects' and engineers' vision. Unfortunately, it does not always work that way with software. Very few large systems are built from scratch, using a single architectural style, one's favorite set of patterns, standard middleware, programming language, operating system, and hardware platform. Instead, a software architect is much more likely to have to mix and even invent styles and patterns, look for new middleware platforms that solve the new problem more effectively, address multilingual development on multiple platforms, and so on. The reasons for this may be legitimate technical considerations. The reasons may also be the many conflicting and changing requirements levied on the architecture and the architect by the other system stakeholders. In many ways, a big element of a software architect's job is deciding which stakeholders to disappoint.

Micromanagement. Another bad habit for a software architect is the impulse to micromanage. An architect produces designs that may result in huge systems developed by many teams, possibly from many organizations, over a significant time period. Making sure that everything goes perfectly and that everyone adheres to the architect's vision at all points in time is simply not possible. It is also not the architect's job. A good architect will recognize that he is surrounded by highly skilled engineers and that many, or even most, of them will be able to do their own jobs much better than he will. Furthermore, trying to meddle in their jobs may create resentment and undermine the architect's goal of leading by example.

Isolationism. Finally, the architect should not isolate himself. Even though the architect may feel that the weight of a project is on his shoulders and that, at least early on in the project, he bears the greatest burden, the architect must remember that he is part of a much larger team, and that an integral part of his job is to ask, watch, listen, and communicate. The architect may get solutions to his specific problems in the process. He will also get the early buy-in from the stakeholders, a sense of joint ownership of the architecture, and the chance to set the stage for the architecture's eventual implementation. Shutting oneself in a room because one is "the architect" will likely achieve the exact opposite effect.

Another aspect of isolating oneself is insisting on always devising and using one's own solutions. Even though at times there may be a legitimate need for an architect to invent new design techniques, notations, patterns, or styles, the accompanying danger is doing this even when it is not necessary. This is often referred to as the "Not invented here" syndrome: Architects and, more broadly, organizations are sometimes unaware of, or even deliberately ignore, known effective solutions and insist on developing their own instead. Closely related to this is the "We have always done it this way" syndrome, where suboptimal or even ineffective solutions are applied repeatedly because they may have been demonstrated to work nominally in the past (possibly in very different contexts and on very different problems). Both of these situations are risky, expensive, and frequently result in duplicating the work someone else has already done or, worse, producing inferior solutions.

The Ultimate
Bad Habit

In many software development organizations, especially start-ups, the chief architect is the person who came up with the original idea upon which the company was founded. That person may hold other titles and responsibilities in such an organization, such as "Chief Technical Officer" or even "Chief Executive Officer." Alternatively, a new owner of an existing company may assume the role of the chief architect of the company's flagship product or its entire line of products.

The responsibility placed on such individuals clearly is greater than it is on "mere" architects: They are responsible for much more than just the technical success of a product. At the same time, these individuals' prior successes, especially if they were big successes —think, for example, Netscape— can become an impediment to doing smart business (and smart architecture). The relatively brief history of the software marketplace teaches us that the fortunes of a product, and of a company, can change rapidly. Therefore, delusions of grandeur is the ultimate bad habit for software architects.

In his fun, insightful, and sobering book, *In Search of Stupidity* (Chapman 2003), Merrill R. (Rick) Chapman chronicles several examples of this ultimate bad habit of software architects from the past few decades. He explains how and why certain companies—including aforementioned Netscape—have gone from being market leaders to historical footnotes through an often rapid succession of missteps, both managerial and architectural. Chapman's book serves as a useful reminder of the need for careful planning, good software architecture, solid engineering practices, and, above all, humility.

17.2 WHAT DO SOFTWARE ARCHITECTS DO?

A software architect's job will require showcasing a number of diverse skills. Being an effective designer is one such skill, but an architect will spend much of his time doing other things. There are four tasks an architect will most likely have to perform regardless of the type of project, his level of experience, the type of organization, the application domain, or the industry segment in which he works. These tasks are developing project strategy, designing systems, communicating with stakeholders, and being a leader. In accomplishing these tasks, the architect repeatedly will have to apply, combine, and extend the skill set described in the preceding section.

17.2.1 Develop Project Strategy

A talented software designer will most often be able to produce an excellent technical solution for the problem at hand. That solution, however, may not be the best one for the *project* or the *organization* solving the problem. A talented software architect will have to recognize the distinction between the two, and make sure always to address the latter. The architect's primary job is to help develop a comprehensive strategy for the project. That strategy, if appropriately implemented, not only will result in a system that is a good technical solution, but also one that becomes a valuable product for the organization.

This requires understanding the economic context of the project and the organization, the competition in the marketplace, and any standards and regulations by which the organization must abide. Perhaps most importantly, the architect must be intimately familiar with the human as well as technical resources at the project's disposal. An otherwise outstanding design will have a high likelihood of failure if it requires purchasing a lot of expensive new technology, retraining the existing engineers, or hiring many new staff.

17.2.2   Design Systems

A central part of overall project strategy is design of the system's architecture. Once an architect is aware of the relevant constraints being faced, he is ready to proceed with solving the problem. This is likely to be the most enjoyable part of architect's job; paradoxically, it may also be the most stressful.

An architect will likely enjoy designing systems because he will get the opportunity to design, use his imagination and creativity, put his stamp on the future systems, and perhaps even to think outside of the proverbial box. However, the architect will still need to be in frequent contact with other stakeholders, gather information from them, and respond to their possibly conflicting requests. He will have to deal with the likelihood that he may not have the complete picture at his disposal and that the picture constantly changes. It has been said that the job of a software architect is a succession of suboptimal decisions made in semidarkness. The architect will also have to avoid letting personal goals, such as producing a clean design in record time, override the other stakeholders' concerns.

17.2.3   Communicate with Stakeholders

Throughout the process of developing the project strategy and producing the architectural design, the architect will be in frequent contact with the system's various stakeholders, which may include developers, testers, technical leads, managers at all levels, customers, and users. One of the main factors in the project's success is whether the architect can project and ensure a continued, coherent vision for the resulting system. In that sense, his job has something in common with that of a salesperson, with the added twist that he is negotiating with and "selling" the project to many different types of customers in many different ways. The architect may need to interact with the various stakeholders repeatedly, especially in a long-lived project, where the overall vision may be temporarily lost in the details. In such situations, the architect may also need to assume the role of the project's cheerleader, maintaining the morale of the different stakeholders. He may also need to show significant awareness and political savvy regarding the competing interests of the various stakeholders in order to carry out this task effectively.

While the architect may use different languages to communicate with different stakeholders and may focus on different aspects of the project depending on the situation, throughout this process he must ensure the architectural integrity of the project. The compromises the architect must inevitably make cannot be allowed to undermine the overall objective or to clash with earlier decisions made for equally valid reasons. Architectural degradation must be avoided throughout this task.

17.2.4   Lead

An architect makes many decisions that are crucial to the project's success and has to convince a broad audience—a part of which that may be skeptical—that those decisions are correct. Some decisions may be unpopular, yet the architect needs to get the buy-in from all the major stakeholders, and must do so continuously throughout the project's life span. In some situations, just getting buy-in may not be good enough; the architect may need to elicit excitement for the project. He will frequently have to assume this responsibility without any explicit authority over the stakeholders.

To do this, the architect must be a leader. While it may be difficult to teach, leadership is a skill that can be nourished and refined. To be an effective leader, an architect must:

1. Show confidence in the project's success.
2. Project conviction in his ideas.
3. Demonstrate readiness to assume full responsibility for any technical problems.
4. Be ready to articulate the technical rationale for design decisions.
5. Be able to further develop the project's detailed architecture.
6. Acknowledge contributions of others.
7. Avoid self-aggrandizement.

At all times, the architect must put the interests of the project before his own, and lead by example. Developing a complex software-intensive system may require sacrifices from engineers, including long hours, working weekends and holidays, and time away from families. An architect who is a true leader will always be prepared to make his share of the sacrifices. He must also know when making such sacrifices is *in*appropriate, and should ensure that project personnel are treated with respect and consideration.

17.3 HOW DO SOFTWARE ARCHITECTS WORK?

An architect may work alone or, more likely, as part of a team. The exact composition of an architecture team and its precise role during the various project stages may vary from one organization to another, and even from one project to another. However, teams should be built with certain generally applicable guidelines and observations in mind, including a balance of skills, allegiance to the project and the organization, and ability to serve for the duration of the project.

17.3.1 Balance of Skills

The software architecture team must be composed from people whose strengths are complementary and cover the range of skills discussed above. It is unlikely that a single person will be an outstanding designer, domain expert, technologist, communicator, *and* leader. More likely, each architect's primary strengths will be in a small number—perhaps only one—of these areas.

Composing the architecture team from people with similar skill sets thus is not helpful. For one, if certain project needs, such as design, are overstaffed, there is a danger that the architects will get in each other's way, while other aspects of the architecture, such as domain expertise, may suffer. At the other extreme, staffing the team with architects whose skills do not sufficiently overlap carries the danger that the information gathered and architectural decisions made will neither be properly understood by different team members nor integrated into a coherent whole.

The architecture team carries a great deal of responsibility for and exerts dominant influence on a project. Thus, it must be staffed with qualified people. A long-time software architecture practioner and researcher, Phillippe Kruchten makes the interesting observation that the architecture team should not become a "retirement home" for aging software engineers (Kruchten 1999). This may seem to be an unnecessary admonition. However, it is not uncommon for engineers with outdated technical skills in large organizations to be "promoted" to software architects. This may be seen as the easiest way of minimizing the negative impact of such engineers' deteriorated abilities, but can be very dangerous and, simply put, it is patently stupid.

The Peter Principle

A failure by an organization to staff its software architecture team with competent people can be viewed through the prism of *The Peter Principle*. This principle was formulated by Laurence J. Peter in his 1969 book of the same name (Peter and Hull 1969), and states that, "In a hierarchy every employee tends to rise to his level of incompetence." In other words, a member of a hierarchical organization eventually is promoted to his highest level of competence; any subsequent promotion will elevate the employee to a position for which he is no longer competent, that is, to his "level of incompetence." Once he reaches his level of incompetence, the employee's chances of further promotion are low. However, from a practical perspective, by that time the damage to the organization may already have been done.

For example, an excellent C programmer within an organization may receive many salary raises and may progress through the company's hierarchy of software engineering positions: "software programmer," "software engineer," "senior software engineer," "principal scientist," and so on. At some point, for reasons discussed in this chapter, the employee may be promoted to a position of "software architect," for which he may be poorly qualified. Such a position is likely too important and carries too much responsibility for the organization to be able to afford letting this employee take the time to learn his new job. However, the organization may have no other choice, unless it wants to demote its otherwise excellent engineer. In the meantime, the likelihood of failed projects will be elevated.

The dire implication of the Peter Principle is that an organization is prone to collapse if a sufficient number of its employees reach their levels of incompetence.

17.3.2 Allegiance to the Project

The software architecture team should be an integral part of the project, and should be associated with the project throughout its life cycle. Both the architecture team and the other stakeholders must understand that the architecture team is invested in the success of the project. To the architects, this is important because of the architecture team's need to exert influence over all principal design decisions whenever required. To the programmers, it is important because they must feel that the software architects are "one of us." To the managers and customers, it is important because they can clearly see accountability for the architectural decisions made.

An alternative to this view is to treat the software architecture team as a consulting entity that jumps in depending on the needs of different projects. This can be dangerous for several reasons. If a project experiences difficulties, an "us versus them" division may result. Furthermore, the implicit lack of accountability and oversight by management in that case makes it less likely to get buy-in from the stakeholders. For example, if developers believe that it is their responsibility alone to build a successful system and that the architecture team is a marginally interested third party, they will be less likely to take and implement the architecture team's advice, thus possibly violating critical architectural decisions. Most importantly, it is highly unlikely that a part-time software architecture team can simply show up whenever needed, understand all the nuances of the system, make appropriate decisions, and move on.

We should recognize the tension that inevitably will appear between the need of the project to have a readily available software architecture team and the need of the organization to leverage the most experienced, talented, and effective architects across multiple projects that may be undertaken simultaneously. There is no easy solution to this problem, and different organizations may try to address it in different ways. For example, more experienced, senior architects may move to another project once a given system's architecture is reasonably stable, while the junior architects would remain with the project, assume additional responsibilities, and further hone their skills.

17.3.3 Allegiance to the Organization

Google the phrase "software architect," and a number of Web sites belonging to consulting firms will appear. These firms specialize in providing software architecture "services" to other software development firms. Their mode of operation is to come into an organization, familiarize themselves with the project and possibly the problem domain, and help develop the appropriate architecture for the system under development. At first blush, this may seem like the part-time software architecture team pitfall mentioned above. However, these teams may be hired to staff the project throughout its duration, alleviating that particular concern.

The real question in this case becomes whether it is preferable to employ a permanent software architecture team that will be part of, and thus fully accountable to, the software development organization, or to outsource this important, but possibly scarce and expensive, capability. The conventional wisdom would suggest that having a native software architecture team is preferable, a stance that probably is influenced by the traditional view of software development in which an organization owns a project and develops it completely in-house. Such organizations and projects still exist in some cases, an obvious example being Microsoft, and this view may be appropriate for them.

The answer to the question of whether to employ or hire a software architecture team becomes more complex in the case of many other development organizations. The reasons are two-fold. First, a typical software project will use a number of off-the-shelf technologies and even application-level components. In such situations, the question becomes, who actually owns and controls the software architecture? It has been shown that such technologies directly impact a system's architecture (Di Nitto and Rosenblum 1999). Therefore, by importing an off-the-shelf capability, an organization, at least in part, imports an architecture as well, and the perception may be that there is less of a need for an in-house architecture team. This may indeed be the case in certain situations. But beware: The danger is that by letting a chosen third-party's technology control the architecture, the organization is, in fact, relinquishing a critical piece of control over the project. And that control is given to people who:

- Did not have that project in mind when they developed their technology.
- May not have taken into account, or even been familiar with, any aspects of the problem domain.

- Are unfamiliar with the organization, the skills of its engineers, the technical and economic context of the project being undertaken, and so on.

In effect, doing this is akin to letting the tail wag the dog.

The second consideration in deciding whether to maintain an internal architecture team has to do with the software development model that has gained increased popularity: outsourcing. Usually a development organization will find it economically advantageous to hire outside developers, often in a foreign country, to implement parts of a system. It might be argued that, by extension, the architecture of the system can be outsourced as well. On the surface, this is similar to hiring an external architecture team. However, relying on an external architecture team assumes that the team would still need to understand the details of the project and its requirements, work in close collaboration with the other system stakeholders, get their buy-in, and oversee the architecture's implementation and evolution. Simply purchasing a putative architecture for a project from a third party usually is not feasible, unless the organization is branching out into a new business area having a well-established existing architecture.

One potentially positive aspect of hiring an external software architecture team or the outright outsourcing of the architecture is that it might be an effective way of avoiding both the "Not invented here," and the "We have always done it this way issues." Even here, however, this risk can never be completely eliminated: The "here" and the "we" may just be shifted to the external team.

17.3.4 Duration of Involvement

The software architecture team does not disband and/or disassociate itself with the project after the architectural design activity is over. There might be an impulse to do so as the team's task is considered to have been completed and other projects may need architectural help. However, moving the team to other projects will have a similar effect to that of treating the team as a consulting entity. More importantly, we have stressed several times throughout this book that it is inappropriate to think of software architecture as a "phase" that is completed early on in a project. While most of the major architectural decisions may be undertaken during the project's early stages, the architecture remains an active, almost organic underpinning for the project that constantly changes and evolves. Cutting off the architecture team from the project can result in many critical architectural decisions being made haphazardly, understood partially at best, and documented poorly, if at all.

Instead, the architecture team must be closely involved with the project throughout the project's life cycle. Once the architecture becomes reasonably stable, it may in fact be possible, and even advisable, to reassign some members of the architecture team to other projects. However, at least a part of the architecture team should remain on the project. In certain cases, members of the architecture team may be assigned as liaisons to the development teams; in other cases, they may become leads of different development teams. This allows the architecture team to have direct oversight of the project's progress, any difficulties encountered, and adherence to the architecture and any needed changes to it. It also helps reinforce the fact that the architecture team's primary allegiance is to the project, thus helping to improve the morale.

17.3.5 Team Structure

Software architecture teams can be structured in different ways, depending on the size of the software development organization, the number and types of projects on which the organization is working concurrently, and the organization's own management structure. We briefly discuss three primary ways of structuring an architecture team. Variations on these models are possible.

Flat Model

The flat model usually works well in small organizations. Architects in it are not stratified in any way and carry comparable clout and responsibility. It is an egalitarian organization that comports well with mature professionals. On the other hand, with less mature or responsible individuals the flat model may cause problems in cases of disagreements, whether within the architecture team or with other stakeholders. It may also overwhelm the architects because of the unspecified or inadequate division of responsibilities. This model may not scale well to large teams and large projects. An extreme case of a flat architecture team model is that of a project staffed by a single software architect.

Hierarchical Model

A more practical model, especially in larger organizations is the hierarchical model. This model was identified as early as Fred Brooks's *The Mythical Man-Month* book (Brooks 1995). In this model, the architecture team is typically headed by a chief architect or senior architect, and staffed with junior architects. In some, typically large, organizations the architecture team may be further stratified. For example, an enterprise architect may be in charge of the software architectures of all of that organization's different projects. The division of responsibilities and authority in the hierarchical model is clearly defined. This makes it more easily scalable to large teams. The potential downside is that the architecture team must in effect assume an internal management structure, in addition to and separate from that in the rest of the organization.

Matrix Model

In the matrix model, architects simultaneously work on multiple projects. A cross-section of skills is applied to a cross-section of projects. A single project may have multiple, changing architecture teams during its life span, depending on the expertise needed. This model can be found in organizations that are understaffed (perhaps unexpectedly) or experience periodic spikes in undertaken, externally funded projects. The matrix model is orthogonal to both the flat and hierarchical models: Architecture teams may, but need not be, stratified. The main advantage of this model is that it is very flexible. However, it should be looked on as a temporary solution. It carries the danger that architects will be oversubscribed and constantly distracted by the many simultaneous problems on which they are working; they may be unable to devote appropriate attention to any of the projects.

17.4 HOW DO SOFTWARE ARCHITECTS RELATE TO OTHER STAKEHOLDERS?

It should be clear by now that a software architect exists neither outside nor above his organization. Instead, an architect is an integral part of a software development team, project, *and* organization. The job of an architect carries with it many responsibilities and to fulfill those responsibilities, the architect is forced to delegate and rely on co-workers; communicate with and garner support from managers; and keep customers and users in the loop as necessary. We now outline the nature of these relationships, and the likely challenges an architect will encounter in maintaining them.

17.4.1 Architects and Engineers

A large project typically will have a number of engineering teams working on it. Different teams may be charged with different facets of the system, and may include specialists in specific software engineering subdisciplines such as requirements, quality assurance, implementation, and cross-application middleware.

The architect must have a close, well-functioning relationship with all engineers. In the case of some, such as requirements engineers, the relationship may be more natural and objectives more mutually aligned than in the case of others, such as software testers. In either case, however, the guiding concern must be the overall success of the project.

Perhaps the most important constituency within the organization to the architect is the programmers. Programmers will realize and refine the architect's vision. They also serve as validators of the architecture: If an architectural design decision has unforeseen consequences, a programmer likely will be the first one to notice. In such cases especially, a close, cooperative relationship between architects and programmers is critical; if it is lacking, architectural degradation will quickly occur.

In many companies, architects also must work closely with systems engineers and, in some projects such as embedded systems projects, hardware engineers. An architect's relationship with these engineers will likely be different from that with software engineers. One reason is that a software architect creates the overall vision and design for the *software* portion of the given system, but does not have analogous control over the remainder of the system. Another reason is that, because systems and hardware engineers lack training in software engineering, they may not have appropriate appreciation for the nuances of the system's software architectural design. They may fall victim to the misconception that, because software is infinitely malleable in principle, it should always change to accommodate the needs of other system components. By now it should be clear that frequent changes to a system, especially if undertaken hastily, tend to invalidate the key architectural design decisions, and result in architectural degradation.

A related, and even bigger, issue that may occur in the relationship between a software architect and nonsoftware engineers is the lack of respect for the architect's importance to the project. This can, of course, happen with software engineers as well. All engineers working on a given project may be highly capable and may qualify as experts in their own focus areas, whether systems, hardware, or some particular specialty. They may thus feel that they understand the nuances of their task much better than the software architect does. Furthermore, they may not see the direct benefit of strictly adhering to the architecture: They frequently are more interested in achieving local optima due to their limited vision of the entire project. In some development organizations software architecture—and software *architects*—still are not held in very high regard. Coupled with a dislike of being told what to do, this can result in significant resistance to the software architect and contribute to a failed project. Avoiding, or identifying and remedying such situations, is one of the main challenges and primary duties of a software architect.

17.4.2 Architects and Managers

At times, an architect must achieve his objectives in the face of skeptical and even uncooperative engineers, and often must do so without any formal authority over those engineers. The architect may have to resort to winning them over with personal competence and leadership. Clearly, things are likely to go more smoothly if he also has the support of the organization's management.

Software development organizations are increasingly beginning to understand the importance of software architectures and software architects. Management must work to ensure a project's success and, in an ideal world, that would mean ensuring that the system's architecture, that is, the architects' vision, is realized fully and effectively. In turn, this requires architects and managers to interact frequently and to closely align their goals. This may mean that the managers must adjust their expectations of a project based on the architects' technical considerations, and it may also require architects to adjust their expectations, and the architecture itself, based on the organization's realities. Schedule and budget constraints, marketplace considerations, personnel turnover, and other such issues must be considered.

Managers and architects do not always work well together, however. There may be many reasons for this, but from a software architect's perspective one reason can be particularly damaging: Understanding the importance of the architect's role in a project does not ensure managerial competence. A project, and an entire organization, may be mismanaged in many ways and for many reasons. The managers also may simply lack the technical know-how to grasp the importance of the architect's design decisions. As a result, while a manager may in principle support the *architect*, he may unwittingly undermine the *architecture*.

Managers may fail to think through all of the consequences of their actions, which may negatively impact the system's architecture. They may commit to purchasing and using third-party components, frameworks, or middleware that are a poor fit for the architecture. They may decide to comply with standards that cannot be easily shoe-horned into the company's existing architectures. They also may commit to delivering too much, too quickly, too cheaply, without understanding the architectural implications of those promises. An architect must always be aware and may be forced to respond to these challenges.

Of course, an even bigger challenge faced by architects is in more traditional software development shops, in which certain techniques, tools, and processes may have ossified over time. In some parts of such organizations, architecture-centric development on the whole may be considered to be a fad, too inefficient, and unnecessary. Likewise, a particular architectural approach—for example, requiring that a developer request a formal architectural design review before he may change a component's interface—may go against the organization's culture, which in the past has relied on, and thus still encourages, a swaggering form of individual initiative. In such situations, architects simultaneously must fight two battles: arriving at an effective architecture for the system under construction while at the same time trying to overcome institutional resistance, ignorance, and hubris.

17.4.3 Other Stakeholders

Software architects must also interact with additional stakeholders, both within and outside of their organization. Of particular importance is their relationship with the marketing department. In many organizations, innovation is frequently driven by market needs and pressures. This is, of course, understandable because a company's primary goal is to sell products. There is nothing inherently wrong or inverted in such an arrangement: The marketing department researches the current marketplace conditions and customers' needs, and reports those to the company's management or engineers; in turn, the software architects employ their skills to design systems that will best take advantage of the market conditions and satisfy customer needs. It is, therefore, not unusual for marketing to drive a product's development, and hence its architecture: It may determine the systems that need to be built, their exact features, development priorities, release dates, and so forth.

At the same time, there are certain pitfalls in this relationship. Both the architects and marketing staff may fail to properly understand the motivations, abilities, and expertise of the other. The architects may resist being told what to do, especially if they fail to appreciate that market conditions will occasionally get in the way of producing the best or preserving the originally envisaged architecture for a system. For example, an architect's task will be directly impacted if a potential competitor has been identified and it becomes imperative to release a product much earlier than originally planned. So, too, if the primary customer base for the system under construction is observed to be moving to a different computing platform, or if the envisioned customer base significantly expands or shrinks. Architects have no choice but to accommodate such nontechnical realities.

On the other hand, the marketing department may cause problems if it fails to understand that a system's architecture cannot be arbitrarily or abruptly modified to incorporate newly identified needs. Marketing may also strive for unrealistic goals and unreasonable deadlines, and may attempt to drive the engineering process without adequate understanding of technical challenges and realities. In the most extreme case, marketing may promise a product that simply cannot be built by the company's engineers at the given time.

In either case, misunderstandings and lack of proper communication between architecture and marketing teams may result in an adversarial, counterproductive relationship. Keeping this relationship healthy should be an important, regular objective.

Somewhat similar to the architect's relationship with the marketing staff will be his relationship with the system's customers and users, with whom the architect may need to interface directly. In fact, he may well be the face of the project as far as the customers and users are concerned: The architect may present the project vision to them, ensure that their requirements are properly reflected in the system's blueprint and eventually in the system itself, address their inquiries, and resolve their concerns and doubts.

If properly established and nurtured, this can be a very productive relationship, helping ensure the system's final acceptance, with all of the major issues addressed as they came up during construction. On the other hand, the customers and users may be very particular in their requests, impatient, and, in the worst case, insufficiently knowledgeable of the nature of software and the nuances of its development. Thus, in addition to providing the rationale behind the architecture to the stakeholders within the organization (developers, testers, managers), the architect may also need to tailor that rationale for the benefit of the technically less savvy customers and users.

17.5 REMAINING CHALLENGES

The architect must possess many skills, from maintaining the system's conceptual integrity to serving as the project's cheerleader, leading by the strength of technical knowledge and character, and interacting effectively with a broad range of stakeholders with frequently competing goals. While some of these skills cannot be taught, they certainly can be nurtured. At the same time, there are several other facets of an architect's job for which he can be trained in a conventional manner—an observation that was a motivation for this textbook as well.

The principal challenge for software development organizations—including, but not restricted to, the traditional software shops that want to introduce software architects and explicit architecture-based software development for the first time—is identifying the best candidates for the software architect positions, the appropriate skill sets they should possess, and the people who can train them. There are several examples in industry of such training programs. One example is NASA Jet Propulsion Laboratory's Software Architect Program (Vickers 2004). Such programs are relatively recent, and their effectiveness and required adjustments will need to be monitored over time.

17.6 END MATTER

A software architect has a multifaceted job, teeming with unique challenges and substantial responsibility. An architect may work alone or, more likely, as part of a team. His job description may be somewhat imprecise, but it will involve many technical skills discussed in this book: architecture modeling and analysis; awareness of and proficiency with architectural styles and patterns; familiarity with product lines and domain-specific architectures; understanding of relevant implementation, deployment, and evolution technologies; and so on. The job of a software architect also requires many skills that, at first blush, may not seem necessary for a software practitioner or that may not be readily learned from a book, including the ability to communicate effectively with many different types of stakeholder; to ensure compliance with relevant laws, regulations, and standards; to lead; to ensure the architecture's economic viability. As an architect, one thus truly has to be a jack-of-all-trades. This is yet another facet of our discipline that distinguishes it from other engineering endeavors.

The Business Case

A critical success factor for a software system is that system's architecture. The skills of the architects and composition of the architecture teams therefore will have a direct and significant impact on the success of a project and of an organization. Each individual architect must possess a large number of diverse skills, while the architecture teams must have a comprehensive balance of those skills.

Fred Brooks has said that great designers must be spotted, selected, and nurtured. However, as we have seen, an architect's job is not restricted to design. He must possess a broad cross-section of skills. Many of those skills can be learned; all can be improved with study and practice. It is thus in a company's interest to provide the appropriate training for its architects. It is also important to strive to achieve a careful balance in the architecture teams.

The bottom line is that a company with skilled architects and carefully composed architecture teams will have a better opportunity to succeed in the marketplace.

17.7 REVIEW QUESTIONS

1. What are the necessary skills a software architect should possess?

2. What are some additional useful skills?

3. This chapter discussed several bad habits a software architect may exhibit. Can you identify any others? Be sure to justify your answers.

4. Your organization has identified an exceptional young software designer and would like to promote him into a software architect. What, if any, additional training would be required to accomplish this? How would you suggest that your organization proceed?

5. Based on the discussion provided in this chapter, present an argument why purchasing an architecture can be a recipe for failure.

6. Outsourcing software development has proven to be a successful strategy for many organizations. Should organizations also outsource architectural design? Be sure to carefully state your argument.

17.8 FURTHER READING

Brooks was one of the first to recognize the importance of a chief designer in a software project in his seminal book, *The Mythical Man-Month* (Brooks 1995). Many of his observations, drawn from the experience of building the IBM 360 operating system in the 1960s, still ring true several decades later and inspired several of the points in this chapter. Brooks followed that with an essay arguing for the importance of software design and of great software designers in tackling the essential difficulties of software engineering (Brooks 1987). The dangers of the Peter Principle—which, as this chapter has argued, has a direct relevance to software organizations and architects—are described in Peter's book of the same name (Peter and Hull 1969).

More recently, a number of authors have tried to answer the questions of who software architects are, what skills they must possess, and how they go about devising a system's architecture. Several of these issues were considered, at least indirectly, by Curtis, Krasner, and Iscoe (Curtis, Krasner, and Iscoe 1988) in the context of designing large-scale software systems, and then more directly by Kruchten (Kruchten 1995, 1999). Kruchten's 1999 paper, in particular, provides an excellent elaboration of the desired skills and responsibilities of software architects. A number of insights from that paper have found their way into this chapter. Several similar observations have also been made by other authors, such as Kari Smolander (Smolander 2002) and Tero Päivärinta (Smolander and Päivärinta 2002).

Elisabetta DiNitto and David Rosenblum (Di Nitto and Rosenblum 1999) provide one of many examples of the manner and extent to which technological solutions (in their case, middleware) impact a software system's architecture, and thereby the system's architects. Will Tracz's work on domain-specific software architectures (Tracz, 1994; Tracz, 1995; Taylor, Tracz, and Coglianese 1995) argues for the other critical facet of an architect's job—domain expertise.

In practice, as argued in this chapter, an effective software architect must possess many additional skills. A number of organizations have established software architect training programs with the objective of molding their architects into well rounded, multifaceted employees. One representative example is NASA Jet Propulsion Laboratory's Software Architect Program (Vickers 2004).

Bibliography

Abbott, Russell J. 1983. Program Design by Informal English Descriptions. *Communications of the ACM* 26 (11): 882–894.

Abdul-Rahman, Alfarez, and Stephen Hailes. 2000. Supporting Trust in Virtual Communities. In Hawaii International Conference on System Sciences, Jan. 4–7, (Maui, HI).

Albin, Stephen T. 2003. *The Art of Software Architecture: Design Methods and Techniques*, Wiley Publishing, Inc.

Alexander, C. 1979. *The Timeless Way of Building*. New York, Oxford University Press.

Alexander, Christopher, Sara Ishikawa, and Murray Silverstein. 1977. *A Pattern Language: Towns, Buildings, Construction*, Oxford University Press, USA.

Allen, Robert. 1997. A Formal Approach to Software Architecture. Ph.D. dissertation, Carnegie Mellon University, Pittsburgh.

Allen, Robert, and David Garlan. 1997. A Formal Basis for Architectural Connection. *ACM Transactions on Software Engineering and Methodology (TOSEM)* 6 (3): 213–249.

Apache Software Foundation. *Apache Derby* (Website). Available from db.apache.org/derby/.

Apollo 11: The NASA Mission Reports. 1999. Edited by R. Godwin, Apogee Books Space Series, Collector's Guide Publishing, Inc.

Argo/UML. 2000. Available from argouml.tigris.org/.

Atria Software. 1992. ClearCase Concepts Manual.

Balek, D., and F. Plasil. 2001. Software Connectors and Their Role in Component Deployment. In *DAIS '01*, Krakow, Kluwer.

Baset, Salman A., and Henning Schulzrinne. 2004. An Analysis of the Skype Peer-to-Peer Internet Telephony Protocol, Columbia University, CUCS-039-04.

Bastarrica, M., A. Shvartsman, and S. Demurjian. 1998. A Binary Integer Programming Model for Optimal Object Distribution. In Second International Conference on Principles of Distributed Systems, December 1998, (Amiens, France), Hermes, pp. 211–226.

Batory, Don, Lou Coglianese, Steve Shafer, and Will Tracz. 1995. The ADAGE Avionics Reference Architecture. In AIAA Computing in Aerospace-10 Conference, March.

Batory, Don, David McAllester, Lou Coglianese, and Will Tracz. 1995. Domain Modeling in Engineering Computer-Based Systems. In 1995 International Symposium and Workshop on Systems Engineering of Computer Based Systems, March, pp. 19–26.

Berners-Lee, Tim, Robert Cailliau, Ari Luotonen, Henrik Frystyk Nielsen, and Arthur Secret. 1994. The World-Wide Web. *Communications of the ACM* 37 (8): 76–82.

Binns, Pam, Matt Englehart, Mike Jackson, and Steve Vestal. 1996. Domain-Specific Software Architectures for Guidance, Navigation and Control. *International Journal of Software Engineering and Knowledge Engineering* 6 (2): 201–227.

Bishop, Matt. 2003. *Computer Security: Art and Science*, Addison-Wesley.

Boehm, B.W. 1988. A Spiral Model of Software Development and Enhancement. *IEEE Computer* 21 (5): 61–72.

Boehm, Barry W. 1981. *Software Engineering Economics*. Upper Saddle River, NJ, Prentice Hall PTR.

Booch, Grady 1986. Object-Oriented Development. *IEEE Transactions on Software Engineering* 12 (2): 211–221.

Booch, Grady, James Rumbaugh, and Ivar Jacobson. 1998. *The Unified Modeling Language User Guide*, *Object Technology Series*. Reading, MA, Addison-Wesley Professional.

———. 2005. *The Unified Modeling Language User Guide*. 2nd ed., Addison-Wesley Object Technology Series. Addison-Wesley Professional, Reading, MA.

Bosch, Jan. 2000. *Design and Use of Software Architectures: Adopting and Evolving a Product-Line Approach*. Reading, MA, ACM Press, Addison-Wesley Professional.

Bowman, Ivan T., Richard C. Holt, and Neil V. Brewster. 1999. Linux as a Case Study: Its Extracted Software Architecture. In Twenty-first International Conference on Software Engineering (ICSE'99), May 16–22, (Los Angeles, CA), pp. 555–563.

Brand, Stewart 1994. *How Buildings Learn: What Happens After They're Built*, Penguin Books.

Bray, Tim, Jean Paoli, and C. M. Sperberg-McQueen. *Extensible Markup Language (XML): Part I. Syntax* (Recommendation). World Wide Web Consortium, February, 1998. Available from www.w3.org/TR/1998/REC-xml.

Briand, Lionel C., and Alexander L. Wolf, eds. 2007. *Future of Software Engineering (FoSE 2007)*. Minneapolis, MN: IEEE Computer Society.

Brooks, Frederick P. Jr. 1995. *The Mythical Man-Month: Essays on Software Engineering*. 2nd ed., Addison-Wesley.

———. 1987. No Silver Bullet: Essence and Accidents of Software Engineering. *IEEE Computer* 20 (4): 10–19.

Brooks, Rodney A. 1986. A Robust Layered Control System for a Mobile Robot. *IEEE Journal of Robotics and Automation* 2 (1): 14–23.

Buschmann, Frank, Regine Meunier, Hans Rohnert, Peter Sommerlad, and Michael Stal. 1996. *Pattern-Oriented Software Architecture: A System of Patterns*. Chichester, West Sussex, UK, Wiley.

Bush, Vannevar. 1996. As We May Think. *interactions* 3 (2): 35–46.

Carzaniga, A., A. Fuggetta, André van der Hoek, R. S. Hall, D. M. Heimbigner, and A. L. Wolf 1998. A Characterization Framework for Software Deployment Technologies, University of Colorado, Boulder, CU-CS-857-98.

Carzaniga, Antonio, David S. Rosenblum, and Alexander L. Wolf. 2001. Design and Evaluation of a Wide-Area Event Notification Service. *ACM Transactions on Computer Systems* 9 (3): 332–383.

The Catalog of Compiler Construction Tools. 2006. Fraunhofer Institute for Computer Architecture and Software Technology. Available from catalog.compilertools.net/.

Chapman, Merrill R. (Rick). 2003. *In Search of Stupidity: Over 20 Years of High-Tech Marketing Disasters*. Apress.

Clements, P., F. Bachmann, L. Bass, David Garlan, J. Ivers, R. Little, R. Nord, and J. Stafford. 2002. *Documenting Software Architectures: Views and Beyond*. Addison-Wesley.

Clements, Paul C., and Linda M. Northrop. 2001. *Software Product Lines: Practices and Patterns*, *The SEI Series in Software Engineering*, Addison-Wesley Professional.

Clements, Paul, Rick Kazman, and Mark Klein. 2002. *Evaluating Software Architectures: Methods and Case Studies*. Addison-Wesley Professional.

Coglianese, Lou, Roy Smith, and Will Tracz. 1992. DSSA Case Study: Navigation, Guidance, and Flight Director Design and Development. In *IEEE Symposium on Computer-Aided Control System Design*, March, pp. 102–109.

Cohen, Bram. *Incentives Build Robustness in BitTorrent*. BitTorrent.org, May 22, 2003. Available from www.bittorrent.org/bittorrentecon.pdf.

Collins-Sussman, Ben, Brian W. Fitzpatrick, and C. Michael Pilato. 2004. *Version Control with Subversion* (HTML), 2004. Available from svnbook.red-bean.com/.

Colouris, G., J. Dollimore, and T. Kindberg. 1994. *Distributed Systems: Concepts and Design*. 2nd. Ed., Addison-Wesley.

Cook, J., and A. Orso. 2005. MonDe: Safe Updating through Monitored Deployment of New Component Versions. In Sixth ESEC/FSE Workshop on Program Analysis for Software Tools and Engineering, September, (Lisbon, Portugal).

Coram, Robert. 2002. *Boyd: The Fighter Pilot Who Changed the Art of War*, Little, Brown, and Company.

Curtis, B., H. Krasner, and N. Iscoe. 1988. A Field Study of the Software Design Process for Large Systems. *Communications of the ACM* 31 (11): 1268–1287.

Damiani, Ernesto, Sabrina De Capitani di Vimercati, Stefano Paraboschi, Pierangela Samarati, and Fabio Violante. 2002. A Reputation-Based Approach for Choosing Reliable Resources in Peer-to-Peer Networks. In Ninth ACM Conference on Computer and Communications Security, November (Washington, DC).

Dashofy, E. M. 2001. Issues in Generating Data Bindings for an XML Schema-Based Language. In Workshop on XML Technologies in Software Engineering (XSE 2001), May 15, (Toronto, Canada).

———. 2003. *xADL 2.0 Distilled: A Guide for Users of the xADL 2.0 Language* (Webpage), January 2003. Available from www.isr.uci.edu/projects/xarchuci/guide.html.

———. 2007. Supporting Stakeholder-Driven, Multi-View Software Architecture Modeling, Ph.D. dissertation, Information and Computer Science, University of California–Irvine. Irvine, CA.

Dashofy, E. M., N. Medvidović, and R. N. Taylor. 1999. Using Off-the-Shelf Middleware to Implement Connectors in Distributed Software Architectures. In Twenty-First International Conference on Software Engineering (ICSE '99), May 16–22, (Los Angeles, CA), pp. 3–12.

Dashofy, Eric M., and André van der Hoek. 2001. Representing Product Family Architectures in an Extensible Architecture Description Language. In International Workshop on Product Family Engineering (PFE-4), October, pp. 330–341.

Dashofy, Eric, André van der Hoek, and Richard N. Taylor. 2005. A Comprehensive Approach for the Development of Modular Software Architecture Description Languages. *ACM Transactions on Software Engineering and Methodology (TOSEM)* 14 (2): 199–245.

Dean, Jeffrey, and Sanjay Ghernawat. 2004. MapReduce: Simplified Data Processing on Large Clusters. In OSDI'04: Sixth Symposium on Operating System Design and Implementation, December (San Francisco, CA).

DeLine, R. 2001. Avoiding Packaging Mismatch with Flexible Packaging. *IEEE Transactions on Software Engineering* 27 (2): 124–143.

DeRemer, Frank, and Hans H. Kron. 1976. Programming-in-the-Large versus Programming-in-the-Small. *IEEE Transactions on Software Engineering* 2 (2): 80–86.

Deutsch, Peter, and James Gosling. *The Eight Fallacies of Distributed Computing*, 1994. Available from blogs.sun.com/jag/resource/Fallacies.html.

Devanbu, Premkumar T., and Stuart Stubblebine. 2000. Software Engineering for Security: A Roadmap. In Proceedings of the Conference on The Future of Software Engineering, (Limerick, Ireland), ACM Press, pp. 227–239.

Di Nitto, Elisabetta, and David S. Rosenblum. 1999. Exploiting ADLs to Specify Architectural Styles Induced by Middleware Infrastructures. In Twenty-First International Conference on Software Engineering, May, (Los Angeles, CA), IEEE Computer Society, pp. 13–22.

Dijkstra, Edsger W. 1968. Letters to the Editor: Go To Statement Considered Harmful. *Communications of the ACM* 11 (3): 147–148.

Dilley, J., B. Maggs, J. Parikh, H. Prokop, R. Sitaraman, and B. Weihl. 2002. Globally Distributed Content Delivery. *IEEE Internet Computing* 6 (5): 50–58.

Dillinger, Marcus, Kambiz Madani, and Nancy Alonistioti. 2003. *Software Defined Radio: Architectures, Systems and Functions*, Wiley.

Dillon, Laura A., George Kutty, P. Michael Melliar-Smith, Louise E. Moser, and Y.S. Ramakrishna. 1992. Graphical Specifications for Concurrent Software Systems. In Fourteenth International Conference on Software Engineering, May, (Melbourne, Australia), pp. 214–224.

Dinda, Peter, Thomas Gross, Roger Karrer, and Bruce Lowekamp. 2001. The Architecture of the Remos System. In IEEE International Symposium on High-Performance Distributed Computing (HPDC 2001), August, (San Francisco, CA).

Dingledine, Roger, Michael Freedman, David Molnar, David Parkes, and Paul Syverson. 2003. Reputation. In The Digital Government Civic Scenario Workshop, April 28–29, (Harvard University, Cambridge, MA, USA).

Dobrica, L., and E. Niemela. 2002. A Survey on Software Architecture Analysis Methods. *IEEE Transactions on Software Engineering* 28 (7): 638–53.

DoD Architecture Framework Working Group. 2004. *DoD Architecture Framework*, Version 1.0, United States Department of Defense.

Doherty, P., P. Haslum, F. Heintz, T. Merz, P. Nyblom, T. Persson, and B. Wingman. 2004. A Distributed Architecture for Autonomous Unmanned Aerial Vehicle Experimentation. In Seventh International Symposium on Distributed Autonomous Systems.

Dwyer, M., J. Hatcliff, C. Pasareanu, Robby, and W. Visser. 2007. Formal Software Analysis: Emerging Trends in Software Model Checking. In Future of Software Engineering 2007, edited by L. Briand and A. Wolf: IEEE-CS Press, pp. 120–136.

Edwards, George, Sam Malek, and Nenad Medvidović. 2007. Scenario-Driven Dynamic Analysis of Distributed Architectures. In Proceedings of the Tenth International Conference on Fundamental Approaches to Software Engineering (FASE), (Braga, Portugal), Springer: Lecture Notes in Computer Science 4422, pp. 125–139.

Emmerich, Wolfgang. 2000. *Engineering Distributed Objects*, Wiley.

Eyles, Don. 2004. Tales from the Lunar Module Guidance Computer. In Twenty-Seventh Annual Guidance and Control Conference of the American Astronautical Society (AAS), February 6, (Breckenridge, CO).

Farrache, Gilles. *bbFTP* (Website), 2005. Available from doc.in2p3.fr/bbftp/.

Feijs, Loe, and Roel De Jong. 1998. 3D Visualization of Software Architectures. *Communications of the ACM* 41 (12): 73–78.

Feiler, Peter H., Bruce Lewis, and Stephen Vestal. 2003. The SAE Avionics Architecture Description Language (AADL) Standard: A Basis for Model-Based Architecture-Driven Embedded Systems Engineering. In RTAS 2003 Workshop on Model-Driven Embedded Systems. May (Washington, DC).

Fielding, R., J. Gettys, J. C. Mogul, H. Frystyk, L. Masinter, P. Leach, and T. Berners-Lee. 1999. Hypertext Transfer Protocol—HTTP/1.1, Internet Engineering Task Force, Request for Comments, RFC 2616.

Fielding, Roy T., and Richard N. Taylor. 2002. Principled Design of the Modern Web Architecture. *ACM Transactions on Internet Technology (TOIT)* 2 (2): 115–150.

Fielding, Roy Thomas. 2000. Architectural Styles and the Design of Network-based Software Architectures. Ph.D. dissertation, Information and Computer Science, University of California–Irvine, Irvine, CA.

Finkelstein, Anthony. 2000. *The Future of Software Engineering 2000*. New York, ACM Press.

Firby, Robert James. 1989. Adaptive Execution in Complex Dynamic Worlds. Doctoral thesis, Computer Science, Yale University.

Fogel, K. 1999. *Open Source Development with CVS*. Scottsdale, Coriolis.

Foote, Brian, and Joseph Yoder. 1997. Big Ball of Mud. In Fouth Conference on Patterns Languages of Programs (PLoP97/EuroPLoP97), (Monticello, IL), Technical Report #WUCS-97-34, Department of Computer Science, Washington University, p. 21.

Formal Systems (Europe) Ltd. 2005. *Failures-Divergence Refinement: FDR2 Users Manual*.

Foster, Ian, Carl Kesselman, and Steven Tuecke. 2001. The Anatomy of the Grid: Enabling Scalable Virtual Organizations. *International Journal of High Performance Computing Applications* 15 (3): 200–222.

Fuggetta, Alfonso, Gian Pietro Picco, and Giovanni Vigna. 1998. Understanding Code Mobility. *IEEE Transactions on Software Engineering* 24 (5): 342–361.

Gambetta, Diego. 2000. Can We Trust Trust? In *Trust: Making and Breaking Cooperative Relations*, edited by D. Gambetta. Oxford: Department of Sociology, University of Oxford, pp. 213–237.

Gamma, Erich, Richard Helm, Ralph Johnson, and John Vlissides. 1995. *Design Patterns: Elements of Reusable Object-Oriented Software*, Addison-Wesley Professional Computing Series. Reading, MA, Addison-Wesley Professional.

Garlan, D., R. Allen, and J. Ockerbloom. 1995. Architectural Mismatch or Why It's Hard to Build Systems Out of Existing Parts. In Seventeenth International Conference on Software Engineering (ICSE), ACM, pp. 179–185.

———. 1994. Exploiting Style in Architectural Design Environments. In Second ACM SIGSOFT '94 Second Symposium on the Foundations of Software Engineering, December 6–9, (New Orleans, LA), ACM Press, pp. 175–188.

———. 1995. Architectural Mismatch: Why Reuse Is So Hard. *IEEE Software* 12 (6): 17–26.

Garlan, David, S. Cheng, and Bradley Schmerl. 2003. Increasing System Dependability through Architecture-Based Self-Repair. In *Architecting Dependable Systems*, edited by R. de Lemos, C. Gacek and A. Romanovsky.

Garlan, David, Robert T. Monroe, and David Wile. 1997. ACME: An Architecture Description Interchange Language. In CASCON '97, November, (Toronto, Ontario, Canada), IBM Center for Advanced Studies, pp. 169–183.

———. 2000. ACME: Architectural Description of Component-Based Systems. In *Foundations of Component-Based Systems*, edited by G. T. Leavens and M. Sitaraman: Cambridge University Press, pp. 47–68.

Gasser, Morrie. 1988. *Building a Secure Computer System*, Van Nostrand Reinhold New York Co.

Georgas, John C., and Richard N. Taylor. 2004. Towards a Knowledge-based Approach to Architectural Adaptation Management. In First ACM SIGSOFT Workshop on Self-Managed Systems (WOSS '04), October (Newport Beach, CA), ACM Press, pp. 59–63.

Georgas, John C., André van der Hoek, and Richard N. Taylor. 2005. Architectural Runtime Configuration Management in Support of Dependable Self-Adaptive Software. In Workshop on Architecting Dependable Systems (WADS '05), in conjunction with ICSE 2005 (St. Louis, MO), pp. 48–53.

Ghemawat, Sanjay, Howard Gobioff, and Shun-Tak Leung. 2003. The Google File System. In Proceedings of the Nineteenth ACM Symposium on Operating Systems Principles, (Bolton Landing, NY), ACM, pp. 29–43.

Ghezzi, Carlo, Mehdi Jazayeri, and Dino Mandrioli. 2003. *Fundamentals of Software Engineering*. 2nd ed., Upper Saddle River, NJ, Prentice Hall.

Gokhale, Swapna. 2007. Architecture-Based Software Reliability Analysis: Overview and Limitations. *IEEE Transactions on Dependable and Secure Computing* 4 (1): 32–40.

Goldman, N., and R. Balzer. 1999. The ISI Visual Design Editor Generator. In IEEE Symposium on Visual Languages (Tokyo), pp. 20–27.

Gomaa, Hassan. 2004. *Designing Software Product Lines with UML: From Use Cases to Pattern-Based Software Architectures*, Addison-Wesley Professional.

Gomaa, Hassan, and Mohamed Hussein. 2004. Software Reconfiguration Patterns for Dynamic Evolution of Software Architectures. In Proceedings of the Fourth Working IEEE/IFIP Conference on Software Architecture, pp. 79–88.

Gorlick, Michael M., and Rami R. Razouk. 1991. Using Weaves for Software Construction and Analysis. In Thirteenth International Conference on Software Engineering, May, pp. 23–34.

Gorton, Ian. 2008. Software Architecture Challenges for Data Intensive Computing. In Seventh Working IEEE/IFIP Conference on Software Architecture, February, (Vancouver, BC), IEEE Computer Society, pp. 4–6.

Gorton, Ian, Adam Wynne, Justin Almquist, and Jack Chatterton. 2008. The MeDICi Integration Framework: A Platform for High Performance Data Streaming Applications. In Seventh Working IEEE/IFIP Conference on Software Architecture, (Vancouver, BC), IEEE Computer Society, pp. 95–104.

Gröne, Bernhard, Andreas Knöpfel, and Rudolf Kugel. 2002. Architecture Recovery of Apache 1.3—A case study. In 2002 International Conference on Software Engineering Research and Practice, (Las Vegas).

Gröne, Bernhard, Andreas Knöpfel, Rudolf Kugel, and Oliver Schmidt. 2004. The Apache Modeling Project, Hasso Plattner Institute for Software Systems Engineering.

Grosso, William. 2001. *Java RMI*. 1st ed., O'Reilly Media, Inc.

Guttag, John V., James J. Horning, and Jeannette M. Wing. 1985. The Larch Family of Specification Languages. *IEEE Software* 2 (5): 24–36.

Guttman, Barbara, and Edward Roback. 1995. An Introduction to Computer Security: The NIST Handbook, edited by Computer Systems Laboratory: National Institute of Standards and Technology: U.S. Government Printing Office.

Haas, R., P. Droz, and B. Stiller. 2003. Autonomic Service Deployment in Networks. *IBM Systems Journal* 42 (1): 150–164.

Hall, Richard S., Dennis Heimbigner, André van der Hoek, and Alexander L. Wolf. 1997. An Architecture for Post-Development Configuration Management in a Wide-Area Network. In

1997 International Conference on Distributed Computing Systems, May, (Baltimore, MD), IEEE Computer Society, pp. 269–278.

Hall, Richard S., Dennis Heimbigner, and Alexander L. Wolf. 1999. A Cooperative Approach to Support Software Deployment Using the Software Dock. In 1999 International Conference on Software Engineering, May, (Los Angeles, CA), ACM Press, pp. 174–183.

Harel, David. 1987. Statecharts: A Visual Formalism for Complex Systems. *Science of Computer Programming* 8: 231–274.

Harold, Elliotte Rusty. 2006. *Java I/O*. 2nd ed., O'Reilly Media, Inc.

Harrison, Michael A., Walter L. Ruzzo, and Jeffrey D. Ullman. 1976. Protection in Operating Systems. *Communications of the ACM* 19 (8): 461–471.

Hayes-Roth, B., K. Pfleger, P. Lalanda, P. Morignot, and M. Balabanovic. 1995. A Domain-Specific Software Architecture for Adaptive Intelligent Systems. *IEEE Transactions on Software Engineering* 21 (4): 288–301.

Heimdahl, Mats P. E. 2007. Safety and Software Intensive Systems: Challenges Old and New. In *Future of Software Engineering 2007*, edited by L. Briand and A. Wolf: IEEE-CS Press, pp. 137–152.

Heineman, George T., and William T. Councill, eds. 2001. *Component-Based Software Engineering: Putting the Pieces Together*. Reading, MA: Addison-Wesley.

Hendrickson, Scott A., Eric M. Dashofy, and Richard N. Taylor. 2005. An (Architecture-Centric) Approach for Tracing, Organizing, and Understanding Events in Event-Based Software Architectures. In Thirteenth International Workshop on Program Comprehension, in conjunction with ICSE 2005, May 15–16, (St. Louis, MO), pp. 227–236.

Hendrickson, Scott A., and André van der Hoek. 2007. Modeling Product Line Architectures through Change Sets and Relationships. In Twenty-Ninth International Conference on Software Engineering (ICSE 2007), May 20–26, (Minneapolis, MN).

Heng, Christopher. *Free Compiler Construction Tools* (Website), October 9, 2007. Available from www.thefreecountry.com/programming/compilerconstruction.shtml.

Hirsch, D., S. Uchitel, and D. Yankelevich. 1999. Towards a Periodic Table of Connectors. In Simposio en Tecnolog´a de Software, (Bueno Aires, Argentina).

Hitchens, Ron. 2002. *Java NIO*, O'Reilly Media, Inc.

Hoare, C. A. R. 1978. Communicating Sequential Processes. *Communications of the ACM* 21 (8): 666–677.

Hofmeister, Christine, R. L. Nord, and D. Soni. 1999. *Applied Software Architecture*, Addison Wesley Longman.

Honeywell, Inc. *MetaH Evaluation and Support Site*, 1998. Available from www.htc.honeywell.com/metah/.

Houston, Peter 1998. Building Distributed Applications with Message Queuing Middleware, Microsoft Corporation, White Paper.

Hunt, Galen C., and Michael L. Scott. 1999. The Coign Automatic Distributed Partitioning System. In Proceedings of the Third Symposium on Operating Systems Design and Implementation, February (New Orleans, LA), USENIX.

IBM. *Autonomic Computing Manifesto* (PDF document), 2001. Available from www.research.ibm.com/autonomic/manifesto/autonomic_computing.pdf.

———. 2002. Autonomic Computing Architecture: A Blueprint for Managing Complex Computing Environments, Whitepaper.

———. 2003. *WebSphere MQ - Product Overview* (Website). IBM. 2003. Available from www-3.ibm. com/software/ts/mqseries/messaging/.

IEEE-SA Standards Board. 2000. *IEEE Recommended Practice for Architectural Description of Software-Intensive Systems.* New York, NY, The Institute of Electrical and Electronics Engineers, Inc.

IEEE. 1991. IEEE Standard Computer Dictionary: A Compilation of IEEE Standard Computer Glossaries: 610. New York: Institute of Electrical and Electronics Engineers, pp. 217.

———. 2004. IEEE Std 1003.1, 2004 Edition.

Immonen, Anne, and Eila Niemela. 2007. Survey of Reliability and Availability Prediction Methods from the Viewpoint of Software Architecture. *Springer Journal of Software and System Modeling.*

InstallShield Corporation. 2000. *InstallShield* (HTML). 2000. Available from www. installshield.com/.

ISO. 1989. LOTOS, A Formal Description Technique Based on the Temporal Ordering of Observational Behavior. (ISO 8807).

ISO/IEC 1998. Information Technology—Open Distributed Processing—Reference Model, ISO/IEC, 10746.

Jackson, Daniel. 2002. Alloy: A Lightweight Object Modelling Notation. ACM *Transactions on Software Engineering and Methodology (TOSEM)* 11 (2): 256–290.

Jackson, M. 2001. *Problem Frames.* Reading, MA, Addison-Wesley Professional.

Jackson, Michael. 1995. *Software Requirements & Specifications: A Lexicon of Practice, Principles and Prejudices,* ACM Press/Addison-Wesley.

———. 2000. Problem Analysis and Structure. In Engineering Theories of Software Construction. NATO Summer School., August, (Marktoberdorf, Germany), IOS Press, pp. 3–20.

———. 2007. *Michael Jackson—Consultancy & Research in Software Development. Past Research Topics.* (Website), 2007. Available from mcs.open.ac.uk/mj665/topics.html.

Jacobson, Ivar. 1992. *Object-Oriented Software Engineering: A Use Case Driven Approach.* 1st ed., Addison-Wesley Professional.

JavaSoft 1996. JavaBeans 1.0 API Specification, Sun Microsystems, Inc., version 1.00-A.

———. 2001. Java Message Service API, Sun Microsystems, Inc., Version 1.0.2b.

Jones, J. Christopher. 1970. *Design Methods: Seeds of Human Futures.* New York, John Wiley & Sons, Ltd.

———. 1992. *Design Methods.* 2nd ed. New York, NY, John Wiley & Sons, Inc. Original edition, J. Christopher Jones, *Design Methods: Seeds of Human Futures.*

Kan, Gene. 2001. Gnutella. In *Peer-to-Peer: Harnessing the Power of Disruptive Technologies,* edited by A. Oram: O'Reilly, pp. 94–122.

Kang, Kyo C., Sholom G. Cohen, James A. Hess, William E. Novak, and A. Spencer Peterson. 1990. Feature-Oriented Domain Analysis (FODA) Feasibility Study, Software Engineering Institute, Technical, CMU/SEI-90-TR-21.

Kelley, Tom, Jonathan Littman, and Tom Peters. 2001. *The Art of Innovation: Lessons in Creativity from IDEO, America's Leading Design Firm.* New York, Currency/Doubleday.

Kephart, Jeffrey O., and David M. Chess. 2003. The Vision of Autonomic Computing. *IEEE Computer* 36 (1): 41–50.

Kernighan, Brian W., and Dennis M. Ritchie. 1988. *The C Programming Language.* 2nd ed., Prentice Hall.

Khare, Rohit, and Richard N. Taylor. 2004. Extending the REpresentational State Transfer Architectural Style for Decentralized Systems. In Twenty-Sixth International Conference on Software Engineering (ICSE 2004), May (Edinburgh, Scotland, UK), pp. 428–437.

Kichkaylo, Tatiana, Anca Ivan, and Vijay Karamcheti. 2003. Constrained Component Deployment in Wide-Area Networks Using AI Planning Techniques. In International Parallel and Distributed Processing Symposium (IPDPS'03).

Klusener, A. S., L. R. Lämmel, and C. Verhoef. 2005. *Architectural Modifications to Deployed Software.* Vol. 54, Elsevier North-Holland, Inc.

Kramer, J., and J. Magee. 1990. The Evolving Philosophers Problem: Dynamic Change Management. *IEEE Transactions on Software Engineering* 16 (11): 1293–1306.

Kramer, Jeff, and Jeff Magee. 1988. Change Management of Distributed Systems. In Proceedings of the Third Workshop on ACM SIGOPS European Workshop: Autonomy or Interdependence in Distributed Systems? (Cambridge, United Kingdom), ACM Press, pp. 1–4.

Kruchten, Philippe. 1995. Mommy: Where Do Software Architectures Come From? In First International Workshop on Architectures for Software Systems, April, (Seattle, WA).

———. 1999. The Software Architect—and the Software Architecture Team. In Software Architecture. Proceedings of TC2 First Working IFIP Conference on Software Architecture, (San Antonio, TX), Kluwer Academic Publishers, pp. 565–583.

———. 2000. *The Rational Unified Process: An Introduction.* Reading, MA: Addison-Wesley Professional.

Kruchten, Phillipe. 2003. *The Rational Unified Process: An Introduction.* 3rd ed.

Lampson, Butler W. 1974. Protection. *ACM SIGOPS Operating Systems Review* 8 (1): 18–24.

Larman, Craig. 2002. *Applying UML and Patterns. An Introduction to Object-Oriented Analysis and Design and the Unified Process.* 2nd ed, Prentice-Hall PTR.

Lazowska, Edward D., John Zahorjan, G. Scott Graham, and Kenneth C. Sevcik. 1984. *Quantitative System Performance: Computer System Analysis Using Queueing Network Models.* Upper Saddle River, NJ, Prentice-Hall, Inc.

Lee, Seungjoon, Rob Sherwood, and Bobby Bhattacharjee. 2003. Cooperative Peer Groups in NICE. In IEEE Infocom, April 1–3, (San Francisco).

Leveson, Nancy G. 1995. *Safeware: System Safety and Computers,* Addison-Wesley Professional.

Liang, Sheng. 1999. *Java Native Interface: Programmer's Guide and Specification.* 1st ed., Prentice Hall PTR.

Littlewood, Bev, and Lorenzo Strigini. 2000. Software Reliability and Dependability: A Roadmap. In *The Future of Software Engineering 2000,* (Limerick, Ireland), ACM Press, pp. 175–188.

Liu, C. L., and James W. Layland. 1973. Scheduling Algorithms for Multiprogramming in a Hard-Real-Time Environment. *Journal of the ACM (JACM)* 20 (1): 46–61.

Luckham, David. 2002. *The Power of Events: An Introduction to Complex Event Processing in Distributed Enterprise Systems,* Addison-Wesley.

Luckham, David C., and Friedrich W. von Henke. 1985. An Overview of Anna, a Specification Language for Ada. *IEEE Software* 2 (2): 9–23.

Luckham, David C., John J. Kenney, Larry M. Augustin, James Vera, Doug Bryan, and Walter Mann. 1995. Specification and Analysis of System Architecture Using Rapide. *IEEE Transactions on Software Engineering* 21 (4): 336–355.

Luckham, David C., and James Vera. 1995. An Event-Based Architecture Definition Language. *IEEE Transactions on Software Engineering* 21 (9): 717–734.

Lutz, Robyn. 2000. Software Engineering for Safety: A Roadmap. In *The Future of Software Engineering 2000*, (Limerick, Ireland), ACM Press, pp. 213–224.

Lyu, Michael. 2007. Software Reliability Engineering: A Roadmap. In *Future of Software Engineering 2007*, edited by L. Briand and A. Wolf: IEEE-CS Press, pp. 153–170.

Magee, Jeff, Naranker Dulay, Susan Eisenbach, and Jeff Kramer. 1995. Specifying Distributed Software Architectures. In Fifth European Software Engineering Conference (ESEC 95), Springer-Verlag, Berlin, pp. 137–153.

Magee, Jeff, Naranker Dulay, and Jeff Kramer. 1994. Regis: A Constructive Development Environment for Distributed Programs. *IEE/IOP/BCS Distributed Systems Engineering* 1 (5): 304–312.

Magee, Jeff, and Jeff Kramer. 1996. Dynamic Structure in Software Architectures. In Fourth ACM SIGSOFT Symposium on Foundations of Software Engineering, October 16–18, (San Francisco), ACM SIGSOFT, pp. 3–14.

———. 2006. *Concurrency: State Models and Java Programs.* 2nd ed., Wiley.

Maier, Mark, and Eberhardt Rechtin. 2000. *The Art of Systems Architecting.* 2nd ed., Boca Raton, FL, CRC Press.

Malek, Sam, Nels Beckman, Marija Mikic-Rakic, and Nenad Medvidović. 2005. A Framework for Ensuring and Improving Dependability in Highly Distributed Systems. In *Architecting Dependable Systems III*, edited by R. de Lemos, C. Gacek and A. Romanowski: Springer Verlag.

Malek, Sam, Marija Mikic-Rakic, and Nenad Medvidović. 2005. A Style-Aware Architectural Middleware for Resource Constrained, Distributed Systems. *IEEE Transactions on Software Engineering* 31 (3): 256–272.

Malek, Sam, Chiyoung Seo, Sharmila Ravula, Brad Petrus, and Nenad Medvidović. 2007. Reconceptualizing a Family of Heterogeneous Embedded Systems via Explicit Architectural Support. In Proceedings of the Twenty-Ninth International Conference on Software Engineering, IEEE Computer Society, pp. 591–601.

Manolescu, Ioana, Marco Brambilla, Stefano Ceri, Sara Comai, and Piero Fraternali. 2005. Model-Driven Design and Deployment of Service-Enabled Web Applications. *ACM Transactions on Internet Technology (TOIT)* 5 (3): 439–479.

Marsh, Stephen. 1994. Formalising Trust as a Computational Concept, Department of Mathematics and Computer Science, University of Stirling, Stirling.

Mattmann, Chris A., Daniel J. Crichton, Nenad Medvidović, and Steve Hughes. 2006. A Software Architecture-Based Framework for Highly Distributed and Data Intensive Scientific Applications. In Proceeding of the Twenty-Eighth International Conference on Software Engineering, (Shanghai, China), ACM Press, pp. 721–730.

Mattmann, Chris A., Nenad Medvidović, Paul M. Ramirez, and Vladimir Jakobac. 2005. Unlocking the Grid. In Component-Based Software Engineering: 8th International Symposium, CBSE 2005, May 14–15, (St. Louis, MO), Lecture Notes in Computer Science.

Mattmann, Chris, Sam Malek, N. Beckman, M. Mikic-Rakic, Nenad Medvidović, and Dan Crichton. 2005. GLIDE: A Grid-Based, Lightweight, Infrastructure for Data-Intensive Environments. In European Grid Conference (EGC2005), February 14–16, (Amsterdam, The Netherlands), pp. 68–77.

Maybee, Mark J., Dennis M. Heimbigner, and Leon J. Osterweil. 1996. Multilanguage Interoperability in Distributed Systems. In Eighteenth International Conference on Software Engineering, March (Berlin, Germany), IEEE Computer Society, pp. 451–463.

Medvidović, Nenad, Eric Dashofy, and Richard N. Taylor. 2007. Moving Architectural Description from Under the Technology Lamppost. *Information and Software Technology* 49 (1): 12–31.

Medvidović, Nenad, Peyman Oreizy, and Richard N. Taylor. 1997. Reuse of Off-the-Shelf Components in C2-Style Architectures. In Nineteenth International Conference on Software Engineering, May (Boston, MA), ACM Press, pp. 692–700.

Medvidović, Nenad, and Richard N. Taylor. 2000. A Classification and Comparison Framework for Software Architecture Description Languages. *IEEE Transactions on Software Engineering* 26 (1): 70–93.

Mehta, Nikunj R., Nenad Medvidović, and Sandeep Phadke. 2000. Towards a Taxonomy of Software Connectors. In 2000 International Conference on Software Engineering, June 4–11 (Limerick, Ireland), ACM Press, pp. 178–187.

Microsoft Corporation. 2007. *PowerPoint Home Page—Microsoft Office Online*, 2007. Available from office.microsoft.com/powerpoint.

———. 2007. *Visio Home Page—Microsoft Office Online*, 2007. Available from office.microsoft.com/visio.

Mitra, Nilo. *Simple Object Access Protocol (SOAP) 1.2: Primer*. W3C, June 24, 2003. Available from www.w3.org/TR/soap12-part0/.

Modular Software-Programmable Radio Consortium 2001. Software Communications Architecture Specification v2.2, Specification, MSRC-5000SCA.

Monroe, Robert T. 1998. Capturing Software Architecture Design Expertise With Armani, School of Computer Science, Carnegie Mellon University, technical report, CMU-CS-98-163.

Moriconi, M., X. Qian, and R.A. Riemenschneider. 1995. Correct Architecture Refinement. *IEEE Transactions on Software Engineering* 21 (4): 356–372.

Mos, A., and J. Murphy. 2004. COMPAS: Adaptive Performance Monitoring of Component-Based Systems. In Workshop on Remote Analysis and Measurement of Software Systems (RAMSS), May (Edinburgh, Scotland).

Mukerji, Jishnu, and Joaquin Miller, eds. 2003. *MDA Guide Version 1.0.1*: Object Management Group.

NASA Jet Propulsion Laboratory. *Cassini-Huygens Mission to Saturn & Titan*. Available from saturn.jpl.nasa.gov/mission/index.cfm.

Nelson, Harold G., and Erik Stolterman. 2003. *The Design Way: Intentional Change in an Unpredictable World—Foundations and Fundamentals of Design Competence*, Educational Technology Publications, Inc.

Nemhauser, G. L., and L. A. Wolsey. 1988. *Integer and Combinatorial Optimization*. New York, NY, Wiley-Interscience.

Nesnas, Issa A.D., Reid Simmons, Daniel Gaines, Clayton Kunz, Antonio Diaz-Calderon, Tara Estlin, Richard Madison, John Guineau, Michael McHenry, I-Hsiang Shu, and David Apfelbaum. 2006. CLARAty: Challenges and Steps Toward Reusable Robotic Software. *International Journal of Advanced Robotic Systems* 3 (1): 23–30.

Ng, Keng, Jeff Kramer, and Jeff Magee. 1996. A CASE Tool for Software Architecture Design. *Journal of Automated Software Engineering* 3: 261–284.

Nilsson, Nils J. 1980. *Principles of Artificial Intelligence*, Tioga Publishing Company.

Norman, Donald A. 2002. *The Design of Everyday Things*. 1st Basic paperback ed. New York, Basic Books. Original edition, *The Psychology of Everyday Things*. New York: Basic Books, 1988.

Nuseibeh, Bashar. 2001. Weaving Together Requirements and Architectures. *IEEE Computer* 34 (2): 115–117.

Nuseibeh, Bashar, and Steve Easterbrook. 2000. Requirements Engineering: A Roadmap. *The Future of Software Engineering* (Limerick, Ireland), ACM Press, pp. 35–46.

Nutaro, Jim. *Adevs: A Discrete EVent System simulator.* Available from www.ornl.gov/~1qn/adevs/index.html.

OASIS. *eXtensible Access Control Markup Language (XACML).* OASIS, 2005. Available from docs.oasis-open.org/xacml/2.0/access_control-xacml-2.0-core-spec-os.pdf.

———. 2007. Web Services Business Process Execution Language Version 2.0, OASIS Standard.

Object Management Group. 2003. *Meta Object Facility (MOF) Specification* (1.4) (PDF), April 2002. Available from www.omg.org/docs/formal/02–04–03.pdf.

———. 2003. *OMG XML Metadata Interchange (XMI) Specification* (1.2) (PDF), January 2002. Available from www.omg.org/docs/formal/02–01–01.pdf.

———. 2005. UML Profile for DODAF/MODAF (UPDM) Request for Proposal, OMG, RFP, OMG document syseng/05–08–01.

———, ed. 2001. *The Common Object Request Broker: Architecture and Specification*: Object Management Group.

Oreizy, Peyman. 1998. Issues in Modeling and Analyzing Dynamic Software Architectures. In International Workshop on the Role of Software Architecture in Testing and Analysis, June 30–July 3, (Marsala, Sicily, Italy).

Oreizy, Peyman, Michael M. Gorlick, Richard N. Taylor, Dennis Heimbigner, Greg Johnson, Nenad Medvidović, Alex Quilici, David S. Rosenblum, and Alexander L. Wolf. 1999. An Architecture-Based Approach to Self-Adaptive Software. *IEEE Intelligent Systems* 14 (3): 54–62.

Oreizy, Peyman, Nenad Medvidović, and Richard N. Taylor. 1998. Architecture-Based Runtime Software Evolution. In Twentieth International Conference on Software Engineering (ICSE '98), April, (Kyoto, Japan), IEEE Computer Society, pp. 177–186.

Oreizy, Peyman, Nenad Medvidovic, and Richard N. Taylor. 2008. Runtime Software Adaptation: Framework, Approaches, and Styles. In Companion of the Thirtieth International Conference on Software Engineering (Leipzig, Germany), ACM, pp. 899–910.

Orfali, Robert, Dan Harkey, and Jeri Edwards. 1996. *The Essential Distributed Objects Survival Guide.* New York, NY, Wiley.

Orso, A., D. Liang, M. J. Harrold, and R. Lipton. 2002. Gamma System: Continuous Evolution of Software after Deployment. In International Symposium on Software Testing and Analysis (ISSTA 2002), July (Rome, Italy).

Paczkowski, B. G., and T. L. Ray. 2004. Cassini Science Planning Process. In SpaceOps 2004, May 17–21, (Montreal, Canada).

Parnas, David L. 1972. On the Criteria to be Used in Decomposing Systems into Modules. *Communications of the ACM* 15 (12): 1053–1058.

Perry, Dewayne E. 1987. Software Interconnection Models. In Ninth International Conference on Software Engineering (ICSE), March, IEEE Computer Society, pp. 61–69.

Perry, Dewayne E., and Alexander L. Wolf. 1992. Foundations for the Study of Software Architecture. *ACM SIGSOFT Software Engineering Notes* 17 (4): 40–52.

Peter, Laurence J., and Raymond Hull. 1969. *The Peter Principle: Why Things Always Go Wrong.* New York, William Morrow & Company, Inc.

Petroski, Henry 1985. *To Engineer Is Human*, St. Martin's Press.

———. 1992. *The Evolution of Useful Things*, Alfred A. Knopf, Inc.

———. 1994. *Design Paradigms: Case Histories of Error and Judgement in Engineering*, Cambridge University Press.

———. 1996. *Invention by Design: How Engineers Get From Thought To Thing*, Harvard University Press.

Pezzè, Mauro, and Michal Young. 2007. *Software Testing and Analysis: Process, Principles, and Techniques*, John Wiley & Sons.

Pfleeger, Charles P., and Shari Lawrence Pfleeger. 2003. *Security in Computing*. 3rd ed., Prentice Hall PTR.

Pohl, Klaus, Günter Böckle, and Frank J. van der Linden. 2005. *Software Product Line Engineering: Foundations, Principles and Techniques*. 1st ed., New York, NY, Springer.

Pollio, Marcus Vitruvius. 2007. *On Architecture* [Website (based on 1826 translation by Joseph Gwilt)], Jan 24, 2006. Available from penelope.uchicago.edu/Thayer/E/Roman/Texts/Vitruvius/home.html.

Polya, G. 1957. *How to Solve It: A New Aspect of Mathematical Method*. 2nd ed., Princeton University Press. Original edition, 1945.

Pooley, Rob. 2000. Software Engineering and Performance: A Roadmap. In *The Future of Software Engineering 2000* (Limerick, Ireland), ACM Press, pp. 189–200.

Rabiner, Lawrence R. 1989. A Tutorial on Hidden Markov Models and Selected Applications in Speech Recognition. *Proceedings of the IEEE* 77 (2): 257–286.

Raggett, Dave, Arnaud Le Hors, and Ian Jacobs 1999. HTML 4.01 Specification, W3C. Available from www.n3.org/TR/REC-html40/.

Rapanotti, Lucia, Jon Hall, Michael Jackson, and Bashar Nuseibeh. 2004. Architecture Driven Problem Decomposition. In Twelfth IEEE International Requirements Engineering Conference (RE'04), September, 2004, (Kyoto, Japan), IEEE, pp. 80–89.

Rational Software Corporation 2003. Rational Rose: Using Rose, IBM Corporation, Report number 800-024462-000.

Reenskaug, Trygve. 1979. Thing-Model-View-Editor—An example from a Planning System, Xerox PARC, Technical note.

———. 2003. The Model-View-Controller (MVC): Its Past and Present. In *Java and Object-Oriented Software Engineering (JAOO)*, September 22–25, (Aarhus, Denmark).

Reiss, Steven P. 1990. Connecting Tools Using Message Passing in the Field Environment. *IEEE Software* 7 (4): 57–66.

Ren, Jie, Richard Taylor, Paul Dourish, and David Redmiles. 2005. Towards An Architectural Treatment of Software Security: A Connector-Centric Approach. In Workshop on Software Engineering for Secure Systems (SESS 05), in conjunction with ICSE 2005, May (St. Louis, MO).

Ren, Jie, and Richard N. Taylor. 2003. Visualizing Software Architecture with Off-The-Shelf Components. In Fifteenth International Conference on Software Engineering and Knowledge Engineering (SEKE 2003), July 1–3, (San Francisco, CA), pp. 132–141.

———. 2005. A Secure Software Architecture Description Language. In Workshop on Software Security Assurance Tools, Techniques, and Metrics, Co-located with the twentieth IEEE/ACM International Conference on Automated Software Engineering (ASE 2005), (Long Beach, CA).

Robbins, Jason, N. Medvidović, David Redmiles, and David Rosenblum. 1998. Integrating Architecture Description Languages with a Standard Design Method. In Twentieth International Conference on Software Engineering (ICSE), April, (Kyoto, Japan), ACM Press, pp. 209–218.

Rosenblum, David S., and Alexander L. Wolf. A Design Framework for Internet-Scale Event Observation and Notification. In Proceedings of the Sixth European Software Engineering Conference held jointly with the Fifth ACM SIGSOFT International Symposium on Foundations of Software Engineering, pp. 344–360, Zurich, Switzerland, September 1997.

Roshandel, Roshanak, André van der Hoek, Marija Mikic-Rakic, and Nenad Medvidović. 2004. Mae - A System Model and Environment for Managing Architectural Evolution. ACM *Transactions on Software Engineering and Methodology (TOSEM)* 13 (2): 240–276.

Rozanski, Nick, and Eoin Woods. 2005. *Software Systems Architecture: Working With Stakeholders Using Viewpoints and Perspectives*. Addison-Wesley Professional.

Rumbaugh, James, Michael Blaha, William Lorensen, Frederick Eddy, and William Premerlani. 1990. *Object-Oriented Modeling and Design*. 1st ed., Prentice Hall.

Sabbagh, Karl. 1989. *Skyscraper*, Viking.

Saltzer, J. H., and M. D. Schroeder. 1975. The Protection of Information in Computer Systems. *Proceedings of the IEEE* 63 (9): 1278–308.

Schach, Stephen R. 2007. *Object-Oriented & Classical Software Engineering*. 7th ed., McGraw Hill Higher Education.

Schneier, Bruce. 1995. *Applied Cryptography: Protocols, Algorithms, and Source Code in C*. 2nd ed., John Wiley & Sons.

———. 2000. *Secrets and Lies: Digital Security in a Networked World*, John Wiley & Sons, Inc.

Schön, Donald. 1983. *The Reflective Practitioner: How Professionals Think in Action*. New York, Basic Books, Inc. Publishers.

Seo, Chiyoung, Sam Malek, and Nenad Medvidović. 2007. An Energy Consumption Framework for Distributed Java-Based Systems. In Twenty-Second IEEE/ACM International Conference on Automated Software Engineering (ASE), November (Atlanta, GA), pp. 421–424.

Sessions, R. 1997. *COM and DCOM: Microsoft's Vision for Distributed Objects*. New York, NY, John Wiley & Sons Inc.

Shaw, M., R. DeLine, and G. Zelesnik. 1996. Abstractions and Implementations for Architectural Connections. In Third International Conference on Configurable Distributed Systems, May (Annapolis, MD), pp. 2–10.

Shaw, Mary. 1994. Procedure Calls Are the Assembly Language of Software Interconnection: Connectors Deserve First-Class Status. In *Studies of Software Design, Proceedings of a 1993 Workshop*, edited by D. A. Lamb: Springer-Verlag, pp. 17–32.

Shaw, Mary, Robert DeLine, Daniel V. Klein, Theodore L. Ross, David M. Young, and Gregory Zelesnik. 1995. Abstractions for Software Architecture and Tools to Support Them. *IEEE Transactions on Software Engineering* 21 (4): 314–335.

Shaw, Mary, and David Garlan. 1996. *Software Architecture: Perspectives on an Emerging Discipline*, Prentice Hall.

Smolander, K. 2002. What is Included in Software Architecture? A Case Study in Three Software Organizations. In Ninth Annual IEEE International Conference and Workshop on the Engineering of Computer-Based Systems, pp. 131–138.

Smolander, K., and T. Päivärinta. 2002. Describing and Communicating Software Architecture in Practice: Observations on Stakeholders and Rationale. In Proceedings of the Fourteenth International Conference on Advanced Information Systems Engineering (CAISE'02), May 27–31, (Toronto, Ontario, Canada), Springer Berlin, pp. 117–133.

Software Engineering Institute. *The Architecture Tradeoff Analysis Method (ATAM)*. Available from www.sei.cmu.edu/architecture/ata_method.html.

Spencer, John 2000. Architecture Description Markup Language (ADML): Creating an Open Market for IT Architecture Tools, The Open Group, White Paper.

Spitznagel, B., and D. Garlan. 2003. A Compositional Formalization of Connector Wrappers. In Twenty-Fifth International Conference on Software Engineering, pp. 374–384.

Spivey, J. M. 1988. *Understanding Z*, Cambridge University Press.

Stewart, W. J. 1994. *Introduction to Numerical Solution of Markov Chains*, Princeton University Press.

Suryanarayana, Girish, Mamadou H. Diallo, Justin R. Erenkrantz, and Richard N. Taylor. 2006. Architecting Trust-Enabled Peer-to-Peer File-Sharing Applications. *ACM Crossroads*, 12 (4): 11–19.

———. 2006. Architectural Support for Trust Models in Decentralized Applications. In Proceedings of the Twenty-eighth International Conference on Software Engineering, May, (Shanghai, China), ACM Press, pp. 52–61.

Suryanarayana, Girish, Justin R. Erenkrantz, and Richard N. Taylor. 2005. An Architectural Approach for Decentralized Trust Management. *IEEE Internet Computing*, November/December, pp. 16–23.

SysML Partners. 2005. Systems Modeling Language (SysML) Specification version 0.9.

SysML.org. 2007. *SysML Partners* (Webpage), 2007. Available from www.sysml.org/partners.htm.

Szyperski, Clemens. 1997. *Component Software: Beyond Object-Oriented Programming*. New York, ACM Press.

———. 2002. *Component Software - Beyond Object-Oriented Programming*. 2nd ed., Addison-Wesley.

Tanenbaum, Andrew S., and Maarten van Steen. 2002. *Distributed Systems: Principles and Paradigms*. Upper Saddle River, NJ: Prentice-Hall.

Taylor, R., W. Tracz, and L. Coglianese. 1995. Software Development Using Domain-Specific Software Architectures. *Software Engineering Notes* 20 (5).

Taylor, Richard N., Nenad Medvidović, Kenneth M. Anderson, E. James Whitehead Jr., Jason E. Robbins, Kari A. Nies, Peyman Oreizy, and Deborah L. Dubrow. 1996. A Component- and Message-Based Architectural Style for GUI Software. *IEEE Transactions on Software Engineering* 22 (6): 390–406.

Taylor, Richard N., and Andre van der Hoek. 2007. Software Design and Architecture. The Once and Future Focus of Software Engineering, In *Future of Software Engineering (FOSE '07)*, edited by A. Wolf and L. Briand: IEEE Computer Society, pp. 226–243.

Telecommunication Standardization Sector of ITU 2002. Specification and Description Language (SDL), ITU Standard Z.100.

Telelogic AB. 2007. *Telelogic System Architect* (Website). 2007. Available from www.telelogic.com/Products/Systemarchitect/.

Telelogic DOORS. Available from www.telelogic.com/products/doors/doors/index.cfm.

The Globus Alliance. *The Globus Alliance* (Website). Available from www.globus.org/.

The Omni Group. 2007. *The Omni Group—Applications—OmniGraffle*, 2007. Available from www.omnigroup.com/applications/omnigraffle/.

The Open Group 2003. TOGAF (The Open Group Architecture Framework) Version 8.1 "Enterprise Edition," The Open Group.

———. 2007. *Distributed Computing Environment Portal*, January 17 2005, Available from www.opengroup.org/dce/.

Tichy, Walter F. 1985. RCS - A System for Version Control. *Software—Practice and Experience* 15 (7): 637–654.

Tierney, B. 2000. A Monitoring Sensor Management System for Grid Environments. In IEEE International Symposium on High Performance Distributed Computing, August (Pittsburgh, PA).

Tracz, W. 1993. LILEANNA: A Parameterized Programming Language. In *Proceedings of the Second International Workshop on Software Reuse*, pp. 66–78.

Tracz, Will. 1994. Domain-Specific Software Architecture (DSSA) Frequently Asked Questions (FAQ). *ACM SIGSOFT Software Engineering Notes* 19 (2): 52–56.

————. 1995. *Confessions of a Used Program Salesman: Institutionalizing Software Reuse.* 1st ed, Addison-Wesley.

————. 1995. DSSA (Domain-Specific Software Architecture): Pedagogical Example. *ACM SIG-SOFT Software Engineering Notes* 20 (3).

Tracz, Will, Lou Coglianese, and Patrick Young. 1993. A Domain-Specific Software Architecture Engineering Process Outline. *ACM SIGSOFT Software Engineering Notes* 18 (2): 40–49.

Tufte, Edward R. 1990. *Envisioning Information,* Graphics Press.

————. 2001. *The Visual Display of Quantitative Information,* Graphics Press.

University of California, Berkeley. 1986. *UNIX Programmer's Manual, 4.3 Berkeley Software Distribution,* Computer Science Division, University of California–Berkeley.

van der Hoek, André. 2000. Capturing Product Line Architectures. In Fourth International Software Architecture Workshop (ISAW-4), June 4–5, (Limerick, Ireland), pp. 95–99.

————. 2004. Design-Time Product Line Architectures for Any-Time Variability. *Science of Computer Programming, Special Issue on Software Variability Management* 53 (30): 285–304.

van Lamsweerde, Axel. 2000. Requirements Engineering in the Year 00: A Research Perspective. In Proceedings of the Twenty-Second International Conference on Software Engineering, (Limerick, Ireland), ACM Press, pp. 5–19.

van Ommering, Rob. 2002. Building Product Populations with Software Components. In Twenty-Fourth International Conference on Software Engineering (ICSE 2002), May 19–25, (Orlando, FL), pp. 255–265.

van Ommering, Rob, Frank van der Linden, Jeff Kramer, and Jeff Magee. 2000. The Koala Component Model for Consumer Electronics Software. *IEEE Computer* 33 (3): 78–85.

van Vliet, Hans. 2000. *Software Engineering: Principles and Practice.* 2nd ed., John Wiley & Sons, LTD.

Vickers, Brian. 2004. Architecting a Software Architect. In IEEE Aerospace Conference, March 6–13, IEEE, pp. 4155–4161.

Vogel, Ed. Cigar Box Guitar. *Make: Technology On Your Time,* 4, pp. 76–82.

Vogels, W. 2003. Web Services Are Not Distributed Objects. *IEEE Internet Computing* 7 (6): 59–66.

Warmer, Jos B., and Anneke G. Kleppe. 1998. *The Object Constraint Language: Precise Modeling with UML,* Addison-Wesley Object Technology Series, Addison-Wesley Professional.

Wing, J. M. 2003. A Call to Action: Look Beyond the Horizon. *IEEE Security & Privacy.* 1 (6): 62–67.

Woodside, Murray, Greg Franks, and Dorina C. Petriu. 2007. The Future of Software Performance Engineering In *Future of Software Engineering 2007,* edited by L. Briand and A. Wolf. IEEE-CS Press, pp. 171–187.

Yellin, D. M., and R. E. Strom. 1994. Interfaces, Protocols, and the Semi-Automatic Construction of Software Adaptors. In OOPSLA '94, October 1994, (Portland, OR).

Zetter, Kim. *Kazaa Delivers More than Tunes,* Jan. 9, 2004. Available from www.wired.com/news/business/0,1367,61852,00.html.

Index

Printed and bound by CPI Group (UK) Ltd, Croydon, CR0 4YY

16/09/2024

14557196-0001